Learning and the Control of Behavior:

Some Principles, Theories,
and Applications of Classical
and Operant Conditioning

David A. Lieberman
University of Illinois

HOLT, RINEHART AND WINSTON, INC.
New York   Chicago   San Francisco   Atlanta   Dallas
Montreal   Toronto   London   Sydney

*To Chris, Mark,
and my parents,
whom I love.*

Library of Congress Cataloging in Publication Data

Lieberman, David A.   comp.
  Learning and the control of behavior.

  Bibliography: p. 532
  1. Conditioned response—Addresses, essays, lectures.
  I. Title. [DNLM: 1. Conditioning, Classical. 2. Conditioning,
  Operant. 3. Learning. LB1051 L716L 1974]
BF319.L53   153.1′52′08   73-14641

ISBN 0-03-001941-9

Preface

When I first began teaching learning, I suffered enormously. Teaching was new to me, there was an enormous amount of preparation to be done, but worst of all my students seemed excruciatingly bored. Aha, I said to myself, this must be because these students are apathetic and unreachable, and anyway learning is inherently less interesting than subjects such as personality and abnormal psychology. I hated to bore my students (there is nothing more painful than an enormous yawn echoing through a classroom), but it was clear to me that a college education should not just be entertaining, that intellectual rigor must also be taught. The behavior of rats in a Skinner box might not be as exciting as the sexual symbolism of dreams, but if the important principles of learning were contained in rat experiments then those were the experiments that I would teach.

Continued teaching experience has not made me abandon my belief in intellectual sophistication or the importance of the experimental method, but I now find myself not a little embarrassed by my earlier faith that these values were to be found only in animal research, and that the applications of learning principles were somehow tainted and impure, of concern only in the less scientific halls of education or even child psychology. With the weight of experience,[1] I now think the effort to base my course solely on the basic principles of learning as developed in the animal laboratory was wrong. Students are reluctant to believe that a white rat, with its 1/10-oz. brain, is an appropriate model for the complexities of human behavior, and their skepticism is justified. Whatever the analytic advantages of exploring behavior in the highly controlled environment of a Skinner box, the principles developed there must ultimately be applied and evaluated in the context of complex human behavior, and these applications are an important part of the study of learning.

This book, then, is not intended solely as a solemn study of basic principles nor as a completely practical guide to training your child. Its purpose is to examine the basic principles of conditioning—how behavior is modified by environmental contingencies—but to examine these principles not only in the controlled conditions of the laboratory but also amid the greater complexity and chaos of the real world. Throughout, the stress has been not only on the principles of learning but on the techniques by which they've been established. The Yale philosopher Paul Weiss tells the story of a baseball fan who arrived during the ninth inning of a game and immediately asked a friend the score. When told that the game was tied, 2 to 2, he replied, "Good, I was afraid I'd missed something." He only missed, of course, the beauty of the game, and hopefully the readings in this book convey not only the results but also the excitement and beauty of experimental research on learning.

[1] Four years of teaching and eight repetitions of my learning course!

Instructor's Preface

Why should you assign this book? To be honest, I don't know if you should. In planning this book I was concerned not with the needs of the "average" or "typical" course in learning, but with the needs of *my* course, and the text and readings thus emphasize my own, very personal view of how learning should be taught. The usefulness of this book for you, therefore, may depend on how closely you share my biases about teaching.

My primary concern in teaching learning has been to convey an appreciation for the nature of scientific analysis. A student will quickly forget the specific facts taught in any learning course, but it will still have lasting value for him if he's learned something of the challenge and excitement of logical analysis. To expose a student to the ambiguities of conflicting evidence, the confusion of opposing explanations, and then to the sheer excitement of an elegant experiment that resolves the apparent contradictions: this seems to me the greatest achievement of any learning course. The first goal of this book, therefore, was to develop an appreciation of scientific analysis in perhaps the only way possible, by directly exposing the student to some of the finest experiments in learning.

A second concern has been to convey to the student that learning is not confined to Skinner boxes or even to classrooms, but is a pervasive process in our everyday lives. "Rat psychology" and "behaviorism" have become terms of veiled and not-so-veiled contempt for many undergraduates, but I think the problem is less with the nature of psychological research than with how it has been presented. It is not enough to simply assert that the principles derived from a rat or a pigeon help explain human behavior: the relevance must be shown. A second criterion in selecting readings, therefore, was to demonstrate how principles developed in the artificial environment of the laboratory can be successfully applied to complex social behavior.

My third concern in teaching, and perhaps the one that will prove most idiosyncratic, has been to demonstrate the usefulness of theory in interpreting and predicting behavior. Most psychologists now accept the advantages of explicit theorizing, but traditionally discussion of learning theory has been deferred to an upper-level course entirely devoted to that subject. It is my belief, however, that some consideration of theory is also useful in an introductory learning course. First, I think a student learns better when he can see how apparently unrelated facts can be fit into a coherent and meaningful theoretical structure. Second, I think the conflict between opposing theories can be one of the most stimulating features of a learning course. Students sometimes literally gasp when they begin to understand how Spence, using only a few simple assumptions, was able to explain transposition. My own theoretical orientation is cognitive, but I have tried in this book to indicate the successes of S-R as well as cognitive theory, and how the differences between them have

iv

sometimes been exaggerated because of the vagueness of their formulations.

These biases—toward methodology, application, and theory—have together largely determined the general outline of this book. Within this framework, my primary selection criterion was whether an article was written in such a way that a beginning student would be able to understand it. Wherever possible, I have tried to include articles that not only made an important point but did so in a clear and even entertaining way. One not entirely anticipated consequence of this criterion was the exclusion of much recent research that was otherwise of considerable interest. The problem with many recent articles is that they presuppose extensive familiarity with the earlier literature! Though they may include a short review, they rarely provide the kind of clear exposition of basic issues available in the earlier papers. Furthermore, they are often concerned with extensions of earlier findings rather than with the basic principles themselves, and the result is that they are often too complex for a beginning student to appreciate or even to understand. I've tried to include recent developments wherever possible (for example, the work of Rescorla, Kamin, and Garcia in classical conditioning), but in general I've been concerned with setting forth the basic issues in learning rather than the most recent solutions.

Another category of research that has been omitted is that on verbal learning. This exclusion is in no way a reflection of my feelings about its importance: I consider the recent development of cognitive models of human memory to be one of the most exciting developments in psychology. Indeed, one of my reasons for wanting to write this book was to show that the dichotomy between conditioning and verbal learning in terms of their complexity was false, in that even simple conditioning situations involve the same complex principles of coding and organization that have been found in verbal learning. My reason for omitting verbal learning, then, was not that I thought it unimportant, but that a number of excellent and inexpensive readers are already available in this area. It seemed to me that a course covering both conditioning and verbal learning would be better served by two readers, covering each area in depth, than by one reader offering reduced coverage of each.

Finally, insofar as conditioning is concerned this book is *not* intended as a supplement to any other text. It can, of course, be used that way, but I have tried through both my selection of articles and the writing of lengthy introductory sections to make this book self-sufficient. The textual material is equivalent in length to a moderate-sized paperback, and it provides all the basic concepts necessary for a student to understand and appreciate the readings. I have tried to make this book a provocative as well as informative introduction to learning, and I hope you and your students find it worth reading.

Champaign, Illinois   D.A.L.
September 1973

Contents

One
Some Basic Assumptions

The Morality of Behavioral Control

The idea of someone manipulating our behavior is repulsive. There is something profoundly evil about the efforts of totalitarian governments to totally control their societies, stifling any artistic or individual creativity, replacing love of the family with loyalty to the state, and using secret police to crush any deviation in political thought from the rigid ideology of the state. Even more modest efforts at control arouse an instinctive resistance in us. Thus when Vance Packard suggested in *The Hidden Persuaders* that advertisers were trying to unconsciously mold our attitudes, to force us to desire their products without our even being aware of it, readers were appalled by the possibility of such covert control, and the book became a widely discussed best seller. The idea of someone trying to control us, to manipulate us, is frightening. It suggests the ultimate horror of George Orwell's *1984*, where people are reduced to colorless automatons manipulated from the top by slogans, rewards, and, when necessary, terrifying punishments.

The idea of controlling behavior is obviously foreign to us, contrary to our most basic and primitive instincts. Or is it? B. F. Skinner (Article 1.1) argues that the debate as to whether or not we should control behavior is pointless, since behavior is already controlled. A parent spanking a child, a teacher awarding grades, a government enforcing tax codes and draft laws, all of these are deliberate efforts at behavioral control. It is not that we haven't been controlled, says Skinner, but that past controls have been haphazard and often ineffective, giving us the illusion of freedom. Advances in behavioral technology, however, are making more effective controls possible, and Skinner argues we must begin rationally planning the best use of these techniques if they are not to be appropriated and perverted by powerful elites. "We are all controlled by the world in which we live, and part

1

of that world has been and will be constructed by man. The question is this: Are we to be controlled by accident, by tyrants, or by ourselves in effective cultural design?"

The extent to which our behavior can be controlled is dramatically demonstrated in Stanley Milgram's research on obedience (Article 1.2). Milgram, using the pretense of a study on the effects of peer-delivered punishment on learning, asked his subjects to deliver electric shocks to their partners whenever the partners made a mistake. Increasingly strong electric shocks were requested by the experimenter as the partner continued to make errors, and Milgram hoped to use the ultimate shock level his subjects were willing to administer as a measure of their obedience to authority (in this case, a scientist in a white lab coat). The astonishing result, which Milgram had not anticipated, was that there were essentially no limits on his subjects' obedience: they continued to administer shocks even when their partners pounded on the wall and refused to answer any questions, and when the switch on the shock control panel was labeled "450 volts" and "Danger: Severe Shock." His subjects became extremely upset as the experiment continued, some laughing hysterically and pleading with the experimenter to let them stop, but almost all continued to administer shocks when ordered to do so by the experimenter.

It would be comforting to think that this willingness to obey authority was somehow anomalous, that people would not really obey authority in this way outside the laboratory; but, if anything, history suggests the opposite. The most recent evidence comes from the My Lai massacre in South Vietnam, in which American soldiers killed hundreds of defenseless women and children. Perhaps the most surprising aspect of this tragedy was not the killing itself but the public reaction. According to polls, almost 75 percent of the public believed that there should be no punishment of the soldiers involved *if they acted under orders*. Social control of our behavior is perhaps not as unacceptable to us, nor as unlikely, as we sometimes think.

Milgram's research supports Skinner's contention that society already controls our behavior, but it also raises in practical form some moral issues that Skinner tends to gloss over. Behavioral controls may be inevitable, but who is to exercise these controls, and to what ends? In the case of Milgram's research, his goal was to find a measure of obedience, leading ultimately to a better understanding of what causes obedience and how society might *reduce* blind obedience to authority; but to attain this goal he deceived his subjects, subjected them to enormous pressures, and risked lasting damage to their personalities when they were forced to confront their willingness to hurt others in what was essentially a frivolous context. Did the potential importance of the research justify the deception and pain of the subjects? Who should decide? Skinner suggests that questions such as these can be simply resolved in designing a new culture: "Let's agree to start with, that health is better than illness, wisdom better than ignorance, love better than hate, and productive energy better than neurotic sloth." The problems raised by Milgram's relatively simple situation, however, suggest that the moral issues may not always be so clear, that definitions of "productive energy" and "neurotic sloth," to take one example, may well become crucial decisions as our techniques of control become increasingly effective.

The Scientific Method

Whether or not you completely accept Skinner's argument, it is clear that much of our behavior is learned, and that a better understanding of principles of learning might be useful in areas as diverse as toilet training children and teaching physics to undergraduates. How, then, can we determine these basic principles of learning?

Historically, the dominant method of study has been introspection, or the observation by a subject of his own thoughts and behavior. The appeal of introspection derives from its apparent simplicity and accessibility to all: no elaborate equipment is required, nor extensive training. Furthermore, its findings seem inherently correct: we tend to have great faith in our own perceptions, and indeed to rely on them as the ultimate test of reality. With Freud's discovery of unconscious motivation, however, confidence in the accuracy of introspective reports began to erode. Freud exposed for the first time the Byzantine world of the unconscious, its primitive swirl of emotions hidden from consciousness behind powerful barriers. The possible existence of such concealed forces challenged the foundation of the introspective technique: its faith in the accessibility of all thought to conscious analysis. Unless every aspect of human thought processes could be traced and analyzed, introspection alone could never adequately explain behavior.

Perhaps even more serious than such theoretical challenges to the limits of conscious analysis was the utter inability of different introspectionists to agree with each other. If one observer says a card is green and the second says it is yellow, it can be very difficult for them to resolve their disagreement, and this was precisely the situation that arose as the introspectionists probed their conscious minds. In the classic controversy over "imageless thought," for example, there were angry debates as to whether or not thinking necessarily involved images, and each side was utterly convinced of the accuracy of its perceptions. If each observer can examine only his own mind, and if their reports differ, there is little hope of reaching agreement on the basic processes of thought.

As psychologists lost faith in the ability of introspection to unravel the complexities of the mind, they turned instead to the experimental analysis of overt behavior. In experimentation, reliance is placed not on subjective analysis but on *objective* reports, observations that can be agreed on by all observers. This necessarily restricts the scope of experimentation—the contents of the mind cannot be directly studied by objective observation—but the possibility of reaching clear and unambiguous conclusions made this sacrifice seem worthwhile to a community of psychologists frustrated by seemingly endless argument.

The logic of experimentation is basically simple: to determine if two events are related, we systematically change one and observe its effects on the other. In the case of lung cancer, for example, we might observe that cancer victims tend to be heavy smokers, and we might infer that smoking causes cancer. Simple observation of a correlation, however, does not prove a causal relationship: perhaps both smoking and cancer are caused by a third factor such as tension. To resolve this issue we can run an experiment, perhaps exposing an experimental group of dogs to cigarette smoke but sparing a control group. If the only difference between the two groups is exposure to cigarette smoke (both groups presumably contain tense dogs), then the appearance of lung cancer in the experimental group would indeed suggest a causal relationship. In a typical experiment, then, one aspect of the environment is manipulated (the independent variable) to see its effects on a particular behavior (the dependent variable). A causal relationship between the independent and dependent variables is called a law.

If experimentation were really so easy, it should be a simple matter to uncover the laws of behavior. All we would have to do is manipulate our independent variables, observe their effects, and combine the resultant laws into a comprehensive account of behavior. The problem, and it is a problem which will be implicit in every experiment in this book, is that we must manipulate *only one independent variable at a time*. In the cancer experiment, for example, if the experimental group had been exposed not only to cigarette smoke but to an accidental dose of radiation, it would obviously be impossible to interpret the results of the experiment. *Some* difference between the experimental and control groups was presumably responsible for the development of cancer, but we can't say whether it was the presence of the smoke or the radiation that was crucial.

It might seem a simple task to design an experiment so that only one independent variable is manipulated, but in fact it is difficult if not impossible. Even when we know the important independent variables it is sometimes difficult to disentangle them. In studying the effects of learning on infant motor coordination, for example, it is impossible to give the infant experience without also allowing the passage of time and thus the possibility that neural maturation rather than learning was responsible for any improvement. In cases such as this where we cannot directly hold constant or control an unwanted variable, we can evaluate its effects indirectly by using a control group. If both experimental and control subjects receive the extraneous variable, then any *difference* between them can no longer be attributed to that variable. If two groups are allowed normal neural development, for example, but only the experimental group is given an opportunity to learn (the control subjects might be given tranquilizers), then any superiority of the experimental group cannot be due to maturation but only to the effects of experience (see Carmichael, 1927). Thus even where a variable cannot be physically eliminated, its effects may still be neutralized through the use of a control group.

Difficult as the problem of separating independent variables may be, it is compounded when we do not even know the relevant variables. Thus if we did not know that neural maturation can affect muscular coordination, we might never realize the need to control for it. The failure to recognize relevant variables has been a recurrent problem in psychological research, one of the classic examples being the case of Clever Hans. Hans was a horse, but a very clever horse indeed. He astonished observers by his ability to add: asked the sum of two plus two, for example, he would paw the ground four times and then stop. Addition, moreover, was only one of his skills, as he was equally proficient at subtraction and, incredibly, multiplication and division. An obvious explanation for his prowess was some sort of signal from his master, but when a blue-ribbon panel of experts was convened to investigate his astonishing abilities, they found that removal of the owner had no effect on Hans' performance. The explanation, discovered after a brilliant series of experiments by the psychologist Oskar Pfungst, turned out to be a variable that no one had thought could possibly be important, and so no one had controlled. The solution, and its practical implications for psychological research, are discussed in Robert Rosenthal's article on "Clever Hans" (Article 1.3).

The Use of Animals

Having decided to study human learning, and to do so by careful experimentation, a final question concerns what species to use as subjects. The answer, of course, is obvious: to understand human behavior you study human subjects. Why, then, given the simplicity of this logic, have some psychologists persisted so stubbornly in studying animals? The reasons are complex, and vary somewhat from psychologist to psychologist, but basically they concern the ease of doing research. We have seen in the previous section that one of the crucial problems in psychological research is manipulating only one independent variable at a time, and this often turns out to be easier when animals are used as subjects. In studying the effects of past experience, for example, it is much simpler to control the past history of a group of rats than of undergraduates, and it may also be easier to control features of the current environment such as hunger or sex drive. In addition, in experiments involving potential pain or injury to the subject, most psychologists believe that it is better to hurt a rat than a human, and thus experiments on punishment or aggression are much more likely to involve animals as subjects.

It may be easier to run experiments with animals as subjects, but is there any reason to think the results of experiments on a rat or even a chimp will have any relevance for human behavior? Before 1858 the answer would have been an emphatic no, but Darwin's theory of evolution suggested for perhaps the first time in Western history that man was not unique, that he was only one animal species among many, subjected to the same environmental forces and evolved from the same common ancestor. Biologically the idea had a certain plausibility, as similarities in such mammalian systems as reproduction and circulation were already known. Behaviorally, on the other hand, the idea of fundamental similarities seemed more farfetched: even if man had once been a simple ape he had long since begun a unique evolutionary path which left him the only animal capable of using tools, of transmitting culture, and, most important of all, capable of symbolic communication. In the years since Darwin, however, evidence has gradually accumulated that man is not unique even in these areas. Jane van Lawick-Goodall, for example, obtained photographic evidence of a chimp preparing and then inserting a stick into a termite's nest in order to lick off those termites foolish enough to adhere to it as he pulled it out, and strikingly similar uses of a twig have been reported in the lowly Galapagos finch. As these and other instances of tool use and even culture were reported, it became increasingly clear that man was not unique in these capacities, although he remained alone in being the only animal with a sophisticated language, with the intellectual capacities this implied.

Perhaps the final step in this evolution of man's self-image may have begun with the publication in 1969 of an article in *Science* magazine by Allen and Beatrice Gardner. The Gardners were determined to teach a chimp English, and they began their research with a young female they named Washoe. Although other researchers had tried and failed to teach chimps to talk, the Gardners felt the problem might be less the general intellectual capacities of chimps than their poor control over their vocal cords. Instead of spoken English, therefore, the Gardners set out to teach Washoe the American Sign Language for the deaf. The exciting and provocative results of their early efforts are reported in "Teaching Sign Language to a Chimpanzee" (Article 1.4).

Even if animal learning is substantially simpler than human learning, the practical advantages of animal research might still make it worthwhile. Precisely because of the simpler processes involved, the basic laws of learning might be easier to isolate in animal subjects, and the interaction of these laws could then be further elaborated with human subjects. The Gardner's research, however, suggests that we may have underestimated the simplicity of animal learning and thus overestimated the gap between animal and human learning processes. A chimp's grasp of a twig or even sign language does not resolve this issue, but it perhaps makes more plausible the unlikely behavior of those psychologists who persist in studying human learning with animal subjects. The ultimate test of the usefulness of animals as subjects, of course, must be whether or not the principles derived from animals can be successfully applied to humans, and hopefully the readings in this book will give you some basis for reaching your own conclusions.

1.1 FREEDOM AND THE CONTROL OF MAN*
B. F. Skinner

The second half of the twentieth century may be remembered for its solution of a curious problem. Although Western democracy created the conditions responsible for the rise of modern science, it is now evident that it may never fully profit from that achievement. The so-called "democratic philosophy" of human behavior to which it also gave rise is increasingly in conflict with the application of the methods of science to human affairs. Unless this conflict is somehow resolved, the ultimate goals of democracy may be long deferred.

I

Just as biographers and critics look for external influences to account for the traits and achievements of the men they study, so science ultimately explains behavior in terms of "causes" or conditions which lie beyond the individual himself. As more and more causal relations are demonstrated, a practical corollary becomes difficult to resist: it should be possible to *produce* behavior according to plan simply by arranging the proper conditions. Now, among the specifications which might reasonably be submitted to a behavioral technology are these: Let men be happy, informed, skillful, well behaved, and productive.

This immediate practical implication of a science of behavior has a familiar ring, for it recalls the doctrine of human perfectibility of eighteenth- and nineteenth-century humanism. A science of man shares the optimism of that philosophy and supplies striking support for the working faith that men can build a better world and, through it, better men. The support comes just in time, for there has been little optimism of late among those who speak from the traditional point of view. Democracy has become "realistic," and it is only with some embarrassment that one admits today to perfectionistic or utopian thinking.

The earlier temper is worth considering, however. History records many foolish and unworkable schemes for human betterment, but almost all the great changes in our culture which we now regard as worthwhile can be traced to perfectionistic philosophies. Governmental, religious, educational, economic, and social reforms follow a common pattern.

* Reprinted from *The American Scholar*, 1955, 25, 47–65. Copyright by B. F. Skinner, and reproduced with the author's permission.

Someone believes that a change in a cultural practice—for example, in the rules of evidence in a court of law, in the characterization of man's relation to God, in the way children are taught to read and write, in permitted rates of interest, or in minimal housing standards—will improve the condition of men: by promoting justice, permitting men to seek salvation more effectively, increasing the literacy of a people, checking an inflationary trend, or improving public health and family relations, respectively. The underlying hypothesis is always the same: that a different physical or cultural environment will make a different and better man.

The scientific study of behavior not only justifies the general pattern of such proposals; it promises new and better hypotheses. The earliest cultural practices must have originated in sheer accidents. Those which strengthened the group survived with the group in a sort of natural selection. As soon as men began to propose and carry out changes in practice for the sake of possible consequences, the evolutionary process must have accelerated. The simple practice of making changes must have had survival value. A further acceleration is now to be expected. As laws of behavior are more precisely stated, the changes in the environment required to bring about a given effect may be more clearly specified. Conditions which have been neglected because their effects were slight or unlooked for may be shown to be relevant. New conditions may actually be created, as in the discovery and synthesis of drugs which affect behavior.

This is no time, then, to abandon notions of progress, improvement or, indeed, human perfectibility. The simple fact is that man is able, and now as never before, to lift himself by his own bootstraps. In achieving control of the world of which he is a part, he may learn at last to control himself.

II

Timeworn objections to the planned improvement of cultural practices are already losing much of their force. Marcus Aurelius was probably right in advising his readers to be content with a haphazard amelioration of mankind. "Never hope to realize Plato's republic," he sighed, ". . . for who can change the opinions of men? And without a change of sentiments what can you make but reluctant slaves and hypocrites?" He was thinking, no doubt, of contemporary patterns of control based upon punishment or the threat of punishment which, as he correctly observed, breed only reluctant slaves of those who submit and hypocrites of those who discover modes of evasion. But we need not share his pessimism, for the opinions of men can be changed. The techniques of indoctrination which were being devised by the early Christian Church at the very time Marcus Aurelius was writing are relevant, as are some of the techniques of psychotherapy and of advertising and public relations. Other methods suggested by recent scientific analyses leave little doubt of the matter.

The study of human behavior also answers the cynical complaint that there is a plain "cussedness" in man which will always thwart efforts to improve him. We are often told that men do not want to be changed, even for the better. Try to help them, and they will outwit you and remain happily wretched. Dostoevsky claimed to see some plan in it. "Out of sheer ingratitude," he complained, or possibly boasted,

> "man will play you a dirty trick, just to prove that men are still men and not the keys of a piano. . . . And even if you could prove that a man is only a piano key, he would still do something out of sheer perversity— he would create destruction and chaos—just to gain his point. . . . And if all this could in turn be analyzed and prevented by predicting that it would occur, then man would deliberately go mad to prove his point."

This is a conceivable neurotic reaction to inept control. A few men may have shown it, and many have enjoyed Dostoevsky's statement because they tend to show it. But that such perversity is a fundamental reaction of the human organism to controlling conditions is sheer nonsense.

So is the objection that we have no way of knowing what changes to make even though we have the necessary techniques. That is one of the great hoaxes of the century—a sort of booby trap left behind in the retreat before the advancing front of science. Scientists themselves have unsuspectingly agreed that there are two kinds of useful propositions about nature—facts and value judgments—and that science must confine itself to "what is," leaving "what ought to be" to others. But with what special sort of wisdom is the non-scientist endowed? Science is only effective knowing, no matter who engages in it. Verbal behavior proves upon analysis to be composed of many different types of utterances, from poetry and exhortation to logic and factual description, but these are not all equally useful in talking about cultural practices. We may classify useful propositions according to the degrees of confidence with which they may be asserted. Sentences about nature range from highly probable "facts" to sheer guesses. In general, future events are less likely to be correctly described than past. When a scientist talks about a projected experiment, for example, he must often resort to statements having only a moderate likelihood of being correct; he calls them hypotheses.

Designing a new cultural pattern is in many ways like designing an experiment. In drawing up a new constitution, outlining a new educational program, modifying a religious doctrine, or setting up a new fiscal policy, many statements must be quite tentative. We cannot be sure that the practices we specify will have the consequences we predict, or that the consequences will reward our efforts. This is in the nature of such proposals. They are not value judgments—they are guesses. To confuse and delay the improvement of cultural practices by quibbling about the word *improve* is itself not a useful practice. Let us agree, to start with, that health is better than illness, wisdom better than ignorance, love better than hate, and productive energy better than neurotic sloth.

Another familiar objection is the "political problem." Though we know what changes to make and how to make them, we still need to control certain relevant conditions, but these have long since fallen into the hands of selfish men who are not going to relinquish them for such purposes. Possibly we shall be permitted to develop areas which at the moment seem unimportant, but at the first signs of success the strong men will move in. This, it is said, has happened to Christianity, democracy, and communism. There will always be men who are fundamentally selfish and evil, and in the long run innocent goodness cannot have its way. The only evidence here is historical, and it may be misleading. Because of the way in which physical science developed, history could until very recently have "proved" that the unleashing of the energy of the atom was quite unlikely, if not impossible. Similarly, because of the order in which processes in human behavior have become available for purposes of control, history may seem to prove that power will probably be appropriated for selfish purposes. The first techniques to be discovered fell almost always to strong, selfish men. History led Lord Acton to believe that power corrupts, but he had probably never encountered absolute power, certainly not in all its forms, and had no way of predicting its effect.

An optimistic historian could defend a different conclusion. The principle that if there are not enough men of good will in the world the first step is to create more seems to be gaining recognition. The Marshall Plan (as originally conceived), Point Four, the offer of atomic materials to power-starved countries—these may or may not be wholly new in the history of international relations, but they suggest an increasing awareness of the power of governmental good will. They are proposals to make certain changes in the environments of men for the sake of consequences which should be rewarding for all concerned. They do not exemplify a disinterested generosity, but an interest which is the interest of everyone. We have not yet seen Plato's philosopher-king, and may not want to, but the gap between real and utopian government is closing.

III

But we are not yet in the clear, for a new and unexpected obstacle has arisen. With a world of their own making almost within reach, men of good will have been seized with distaste for their achievement. They have uneasily rejected opportunities to apply the techniques and findings of science in the service of men, and as the import of effective cultural design has come to be understood, many of them have voiced an outright refusal to have any part in it. Science has been challenged before when it has encroached upon institutions already engaged in the control of human behavior; but what are we to make of benevolent men, with no special interests of their own to defend, who nevertheless turn against the very means of reaching long-dreamed-of goals?

What is being rejected, of course, is the scientific conception of man and his place in nature. So long as the findings and methods of science are applied to human affairs only in a sort of remedial patchwork, we may continue to hold any view of human nature we like. But as the use of science increases, we are forced to accept the theoretical structure with which science represents its facts. The difficulty is that this structure is clearly at odds with the traditional democratic conception of man. Every discovery of an event which has a part in shaping a man's behavior seems to leave so much the less to be credited to the man himself; and as such explanations become more and more comprehensive, the contribution which may be claimed by the individual himself appears to approach zero. Man's vaunted creative powers, his original accomplishments in art, science, and morals, his capacity to choose and our right to hold him responsible for the consequences of his choice—none of these is conspicuous in this new self-portrait. Man, we once believed, was free to express himself in art, music, and literature, to inquire into nature, to seek salvation in his own way. He could initiate action and make spontaneous and capricious changes of course. Under the most extreme duress some sort of choice remained to him. He could resist any effort to control him, though it might cost him his life. But science insists that action is initiated by forces impinging upon the individual, and that caprice is only another name for behavior for which we have not yet found a cause.

In attempting to reconcile these views it is important to note that the traditional democratic conception was not designed as a description in the scientific sense but as a philosophy to be used in setting up and maintaining a governmental process. It arose under historical circumstances and served political purposes apart from which it cannot be properly understood. In rallying men against tyranny it was necessary that the individual be strengthened, that he be taught that he had rights and could govern himself. To give the common man a new conception of his worth, his dignity, and his power to save himself, both here and hereafter, was often the only resource of the revolutionist. When democratic principles were put into practice, the same doctrines were used as a working formula. This is exemplified by the notion of personal responsibility in Anglo-American law. All governments make certain forms of punishment contingent upon certain kinds of acts. In democratic countries these contingencies are expressed by the notion of responsible choice. But the notion may have no meaning under governmental practices formulated in other ways and would certainly have no place in systems which did not use punishment.

The democratic philosophy of human nature is determined by certain political exigencies and techniques, not by the goals of democracy. But exigencies and techniques change; and a conception which is not supported for its accuracy as a likeness—is not, indeed, rooted in fact at all—may be expected to change too. No matter how effective we judge current democratic practices to be, how highly we value them or how long we expect them to survive, they are almost certainly not the *final* form of government. The philosophy of human nature which has been useful in implementing them is also almost certainly not the last word. The ultimate achievement of democracy may be long deferred unless we emphasize the real aims rather than the verbal devices of democratic thinking. A philosophy which has been appropriate to one set of political exigencies will defeat its purpose if, under other circumstances, it prevents us from applying to human affairs the science of man which probably nothing but democracy itself could have produced.

IV

Perhaps the most crucial part of our democratic philosophy to be reconsidered is our attitude toward freedom—or its reciprocal, the control of human behavior. We do not oppose all forms of control because it is "human nature" to do so. The reaction is not characteristic of all men under all conditions of life. It is an attitude which has been carefully engineered, in large part by what we call the "literature" of democracy. With respect to some methods of control (for example, the threat of force), very little engineering is needed, for the techniques or their immediate consequences are objectionable. Society has suppressed these methods by branding them "wrong," "illegal," or "sinful." But to encourage these attitudes toward objectionable forms of control, it has been necessary to disguise the real nature of certain indispensable techniques, the commonest examples of which are education, moral discourse, and persuasion. The actual procedures appear harmless enough. They consist of supplying information, presenting opportunities for action, pointing out logical relationships, appealing to reason or "enlightened understanding," and so on. Through a masterful piece of misrepresentation, the illusion is fostered that these procedures do not involve the control of behavior; at most, they are simply ways of "getting someone to change his mind." But analysis not only reveals the presence of well-defined behavioral processes, it demonstrates a kind of control no less inexorable, though in some ways more acceptable, than the bully's threat of force.

Let us suppose that someone in whom we are interested is acting unwisely—he is careless in the way he deals with his friends, he drives too fast, or he holds his golf club the wrong way. We could probably help him by issuing a series of commands: don't nag, don't drive over sixty, don't hold your club that way. Much less objectionable would be "an appeal to reason." We could show him how people are affected by his treatment of them, how accident rates rise sharply at higher speeds, how a particular grip on the club alters the way the ball is struck and corrects a slice. In doing so we resort to verbal mediating devices which emphasize and support certain "contingencies of reinforcement"—that is, certain relations between behavior and its consequences—which strengthen the behavior we wish to set up. The same consequences would possibly set up the behavior without our help, and they eventually take control no matter which form of help we give. The appeal to reason has certain advantages over the authoritative command. A threat of punishment, no matter how subtle, generates emotional reactions and tendencies to escape or revolt. Perhaps the controllee merely "feels resentment" at being made to act in a given way, but even that is to be avoided. When we "appeal to reason," he "feels freer to do as he pleases." The fact is that we have exerted *less* control than in using a threat; since other conditions may contribute to the result, the effect may be delayed or, possibly in a given instance, lacking. But if we have worked a change in his behavior at all, it is because we have altered relevant environmental conditions, and the processes we have set in motion are just as real and just as inexorable, if not as comprehensive, as in the most authoritative coercion.

"Arranging an opportunity for action" is another example of disguised control. The power of the negative form has already been exposed in the analysis of censorship. Restriction of opportunity is recognized as far from harmless. As Ralph Barton Perry said in an article which appeared in the Spring, 1953, *Pacific Spectator*, "Whoever determines what alternatives shall be made known to man controls what that man shall choose *from*. He is deprived of freedom in proportion as he is denied access to *any* ideas, or is confined to any range of ideas short of the totality of relevant possibilities." But there is a positive side as well. When we present a relevant state of affairs, we increase the likelihood that a given form of behavior will be emitted. To the extent that the probability of action has changed, we have made a definite contribution. The teacher of history controls a student's behavior (or, if the reader prefers, "deprives him of freedom") just as much in *presenting* historical facts as in suppressing them. Other conditions will no doubt affect the student, but the contribution made to his behavior by the presentation of material is fixed and, within its range, irresistible.

The methods of education, moral discourse, and persuasion are acceptable not because they recognize the freedom of the individual or his right to dissent, but because they make only *partial* contributions to the control of his behavior. The freedom they recognize is freedom from a more coercive form of control. The dissent which they tolerate is the possible effect of other determiners of action. Since these sanctioned methods are frequently ineffective, we have been able to convince ourselves that they do not represent control at all. When they show too much strength to permit disguise, we give them other names and suppress them as energetically as we suppress the use of force. Education grown too powerful is rejected as propaganda or "brain-washing," while really effective persuasion is decried as "undue influence," "demagoguery," "seduction," and so on.

If we are not to rely solely upon accident for the innovations which give rise to cultural evolution, we must accept the fact that some kind of control of human behavior is inevitable. We cannot use good sense in human affairs unless someone engages in the design and construction of environmental conditions which affect the behavior of men. Environmental changes have always been the condition for the improvement of cultural patterns, and we can hardly use the more effective methods of science without making changes on a grander scale. We are all controlled by the world in which we live, and part of that world has been and will be constructed by men. The question is this: Are we to be controlled by accident, by tyrants, or by ourselves in effective cultural design?

The danger of the misuse of power is possibly greater than ever. It is not allayed by disguising the facts. We cannot make wise decisions if we continue to pretend that human behavior is not controlled, or if we refuse to engage in control when valuable results might be forthcoming. Such measures weaken only ourselves, leaving the strength of science to others. The first step in a defense against tyranny is the fullest possible exposure of controlling techniques. A second step has already been taken successfully in restricting the use of physical force. Slowly, and as yet imperfectly, we have worked out an ethical and governmental design in which the strong man is not allowed to use the power deriving from his strength to control his fellow men. He is restrained by a superior force created for that purpose—the ethical pressure of the group, or more explicit religious and governmental measures. We tend to distrust superior forces, as we currently hesitate to relinquish sovereignty in order to set up an international police force. But it is only through such counter-control that we have achieved what we call peace—a condition in which men are not permitted to control each other through force. In other words, control itself must be controlled.

Science has turned up dangerous processes and materials before. To use the facts and techniques of a science of man to the fullest extent without making some monstrous mistake will be difficult and obviously perilous. It is no time for self-deception, emotional indulgence, or the assumption of attitudes which are no longer useful. Man is facing a difficult test. He must keep his head now, or he must start again—a long way back.

V

Those who reject the scientific conception of man must, to be logical, oppose the methods of science as well. The position is often supported by predicting a series of dire consequences which are to follow if science is not checked. A recent book by Joseph Wood Krutch, *The Measure of Man*, is in this vein. Mr. Krutch sees in the growing science of man the threat of an unexampled tyranny over men's minds. If science is permitted to have its way, he insists, "we may never be able really to think again." A controlled culture will, for example, lack some virtue inherent in disorder. We have emerged from chaos through a series of happy accidents, but in an engineered culture it will be "impossible for the unplanned to erupt again." But there is no virtue in the accidental character of an accident, and the diversity which arises from disorder can not only be duplicated by design but vastly extended. The experimental method is superior to simple observation just because it multiplies "accidents" in a systematic coverage of the possibilities. Technology offers many familiar examples. We no longer wait for immunity to disease to develop from a series of accidental exposures, nor do we wait for natural mutations in sheep and cotton to produce better fibers; but we continue to make use of such accidents when they occur, and we certainly do not prevent them. Many of the things we value have emerged from the clash of ignorant armies on darkling plains, but it is not therefore wise to encourage ignorance and darkness.

It is not always disorder itself which we are told we shall miss but certain admirable qualities in men which flourish only in the presence of disorder. A man rises above an unpropitious childhood to a position of eminence, and since we cannot give a plausible account of the action of so complex an environment, we attribute the achievement to some admirable faculty in the man himself. But such "faculties" are suspiciously like the explanatory fictions against which the history of science warns us. We admire Lincoln for rising above a deficient school system, but it was not necessarily something *in him* which permitted him to become an educated man in spite of it. His educational environment was certainly unplanned, but it could nevertheless have made a full contribution to his mature behavior. He was a rare man, but the circumstances of his childhood were rare too. We do not give Franklin Delano Roosevelt the same credit for becoming an educated man with the help of Groton and Harvard, although the same behavioral processes may have been involved. The founding of Groton and Harvard somewhat reduced the possibility that fortuitous combinations of circumstances would erupt to produce other Lincolns. Yet the founders can hardly be condemned for attacking an admirable human quality.

Another predicted consequence of a science of man is an excessive uniformity. We are told that effective control—whether governmental, religious, educational, economic, or social—will produce a race of men who differ from each other only through relatively refractory genetic differences. That would probably be bad design, but we must admit that we are not now pursuing another course from choice. In a modern school, for example, there is usually a syllabus which specifies what every student is to learn by the end of each year. This would be flagrant regimentation if anyone expected every student to comply. But some will be poor in particular subjects, others will not study, others will not remember what they have been taught, and diversity is assured. Suppose, however, that we someday possess such effective educational techniques that every student will in fact be put in possession of all the behavior specified in a syllabus. At the end of the year, all students will correctly answer all questions on the final examination and "must all have prizes." Should we reject such a system on the grounds that in making all students excellent it has made them all alike? Advocates of the theory of a special faculty might contend that an important advantage of the present system is that the good student learns in spite of a system which is so defective that it is currently producing bad students as well. But if really effective techniques are available, we cannot avoid the problem of design simply by preferring the status quo. At what point should education be deliberately inefficient?

Such predictions of the havoc to be wreaked by the application of science to human affairs are usually made with surprising confidence. They not only show a faith in the orderliness of human behavior; they presuppose an established body of knowledge with the help of which it can be positively asserted that the changes which scientists propose to make will have quite specific results—albeit not the results they foresee. But the predictions made by the critics of science must be held to be equally fallible and subject also to empirical test. We may be sure that many steps in the scientific design of cultural patterns will produce unforeseen consequences. But there is only one way to find out. And the test must be made, for if we cannot advance in the design of cultural patterns with absolute certainty, neither can we rest completely confident of the superiority of the status quo.

VI

Apart from their possibly objectionable consequences, scientific methods seem to make no provision for certain admirable qualities and faculties which seem to have flourished in less explicitly. planned cultures; hence they are called "degrading" or "lacking in dignity." (Mr. Krutch has called the author's *Walden Two* an "ignoble Utopia.") The conditioned reflex is the current whipping boy. Because conditioned reflexes may be demonstrated in animals, they are spoken of as though they were exclusively subhuman. It is implied, as we have seen, that no behavioral processes are involved in education and moral discourse or, at least, that the processes are exclusively human. But men do show conditioned reflexes (for example, when they are frightened by all instances of the control of human behavior because some instances engender fear), and animals do show processes similar to the human behavior involved in instruction and moral discourse. When Mr. Krutch asserts that " 'Conditioning' is achieved by methods which by-pass or, as it were, short-circuit those very reasoning faculties which education proposes to cultivate and exercise," he is making a technical statement which needs a definition of terms and a great deal of supporting evidence.

If such methods are called "ignoble" simply because they leave no room for certain admirable attributes, then perhaps the practice of admiration needs to be examined. We might say that the child whose education has been skillfully planned has been deprived of the right to intellectual heroism. Nothing has been left to be admired in the way he acquires an education. Similarly, we can conceive of moral training which is so adequate to the demands of the culture that men will be good practically automatically, but to that extent they will be deprived of the right to moral heroism, since we seldom admire automatic goodness. Yet if we consider the end of morals rather than certain virtuous means, is not "automatic goodness" a desirable state of affairs? Is it not, for example, the avowed goal of religious education? T. H. Huxley answered the question unambiguously: "If some great power would agree to make me always think what is true and do what is right, on condition of being a sort of clock and wound up every morning before I got out of bed, I should close instantly with the offer." Yet Mr. Krutch quotes this as the scarcely credible point of view of a "proto-modern" and seems himself to share T. S. Eliot's contempt for ". . . systems so perfect / That no one will need to be good."

"Having to be good" is an excellent example of an expendable honorific. It is inseparable from a particular form of ethical and moral control. We distinguish between the things we *have* to do to avoid punishment and those we *want* to do for rewarding consequences. In a culture which did not resort to punishment we should never "have" to do anything except with respect to the punishing contingencies which arise directly in the physical environment. And we are moving toward such a culture, because the neurotic, not to say psychotic, by-products of control through punishment have long since led compassionate men to seek alternative techniques. Recent research has explained some of the objectionable results of punishment and has revealed resources of at least equal power in "positive reinforcement." It is reasonable to look forward to a time when man will seldom "have" to do anything, although he may show interest, energy, imagination, and productivity far beyond the level seen under the present system (except for rare eruptions of the unplanned).

What we have to do we do with *effort*. We call it "work." There is no other way to distinguish between exhausting labor and the possibly equally energetic but rewarding activity of play. It is presumably good cultural design to replace the former with the latter. But an adjustment in attitudes is needed. We are much more practiced in admiring the heroic labor of a Hercules than the activity of one who works without having to. In a truly effective educational system the student might not "have to work" at all, but that possibility is likely to be received by the contemporary teacher with an emotion little short of rage.

We cannot reconcile traditional and scientific views by agreeing upon *what* is to be admired or condemned. The question is whether anything is to be so treated. Praise and blame are cultural practices which have been adjuncts of the prevailing system of control in Western democracy. All peoples do not engage in them for the same purposes or to the same extent, nor, of course, are the same behaviors always classified in the same way as subject to praise or blame. In admiring intellectual and moral heroism and unrewarding labor, and in rejecting a world in which these would be uncommon, we are simply demonstrating our own cultural conditioning. By promoting certain tendencies to admire and censure, the group of which we are a part has arranged for the social reinforcement and punishment needed to assure a high level of intellectual and moral industry. Under other and possibly better controlling systems, the behavior which we now admire would occur, but not under those conditions which make it admirable, and we should have no reason to admire it because the culture would have arranged for its maintenance in other ways.

To those who are stimulated by the glamorous heroism of the battlefield, a peaceful world may not be a better world. Others may reject a world without sorrow, longing, or a sense of guilt because the relevance of deeply moving works of art would be lost. To many who have devoted their lives to the struggle to be wise and good, a world without confusion and evil might be an empty thing. A nostalgic concern for the decline of moral heroism has been a dominating theme in the work of Aldous Huxley. In *Brave New World* he could see in the application of science to human affairs only a travesty on the notion of the Good (just as George Orwell, in *1984*, could foresee nothing but horror). In a recent issue of *Esquire*, Huxley has expressed the point this way: "We have had religious revolutions, we have had political, industrial, economic and nationalistic revolutions. All of them, as our descendants will discover, were but ripples in an ocean of conservatism—trivial by comparison with the psychological revolution toward which we are so rapidly moving. *That* will really be a revolution. When it is over, the human race will give no further trouble." (Footnote for the reader of the future: This was not meant as a happy ending. Up to *1956* men had been admired, if at all, for causing trouble or alleviating it. Therefore—)

It will be a long time before the world can dispense with heroes and hence with the cultural practice of admiring heroism, but we move in that direction whenever we act to prevent war, famine, pestilence, and disaster. It will be a long time before man will never need to submit to punishing environments or engage in exhausting labor, but we move in that direction whenever we make food, shelter, clothing, and labor-saving devices more readily available. We may mourn the passing of heroes but not the conditions which make for heroism. We can spare the self-made saint or sage as we spare the laundress on the river's bank struggling against fearful odds to achieve cleanliness.

VII

The two great dangers in modern democratic thinking are illustrated in a paper by former Secretary of State Dean Acheson. "For a long time now," writes Mr. Acheson,

> "we have gone along with some well-tested principles of conduct: That it was better to tell the truth than falsehoods; . . . that duties were older than and as fundamental as rights; that, as Justice Holmes put it, the mode by which the inevitable came to pass was effort; that to perpetrate a harm was wrong no matter how many joined in it . . . and so on. . . . Our institutions are founded on the assumption that most people follow these principles most of the time because they want to, and the institutions work pretty well when this assumption is true. More recently, however, bright people have been fooling with the machinery in the human head and they have discovered quite a lot. . . . Hitler introduced new refinements [as the result of which] a whole people have been utterly confused and corrupted. Unhappily neither the possession of this knowledge nor the desire to use it was confined to Hitler. . . . Others dip from this same devil's cauldron."

The first dangerous notion in this passage is that most people follow democratic principles of conduct "because they want to." This does not account for democracy or any other form of government if we have not explained why people *want* to behave in given ways. Although it is tempting to assume that it is human nature to believe in democratic principles, we must not overlook the "cultural engineering" which produced and continues to maintain democratic practices. If we neglect the conditions which produce democratic *behavior*, it is useless to try to maintain a democratic *form* of government. And we cannot expect to export a democratic form of government successfully if we do not also provide for the cultural practices which will sustain it. Our forebears did not discover the essential nature of man; they evolved a pattern of behavior which worked remarkably well under the circumstances. The "set of principles" expressed in that pattern is not the only true set or necessarily the best. Mr. Acheson has presumably listed the most unassailable items; some of them are probably beyond question, but others— concerning duty and effort—may need revision as the world changes.

The second—and greater—threat to the democracy which Mr. Acheson is defending is his assumption that knowledge is necessarily on the side of evil. All the admirable things he mentions are attributed to the innate goodness of man, all the detestable to "fooling with the machinery in the human head." This is reminiscent of the position, taken by other institutions engaged in the control of men, that certain forms of knowledge are in themselves evil. But how out of place in a democratic philosophy! Have we come this far only to conclude that well-intentioned people cannot study the behavior of men without becoming tyrants or that informed men cannot show good will? Let us for once have strength and good will on the same side.

VIII

Far from being a threat to the tradition of Western democracy, the growth of a science of man is a consistent and probably inevitable part of it. In turning to the external conditions which shape and maintain the behavior of men, while questioning the reality of inner qualities and faculties to which human achievements were once attributed, we turn from the ill-defined and remote to the observable and manipulable. Though it is a painful step, it has far-reaching consequences, for it not only sets higher standards of human welfare but shows us how to meet them. A change in a theory of human nature cannot change the facts. The achievements of man in science, art, literature, music, and morals will survive any interpretation we place upon them. The uniqueness of the individual is unchallenged in the scientific view. Man, in short, will remain man. (There will be much to admire for those who are so inclined. Possibly the noblest achievement to which man can aspire, even according to present standards, is to accept himself for what he is, as that is revealed to him by the methods which he devised and tested on a part of the world in which he had only a small personal stake.)

If Western democracy does not lose sight of the aims of humanitarian action, it will welcome the almost fabulous support of its own science of man and will strengthen itself and play an important role in building a better world for everyone. But if it cannot put its "democratic philosophy" into proper historical perspective—if, under the control of attitudes and emotions which it generated for other purposes, it now rejects the help of science—then it must be prepared for defeat. For if we continue to insist that science has nothing to offer but a new and more horrible form of tyranny, we may produce just such a result by allowing the strength of science to fall into the hands of despots. And if, with luck, it were to fall instead to men of good will in other political communities, it would be perhaps a more ignominious defeat; for we should then, through a miscarriage of democratic principles, be forced to leave to others the next step in man's long struggle to control nature and himself.

1.2 BEHAVIORAL STUDY OF OBEDIENCE*
Stanley Milgram

Obedience is as basic an element in the structure of social life as one can point to. Some system of authority is a requirement of all communal living, and it is only the man dwelling in isolation who is not forced to respond, through defiance or submission, to the commands of others. Obedience, as a determinant of behavior, is of particular relevance to our time. It has been reliably established that from 1933–45 millions of innocent persons were systematically slaughtered on command. Gas

* Stanley Milgram, "Behavioral Study of Obedience," *The Journal of Abnormal and Social Psychology*, 1963, 67, 371–378. Copyright 1963 by the American Psychological Association, and reproduced by permission. This research was supported by a grant (NSF G-17916) from the National Science Foundation. Exploratory studies conducted in 1960 were supported by a grant from the Higgins Fund at Yale University. The research assistance of Alan C. Elms and Jon Wayland is gratefully acknowledged.

chambers were built, death camps were guarded, daily quotas of corpses were produced with the same efficiency as the manufacture of appliances. These inhumane policies may have originated in the mind of a single person, but they could only be carried out on a massive scale if a very large number of persons obeyed orders.

Obedience is the psychological mechanism that links individual action to political purpose. It is the dispositional cement that binds men to systems of authority. Facts of recent history and observation in daily life suggest that for many persons obedience may be a deeply ingrained behavior tendency, indeed, a prepotent impulse overriding training in ethics, sympathy, and moral conduct. C. P. Snow (1961) points to its importance when he writes:

> When you think of the long and gloomy history of man, you will find more hideous crimes have been committed in the name of obedience than have ever been committed in the name of rebellion. If you doubt that, read William Shirer's *Rise and Fall of the Third Reich*. The German Officer Corps were brought up in the most rigorous code of obedience . . . in the name of obedience they were party to, and assisted in, the most wicked large-scale action in the history of the world [p. 24].

While the particular form of obedience dealt with in the present study has its antecedents in these episodes, it must not be thought all obedience entails acts of aggression against others. Obedience serves numerous productive functions. Indeed, the very life of society is predicated on its existence. Obedience may be ennobling and educative and refer to acts of charity and kindness, as well as to destruction.

GENERAL PROCEDURE

A procedure was devised which seems useful as a tool for studying obedience (Milgram, 1961). It consists of ordering a naive subject to administer electric shock to a victim. A simulated shock generator is used, with 30 clearly marked voltage levels that range from 15 to 450 volts. The instrument bears verbal designations that range from Slight Shock to Danger: Severe Shock. The responses of the victim, who is a trained confederate of the experimenter, are standardized. The orders to administer shocks are given to the naive subject in the context of a "learning experiment" ostensibly set up to study the effects of punishment on memory. As the experiment proceeds the naive subject is commanded to administer increasingly more intense shocks to the victim, even to the point of reaching the level marked Danger: Severe Shock. Internal resistances become stronger, and at a certain point the subject refuses to go on with the experiment. Behavior prior to this rupture is considered "obedience," in that the subject complies with the commands of the experimenter. The point of rupture is the act of disobedience. A quantitative value is assigned to the subject's performance based on the maximum intensity shock he is willing to administer before he refuses to participate further. Thus for any particular subject and for any particular experimental condition the degree of obedience may be specified with a numerical value. The crux of the study is to systematically vary the factors believed to alter the degree of obedience to the experimental commands.

The technique allows important variables to be manipulated at several points in the experiment. One may vary aspects of the source of command, content and form of command, instrumentalities for its execution, target object, general social setting, etc. The problem, therefore, is not one of designing increasingly more numerous experimental conditions, but of selecting those that best illuminate the *process* of obedience from the socio-psychological standpoint.

RELATED STUDIES

The inquiry bears an important relation to philosophic analyses of obedience and authority (Arendt, 1958; Friedrich, 1958; Weber, 1947), an early experimental study of obedience by Frank (1944), studies in "authoritarianism" (Adorno, Frenkel-Brunswik, Levinson, and Sanford, 1950; Rokeach, 1961), and a recent series of analytical and empirical studies in social power (Cartwright, 1959). It owes much to the long concern with *suggestion* in social psychology, both in its normal forms (e.g., Binet, 1900) and in its clinical manifestations (Charcot, 1881). But it derives, in the first instance, from direct observation of a social fact; the individual who is commanded by a legitimate authority ordinarily obeys. Obedience comes easily and often. It is a ubiquitous and indispensable feature of social life.

METHOD

Subjects

The subjects were 40 males between the ages of 20 and 50, drawn from New Haven and the surrounding communities. Subjects were obtained by a newspaper advertisement and direct mail solicitation. Those who responded to the appeal believed they were to participate in a study of memory and learning at Yale University. A wide range of occupations is represented in the sample. Typical subjects were postal clerks, high school teachers, salesmen, engineers, and laborers. Subjects ranged in educational level from one who had not finished elementary school, to those who had doctorate and other professional degrees. They were paid $4.50 for their participation in the experiment. However, subjects were told that payment was simply for coming to the laboratory, and that the money was theirs no matter what happened after they arrived. Table 1.2–1

TABLE 1.2–1   Distribution of Age and Occupational Types in the Experiment

Occupations	20–29 Years N	30–39 Years N	40–50 Years N	Percentage of Total (Occupations)
Workers, skilled and unskilled	4	5	6	37.5
Sales, business, and white-collar	3	6	7	40.0
Professional	1	5	3	22.5
Percentage of total (age)	20	40	40	

Note.—Total $N = 40$.

shows the proportion of age and occupational types assigned to the experimental condition.

Personnel and Locale

The experiment was conducted on the grounds of Yale University in the elegant interaction laboratory. (This detail is relevant to the perceived legitimacy of the experiment. In further variations, the experiment was dissociated from the university, with consequences for performance.) The role of experimenter was played by a 31-year-old high school teacher of biology. His manner was impassive, and his appearance somewhat stern throughout the experiment. He was dressed in a gray technician's coat. The victim was played by a 47-year-old accountant, trained for the role; he was of Irish-American stock, whom most observers found mild-mannered and likeable.

Procedure

One naive subject and one victim (an accomplice) performed in each experiment. A pretext had to be devised that would justify the administration of electric shock by the naive subject. This was effectively accomplished by the cover story. After a general introduction on the presumed relation between punishment and learning, subjects were told:

> But actually, we know *very little* about the effect of punishment on learning, because almost no truly scientific studies have been made of it in human beings.
>
> For instance, we don't know how *much* punishment is best for learning—and we don't know how much difference it makes as to who is giving the punishment, whether an adult learns best from a younger or an older person than himself—or many things of that sort.

So in this study we are bringing together a number of adults of different occupations and ages. And we're asking some of them to be teachers and some of them to be learners.

We want to find out just what effect different people have on each other as teachers and learners, and also what effect *punishment* will have on learning in this situation.

Therefore, I'm going to ask one of you to be the teacher here tonight and the other one to be the learner.

Does either of you have a preference?

Subjects then drew slips of paper from a hat to determine who would be the teacher and who would be the learner in the experiment. The drawing was rigged so that the naive subject was always the teacher and the accomplice always the learner. (Both slips contained the word "Teacher.") Immediately after the drawing, the teacher and learner were taken to an adjacent room and the learner was strapped into an "electric chair" apparatus.

The experimenter explained that the straps were to prevent excessive movement while the learner was being shocked. The effect was to make it impossible for him to escape from the situation. An electrode was attached to the learner's wrist, and electrode paste was applied "to avoid blisters and burns." Subjects were told that the electrode was attached to the shock generator in the adjoining room.

In order to improve credibility the experimenter declared, in response to a question by the learner: "Although the shocks can be extremely painful, they cause no permanent tissue damage."

Learning Task. The lesson administered by the subject was a paired-associate learning task. The subject read a series of word pairs to the learner, and then read the first word of the pair along with four terms. The learner was to indicate which of the four terms had originally been paired with the first word. He communicated his answer by pressing one of four switches in front of him, which in turn lit up one of four numbered quadrants in an answer-box located atop the shock generator.

Shock Generator. The instrument panel consists of 30 lever switches set in a horizontal line. Each switch is clearly labeled with a voltage designation that ranges from 15 to 450 volts. There is a 15-volt increment from one switch to the next going from the left to right. In addition, the following verbal designations are clearly indicated for groups of four switches going from left to right: Slight Shock, Moderate Shock, Strong Shock, Very Strong Shock, Intense Shock, Extreme Intensity Shock, Danger: Severe Shock. (Two switches after this last designation are simply marked XXX.)

Upon depressing a switch: a pilot light corresponding to each switch is illuminated in bright red; an electric buzzing is heard; an electric blue light, labeled "voltage energizer," flashes; the dial on the voltage meter swings to the right; various relay clicks are sounded.

The upper left-hand corner of the generator is labeled Shock Generator, Type ZLB, Dyson Instrument Company, Waltham, Mass. Output 15 Volts—450 Volts.

Details of the instrument were carefully handled to insure an appearance of authenticity. The panel was engraved by precision industrial engravers, and all components were of high quality. No subject in the experiment suspected that the instrument was merely a simulated shock generator.[1]

Sample Shock. Each naive subject is given a sample shock on the shock generator, prior to beginning his run as teacher. This shock is always 45 volts, and is applied by pressing the third switch of the generator. The shock is applied to the wrist of the naive subject, and has its source in a 45-volt battery wired into the generator. This further convinces the subject of the authenticity of the generator.

Shock Instructions. The subject is told to administer a shock to the learner each time he gives a wrong response. Moreover—and this is the key command—the subject is instructed to "move one level higher on the shock generator each time the learner flashes a wrong answer." He is also instructed to announce the voltage level before administering a shock. This serves to continually remind subjects of the increasing intensity of shocks administered to the learner.

Preliminary and Regular Run. Pretests revealed that the procedure of reading words and administering shocks requires some practice before it can be handled smoothly. Therefore, immediately preceding the regular run, the teacher is given a preliminary series of 10 words to read to the learner. There are 3 neutral words in the practice series (i.e., words that the learner answers correctly), so that shocks are administered for 7 of the words, with the maximum shock at 105 volts (moderate shock). Almost all subjects master the procedure by the time the preliminary run is over.

Subjects are then presented with a second list, and are told that the procedure is the same as for the first list; the experimenter adds, however:

When you get to the bottom of the list, repeat it over again, and continue giving shocks, until the learner has learned all the pairs correctly.

The experimenter instructs the subject to,

start from 15 volts and increase the shock level one step each time the learner gives a wrong answer.

Feedback from the Victim. In all conditions the learner gives a pre-determined set of responses to the word pair test, based on a schedule of approximately three wrong answers to one correct answer. In the present experimental condition no vocal response or other sign of protest is heard from the learner until Shock Level 300 is reached. When the 300-volt shock is administered, the learner pounds on the wall of the room in which he is bound to the electric chair. The pounding can be heard by the subject. From this point on, the learner's answers no longer appear on the four-way panel.

At this juncture, subjects ordinarily turn to the experimenter for guidance. The experimenter instructs the subject to treat the absence of a response as a wrong answer, and to shock the subject according to the usual schedule. He advises the subjects to allow 5–10 seconds before considering no response as a wrong answer, and to increase the shock level one step each time the learner fails to respond correctly. The learner's pounding is repeated after the 315-volt shock is administered; afterwards he is not heard from, nor do his answers reappear on the four-way signal box.

Experimenter Feedback. At various points in the experiment the subject may turn to the experimenter for advice on whether he should continue to administer shocks. Or he may indicate that he does not wish to go on. It was important to standardize the experimenter's responses to these inquiries and reactions.

If the subject indicated his unwillingness to go on. the experimenter responded with a sequence of "prods," using as many as necessary to bring the subject into line.

Prod 1: Please continue, *or* Please go on.
Prod 2: The experiment requires that you continue.
Prod 3: It is absolutely essential that you continue.
Prod 4: You have no other choice, you *must* go on.

The prods were always made in sequence: Only if Prod 1 had been unsuccessful, could Prod 2 be used. If the subject refused to obey the experimenter after Prod 4, the experiment was terminated. The experimenter's tone of voice was at all times firm, but not impolite. The sequence was begun anew on each occasion that the subject balked or showed reluctance to follow orders.

Special Prods. If the subject asked if the learner was liable to suffer permanent physical injury, the experimenter said:

Although the shocks may be painful, there is no permanent tissue damage, so please go on. [Followed by Prods 2, 3, and 4 if necessary.]

If the subject said that the learner did not want to go on, the experimenter replied:

Whether the learner likes it or not, you must go on until he has learned all the word pairs correctly. So please go on. [Followed by Prods 2, 3, and 4 if necessary.]

Dependent Measures

The primary dependent measure for any subject is the maximum shock he administers before he refuses to go any further. In principle this may vary from 0 (for a subject who refuses to administer even the first shock) to 30 (for a subject who administers the highest shock on the generator). A subject who breaks off the experiment at any point prior to administering the thirtieth shock level is termed a *defiant* subject. One who complies with experimental commands fully, and proceeds to administer all shock levels commanded, is termed an *obedient* subject.

Further Records. With few exceptions, experimental sessions were recorded on magnetic tape. Occasional photographs were taken through one-way mirrors. Notes were kept on any unusual behavior occurring during the course of the experiments. On occasion, additional observers were directed to write objective descriptions of the subjects' behavior. The latency and duration of shocks were measured by accurate timing devices.

Interview and Dehoax. Following the experiment, subjects were interviewed; open-ended questions, projective measures, and attitude scales were employed. After the interview, procedures were undertaken to assure that the subject would leave the laboratory in a state of well being. A friendly reconciliation was arranged between the subject and the victim, and an effort was made to reduce any tensions that arose as a result of the experiment.

RESULTS

Preliminary Notions

Before giving an account of the experimental results, it is instructive to consider how persons predict others will perform when commanded to administer powerful shocks to another person. Fourteen Yale seniors, all psychology majors, were provided with a detailed description of the experimental situation. They were asked to reflect carefully on it, and to predict the behavior of 100 hypothetical subjects. More specifically, they were instructed to plot the distribution of obedience of "100 Americans of diverse occupations, and ranging in age from 20 to 50 years," who were placed in the experimental situation.

There was considerable agreement among the respondents on the expected behavior of hypothetical subjects. All respondents predicted that only an insignificant minority would go through to the end of the shock series. (The estimates ranged from 0 to 3 per cent; i.e., the most "pessimistic" member of the class predicted that of 100 persons, 3 would continue through to the most potent shock available on the shock generator—450 volts.) The class mean was 1.2 per cent. The question was also posed informally to colleagues of the author, and the most general feeling was that few if any subjects would go beyond the designation Very Strong Shock.

Result of Experiment I

Subjects Accept Situation. With few exceptions subjects were convinced of the reality of the experimental situation, that they were administering shocks to another person, and the most potent shocks were extremely painful. In the post-experimental interview subjects were asked: "How painful to the learner were the last few shocks that you administered to him?" Subjects were instructed to indicate their answers on a printed 14-point scale ranging from "Not at all painful" to "Extremely painful." The modal response was 14 (Extremely painful) with the mean at 13.42.

Signs of Extreme Tension. Many subjects showed signs of nervousness in the experimental situation, and especially upon administering the more powerful shocks. In a large number of cases the degree of tension reached extremes that are rarely seen in sociopsychological laboratory studies. Subjects were observed to sweat, tremble, stutter, bite their lips, groan, and dig their fingernails into their flesh. These were characteristic rather than exceptional responses to the experiment.

One sign of tension was the regular occurrence of nervous laughing fits. Fourteen of the 40 subjects showed definite signs of nervous laughter and smiling. The laughter seemed entirely out of place, even bizarre. Full-blown, uncontrollable seizures were observed for 3 subjects. On one occasion we observed a seizure so violently convulsive that it was necessary to call a halt to the experiment. The subject, a 46-year-old encyclopedia salesman, was seriously embarrassed by his untoward and uncontrollable behavior. In the post-experimental interviews subjects took pains to point out that they were not sadistic types, and that the laughter did not mean they enjoyed shocking the victim.

Distribution of Scores. It had been conjectured that persons would not, in general, agree to administer shocks beyond the level designated as Very Strong Shock. The distribution of maximum shocks for this experiment is shown in Table 1.2–2. The obtained distribution of scores deviates radically from the prediction.

Upon command of the experimenter, each of the 40 subjects went

TABLE 1.2–1 Distribution of Breakoff Points

Verbal Designation and Voltage Indication	Number of Subjects for Whom This Was Maximum Shock
Slight Shock	
15	0
30	0
45	0
60	0
Moderate Shock	
75	0
90	0
105	0
120	0
Strong Shock	
135	0
150	0
165	0
180	0
Very Strong Shock	
195	0
210	0
225	0
240	0
Intense Shock	
255	0
270	0
285	0
300	5
Extreme Intensity Shock	
315	4
330	2
345	1
360	1
Danger: Severe Shock	
375	1
390	0
405	0
420	0
XXX	
435	0
450	26

beyond the expected breakoff point. No subject stopped prior to administering Shock Level 20. (At this level—300 volts—the victim kicks on the wall and no longer provides answers to the teacher's multiple-choice questions.)

Of the 40 subjects, 5 refused to obey the experimental commands beyond the 300-volt level. Four more subjects administered one further shock, and then refused to go on. Two broke off at the 330-volt level, and 1 each at 345, 360, and 375 volts. Thus a total of 14 subjects defied the experimenter. It is instructive to reprint their remarks at the point of defiance, as transcribed from the tape recording:

[0124] I think he's trying to communicate, he's knocking. . . . Well it's not fair to shock the guy . . . these are terrific volts. I don't think this is very humane. . . . Oh, I can't go on with this; no, this isn't right. It's a hell of an experiment. The guy is suffering in there. No, I don't want to go on. This is crazy. [Subject refused to administer more shocks.]

[0123] He's banging in there, I'm gonna chicken out. I'd like to continue, but I can't do that to a man. . . . I'm sorry I can't do that to a man. I'd hurt his heart. You take your check . . . No really, I couldn't do it.

These subjects were frequently in a highly agitated and even angered state. Sometimes, verbal protest was at a minimum and the subject simply got up from his chair in front of the shock generator and indicated that he wished to leave the laboratory.

Of the 40 subjects, 26 obeyed the orders of the experimenter to the end, proceeding to punish the victim until they reached the most potent shock available on the shock generator. At that point, the experimenter called a halt to the session. (The maximum shock is labeled 450 volts, and is two steps beyond the designation: Danger: Severe Shock.) Although obedient subjects continued to administer shocks, they often did so under extreme stress. Some expressed reluctance to administer shocks beyond the 300-volt level, and displayed fears similar to those who defied the experimenter; yet they obeyed.

After the maximum shocks had been delivered, and the experimenter called a halt to the proceedings, many obedient subjects heaved sighs of relief, mopped their brows, rubbed their fingers over their eyes, or nervously fumbled cigarettes. Some shook their heads, apparently in regret. Some subjects had remained calm throughout the experiment, and displayed only minimal signs of tension from beginning to end.

DISCUSSION

The experiment yielded two findings that were surprising. The first finding concerns the sheer strength of obedient tendencies manifested in this situation. Subjects have learned from childhood that it is a fundamental breach of moral conduct to hurt another person against his will. Yet, 26 subjects abandon this tenet in following the instructions of an authority who has no special powers to enforce his commands. To disobey would bring no material loss to the subject; no punishment would ensue. It is clear from the remarks and outward behavior of many participants that in punishing the victim they are often acting against their own values.

Subjects often expressed deep disapproval of shocking a man in the face of his objections, and others denounced it as stupid and senseless. Yet the majority complied with the experimental commands. This outcome was surprising from two perspectives: first, from the standpoint of predictions made in the questionnaire described earlier. (Here, however, it is possible that the remoteness of the respondents from the actual situation, and the difficulty of conveying to them the concrete details of the experiment, could account for the serious underestimation of obedience.)

But the results were also unexpected to persons who observed the experiment in progress, through one-way mirrors. Observers often uttered expressions of disbelief upon seeing a subject administer more powerful shocks to the victim. These persons had a full acquaintance with the details of the situation, and yet systematically underestimated the amount of obedience that subjects would display.

The second unanticipated effect was the extraordinary tension generated by the procedures. One might suppose that a subject would simply break off or continue as his conscience dictated. Yet, this is very far from what happened. There were striking reactions of tension and emotional strain. One observer related:

I observed a mature and initially poised businessman enter the laboratory smiling and confident. Within 20 minutes he was reduced to a twitching, stuttering wreck, who was rapidly approaching the point of nervous collapse. He constantly pulled on his earlobe, and twisted his hands. At one point he pushed his fist into his forehead and muttered: "Oh God, let's stop it." And yet he continued to respond to every word of the experimenter, and obeyed to the end.

Any understanding of the phenomenon of obedience must rest on an analysis of the particular conditions in which it occurs. The following features of the experiment go some distance in explaining the high amount of obedience observed in the situation.

1. The experiment is sponsored by and takes place on the grounds of an institution of unimpeachable reputation, Yale University. It may be reasonably presumed that the personnel are competent and reputable. The importance of this background authority is now being studied by conducting a series of experiments outside of New Haven, and without any visible ties to the university.

2. The experiment is, on the face of it, designed to attain a worthy purpose—advancement of knowledge about learning and memory. Obedience occurs not as an end in itself, but as an instrumental element in a situation that the subject construes as significant and meaningful. He may not be able to see its full significance, but he may properly assume that the experimenter does.

3. The subject perceives that the victim has voluntarily submitted to

the authority system of the experimenter. He is not (at first) an unwilling captive impressed for involuntary service. He has taken the trouble to come to the laboratory presumably to aid the experimental research. That he later becomes an involuntary subject does not alter the fact that, initially, he consented to participate without qualification. Thus he has in some degree incurred an obligation toward the experimenter.

4. The subject, too, has entered the experiment voluntarily, and perceives himself under obligation to aid the experimenter. He has made a commitment, and to disrupt the experiment is a repudiation of this initial promise of aid.

5. Certain features of the procedure strengthen the subject's sense of obligation to the experimenter. For one, he has been paid for coming to the laboratory. In part this is canceled out by the experimenter's statement that:

> Of course, as in all experiments, the money is yours simply for coming to the laboratory. From this point on, no matter what happens, the money is yours.[2]

6. From the subject's standpoint, the fact that he is the teacher and the other man the learner is purely a chance consequence (it is determined by drawing lots) and he, the subject, ran the same risk as the other man in being assigned the role of learner. Since the assignment of positions in the experiment was achieved by fair means, the learner is deprived of any basis of complaint on this count. (A similar situation obtains in Army units, in which—in the absence of volunteers—a particularly dangerous mission may be assigned by drawing lots, and the unlucky soldier is expected to bear his misfortune with sportsmanship.)

7. There is, at best, ambiguity with regard to the prerogatives of a psychologist and the corresponding rights of his subject. There is a vagueness of expectation concerning what a psychologist may require of his subject, and when he is overstepping acceptable limits. Moreover, the experiment occurs in a closed setting, and thus provides no opportunity for the subject to remove these ambiguities by discussion with others. There are few standards that seem directly applicable to the situation, which is a novel one for most subjects.

8. The subjects are assured that the shocks administered to the subject are "painful but not dangerous." Thus they assume that the discomfort caused the victim is momentary, while the scientific gains resulting from the experiment are enduring.

9. Through Shock Level 20 the victim continues to provide answers on the signal box. The subject may construe this as a sign that the victim is still willing to "play the game." It is only after Shock Level 20 that the victim repudiates the rules completely, refusing to answer further.

These features help to explain the high amount of obedience obtained in this experiment. Many of the arguments raised need not remain matters of speculation, but can be reduced to testable propositions to be confirmed or disproved by further experiments.[3]

The following features of the experiment concern the nature of the conflict which the subject faces.

10. The subject is placed in a position in which he must respond to the competing demands of two persons: the experimenter and the victim. The conflict must be resolved by meeting the demands of one or the other; satisfaction of the victim and the experimenter are mutually exclusive. Moreover, the resolution must take the form of a highly visible action, that of continuing to shock the victim or breaking off the experiment. Thus the subject is forced into a public conflict that does not permit any completely satisfactory solution.

11. While the demands of the experimenter carry the weight of scientific authority, the demands of the victim spring from his personal experience of pain and suffering. The two claims need not be regarded as equally pressing and legitimate. The experimenter seeks an abstract scientific datum; the victim cries out for relief from physical suffering caused by the subject's actions.

12. The experiment gives the subject little time for reflection. The conflict comes on rapidly. It is only minutes after the subject has been seated before the shock generator that the victim begins his protests. Moreover, the subject perceives that he has gone through but two-thirds of the shock levels at the time the subject's first protests are heard. Thus he understands that the conflict will have a persistent aspect to it, and may well become more intense as increasingly more powerful shocks are required. The rapidity with which the conflict descends on the subject, and his realization that it is predictably recurrent may well be sources of tension to him.

13. At a more general level, the conflict stems from the opposition of two deeply ingrained behavior dispositions: first, the disposition not to harm other people, and second, the tendency to obey those whom we perceive to be legitimate authorities.

NOTES

1. A related technique, making use of a shock generator, was reported by Buss (1961) for the study of aggression in the laboratory. Despite the considerable similarity of technical detail in the experimental procedures, both investigators proceeded in ignorance of the other's work. Milgram provided plans and photographs of his shock generator, experimental procedure, and first results in a report to the National Science Foundation in January 1961. This report received only limited circulation. Buss reported his procedure 6 months later, but to a wider audience. Subsequently, technical information and reports were exchanged. The

present article was first received in the Editor's office on December 27, 1961; it was resubmitted with deletions on July 27, 1962.

2. Forty-three subjects, undergraduates at Yale University, were run in the experiment without payment. The results are very similar to those obtained with paid subjects.

3. A series of recently completed experiments employing the obedience paradigm is reported in Milgram (1964).

REFERENCES

Adorno, T., Else Frenkel-Brunswick, D. J. Levinson, and R. N. Sanford. *The authoritarian personality*. New York: Harper, 1950.

Arendt, H. What was authority? In C. J. Friedrich (Ed.), *Authority*. Cambridge: Harvard University Press, 1958, pp. 81–112.

Binet, A. *La suggestibilité*. Paris: Schleicher, 1900.

Buss, A. H. *The psychology of aggression*. New York: Wiley, 1961.

Cartwright, S. (Ed.) *Studies in social power*. Ann Arbor: University of Michigan Institute for Social Research, 1959.

Charcot, J. M. *Oeuvres complètes*. Paris: Bureaux du Progrès Médical, 1881.

Frank, J. D. Experimental studies of personal pressure and resistance. *J. gen. Psychol.*, 1944, *30*, 23–64.

Friedrich, C. J. (Ed.) *Authority*. Cambridge: Harvard University Press, 1958.

Milgram, S. Dynamics of obedience. Washington: National Science Foundation, 25 January 1961. (Mimeo)

———. Some conditions of obedience and disobedience to authority. *Hum. Relat.*, *18*, 1964, 57–76.

Rokeach, M. Authority, authoritarianism, and conformity. In I. A. Berg & B. M. Bass (Eds.), *Conformity and deviation*. New York: Harper, 1961, pp. 230–257.

Snow, C. P. Either-or. *Progressive*, 1961 (Feb.), 24.

Weber, M. *The theory of social and economic organization*. Oxford: Oxford University Press, 1947.

1.3   CLEVER HANS: A CASE STUDY OF SCIENTIFIC METHOD*

Robert Rosenthal

I

Ever since the Byzantine Empire was ruled by Justinian (A.D. 483–565) there have been reports of learned animals. But no animal intelligence so captured the imagination of layman and scholar alike as that attributed

* Robert Rosenthal. Introduction. In Oskar Pfungst, *Clever Hans: The Horse of Mr. von Osten*. New York: Holt, Rinehart and Winston, Inc., 1965. Used in excerpted form.

to Clever Hans, the horse of Mr. von Osten. Hans gave every evidence of being able to add and subtract, multiply and divide—operations performed with equal accuracy upon integers or fractions. He was also able to read and spell, to identify musical tones, and to state the relationship of tones to one another. His preferred mode of communication with his questioners was by means of converting all answers into a number and tapping out these numbers with his foot.

What Clever Hans and Mr. von Osten did for science (and for love), Clever Rosa, the mare of Berlin, and her owner did for entertainment (and for money). Any expert on animal training could observe that Rosa's behavior was under the strict control of her trainer. Rosa gave correct answers because her trainer had only to bend forward in order to stop her tapping at the correct point, but no such signals could be observed to control Hans's tapping responses. In fact, on September 12, 1904, thirteen men risked their professional reputations by certifying that Hans was receiving no intentional cues from his owner or from any other questioner. Furthermore, these men, including in their number a psychologist, a physiologist, a veterinarian, a director of the Berlin Zoo, and a circus manager, certified that their investigation revealed no presence of signs or cues of even an unintentional nature. "This is a case," the investigating committee wrote, "which appears in principle to differ from any hitherto discovered." A "serious and incisive" inquiry into the cleverness of Hans was recommended and subsequently conducted. This book is the report by Oskar Pfungst of the procedure and the results of that inquiry which was undertaken in collaboration with Carl Stumpf, the eminent psychologist.[1]

Clever Hans constitutes a famous "case" in this history of psychology. One wishes to know about it for its own sake. There is, however, another reason for reprinting this book, long so difficult to obtain. The investigation of Hans's abilities is also a classic in respect of method, for it is a first-rate scientific inquiry into what began as an incomprehensible case history.

Pfungst's work is ideal as a paradigm for this kind of inquiry. First, he did careful and sophisticated work. Second, he described his procedures and his thinking in such detail that anyone, layman or student, can understand what goes on in a scientific inquiry. Third, the subject of his investigation has great intrinsic interest.[2]

First Pfungst established that Hans was, in fact, clever, and that his cleverness did not depend on the presence of his master, Mr. von Osten. Anyone, or almost anyone, could put a question to Hans, and the chances were good that an accurate answer would be forthcoming. Next, Pfungst employed a control condition in fitting Hans with blinders so that he could not see his questioners. This experimental addition reduced Hans's cleverness. There was another experimental change that cramped Hans's style: The questioners asked questions to which they did not know the answers. Pfungst also noted that Hans's accuracy diminished as the physical distance between him and his questioners increased. The closer the questioner, the more impressive was Hans's performance. From these data Pfungst could see that Hans was clever only when he had visual access to a source of the correct answer. In this indirect manner the likelihood had been increased that visual cues were involved, despite the fact that no specific visual cues had as yet been discovered.[3]

Eventually Pfungst noticed that the slight forward inclination of the questioner's head, to better see Hans's hoof tapping, was the signal for Hans to begin tapping. This forward inclination of the head did not need to be accompanied by a question for it to serve as a stimulus to tapping by Hans. When a correct answer required a long series of taps Hans would tap at a faster rate, as though he knew he had a lot of work ahead of him. This accommodation to the task at hand, which greatly added to the intellectual status ascribed to Hans, also came to be understood by Pfungst: He found that the interrogator, when putting a question to Hans, tended to lean further forward when the number that was the answer was a large one—as though he were settling down for a long wait. Hans's rate of tapping apparently depended on the angle of the questioner's forward inclination. Similarly, the cue for Hans to stop tapping also turned out to be derived from the questioner's expectancy for a correct answer; for when Hans reached the correct number of taps, the questioner tended to straighten up—and that was the cue for Hans to stop. Hans was sensitive to tiny upward motions of the head, even to the raising of eyebrows or the dilation of nostrils, any of which was sufficient to stop his tapping. Pfungst showed that anyone could start Hans tapping, and that anyone else could then stop his tapping at any time by the use of these cues. Most interesting was the finding that even after he had learned the cueing system very well Pfungst still cued Hans unintentionally, though he was consciously trying to suppress sending the crucial visual messages.

When Pfungst had learned all this about this man-horse communication system, he did a very modern thing indeed. He took his discoveries to the laboratory for further confirmation. As he put it, "Thus, artificial synthesis became the test of the correctness of analytical observation." In order to increase the generality of his findings at this point he not only increased his sample size but sampled from a different species—people, instead of horses. Pfungst took the part of Hans, inviting questions to which he tapped out his answers.

Of 25 subjects, 23 unintentionally cued Pfungst as to when he should stop tapping! When errors did occur, they tended to be errors of either one too many or one too few taps—the kind of errors Hans was most likely to make. The subjects, including men and women of assorted ages and occupations, had of course not been told the intent of the experiment. One of the subjects was a psychologist trained in introspection, but even he was unable to discover that he was emitting cues to Pfungst, Hans's surrogate.

To record his subjects' responses permanently and for leisurely study, as well as to amplify their very subtle cues, Pfungst developed an ingenious system of instrumentation. The questioner-subjects were hooked into a series of recording devices which would record an amplification of their head movements on three planes. In addition he undertook to measure the changes in his subjects' respiration. In interpreting the results of these recordings, Pfungst postulated a build-up of tension in his subjects that was released as a motor response to the perception of the correct answer as the experimenter tapped it out. . . .

III

In many of the cases of the Clever Hans phenomenon the subtle and unintentional cueing of the subject by the experimenter could be attributed to the experimenter's expectancy. Pfungst, for example, considered expectation and its attendant tension as helping him to account for the communication of correct responses to Clever Hans.

In general Hans performed accurately only for those questioners who consciously or unconsciously believed he could. Merton's (1948) concept of the self-fulfilling prophecy seems relevant: one behaves in such a way as to increase the likelihood of the prophesied event. That many experimenters over the years may have fulfilled their experimental prophecies by unintentionally communicating information to their subjects may be a disquieting proposition. We will probably never know what proportion of behavioral researches have been affected by the unintended communication of experimenter expectancies. This problem, the Clever Hans phenomenon, has occupied the present writer's attention for most of the last decade.

With horses so hard to come by and troublesome as laboratory animals, rats will do. A dozen students of experimental psychology served as experimenters in a study of the learning of a brightness discrimination in which rats were purported to have been specially bred for cleverness (Rosenthal and Fode, 1963). Each experimenter trained five animals a day for five days. Half the experimenters were told that their animals were from the "Berkeley Colony: Maze Bright Division," and the remaining experimenters were told that their animals were from the "Maze Dull Division." The experimenter's expectations were thus manipulated by alleged reference to the subjects' genetic history. All the rats were, of course, from a homogeneous population and were assigned at random to experimenters. At the end of the first day's running the animals used by experimenters expecting better performance outperformed the animals used by experimenters expecting poorer performance. The difference found was statistically significant and held up over the full five-day schedule. Animals believed to be bright made half again as many correct responses as those believed to be dull. The particular discrimination employed was a difficult one, and the animals often refused to make any response at all. Moreover, among animals used by experimenters expecting good performance no running at all occurred on 11% of the trials, whereas the animals used by experimenters expecting poor performance refused to run on 29% of the trials.

What cues could have been given the rats by their experimenters to account for the results of this experiment? It would be preposterous to suppose that the rats carefully observed the head movements of the experimenters as Hans had done, or listened for auditory cues as Johnson's dogs may have done. Still cues can operate, as it were, automatically. To this writer it seems more likely that these experimenters handled their rats differentially as a function of their expectancy about their abilities and that the differences in handling these animals led to the differences in their performance. How does one handle a rat believed to be bright? Perhaps more often and more gently; perhaps more "warmly" and enthusiastically than one handles an animal believed to be dull. Associated with the perception of animals' brightness in our sample of experimenters was the perception of animals' "character." Rats believed to be brighter were described by their experimenters as cleaner, tamer, and generally more pleasant. It may have been these associated characteristics that led the experimenters to handle their brighter-perceived animals differentially. In any case, experimenters who believed their subjects to be bright stated that they did handle these subjects more often and more gently than did the experimenters who expected less of their subjects.[4]

If, as Pfungst and others found, the expectancies of experimenters are communicated so readily to their animal subjects, we might expect that they can also be communicated to their human subjects. For this reason a series of studies was undertaken to learn the role of the experimenters' expectancy in influencing the responses of their human subjects. A task of person-perception was employed in many of these investigations (Rosenthal, 1963). Subjects were asked to judge what degree of success had been experienced by each person pictured in a series of photographs. The subjects rated each photo from very unsuccessful (-10) to mildly unsuccessful (-1) to mildly successful ($+1$) to very successful ($+10$). The photos, cut from a magazine, had been standardized to evoke average ratings of zero (neither successful nor unsuccessful). The basic procedure employed in many of these studies was to draw a random sample of experimenters and to lead half of them to expect that the subjects assigned to them would tend to see the people pictured as failures. The remaining experimenters were led to expect that their subjects would tend to see the people pictured as successes. Actually, of course, subjects were simply assigned to their experimenters at random. All experimenters were given identical instructions to read to their subjects. Nevertheless, in three studies in which 30 experimenters each used about a dozen subjects, the lowest average rating obtained by any experimenter expecting high ratings was higher than the highest average rating obtained by any experimenter expecting low ratings from his subjects. In all three studies these nonoverlapping distributions of experimental results differed very significantly from any results that could be attributed to chance.

The conclusion to be drawn from these and subsequent studies (Rosenthal, 1964) is that in some subtle, unintentional way experimenters do communicate their expectations to their human subjects, whose performance is then significantly altered. There remains, however, the most urgent question: How do the experimenters communicate to their subjects what it is they expect of them?

The exquisite sensitivity of human subjects to these "demand characteristics" has been amply documented by Martin Orne (1962). Data from several experiments, including a careful analysis of sound motion pictures of interactions between the experimenter and his subject, suggest that no gross procedural errors are responsible; neither words nor readily perceptible gestures carry the burden of communication. The explanation does not lie in the infrequent occurrence of biased errors of observation, recording, and computation. . . .

Following closely in Pfungst's footsteps, Fode (1960) undertook a study directed at learning the relative contribution of visual and auditory cues to the process by which an experimenter unintentionally communicates his expectancy to his subjects. The standard photo-rating task was administered by 24 experimenters to 180 men and women subjects. The 24 experimenters were randomly assigned to one of four groups. One group of six experimenters, the *control* group, was led to expect their subjects to rate the photos as being of unsuccessful people. The remaining three experimental groups of six experimenters each were led to expect their subjects to rate the photos as being of successful people. The experimental groups differed from each other in the types of cues they unwittingly sent their subjects. The experimenters permitting *visual cues* were visible to their subjects, but remained entirely silent except for greeting their subjects and handing them written instructions. The experimenters permitting *auditory cues* read their instructions to subjects aloud, but were hidden from their subjects' view by an interposed screen.

Those free to give both *visual and auditory cues* read their instructions to their subjects and also remained in full view. This group differed from the control group only in the induced expectancy.

The results of this study showed no difference in obtained photo-ratings between the group permitted visual cues and the control group, a result which suggested, among other interpretations, that visual cues alone were insufficient to carry the burden of the unintended communication or that the strangeness to the subjects of an apparently unnecessarily aloof and mute experimenter led to their rating the photos as more unsuccessful. The group permitted auditory cues obtained significantly more ratings of success than did the control group, a result suggesting that auditory-paralinguistic cues alone might be sufficient to communicate experimenters' expectancies to subjects. The group permitted both visual and auditory cues obtained significantly more ratings of success than did the group permitted only auditory cues. It appeared, then, that the effects of auditory cues, although sufficient, could be significantly increased (approximately "doubled") by the addition of visual cues, even though the effect of visual cues alone was at best only equivocal. In any case, it seems clear that neither the strategy nor the tactics of inquiry employed by Pfungst are in any way outmoded or irrelevant to contemporary psychology.

NOTES

1. The book which lies ahead is Pfungst's, yet in noting that Stumpf was both a collaborator of Pfungst and eminent as well, more should be said about him. What could and should be said has been said by Boring (1950). One of the most important (but clearly not *the* most important) of the German psychologists of the waning years of the last century, Stumpf nevertheless held the most important chair of psychology in all Germany, the one at the University of Berlin. Oskar Pfungst was one of his outstanding students. That Pfungst should have conducted the investigation of Clever Hans at Stumpf's suggestion made sense, for Stumpf often turned experimental enterprises over to students who would accept them. As Boring (1950) put it: "Stumpf was an experimentalist by philosophical conviction but not by temperament" (p. 371).

   Stumpf, of course, was one of the thirteen courageous men who risked their professional reputations by absolving Hans from the reception of any observed cues, and Albert Moll in an acrimonious context (1910), refers to the "September Report" of 1904 as that "deplorable report," for he claimed to have known all along, on the basis of his own study of Hans, what was really going on. Poor Stumpf was berated for not having known, as Moll thought any worker in the area of hypnosis would, that small cues can be effective communicating agents even when unobserved by the sender or bystanders. Moll further implied that the research program carried out by Pfungst owed much of its technique to Moll's experiments with Hans, experiments which he said had already been reported to the Psychological Society of Berlin. Ultimately Moll called Stumpf a liar (p. 458), but Stumpf survived the attack (by some 30 years, in fact) and even got in some thrusts of his own, as can be seen in some of Stumpf's supplementary sections included in this book. (When reading these sections such phrases as "obscure irresponsibles" are best read as "Albert Moll".) H. M. Johnson (1911) was right when he remarked that the name-calling aspects of the controversy did "scant credit to either of the parties" (p. 666).

Less fortunate in the matter of survival was Mr. von Osten, nor is it here quite so easy to view the controversy as somewhat quaint. Mr. von Osten, unlike scientific antagonists, had everything to lose and nothing comparable to gain by having his Hans investigated. He must indeed have been completely honest and sincere and the findings in this book grieved him deeply, nor could he accept them. Within a few months he died. (Johnson, 1911).

2. Of Pfungst's work H. M. Johnson (1911) said: "His account may be read with the interest of an exciting novel, and yet with great and lasting profit by anyone at all interested in animal behavior or in the problems of animal consciousness, whether his interest be that of the comparative psychologist, the naturalist, or the mere lover of domestic animals" (see page 633).

3. The teacher of psychology can nicely employ Pfungst's inquiry as an illustration of John Stuart Mill's major principles of scientific method as set forth in his *Logic* of 1843. Mill's method of agreement, the observation of systematic consequences of an event, is illustrated by Pfungst's observation that Hans's cleverness followed his viewing a questioner who knew the answer to the question posed. Mill's method of difference, the more powerful principle, requires not only systematic consequences of an event but also the *absence* of these consequences in the *absence* of the event. This principle is illustrated by Pfungst's employment of blinders and of questioners who did not know the answers to their questions. Mill's method of concomittant variations, an extension of the method of difference, requires that changes in the magnitude of the consequences are systematically related to changes in the magnitude of the antecedent. This principle is illustrated by Pfungst's observation of the relationship between the questioner's distance from Hans and Hans's cleverness. (See also the discussion of Mill's methods by Boring [1954].)

4. A second experiment was conducted to check on the results of this first one and to extend the generality of its findings (Rosenthal and Lawson, 1964). The learning tasks for the animals were posed within the context of Skinner boxes; half the experimenters were told that their animals were "Skinner-box dull," while the remainder were told that their animals were "Skinner-box bright." Subjects were again labeled bright and dull at random and assigned to the research groups at random. This was a more longitudinal experiment in that experimenters worked with the same animals over the course of an entire academic quarter. Seven specific experiments were performed: magazine training, operant acquisition, extinction and spontaneous recovery, secondary reinforcement, stimulus discrimination, stimulus generalization, and chaining of responses.

In this experiment, as in the earlier one, those experimenters who believed their animals were the better performers obtained significantly better performance than did the experimenters who believed their subjects to be the poorer performers. In this study, too, experimenters who believed their subjects to be brighter rated themselves as more pleasant vis-à-vis their animals and reported that they handled them more. Although less handling of subjects occurred generally in this Skinner-box study than in the maze-learning study, there was still opportunity for handling animals in transporting them from home cage to Skinner box and then back again at the end of the day's work. At the present time, and on the basis of the two studies described, we can conclude that experiments' expectancy may be a significant determinant of their subjects' performance when those subjects are laboratory rats. Our best guess about the "cues" involved is they are mediated to the subject by differential handling patterns. Visual and auditory cues have not been definitively ruled out for rat subjects, but they seem less likely to play the major role they have played in the experimenter-determined performances of horses, dogs, and pigs.

REFERENCES

Alexander, R. D., Communicative systems of animals: acoustic behavior. *Science*, 1964, 144, 713–715.

Boring, E. G., *A History of Experimental Psychology*, 2d ed. New York: Appleton-Century-Crofts, 1950.

Boring, E. G., The nature and history of experimental control. *Amer. J. Psychol.*, 1954, 67, 573–589.

Boring, E. G., and Boring, Mollie D., Masters and pupils among the American psychologists. *Amer. J. Psychol.*, 1948, 61, 527–534. Also reprinted in E. G. Boring, *History, Psychology, and Science: Selected Papers*. New York and London: Wiley, 1963, pp. 132–139.

Broadhurst, P. L., *The Science of Animal Behavior*. Baltimore, Md.: Penguin, 1963.

Brown, R., *Words and Things*. New York: Free Press of Glencoe, 1958.

Fode, K. L., The effect of non-visual and non-verbal interaction on experimenter bias. Unpublished master's thesis, University of North Dakota, 1960.

Foster, W. S., Experiments on rod-divining. *J. appl. Psychol.*, 1923, 7, 303–311.

Friedman, Pearl, A second experiment on interviewer bias. *Sociometry*, 1942, 5, 378–379.

Geldard, F. A., Some neglected possibilities of communication. *Science*, 1960, 131, 1583–1588.

Gruenberg, B. C., *The Story of Evolution*. Princeton, N.J.: Van Nostrand, 1929.

Hansen, F. C. C., and Lehman, A., Ueber Unwillkürliches Flüstern. *Phil. Stud.*, 1895, 11, 471–530.

Johnson, H. M., Review of Pfungst, O., *Clever Hans* (New York: Holt, 1911). *J. Philos., Psychol. & Scientific Methods*, 1911, 8, 663–666.

Johnson, H. M., The talking dog. *Science*, 1912, 35, 749–751.

Johnson, H. M., Audition and habit formation in the dog. *Behav. Monogr.*, 1913, 2, no. 3, serial no. 8.

Kellogg, W. N., Sonar system of the blind. *Science*, 1962, 137, 399–404.

Kennedy, J. L., Experiments on "unconscious whispering." *Psychol. Bull.*, 1938, 35, 526. (Abstract)

Kennedy, J. L., A methodological review of extra-sensory perception. *Psychol. Bull.*, 1939, 36, 59–103.

Lindzey, G., A note on interviewer bias. *J. appl. Psychol.*, 1951, 35, 182–184.

Merton, R. K., The self-fulfilling prophecy. *Antioch Rev.*, 1948, 8, 193–210.

Mill, J. S., *A System of Logic, Ratiocinative and Inductive*. London: Longmans, 1925 (1843).

Miller, J. G., *Unconsciousness*. New York: Wiley, 1942.

Moll, A., *Hypnotism*, 4th ed. New York: Scribner's, 1898.

Moll, A., *Hypnotism*, 4th enlarged ed., trans. A. F. Hopkirk. New York: Scribner's, 1910; London: Walter Scott.

Orne, M. T., On the social psychology of the psychological experiment: with particular reference to demand characteristics and their implications. *Amer. Psychologist*, 1962, 17, 776–783.

Polanyi, M., *Personal Knowledge*. Chicago: University of Chicago Press, 1958.

Razran, G., Pavlov the empiricist. *Science*, 1959, 130, 916.

Rosenthal, R., The effect of the experimenter on the results of psychological research. In B. Maher, ed. *Progress in Experimental Personality Research*. Vol. I. New York: Academic Press, 1964.

Rosenthal, R., On the social psychology of the psychological experiment: the experimenter's hypothesis as unintended determinant of experimental results. *Amer. Scientist*, 1963, 51, 268–283.

Rosenthal, R., The control of experimenter expectancy effects. Unpublished manuscript, Harvard University, 1964a.

Rosenthal, R., and Fode, K. L., The effect of experimenter bias on the performance of the albino rat. *Behav. Sci.*, 1963, 8, 183–189.

Rosenthal, R., and Lawson, R., A longitudinal study of the effects of experimenter bias on the operant learning of laboratory rats. *J. Psychiat. Res.*, 1964, 2, 61–72.

Sebeok, T. A., Hayes, A. S., and Bateson, Mary C., eds. *Approaches to Semiotics*. The Hague: Moulton, 1964.

Stanton, F., Further contributions at the twentieth anniversary of the psychological corporation and to honor its founder, James McKeen Cattel. *J. appl. Psychol.*, 1942a, 26, 16–17.

Stanton, F., and Baker, K. H., Interviewer bias and the recall of incompletely learned materials. *Sociometry*, 1942, 5, 123–134.

Stratton, G. M., The control of another person by obscure signs. *Psychol. Rev.*, 1921, 28, 310–314.

Warner, L., and Raible, Mildred, Telepathy in the psychophysical laboratory. *J. Parapsychol.*, 1937, 1, 44–51.

Wilson, E. B., *An Introduction to Scientific Research*. New York: McGraw-Hill, 1952.

Zirkle, C., Pavlov's beliefs. *Science*, 1958, 128, 1476.

1.4 | TEACHING SIGN LANGUAGE TO A CHIMPANZEE*

R. Allen Gardner and Beatrice T. Gardner

The extent to which another species might be able to use human language is a classical problem in comparative psychology. One approach to this problem is to consider the nature of language, the processes of learning,

* Reprinted from *Science*, 1969, *165*, 664–672. Copyright 1969 by the American Association for the Advancement of Science, and reproduced by permission.

the neural mechanisms of learning and of language, and the genetic basis of these mechanisms, and then, while recognizing certain gaps in what is known about these factors, to attempt to arrive at an answer by dint of careful scholarship (1). An alternative approach is to try to teach a form of human language to an animal. We chose the latter alternative and, in June 1966, began training an infant female chimpanzee, named Washoe, to use the gestural language of the deaf. Within the first 22 months of training it became evident that we had been correct in at least one major aspect of method, the use of a gestural language. Additional aspects of method have evolved in the course of the project. These and some implications of our early results can now be described in a way that may be useful in other studies of communicative behavior. Accordingly, in this article we discuss the considerations which led us to use the chimpanzee as a subject and American Sign Language (the language used by the deaf in North America) as a medium of communication; describe the general methods of training as they were initially conceived and as they developed in the course of the project; and summarize those results that could be reported with some degree of confidence by the end of the first phase of the project.

PRELIMINARY CONSIDERATIONS

The Chimpanzee as a Subject

Some discussion of the chimpanzee as an experimental subject is in order because the species is relatively uncommon in the psychological laboratory. Whether or not the chimpanzee is the most intelligent animal after man can be disputed; the gorilla, the orangutan, and even the dolphin have their loyal partisans in this debate. Nevertheless, it is generally conceded that chimpanzees are highly intelligent, and that members of this species might be intelligent enough for our purposes. Of equal or greater importance is their sociability and their capacity for forming strong attachments to human beings. We want to emphasize this trait of sociability; it seems highly likely that it is essential for the development of language in human beings, and it was a primary consideration in our choice of a chimpanzee as a subject.

Affectionate as chimpanzees are, they are still wild animals, and this is a serious disadvantage. Most psychologists are accustomed to working with animals that have been chosen, and sometimes bred, for docility and adaptability to laboratory procedures. The difficulties presented by the wild nature of an experimental animal must not be underestimated. Chimpanzees are also very strong animals; a full-grown specimen is likely to weigh more than 120 pounds (55 kilograms) and is estimated to be from three to five times as strong as a man, pound-for-pound. Coupled with the wildness, this great strength presents serious difficulties for a procedure that requires interaction at close quarters with a free-living animal. We have always had to reckon with the likelihood that at some point Washoe's physical maturity will make this procedure prohibitively dangerous.

A more serious disadvantage is that human speech sounds are unsuitable as a medium of communication for the chimpanzee. The vocal apparatus of the chimpanzee is very different from that of man (2). More important, the vocal behavior of the chimpanzee is very different from that of man. Chimpanzees do make many different sounds, but generally vocalization occurs in situations of high excitement and tends to be specific to the exciting situations. Undisturbed, chimpanzees are usually silent. Thus, it is unlikely that a chimpanzee could be trained to make refined use of its vocalizations. Moreover, the intensive work of Hayes and Hayes (3) with the chimpanzee Viki indicates that a vocal language is not appropriate for this species. The Hayeses used modern, sophisticated, psychological methods and seem to have spared no effort to teach Viki to make speech sounds. Yet in 6 years Viki learned only four sounds that approximated English words (4).

Use of the hands, however, is a prominent feature of chimpanzee behavior; manipulatory mechanical problems are their forte. More to the point, even caged, laboratory chimpanzees develop begging and similar gestures spontaneously (5), while individuals that have had extensive contact with human beings have displayed an even wider variety of communicative gestures (6). In our choice of sign language we were influenced more by the behavioral evidence that this medium of communication was appropriate to the species than by anatomical evidence of structural similarity between the hands of chimpanzees and of men. The Hayeses point out that human tools and mechanical devices are constructed to fit the human hand, yet chimpanzees have little difficulty in using these devices with great skill. Nevertheless, they seem unable to adapt their vocalizations to approximate human speech.

Psychologists who work extensively with the instrumental conditioning of animals become sensitive to the need to use responses that are suited to the species they wish to study. Lever-pressing in rats is not an arbitrary response invented by Skinner to confound the mentalists; it is a type of response commonly made by rats when they are first placed in a Skinner box. The exquisite control of instrumental behavior by schedules of reward is achieved only if the original responses are well chosen. We chose a language based on gestures because we reasoned that gestures for the chimpanzee should be analogous to bar-pressing for rats, key-pecking for pigeons, and babbling for humans.

American Sign Language

Two systems of manual communication are used by the deaf. One system is the manual alphabet, or finger spelling, in which configurations of the hand correspond to letters of the alphabet. In this system the words of a spoken language, such as English, can be spelled out manually. The other system, sign language, consists of a set of manual configurations and gestures that correspond to particular words or concepts. Unlike finger spelling, which is the direct encoding of a spoken language, sign languages have their own rules of usage. Word-for-sign translation between a spoken language and a sign language yields results that are similar to those of word-for-word translation between two spoken languages; the translation is often passable, though awkward, but it can also be ambiguous or quite nonsensical. Also, there are national and regional variations in sign languages that are comparable to those of spoken languages.

We chose for this project the American Sign Language (ASL), which with certain regional variations, is used by the deaf in North America. This particular sign language has recently been the subject of formal analysis (7). The ASL can be compared to pictograph writing in which some symbols are quite arbitrary and some are quite representational or iconic, but all are arbitrary to some degree. For example, in ASL the sign for "always" is made by holding the hand in a fist, index finger extended (the pointing hand), while rotating the arm at the elbow. This is clearly an arbitrary representation of the concept "always." The sign for "flower," however, is highly iconic; it is made by holding the fingers of one hand extended, all five fingertips touching (the tapered hand), and touching the fingertips first to one nostril then to the other, as if sniffing a flower. While this is an iconic sign for "flower," it is only one of a number of conventions by which the concept "flower" could be iconically represented; it is thus arbitrary to some degree. Undoubtedly, many of the signs of ASL that seem quite arbitrary today once had an iconic origin that was lost through years of stylized usage. Thus, the signs of ASL are neither uniformly arbitrary nor uniformly iconic; rather the degree of abstraction varies from sign to sign over a wide range. This would seem to be a useful property of ASL for our research.

The literate deaf typically use a combination of ASL and finger spelling; for purposes of this project we have avoided the use of finger spelling as much as possible. A great range of expression is possible within the limits of ASL. We soon found that a good way to practice signing among ourselves was to render familiar songs and poetry into signs; as far as we can judge, there is no message that cannot be rendered faithfully (apart from the usual problems of translation from one language to another). Technical terms and proper names are a problem when first introduced, but within any community of signers it is easy to agree on a convention for any commonly used term. For example, among ourselves we do not finger-spell the words *psychologist* and *psychology*, but render them as "think doctor" and "think science." Or, among users of ASL, "California" can be finger-spelled but is commonly rendered as "golden playland." (Incidentally, the sign for "gold" is made by plucking at the earlobe with thumb and forefinger, indicating an earring—another example of an iconic sign that is at the same time arbitrary and stylized.)

The fact that ASL is in current use by human beings is an additional advantage. The early linguistic environment of the deaf children of deaf parents is in some respects similar to the linguistic environment that we could provide for an experimental subject. This should permit some comparative evaluation of Washoe's eventual level of competence. For example, in discussing Washoe's early performance with deaf parents we have been told that many of her variants of standard signs are similar to the baby-talk variants commonly observed when human children sign.

Washoe

Having decided on a species and a medium of communication, our next concern was to obtain an experimental subject. It is altogether possible that there is some critical early age for the acquisition of this type of behavior. On the other hand, newborn chimpanzees tend to be quite helpless and vegetative. They are also considerably less hardy than older infants. Nevertheless, we reasoned that the dangers of starting too late were much greater than the dangers of starting too early, and we sought the youngest infant we could get. Newborn laboratory chimpanzees are very scarce, and we found that the youngest laboratory infant we could get would be about 2 years old at the time we planned to start the project. It seemed preferable to obtain a wild-caught infant. Wild-caught infants are usually at least 8 to 10 months old before they are available for research. This is because infants rarely reach the United States before they are 5 months old, and to this age must be added 1 or 2 months before final purchase and 2 or 3 months for quarantine and other medical services.

We named our chimpanzee Washoe for Washoe County, the home of the University of Nevada. Her exact age will never be known, but from her weight and dentition we estimated her age to be between 8 and 14 months at the end of June 1966, when she first arrived at our laboratory. (Her dentition has continued to agree with this initial estimate, but her weight has increased rather more than would be expected.) This is very young for a chimpanzee. The best available information indicates that infants are completely dependent until the age of 2 years and semi-dependent until the age of 4; the first signs of sexual maturity (for example, menstruation, sexual swelling) begin to appear at about 8 years, and full adult growth is reached between the ages of 12 and 16 (8). As for the complete life span, captive specimens have survived for well over 40 years. Washoe was indeed very young when she arrived; she did not have her first canines or molars, her hand-eye coordination was rudimentary, she had only begun to crawl about, and she slept a great deal. Apart from making friends with her and adapting her to the daily routine, we could accomplish little during the first few months.

Laboratory Conditions

At the outset we were quite sure that Washoe could learn to make various signs in order to obtain food, drink, and other things. For the project to be a success, we felt that something more must be developed. We wanted Washoe not only to ask for objects but to answer questions about them and also to ask us questions. We wanted to develop behavior that could be described as conversation. With this in mind, we attempted to provide Washoe with an environment that might be conducive to this sort of behavior. Confinement was to be minimal, about the same as that of human infants. Her human companions were to be friends and playmates as well as providers and protectors, and they were to introduce a great many games and activities that would be likely to result in maximum interaction with Washoe.

In practice, such an environment is readily achieved with a chimpanzee; bonds of warm affection have always been established between Washoe and her several human companions. We have enjoyed the interaction almost as much as Washoe has, within the limits of human endurance. A number of human companions have been enlisted to participate in the project and relieve each other at intervals, so that at least one person would be with Washoe during all her waking hours. At first we feared that such frequent changes would be disturbing, but Washoe seemed to adapt very well to this procedure. Apparently it is possible to provide an infant chimpanzee with affection on a shift basis.

All of Washoe's human companions have been required to master ASL and to use it extensively in her presence, in association with interesting activities and events and also in a general way, as one chatters at a human infant in the course of the day. The ASL has been used almost exclusively, although occasional finger spelling has been permitted. From time to time, of course, there are lapses into spoken English, as when medical personnel must examine Washoe. At one time, we considered an alternative procedure in which we would sign and speak English to Washoe simultaneously, thus giving her an additional source of informative cues. We rejected this procedure, reasoning that, if she should come to understand speech sooner or more easily than ASL, then she might not pay sufficient attention to our gestures. Another alternative, that of speaking English among ourselves and signing to Washoe, was also rejected. We reasoned that this would make it seem that big chimps talk and only little chimps sign, which might give signing an undesirable social status. The environment we are describing is not a silent one. The human beings can vocalize in many ways, laughing and making sounds of pleasure and displeasure. Whistles and drums are sounded in a variety of imitation games, and hands are clapped for attention. The rule is that all meaningful sounds, whether vocalized or not, must be sounds that a chimpanzee can imitate.

TRAINING METHODS

Imitation

The imitativeness of apes is proverbial, and rightly so. Those who have worked closely with chimpanzees have frequently remarked on their readiness to engage in visually guided imitation. Consider the following typical comment of Yerkes (9): "Chim and Panzee would imitate many of my acts, but never have I heard them imitate a sound and rarely make a sound peculiarly their own in response to mine. As previously stated, their imitative tendency is as remarkable for its specialization and limitations as for its strength. It seems to be controlled chiefly by visual stimuli. Things which are seen tend to be imitated or reproduced. What is heard is not reproduced. Obviously an animal which lacks the tendency to reinstate auditory stimuli—in other words to imitate sounds—cannot reasonably be expected to talk. The human infant exhibits this tendency to a remarkable degree. So also does the parrot. If the imitative tendency of the parrot could be coupled with the quality of intelligence of the chimpanzee, the latter undoubtedly could speak."

In the course of their work with Viki, the Hayeses devised a game in which Viki would imitate various actions on hearing the command "Do this" (10). Once established, this was an effective means of training Viki to perform actions that could be visually guided. The same method should be admirably suited to training a chimpanzee to use sign language; accordingly we have directed much effort toward establishing a version of the "Do this" game with Washoe. Getting Washoe to imitate us was not difficult, for she did so quite spontaneously, but getting her to imitate on command has been another matter altogether. It was not until the 16th month of the project that we achieved any degree of control over Washoe's imitation of gestures. Eventually we got to a point where she would imitate a simple gesture, such as pulling at her ears, or a series of such gestures—first we make a gesture, then she imitates, then we make a second gesture, she imitates the second gesture, and so on—for the reward of being tickled. Up to this writing, however, imitation of this sort has not been an important method for introducing new signs into Washoe's vocabulary.

As a method of prompting, we have been able to use imitation extensively to increase the frequency and refine the form of signs. Washoe sometimes fails to use a new sign in an appropriate situation, or uses another, incorrect sign. At such times we can make the correct sign to Washoe, repeating the performance until she makes the sign herself. (With more stable signs, more indirect forms of prompting can be used— for example, pointing at, or touching, Washoe's hand or a part of her body that should be involved in the sign; making the sign for "sign," which is equivalent to saying "Speak up"; or asking a question in signs, such as "What do you want?" or "What is it?") Again, with new signs, and often with old signs as well, Washoe can lapse into what we refer to as poor "diction." Of course, a great deal of slurring and a wide range of variants are permitted in ASL as in any spoken language. In any event, Washoe's diction has frequently been improved by the simple device of repeating, in exaggeratedly correct form, the sign she has just made, until she repeats it herself in more correct form. On the whole, she has responded quite well to prompting, but there are strict limits to its use with a wild animal—one that is probably quite spoiled, besides. Pressed too hard, Washoe can become completely diverted from her original object; she may ask for something entirely different, run away, go into a tantrum, or even bite her tutor.

Chimpanzees also imitate, after some delay, and this delayed imitation can be quite elaborate (10). The following is a typical example of Washoe's delayed imitation. From the beginning of the project she was bathed regularly and according to a standard routine. Also, from her 2nd month with us, she always had dolls to play with. One day, during the 10th month of the project, she bathed one of her dolls in the way we usually bathed her. She filled her little bathtub with water, dunked the doll in the tub, then took it out and dried it with a towel. She has repeated the entire performance, or parts of it, many times since, sometimes also soaping the doll.

This is a type of imitation that may be very important in the acquisition of language by human children, and many of our procedures with Washoe were devised to capitalize on it. Routine activities—feeding, dressing, bathing, and so on—have been highly ritualized, with appropriate signs figuring prominently in the rituals. Many games have been invented which can be accompanied by appropriate signs. Objects and activities have been named as often as possible, especially when Washoe seemed to be paying particular attention to them. New objects and new examples of familiar objects, including pictures, have been continually brought to her attention, together with the appropriate signs. She likes to ride in automobiles, and a ride in an automobile, including the preparations for a ride, provides a wealth of sights that can be accompanied by signs. A good destination for a ride is a home or the university nursery school, both well stocked with props for language lessons.

The general principle should be clear: Washoe has been exposed to a wide variety of activities and objects, together with their appropriate signs, in the hope that she would come to associate the signs with their referents and later make the signs herself. We have reason to believe that she has come to understand a large vocabulary of signs. This was expected, since a number of chimpanzees have acquired extensive understanding vocabularies of spoken words, and there is evidence that even dogs can acquire a sizable understanding vocabulary of spoken words (11). The understanding vocabulary that Washoe has acquired, however, consists of signs that a chimpanzee can imitate.

Some of Washoe's signs seem to have been originally acquired by delayed imitation. A good example is the sign for "toothbrush." A part of the daily routine has been to brush her teeth after every meal. When this routine was first introduced Washoe generally resisted it. She gradually came to submit with less and less fuss, and after many months she would even help or sometimes brush her teeth herself. Usually, having finished her meal, Washoe would try to leave her highchair; we would restrain her, signing "First, toothbrushing, then you can go." One day, in the 10th month of the project, Washoe was visiting the Gardner home and found her way into the bathroom. She climbed up on the counter, looked at our mug full of toothbrushes, and signed "toothbrush." At the time, we believed that Washoe understood this sign but we had not seen her use it. She had no reason to ask for the toothbrushes, because they were well within her reach, and it is most unlikely that she was asking to have her teeth brushed. This was our first observation, and one of the clearest examples, of behavior in which Washoe seemed to name an object or an event for no obvious motive other than communication.

Following this observation, the toothbrushing routine at mealtime was altered. First, imitative prompting was introduced. Then as the sign became more reliable, her rinsing-mug and toothbrush were displayed prominently until she made the sign. By the 14th month she was making the "toothbrush" sign at the end of meals with little or no prompting; in fact she has called for her toothbrush in a peremptory fashion when its appearance at the end of a meal was delayed. The "toothbrush" sign is not merely a response cued by the end of a meal; Washoe retained her ability to name toothbrushes when they were shown to her at other times.

The sign for "flower" may also have been acquired by delayed imitation. From her first summer with us, Washoe showed a great interest in flowers, and we took advantage of this by providing many flowers and pictures of flowers accompanied by the appropriate sign. Then one day in the 15th month she made the sign, spontaneously, while she and a companion were walking toward a flower garden. As in the case of "tooth-brush," we believed that she understood the sign at this time, but we had made no attempt to elicit it from her except by making it ourselves in appropriate situations. Again, after the first observation, we proceeded to elicit this sign as often as possible by the variety of methods, most frequently by showing her a flower and giving it to her if she made the sign for it. Eventually the sign became very reliable and could be elicited by a variety of flowers and pictures of flowers.

It is difficult to decide which signs were acquired by the method of delayed imitation. The first appearance of these signs is likely to be sudden and unexpected; it is possible that some inadvertent movement of Washoe's has been interpreted as meaningful by one of her devoted companions. If the first observer were kept from reporting the observation and from making any direct attempts to elicit the sign again, then it might be possible to obtain independent verification. Quite understandably, we have been more interested in raising the frequency of new signs than in evaluating any particular method of training.

Babbling

Because the Hayeses were attempting to teach Viki to speak English, they were interested in babbling, and during the first year of their project they were encouraged by the number and variety of spontaneous vocaliza-tions that Viki made. But, in time, Viki's spontaneous vocalizations de-creased further and further to the point where the Hayeses felt that there was almost no vocal babbling from which to shape spoken language. In planning this project we expected a great deal of manual "babbling," but during the early months we observed very little behavior of this kind. In the course of the project, however, there has been a great increase in manual babbling. We have been particularly encouraged by the increase in movements that involve touching parts of the head and body, since these are important components of many signs. Also, more and more frequently, when Washoe has been unable to get something that she wants, she has burst into a flurry of random flourishes and arm-waving.

We have encouraged Washoe's babbling by our responsiveness; clapping, smiling, and repeating the gesture much as you might repeat "goo goo" to a human infant. If the babbled gesture has resembled a sign in ASL, we have made the correct form of the sign and have attempted to engage in some appropriate activity. The sign for "funny" was probably acquired in this way. It first appeared as a spontaneous babble that lent itself readily to a simple imitation game—first Washoe signed "funny," then we did, then she did, and so on. We would laugh and smile during the interchanges that she initiated, and initiate the game ourselves when something funny happened. Eventually Washoe came to use the "funny" sign spontaneously in roughly appropriate situations.

Closely related to babbling are some gestures that seem to have appeared independently of any deliberate training on our part, and that resemble signs so closely that we could incorporate them into Washoe's repertoire with little or no modification. Almost from the first she had a begging gesture—an extension of her open hand, palm up, toward one of us. She made this gesture in situations in which she wanted aid and in situations in which we were holding some object that she wanted. The ASL sign for "give me" and "come" are very similar to this, except that they involve a prominent beckoning movement. Gradually Washoe came to incorporate a beckoning wrist movement into her use of this sign. In Table 1.4–1 we refer to this sign as "come-gimme." As Washoe has come to use it, the sign is not simply a modification of the original begging gesture. For example, very commonly she reaches forward with one hand (palm up) while she gestures with the other hand (palm down) held near her head. (The result resembles a classic fencing posture.)

Another sign of this type is the sign for "hurry," which, so far, Washoe has always made by shaking her open hand vigorously at the wrist. This first appeared as an impatient flourish following some request that she had made in signs; for example, after making the "open" sign before a door. The correct ASL for "hurry" is very close, and we began to use it often, ourselves, in appropriate contexts. We believe that Washoe has come to use this sign in a meaningful way, because she has frequently used it when she, herself, is in a hurry—for example, when rushing to her nursery chair.

TABLE 1.4–1   Signs Used Reliably by Chimpanzee Washoe within 22 Months of the Beginning of Training. The signs are listed in the order of their original appearance in her repertoire (see text for the criterion of reliability and for the method of assigning the date of original appearance).

Signs	Description	Context
Come-gimme	Beckoning motion, with wrist or knuckles as pivot.	Sign made to persons or animals, also for objects out of reach. Often combined: "come tickle," "gimme sweet," etc.
More	Fingertips are brought together, usually overhead. (Correct ASL form: tips of the tapered hand touch repeatedly.)	When asking for continuation or repetition of activities such as swinging or tickling, for second helpings of food, etc. Also used to ask for repetition of some performance, such as a somersault.

TABLE 1.4–1   (Continued)

Signs	Description	Context
Up	Arm extends upward, and index finger may also point up.	Wants a lift to reach objects such as grapes on vine, or leaves; or wants to be placed on someone's shoulders; or wants to leave potty chair.
Sweet	Index or index and second fingers touch tip of wagging tongue. (Correct ASL form: index and second fingers extended side by side.)	For dessert; used spontaneously at end of meal. Also, when asking for candy.
Open	Flat hands are placed side by side, palms down, then drawn apart while rotated to palms up.	At door of house, room, car, refrigerator, or cupboard; on containers such as jars; and on faucets.
Tickle	The index finger of one hand is drawn across the back of the other hand. (Related to ASL "touch.")	For tickling or for chasing games.
Go	Opposite of "come-gimme."	While walking hand-in-hand or riding on someone's shoulders. Washoe usually indicates the direction desired.
Out	Curved hand grasps tapered hand; then tapered hand is withdrawn upward.	When passing through doorways; until recently, used for both "in" and "out." Also, when asking to be taken outdoors.
Hurry	Open hand is shaken at the wrist. (Correct ASL form: index and second fingers extended side by side.)	Often follows signs such as "come-gimme," "out," "open," and "go," particularly if there is a delay before Washoe is obeyed. Also, used while watching her meal being prepared.
Hear-listen	Index finger touches ear.	For loud or strange sounds: bells, car horns, sonic booms, etc. Also, for asking someone to hold a watch to her ear.
Toothbrush	Index finger is used as brush, to rub front teeth.	When Washoe has finished her meal, or at other times when shown a toothbrush.
Drink	Thumb is extended from fisted hand and touches mouth.	For water, formula, soda pop, etc. For soda pop, often combined with "sweet."
Hurt	Extended index fingers are jabbed toward each other. Can	To indicate cuts and bruises on herself or on others. Can be

TABLE 1.4–1   (Continued)

Signs	Description	Context
	be used to indicate location of pain.	elicited by red stains on a person's skin or by tears in clothing.
Sorry	Fisted hand clasps and unclasps at shoulder. (Correct ASL form: fisted hand is rubbed over heart with circular motion.)	After biting someone, or when someone has been hurt in another way (not necessarily by Washoe). When told to apologize for mischief.
Funny	Tip of index finger presses nose, and Washoe snorts. (Correct ASL form: index and second fingers used; no snort.)	When soliciting interaction play, and during games. Occasionally, when being pursued after mischief.
Please	Open hand is drawn across chest. (Correct ASL form: finger-tips used, and circular motion.)	When asking for objects and activities. Frequently combined: "Please go," "Out, please," "Please drink."
Food-eat	Several fingers of one hand are placed in mouth. (Correct ASL form: fingertips of tapered hand touch mouth repeatedly.)	During meals and preparation of meals.
Flower	Tip of index finger touches one or both nostrils. (Correct ASL form: tips of tapered hand touch first one nostril, then the other.)	For flowers.
Cover-blanket	Draws one hand toward self over the back of the other.	At bedtime or naptime, and, on cold days, when Washoe wants to be taken out.
Dog	Repeated slapping on thigh.	For dogs and for barking.
You	Index finger points at a person's chest.	Indicates successive turns in games. Also used in response to questions such as "Who tickle?" "Who brush?"
Napkin-bib	Fingertips wipe the mouth region.	For bib, for washcloth, and for Kleenex.
In	Opposite of "out."	Wants to go indoors, or wants someone to join her indoors.
Brush	The fisted hand rubs the back of the open hand several times. (Adapted from ASL "polish.")	For hairbrush, and when asking for brushing.
Hat	Palm pats top of head.	For hats and caps.
I-me	Index finger points at, or touches, chest.	Indicates Washoe's turn, when she and a companion share

TABLE 1.4–1   (Continued)

Signs	Description	Context
		food, drink, etc. Also used in phrases, such as "I drink," and in reply to questions such as "Who tickle?" (Washoe: "you"); "Who I tickle?" (Washoe: "Me.")
Shoes	The fisted hands are held side by side and strike down on shoes or floor. (Correct ASL form: the sides of the fisted hands strike against each other.)	For shoes and boots.
Smell	Palm is held before nose and moved slightly upward several times.	For scented objects: tobacco, perfume, sage, etc.
Pants	Palms of the flat hands are drawn up against the body toward waist.	For diapers, rubber pants, trousers.
Clothes	Fingertips brush down the chest.	For Washoe's jacket, nightgown, and shirts; also for our clothing.
Cat	Thumb and index finger grasp cheek hair near side of mouth and are drawn outward (representing cat's whiskers).	For cats.
Key	Palm of one hand is repeatedly touched with the index finger of the other. (Correct ASL form: crooked index finger is rotated against palm.)	Used for keys and locks and to ask us to unlock a door.
Baby	One forearm is placed in the crook of the other, as if cradling a baby.	For dolls, including animal dolls such as a toy horse and duck.
Clean	The open palm of one hand is passed over the open palm of the other.	Used when Washoe is washing or being washed, or when a companion is washing hands or some other object. Also used for "soap."

Instrumental Conditioning

It seems intuitively unreasonable that the acquisition of language by human beings could be strictly a matter of reiterated instrumental conditioning—that a child acquires language after the fashion of a rat that is conditioned, first, to press a lever for food in the presence of one stimulus, then to turn a wheel in the presence of another stimulus, and so on until a large repertoire of discriminated responses is acquired. Nevertheless, the so-called "trick vocabulary" of early childhood is probably acquired in this way, and this may be a critical stage in the acquisition of language by children. In any case, a minimal objective of this project was to teach Washoe as many signs as possible by whatever procedures we could enlist. Thus, we have not hesitated to use conventional procedures of instrumental conditioning.

Anyone who becomes familiar with young chimpanzees soon learns about their passion for being tickled. There is no doubt that tickling is the most effective reward that we have used with Washoe. In the early months, when we would pause in our tickling, Washoe would indicate that she wanted more tickling by taking our hands and placing them against her ribs or around her neck. The meaning of these gestures was unmistakable, but since we were not studying our human ability to interpret her chimpanzee gestures, we decided to shape an arbitrary response that she could use to ask for more tickling. We noted that, when being tickled, she tended to bring her arms together to cover the place being tickled. The result was a very crude approximation of the ASL sign for "more" (see Table 1.4-1). Thus, we would stop tickling and then pull Washoe's arms away from her body. When we released her arms and threatened to resume tickling, she tended to bring her hands together again. If she brought them back together, we would tickle her again. From time to time we would stop tickling and wait for her to put her hands together by herself. At first, any approximation to the "more" sign, however crude, was rewarded. Later, we required closer approximations and introduced imitative prompting. Soon, a very good version of the "more" sign could be obtained, but it was quite specific to the tickling situation.

In the 6th month of the project we were able to get "more" signs for a new game that consisted of pushing Washoe across the floor in a laundry basket. In this case we did not use the shaping procedure but, from the start, used imitative prompting to elicit the "more" sign. Soon after the "more" sign became spontaneous and reliable in the laundry-basket game, it began to appear as a request for more swinging (by the arms)—again, after first being elicited with imitative prompting. From this point on, Washoe transferred the "more" sign to all activities, including feeding. The transfer was usually spontaneous, occurring when there was some pause in a desired activity or when some object was removed. Often we ourselves were not sure that Washoe wanted "more" until she signed to us.

The sign for "open" had a similar history. When Washoe wanted to get through a door, she tended to hold up both hands and pound on the door with her palms or her knuckles. This is the beginning position for the "open" sign (see Table 1.4-1). By waiting for her to place her hands on the door and then lift them, and also by imitative prompting, we were able to shape a good approximation of the "open" sign, and would reward this by opening the door. Originally she was trained to make this sign for three particular doors that she used every day. Washoe transferred this sign to all doors; then to containers such as the refrigerator, cupboards, drawers, briefcases, boxes, and jars; and eventually—an invention of Washoe's—she used it to ask us to turn on water faucets.

In the case of "more" and "open" we followed the conventional laboratory procedure of waiting for Washoe to make some response that could be shaped into the sign we wished her to acquire. We soon found that this was not necessary; Washoe could acquire signs that were first elicited by our holding her hands, forming them into the desired configuration, and then putting them through the desired movement. Since this procedure of guidance is usually much more practical than waiting for a spontaneous approximation to occur at a favorable moment, we have used it much more frequently.

RESULTS

Vocabulary

In the early stages of the project we were able to keep fairly complete records of Washoe's daily signing behavior. But, as the amount of signing behavior and the number of signs to be monitored increased, our initial attempts to obtain exhaustive records became prohibitively cumbersome. During the 16th month we settled on the following procedure. When a new sign was introduced we waited until it had been reported by three different observers as having occurred in an appropriate context and spontaneously (that is, with no prompting other than a question such as "What is it?" or "What do you want?"). The sign was then added to a checklist in which its occurrence, form, context, and the kind of prompting required were recorded. Two such checklists were filled out each day, one for the first half of the day and one for the second half. For a criterion of acquisition we chose a reported frequency of at least one appropriate and spontaneous occurrence each day over a period of 15 consecutive days.

In Table 1.4–1 we have listed 30 signs that met this criterion by the end of the 22nd month of the project. In addition, we have listed four signs ("dog," "smell," "me," and "clean") that we judged to be stable, despite the fact that they had not met the stringent criterion before the end of the 22nd month. These additional signs had, nevertheless, been reported to occur appropriately and spontaneously on more than half of the days in a period of 30 consecutive days. An indication of the variety of signs that Washoe used in the course of a day is given by the following data: during the 22nd month of study, 28 of the 34 signs listed were reported on at least 20 days, and the smallest number of different signs reported for a single day was 23, with a median of 29 (12).

The order in which these signs first appeared in Washoe's repertoire is also given in Table 1.4–1. We considered the first appearance to be the date on which three different observers reported appropriate and spontaneous occurrences. By this criterion, 4 new signs first appeared during the first 7 months, 9 new signs during the next 7 months, and 21 new signs during the next 7 months. We chose the 21st month rather than the 22nd month as the cutoff for this tabulation so that no signs would be included that do not appear in Table 1.4–1. Clearly, if Washoe's rate of acquisition continues to accelerate, we will have to assess her vocabulary on the basis of sampling procedures. We are now in the process of developing procedures that could be used to make periodic tests of Washoe's performance on samples of her repertoire. However, now that there is evidence that a chimpanzee can acquire a vocabulary of more than 30 signs, the exact number of signs in her current vocabulary is less significant than the order of magnitude—50, 100, 200 signs, or more—that might eventually be achieved.

Differentiation

In Table 1.4–1, column 1, we list English equivalents for each of Washoe's signs. It must be understood that this equivalence is only approximate, because equivalence between English and ASL, as between any two human languages, is only approximate, and because Washoe's usage does differ from that of standard ASL. To some extent her usage is indicated in the column labeled "Context" in Table 1.4–1, but the definition of any given sign must always depend upon her total vocabulary, and this has been continually changing. When she had very few signs for specific things, Washoe used the "more" sign for a wide class of requests. Our only restriction was that we discouraged the use of "more" for first requests. As she acquired signs for specific requests, her use of "more" declined until, at the time of this writing, she was using this sign mainly to ask for repetition of some action that she could not name, such as a somersault. Perhaps the best English equivalent would be "do it again." Still, it seemed preferable to list the English equivalent for the ASL sign rather than its current referent for Washoe, since further refinements in her usage may be achieved at a later date.

The differentiation of the signs for "flower" and "smell" provides a further illustration of usage depending upon size of vocabulary. As the "flower" sign became more frequent, we noted that it occurred in several inappropriate contexts that all seemed to include odors; for example, Washoe would make the "flower" sign when opening a tobacco pouch or when entering a kitchen filled with cooking odors. Taking our cue from this, we introduced the "smell" sign by passive shaping and imitative prompting. Gradually Washoe came to make the appropriate distinction between "flower" contexts and "smell" contexts in her signing, although "flower" (in the single-nostril form) (see Table 1.4–1) has continued to occur as a common error in "smell" contexts.

Transfer

In general, when introducing new signs we have used a very specific referent for the initial training—a particular door for "open," a particular hat for "hat." Early in the project we were concerned about the possibility that signs might become inseparable from their first referents. So far, however, there has been no problem of this kind: Washoe has always been able to transfer her signs spontaneously to new members of each class of referents. We have already described the transfer of "more" and "open." The sign for "flower" is a particularly good example of transfer, because flowers occur in so many varieties, indoors, outdoors, and in pictures, yet Washoe uses the same sign for all. It is fortunate that she has responded well to pictures of objects. In the case of "dog" and "cat" this has proved to be important because live dogs and cats can be too exciting, and we have had to use pictures to elicit most of the "dog" and "cat" signs. It is noteworthy that Washoe has transferred the "dog" sign to the sound of barking by an unseen dog.

The acquisition and transfer of the sign for "key" illustrates a further point. A great many cupboards and doors in Washoe's quarters have been kept secure by small padlocks that can all be opened by the same simple key. Because she was immature and awkward, Washoe had great difficulty in learning to use these keys and locks. Because we wanted her to improve her manual dexterity, we let her practice with these keys until she could open the locks quite easily (then we had to hide the keys). Washoe soon transferred this skill to all manner of locks and keys, including ignition keys. At about the same time, we taught her the sign for "key," using the original padlock keys as a referent. Washoe came to use this sign both to name keys that were presented to her and to ask for the keys to various locks when no key was in sight. She readily transferred the sign to all varieties of keys and locks.

Now, if an animal can transfer a skill learned with a certain key and lock to new types of key and lock, it should not be surprising that the same animal can learn to use an arbitrary response to name and ask for a certain key and then transfer that sign to new types of keys. Certainly, the relationship between the use of a key and the opening of locks is as arbitrary as the relationship between the sign for "key" and its many referents. Viewed in this way, the general phenomenon of transfer of training and the specifically linguistic phenomenon of labeling become very similar, and the problems that these phenomena pose for modern learning theory should require similar solutions. We do not mean to imply that the problem of labeling is less complex than has generally been supposed; rather, we are suggesting that the problem of transfer of training requires an equally sophisticated treatment.

Combinations

During the phase of the project covered by this article we made no deliberate attempts to elicit combinations or phrases, although we may have responded more readily to strings of two or more signs than to single signs. As far as we can judge, Washoe's early use of signs in strings was spontaneous. Almost as soon as she had eight or ten signs in her repertoire, she began to use them two and three at a time. As her repertoire increased, her tendency to produce strings of two or more signs also increased, to the point where this has become a common mode of signing for her. We, of course, usually signed to her in combinations, but if Washoe's use of combinations has been imitative, then it must be a generalized sort of imitation, since she has invented a number of combinations, such as "gimme tickle" (before we had ever asked her to tickle us), and "open food drink" (for the refrigerator—we have always called it the "cold box").

Four signs—"please," "come-gimme," "hurry," and "more"—used with one or more other signs, account for the largest share of Washoe's early combinations. In general, these four signs have functioned as emphasizers, as in "please open hurry" and "gimme drink please."

Until recently, five additional signs—"go," "out," "in," "open," and "hear-listen"—accounted for most of the remaining combinations. Typical examples of combinations using these four are, "go in" or "go out" (when at some distance from a door), "go sweet" (for being carried to a raspberry bush), "open flower" (to be let through the gate to a flower garden), "open key" (for a locked door), "listen eat" (at the sound of an alarm clock signaling mealtime), and "listen dog" at the sound of barking by an unseen dog). All but the first and last of these six examples were inventions of Washoe's. Combinations of this type tend to amplify the meaning of the single signs used. Sometimes, however, the function of these five signs has been about the same as that of the emphasizers, as in "open out" (when standing in front of a door).

Toward the end of the period covered in this article we were able to introduce the pronouns "I-me" and "you," so that combinations that resemble short sentences have begun to appear.

CONCLUDING OBSERVATIONS

From time to time we have been asked questions such as, "Do you think that Washoe has language?" or "At what point will you be able to say that Washoe has language?" We find it very difficult to respond to these questions because they are altogether foreign to the spirit of our research. They imply a distinction between one class of communicative behavior that can be called language and another class that cannot. This in turn implies a well-established theory that could provide the distinction. If our objectives had required such a theory, we would certainly not have been able to begin this project as early as we did.

In the first phase of the project we were able to verify the hypothesis that sign language is an appropriate medium of two-way communication for the chimpanzee. Washoe's intellectual immaturity, the continuing acceleration of her progress, the fact that her signs do not remain specific to their original referents but are transferred spontaneously to new referents, and the emergence of rudimentary combinations all suggest that significantly more can be accomplished by Washoe during the subsequent phases of this project. As we proceed, the problems of these subsequent phases will be chiefly concerned with the technical business of measurement. We are now developing a procedure for testing Washoe's ability to name objects. In this procedure, an object or a picture of an object is placed in a box with a window. An observer, who does not know what is in the box, asks Washoe what she sees through the window. At present, this method is limited to items that fit in the box; a more ingenious method will have to be devised for other items. In particular, the ability to combine and recombine signs must be tested. Here, a great deal depends upon reaching a stage at which Washoe produces an extended series of signs in answer to questions. Our hope is that Washoe can be brought to the point where she describes events and situations to an observer who has no other source of information.

At an earlier time we would have been more cautious about suggesting that a chimpanzee might be able to produce extended utterances to communicate information. We believe now that it is the writers—who would predict just what it is that no chimpanzee will ever do—who must proceed with caution. Washoe's accomplishments will probably be exceeded by another chimpanzee, because it is unlikely that the conditions of training have been optimal in this first attempt. Theories of language that depend upon the identification of aspects of language that are exclusively human must remain tentative until a considerably larger body of intensive research with other species becomes available.

SUMMARY

We set ourselves the task of teaching an animal to use a form of human language. Highly intelligent and highly social, the chimpanzee is an obvious choice for such a study, yet it has not been possible to teach a member of this species more than a few spoken words. We reasoned that a spoken language, such as English, might be an inappropriate medium of communication for a chimpanzee. This led us to choose American Sign Language, the gestural system of communication used by the deaf in North American, for the project.

The youngest infant that we could obtain was a wild-born female, whom we named Washoe, and who was estimated to be between 8 and 14 months old when we began our program of training. The laboratory conditions, while not patterned after those of a human family (as in the studies of Kellogg and Kellogg and of Hayes and Hayes), involved a minimum of confinement and a maximum of social interaction with human companions. For all practical purposes, the only verbal communication was in ASL, and the chimpanzee was maximally exposed to the use of this language by human beings.

It was necessary to develop a rough-and-ready mixture of training methods. There was evidence that some of Washoe's early signs were acquired by delayed imitation of the signing behavior of her human companions, but very few if any, of her early signs were introduced by immediate imitation. Manual babbling was directly fostered and did increase in the course of the project. A number of signs were introduced by shaping and instrumental conditioning. A particularly effective and convenient method of shaping consisted of holding Washoe's hands, forming them into a configuration, and putting them through the movements of a sign.

We have listed more than 30 signs that Washoe acquired and could use spontaneously and appropriately by the end of the 22nd month of the project. The signs acquired earliest were simple demands. Most of the later signs have been names for objects, which Washoe has used both as demands and as answers to questions. Washoe readily used noun signs to name pictures of objects as well as actual objects and has frequently called the attention of her companions to pictures and objects by naming them. Once acquired, the signs have not remained specific to the original referents but have been transferred spontaneously to a wide class of appropriate referents. At this writing, Washoe's rate of acquisition of new signs is still accelerating.

From the time she had eight or ten signs in her repertoire, Washoe began to use them in strings of two or more. During the period covered by this article we made no deliberate effort to elicit combinations other than by our own habitual use of strings of signs. Some of the combined forms that Washoe has used may have been imitative, but many have been inventions of her own. Only a small proportion of the possible combinations have, in fact, been observed. This is because most of Washoe's combinations include one of a limited group of signs that act as combiners. Among the signs that Washoe has recently acquired are the pronouns "I-me" and "you." When these occur in combinations the result resembles a short sentence. In terms of the eventual level of communication that a chimpanzee might be able to attain, the most promising results have been spontaneous naming, spontaneous transfer to new referents, and spontaneous combinations and recombinations of signs.

REFERENCES AND NOTES

1. See, for example, E. H. Lenneberg, *Biological Foundations of Language* (Wiley, New York, 1967).
2. A. L. Bryan, *Curr. Anthropol.* 4, 297 (1963).
3. K. J. Hayes and C. Hayes, *Proc. Amer. Phil. Soc.* 95, 105 (1951).
4. K. J. Hayes, personal communication. Dr. Hayes also informed us that Viki used a few additional sounds which, while not resembling English words, were used for specific requests.
5. R. M. Yerkes, *Chimpanzees* (Yale Univ. Press, New Haven, 1943).
6. K. J. Hayes and C. Hayes, in *The Non-Human Primates and Human Evolution*, J. A. Gavan, Ed. (Wayne Univ. Press, Detroit, 1955), p. 110; W. N. Kellogg and L. A. Kellogg, *The Ape and the Child* (Hafner, New York, 1967; originally published by McGraw-Hill, New York, 1933); W. N. Kellogg, *Science* 162, 423 (1968).
7. W. C. Stokoe, D. Casterline, C. G. Croneberg, *A Dictionary of American Sign Language* (Gallaudet College Press, Washington, D. C., 1965); E. A. McCall, thesis, University of Iowa (1965).
8. J. Goodall, in *Primate Behavior*, I. DeVore, Ed. (Holt, Rinehart & Winston, New York, 1965), p. 425; A. J. Riopelle and C. M. Rogers, in *Behavior of Nonhuman Primates*, A. M. Schrier, H. F. Harlow, F. Stollnitz, Eds. (Academic Press, New York, 1965), p. 449.
9. R. M. Yerkes and B. W. Learned, *Chimpanzee Intelligence and Its Vocal Expression* (Williams & Wilkins, Baltimore, 1925), p. 53.
10. K. J. Hayes and C. Hayes, *J. Comp. Physiol. Psychol.* 45, 450 (1952).
11. C. J. Warden and L. H. Warner, *Quart. Rev. Biol.* 3, 1 (1928).
12. The development of Washoe's vocabulary of signs is being recorded on motion-picture film. At the time of this writing, 30 of the 34 signs listed in Table 1.4-1 are on film.
13. The research described in this article has been supported by National Institute of Mental Health grants MH-12154 and MH-34953 (Research Scientist Development Award to B. T. Gardner) and by National Science Foundation grant GB-7432. We acknowledge a great debt to the personnel of the Aero-medical Research Laboratory, Holloman Air Force Base, whose support and expert assistance effectively absorbed all of the many difficulties attendant upon the acquisition of a wild-caught chimpanzee. We are also grateful to Dr. Frances L. Fitz-Gerald of the Yerkes Regional Primate Research Center for detailed advice on the care of an infant chimpanzee. Drs. Emanual Berger of Reno, Nevada, and D. B. Olsen of the University of Nevada have served as medical consultants, and we are grateful to them for giving so generously of their time and medical skills. The faculty of the Sarah Hamilton Fleischmann School of Home Economics, University of Nevada, has generously allowed us to use the facilities of their experimental nursery school on weekends and holidays.

Two
Classical
Conditioning

A dog stands motionless in the middle of the room, immobilized by a leather harness. The room is very quiet, all outside sound blocked by concrete walls six inches thick. A bell rings, the dog turns toward it but otherwise shows little reaction. Five seconds later food powder is presented to the dog through a long rubber tube. The silence returns. Ten minutes later the bell again sounds and is again followed by food. Ten more minutes pass. The bell sounds for a third time but now the dog begins to move restlessly in his harness, saliva dripping from his mouth. As the trials continue, the dog becomes increasingly excited at the sound of the bell, more and more saliva flowing into a surgically implanted tube in his mouth and then into an adjoining room where technicians record the number of drops.

This simple experiment by Ivan Petrovitch Pavlov is probably the most important psychological experiment ever done, and it quickly made him one of the most famous scientists of all time. Why did this research generate such excitement? What is so *interesting* about a hungry dog salivating in anticipation of food? The answer has its roots in the complex history of Western intellectual thought, and we must briefly trace that history to appreciate the significance of Pavlov's research.

Early explanations of human behavior were generally religious in character: behavior is unpredictable, determined by fate or the whim of the gods. The advent of Christianity introduced a number of changes, but behavior was still seen as fundamentally unpredictable, every man having free will because of his possession of a soul. For about 2000 years there were no significant departures from this theme, until the publication in 1650 of *The Passions of the Soul* by René Descartes. Descartes was a mathematician (Cartesian geometry), but he was also a brilliant philosopher, of such eminence that he was invited to Sweden to serve as the personal tutor to Queen Christina. His first reaction was to say no, but she dispatched a warship to escort him, at which point he apparently found the honor too great to be refused. Conditions, however, proved to be less than ideal: classes were held three times a week at 5 o'clock in the morning, and took place in the unheated library of her castle. We are told that it was an unusually rigorous Swedish winter, and he died before it was over of pneumonia, at the age of 54 (see Boring, 1950).

Aside from its rather somber implications for students of philosophy, Descartes' life is important to us because he was the first philosopher in Western civilization to offer a detailed, mechanistic explanation for human behavior. According to Descartes our senses and muscles are interconnected by a complex network of nerves, and it is the flow of "animal spirits" through these nerves that makes possible the instinctive reactions necessary for survival. If the foot is burned, for example, the senses in the foot are stimulated and release into the nerve a vapor that then travels to the calf muscle and causes it to contract, resulting in the foot's withdrawal from the fire. This simple mechanism, a receptor activating a muscle via a direct neural connection, Descartes called a *reflex*, and he proposed that these reflexes underlie all our automatic, involuntary reactions, though not our higher processes. Thought for Descartes was still divinely inspired, guided by the soul, which was located in the pineal gland.

Descartes' analysis showed how simple, mechanical principles might explain the seemingly complex operations of the body, but he was not yet ready to allow a similar determinism in the operation of the mind. This next step was taken some forty years later by a British scholar and physician named John Locke. Locke's principal occupation was as a secretary to the Earl of Shaftesbury, but in the custom of those times he also met weekly with friends to discuss current issues in areas such as science and theology. At one of these meetings the disagreements became particularly intense, and it puzzled Locke how intelligent men could hold such different opinions regarding the same basic facts. He resolved, therefore, to prepare a brief paper for the next meeting, analyzing how each of us form our ideas of the world, and why they are so different. Twenty years later he finally completed this analysis, and it was published as a 400-page book, *An Essay Concerning Human Understanding*. The ideas of this essay were elaborated by subsequent philosophers such as David Hartley and James Mill, and together they form the doctrine of Associationism.

The fundamental principle of this approach was that any two sensations which repeatedly occur together will become *associated*, so that the later occurrence of one will invariably elicit the other. A stone, for example, produces a variety of visual and tactile sensations, and through repeated pairings they become associated together, and this compound sensation forms our "idea" of a stone:

From a stone I have had, (simultaneously), the sensation of colour, the sensation of hardness, the sensations of shape, and size, the sensation of weight. When the idea of one of these sensations occurs, the ideas of all of them occur. They exist in my mind (simultaneously); and their (simultaneous) existence is called the idea of the stone [James Mill, *Analysis of the Phenomena of the Human Mind*, 1829].

In addition to these associations among sensations which occur simultaneously, there are also sensations formed between *successive* ideas:

Our ideas spring up, or exist, in the order in which the sensations existed, of which they are the copies. This is the general law of the "Association of Ideas" . . . of the successive order of our ideas, many remarkable instances might be adduced. Of these none seems better adapted to the learner than the repetition of any passage, or words; the Lord's Prayer, for example, committed to memory. In learning the passage, we repeat it; that is, we pronounce the words, in successive order, from the beginning to the end. The order of the sensations is successive. When we proceed to repeat the passage, the ideas of the words also rise in succession, the preceding always suggesting the succeeding, and no other. *Our* suggests *father, father* suggests *which, which* suggests *art*; and so on, to the end. How remarkably this is the case, anyone may convince himself, by trying to repeat backwards, even a passage with which he is as familiar as the Lord's Prayer [James Mill, *Analysis of the Phenomena of the Human Mind*, 1829].

Not only the existence of ideas, therefore, but their order of occurrence can be explained through the Law of Association. The basic principle of this law is that of *contiguity*—associations are formed between events which occur together—but the strength of any association also depends on the *frequency* with which the events are paired:

Learning to play on a musical instrument is another remarkable illustration of the effect of repetition in strengthening associations, in rendering those sequences, which, at first, are slow, and difficult, afterwards, rapid, and easy. At first, the learner, after thinking of each successive note, as it stands in his book, has each time to look out with care for the key or the string which he is to touch, and the finger he is to touch it with, and is every moment committing mistakes. Repetition is well known to be the only means of overcoming these difficulties. As the repetition goes on, the sight of the note, or even the idea of the note, becomes associated with the place of the key or the string; and that of the key or the string with the proper finger. The association for a time is imperfect, but at last becomes so strong, that it is performed with the greatest rapidity, without an effort, and almost without consciousness [James Mill, *Analysis of the Phenomena of the Human Mind*, 1829].

And finally, the strength of an association depends on the *intensity* of the feelings it evokes in us:

> Attention and repetition help much to the fixing any ideas in the memory: but those which naturally at first make the deepest and most lasting impression, are those which are accompanied with pleasure or pain. . . . A man receives a sensible injury from another, thinks on the man and that action over and over, and by ruminating on them strongly or much in his mind, so cements two ideas together, that he makes them almost one; never thinks on the man, but the pain and displeasure he suffered comes into his mind with it, so that he scarce distinguishes them, but has as much an aversion for the one as the other. Thus hatreds are often begotten from slight and almost innocent occasions, and quarrels propagated and continued in the world. A man has suffered pain or sickness in any place; he saw his friend die in such a room. Though these have in nature nothing to do with one another, yet when the idea of the place occurs to his mind, it brings that of the pain and displeasure with it; he counfounds them in his mind, and can as little bear the one as the other [John Locke, *An Essay Concerning Human Understanding*, 1690].

Thus by the time of Pavlov the historical groundwork had been laid for a theory of behavior based on associations. Descartes had shown how seemingly complex reactions of the body could be explained in terms of simple, reflexive connections between a stimulus and a response, but he had restricted his explanation to so-called involuntary behavior. Pavlov's discovery of *conditioned* reflexes, however, suggested that learned behavior might also be due to stimulus-response associations. If the principles of conditioning were understood, therefore, it should be possible to explain *all* bodily movement, and, if the British Associationists were right, the operation of the mind as well.

Even beyond an abstract understanding of the body, however, discovery of the laws of conditioning should allow practical control over its operations. Salivation had always been considered an involuntary response largely beyond an individual's control, but now Pavlov's research showed that this automatic reaction to food in the mouth could be arbitrarily transferred to any stimulus of the experimenter's choice. If salivation could be so readily conditioned, what of our other involuntary responses, might not they too be controlled through the procedures of conditioning? Could we learn to control our emotions, to react with courage instead of fear, love instead of hate?

In this chapter we will seek some of the answers to these questions, looking first at research directed toward discovering the laws of conditioning, and then at experimental attempts to apply them.

First, however, a note on terminology. Pavlov called the salivation elicited by food an *unconditioned response,* since it occurred without any training, while salivation to a bell was a *conditioned response,* since it was learned. Similarly, the food powder was an *unconditioned stimulus* for salivation while the bell was a *conditioned stimulus.* The entire process, the development of a conditioned response as a result of pairings of a conditioned and an unconditioned stimulus, is what is now referred to as *classical conditioning.*

Intensity

One of the three basic laws of the British Associationists was that associations involving intense stimuli seem to be remembered more easily. If true, the effectiveness of classical conditioning should also depend on the intensity of the stimuli. Suppose, for example, that we conditioned two groups of subjects with a tone as the conditioned stimulus (CS) and a puff of air in the eye as the unconditioned stimulus (US) eliciting an eyeblink. We might use a mild puff of air as the US for our first group, and an intense puff of air for the second. If we now found stronger conditioning in the high-intensity group, could we conclude that intensity does indeed determine the strength of classical conditioning? The perhaps surprising answer is no, not necessarily.

Learning generally refers to a change in behavior as a result of experience, *but not all changes in behavior are due to learning.* A trivial example would be the development of a limp because of a leg injury, but more troublesome would be a change in the probability of eating as the result of having been deprived of food for twenty-four hours. This would be a change in behavior as a result of past experience, but it somehow is not what we really intend by the term learning. Changes due to hunger seem to be temporary and tied to the immediate conditions of the organism, whereas learning seems to imply a more permanent change in behavior. The criterion of permanence has its problems (for example, rapid forgetting), but it does seem reasonable to try to exclude phenomena that are temporary or due only to changes in motivation from our definition of learning.

Returning to our classical conditioning experiment, enhanced performance in the group with the more intense air puff might not necessarily be due to learning. The harsher air puff might have dried out the subject's eye, for example, or made him more nervous, thus making him more likely to blink in the future but not because of any direct conditioning to the tone. In fact, experiments have shown that if we presented an intense air puff *by itself*, never pairing it with the tone, we might still find an increase in the probability of blinking on test trials with the tone. This phenomenon is called *pseudoconditioning*, and it's possible that the intensity of the US affects pseudoconditioning rather than having any direct effect on conditioning.

How, then, can we tell whether the intensity of the US affects conditioning or only pseudoconditioning? One very clever solution is discussed in the article by Spence, Haggard, and Ross (Article 2.1), and it ultimately led to the conclusion that there is a genuine effect on conditioning. The authors discuss the problem in terms of separating the effects of drive and habit rather than conditioning and pseudoconditioning, but the logic in both cases is similar. The terms Drive (D) and Habit (H) are derived from the theoretical system of Clark Hull, which assumes that the probability of a response is a joint function of the subject's drive level (his general level of motivation or excitement) and habit strength (how well he has learned the response). An intensity effect involving drive would be an example of what we have called pseudoconditioning, while an effect on habit would correspond to conditioning.

An incidental point to notice in the Spence *et al.* article is the effect of trials. James Mill in 1829 wrote that "the causes of strength in conditioning seem all to be resolvable into two: the vividness of the associated feelings; and the frequency of the association," and Spence's results reveal the effects of both variables.

Having shown that the intensity of the US affects conditioning, we might also expect a similar effect of CS intensity. In the case of the CS, however, more intense stimuli seem to enhance only immediate performance, with no permanent effect on conditioning (see Beecroft, 1966). One interpretation of this finding is that CS intensity has a motivational effect, with more intense stimuli increasing the subject's arousal level and thus increasing the vigor of the subsequent conditioned response. Alternatively, the effect of CS intensity might be perceptual, with more intense stimuli being easier to detect.

It is not clear, in other words, whether it is the absolute intensity of the CS that determines performance, or only the amount of stimulus change. If, for example, a 100-db tone is more effective in eliciting response than a 50-db tone, is this because of the absolute decibel level, 100 db being stronger than 50 db, or because of the amount of stimulus change, a change from silence to 100 db being easier to detect than a change from silence to 50 db? One way to resolve this issue would be to use *decreases* in intensity as the CS. If the absolute intensity of the stimulus preceding the US is important, then a 25-db increase over background noise should be more effective than a 25-db decrease, but if it is stimulus change that is important, then both conditioned stimuli should be equally effective. Logan and Wagner (Article 2.2) report an experiment using essentially this design, and their results together with those of Grice, Masters, and Kohfeld (1966) support a stimulus change interpretation. Unlike US intensity, then, CS intensity seems to affect performance rather than learning. We seem more likely to notice large changes in the environment, and thus the probability of our responding is greater.

Contiguity

The most important principle in forming associations, according to the British Associationists, was contiguity. The strength of an association might be influenced by the intensity of the stimuli or by the frequency of their pairing, but the fundamental law of association was that of temporal contiguity. Again, translating this idea to conditioning, we would expect the effectiveness of conditioning to depend on the time separating the CS and US, shorter intervals yielding better conditioning. McAllister (Article 2.3) confirmed this relationship for eyelid conditioning, showing that conditioning increased as CS-US contiguity increased, up to an optimal separation of approximately one half a second. Although experiments with other conditioned responses have revealed some variability in the optimal CS-US interval, and also in the maximum interval at which conditioning is possible (see Revusky, 1971), they have generally confirmed the importance of contiguity, conditioning being strongest when the conditioned and unconditioned stimuli follow each other closely in time.

Contingency

Until recently the three major principles of the British Associationists, contiguity, frequency, and intensity, were thought to provide an essentially complete account of the basic laws of conditioning, but in 1967 a graduate student at the University of Pennsylvania presented provocative evidence that a fourth principle might be necessary. Robert Rescorla, in a preliminary report published in *Psychonomic Science* (Article 2.4), suggested that conditioning depended not only on the

contiguity of the CS and US but on their *contingency*. The presence
of a contingency between two events essentially means that the
occurrence of one event depends or is contingent on the occurrence of
the other, regardless of their temporal relationship. Nausea, for example,
is often contingent on eating rotten meat, even though its onset may
be delayed many hours. In classical conditioning, however, the US is
usually both contiguous with the CS and contingent on it, since it is
presented when the CS has already occurred. It had always been
assumed that it was only the contiguity of the two stimuli that mattered,
not their contingency, until Rescorla raised the interesting question of
what would happen if that contingency were eliminated.

Specifically, Rescorla exposed two groups of dogs to contiguous
pairings of tone and shock, but for one of these groups, the random
control, shock also occurred in the *absence* of the tone. The extra shock
presentations should not affect CS-US contiguity, since every tone
presentation is still closely followed by shock. This procedure would,
however, eliminate the contingency between the CS and US, since
shock was now equally probable in the presence or absence of the tone.
For the random control subjects, then, the CS was still closely
followed by the US, but it no longer reliably predicted when the US
would occur. If contiguity is sufficient for conditioning, fear should be
conditioned to the tone in both groups, but if a contingency is also
necessary then there should be no fear conditioning in the random control.

To measure fear Rescorla used an indirect procedure in which the
CS is presented as the subject is responding on a Sidman Avoidance
Task. In Sidman Avoidance subjects must respond periodically if they
are to avoid an electric shock, and they usually learn to respond at a rate
sufficient to avoid all shocks. Presenting a fear-evoking CS in this
situation has been found to increase the rate of avoidance responding,
and this change in rate provides a sensitive index of the subject's
fear. Using this procedure Rescorla found strong fear conditioning in
the experimental group where there was a contingency, but none in
the random control.

Merely pairing a CS and US, then, is not sufficient for conditioning:
the CS must have some genuine predictive value if it is to elicit a
conditioned response. Once recognized this principle makes sense, in
that it allows for better adaptation to the environment than would
contiguity alone. In Rescorla's random control group, for example, it
might make sense for the dog to become afraid of the box and later
avoid it, since that was the only place he ever received shock, but it
would be useless and perhaps even harmful for him to become
frightened whenever he heard the tone, as it was simply an incidental
stimulus that didn't differentiate between periods of shock and safety.

Another interesting finding of Rescorla's experiment was that a stimulus explicitly *unpaired* with shock, that is, one that predicted a period of safety, could reduce fear in a later avoidance test. Pavlov was the first to suggest that conditioning involves two opposing processes, excitation and inhibition, and that while a stimulus predicting a US would come to elicit a conditioned response, a stimulus predicting the absence of that US would come to actively inhibit the conditioned response. We will encounter the concept of inhibition again later, but it is worth noting at this point that conditioning can be used not only to increase fear but to decrease it.

Applications

Until recently, American research on conditioning has been largely confined to studying the eyeblink, in the hopes of thoroughly developing the laws of conditioning in one system and only then extrapolating those laws to other behaviors. Within the last decade, however, there has been a growing interest in the range of behaviors which can be conditioned, and there is now evidence for the conditioning of complex instincts as well as such relatively simple responses as salivation. Farris (1967), for example, was able to condition the courting response in Japanese quail to a buzzer, and aggression has been conditioned in both rats (Vernon and Ulrich, 1966) and Siamese fighting fish (Adler and Hogan, 1963). The most dramatic research, however, has been reported by the Russians, who have claimed successful conditioning of an extraordinary variety of internal processes. Although there are still only fragmentary accounts available in the West, they have reported conditioning of such vital processes as the movement of white blood corpuscles to the site of an injury, and the production of blood by bone marrow! On a somewhat lighter note, the Russians have also conditioned urination to cues controlled by the experimenter, using as subjects hospital patients who had undergone kidney surgery (see Razran, 1961).

These experiments suggest that conditioning is a pervasive process, by no means limited to salivation or blinking, but they still leave a number of practical questions unanswered. Can we condition emotions or instincts in man as well as in animals? If so, can we practically apply the principles of classical conditioning to reduce paralyzing anxieties or perhaps even to increase fear in those situations where it would be adaptive?

The first experimental attempt to answer these questions was by

John Broadus Watson, the founder of Behaviorism. Watson was one of the first to argue that psychologists should be more concerned with overt behavior than with the hidden processes of the mind, and as part of his emphasis on behavior he argued for a greater concern with practical applications. Thus in 1920, together with Rosalie Raynor, Watson attempted to directly condition fear in a human infant, the "stolid and unemotional" Albert B. (Article 2.5). Using a white rat as the conditioned stimulus (Albert initially showed no signs of fear in its presence) and a loud noise as the unconditioned stimulus, they found that fear was not only quickly conditioned in an infant but seemed to persist over long periods. They hypothesized that such fear conditioning might explain many of the phobias and anxieties of adults, and offered some interesting suggestions for eliminating such fears. Their experimental efforts, however, had to be abruptly terminated when Albert was removed by his mother from the hospital where they had been testing him.

One of their suggestions for eliminating fear was to associate the fearful stimulus with a pleasurable event such as food or sexual stimulation. The pleasant emotions associated with these events are incompatible with fear, and thus if they could be strongly conditioned fear might be suppressed. This procedure was first investigated by Pavlov, who called it *counterconditioning*, but its first human application was in an experiment by Mary Carver Jones (1924). One of her subjects, Peter, was afraid of rabbits, and following Watson and Raynor's suggestion she introduced a rabbit while Peter was eating. Gradually, so as not to frighten the child, she moved the rabbit closer and closer to his chair as he ate, and the eventual result was that Peter not only lost his fear of the rabbit but actively sought out opportunities to play with it.

By 1924, then, both conditioning and elimination of fear had been successfully demonstrated with human subjects, but for the next several decades there was little further effort at practical applications of conditioning. The reasons for this gap are somewhat obscure (see Franks, 1969), but the next important development did not come until the mid-1950s, when Joseph Wolpe reported on a new therapy he called *systematic desensitization*. Wolpe's technique was very similar to that of Jones, except that he used relaxation as the conditioned response instead of eating, and he asked his subjects to imagine fearful stimuli instead of actually presenting them. In Wolpe's procedure subjects were first asked to describe the kinds of stimuli they feared, and then together with the therapist to arrange these stimuli in a hierarchy based on their fearfulness. Someone with a fear of snakes, for example, might find the idea of looking at a toy snake least threatening, with other situations arranged in ascending order to the most fearful, actually picking up a live snake. The patient is then instructed in relaxation techniques, and starting with the first stimulus in the hierarchy is asked to alternately visualize the scene and relax. Only when relaxation is completely conditioned to that scene will the therapist mention the next image in the hierarchy, and so on. Using this technique Wolpe reported extraordinary success in eliminating phobias, and in more recent controlled studies substantial improvement has been reported in as many as 86 percent of the patients, as opposed to 0 to 20 percent in control groups involving standard therapy or no treatment (see Paul, 1969).

There is thus substantial evidence that systematic desensitization is effective, but why it works is still not clear. The basic rationale for the therapy is that phobias and other neurotic behaviors are really learned, acquired in part through classical conditioning. To the extent these responses are learned, then, we should be able to use the principles of learning to help eliminate them. A very different interpretation of neuroses was that of Sigmund Freud, who saw them as external manifestations of fundamental conflicts within the mind. The mind, according to Freud, was composed of three major forces, the id, the ego, and the superego, and the goals of these forces were often in opposition. The intense conflicts between them sometimes become too great to be contained, and they then appear in symbolic form in behaviors such as dreams or phobias. The important point in this interpretation is that phobias are only *symptoms* of underlying disturbances, much as yellow skin is a symptom of jaundice rather than the disease itself. To treat only the external behavior, the Freudians argue, is useless, since the underlying malaise will still be present and the elimination of one symptom will only result in its replacement by another. Snakes, for example, were seen by Freud as a sexual symbol, and fear of snakes was thus an external manifestation of anxiety about sex. Systematic desensitization might succeed in eliminating the fear of snakes, but the underlying fear of sex would still be present and would emerge in some other form, perhaps as a facial tic.

The debate as to whether phobias are learned behaviors or only symptoms is not easily resolved, but we can say that the Freudian prediction of symptom substitution has not been supported. There is now an extensive literature of phobic desensitization in which patients have been observed for up to four years after treatment, and there have been few cases involving either recurrence of the old symptom or the development of new ones (see Paul, 1969). In the treatment of phobias, then, systematic desensitization appears to be a highly successful therapy.

A more troublesome question from the point of view of learning theory is whether this success is really due to a straightforward application of the principles of classical conditioning. For one thing, the stimuli employed are very different from those usually studied in the laboratory. The CS, for example, is *imagining* a fearful event rather than having it actually presented, and the US involves instructions to relax, which are very different from the involuntary unconditioned stimuli normally employed. Furthermore, even if these stimuli do correspond to more traditional conditioned and unconditioned stimuli, the success of the therapy is not necessarily due to their associative pairing. It might be that relaxation training alone results in a general lessening of anxiety, or perhaps it is the friendly interest and encouragement of the therapist. Davison (Article 2.6) presents evidence from a well-controlled experiment that the association of the fearful stimuli and relaxation is in fact crucial, but because of its importance this area is likely to remain controversial for some time.

In desensitization, the goal is elimination of fear, but in *aversion therapy* the aim is to actively encourage fear, to make some harmful stimulus sufficiently aversive that it will be avoided in the future. The principles of aversion therapy have long been known, and some of the most imaginative applications stem from ancient times. Pliny the Elder, for example, recommended putting putrid spiders in the bottom of an alcoholic's cup, so that the feeling of extreme revulsion he would experience when he first tipped the tankard would effectively deter any further efforts at drinking. Raymond (Article 2.7) reports a somewhat more modern attempt to condition aversions, inducing nausea with the drug apomorphine rather than with putrid spiders. In order to eliminate cigarette smoking, for example, he conditioned nausea to the act of smoking, and obtained some dramatic changes. In general, however, attempts to eliminate such strong behaviors as addiction and homosexuality have had mixed success, and it is not yet clear whether the fault lies in the learning principles involved, or in the inability of the therapist to maintain the appropriate contingencies when the subject returns to the real world. Cigarette smoking may be paired with aversive stimuli in the laboratory, but if it is still pleasurable outside the lab the patient will quickly learn that discrimination, much as Rescorla's dogs learned to distinguish between a tone paired with the presence of shock and one paired with its absence. There are ways to circumvent such problems—alcoholics, for example, can be administered drugs which will result in severe nausea whenever they drink—so that with further research these applications may prove increasingly effective.

2.1 UCS INTENSITY AND THE ASSOCIATIVE (HABIT) STRENGTH OF THE EYELID CR*

K. W. Spence, D. F. Haggard, and L. E. Ross

In a recent series of lectures (7) the senior author tentatively suggested the theoretical possibility that classical aversive conditioning is governed by a reinforcement principle, whereas instrumental appetional (reward) conditioning does not involve such a principle. Contiguity of the stimulus and behavior events was considered to be a sufficient condition for learning, i.e., habit formation, to occur in this latter type of situation. That is, the increment of habit strength (H) of the instrumental response was assumed to depend only on the occurrence of the response and not be a function of the reinforcer and its properties. In contrast, the increment of H of the conditioned aversive response was interpreted as being a function of the occurrence and properties of the reinforcing UCS. The present study is concerned with evidence as to whether classical aversive conditioning requires the assumption of a reinforcement principle, or more specifically, whether the habit strength (H) of a defense CR is a function of the intensity of the UCS.

On the basis of the experimental finding that level of performance in classical aversive conditioning varies directly with the intensity of the UCS it has been assumed that drive strength, D, is a function of the intensity (noxiousness) of the UCS. According to a reinforcement interpretation of this kind of learning the habit strength (H) would also be assumed to be a function of the UCS. Thus, according to this conception, performance differences with different intensities of the UCS reflect differences both in H and in level of D.

The experimental problem involved in testing this theory is to find some way of separating out these two factors. A previous study by Spence (6) attempted to accomplish this by employing the factorial design type of experiment. While the results of this experiment were in agreement with the reinforcement interpretation that different amounts of habit strength develop with different intensities of the UCS, as was

* K. W. Spence, D. F. Haggard, and L. E. Ross, "UCS Intensity and the Associative (Habit) Strength of the Eyelid CR," *The Journal of Experimental Psychology*, 55, 1958, 404–411. Copyright 1958 by the American Psychological Association, and reproduced by permission. This study was carried out as part of a project concerned with the role of motivation in learning under Contract N9 onr-93802, Project NR 154-107 between the State University of Iowa and the Office of Naval Research.

pointed out, it was also possible to interpret the findings in terms of a differential drive (D) level based on fear responses of different strength that become conditioned to the cues of the experimental situation.

The present studies represent a different type of attack on this problem. In these experiments an attempt is made to equate S's level of drive during the course of the conditioning and at the same time provide for differential reinforcement. In order to understand the logic of these experiments, it is necessary first to consider further the source of drive in classical defense conditioning. In the other main types of conditioning situations, classical and instrumental reward, and instrumental escape conditioning, the drive level (D) is a function of some relevant need produced by the manipulation of a maintenance schedule or by presentation of a noxious stimulus. The need in these instances is active (present) at the moment of the occurrence of the response and thus provides a certain level of D which, in combination with habit strength, determines the excitatory strength of the response. But what determines the need (drive state) and hence the level of D in the case of the conditioned anticipatory response on a particular trial in the classical defense type of conditioning? One cannot say that it is the noxious UCS on that particular trial for the CR anticipates this stimulus event. Furthermore, one cannot appeal to a conditioned emotional (fear) response that presumably would be established to the CS. The latency of such a response, mediated as it is by the autonomic nervous system, is much longer than the half-second or less interval of time that has typically been used and found optimal for conditioning such defense reactions. Thus in such instances the conditioned skeletal response, occurring as it does in from 200 to 500 msec., and lasting only briefly, has presumably taken place long before the fear response would even get started.

Because of these considerations it has generally been assumed that the level of drive (D) in this type of conditioning experiment is determined by the previous unconditioned stimuli; that is, those given on previous trials. These stimuli, depending upon their intensity, have been assumed to elicit hypothetical emotional responses (r_e) of varying magnitude (7). The latter have been thought of as persisting in their effects, lasting at least until the ensuing trial. As a number of writers have pointed out, this persisting emotional response may also get established as a CR to other cues in the general situation, possibly even to S's own verbal responses. These expectations, or fears, are assumed to keep a persisting level of emotional activity present that is, to an important degree, a function of the intensity of the UCS employed in the experiment. We have assumed that the level of D is directly related to this level of hypothetical emotional activity.

In the two experiments to be reported the drive level (D) of two groups for whom reinforcement was differential was equated by employing two different intensities of the UCS (air puff). For the low-reinforcement group a weak puff always occurred on a conditioning trial, while a strong puff was always presented on a trial on which no conditioning could occur. For the high-reinforcement group these conditions were reversed, the strong puff being presented on the conditioning trials and the weak puff being presented under the conditions in which no learning could take place. Since the two groups received the same average intensity of the noxious puff stimulus throughout the training period, their drive levels would be equal. However, the intensity of the puff on the trials on which conditioning could occur differed for the two groups. According to the present reinforcement interpretation the group that had the strong puff on a trial on which conditioning could occur should develop a greater amount of habit strength than the group that had a weak puff on a conditioning trial. Multiplication of these different H values by the same D values (since drive level was equal) implies that the excitatory potential (E) and, hence, response strength should be greater for the high-reinforcement group than for the low-reinforcement group.

EXPERIMENT I

Subjects

A total of 164 men and women students from an introductory course in psychology were used. Ten of these were eliminated because they met the criteria employed in previous studies in this laboratory defining a voluntary responder (6, 8). The data of four other Ss were discarded, two because they gave CR's in the pretest trials and two for reasons of equipment failure. The remaining 150 Ss provided three groups, each of which contained 25 men and 25 women.

Apparatus and Method of Recording

The S was seated in a dental chair in a semidarkened room. The E was in an adjoining room in which the stimulus controls and recording equipment were located. The apparatus for recording the eyeblinks and presenting the stimuli was identical with that used in recent studies from this laboratory (see 6).

The CS consisted of an increase in the brightness of a 6-cm. circular disc from a level of .004 to .506 apparent ft.-candle. The duration of the CS was .500 msec., with the UCS occurring 450 msec. after the onset of the CS. The duration of the UCS, an air puff of either .33 or 2.0 lb./sq. in. applied to the right eye through a .062-in. diameter orifice, was limited to 50 msec., by a 100-V., 60-cycle AC-operated solenoid valve controlled by an electronic timer.

The word "ready" preceded each presentation of the CS by 2, 3, or

4 sec. according to a prearranged schedule. The Ss were instructed to blink upon presentation of the ready signal and then fixate the circular disc in front of them. A CR was recorded whenever the record showed a deflection of 1 mm. or more in the interval 200 to 450 msec. following the onset of the CS. Responses with a latency of less than 200 msec., which were infrequent, were classified as original responses and were not included in the data.

Conditioning Procedure

Following the reading of instructions, each S received three presentations of the CS alone. A single presentation of the UCS alone was then given. Immediately following these preliminary trials each S received 100 trials, 50 conditioning trials which involved the paired presentation after the ready signal of the CS and the UCS and 50 trials which involved the presentation of only the UCS. The order of presentation of these paired and unpaired trials was prearranged according to an irregular order in which the number of each was equalized in blocks of four trials. Intertrial intervals of 15, 20, and 25 sec., averaging 20 sec. and arranged according to a fixed schedule, were used throughout the 100 trials. At the end of the experiment Ss were warned not to discuss the experiment with other members of the class.

In the case of the high-reinforcement group (Group H) the CS was always paired with the strong puff, whereas the weak puff was always presented alone, i.e., without the CS. The reverse conditions held for Group L (low reinforcement), the weak puff always being paired with the CS and the strong puff always being presented alone. A third group designated Group LL (low reinforcement and low drive) was also run in which a weak puff was used on both the paired (conditioning) trials and the trials on which the air puff was given alone.

Results

Figure 2.1–1 presents the frequency curves of conditioning for the three groups of Ss, 50 in each group. As may be seen, the curve for Group H rises well above that for Group L, whereas the latter is above that for Group LL. Evaluation of the performance levels over the last two points of the curves by means of the Mann-Whitney U test indicated that the difference between Groups H and L was highly significant ($P = .0014$), while the difference between Groups L and LL was significant at the .05 level.

Since the level of D, defined in terms of the intensities of the UCS employed, was equated for Groups H and L, the significant difference in the performance levels of these two groups presumably reflects a differential strength of H. The latter is, of course, related to the different intensities of the puff strengths on the paired conditioning trials. The

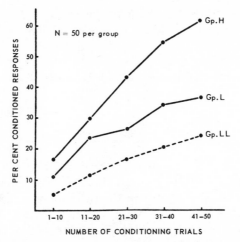

FIGURE 2.1–1   Acquisition curves showing the percentage of CR's in successive blocks of ten conditioning trials.

difference in the curves of Groups L and LL, on the other hand, presumably reflects a difference in the level of D only, since these two groups had equated puff strengths on the conditioning, i.e., H-producing, trials. The difference between Groups H and LL, which was also highly significant ($P = .0002$), would be interpreted by the present theory as reflecting differences in both habit strength and drive level.

The findings of this experiment are thus seen to be in accord with those reported in a preliminary experiment in which a regular order of presentation of the paired (P) and unpaired (U) trials (repeated blocks of UPPU) was employed (7, p. 177). The irregular order of presentation employed in the present experiment rules out the possibility that the difference between the high- and low-reinforcement groups could have resulted from the conditioning of the S's emotional response to the temporal order.

In order to investigate the possibility that the performance difference between the high- and low-reinforcement groups (H and L) might be due either to a difference in the magnitude of the UCS's made to the different intensities of the UCS on their respective conditioning trials, or to adaptation of the response to the weaker UCS during the conditioning trials, a further analysis of the data was made. Measurement of the amplitudes of the UCR's made to the air puff on the conditioning trials on which no CR occurred over the first 10 and last 10 paired trials revealed the fact that some Ss did show considerable adaptation of the eyeblink to the puff, and also that there was a marked difference in Groups H and L in this respect. Accordingly, all Ss whose UCR's during the last 10 paired trials averaged less than 50% of their magnitudes in the first 10 paired trials were eliminated. On the basis of this criterion 1 S was eliminated from Group H and 11 from Group L, leaving 49 and 39, respectively, in these two groups.[1]

TABLE 2.1–1   Mean Percentage of CR's in Last 20 Conditioning Trials

Group	N	Mean	σ_m
H	49	59.6	4.43
L	39	43.8	5.06

Table 2.1–1 gives the mean percentage of CR's made in the last 20 conditioning trials (31–50) by Groups H and L after elimination of these 12 Ss. While the difference between the two groups was reduced, it was still significant as tested by the Mann-Whitney U test ($.02 < P < .05$). Thus the performance difference in the case of these Ss is shown not to be accountable for in terms of failure of the low-reinforcement Ss to respond with adequate UCR's on the conditioning trials.

EXPERIMENT II

Instead of using the UCS alone on the nonconditioning trials the CS was presented on all trials in this experiment. On half of the trials the UCS was administered at a CS-UCS interval (500 msec.) known to produce optimal conditioning, whereas on the other half of the trials this interval was 2650 msec., a duration known to produce little or no conditioning, and to result in extinction when introduced after establishing a CR at a shorter, optimal interval (2, 3).

It will be seen that this procedure involved a kind of partial reinforcement for both groups, with half of the trials being reinforced and half nonreinforced. In the case of the high reinforcement Ss the reinforcing, H-producing trials (short CS-UCS interval) always involved the strong UCS, whereas the weak UCS was present on the nonreinforcing trials. The reverse conditions held for the low-reinforcement Ss. According to a reinforcement interpretation the group which received the strong UCS on the short CS-UCS (i.e., reinforcing) trials should show a higher frequency of CR's than the group which received the weak UCS on these trials. Again, since the intensity of the air puffs administered was equated for the two groups during the training period, the performance difference cannot be interpreted as reflecting a difference in D and hence would be considered as due to a difference in H.

Subjects

The Ss were 47 women and 44 men from an introductory course in psychology. The data of seven Ss who were identified by criteria described previously (8) as defining voluntary responders were eliminated from the experiment along with that of two Ss who gave CR's to initial test trial presentations of the CS alone. Two additional Ss were excluded due to E's error. The remaining 80 Ss provided two groups, each of which contained 20 men and 20 women.

Apparatus and Method of Recording

The experimental apparatus and recording procedures used in this experiment were identical with those employed in the first experiment.

Conditioning Procedure

The instructions and preliminary trials were the same as those used in Exp. I, as was the employment of a 15-, 20-, or 25-sec. intertrial interval, a ready signal which preceded the CS, again an increase in the brightness of a 6-in. circular disk, by 2, 3, or 4 sec. Each S received 100 trials, 50 reinforcing trials with a 500-msec. CS-UCS interval, and 50 nonreinforcing trials with a 2650 msec. CS-UCS interval. The order of the two kinds of trials was irregular with the number of each type equalized in blocks of four trials. One group of Ss (H-50%) received a 2-lb./sq. in. air puff on the 500-msec. trials and a .33-lb./sq. in. air puff on the 2650-msec. trials, while the other group (L-50%) receive the reverse pairing, i.e., a .33-lb. puff on the 500-msec. trials and a 2-lb. puff on the 2650-msec. trials.

Results

The dotted curves in Fig. 2.1–2 present the data obtained in this experiment. They represent the frequency curves of conditioning in terms of the number of conditioning (i.e., reinforcing) trials for the high-reinforcement group (H-50%) and the low-reinforcement group (L-50%). Also presented for comparative purposes are the frequency conditioning curves obtained for high- and low-reinforcement conditions in Exp. I. Corroborating the results of Exp. I in which 100% reinforcement was involved, the curve for Group H-50% exhibited a gradual divergence from that of Group L-50%. Over the last 20 trials the difference in performance level in favor of the high-reinforcement group, tested by means of the Mann-Whitney U test, was highly significant ($P < .01$).

The relative position of the conditioning curves obtained in the present experiment with respect to those of Exp. I is of some interest. Unfortunately, through an error in calibration, the CS-UCS interval employed in the two experiments differed by 50 msec. The interval employed in Exp. I was 450 msec., while that used in the present one was 500 msec. With the exception, however, of this difference and the difference in reinforcing procedure, the experimental conditions in the two studies were the same. Since we know from other unpublished data obtained in our laboratory that a 500-msec. interval produces just as high, if not slightly higher, level of performance than 450 msec., the

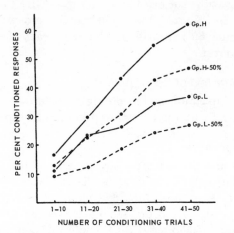

FIGURE 2.1–2   Acquisition curves showing percentage of CR's in successive blocks of ten conditioning trials for high- and low-reinforcement groups. The curves for both Exp. I (solid) and Exp. II (broken) are shown in order to reveal the decremental effects of the partial reinforcement schedule used in Exp. II.

depressed levels of performance shown by the high- and low-reinforcement groups in the present experiment, as compared with the groups from the first, reflect the inhibitory effects of the nonreinforcing trials.

The findings of this experiment further preclude the possibility that the performance difference in the two previous experiments might have been due to the operation of some kind of differential set with respect to the CS that could have been established in the two reinforcement groups by virtue of the fact that the CS was paired with a UCS of different strength. In the present experiment there presumably was no possibility of such a differential set being present since the CS was followed equally often in both groups by the two different puff intensities. Furthermore, S was never aware of which puff intensity would follow the CS on any particular trial.[2]

As in Exp. I, an analysis of the data was also carried out in which Ss who exhibited adaptation to the UCS were eliminated. Thus all Ss whose UCR's during the last 10 reinforcing trials averaged less than 50% of the magnitudes in the first 10 reinforcing trials were eliminated. In the case of the high-reinforcement group these were UCR's made to the 2.0-lb. puff, whereas in the case of the weak-reinforcement group they were responses given to the weak (.33 lb.) puff. On the basis of the criterion of elimination, one S was eliminated from Group H-50% and nine from Group L-50%, leaving 39 and 31 Ss, respectively, in the two groups.

Table 2.1–2 shows the mean percentage of CR's made in the last 20 conditioning trials (last 40 trials) by the two groups of Ss after elimination of the 10 adapters. Again, as in the previous experiment, the differ-

TABLE 2.1–2   Mean Percentage of CR's in Last 20 Conditioning Trials

Group	N	Mean	σ_m
H-50%	39	47.8	5.4
L-50%	31	31.6	3.9

ence between the two groups was reduced, but was still significant at the .05 level. That there was no relation within these Ss between the amplitude of the UCR made to the reinforcing UCS and the percentage of CR's is shown by the fact that the correlation coefficient between them was —.046. In the case of all Ss this coefficient was .245.

This finding thus confirms the previous experiment in showing that the performance difference between the two groups is not due to a failure of the low-reinforcement Ss to respond with an adequate UCR on the conditioning trials. Perhaps attention should also be called here to the point that the failure of the Ss whose UCS adapts out to show conditioning is quite in accord with a reinforcement interpretation that learning (i.e., growth of H) is a function of the intensity of the reinforcing aversive stimulus. Such Ss, according to this interpretation, should show relatively little, if any, conditioning.

DISCUSSION

The evidence of these two experiments and the similar experiment previously reported by Spence (7, p. 177) shows clearly that, with level of drive (D) equated, performance in classical aversive conditioning is a function of the intensity of the UCS occurring on the reinforced trials. This finding may be interpreted as lending support to a reinforcement-type theory that habit strength (H) in such aversive conditioning is a function of the intensity of the UCS. One version of such a reinforcement theory is the drive-stimulus reduction conception of Hull (1) and Miller and Dollard (4). According to this view the cessation of a strong UCS in aversive conditioning would provide greater reinforcement than cessation of a weak UCS and thus should lead to a greater increment of H per trial. The present writers would prefer to confine their interpretation to the more general conception that habit strength (H) is some function of the intensity of the UCS, leaving the nature of the reinforcing mechanism out of consideration.

In connection with the decremental effects of the partial reinforcement procedure employed in Exp. II, attention should be directed to the evidence provided in Fig. 2.1–2 by a comparison of the upper two curves that the inhibitory effect developed gradually and consistently over the 50 trials of conditioning and 50 reinforced trials. In contrast, the two lower curves suggest that the inhibitory effect reached a maximum much earlier in the low-reinforcement condition, possibly as soon as 20 conditioning trials or a total of 40 trials. Further data providing such comparisons are needed so that we may ascertain the nature of the development of such inhibitory effects on performance level during conditioning under partial schedules of reinforcement.

SUMMARY

This study was concerned with the problem of whether habit strength (H) is a function of the intensity of the UCS in classical aversive (eyelid) conditioning. In Exp. I one group (high reinforcement) always had the CS paired with a strong UCS and in the other group (low reinforcement) with a weak UCS. The drive (D) level was equated (on the average) in the two groups by interspersing among the conditioning trials an equal number of trials with the UCS alone. Thus the high-reinforcement group was presented with the weak UCS on such trials and the low-reinforcement group the strong UCS. Comparison of the frequency of CR's in the last 20 conditioning trials revealed a significant difference between the high- and low-reinforcement groups. This result was shown to hold even with Ss equated for the magnitudes of their UCR's.

In Exp. II one group (high reinforcement) had the CS, a light, paired on half the trials with a strong UCS at an optimal CS-UCS interval (500 msec.). On the other half of the trials the CS was paired with a weak UCS at an interval (2650 msec.) known not to lead to conditioning. The conditions for low-reinforcement group were the reverse, the CS being paired with the weak UCS on the conditioning (i.e., reinforcing) trials and the strong UCS on the nonconditioning trials. Performance measured over the last 20 conditioning trials (40 total trials) revealed that the high-reinforcement group gave a significantly greater number of CR's than the low-reinforcement group.

Since the drive levels of the high- and low-reinforcement groups in each experiment were equated, the performance differences between them were interpreted as reflecting a difference in the learning factor (H) and hence as supporting a reinforcement type of learning theory as far as aversive conditioning is concerned.

NOTES

1. Examination of the amplitudes of the UCR's given by the two curtailed groups during the last 10 paired trials on which no CR's occurred revealed a slight, but insignificant, difference in their mean magnitudes (H = 25.9 mm., L = 24.0 mm.). Within these groups there was no evidence of any relation between the level of conditioning performance and magnitude of the UCR.

2. It is of some interest to note that Ss did not acquire a set to respond differentially at the longer interval. Thus, there was no difference between the two groups of the present experiment in the number of anticipatory responses occurring 1 sec. prior to the UCS in the long-interval trials. Such responses are, for the most part, random blinks, for we know that there is little, if any, conditioning at this long interval.

REFERENCES

1. Hull, C. L. *Principles of behavior*. New York: Appleton-Century, 1943.
2. McAllister, W. R. The effect on eyelid conditioning of shifting the CS-US interval. *J. exp. Psychol.*, 1953, 45, 423–428.
3. McAllister, W. R. Eyelid conditioning as a function of the CS-US interval. *J. exp. Psychol.*, 1953, 45, 417–422.
4. Miller, N. E., & Dollard, J. *Social learning and imitation*. New Haven: Yale Univer. Press, 1941.
5. Passey, G. E. The influence of the intensity of unconditioned stimulus upon acquisition of a conditioned response. *J. exp. Psychol.*, 1948, 38, 420–428.
6. Spence, K. W. Learning and performance in eyelid conditioning as a function of the intensity of the UCS. *J. exp. Psychol.*, 1953, 45, 57–63.
7. Spence, K. W. *Behavior theory and conditioning*. New Haven: Yale Univer. Press, 1956.
8. Spence, K. W., & Taylor, J. A. Anxiety and strength of the UCS as determiners of the amount of eyelid conditioning. *J. exp. Psychol.*, 1951, 42, 183–188.

2.2 SUPPLEMENTARY REPORT: DIRECTION OF CHANGE IN CS IN EYELID CONDITIONING*

Frank A. Logan and Allan R. Wagner

The assumption that the important parameter of the CS is the amount of change from the pre-CS condition to the CS condition (e.g., Logan, 1954; Perkins, 1953) implies that a decrease in intensity should be as effective a CS as the corresponding increase in intensity. The assumption that the absolute value of the CS has a motivational (dynamogenic) property (e.g., Hull, 1952) implies that an increase in intensity should be more effective. Kish (1955) found tone-off to be a less effective CS than tone-on for avoidance conditioning in rats but Schwartz and Goodson (1958), using a comparable situation, found these events to be equally effective. Hansche and Grant (1960) concluded that light-off was as effective as light-on for eyelid conditioning under a procedure in which the light was off between trials for all Ss. The present study compares an increase with a decrease in intensity between two nonzero values treated symmetrically.

* Frank A. Logan and Allan R. Wagner, "Supplementary Report: Direction of Change in CS in Eyelid Conditioning," *The Journal of Experimental Psychology, 64*, 1962, 325–326. Copyright 1962 by the American Psychological Association, and reproduced by permission. Supported in part by Grants G-9014 and G-13080 from the National Science Foundation.

METHOD

The general features of the eyelid conditioning apparatus, recording equipment, and procedures have been described elsewhere (Dufort & Kimble, 1958). The CS was provided by a circular milk glass disk, 2.25 in. in diameter, set in a flat black ground, and illuminated from behind by General Electric NE30 neon bulbs. The onset of the CS was either an increase from two to four bulbs or a decrease from four to two bulbs. In each case, the CS intensity lasted for 600 msec. during the last 100 msec. of which a 2-lb. air-puff CS was delivered to the corner of the eye. The non-CS intensity remained on during the intertrial interval which averaged 20 sec. in length.

Five test trials of CS or UCS alone were followed by 60 conditioning trials. During these trials the CS for half of the Ss was an increase while for the other half it was a decrease in illumination. All Ss were then given 20 additional conditioning trials with the opposite CS. The results from 16 female student nurses were combined with those from 40 male undergraduates since they were virtually identical.

RESULTS AND DISCUSSION

The results are shown in Fig. 2.2–1. Both the increase and decrease in intensity were clearly and equally effective CSs in producing a relatively high level of conditioning. Although the null hypothesis cannot be proven statistically, the standard error of the difference between the groups at the end of training was only 7% and hence it is unlikely that the true difference deviates very much from zero. The data thus indicate the greater relative importance of the change parameter of the CS rather than its absolute intensity.

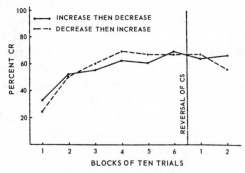

FIGURE 2.2–1 Percentages of conditioned responses during training. (The solid curve refers to Ss for whom the CS was an increase from the between-trials intensity during the first sixty trials and a decrease during the next twenty trials, while the dashed curve refers to Ss who received these CS conditions in the reverse order.)

The degree of transfer when the direction of change was reversed is remarkable. Indeed, a slight drop in performance would be expected because of the "extinction trial" given inadvertently when the non-CS intensity was reversed between the last acquisition trial and the first reversal trial. This finding suggests that generalization should be viewed in terms of a surface including the non-CS condition as well as the CS condition. However, it will require a large parametric study adequately to characterize this surface.

REFERENCES

Dufort, R. H., & Kimble, G. A. Ready signals and the effect of interpolated UCS presentations in eyelid conditioning. *J. exp. Psychol.*, 1958, 56, 1–7.

Hansche, W. J., & Grant, D. A. Onset versus termination of a stimulus as the CS in eyelid conditioning. *J. exp. Psychol.*, 1960, 59, 19–26.

Hull, C. L. *A behavior system.* New Haven: Yale Univer. Press, 1952.

Kish, G. B. Avoidance learning to the onset and cessation of conditioned stimulus energy. *J. exp. Psychol.*, 1955, 50, 31–38.

Logan, F. A. A note on stimulus intensity dynamism (V). *Psychol. Rev.*, 1954, 61, 77–80.

Perkins, C. C., Jr. The relation between conditioned stimulus intensity and response strength. *J. exp. Psychol.*, 1953, 46, 225–231.

Schwartz, M., & Goodson, J. E. Direction and rate of conditioned stimulus change in avoidance performance. *Psychol. Rep.*, 1958, 4, 499-502.

2.3 | EYELID CONDITIONING AS A FUNCTION OF THE CS–US INTERVAL*

Wallace R. McAllister

The length of the time interval between the onsets of the conditioned stimulus (CS) and the unconditioned stimulus (US) has long been considered one of the important variables determining the frequency of

* Wallace R. McAllister, "Eyelid Conditioning as a Function of the CS-US Interval," *The Journal of Experimental Psychology*, 45, 1953, 417–422. Copyright 1953 by the American Psychological Association, and reproduced by permission. This article is based on a portion of a dissertation submitted to the Graduate College of the State University of Iowa in partial fulfillment of the requirements for the Ph.D. degree. The writer wishes to express his appreciation to Professor Kenneth W. Spence for valuable aid and advice offered throughout the course of the experiment. The writer is also indebted to Mr. John P. Dolch for technical assistance.

conditioned responses (CR's) and has been studied in a number of experiments. Of those employing the delayed-conditioning procedure (6, 7, 9), all but one (6) have used a visual CS.[1] On the other hand, investigators using the trace procedure (1, 10, 13, 14) have all utilized a brief, auditory CS. With the exception of three (6, 13, 14), all of these experiments involved eyelid conditioning.

The optimal interval was found to be around 400 to 500 msec. in all but three of the above studies. In the exceptions (1, 6, 14), the optimal intervals lay at 300, 666, and 200 msec., respectively. However, only the first of these involved the eyelid response. Thus it is apparent that the results have been quite consistent, at least for eyelid conditioning. Nevertheless, in the studies involving eyelid conditioning, a different CS was used for each of the two conditioning techniques. Thus, it is not known whether the relationship between conditioning and the interstimulus interval is the same for different types of CS's (i.e., for stimulation of different sensory modalities) when the same conditioning technique is used.

The purpose of this experiment was to study the relationship between the conditioning of the eyelid response and the length of the time interval between the onset of the CS (tone) and the US (puff of air) using the delayed-conditioning technique.

METHOD

Subjects and Design

The Ss were 105 members of an introductory course in psychology at the State University of Iowa. Each S was assigned at random to one of five groups, each group being conditioned with one of the following CS–US intervals: 100, 250, 450, 700, and 2500 msec. Forty-five Ss were assigned to the 450-msec. group and 15 to each of the others.[2] For all conditions the proportion of women to men was fixed at a ratio of eight to seven. Subsequent to the main experiment, 30 additional Ss were run, 15 under the 250-msec. condition and 15 under the 450-msec. condition. The reason for running them will be discussed later.

Apparatus

The CS was a tone of 1000 cycles, 50 db above each S's threshold,[3] generated by a Hewlitt-Packard audio oscillator, Model 200D, and delivered to S through a set of Permoflux headphones, P.D.R.-8.

The US was a puff of air, of approximately 1.6 lb./sq. in., produced by the fall of a column of mercury through a distance of 80 mm., and delivered to the right cornea. The onsets and durations of the CS and the US were controlled by two Hunter-Brown decade-type electronic interval timers (5). After its onset, the US continued for 400 msec., and the CS was extended to overlap it so that both stimuli terminated simultaneously. The onset and offset of the stimuli were recorded on a polygraph by means of a signal marker.

The eyelid movement was recorded by a combination of electrical and mechanical means which has been described elsewhere (11). Briefly, the method of recording involved (a) a small plastic lever fastened to the eyelid with adhesive tape, (b) a light-weight microtorque potentiometer, the variable (rotating) arm of which was connected to the plastic lever by a silk thread, (c) a fixed-frequency oscillator, (d) an audio-frequency amplifier, (e) a full-wave rectifier for rectifying the amplified signal, (f) a Brush BL 902 pen recorder, and (g) a polygraph.

The Ss were seated in an adjustable dental chair which was in a semisoundproof room adjoining that in which the recording apparatus and stimulus controls were located. The room was under a constant illumination of .15 ft.-candles.

Conditioning Procedure

After S was seated comfortably in the chair, instructions designed to induce a neutral set were read to him, and any questions about the procedure were answered. Prior to the conditioning trials, three presentations of the CS alone were given to insure that S was following instructions and to determine whether S's eyelid response was already conditioned to the stimulus. If S gave three CR's to the tone, he was eliminated. Two Ss were discarded for this reason.

At random intervals of 2, 3, or 4 sec. before the CS was presented, a weak buzzer was sounded to serve as a ready signal. At this signal S was instructed to fixate a lighted disk (.19 apparent ft.-candles) located about 92 in. from his eye and approximately 4.5 in. above eye level. Upon fixating the light, S was instructed to blink once. The trial was then given. The intertrial interval averaged 20 sec., varying in a fixed, irregular order of 15, 20, or 25 sec. One hundred conditioning trials were given to each S during one experimental session.

Measurement of the CR

In defining and counting CR's, certain problems arise. In the first place, as interstimulus intervals become shorter, there is less opportunity for a response to anticipate the onset of the US. Therefore, if only anticipatory responses were counted as CR's, poorer performance might be found for shorter interstimulus interval groups merely because of this restriction in measurement. In order to lessen this possibility, test trials, in which no

US was presented, were used on 20% of the trials for each group, and on the test trials the time interval in which CR's were counted was lengthened. For each S one-third of the test trials occurred on the trial prior to each successive fifth trial, one-third on each successive fifth trial, and one-third on the trial following each successive fifth trial. The order was counterbalanced within each group. This procedure was adopted to prevent Ss from determining which trial would be unreinforced and to keep the average ordinal number of each test trial a multiple of five.

For most groups it was also possible to count anticipatory CR's. Thus two measures of a CR were obtained—one in terms of anticipatory responses and one in terms of responses made in a longer interval on the test trials. For each group the longer interval extended 200 msec. beyond the usual point of onset of the US. This value was selected arbitrarily. The time intervals in which a movement of the penwriter 1 mm. or more was counted as a CR are given in Table 2.3–1. In recording the anticipatory CR data, responses on the test trials were counted only if the response fell within the latencies designated for anticipatory CR's.

TABLE 2.3–1   Intervals (in Milliseconds) in which Responses Were Counted as CR's

CS–US Intervals	Intervals Used for Anticipatory Responses	Intervals Used for Test Trial Responses
100	—	100–300
250	100–250	100–450
450	100–450	100–650
700	100–700	100–900
2500	100–2500	100–2700

The fact that the eye often makes an unconditioned blink (an original response) to the onset of a tone constitutes a second problem. Since these original responses occur with a very short latency, it was decided to count no response which occurred within the first 100 msec. as a CR and in this manner to avoid introducing original responses into the data. Thus it was impossible to count anticipatory CR's for the 100-msec. group.

A further problem lies in the fact that the eye blinks randomly. This means that the longer CS–US intervals will include a greater number of such random blinks than the shorter intervals and will artificially increase the number of CR's counted for those groups. In an attempt to solve this problem, the percentage of CR's occurring on the first block of trials was subtracted from the percentage of CR's occurring on each subsequent block of trials.

RESULTS

Acquisition of CR

Performance curves showing the percentage of CR's made on the test trials plotted against blocks of two test trials are given in Fig. 2.3–1. The fact that the percentage of CR's on the first block of trials tends to be larger the longer the CS–US interval is to be expected because the longer CS–US intervals permit more random blinks to occur. To take this factor into account, the correction for random blinking mentioned above (which amounts to using each S as his own control) was made. The curves, after this correction was carried out, are shown in Fig. 2.3–2. It is apparent that

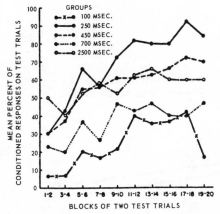

FIGURE 2.3–1 Mean percentage of CR's in successive blocks of two trials for each group.

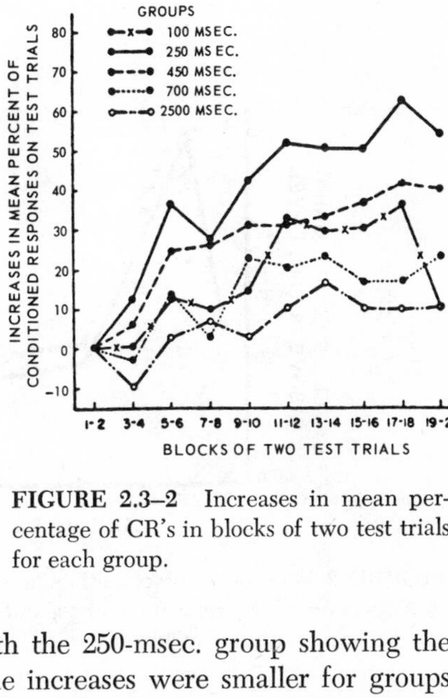

FIGURE 2.3–2 Increases in mean percentage of CR's in blocks of two test trials for each group.

each curve grows systematically, with the 250-msec. group showing the greatest increase in performance. The increases were smaller for groups run with shorter or with longer CS–US intervals. The sharp drop in the curve at the last point of the 100-msec. group is probably a chance occurrence only. Since the results obtained with the anticipatory CR measure were so similar to these results, those data are not presented in this paper.[4]

At the completion of the experiment it was discovered that through random sampling a greater proportion of Ss scoring high on a scale of manifest anxiety had been included in the 250-msec. group. Since it has been shown that such Ss condition better than other Ss (11, 12), the high level of performance reached by the 250-msec. group might be accounted for by that fact. To check on this possibility, 30 additional Ss, all scoring in the middle range of the anxiety scale, were run, 15 under each of the 250- and 450-msec. conditions. The final level reached by these two groups was similar but the 250-msec. group conditioned much more rapidly.

Conditioning Level as a Function of Time Interval

To examine the effect of the CS–US interval upon the final level of conditioning reached, the mean percentage of increases (i.e., the percentage of CR's remaining after the correction for random blinking) in anticipatory CR's for the last 30 trials and in test trial CR's for the last 6 test trials was computed for each group. In Fig. 2.3–3 these percentages

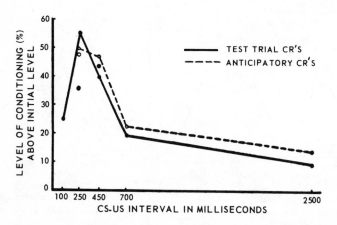

FIGURE 2.3–3   Level of conditioning (%) above the initial level of conditioning as a function of the time interval separating the onsets of the CS and the US. (See text for explanation of unjoined circles.)

are plotted against CS–US intervals. Inspection of the figure reveals that the 250-msec. group reached a higher level of conditioning than did any other group. The longer the interval beyond the 250-msec., the poorer was the performance; the one shorter interval was also inferior.

The same computations were made on the data obtained in the follow-up study. In Fig. 2.3–3 the results obtained are plotted as unjoined circles; the open circles represent anticipatory CR's, the closed circles, test-trial CR's. Again the 250-msec. group was found superior to the 450-msec. group with respect to the anticipatory CR's, although the difference was not as great as in the original experiment. In terms of the test-trial data, the 450-msec. group was superior. However, more weight should be given the anticipatory CR data for two reasons: (*a*) the data are based on 30 measures instead of 6 and thus are probably more reliable; and (*b*) the 30 trials from which the anticipatory CR data were obtained include the 6 test trials.

In order to evaluate the differences between the final levels of conditioning and to check on possible sex differences, a factorial analysis of variance was carried out on the data from the main experiment with the CS–US interval as one factor and sex as the other.[5] For the anticipatory CR's, the differences in the final level of the corrected scores were significant beyond the .1% level for CS–US intervals; for sex, beyond the 1% level (with women superior); for interaction, at more than the 50% level ($F = 7.02$, 4.79, and .05, with 3 and 82, 1 and 82, and 3 and 82 df, respectively). A similar analysis was made on the test-trial data. The differences in the final level of the corrected scores were found to be significant between the 1% and 5% levels for the interval factor; for sex, between the 20% and 30% levels (with women superior); for interaction, at more than the 50% level ($F = 2.91$, 1.32, and .90, with 4 and 95, 1 and 95, and 4 and 95 df, respectively).

Since the superiority of the 250-msec. group over the 450-msec. group was contrary to previous findings, it was of interest to determine whether the difference was statistically significant. Therefore, t tests (using the within-cells variance estimates from the above analyses) were computed between the increases in anticipatory CR's and between the increases in test-trial CR's for the 250- and 450-msec. groups. For the anticipatory-CR data t was .32, and for the test-trial CR data t was 1.35. Thus, the differences between the 250- and 450-msec. groups were not reliable.

A similar analysis (with CS–US interval and sex as factors) was carried out with the data collected in the follow-up study. The F ratios obtained were all less than unity regardless of whether the anticipatory-CR data or the test-trial CR data were used. Thus, the differences between the 250- and 450-msec. groups again were not statistically significant. Although not significant, the sex difference was in favor of the men.

DISCUSSION

Effects of CS–US Interval

Several comments should be made concerning the values plotted in Fig. 2.3–3. In the first place, the value plotted for the 100-msec. group is probably low because of the sharp drop obtained, for no known reason, on the last two test trials. Secondly, it seems unusual that the level of conditioning should be so much lower in the 700-msec. group than that usually obtained with a visual CS. It is possible that the low level is due to random sampling. In the third place, two compensating artifacts affect the value plotted in Fig. 2.3–3 for the 2500-msec. group. Myers (9) found that the number of eyelid responses increased (14% in 80 trials) as a function of the number of times the eye was puffed without being paired with a neutral stimulus. Thus, the slight increase in performance found for the 2500-msec. group in this study might be attributed, in part at least, to that fact. Offsetting such a possibility, however, is another circumstance. Only one CR was counted per trial no matter how many blinks occurred, and to correct for random blinks the percentage of responses on the first block of ten trials was subtracted from every subsequent block. Thus, if Ss began to condition, there would be less opportunity for an increase in conditioning to be demonstrated for that interval because of the correction. The performance curve would in this way be artificially lowered. It is difficult to determine to what extent these two factors offset one another. However, on the basis of these data and those of Myers,[6] it appears safe to conclude that eyelid conditioning under as long an interval as 2500 msec. is poor or negligible.

The results of the present experiment are in agreement with those of previous studies in showing that the level of conditioning varies with the time interval between the onsets of the CS and the US. They differ from most earlier studies in suggesting that intervals as short as 250 msec. may result in superior performance. It will be recalled that in the majority of previous studies maximum conditioning was found in the neighborhood of 400–500 msec. Many of these studies, however, employed a visual CS, and when an auditory CS was used, the conditioning was of the trace variety. The results of this study suggest that the optimal CS–US interval may be shorter than hitherto supposed (e.g., 3, 4), at least when an auditory stimulus is used as a CS under the delayed-conditioning procedure.

Effects of Sex

Although a significant sex difference in favor of women was found with one of the two measures in the major experiment, in the follow-up study the difference was in the opposite direction but was not significant. The over-all results, therefore, do not support the conclusion that there is a true sex difference in conditioning.

SUMMARY

The eyelid response of five groups of Ss was conditioned, by the delayed-conditioning technique, with CS–US intervals of 100, 250, 450, 700, and 2500 msec., respectively. A 1000-cycle tone, set 50 db above each S's threshold, was the CS; a fall of mercury in a manometer through a distance of 80 mm., the US. Twenty of the 100 trials were nonreinforced; i.e., were test trials. Two measures were obtained, anticipatory CR's and CR's counted in a longer interval on the test trials.

Subsequent to the main experiment 30 additional Ss were run, 15 under the 250- and 15 under the 450-msec. condition. This second study was conducted when it was found that through random sampling a disproportionate number of Ss scoring high on a test of manifest anxiety had been included in the 250-msec. group. A check on possible sex differences was also made when the data were analyzed. The main findings are listed below.

1. The level of conditioning was found to vary with the time interval between the onsets of the CS and the US. The optimal interval was found to be 250-msec. although the difference between the 250- and 450-msec. groups was not significant.

2. Conditioning with intervals as long as 2500 msec. was markedly inferior, possibly negligible.

3. Little evidence for sex differences in conditioning was found.

NOTES

1. *Delayed conditioning* here refers to the technique in which some time greater than zero intervenes between the onset of the CS and the onset of the US and in which the CS overlaps (some portion of) the US. *Trace conditioning* here refers to the technique in which the offset of the CS occurs before the onset of the US at a time interval greater than zero. This use of terms is somewhat at variance with others' terminology. (Cf. 2, p. 575).

2. The Ss in the 450-msec. group were subdivided into three groups of 15 Ss each at the end of the conditioning trials and were then given differential treatment. The results obtained will be published elsewhere (8).

3. The auditory threshold of each Ss was roughly determined before the conditioning trials by presenting one descending and one ascending series of a continuously sounding, 1000-cycle tone (method of limits). The S was instructed to lower his finger when he no longer heard the tone (descending series) and to raise his finger as soon as he heard the tone (ascending series). The attenuation of the tone when S thus responded was noted for both series, the mean attenuation being taken as the threshold. The tone (CS) was set 50 db above this value for the conditioning trials.

4. A two-page table giving anticipatory CR data of the main and the follow-up experiment and the test-trial data of the latter study has been deposited with the American Documentation Institute. Order Document No. 3919 from American Documentation Institute, Auxiliary Publications project, Photoduplication Service, c/o Library of Congress, Washington 25, D. C., remitting $1.25 for microfilm (images 1 inch high on standard 35 mm. motion picture film) or $1.25 for photoprint readable without optical aid.

5. Before these analyses were made, the assumption of homogeneity of population variances was checked by computing Bartlett's test. In no case were the chi-square values significant at the 5% level. The assumption of normality of the population distribution was assumed to be tenable from inspection of the data.

6. Using an increase in brightness as the CS, a blow from an electromagnetic hammer to the corner of the eye as the US, and running Ss under 500-, 1000-, 1500-, and 2500-msec. inter-stimulus intervals, Myers (9) found that the final level of conditioning (corrected for random blinking) decreased monotonically beyond the 500-msec. interval. The curve started approximately at 33% CR's for the 500-msec. interval and decreased to about 5% for the 2500-msec. interval. To correct for an increase in CR's attributable merely to stimulation by the US, he subtracted the increase in CR's found in a control group to which only the US was administered.

REFERENCES

1. Bernstein, A. L. Temporal factors in the formation of conditioned eyelid reactions in human subjects. *J. gen. Psychol.*, 1934, 10, 173–197.
2. Brogden, W. J. Animal studies of learning. In S. S. Stevens (Ed.), *Handbook of experimental psychology.* New York: Wiley, 1951.
3. Hull, C. L. *Principles of behavior.* New York: D. Appleton-Century, 1943.
4. Hull, C. L. *Essentials of behavior.* New Haven: Yale Univer. Press, 1951.
5. Hunter, T. A., & Brown, J. S. A decade-type electronic interval-timer. *Amer. J. Psychol.*, 1949, 62, 570–575.
6. Kappauf, W. E., & Schlosberg, H. Conditioned responses in the white rat: III. Conditioning as a function of the length of the period of delay. *J. genet. Psychol.*, 1937, 50, 27–45.
7. Kimble, G. A. Classical conditioning as a function of the time between conditioned and unconditioned stimuli. *J. exp. Psychol.*, 1947, 37, 1–16.
8. McAllister, W. R. The effect on eyelid conditioning of shifting the CS–US interval. *J. exp. Psychol.*, 1953, 45, 423–428.
9. Myers, J. A. An experimental investigation of the effect of varying the time between the onsets of the conditioned and unconditioned stimuli on the conditioned eyelid response. Unpublished doctor's dissertation, Univer. of Iowa, 1950.
10. Reynolds, B. The acquisition of a trace conditioned response as a function of the magnitude of the stimulus trace. *J. exp. Psychol.*, 1945, 35, 15–30.
11. Spence, K. W., & Taylor, J. A. Anxiety and strength of the UCS as determiners of the amount of eyelid conditioning. *J. exp. Psychol.*, 1951, 42, 183–188.
12. Taylor, J. A. The relationship of anxiety to the conditioned eyelid response. *J. exp. Psychol.*, 1951, 41, 81–92.
13. Wolfle, H. M. Time factors in conditioning finger-withdrawal. *J. gen. Psychol.*, 1930, 4, 372–379.
14. Wolfle, H. M. Conditioning as a function of the interval between the conditioned and the original stimulus. *J. gen. Psychol.*, 1932, 7, 80–103.

2.4 PREDICTABILITY AND NUMBER OF PAIRINGS IN PAVLOVIAN FEAR CONDITIONING*

Robert A. Rescorla

Three groups of dogs were Sidman avoidance trained. They then received different kinds of Pavlovian fear conditioning. For one group CSs and USs occurred randomly and independently; for a second group, CSs predicted the occurrence of USs; for a third group, CSs predicted the absence of the USs. The CSs were subsequently presented while S performed the avoidance response. CSs which had predicted the occurrence or the absence of USs produced, respectively, increases and decreases in avoidance rate. For the group with random CSs and USs in conditioning, the CS had no effect upon avoidance.

Traditional conceptions of Pavlovian conditioning have emphasized the pairing of CS and US as the essential condition for the development of a CR. As long as the CS and US occur in temporal contiguity, the conditions for Pavlovian conditioning are assumed to be met. In contrast, another view of Pavlovian conditioning argues that conditioning depends upon the degree to which the CS allows S to *predict* the occurrence of the US. If the CS is followed by a change in the probability of the US, Pavlovian conditioning will occur. If the CS forecasts an *increased* likelihood of the US, excitatory conditioning will occur; if the CS forecasts a *decreased* likelihood of the US, the CS will take on inhibitory properties. According to this view, the number of CS–US pairings may be irrelevant to the development of a CR if the CS does not predict a change in the probability of occurrence of the US.

The experiment reported here explores the fruitfulness of this second approach to Pavlovian fear conditioning. Three groups of dogs received different kinds of Pavlovian conditioning. For one group, CSs and USs occurred randomly and independently in such a way that CS occurrences provided no information about US occurrences. In a second group, CS occurrences were followed by an increase in the probability of US occurrences; however, Ss in this group received the same number of CS–US pairings as did Ss in the first group. For a third group, CS occurrences predicted the *absence* of USs. These CSs were then presented while S

* Reprinted from *Psychonomic Science*, 1966, *4*, 383–384. Copyright 1966 by the Psychonomic Society, and reproduced by permission. This research was supported by United States Public Health Service Grant MH-04202 to Richard L. Solomon. The author thanks Dr. Solomon for his advice and criticism.

101

performed a previously trained avoidance response. Increases in the rate of avoidance responding produced by CSs were taken as evidence for excitatory fear conditioning and decreases were taken as indicating inhibition of fear. Such changes in rate of avoidance responding have been shown by Rescorla & LoLordo (1965) to be a sensitive index of the level of conditioned fear.

METHOD

Ss were 18 mongrel dogs, individually housed and maintained on ad lib food and water throughout the experiment. The apparatus was a two-compartment dog shuttlebox described in detail by Solomon & Wynne (1953). The two compartments were separated by a barrier of adjustable height and by a drop gate which, when lowered, prevented S from crossing from one compartment into the other. The floor was composed of stainless steel grids which could be electrified through a scrambler. Speakers, mounted above the hardware-cloth ceiling, provided a continuous white noise background and permitted the presentation of tonal stimuli.

The training procedure was similar to that described by Rescorla & LoLordo (1965). Each S was trained to jump the barrier, separating the two sides of the shuttlebox, to avoid electric shock. Brief shocks, 0.25 sec., were programmed on a Sidman avoidance schedule; the shock-shock interval was 10 sec. and the response-shock interval was 30 sec. The Ss received three initial days of avoidance training. On the first day the barrier height was 9 in. and the shock level 6 ma; on all subsequent days, the barrier height was 15 in. and the shock set at 8 ma.

Beginning with the fourth experimental day, S was confined to one-half of the shuttlebox and given Pavlovian fear conditioning. For the six dogs in Group R (random), 24, 5-sec., 3 ma shocks were programmed on a variable interval schedule with a mean of 2.5 min. Twenty-four, 5-sec., 400 cps tones were independently programmed randomly throughout the session in such a way that a tone onset was equiprobable at any time in the session. This was accomplished by a VI timer and a series of tapes. The six dogs in Group P (positive prediction) received a treatment identical to that of Group R except that they received only those shocks which were programmed to occur during the 30 sec. following each tone onset. The six dogs in Group N (negative prediction) received a treatment identical to that of Group R except that they received only those shocks which were *not* programmed to occur within 30 sec. after a tone onset. The treatments for Groups P and N were accomplished by having each CS onset reset a 30 sec. timer through which the pre-programmed shocks were gated. Thus, for Group P, CS occurrences predicted US occurrences; and for Group N, CS occurrences predicted absence of USs.

Pavlovian conditioning and Sidman avoidance training days were then alternated until S had received a total of seven avoidance and five conditioning sessions. On day 13 a single test session was given. During this session, S performed the avoidance response with the Sidman schedule remaining in effect. In addition, 24, 5-sec., 400 cps tones were superimposed upon the avoidance behavior with a mean intertrial interval of 2.5 min. Changes in the rate of avoidance induced by these CSs were used as an index of the conditioned excitatory and inhibitory effects of the tones.

RESULTS

The Sidman avoidance response was rapidly acquired by most animals and after several sessions all Ss were reliable responders. Figure 2.4–1 shows the results of the test session. Plotted in this figure are the mean

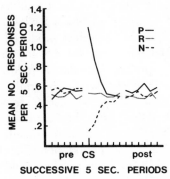

FIGURE 2.4–1   Mean number of responses per 5-sec. period in successive periods prior to CS onset, during the CS and the subsequent 25 sec. of differential conditioning treatment, and after the expiration of the 25-sec. period.

number of responses per 5-sec. period of time over successive 5-sec. periods. Prior to the occurrence of a CS, all groups responded at approximately the same rate. However, the occurrence of a CS led the markedly different results in the three groups. For Group P, CS onset produced an abrupt increase in response rate followed by a return to base rate. The rate increase was confined to the first few 5-sec. periods following CS onset. In contrast, the CS produced a sharp decrease in rate in Group N. Again the rate change was maximal immediately following CS onset. For Group R, the occurrence of a CS produced very little effect.

Comparisons among the groups were made with the help of suppression ratios. These ratios are of the form $^{A}/_{(A + B)}$ where B is the mean rate in the 30 sec. prior to CS onset and A is the rate for the period on which the two groups are to be compared. Using this measure, the rate increase during the CS was reliably greater for Group P than for Group R($U = 0$;

p < .01). Group R, in turn, responded more frequently during CS than did Group N (U = 0; p < .01). Similar conclusions result if the groups are compared on the rate during the entire 30 sec. following CS onset.

DISCUSSION

The results of this experiment indicate that the degree to which a CS allows S to predict US occurrences is an important variable in Pavlovian fear conditioning. Stimuli which signalled increased probability of the US became elicitors of fear, resulting in an increased jumping rate, and stimuli which signalled decreased probability of the US became inhibitors of fear, resulting in a decreased jumping rate. The results, therefore, substantiate the findings of Rescorla & LoLordo (1965), that active inhibition and excitation of fear can be induced by Pavlovian methods. However, these effects seem to be independent of the more traditionally emphasized effects of number of CS–US pairings. Despite the fact that Ss in Group R received at least as many pairings of the CS and US as Ss in Group P, only the Ss in Group P showed evidence of Pavlovian fear conditioning.

The temporal location of the effect produced by the CS is also of interest. The differential effects of the CS for the three groups were primarily confined to the periods immediately following CS onset. Perhaps this happened because shocks were uniformly distributed, and for Group P the probability of a US in the next 30 sec. was maximal just after CS onset and declined as time since the CS increased; but for Group N, the probability of a shock was minimal immediately after CS onset. Another possibility is that the period immediately after CS onset is simply more discriminable from the baseline conditions than are subsequent periods.

These results suggest that we consider as a basic dimension of Pavlovian conditioning the degree to which the US is contingent upon prior CSs. From this point of view, the appropriate control procedure for nonassociative effects of Pavlovian conditioning, such as sensitization or pseudoconditioning, is one in which there is *no* contingency between CS and US. The two extremes in which CS predicts either the increased or the decreased probability of a US are seen in the present experiment to produce, respectively, excitation and inhibition. A procedure such as that of Group R in which there is *no contingency* between CS and US provides an appropriate control procedure against which to evaluate both of these effects.

REFERENCES

Rescorla, R. A., & LoLordo, V. M. Inhibition of avoidance behavior. *J. Comp. physiol. Psychol.*, 1965, 59, 406–412.

Solomon, R. L., & Wynne, L. C. Traumatic avoidance learning: Acquisition in normal dogs. *Psychol. Monogr.*, 1953, 67, No. 4 (Whole No. 354).

2.5 | CONDITIONED EMOTIONAL REACTIONS*
John B. Watson and Rosalie Rayner

In recent literature various speculations have been entered into concerning the possibility of conditioning various types of emotional response, but direct experimental evidence in support of such a view has been lacking. If the theory advanced by Watson and Morgan[1] to the effect that in infancy the original emotional reaction patterns are few, consisting so far as observed of fear, rage and love, then there must be some simple method by means of which the range of stimuli which can call out these emotions and their compounds is greatly increased. Otherwise, complexity in adult response could not be accounted for. These authors without adequate experimental evidence advanced the view that this range was increased by means of conditioned reflex factors. It was suggested there that the early home life of the child furnishes a laboratory situation for establishing conditioned emotional responses. The present authors have recently put the whole matter to an experimental test.

Experimental work has been done so far on only one child, Albert B. This infant was reared almost from birth in a hospital environment; his mother was a wet nurse in the Harriet Lane Home for Invalid Children. Albert's life was normal: he was healthy from birth and one of the best developed youngsters ever brought to the hospital, weighing twenty-one pounds at nine months of age. He was on the whole stolid and unemotional. His stability was one of the principal reasons for using him as a subject in this test. We felt that we could do him relatively little harm by carrying out such experiments as those outlined below.

At approximately nine months of age we ran him through the emotional tests that have become a part of our regular routine in determining whether fear reactions can be called out by other stimuli than sharp noises and the sudden removal of support. Tests of this type have been described by the senior author in another place.[2] In brief, the infant was confronted suddenly and for the first time successively with a white rat, a rabbit, a dog, a monkey, with masks with and without hair, cotton wool, burning newspapers, etc. A permanent record of Albert's reactions to these objects and situations has been preserved in a motion picture study. Manipulation was the most usual reaction called out. *At no time did this infant ever show fear in any situation.* These experimental records were

* John B. Watson and Rosalie Rayner, "Conditioned Emotional Reactions," *The Journal of Experimental Psychology*, 3, 1920, 1–14. Copyright 1920 by the American Psychological Association, and reproduced by permission. Used in excerpted form.

confirmed by the casual observations of the mother and hospital attendants. No one had ever seen him in a state of fear and rage. The infant practically never cried.

Up to approximately nine months of age we had not tested him with loud sounds. The test to determine whether a fear reaction could be called out by a loud sound was made when he was eight months, twenty-six days of age. The sound was that made by striking a hammer upon a suspended steel bar four feet in length and three-fourths of an inch in diameter. The laboratory notes are as follows:

> One of the two experimenters caused the child to turn its head and fixate her moving hand; the other, stationed back of the child, struck the steel bar a sharp blow. The child started violently, his breathing was checked and the arms were raised in characteristic manner. On the second stimulation the same thing occurred, and in addition the lips began to pucker and tremble. On the third stimulation the child broke into a sudden crying fit. This is the first time an emotional situation in the laboratory has produced any fear or even crying in Albert.

We had expected just these results on account of our work with other infants brought up under similar conditions. It is worth while to call attention to the fact that removal of support (dropping and jerking the blanket upon which the infant was lying) was tried exhaustively upon this infant on the same occasion. It was not effective in producing the fear response. This stimulus is effective in younger children. At what age such stimuli lose their potency in producing fear is not known. Nor is it known whether less placid children ever lose their fear of them. This probably depends upon the training the child gets. It is well known that children eagerly run to be tossed into the air and caught. On the other hand it is equally well known that in the adult fear responses are called out quite clearly by the sudden removal of support, if the individual is walking across a bridge, walking out upon a beam, etc. There is a wide field of study here which is aside from our present point.

The sound stimulus, thus, at nine months of age, gives us the means of testing several important factors. I. Can we condition fear of an animal, e.g., a white rat, by visually presenting it and simultaneously striking a steel bar? II. If such a conditioned emotional response can be established, will there be a transfer to other animals or other objects? III. What is the effect of time upon such conditioned emotional responses? IV. If after a reasonable period such emotional responses have not died out, what laboratory methods can be devised for their removal?

I. The establishment of conditioned emotional responses. At first there was considerable hesitation upon our part in making the attempt to set up fear reactions experimentally. A certain responsibility attaches to such a procedure. We decided finally to make the attempt, comforting ourselves by the reflection that such attachments would arise anyway as soon as the child left the sheltered environment of the nursery for the rough and tumble of the home. We did not begin this work until Albert was eleven months, three days of age. Before attempting to set up a conditioned response we, as before, put him through all of the regular emotional tests. *Not the slightest sign of a fear response was obtained in any situation.*

The steps taken to condition emotional responses are shown in our laboratory notes.

11 Months 3 Days

1. White rat suddenly taken from the basket and presented to Albert. He began to reach for rat with left hand. Just as his hand touched the animal the bar was struck immediately behind his head. The infant jumped violently and fell forward, burying his face in the mattress. He did not cry, however.

2. Just as the right hand touched the rat the bar was again struck. Again the infant jumped violently, fell forward and began to whimper.

In order not to disturb the child too seriously no further tests were given for one week.

11 Months 10 Days

1. Rat presented suddenly without sound. There was steady fixation but no tendency at first to reach for it. The rat was then placed nearer, whereupon tentative reaching movements began with the right hand. When the rat nosed the infant's left hand, the hand was immediately withdrawn. He started to reach for the head of the animal with the forefinger of the left hand, but withdrew it suddenly before contact. It is thus seen that the two joint stimulations given the previous week were not without effect. He was tested with his blocks immediately afterwards to see if they shared in the process of conditioning. He began immediately to pick them up, dropping them, pounding them, etc. In the remainder of the tests the blocks were given frequently to quiet him and to test his general emotional state. They were always removed from sight when the process of conditioning was under way.

2. Joint stimulation with rat and sound. Started, then fell over immediately to right side. No crying.

3. Joint stimulation. Fell to right side and rested upon hands, with head turned away from rat. No crying.

4. Joint stimulation. Same reaction.

5. Rat suddenly presented alone. Puckered face, whimpered and withdrew body sharply to the left.

6. Joint stimulation. Fell over immediately to right side and began to whimper.

7. Joint stimulation. Started violently and cried, but did not fall over.

8. Rat alone. *The instant the rat was shown the baby began to cry. Almost instantly he turned sharply to the left, fell over on left side, raised himself on all fours and began to crawl away so rapidly that he was caught with difficulty before reaching the edge of the table.*

This was as convincing a case of a completely conditioned fear response as could have been theoretically pictured. In all seven joint stimulations were given to bring about the complete reaction. It is not unlikely had the sound been of greater intensity or of a more complex clang character that the number of joint stimulations might have been materially reduced. Experiments designed to define the nature of the sounds that will serve best as emotional stimuli are under way.

II. When a conditioned emotional response has been established for one object, is there a transfer? Five days later Albert was again brought back into the laboratory and tested as follows:

11 Months 15 Days

1. Tested first with blocks. He reached readily for them, playing with them as usual. This shows that there has been no general transfer to the room, table, blocks, etc.

2. Rat alone. Whimpered immediately, withdrew right hand and turned head and trunk away.

3. Blocks again offered. Played readily with them, smiling and gurgling.

4. Rat alone. Leaned over to the left side as far away from the rat as possible, then fell over, getting up on all fours and scurrying away as rapidly as possible.

5. Blocks again offered. Reached immediately for them, smiling and laughing as before.

The above preliminary test shows that the conditioned response to the rat had carried over completely for the five days in which no tests were given. The question as to whether or not there is a transfer was next taken up.

6. Rabbit alone. The rabbit was suddenly placed on the mattress in front of him. The reaction was pronounced. Negative responses began at once. He leaned as far away from the animal as possible, whimpered, then burst into tears. When the rabbit was placed in contact with him he buried his face in the mattress, then got up on all fours and crawled away, crying as he went. This was a most convincing test.

7. The blocks were next given him, after an interval. He played with them as before. It was observed by four people that he played far more energetically with them than ever before. The blocks were raised high over his head and slammed down with a great deal of force.

8. Dog alone. The dog did not produce as violent a reaction as the

rabbit. The moment fixation occurred the child shrank back and as the animal came nearer he attempted to get on all fours but did not cry at first. As soon as the dog passed out of his range of vision he became quiet. The dog was then made to approach the infant's head (he was lying down at the moment). Albert straightened up immediately, fell over to the opposite side and turned his head away. He then began to cry.

9. The blocks were again presented. He began immediately to play with them.

10. Fur coat (seal). Withdrew immediately to the left side and began to fret. Coat put close to him on the left side, he turned immediately, began to cry and tried to crawl away on all fours.

11. Cotton wool. The wool was presented in a paper package. At the end the cotton was not covered by the paper. It was placed first on his feet. He kicked it away but did not touch it with his hands. When his hand was laid on the wool he immediately withdrew it but did not show the shock that the animals or fur coat produced in him. He then began to play with the paper, avoiding contact with the wool itself. He finally, under the impulse of the manipulative instinct, lost some of his negativism to the wool.

12. Just in play W. put his head down to see if Albert would play with his hair. Albert was completely negative. Two other observers did the same thing. He began immediately to play with their hair. W. then brought the Santa Claus mask and presented it to Albert. He was again pronouncedly negative . . .

III. The effect of time upon conditioned emotional responses. We have already shown that the conditioned emotional response will continue for a period of one week. It was desired to make the time test longer. In view of the imminence of Albert's departure from the hospital we could not make the interval longer than one month. Accordingly no further emotional experimentation was entered into for thirty-one days after the above test. During the month, however, Albert was brought weekly to the laboratory for tests upon right and left-handedness, imitation, general development, etc. No emotional tests whatever were given and during the whole month his regular nursery routine was maintained in the Harriet Lane Home. The notes on the test given at the end of this period are as follows:

1 Year 21 Days

1. Santa Claus mask. Withdrawal, gurgling, then slapping at it without touching. When his hand was forced to touch it, he whimpered and cried. His hand was forced to touch it two more times. He whimpered and cried on both tests. He finally cried at the mere visual stimulus of the mask.

2. Fur coat. Wrinkled his nose and withdrew both hands, drew

back his whole body and began to whimper as the coat was put nearer. Again there was the strife between withdrawal and the tendency to manipulate. Reached tentatively with left hand but drew back before contact had been made. In moving his body to one side his hand accidentally touched the coat. He began to cry at once, nodding his head in a very peculiar manner (this reaction was an entirely new one). Both hands were withdrawn as far as possible from the coat. The coat was then laid on his lap and he continued nodding his head and whimpering, withdrawing his body as far as possible, pushing the while at the coat with his feet but never touching it with his hands.

3. Fur coat. The coat was taken out of his sight and presented again at the end of a minute. He began immediately to fret, withdrawing his body and nodding his head as before.

4. Blocks. He began to play with them as usual.

5. The rat. He allowed the rat to crawl towards him without withdrawing. He sat very still and fixated it intently. Rat then touched his hand. Albert withdrew it immediately, then leaned back as far as possible but did not cry. When the rat was placed on his arm he withdrew his body and began to fret, nodding his head. The rat was then allowed to crawl against his chest. He first began to fret and then covered his eyes with both hands.

6. Blocks. Reaction normal.

7. The rabbit. The animal was placed directly in front of him. It was very quiet. Albert showed no avoiding reactions at first. After a few seconds he puckered up his face, began to nod his head and to look intently at the experimenter. He next began to push the rabbit away with his feet, withdrawing his body at the same time. Then as the rabbit came nearer he began pulling his feet away, nodding his head, and wailing "da da." After about a minute he reached out tentatively and slowly and touched the rabbit's ear with his right hand, finally manipulating it. The rabbit was again placed in his lap. Again he began to fret and withdrew his hands. He reached out tentatively with his left hand and touched the animal, shuddered and withdrew the whole body. The experimenter then took hold of his left hand and laid it on the rabbit's back. Albert immediately withdrew his hand and began to suck his thumb. Again the rabbit was laid in his lap. He began to cry, covering his face with both hands.

8. Dog. The dog was very active. Albert fixated it intensely for a few seconds, sitting very still. He began to cry but did not fall over backwards as on his last contact with the dog. When the dog was pushed closer to him he at first sat motionless, then began to cry, putting both hands over his face.

These experiments would seem to show exclusively that directly conditioned emotional responses as well as those conditioned by transfer persist, although with a certain loss in the intensity of the reaction, for a longer period than one month. Our view is that they persist and modify personality throughout life. It should be recalled again that Albert was of an extremely phlegmatic type. Had he been emotionally unstable probably both the directly conditioned response and those transferred would have persisted throughout the month unchanged in form.

IV. "Detachment" or removal of conditioned emotional responses. Unfortunately Albert was taken from the hospital the day the above tests were made. Hence the opportunity of building up an experimental technique by means of which we could remove the conditioned emotional responses was denied us. Our own view, expressed above, which is possibly not very well grounded, is that these responses in the home environment are likely to persist indefinitely, unless an accidental method for removing them is hit upon. The importance of establishing some method must be apparent to all. Had the opportunity been at hand we should have tried out several methods, some of which we may mention. (1) Constantly confronting the child with those stimuli which called out the responses in the hopes that habituation would come in corresponding to "fatigue" of reflex when differential reactions are to be set up. (2) By trying to "recondition" by showing objects calling out fear responses (visual) and simultaneously stimulating the erogenous zones (tactual). We should try first the lips, then the nipples and as a final resort the sex organs. (3) By trying to "recondition" by feeding the subject candy or other food just as the animal is shown. This method calls for the food control of the subject. (4) By building up "constructive" activities around the object by imitation and by putting the hand through the motions of manipulation. At this age imitation of overt motor activity is strong, as our present but unpublished experimentation has shown.

INCIDENTAL OBSERVATIONS

(a) Thumb sucking as a compensatory device for blocking fear and noxious stimuli. During the course of these experiments, especially in the final test, it was noticed that whenever Albert was on the verge of tears or emotionally upset generally he would continually thrust his thumb into his mouth. The moment the hand reached the mouth he became impervious to the stimuli producing fear. Again and again while the motion pictures were being made at the end of the thirty-day rest period, we had to remove the thumb from his mouth before the conditioned response could be obtained. This method of blocking noxious and emotional stimuli (fear and rage) through erogenous stimulation seems to persist from birth onward. Very often in our experiments upon the work adders with infants under ten days of age the same reaction appeared. When at work upon the adders both of the infants arms are under slight restraint. Often rage appears. They begin to cry, thrashing their arms and legs about. If the finger gets into the mouth crying ceases at once. The organism thus apparently from birth, when under the influence of love stimuli is blocked to all others.[3] This resort to sex stimulation when under the influence of noxious and emotional situations, or when the individual is restless and idle, persists throughout adolescent and adult life. Albert, at any rate, did not resort to thumb sucking execpt in the presence of such stimuli. Thumb sucking could immediately be checked by offering him his blocks. These invariably called out active manipulation instincts. It is worth while here to call attention to the fact that Freud's conception of the stimulation of erogenous zones as being the expression of an original "pleasure" seeking principle may be turned about and possibly better described as a compensatory (and often conditioned) device for the blockage of noxious and fear and rage producing stimuli.

(b) Equal primacy of fear, love and possibly rage. While in general the results of our experiment offer no particular points of conflict with Freudian concepts, one fact out of harmony with them should be emphasized. According to proper Freudians sex (or in our terminology, love) is the principal emotion in which conditioned responses arise which later limit and distort personality. We wish to take sharp issue with this view on the basis of the experimental evidence we have gathered. Fear is as primal a factor as love in influencing personality. Fear does not gather its potency in any derived manner from love. It belongs to the original and inherited nature of man. Probably the same may be true of rage although at present we are not so sure of this.

The Freudians twenty years from now, unless their hypotheses change, when they come to analyze Albert's fear of a seal skin coat—assuming that he comes to analysis at that age—will probably tease from him the recital of a dream which upon their analysis will show that Albert at three years of age attempted to play with the pubic hair of the mother and was scolded violently for it. (We are by no means denying that this might in some other case condition it.) If the analyst has sufficiently prepared Albert to accept such a dream when found as an explanation of his avoiding tendencies, and if the analyst has the authority and personality to put it over, Albert may be fully convinced that the dream was a true revealer of the factors which brought about the fear.

It is probable that many of the phobias in psychopathology are true conditioned emotional reactions either of the direct or the transferred type. One may possibly have to believe that such persistence of early conditioned responses will be found only in persons who are constitutionally inferior. Our argument is meant to be constructive. Emotional disturbances in adults cannot be traced back to sex alone. They must be retraced along at least three collateral lines—to conditioned and transferred responses set up in infancy and early youth in all three of the fundamental human emotions.

NOTES

1. "Emotional Reactions and Psychological Experimentation," *American Journal of Psychology*, April, 1917, Vol. 28, pp. 163–174.
2. "Psychology from the Standpoint of a Behaviorist," p. 202.
3. The stimulus to love in infants according to our view is stroking of the skin, lips, nipples and sex organs, patting and rocking, picking up, etc. Patting and rocking (when not conditioned) are probably equivalent to actual stimulation of the sex organs. In adults of course, as every lover knows, vision, audition and olfaction soon become conditioned by joint stimulation with contact and kinæsthetic stimuli.

2.6
SYSTEMATIC DESENSITIZATION AS A COUNTERCONDITIONING PROCESS*
Gerald C. Davison

Systematic desensitization, demonstrated in both clinical and experimental studies to reduce avoidance behavior, entails the contiguous pairing of aversive imaginal stimuli with anxiety-competing relaxation. If, as is widely assumed, the efficacy of the procedure derives from a genuine counterconditioning process, a disruption of the pairing between graded aversive stimuli and relaxation should render the technique ineffective in modifying avoidance behavior. This hypothesis was strongly confirmed: significant reduction in avoidance behavior was observed only in densensitization Ss, with none occurring either in yoked Ss for whom relaxation was paired with irrelevant stimuli or in yoked Ss who were gradually exposed to the imaginal aversive stimuli without relaxation. Other theoretical issues were raised, especially the problem of transfer from imaginal to actual stimulus situations.

Recent years have witnessed increasing application of the systematic desensitization procedure, as developed by Wolpe (1958), to the modification of a wide range of neurotic disorders. In this therapeutic method the

* Gerald C. Davison, "Systematic Desensitization as a Counterconditioning Process," *The Journal of Abnormal Psychology*, 73, 1968, 91–99. Copyright 1968 by the American Psychological Association, and reproduced by permission. This paper is based on the author's doctoral dissertation written at Stanford University under Albert Bandura, whose invaluable advice and direction at every stage of the research and composition he is pleased to acknowledge. For their aid and encouragement, sincere thanks are also rendered to Arnold A. Lazarus and Gordon L. Paul. The author is especially grateful to O. B. Neresen, who made available both the physical facilities and human resources at Foothill Junior College, Los Altos, California.

client is deeply relaxed and then instructed to imagine scenes from a hierarchy of anxiety-provoking stimuli. Initially he is asked to imagine the weakest item in the list and, if relaxation is unimpaired, is gradually presented incremental degrees of aversive stimuli until eventually he is completely desensitized to the most upsetting scene in the anxiety hierarchy.

In numerous publications, both Wolpe (e.g., 1952, 1958) and other clinical workers (e.g., Geer, 1964; Lang, 1965; Lazarus, 1963; Lazarus & Rachman, 1957; Rachman, 1959) have claimed a high degree of success in eliminating diverse forms of anxiety disorders by means of this therapeutic technique.

These clinical claims of efficacy find some support in recent laboratory investigations conducted under more controlled conditions and with more objective assessment of therapeutic outcomes (e.g., Lang and Lazovik, 1963; Lang, Lazovik, & Reynolds, 1965; Lazarus, 1961; Paul, 1966; Paul & Shannon, 1966). Although results from these experiments have confirmed the effectiveness of systematic desensitization, they do not provide direct information on the relative contributions to the observed outcomes of the different variables in the treatment procedure (e.g., relaxation, graded exposure to aversive stimuli, temporal contiguity of stimulus events). Moreover, the learning process governing the behavioral changes has not been adequately elucidated. There is some suggestive evidence from Lang et al. (1965) that extensive contact with an E, along with relaxation training, does not effect behavior change. However, one can raise questions about the suitability of their control for relaxation, inasmuch as Ss in this condition began imagining snake-aversive items, but were then led away from this theme by means of subtle manipulation of content by E. It is possible that this imaginal snake avoidance may have counteracted the nonspecific effects built into the control.

Wolpe's (1958) theoretical formulation of the desensitization process as "reciprocal inhibition" is based on Hull's (1943) drive-reduction theory of classical conditioning, a fatigue theory of extinction ("conditioned inhibition"), and Sherrington's (1906) concept of reciprocal inhibition, whereby the evocation of one reflex suppresses the evocation of other reflexes. The conditions which Wolpe (1958) specified for the occurrence of reciprocal inhibition were succinctly stated in his basic principle:

If a response antagonistic to anxiety can be made to occur in the presence of anxiety-evoking stimuli so that it is accompanied by a complete or partial suppression of the anxiety responses, the bond between these stimuli and the anxiety responses will be weakened [p. 71].

This statement appears indistinguishable from Guthrie's (1952) view of counterconditioning, according to which notion the elimination of a response can be achieved by eliciting a strong incompatible response in the presence of cues that ordinarily elicit the undesirable behavior: "Here . . . the stimulus is present, but other responses are present shutting out the former response, and the stimulus becomes a conditioner of these and an inhibitor of its former response [p. 62]." Wolpe, in fact, used the terms "reciprocal inhibition" and "counterconditioning" interchangeably, but clearly indicated a preference for the former in view of his inferences about the neurological process accounting for the observed changes in behavior. However, aside from the fact that he has as yet provided no independent evidence for the existence of reciprocal inhibition at the complex behavioral level that he is dealing with, one must be wary of basing a neurological hypothesis, albeit an ingenious one, upon a behavioral system which, itself, has been shown to have serious short-comings (Gleitman, Nachmias, & Neisser, 1954; Kimble, 1961; Lawrence & Festinger, 1962; Mowrer, 1960; Solomon & Brush, 1956).

At the present time, it appears both unnecessary and premature to "explain" behavioral phenomena in terms of an underlying neural process whose existence is inferrable solely from the very psychological data which it is invoked to explain. It appears to this writer more fruitful to stay closer to the empirical data and to conceptualize the process of systematic desensitization in terms of counterconditioning, according to which the neutralization of aversive stimuli results from the evocation of incompatible responses which are strong enough to supersede anxiety reactions to these stimuli (cf. Bandura, 1969).

PROBLEM

In view of the fact that the behavioral outcomes associated with systematic desensitization are assumed to result from counterconditioning, evidence that such a process does in fact occur is particularly essential (cf. Breger & McGaugh, 1965). To the extent that desensitization involves counter-conditioning, the contiguous association of graded anxiety-provoking stimuli and incompatible relaxation responses would constitute a necessary condition for fear reduction. It is possible, however, that the favorable outcomes produced by this method are primarily attributable to relaxation alone, to the gradual exposure to aversive stimuli, or to nonspecific relationship factors. The present experiment was therefore designed to test directly the hypothesis that systematic desensitization involves a genuine counterconditioning process.

The Ss were indiivdually matched in terms of strength of their snake-avoidance behavior and assigned to one of four conditions. For one group of Ss (desensitization), a graded series of aversive stimuli was contiguously paired in imagination with deep muscle relaxation, as in the standard clinical technique. The Ss in a second group participated in a "pseudodesensitization" treatment that was identical to the first procedure except that the content of the imaginal stimuli paired with relaxation was essentially neutral and completely irrelevant to snakes. This group provided a control for the effects of relationship factors, expectations of beneficial outcomes, and relaxation per se. A third group (exposure) was presented the same series of graded aversive items, but in the absence of deep relaxation. This condition served as a control for the effects of mere repeated exposure to the aversive stimuli. A fourth group (no treatment) participated only in the pre- and posttreatment assessments of snake avoidance.

In order to ensure comparability of stimulus events, Ss in the pseudo-desensitization and exposure groups were *yoked* to their matched partners in the desensitization group, whose progress determined the number of treatment sessions, the duration of each session, the number of stimulus exposures per session, and the duration of each exposure.

Within 3 days following the completion of treatment, all Ss were tested for snake avoidance as well as for the amount of anxiety accompanying each approach response.

On the assumption that the temporal conjunction of relaxation and anxiety-provoking stimuli is essential for change, it was predicted that only Ss in the desensitization condition would display significant decrements in avoidance behavior, and would also be superior in this respect to Ss in the three control groups.

METHOD

Subjects

The Ss were 28 female volunteers drawn from introductory psychology courses at a junior college. Students who reported themselves very much afraid of nonpoisonous snakes were asked to assist in a study investigating procedures for eliminating common fears. In order to minimize suggestive effects, the project was presented as an experiment, rather than as a clinical study, and no claims were made for the efficacy of the procedure to be employed. To reduce further the development of strong expectation of beneficial outcomes, which might in itself produce some positive change, E was introduced as a graduate student rather than as an experienced psychotherapist. To some extent, the results from all the experiments cited above might have been confounded by these variables.

Pre- and Posttreatment Assessments of Avoidance Behavior

These assessments were conducted by an E (E_1) who did not participate in the treatment phases of the study and had no knowledge of the conditions to which Ss were assigned. The avoidance test was similar to that employed by Lang and Lazovik (1963) except for several important changes that were introduced in order to provide a more stringent and sensitive test of the efficacy of the various treatment procedures. First, whereas Lang and Lazovik used essentially a 3-item test, the present behavioral test consisted of 13 items requiring progressively more intimate interaction with the snake (e.g., placing a gloved hand against the glass near the snake, reaching into the cage and touching the snake once, culminating with holding the snake barehanded for 30 sec.). Second, rather than obtaining a single overall estimate of felt anxiety following the entire approach test, the examiner in the present study asked S to rate herself on a 10-point scale following the successful performance of each task. Third, the examiner stood at all times not closer than 2 ft. from the cage, whereas the tester in Lang and Lazovik's study touched and held the snake before requesting an S to do so. Evidence that avoidance behavior can be reduced through observation of model approach responses (Bandura, Grusec, & Menlove, 1967) suggests that the behavioral changes obtained by Lang and Lazovik may reflect the effects of both vicarious extinction and counterconditioning via systematic desensitization.

Any S who, on the pretreatment assessments, succeeded in touching the snake barehanded was excluded from the study. Eligible Ss were matched individually on the basis of their approach behavior and then assigned randomly to the different treatment conditions so as to constitute "clusters" of equally avoidant Ss across groups. Initially it had been planned to include an equal number of matched Ss in the no treatment control group. However, since preliminary findings, as well as data reported by Lang and Lazovik (1963), revealed virtually no changes in nontreated controls, it was decided to enlarge the size of the three treatment conditions. Therefore, eight Ss were assigned to each of the three treatment groups, while the nontreated control group contained four cases. The experimental design is summarized in Table 2.6–1.

Treatment Procedures

The treatment sessions were conducted in a room other than the one in which the avoidance behavior was measured. The Ss in conditions employing relaxation training reclined in a lounger, whereas for Ss in the exposure group the chair was set in an upright position to minimize the development of relaxed states.

Relaxation Paired with Graded Aversive Stimuli (Systematic Desensitization). During the first session, these Ss received training in deep muscular relaxation by means of a 30-min. tape recording consisting of instructions to tense and to relax alternately the various muscle groups of the body, interspersed with suggestions of heaviness, calm, and

TABLE 2.6–1   Summary of Experimental Design

Group	Pretreatment assessment (E_1)	Treatment procedure (E_2)	Posttreatment assessment (E_1)
Desensitization[a]	Avoidance test with anxiety self-reports	Relaxation paired with graded aversive stimuli	Avoidance test with anxiety self-reports
Pseudodesensitization[a]	Same	Relaxation paired with snake-irrelevant stimuli	Same
Exposure[a]	Same	Exposure to graded aversive stimuli without relaxation	Same
No treatment[b]	Same	No treatment	Same

[a] $N = 8$.
[b] $N = 4$.

relaxation. This procedure, used earlier by the author (Davison, 1965b), is based on Lazarus' (1963) accelerated training in Jacobsonian relaxation and is very similar to the technique used by Paul (1966).

In the second session Ss ranked 26 cards each describing snake scenes in order of increasing aversiveness, for example, "Picking up and handling a toy snake," "Standing in front of the cage, looking down at the snake through the wire cover, and it is moving around a little," "Barehanded, picking the snake up, and it is moving around." The desensitization procedure, modeled after Lazarus (1963), Paul (1966), and Wolpe (1961), was administered in a standardized fashion, with a criterion of 15 sec. without signaling anxiety on each item. (For specifics of the procedure, see Davison, 1965a.) A maximum of nine sessions, each lasting about 45 min., was allowed for completing the anxiety hierarchy.

Relaxation Paired with Snake-Irrelevant Stimuli (Pseudodesensitization). The Ss assigned to this group received the same type and amount of relaxation training as Ss in the above-mentioned group. Similarly, in the second session they also ranked 26 stimulus items, except that the depicted scenes were entirely unrelated to snakes. Because of the widespread belief that exploration of childhood experiences may be important in alleviating objectively unrealistic fears, it was decided to employ descriptions of common childhood events, which Ss were asked to rank chronologically. Some of the items were essentially neutral in content ("You are about age six, and your family is discussing where to go for a ride on Sunday afternoon, at the dinner table."), while the others had mild affective properties ("You are about five years old, and you are sitting on the floor looking sadly at a toy that you have just broken."). The use of generic content thus made it possible to use snake-irrelevant stimuli without reducing the credibility of the treatment procedure.

As in the desensitization condition, Ss were deeply relaxed and asked to imagine vividly each scene presented by the E until told to discontinue the visualization. Each S in this condition, it will be recalled, was yoked to her matched partner in the desensitization group, whose progress defined the number of treatment sessions, the length of each session, as well as the number and duration of each imaginal exposure. Thus, Ss undergoing pseudodesensitization received the same number and duration of pairings during each session as their desensitization mates, with the important exception that snake-irrelevant stimuli were contiguously associated with relaxation.

Exposure to Graded Aversive Stimuli without Relaxation (Exposure). The Ss in this group were administered the same series of snake-aversive stimuli in the same order and for the same durations as determined by their respective partners in the desensitization group to whom they were yoked. However, exposure Ss received no relaxation training (hence, had one session less with E), nor did they engage in anxiety-competing relaxation while visualizing the aversive situations. Because of the yoking requirements, on those occasions when Ss signaled anxiety, they were instructed to maintain the images until E asked them to discontinue. Cooperation in this obviously unpleasant task was obtained through friendly but cogent reminders that such visualization was important for the experimental design.

No Treatment Group. The Ss assigned to this group merely participated in the assessments of avoidance behavior at the same time as their matched partners in the desensitization condition.

RESULTS

Table 2.6–2 presents the change scores in approach behavior for each S in each of the eight matched clusters.

Between-Group Differences

Because of the unequal number of Ss in the no treatment group, these data were not included in the overall statistical analysis. Two-way analysis of variance of the change scores obtained by the three matched treatment groups yielded a highly significant treatment effect ($F = 6.84$; $p < .01$).

Further, one-tailed comparisons of pairs of treatment conditions by t tests for correlated means revealed that Ss who had undergone systematic desensitization subsequently displayed significantly more snake-approach behavior than Ss in either the pseudodesensitization group ($t = 2.57$; $p < .01$), the exposure group ($t = 3.60$; $p < .005$), or the no treatment control group ($t = 3.04$; $p < .01$). The pseudodesensitization and exposure groups did not differ significantly in approach behavior from the no treatment controls (t's $= .92$, $.21$, respectively), nor did they differ from each other.

TABLE 2.6–2   Changes in Snake-Approach Behavior Displayed by Subjects in Each of the Treatment Conditions

	Condition			
Matched cluster	Desensi- tization	Pseudo- desensi- tization	Exposure	No treat- ment
1	3	2	2	0
2	3	−1	0	—
3	6	0	−1	−1
4	5	1	−5	0
5	0	1	2	—
6	6	8	1	0
7	12	0	0	—
8	7	1	1	—
M	5.25	1.50	0.0	−0.25

Within-Group Differences

Within-group changes in avoidance behavior were evaluated by t tests for correlated means. Results of this analysis likewise disclosed that only Ss in the desensitization condition achieved a significant reduction in avoidance behavior ($t = 4.20$; $p < .005$).

Performance of the Criterion Behavior in Posttreatment Assessment

If the desensitization treatment does, in fact, involve a genuine counterconditioning process, then one would expect to find relationships between factors that are known to affect the conditioning process (e.g., number of aversive stimuli that have been neutralized) and degree of behavioral change. In this connection, of the eight Ss in the desensitization group, five completed their anxiety hierarchies within the allotted nine sessions. It is of interest to note that four of these five Ss performed the terminal behavior at the posttreatment assessment, whereas not a single S whose desensitization had to be terminated before all anxiety items had been successfully neutralized was able to hold the snake barehanded. Moreover, no S in the exposure or no treatment groups performed the terminal behavior, and only one out of the eight pseudodesensitization Ss attained the criterion performance.

Anxiety-Inhibiting Function of Relaxation

The Ss in both the desensitization and exposure conditions had been instructed to signal to E by raising their index finger whenever a particular imagined scene aroused anxiety. Since Ss in these two groups were matched for the order, number, and duration of stimulus exposures, any differences in the frequency of anxiety signaling provide suggestive evidence for the efficacy of relaxation in counteracting the development of emotional arousal during systematic desensitization (but see methodological problem raised in Discussion below).

The Ss in the desensitization group signaled anxiety on 27% of the stimulus presentations, whereas the corresponding figure for the exposure group was 61%. This highly significant difference ($t = 3.30$; $p < .01$, two-tailed test) not only furnishes an independent check on the relaxation training, but also attests to the anxiety-inhibiting capabilities of relaxation procedures.

Relationship between Anxiety Decrements and Approach Behavior

All Ss except those in the first cluster rated the degree of emotional disturbance that they experienced during the successful performance of each task in the pre- and posttreatment assessments. Since all but one S in the desensitization treatment surpassed their initial approach performance, it is possible to obtain a measure of anxiety decrement at the point at which Ss were unable to proceed any further during the pretreatment assessment. Thus, for example, an S who, on the first test, went so far as to look down at the snake with the wire cover drawn back and reported an anxiety rating of 9, but subsequently performed this same task with an anxiety rating of 2, would receive a decrement score of 7 points. These self-report data were analyzed in order to determine whether desensitization, in addition to increasing approach behavior, also reduces the degree of emotional disturbance accompanying the overt responses.

Except for one S who exhibited no behavioral change and reported a 1-point increase in anxiety, the remaining six cases all showed decreases, the mean decrement being 3.28. The t value for the correlated differences is 3.31, significant beyond the .04 level, two-tailed test.

It will be recalled that some Ss in the pseudodesensitization group showed small but nonsignificant increases in approach behavior (Table 2.6–2). These Ss also displayed some decrease in anxiety ($M = 2.67$), but not of a statistically significant magnitude ($t = 1.76$).

A within-group correlational analysis for Ss in the desensitization condition further revealed that the magnitude of anxiety decrement is highly predictive of the degree of increase exhibited by Ss in approach behavior. The product-moment correlation obtained between these two measures is $r = .81$, significant beyond the .05 level. This strong relationship indicates that Ss who experienced the greatest amount of anxiety reduction also showed the most behavioral improvement.

Anxiety Accompanying Strong Approach Responses

Although Ss who had undergone systematic desensitization exhibited highly significant improvement in overt approach to the snake, it is evident from the data that the bold approach responses performed in the posttest were accompanied by considerable anxiety, ranging from 4 to 10 on the 10-point self-report scale, with a mean of 7.75. These findings, which are consistent with results obtained by Lang and Lazovik (1963) and Lang et al. (1965), will be discussed later.

DISCUSSION

The results of the present study provide strong support for the hypothesis that behavioral changes produced by systematic desensitization reflect a counterconditioning process. This is shown in the finding that only Ss for whom aversive stimuli were contiguously associated in imagination with the anxiety-competing response of relaxation (i.e., Ss in the desensitization group) displayed significant reduction in avoidance behavior; this reduction was also significantly greater than the nonsignificant changes observed in the pseudodesensitization, exposure, and no treatment control groups. The fact that Ss who were merely exposed to the aversive stimuli, and those for whom relaxation was paired with snake-irrelevant stimuli, showed no significant changes in snake avoidance indicates that neither graded exposure alone nor relaxation and expectations of beneficial effects were determinants of the outcomes yielded by the desensitization treatment. Moreover, the desensitization–no treatment comparison replicates Lang and Lazovik (1963), while the desensitization–pseudodesensitization comparison provides some manner of confirmation of Lang et al. (1965).

In evaluating the treatment involving mere exposure to the graded aversize stimuli, it should be noted that, in order to control for duration of visualization, Ss were often required to continue imagining a scene after they had signaled anxiety. It is possible that, had Ss been allowed to control their own exposures to the aversive items, they might have produced some extinction of fear. In a pilot study by the author (Davison, 1965b), considerable extinction was observed when Ss controlled their own exposures to aversive stimuli. In comparison, it should be pointed out that Davison's experiment, as well as the earlier observations of Grossberg (1965), Herzberg (1941), and Jones (1924), used actual rather than symbolic stimuli. Nonetheless, it would be of considerable interest and importance to determine whether self-controlled exposure to aversive stimuli in imaginal form also effects significant reduction in avoidance.

In addition, this issue of forced versus self-controlled exposure necessitates caution in interpreting the finding that desensitization Ss signaled anxiety significantly less often than their matched and yoked exposure mates. This difference may be due not only to the anxiety-competing properties of deep muscular relaxation, but also to the aversive nature of being unable to perform a response that will remove one from a fearful situation (cf. Mowrer & Viek, 1948).

Suggestive evidence was obtained indicating that the increased approach behavior of the desensitization group was due to a decrease in anxiety; that is, the actual avoidance gradient seems to have been lowered to allow for more approach. While performing on the posttreatment assessment the most difficult behavior encountered at the pretreatment assessment, desensitization Ss rated themselves as significantly less anxious; furthermore, a high positive and significant correlation was found in this group between decrements in self-reported anxiety and amount of overt behavioral improvement. These findings are consistent with the anxiety-avoidance paradigm of Mowrer (1940, 1947) and Miller (1948), as well as with theories of psychopathology based on animal learning experiments (Dollard & Miller, 1950; Mowrer, 1950)—all of which at least implicitly form the basis of Wolpian behavior therapy. According to this general view, avoidance responses are mediated by a secondary drive of fear; to the extent that a treatment method successfully reduces this fear, formerly inhibited approach responses will become manifest with the reduction of fear.

However, this anxiety-reduction analysis of the data is subject to several qualifications. First, questions can be raised as to the validity of self-report data on a numerical scale as a measure of anxiety (cf. Martin, 1961). Asking a naive S to rate herself on a scale from 1 to 10 may be making undue demands for rather fine discriminations among degrees of emotional arousal. A second problem is that Ss rated their anxiety *after* they performed a given behavior. In order to infer the role of fear in inhibiting a given behavior, a logical requirement is that such measures be taken before or during the behavior. Although Ss had been asked to rate the anxiety they were experiencing while performing the behavior, it is impossible to estimate the effect of actually performing the behavior on their self-reported ratings. A third consideration is of a theoretical nature. The experiments of Solomon and Wynne (1954) and Wynne and Solomon (1955) raise doubts about a straightforward interpretation of avoidance behavior as mediated by covert fear responses. Indeed, the data reported in the present study are amenable to at least one alternative explanation, namely, that anxiety and avoidance responses are *both* conditioned to the aversive stimuli, therefore being correlated classes of responses but not necessarily causally related. Systematic desensitization, then, may be reducing both components of avoidance behavior. Indeed, some suggestive evidence for the partial independence of anxiety and avoidance is the fact that Ss characteristically experienced high emotional arousal while successfully executing the terminal approach response, even after having completed their anxiety hierarchies. Unfortunately, these data, it will be seen below, may also be considered in support of the anxiety-avoidance hypothesis.

Limitations of Systematic Desensitization

Having confirmed that systematic desensitization significantly reduces avoidance behavior, and having provided evidence that an actual process of counterconditioning underlies these effects, it would seem valuable at this point to examine both the practical and theoretical limitations of the technique.

The practical limitations concern levels of relaxation achieved, the clarity of aversive images, and the signaling of anxiety. In the present study, as in clinical uses of the procedure, extensive reliance was placed on Ss' self-reports. It is clear that the outcome of any desensitization study will greatly depend on how satisfactorily these problems are dealt with.

Perhaps more intriguing are the theoretical limitations. It will be recalled that desensitization Ss experienced considerable anxiety while performing the terminal behavior or approach responses high in the graduated series of tasks during the posttreatment assessment. Inasmuch as five of eight Ss in this group had been successfully desensitized in imagination, their anxiety reactions in the posttreatment assessment situation raise an interesting theoretical question regarding transfer effects.

One would expect, on the basis of the principle of stimulus generalization (Kimble, 1961), that the degree of transfer of counterconditioning effects from one stimulus situation to another is determined by the number of common elements. According to Guthrie's (1952) notion, for example, a complex stimulus (like a snake) consists of a finite number of stimulus elements, each of which can be attached to only one molecular fear response at any given time. The desensitization procedure, as the present author has heuristically viewed it, operates in two ways to render a given molar stimulus incapable of arousing the molar response of fear. First, by beginning with the weakest items of an anxiety hierarchy one is presumably taking a very small sample of the "snake-object population of stimulus elements." Since this limited "amount of snake" elicits a limited "amount of fear," an incompatible response can be made dominant over the minimal fear response. This is why, second, deep muscular relaxation responses are induced prior to the introduction of the small dose of aversive stimuli. It is in this fashion that one "alienates" the small sample of fear stimuli from the limited number of molecular fear responses.

When a given anxiety item has been neutralized (defined as visualizing it for 15 sec. without signaling anxiety), another sample from the population of fear stimuli is presented, the incompatible relaxation response being set against that part of the total fear response which would ordinarily be elicited by the sample of fear stimuli. This process continues up the anxiety hierarchy until all items have been successfully desensitized.

When viewed in this fashion, the process of systematic desensitization would not be expected to effect complete transfer from the imaginal to the real-life situation. For, even though an S succeeds in imagining the various anxiety items without becoming anxious, the facts remain that: (a) The visualization is unlikely to involve all the stimulus elements for the respective level of the hierarchy; and (b) the hierarchy itself cannot possibly provide an exhaustive sampling of the population of fear elements.

In the studies of Lang and Lazovik (1963), Lang et al. (1965), and Paul (1966), there was also a failure to find complete fearlessness on the part of successfully desensitized Ss. On the other hand, the clinical literature would lead one to expect perfect transfer, namely, "It has consistently been found that at every stage a stimulus that evokes no anxiety when imagined in a state of relaxation evokes no anxiety when encountered in reality [Wolpe, 1961, p. 191]." This discrepancy may in some measure be due to the unreliability of clinical reports. However, assuming that the clinical data are, in fact, valid, the greater generalization of counterconditioning effects in actual clinical practice may be a function of several factors which were intentionally excluded from the present experimental design. Among these would be in vivo desensitization based on differential relaxation (Davison, 1965b; Wolpe & Lazarus, 1966), the positive reinforcement of approach responses in interaction with presumed counterconditioning (Bower & Grusec, 1964; Davison, 1964; Lazarus, Davison, & Polefka, 1965), the vicarious extinction of avoidance responses by means of modeling procedures (Bandura et al., 1967; Jones, 1924), "placebo effect" (Frank, 1961; Paul, 1966), and the so-called "nonspecifics" of a therapeutic relationship (cf. Lazarus, 1963).

Etiology versus Treatment

Having furnished evidence in favor of a conditioning interpretation of a particular technique of behavior modification, it would seem appropriate to comment briefly on the implications which these findings have for the development of neurotic anxiety. An error in logic is committed if one adduces data such as these as evidence in support of a conditioning model of the *acquisition* of inappropriate anxiety: from evidence regarding efficacy in changing behavior, one cannot claim to have demonstrated that the problem evolved in an analogous fashion (cf. Rimland, 1964). Whether in the present instance neurotic disorders, modifiable via counterconditioning techniques, originate in situations conceptualized in classical conditioning terms is a very important research and preventive therapy question; it is, however, separate from the corrective therapy issue. In fact, the author has sought vainly in the experimental literature for paradigms which illustrate the acquisition of *stable* fear responses in human beings under conditions bearing even a remote resemblance to what would likely hold in real life.[1]

NOTE

1. The author is indebted to Gordon L. Paul and Bernard Rimland for first pointing out these issues.

REFERENCES

Bandura, A. *Principles of behavior modification.* New York:, Holt Rinehart and Winston, 1969.

Bandura, A., Grusec, J. E., & Menlove, F. Vicarious extinction of avoidance responses. *Journal of Personality and Social Psychology,* 1967, 5, 16–23.

Bower, G. H., & Grusec, T. Effect of prior Pavlovian discrimination training upon learning an operant discrimination. *Journal of Experimental Analysis of Behavior,* 1964, 7, 401–404.

Breger, L., & McGaugh, J. L. A critique and reformulation of "learning theory" approaches to psychotherapy and neurosis. *Psychological Bulletin,* 1965, 63, 338–358.

Davison, G. C. A social learning therapy programme with an autistic child. *Behaviour Research and Therapy,* 1964, 2, 149–159.

Davison, G. C. The influence of systematic desensitization, relaxation, and graded exposure to imaginal aversive stimuli on the modification of phobic behavior. Unpublished doctoral dissertation, Stanford University, 1965. (a)

Davison, G. C. Relative contributions of differential relaxation and graded exposure to the in vivo desensitization of a neurotic fear. In, *Proceedings of the 73rd annual convention of the American Psychological Association, 1965.* Washington, D. C.: American Psychological Association, 1965. (b)

Dollard, J., & Miller, N. E. *Personality and psychotherapy.* New York: McGraw-Hill, 1950.

Frank, J. D. *Persuasion and healing.* Baltimore: Johns Hopkins Press, 1961.

Geer, J. Phobia treated by reciprocal inhibition. *Journal of Abnormal and Social Psychology,* 1964, 69, 642–645.

Gleitman, H., Nachmias, J., & Neisser, U. The S-R reinforcement theory of extinction. *Psychological Review,* 1954, 61, 23–33.

Grossberg, J. M. Successful behavior therapy in a case of speech phobia ("stage fright"). *Journal of Speech and Hearing Disorders,* 1965, 30, 285–288.

Guthrie, E. R. *The psychology of learning.* New York: Harper, 1952.

Herzberg, A. Short treatment of neuroses by graduated tasks. *British Journal of Medical Psychology,* 1941, 19, 36–51.

Hull, C. L. *Principles of behavior.* New York: Appleton, 1943.

Jones, M. C. The elimination of children's fears. *Journal of Experimental Psychology,* 1924, 7, 382–390.

Kimble, G. A. *Hilgard and Marquis' conditioning and learning.* New York: Appleton-Century-Crofts, 1961.

Lang, P. J. Behavior therapy with a case of nervous anorexia. In L. P. Ullmann & L. Krasner (Eds.), *Case studies in behavior modification.* New York: Holt, 1965.

Lang, P. J., & Lazovik, A. D. Experimental desensitization of a phobia. *Journal of Abnormal and Social Psychology,* 1963, 66, 519–525.

Lang, P. J., Lazovik, A. D., & Reynolds, D. J. Desensitization, suggestibility, and pseudotherapy. *Journal of Abnormal Psychology,* 1965, 70, 395–402.

Lawrence, D. H., & Festinger, L. *Deterrents and reinforcement: The psychology of insufficient reward.* Stanford: Stanford University Press, 1962.

Lazarus, A. A. Group therapy of phobic disorders by systematic desensitization. *Journal of Abnormal and Social Psychology,* 1961, 63, 504–510.

Lazarus, A. A. The results of behavior therapy in 126 cases of severe neurosis. *Behaviour Research and Therapy,* 1963, 1, 69–79.

Lazarus, A. A., Davison, G. C., & Polefka, D. Classical and operant factors in the treatment of a school phobia. *Journal of Abnormal Psychology,* 1965, 70, 225–229.

Lazarus, A. A., & Rachman, S. The use of systematic desensitization in psychotherapy. *South African Medical Journal,* 1957, 31, 934–937.

Martin, B. The assessment of anxiety by physiological behavioral measures. *Psychological Bulletin,* 1961, 58, 234–255.

Miller, N. E. Studies of fear as an acquirable drive: I. Fear as motivation and fear-reduction as reinforcement in the learning of new responses. *Journal of Experimental Psychology,* 1948, 38, 89–101.

Mowrer, O. H. Anxiety-reduction and learning. *Journal of Experimental Psychology,* 1940, 27, 497–516.

Mowrer, O. H. On the dual nature of learning—a reinterpretation of "conditioning" and "problem solving." *Harvard Education Review,* 1947, 17, 102–148.

Mowrer, O. H. *Learning theory and personality dynamics.* New York: Ronald Press, 1950.

Mowrer, O. H. *Learning theory and behavior.* New York: Wiley, 1960.

Mowrer, O. H., & Viek, P. An experimental analogue of fear from a sense of helplessness. *Journal of Abnormal and Social Psychology,* 1948, 43, 193–200.

Paul, G. L. *Insight versus desensitization in psychotherapy: An experiment in anxiety-reduction.* Stanford: Stanford University Press, 1966.

Paul, G. L., & Shannon, D. T. Treatment of anxiety through systematic desensitization in therapy groups. *Journal of Abnormal Psychology,* 1966, 71, 124–135.

Rachman, S. The treatment of anxiety and phobic reactions by systematic desensitization psychotherapy. *Journal of Abnormal and Social Psychology,* 1959, 58, 259–263.

Rimland, B. *Infantile autism.* New York: Appleton-Century-Crofts, 1964.

Sherrington, C. S. *The integrative action of the central nervous system.* Cambridge: Cambridge University Press, 1906.

Solomon, R. L., & Brush, E. S. Experimentally derived conceptions of anxiety and aversion. In M. R. Jones (Ed.), *Nebraska symposium on motivation: 1956.* Lincoln: University of Nebraska Press, 1956.

Solomon, R. L., & Wynne, L. C. Traumatic avoidance learning: The principles of anxiety conservation and partial irreversibility. *Psychological Review,* 1954, 61, 353–395.

Wolpe, J. Objective psychotherapy of the neuroses. *South African Medical Journal,* 1952, 26, 825–829.

Wolpe, J. *Psychotherapy by reciprocal inhibition.* Stanford: Stanford University Press, 1958.

Wolpe, J. The systematic desensitization treatment of neurosis. *Journal of Nervous and Mental Disease,* 1961, 132, 189–203.

Wolpe, J., & Lazarus, A. A. *Behavior therapy techniques.* New York: Pergamon, 1966.

Wynne, L. C., & Solomon, R. L. Traumatic avoidance learning: Acquisition and extinction in dogs deprived of normal peripheral autonomic functioning. *Genetic Psychology Monographs,* 1955, 52, 241–284.

THE TREATMENT OF ADDICTION BY AVERSION
CONDITIONING WITH APOMORPHINE*

M. J. Raymond

Summary—*An account is given of the techniques employed in using
apomorphine for the treatment of chronic alcoholism, addiction to other
drugs and addiction to cigarette smoking. No evaluation is made here
but each technique is illustrated by the report of a case in which the
result is considered, after a reasonable follow-up period, to be
highly satisfactory.*

INTRODUCTION

Apomorphine is derived from morphia by the removal of a molecule of
water and was first prepared in 1869 by Matthieson & Wright. It is a
centrally acting emetic and, less powerfully, a hypnotic. Tolerance to it
rarely if ever develops. Its value in the treatment of alcoholism was first
described by Hare (1912) who was particularly concerned with its seda-
tive and hypnotic action. Hare stated that it produced a prompt though
fleeting "freedom from the dipsomaniac craving". Dent (1934) also
stressed the value of the drug in the relief of the anxiety underlying
addiction. Originally he produced vomiting by means of apomorphine
given in conjunction with alcohol, but he subsequently modified his
technique, and stated that the need for alcohol could be suppressed
without nausea or vomiting, simply by the action of apomorphine on the
fore-brain and the hind-brain, to correct inbalance.

Voegtlin (1947) and his collaborators began to treat alcoholics with
apomorphine in 1936 but for them the essence of the treatment was the
establishment of a conditioned reflex of aversion to the sight, taste and
smell of alcohol. They stressed the importance of working with the
same precision as the physiologist requires when creating conditioned
reflexes in laboratory animals. In subsequent work Voegtlin discarded
apomorphine in favour of emetine because he regarded the hypnotic
effect of apomorphine as a hindrance to conditioning.

* Reprinted from *Behaviour Research and Therapy*, 1, 1964, 287–291. Copyright 1964
by the Pergamon Press, and reproduced by permission.

ALCOHOLISM

It is not our practice to treat any patient until he has accepted the fact that alcohol is for him a serious problem and that he must avoid it for the rest of his life. The treatment and its rationale are discussed with him, and he must undertake it voluntarily. We no longer consider it necessary to segregate the patient during the period of his treatment, or to subject him to the rigours of many treatments during day and night. He lives in the therapeutic community, joining in the same occupational, social and dietary regime as the other patients. Usually he has two or three treatments during the day, but the times are varied at random. It is important to correct the idea, common among patients who have heard of the treatment or who have perhaps had some experience of it, that success is going to be estimated as in direct proportion to the volume of vomitus. In fact, all that is required is a definite period of nausea, and this need not be prolonged. The dose of apomorphine is kept to a minimum: we start with 1/20g and do not often exceed 1/10g. The dose is dissolved in 1 cm³ of normal saline and injected subcutaneously. Seven minutes after the first injection the patient is taken to the treatment room. He should on the first occasion take one small drink only, the prime object being to determine (a) the "nausea time", and (b) the "vomiting time", if in fact vomiting ensues. The patient is told to report any feeling of nausea, or queasiness he feels, and the times are noted most carefully. He must be observed for blanching, sweating, and the increased swallowing which may denote increased salivation. This must not be confused with the tongue movements of the anxious patient with a dry mouth. It may be necessary to ask the patient, perhaps repeatedly, when those signs are observed, whether he feels nauseated. It is important to realise that the nausea may be very mild and fleeting, but that once it is defined with certainty, it can be expanded quite quickly in subsequent sessions without increasing the dose. If no reaction at all is produced, the session is discontinued after half an hour. At the next session 1/10g is employed, the procedure is repeated, and all observations carefully noted. If again no nausea is produced, then the third session will be preceded by a dose of emetine hydrochloride 1½g. This is given in a tumblerful of weak saline ten minutes before the subcutaneous injection of apomorphine 1/20g. The average nausea time after emetine is twenty minutes, and the average nausea time after apomorphine is ten minutes. The time intervals recorded are measured from the time of the injection. If this manoeuvre is successful, the next session will be with apomorphine 1/10g and if this is successful the dose may subsequently be dropped to 1/20g. On each occasion the patient does not start to drink until just before the nausea is predicted.

The treatment room and its environs must be quiet, and in addition to the obviously essential furnishings it should contain a bed or couch. An oxygen cylinder and a resuscitation tray containing syringes and Cora-mine should be placed within easy reach as a matter of routine. The patient is not allowed to smoke. Conversation and jocularity are dis-couraged. The use of "familiar bar clichés" and dramatic accoutrements such as the spotlight are impediments which have no place in the treat-ment. We usually insist that the patient continues to drink during the early part of the nausea period, but this does not necessitate the harsh, bullying technique one has sometimes observed. Above all, noise is to be avoided, and encouragement may be quite effectively given by gesture or by whispered instructions. It is most important that he should not be pressed or allowed to continue drinking once the nausea has passed. If alcohol is taken as the nausea subsides, the foregoing treatment will be largely vitiated, and at best aversion will take much longer to produce. It is our practice to withhold alcohol as soon as the patient's resistance to it begins to relax, and if there is any doubt about the end point, it is better to withhold alcohol as soon as nausea occurs, rather than risk "drinking through". We believe that neglect of this principle is one of the chief reasons for failures with this treatment. The amount of alcohol given should be small. If the patient becomes drunk, conditioning will not occur. It is not necessary to employ a wide range of beverages, but a variety should be available, and should of course include the patient's favourite drink. One to which he is normally somewhat averse is often most valuable in the initial stages of establishing nausea. An inferior brand of rum is very useful in this respect.

During the post nausea period the patient is usually in a drowsy state and may often be observed to yawn. It is at this stage that one can profitably discuss his revaluation of alcohol and his unique circumstances. The hazards of alcohol are repeatedly put to him, and he is repeatedly told that it will now be possible for him to live without alcohol.

The "Choice" Reaction

After nausea has been quite regularly produced for a week or ten days, and the patient is beginning to show and express distaste for alcohol, he is quite unexpectedly given a choice. Without his knowledge of the changed routine, he is given an injection of 1 cm^3 of normal saline sub-cutaneously, and when he arrives in the treatment room seven minutes later, he finds among the alcohol various soft drinks such as tonic water, bitter lemon, tomato juice, etc. He usually comments on this immediately, but in any case is told that he may drink whatever he chooses. When he chooses a soft drink, and we have not yet had a patient who did not, the atmosphere is immediately relaxed, conversation is encouraged, and the patient, lest he remain apprehensive, is assured that he will certainly not feel in any way ill. The next two or three treatments will be with apo-morphine and alcohol, with continuing careful attention to timing. Further "choice" reactions are provoked, but care is taken to avoid any regular sequence which would enable the patient to predict that a choice will be available.

Rationale Underlying the "Choice" Reaction

The ultimate aim of our therapy is to enable the patient to achieve a new, positive, and successful adaptation to the drinking situation which the average patient cannot avoid encountering recurrently in numerous and varied forms as part of the social complex. Aversion produced by classical conditioning is accompanied by considerable anxiety as may be readily observed after only a few sessions. The immediate relaxation of tension as described above strongly reinforces the conditioned aversion to alcohol and is contingent upon the patient's correct response in choosing a non-alcoholic drink. Moreover, this incorporation of free operant conditioning into the treatment establishes the patient in active control where formerly he considered himself passively controlled.

The average length of treatment is three weeks. After treatment the patient is given Antabuse and advised to take it regularly in order to guard against the possibility of the "first drink". Its action is carefully explained to him. It may be helpful if with the consent of the patient, a relative or employer is asked to see that the dose is given each morning.

Case Report

A 63-year-old man who had been a heavy drinker for many years, had for five years correctly regarded himself as an alcoholic. He had attended meetings of A.A., but was finding it increasingly difficult to manage without alcohol. He was still actively employed as a company director, but his colleagues, though they greatly valued his experience and technical advice, now anxiously sought his resignation as the only solution to an embarrassing situation. He said that he wanted treatment, and despite his age, he was advised to have aversion therapy. Characteristically, he found it impossible to start for "a week or two" because of pressure of business. He and his relatives were told that it was pointless to force the issue, but were instructed exactly how to proceed when he really accepted the necessity. He arrived at the hospital ten days later, relatively sober, and declared that he was thoroughly frightened by what was probably an attempt at suicide during a period of exceptional drinking, for which he had no clear memory. Physical examination revealed hypertension, emphysema and bronchitis, multiple extra-systoles, and a fractured clavicle. Within three weeks of admission he was considered to be fit enough to start aversion therapy, though it was thought wise to start with apo-morphine 1/40 g. This was subsequently increased to 1/20 g, which was the maximum dose he received throughout his treatment. The lower dose produced vomiting without appreciable nausea, but the nausea time was with the larger dose established at eight minutes, often without any vomiting at all. He received only two treatments each day, and on the 17th day was given his first "choice", to which he readily responded with the required reaction. After a further three days' treatment he was again allowed a choice, and this was repeated on the 24th and the 27th days. Treatment was concluded after 31 days. Three days later he started taking Antabuse and was discharged after a further week.

It is now almost three years since his treatment, and he reports that he has never taken alcohol since. His family confirm this and say that he is very active and successful in his business.

DRUG ADDICTION

Aversion conditioning may be used in the treatment of any drug addiction. The treatment is similar to that already described, and the patient administers his own drug of addiction immediately before the predicted nausea produced by an injection of apomorphine. When the drug of addiction is taken orally, it is necessary to produce vomiting in addition to nausea, and it may be necessary to use emetine hydrochloride before each session, in the manner described above. When the drug of addiction is taken by injection, part of the contents of the ampoule is discarded and replaced by normal saline, as described in the following case:

A Case of Physeptone Addiction

A 30-year-old woman (Mrs. C.) had been addicted to injections of Physeptone for six years. The drug was originally prescribed for the relief of migrainous headaches, but she now found it a necessary stimulant without which she became anergic and deeply depressed. Her average daily dose was three ampoules (30 mg) but at times she had been known to take as many as 200 ampoules (2000 mg) in a month. There had been a striking personality change, and she was described as having become furtive, and dishonest. She had been persuaded to enter hospital for treatment following a Home Office enquiry into her case.

Before the first treatment, part of the contents of an ampoule of Physeptone was withdrawn and replaced by sterile normal saline. This ampoule was placed in its box with unopened ampoules in the treatment room. Seven minutes after an injection of apomorphine 1/40 g, the patient was taken to the treatment room and told to give herself an injection of Physeptone, it being explained that she would be allowed only one ampoule, which had been already opened for her. Nausea occurred five minutes after the Physeptone injection (12 min. after the apomorphine injection). The amount of Physeptone replaced by normal saline was very gradually increased with each session. The empty ampoules were not discarded, but placed in the box so that it might be evident to the patient that a fresh ampoule was used for each session. In this way Physeptone was gradually withdrawn without the patient's knowledge. After eight days, treatment had to be discontinued because of severe depression. The patient expressed guilt and shame, and thought that her family would be better without her. She was considered to be potentially suicidal, and over the next three weeks was treated with E.C.T. During this period no Physeptone was given. The profuse perspiration, tremor, diarrhea, and depression which had marked the withdrawal phase had now disappeared. It thus appeared that there was no longer any autonomic dependence on the drug, but she said, however, that she still felt the craving for Physeptone. Aversion therapy was therefore resumed, and at the second session of the third day after resumption, she showed reluctance to inject herself. On the fifth day she deliberately smashed her syringe. During the post nausea period the patient was encouraged to discuss some of her problems and the family tensions in relation to her headaches. It was repeatedly suggested to her that Physeptone had simply aggravated these problems, as would be the case if she had recourse to other similar drugs. Aversion therapy was concluded on the ninth day. She was finally discharged from hospital seven weeks later, although her headaches had returned during a ten-day period at home. She was subsequently seen regularly as an outpatient for six months.

Two and a half years after her discharge from hospital, she wrote the following: "I never get any headaches now, and have never once had any desire for Physeptone. My general health has been better than I have ever known it and I feel wonderfully well". Her general practitioner writes: "Mrs. C. is very well and not taking any medicine or drugs of any kind".

A Case of Cigarette Addiction

A fourteen-year-old boy was said by his parents to have started smoking at the age of seven, and to be spending every penny of his pocket money on cigarettes. He had at one time regularly smoked 40 cigarettes per day, but was now averaging about half that number because his pocket money had been reduced. He said he wanted to give up smoking because he had a smoker's cough, was breathless on exertion, and because it was costing so much money. Physical examination and chest X-ray were normal. Treatment was given in the outpatient department. On the first occasion he was given an injection of apomorphine 1/20 g, and after seven minutes he was told to start smoking. At eleven minutes he became nauseated and vomited copiously. Four days later he came for the second treatment, and said that he still had the craving for cigarettes, but had not in fact smoked since the previous session because he felt nauseated when he tried to light one. He was given an injection of apomorphine 1/20 g, and after seven minutes he lit a cigarette reluctantly, and immediately said he felt ill. He was encouraged to continue smoking, and he collapsed. He was given oxygen and an injection of Coramine. When he recovered he was very hungry and asked for food, which he ate voraciously. Four days later he was given apomorphine 1/40 g, and vomited as soon as he attempted to light a cigarette seven minutes later. When he next attended he said he no longer had any craving for cigarettes, and he made two interesting comments: "When I see an advert on T.V. for cigarettes it seems like a dead advert, like Omo." "Just smoke from my father's cigarette makes me feel ill." Two months later he left school and started working. He said he had "got a bit down" at work and wanted to "keep in with the others", so he had accepted a proffered cigarette. He immediately felt faint and hot, and was unable to smoke. It is now a year since his treatment, and his parents confirm that he no longer smokes.

REFERENCES

Dent, J. Y. (1934) Apomorphine in the treatment of anxiety states with special reference to alcoholism. *Brt. J. Inebr.* 43, 65–69; (1944) Self-treatment of anxiety and craving by apomorphine through the nose. *Brit. J. Addict.* 41, 78–84; (1949) Apomorphine treatment of addiction. *Brit. J. Addict.* 46, 1528; (1955) *Anxiety and its Treatment with Special Reference to Alcoholism.* Skeffington, London.

Hare F. (1912) *On Alcoholism, its Clinical Aspects and Treatment.* Churchill, London.

Voegtlin W. (1947) The conditioned reflex treatment of alcoholism. *Arch. Neurol. Psychiat.* 57, 514–516.

Three
The Generality
of Reinforcement

Rewards strengthen behavior. Few principles are simpler or better known, and yet . . . if the principle of reward is so obvious, why is behavior so hard to control? Why do mothers have such trouble getting their children to clean their rooms or their husbands to wash the dishes? Why do teachers have to repeat lessons over and over and still find average exam scores of only 75 percent?

In the following chapters, we will argue that there are two explanations: the principles of reward are not quite as obvious as they appear, and even when we do understand them, we too often fail to apply them systematically. In this chapter, we will look at the enormous potential of rewards for controlling behavior: the wide range of events that can be used as rewards, and the variety of responses that they can strengthen. Then in the following chapter we will examine some of the principles of reward, and how failure to follow them explains why seemingly powerful rewards sometimes have little or no effect on behavior. Finally, we will look at two situations in which these principles have been consistently followed, and the dramatic behavioral changes that resulted.

Before we begin, a note on terminology. Rewards are events which strengthen or reinforce behavior, and it has become customary among psychologists to refer to them as *reinforcers*. A reinforcer is technically defined as an event that increases the probability of a response when made contingent on that response. The actual presentation of a reinforcer after a response is called *reinforcement*.

Primary Reinforcement

The Peppered Moth is a white moth with dark spots which can be found in many areas of Great Britain. It was white, at any rate, until 1848 when the first black Peppered Moth was caught near Manchester.

By 1895, 95 percent of all Peppered Moths in this region of England had become black, a percentage which has remained largely stable since. What could have caused the sudden shift in the moth's coloration? The period from 1850 to 1900 was also a time of heavy industrialization in this region, and great quantities of soot and other industrial wastes were being deposited in what was once a quiet, rural area. It seemed reasonable to scientists that the environmental change and the color change were somehow related, but the nature of the relationship could only be guessed at. One suggestion was that the industrial wastes were somehow affecting the rate of mutation among the moths, and that by chance the mutant gene controlling blackness became the most common. Another explanation was that the soot was turning the trees in the area black, and that the white moths were less likely to survive because they were more easily detected against the black background, and thus more likely to be eaten by predators. The plausibility of this explanation was weakened, however, by the fact that the Peppered Moth had no predators!

This mystery was finally solved in a series of experiments by H. B. D. Kettlewell (1959), who took motion pictures of the moths in their natural habitat. The slow-motion pictures revealed what the eye had not seen, that the moths were indeed being eaten by a wide variety of bird species, and that a moth's chances of being caught seemed to depend on his color. To confirm this, Kettlewell released an equal number of black and white moths into an industrial area where the trees were dark, and found that 74 percent of the moths caught by birds were white. Repeating the same experiment in a rural area where the trees were still light, he found that only 14 percent of those caught were white. These results strongly suggested that the moths' change in coloration was due to the differential vulnerability of the black and white varieties to predators, and provide some of the clearest evidence of how natural selection acts to adapt species to their environment.

This principle, that those traits that increase the chances of survival are selectively strengthened in the course of evolution, applies to behavior as well as morphology. A bird that doesn't fly south may be less likely to survive the winter; a predator that periodically roars while stalking his prey is less likely to catch it. Similarly in the case of reinforcement, an animal that repeats actions that have led to food in the past is more likely to be successful than one who searches randomly. In the course of evolution, then, it seems reasonable to suppose that animals have become specialized so as to repeat actions leading to food, water, or other substances necessary for survival.

Following just this logic, psychologists assumed that all primary reinforcers would be events that directly affect the likelihood of individual or species survival. Starting around 1950, however, evidence began to accumulate that traditional conceptions of reinforcement might be too narrow. Light, for example, hardly seems to be a substance necessary for an individual's survival, but George Kish (Article 3.1) found that mice would repeatedly press a bar in order to increase the illumination in their cage. But does this prove that light is a reinforcer? It might seem that Kish's results completely satisfy our definition—a reinforcer is an event that strengthens the response on which it is contingent—but it is necessary not only to establish a contingency but to prove that the results are due to that contingency! Imagine, for example, a crooked-but-college-educated fight manager who wanted to train his dumb-but-honest boxer to lose a fight. Persuasion having failed, the manager resorts to reinforcement, giving him a pint of alcohol as a reward after every bad round during training. If the fighter's performance then steadily deteriorates, could the manager safely conclude that the fighter has learned bad boxing habits? Obviously the alcohol might only be having a temporary effect on performance rather than a permanent effect on learning, and exactly the same might be true of the light's effect on the mice. The light might have been producing a general increase in activity (most mammals are more active in the light than in the dark), and bar-pressing might have been only an incidental by-product of this heightened activity.

To test this possibility, Kish used two separate control procedures. In the first, he *extinguished* bar-pressing by no longer presenting the light. If the light were having only a temporary effect on performance, he reasoned, then responding should cease when the light was removed, whereas if the effect was on learning, then responding should continue until subjects learned the altered contingencies. The result during extinction was that the subjects did continue responding for several sessions, supporting a reinforcement interpretation. As a further test Kish then presented the light *noncontingently*, regardless of whether the mice pressed the bar. The light's eliciting properties should be the same whether presented contingently or noncontingently, but if the light was truly a reinforcer then it should strengthen bar-pressing only when contingent on it. The results again supported the reinforcement interpretation, as the noncontingent light presentations had no effect on responding.

Light now appears to be only one example of a broad category of events that Kish (1965) has called "sensory reinforcers." Sensory reinforcers are stimuli whose physical effects seem limited to the neural structures involved in their detection, having little or no effect on general metabolism. Intuitively, their most important characteristic seems to be that they provide variety in our perceptual environment. Rats, for example, prefer complex mazes with many turns to simple ones (Montgomery, 1954), and monkeys in a cage will work for up to nine consecutive hours to open a window that allows them to see a toy train or another monkey (Butler, 1954). In a comparable human study, subjects confined in a dark room responded repeatedly to turn on a series of flashing lights, and their response rates increased significantly with their period of confinement (Jones, Wilkinson, and Braden, 1961). We seem to have a genuine need for variety or novelty, and future research may help us to better understand this need, and why a painting by Picasso or Rembrandt fills it so much better than a series of randomly flashing lights.

Another potent reinforcement class that we have only recently begun to explore is that of social reinforcers, sensory stimuli originating from the presence of conspecifics (members of the same species). It's obvious that our behavior is heavily influenced by social approval such as praise from parents or friends, but it's not clear why these stimuli are effective. Do we have an instinctive need for affection, or do we only learn to covet approval because it is associated with other, more desirable consequences (for example, ice cream or candy)?

Animal research provides tantalizing hints that the need for social contact may be at least in part innate. In some species of birds, for example, a need for social proximity seems to exist from the moment of birth, although the object of that need seems to be learned by a process called *imprinting*. During a brief critical period in their first hours of life these birds seem to be uniquely prepared to form social attachments, and they quickly learn to follow the first moving object they see. Normally this would be their mothers, but laboratory experiments have resulted in successful imprinting on wooden duck decoys and even rotating watering cans! Once imprinted, the birds look as if they're comforted by the presence of the imprinted stimulus, following it wherever it goes and emitting distress cries when it is taken away. To test whether the imprinted stimulus really does become reinforcing, Hoffman, Searle, Toffey, and Kuzma (1966) imprinted chicks on a milk bottle moved along a tiny railroad track, and then made presentation of the milk bottle contingent on pecking a key. They found that the bottle was an effective reinforcer for chicks imprinted to it during the critical period. They also found that raising the chicks' fear level by giving them electric shocks resulted in increases in both distress cries and efforts to obtain the milk bottle. Even more remarkable, imprinting seems to determine the birds' sexual preferences, so that a turkey imprinted on a human being will later prefer to court human beings rather than other turkeys (Schein and Hale, 1959), and this preference may persist even after sexual experience with other turkeys (Schein, 1963).

Evidence of imprinting in birds and other species suggests an innate need for social contact, even though its object may be partly learned. We don't know if there is a similar process in humans, but there is evidence that at least some forms of social reinforcement may be innate. Rheingold, Gewirtz, and Ross (Article 3.2) studied the effects of smiling on three-month-old infants, and found the infants would increase their rate of vocalizations when an adult's smiling was made contingent on that response. In a follow-up study, Weisberg (1963) confirmed this result, and further showed that smiling was not simply eliciting activity nor acting as a sensory reinforcer. We still know very little about social reinforcement, but this evidence suggests that our need for social contact and approval may be as basic as our need for food.

As important as food and social reinforcement are, perhaps the most powerful reinforcers are those which directly affect the regulatory centers of the brain. Drugs such as alcohol or LSD could perhaps be classified in this category, but the reinforcer most studied in the laboratory has been intracranial self-stimulation, or ICS. The cranium is the skull, and intracranial self-stimulation refers to direct electrical stimulation of the brain. A small hole is drilled in the skull and then two tiny wires are implanted in the brain. If they have been placed in the proper area, rats will repeatedly press a bar to turn on an electric current through these wires. The potency of this stimulation can be unbelievable: rats will press a bar as often as twice a second for up to 24 hours, and monkeys have emitted more than 200,000 consecutive responses before finally quitting in apparent exhaustion. In some experiments subjects have totally ignored food and water in order to keep responding for ICS, and have been willing to cross electrified barriers in order to reach the bar. For obvious reasons there has been little research on ICS with humans, but there is some evidence that its effects may be equally potent. Dr. Robert G. Heath has reported on some therapeutic uses of ICS with psychotic patients (Article 3.3) and his patients showed signs of intense pleasure at stimulation, including what Heath described as the onset of a "sexual motive state." It's difficult to take ICS seriously—it sounds too much like science fiction, with its overtones of artificial ecstasy and thought control— but it's at least possible that we will be seeing an increasing use of ICS in the future.

Sensory, social, and physiological reinforcers all represent a considerable expansion of the list of reinforcers studied by psychologists twenty years ago, but perhaps the most dramatic reversal of traditional conceptions of reinforcement is due to the work of David Premack. When we reinforce a rat's bar-pressing by giving him food, it seems obvious the reinforcer is food, but Premack argued that the reinforcing event is not the stimulus of food, but the response of eating, and that *any* response will act as a reinforcer if it is more probable than the response on which it is contingent. In one experiment Premack (1962) first established a typical contingency in which a thirsty rat had to run a certain number of feet in a running wheel in order to obtain water. After obtaining the typical result—water reinforced running—Premack then reversed the contingency, so that the rat was deprived of opportunities to run and had to drink a certain amount of water in order to be allowed to run. By manipulating deprivation conditions Premack was making running a relatively more probable response than drinking, and the result was a threefold increase in the rat's drinking!

One lesson to be learned from Premack's work is not to think of reinforcers as a discrete category of events but as a relative condition, varying from moment to moment and individual to individual. Instead of consulting a handbook of approved reinforcers, we need only observe behavior and see what people enjoy doing. Whatever people enjoy, *that* is reinforcing. The practical advantages of this approach are imaginatively demonstrated in an experiment by Homme, de Baca, Devine, Steinhorst, and Rickert (Article 3.4), who were able to train nursery children to behave using some *very* unusual reinforcers.

Secondary Reinforcement

All the reinforcers we've discussed up to this point have been *primary reinforcers*, requiring no special training to be effective. Light, for example, is an effective reinforcer with infants as young as three weeks (Siqueland and DeLucia, 1969). Another important category of reinforcers is *secondary reinforcers*, initially neutral stimuli which acquire their reinforcing properties, usually through pairing with a primary reinforcer (but see Lieberman, 1972).

One of the earliest experiments on secondary reinforcement was by Cowles (1937), who in the first part of his experiment trained two chimpanzees to put a metal token into a slot in order to obtain raisins. To test whether the token had become a secondary reinforcer through its pairing with food, Cowles then gave his subjects a discrimination problem in which they received a token for selecting the correct alternative from among five boxes. After several preliminary training trials, Cowles found that the chimps made the correct response on 74 percent of the trials, which compared favorably with a success rate of 93 percent when the raisins themselves were used as the reinforcer.

Why did a metal token of no intrinsic value become such an effective reinforcer? One obvious explanation is that the chimps knew that they could later exchange the token for food, but psychologists are reluctant to use words like "know" when there is no possible way to directly evaluate mental states. An alternative explanation, phrased in more objective language, is that the token became a secondary reinforcer because of its pairing with food. This translation may seem awkward at first because of its more formal and colorless language, but it does raise the interesting question of whether the associative process involved in establishing a secondary reinforcer is the same as in classical conditioning.

If the same process was involved, we should expect the same laws to hold in both cases, and in fact the strength of a secondary reinforcer does depend on the intensity of the primary reinforcer, the contiguity of the two stimuli during pairing, and the frequency of the pairing (see Wike, 1966). The effects of contingency have not been discussed in those terms, but Egger and Miller (Article 3.5) have examined the identical issue phrased in terms of information. In classical conditioning the CS and US occur together, and we can express this relationship either by saying the US is contingent on the CS, or by saying the CS gives us information about the US (that is, it predicts when it will occur). Similarly if we start presenting the US in the absence of the CS as well as in its presence, we can either say the US is no longer contingent on the CS, or that the CS is no longer informative about the US. The concepts of information and contingency are almost identical, even though in one case we seem to emphasize a property of the CS and in the other case a property of the US. The important point in both cases is that we are really measuring the extent to which the occurrence of two events is related.

The concepts of information and contingency differ in one respect, but to understand this difference we need to define information more precisely. In information theory, which was originally developed by engineers to describe ideal communication systems, the amount of information in a message is determined by how much it reduces the recipient's uncertainty. The words in a sentence, for example, do not completely determine the information content of the sentence: we must also know the subject's initial uncertainty. The same sentence, "Hot Horse Harry won in the fifth," may convey a lot of information to a naive bettor, but only a little to a trainer, depending on their initial uncertainty about the outcome. In the extreme, where the initial uncertainty is zero (for example, to a man who fixed the race) a message about the outcome will have no information, and is said to be *redundant*.

This dependence of information on a subject's initial uncertainty, and thus the possibility that a message of genuine predictive power may be said to have no information, are concepts not shared with contingency. Consider, for example, a situation in which two conditioned stimuli are presented on every trial before the US. If CS_1 always precedes CS_2, then CS_1 will be informative (it reduces uncertainty), but CS_2 will be redundant (there is no uncertainty left to reduce). In terms of contingency, however, the US is contingent on both stimuli, since it occurs in their presence but not in their absence. The concepts of information and contingency, then, are both concerned with measuring the relationship between two stimuli, but contingency is totally determined by the conditional probability of the two stimuli, whereas the amount of information also depends on what other stimuli may be present.

Egger and Miller used exactly the situation we have just described to evaluate the role of information in secondary reinforcement. In their basic experimental condition they presented two successive stimuli, S_1 and S_2, closely followed by a pellet of food. According to the law of contiguity S_2 should be the better conditioned stimulus since it is more closely associated with the US. According to an information analysis, however, S_2 is redundant, so that if information is important only S_1 should be conditioned. In this and other situations Egger and Miller found that predictions based on information concepts were correct, suggesting that the development of a secondary reinforcer depends on its information value as well as its contiguity with the primary reinforcer.

In theoretical terms, this experiment provides further evidence for the operation of similar laws in classical conditioning and secondary reinforcement, and thus the argument that the same basic process underlies both. In practical terms, it also suggests the limitations of secondary reinforcement in controlling behavior. Information did indeed have a large and significant effect on secondary reinforcement, but secondary reinforcement had only a marginal effect on responding. In testing, the experimental subjects received a secondary reinforcer every time they pressed a bar, and the result was an increase of only about 20 or 30 bar presses over control subjects who received no secondary reinforcement. The lesson from this and similar experiments is that a secondary reinforcer must at least occasionally be paired with a primary reinforcer if it is to maintain its effectiveness, for when presented alone it quickly loses all power. In Cowles' research, on the other hand, tokens could be exchanged for food at intervals throughout the experiment, and even though the exchange periods were sometimes substantially delayed, the tokens remained effective indefinitely.

The Response

Are there any limits to the effectiveness of reinforcement? Can we be reinforced for controlling our kidneys or believing in God as readily as for pressing a bar? The traditional answer to such questions has been "No," that reinforcement affects only those muscles involved in locomotion. Our behavior is determined by two partially independent control systems: the *skeletal nervous system,* which controls the striped muscles involved in locomotion, and the *autonomic nervous system,* which controls our glands and smooth muscles (those involved in intestinal contractions, blood vessel diameter, etc). The internal processes controlled by the autonomic nervous system have generally been thought to be modified only through classical conditioning, with the effects of reinforcement limited to the skeletal nervous system.

This is not to say that there have been no reports of autonomic responses modified by reinforcement—there have in fact been several such experiments, but each has raised difficult problems of interpretation. Imagine, for example, an experimenter who rigs a sophisticated recording system so that he can continuously monitor heart rate in a rat, and then reinforces the rat with food pellets every time he increases his heart rate. The experimenter might very well find a significant increase in heart rate, but would that prove that he had directly reinforced heart rate? An equally plausible explanation might be that he had reinforced some skeletal response such as running or breathing hard, and that the change in heart rate was only an indirect result of this skeletal activity. Similar explanations based on skeletal mediation could be given for almost any autonomic response because of the complex relationships between the two systems.

In order to demonstrate reinforcement of autonomic behavior, then, it is necessary to eliminate any possibility of skeletal mediation, to somehow block skeletal responses while not interfering with autonomic activity. This may sound impossible, but in fact psychologists have long known of a drug with exactly these properties. *Curare* is a deadly poison used by South American Indians, but in small doses it results in the selective paralysis of all skeletal muscles. Curare would thus appear to be the ideal solution for the problem of eliminating skeletal mediation, except for some rather serious practical problems. For one thing, it is difficult to keep a curarized subject alive—he cannot breathe since the chest muscles are paralyzed, and since he cannot swallow he is in constant danger of choking on his own saliva! Furthermore, there is a delicate problem of presenting a reinforcer—a paralyzed subject is in no position to eat or drink.

These problems were finally overcome in a brilliant series of experiments by Neal Miller and his colleagues at Yale and then Rockefeller Universities. Using rats as subjects and modern surgical procedures to keep them alive (artificial respiration and the like), they used electrical stimulation of the brain as their reinforcer. In one of the first experiments with these techniques, Jay Trowell made ICS contingent on an increase in heart rate and found a small but significant increase. To show that the ICS was not simply eliciting this heart rate change, he also reinforced subjects for *decreasing* their heart rate, and demonstrated that he could decrease heart rate as well as increase it. In a follow-up study, Miller and DiCara (1967) shaped their subjects so that a progressively larger rate change was required for reinforcement as the session continued, and were able to increase or decrease heart rate by as much as 25 percent over a 90-minute session. In perhaps the most dramatic experiment of all, DiCara and Miller (Article 3.6) looked at the specificity of autonomic control, and found they could selectively reinforce the rate of blood flow in *one ear* of a rat. Using a photocell to determine the rate of blood flow (the more blood, the less light will pass through the ear), they reinforced their subjects for *vasodilation* (an increase in capillary size) in either the right or left ear. The results showed changes only in the ear that was reinforced, and measurements from the paws indicated that other areas of the body were not affected.

The practical implications of such precise control could be enormous. In research already under way, Miller and his colleagues are trying to train epileptics to control their brain waves by giving them informative feedback ("biofeedback") whenever they produce the desired response pattern. The feedback is intended to serve as a form of secondary reinforcement for the subject, and Miller hopes that patients will learn to suppress abnormal spikes in the brain wave record and thus prevent seizures. In similar studies patients are being trained to reduce their high blood pressure and to control cardiac irregularities. It is still too early to evaluate these efforts (Miller himself has had some difficulty not only in training human subjects but in replicating his original rat studies), but anecdotal evidence provides some basis for optimism. Hindu mystics are said to have extraordinary control over their metabolic functions, and similar control may be involved in psychosomatic illnesses and in hysterical pregnancies where almost all of the symptoms of pregnancy are mimicked except for the fetus! If the techniques involved could be taught on a systematic basis, Miller's research may someday be seen as one of the great breakthroughs in psychological research.

A second controversial issue concerning the generality of reinforcement has been whether cognitive processes such as attitudes can be reinforced. There is little question that people can be reinforced for *saying* certain things ("I just love Wheaties"; "If elected, I promise . . ."), but can fundamental attitudes be modified by reinforcement? There are serious problems in defining and measuring attitudes, but there has been some provocative research suggesting that attitudes really can be strengthened by reinforcement. Scott (Article 3.7) reports the results of one such experiment, and you might try to imagine other situations in which social approval is contingent on certain attitudes, and how you think you would react in those situations.

3.1 LEARNING WHEN THE ONSET OF ILLUMINATION IS USED AS REINFORCING STIMULUS*

George Bela Kish

The concept of reinforcement holds a key explanatory position in several major theories of behavior. Behaviorally, reinforcement is judged to have occurred if (*a*) the reinforcer occurs as a result of, or in close temporal contiguity with, a response of an organism, (*b*) the occurrence of the reinforcer increases the performance strength of the response, and (*c*) occurrence of the reinforcer leads to learning.

On the basis of these criteria, the major classes of events which have been demonstrated to be reinforcers are: (*a*) the presentation of a substance which can reduce an existing need of the organism (food, water, etc.), (*b*) the removal of an aversive stimulus (bright light, electric shock, etc.), (*c*) the presentation of a stimulus which has had prior association with the conditions in *a*, and (*d*) the removal of a stimulus which has had prior association with the conditions in *b*.

These classes of reinforcers have been integrated by Hull (4), in his postulates of primary and secondary reinforcement, under the concept of need reduction. According to this conception, to be a reinforcer an event must either reduce an existing need or have been previously associated with the reduction of an existing need.

A class of events that appears neither to be need-reducing nor previously associated with need reduction has been investigated by Kish and Antonitis (5). They found that such stimuli as microswitch clicks, relay noises, and stimuli produced by a moving platform exerted what appeared to be reinforcing effects on the unconditioned operant behavior of mice. These findings suggested the following hypothesis: A perceptible environmental change, which is unrelated to such need states as hunger and thirst, will reinforce any response that it follows.

The present experiment was designed to provide a direct test of this hypothesis in the light of the criteria for reinforcement presented above. Utilizing the onset of dim illumination as the stimulus to be tested for

* George Bela Kish, "Learning When the Onset of Illumination Is Used as Reinforcing Stimulus," *The Journal of Comparative and Physiological Psychology,* 48, 1955, 261–264. Copyright 1955 by the American Psychological Association, and reproduced by permission. This work was done under the Summer Research Apprentice Program of the R. B. Jackson Memorial Laboratory during the summer of 1952. Grateful thanks are extended to Dr. J. P. Scott and members of the staff of the Jackson Laboratory for their interest and encouragement during the course of this investigation. Thanks are also extended to Dr. J. J. Antonitis for critical reading of the manuscript.

reinforcing properties, the several possible effects measured were: (a) the effect of the introduction of the stimulus as a consequence of a bar-touch response upon the rate of emission of that response, (b) the establishment or nonestablishment by such stimulation of learning structures, as evidenced by a significant amount of extinction-responding, and (c) the effect upon the response rate of the presentation of this stimulus uncorrelated with the behavior of the subjects.

METHOD

Apparatus

A modified Skinner box was used. It consisted of a cubic experimental compartment of ¼-in. plywood with 6- by 6- by 6-in. inside dimensions, a wire-mesh floor, and a removable wooden cover which contained a 6- by 6-in. Plexiglas window. The Ss were placed in the compartment by removing this cover. The four walls of the compartment were painted with gray enamel.

A nonmovable U-shaped bar of ⅛-in. brazing brass protruded into the experimental compartment 1½ in. above the floor and ¾ in. from the wall. This bar was insulated from the wall of the box by ⅛ in. of solid rubber. Contacts with this bar were recorded by means of an electronic contact relay (6). Recording was accomplished with a rigid bar which offered a minimum of perceptible stimulation, other than tactual, to the Ss during the recording process.

This experimental compartment was placed within a sound-resisting box, the inside dimensions of which were in inches 14 by 14 by 14, made of ¼-in. plywood with 4 in. of Rockwool insulation. Ventilation of this and the experimental compartment was achieved by drawing air through these compartments with a Cenco water aspirator.

Three identical apparatus units were operated simultaneously, and the Ss were rotated among these on successive experimental days to counterbalance possible apparatus differences.

Recording equipment consisted of three Mercury 115 VAC 60-cycle counters.

The light stimulus was provided by a frosted 7½-w. GE bulb operating at 115 VAC. This bulb was placed in a wooden lampshade 6 by 6 by 5 in. which fitted in the cover of the experimental compartment. The intensity of the light was reduced by filtering it through three sheets of white mimeographed paper. The light circuit was operated through the relay of the electronic circuit. Each closure of the relay activated the light and recorder circuits simultaneously. Both light and recorder circuits were so designed that they remained closed as long as contact with the bar was maintained. No other source of illumination was provided. The animals were in total darkness at all times except when the light stimulus was presented. The light stimulus could also be presented for ½ sec. at a number of different time intervals by means of a timing device which was incorporated into the circuit.

Subjects

The Ss were 16 experimentally naive female C57 Black Subline 10 mice approximately 56 days of age at the beginning of experimentation.

The mice were individually housed in the standard wooden boxes in use at the Jackson Laboratory and had free access to food and water at all times except during the 25-min. testing period. The laboratory was lighted from 9 A.M. to 5 P.M. During this period, once each week, the food hoppers and water bottles were refilled. This was done while food and water still remained from the previous filling.

Procedure

Phase 1—Habituation. Since preliminary experiments seemed to indicate that the effects of introduction of the stimulus were enhanced by an habituation period, days 1 through 7 were devoted to an operant level determination and habituation to the experimental compartment. All 16 Ss were run for 25 min. per day in total darkness. Touches upon the bar were recorded but did not result in the onset of illumination. The animals were then divided into two groups of eight mice each, the groups equated on the basis of mean total numbers of responses emitted during 5, 6, and 7.

Phase 2—Conditioning. On day 8, the Ss of the experimental group (stimulus group) received the onset of illumination as the consequence of each bar contact. The Ss of the control group (nonstimulus group) continued as in phase 1.

Phase 3—Extinction. On days 9 through 12, all Ss were tested under the conditions of phase 1.

Phase 4—Uncorrelated Stimulation. On day 13, the control group received 150 ½-sec. presentations of light at 10-sec. intervals. The light flashes were not correlated with the behavior of the Ss. The experimental group continued as in phases 1 and 3.

Total number of bar contacts during each 25-min. experimental period was recorded for each S.

RESULTS

The results are presented graphically in Figure 3.1–1. The graph shows the mean numbers of bar touches emitted by the stimulus and nonstimulus groups during each of the 13 experimental sessions. It is apparent that the

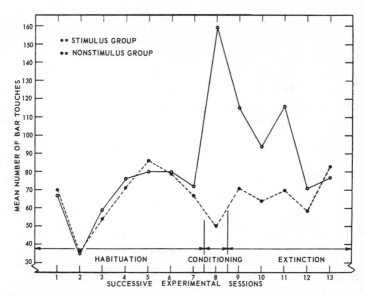

FIGURE 3.1–1 The mean number of bar-touch responses for the stimulus and nonstimulus groups plotted as a function of successive 25-min. experimental sessions.

two groups were well matched since the group means differed but slightly during the seven days of the habituation period.

On day 8, the mean number of responses emitted by the stimulus group is more than twice that emitted by this group on day 7. The resulting difference between the stimulus and nonstimulus groups on day 8 is significant beyond the .005 level for a two-tailed t test ($t = 4.14$, $df = 8$). An F test for homogeneity of variance between the two groups on day 8 showed that the stimulus group was significantly more variable than the nonstimulus group ($F = 19$, $df = 7, 7$, $p < .01$). For this reason the t test used above is an appropriate test indicated for use when the assumption of homogeneity of variance cannot be met.

During the four extinction days, the mean number of responses emitted by the stimulus group remained greater than that of the non-stimulus group, but the difference between the two groups decreased over the four days. On day 9 the difference was still significant at the .005 level ($t = 3.06$, $df = 14$). On day 10 the difference was not significant ($t = 1.98$, $df = 14$, $p = .10$). On day 11, due to an increase in the responses emitted by the stimulus group, the difference approached significance ($t = 2.11$, $df = 14$, $p > .05$). The difference on day 12 was extremely small and not statistically significant. The variance of the two groups was found to be homogeneous throughout the extinction period.

On day 13 the mean number of responses emitted by the nonstimulus group increased slightly over day 12. This increase presumably is due to the presentation of 150 light flashes which were uncorrelated with the behavior of the Ss. This increase from day 12 to 13 results in a t value of .80 which is not significant. Analysis of the data of individual Ss in this group on day 13 revealed that this increase in mean number of responses was primarily contributed by three animals whose initial response rates were high. With Ss having high response rates, chance correlations of responses and light flashes become more probable.

DISCUSSION

The data clearly demonstrate that the onset of dim illumination occurring as the consequence of a response, leads to behavioral effects which correspond to those noted as the criteria for the occurrence of reinforcement. The onset of illumination when presented as the direct consequence of a bar-touching response produced a marked and significant increase in the bar-touching rate. Furthermore, a significant amount of extinction-responding was demonstrated as an aftereffect of exposure to such stimulation. These results, therefore, appear to support the hypothesis that a perceptible environmental change, which is unrelated to such need states as hunger and thirst, will reinforce any response which it follows. Several problems, however, are raised by the statement of the hypothesis in such a general form.

1. No restrictions, other than perceptibility, are placed upon the modality which the environmental change must stimulate in order to function in a reinforcing manner. Thus, light onset is assumed to be representative of stimulation in other sense modalities. Some evidence can be marshalled in favor of this assumption from published experiments which utilize stimuli in various sense modalities and which report results similar to those reported here. Sharpe (7), using the sound of a chime as the reinforcer, reported significant increments in the chain-pulling rate of preschool children. In a situation similar to that of the present experiment, Girdner (2) reported increases in the bar-touching rate by rats when each response was reinforced by either the appearance of a dim spot of light above the animal or the onset of a buzzer noise.

2. Phase 4 of the present experiment was included as a test of an alternative to the conditioning-reinforcement interpretation. According to this alternative interpretation, the increase in bar-touching rate was not the result of a direct reinforcement of that response, but the reflection of an increase in general activity resulting from stimulation by the repeated onset of light. This hypothesis was tested by presenting the onset of light uncorrelated with any specific response of the S and measuring the specific response of bar-touching. Since the effect of this procedure

was not significant, the activity-increase interpretation does not appear to account for the present findings.

3. The hypothesis does not specify whether the process involved here is one of primary or secondary reinforcement. Several considerations, however, would appear to indicate that this process is not one of secondary reinforcement. The Ss were given no training associating the onset of light with primary reinforcement. Organic drives were kept at minimal strength by allowing the Ss free access to food and water at all times except for the 25-min. experimental period. Furthermore, the nocturnal habits of the mouse would make the association of primary reinforcement and light less probable than such an association with darkness.

Apparently, the process involved in this experiment is that of primary reinforcement. The term, in this case, is used in its broadest sense as referring to a process for the operation of which a minimum of previous learning is necessary. The term is not used here to denote the process defined by Hull (4) as involving the reduction of a need. Such usage with reference to the present phenomenon appears to be decidedly premature. In the present study, at least, there is no evidence for any drive or need that could be reduced by the onset of light.

Such a drive, however, has been postulated. Harlow (3) has integrated the results of a number of studies, similar to the present one, under the concept of exploratory drive. It is conceivable that the onset of light in the present experiment was acting as a reinforcer with respect to an exploratory or curiosity motive. Behavioral data of the type presented here, however, do not constitute sufficient evidence for a demonstration of the operation of a drive. Such evidence might be offered by experiments in which the reinforcer is held constant and the influence of other non-stimulus variables, such as deprivation from stimulation, upon the magnitude of the reinforcement effects is studied.

SUMMARY

Two groups of eight female C57 Black 10 mice each were tested in a modified Skinner box to examine the hypothesis that: A perceptible environmental change which is unrelated to such need states as hunger and thirst will reinforce any response which it follows. The effect, upon the emission rate of a bar-contact response, of the onset of dim illumination which followed this response was tested.

Introduction of the stimulus significantly increased the rate of emission of this response. Significant extinction effects were also noted when stimulation was discontinued. The results were considered to be in agreement with the initial hypothesis and were discussed with reference to the general implications of the hypothesis.

REFERENCES

1. Dixon, W. J., & Massey, F. J. *Introduction to statistical analysis.* New York: McGraw-Hill 1951, p. 105.
2. Girdner, J. B. An experimental analysis of the behavioral effects of a perceptual consequence unrelated to organic drive states. Unpublished doctor's dissertation, Duke University, 1953.
3. Harlow, H. F. Motivation as a factor in the acquisition of new responses. In J. S. Brown *et al., Current theory and research in motivation.* Lincoln: Univer. of Nebraska Press, 1963, pp. 24–49.
4. Hull, C. L. *Principles of behavior: an introduction to behavior theory.* New York: D. Appleton-Century, 1943.
5. Kish, G. B., & Antonitis, J. J. Unconditioned operant behavior in two homozygous strains of mice. *J. genet. Psychol.,* 1956, *88,* 121–129.
6. Pilgrim, F. J. A simple electronic relay for counting, timing, or automatic control. *J. Psychol.,* 1948, *26,* 537–540.
7. Sharpe, P. B. The effect of delayed introduction of a novel stimulus on the rate of responding in children. Unpublished master's thesis, Univer. of Maine, 1951.

3.2 | SOCIAL CONDITIONING OF VOCALIZATIONS IN THE INFANT*

Harriet L. Rheingold, Jacob L. Gewirtz, and Helen W. Ross

By three months of age the infant gives a well-defined social response to the appearance of adults. He looks at them intently, smiles, becomes active, and vocalizes. This behavior is repeated again and again in sequence. Adults often respond to these acts of the infant; they may only look at the child, but they may also smile to him, touch or caress him, or vocalize in return. Frequently one observes "answering" social and, in particular, vocal play between mother and child. The adults' responses may therefore play an important part in maintaining and developing social responsiveness in the child (Rheingold, 1956). The principles of operant conditioning (Skinner, 1953) suggest that some of these adult

* Harriet L. Rheingold, Jacob L. Gewirtz, and Helen W. Ross, "Social Conditioning of Vocalizations in the Infant," *The Journal of Comparative and Physiological Psychology,* 52, 68–73. Copyright 1959 by the American Psychological Association, and reproduced by permission.

responses, functioning as reinforcers, may affect the development of the child's social behavior (Gewirtz, 1956). Thus, smiling in the infant has been shown to respond to conditioning (Brackbill, 1958).

The present study was an attempt to condition vocalizations in infants. Vocalizations were selected for study because they seem to provide an index of the whole social response (Rheingold, 1956). The reinforcing stimulus was a complex of social acts which resembled those an attentive adult might naturally make when a child vocalizes. If temporal contiguity between the infant's vocalization and the reinforcing stimulus, which follows it, brings about an increase in the vocalizations, conditioning may be said to have occurred. The possibility that the reinforcing stimulus may also have functioned as an arouser of vocalizations will be considered. In any case, the results of the study should provide further understanding about the development of social responsiveness, as well as of speech.

METHOD

Two parallel experiments were carried out in sequence. In the first, 11 babies (Ss) were studied, with one experimenter (E) and one observer-recorder (O), both women. In the second, 10 other Ss and one S from Experiment I were studied with the E and O of the first experiment exchanging roles. An experiment was composed of three successive units in each of which three or four Ss were studied at one time.

Subjects

The Ss were 21 infants, all residents almost from birth in the same institution. (We are grateful to Sister Thecla and the staff of St. Ann's Infant Asylum, Washington, D.C., for their generous cooperation.) Their median age was 3.0 months; three-quarters of them were no more than three days older or younger than the median. In each experiment six Ss were male, five were female. Age was the main criterion for selection. Four possible Ss were rejected: one seemed immature, two had a very high rate of vocalizing during the first baseline measure, and one was markedly fussy.

The institution offers excellent care and, as is characteristic of institutions, there are multiple caretakers. In general, the Ss were well developed, healthy, alert, and socially responsive. The Es asked for no modifications in the usual caretaking routines. The caretakers knew that the Es were observing the development of social behavior, but they did not know the details of the experiment. The caretakers' usual behavior toward the Ss appeared not to be modified by the conditions of the experiment.

Experimental Conditions

Baseline. In experimental Day 1 and 2 (first and second Baseline days) E leaned over the crib with her face about 15 in. above S's and looked at him with an expressionless face, while O tallied vocalizations, out of S's sight. The E moved her head as necessary to remain in S's line of vision, a condition which obtained throughout the experiments.

Conditioning. During experimental Days 3 and 4 (first and second Conditioning days), E again leaned over the crib with an expressionless face except that when S vocalized, E made an immediate response and then resumed the expressionless face until the next vocalization. The response, or *reinforcing stimulus*, consisted of three acts executed by E simultaneously, quickly, and smoothly. They were a broad smile, three "tsk" sounds, and a light touch applied to the infant's abdomen with thumb and fingers of the hand opposed. No more than a second of time was acquired to administer the reinforcer.

At the beginning of the conditioning periods each vocalization was reinforced. Sometimes, as the rate of vocalizing increased, only every second, and later, every third, vocalization was reinforced. In Experiment I, 72% of the reinforcers occurred after *each* vocalization, in Experiment II, 94%. Less frequent reinforcing seemed to depress the rate, at least initially, and, because of the rather severe time restrictions, was abandoned altogether by the end of the study.

Extinction. Experimental Days 5 and 6 (first and second Extinction days) were the same as Days 1 and 2; E leaned over the crib with an expressionless face and made no response to S's vocalizations.

The Vocal Response

Every discrete, voiced sound produced by S was counted as a *vocalization*. A number of other sounds characteristically made by very young infants, e.g., straining sounds and coughs, and the whistles, squeaks, and snorts of noisy breathing, were not counted as vocalizations. Sounds falling under the categories of protests, fusses, and cries (see Emotional Behavior below) were recorded separately. No attempt was made to record the phonetic characteristics of any of the sounds or their duration.

Observer Agreement. Agreement between two Os on the number of vocalizations produced by Ss in 3-min. periods was high. Counts for 27 periods, using 13 different Ss, yielded a median percentage agreement of 96 (range, 67 to 100). About half of these reliability measures were obtained at the Ss' cribs, and the rest from tape recordings made during the experiment. These two techniques yielded similar percentages of observer agreement.

The Unit of Measurement. The unit for statistical analysis was the number of vocalizations an S gave in a 3-min. period. The counts were recorded by half-minutes and these were summed to give the score for the 3-min. period. After a rest period of 2 min., in which both E and O walked away from the baby's crib, another 3-min. count was made. After a second rest period a third count was made.

In each day nine such 3-min. counts were planned, distributed thus: one block of three in the first part of the morning, the second block of three in the late morning, and the third block of three after the midday meal. The minimum amount of time between blocks was 10 min., although usually an hour or more elapsed.

Actually, nine periods of observations were obtained during only 80% of the 132 subject-days (22 Ss $\times$ 6 experimental days). Since three or four Ss were studied at a time, it was not always possible to find nine periods in a day when each was awake, alert, and content. Further, because the experiments were carried out in the nursery which the Ss shared with 12 other infants, the presence and activities of these other babies, and of the caretakers in carrying out their routines, sometimes made it impossible to obtain the desired number of periods.

Emotional Behavior

A number of responses which seemed to be "emotional" were recorded during the observation periods. These were: "protests," discrete sounds of a whining nature; "fusses," a series of sounds separated by a catch in the voice, whimpering; "cries" continuous loud, wailing sounds; "persistent looking away from E," rolling of the head from side to side or staring to one side or the other of E; and "marked hand activity," hand play, finger sucking, or face or head rubbing. The last two activities seemed to be attempts to avoid E. Measures of observer-agreement in the recording of these responses were not made.

Each of these responses was given a credit of one for each half-minute in which it occurred. From the sum for each S a mean score was obtained for each experimental day.

RESULTS

Similarity between Experiments

Figure 3.2–1 presents the means of both experiments for the six experimental days. Each point represents the mean of 11 individual means. It was expected that the effect of the experimental conditions would be similar from experiment to experiment, but the extent to which the slopes of the curves would be congruent was not predicted.

The amount of similarity between the two experiments was estimated by an analysis of variance (Table 3.2–1), using Lindquist's Type VI design

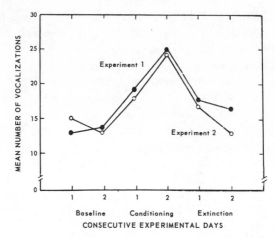

FIGURE 3.2–1 Mean number of vocalizations on consecutive experimental days.

(1953). The analysis reveals no evidence of a difference between Experiments. Further, no source of variation involving Experiments is significant. (The difference between the two experiments in second Extinction day means is not significant; it suggests, however, that the less frequent reinforcement in Experiment I may have made the behavior more resistant to extinction.)

Three conclusions may be drawn from such close agreement in the results of two parallel experiments, each using different Ss and different

TABLE 3.2–1 Analysis of Variance of Effect of Consecutive Experimental Days

Source of Variation	df	MS	F
Between Subjects	21		
Experiments (1 vs. 2)	1	1218	0.03
Error	20	45322	
Within Subjects	110		
Conditions (Baseline vs. Conditioning vs. Extinction)	2	71243 (1)[a]	10.63*
Days within Conditions (1 vs. 2)	1	4205 (2)[a]	1.88
Conditions × Days	2	22917 (3)[a]	9.24*
Days × Experiments	1	1738 (2)[a]	0.78
Conditions × Experiments	2	2031 (1)[a]	0.30
Conditions × Days × Experiments	2	866 (3)[a]	0.35
Error 1	40	6703	
Error 2	20	2233	
Error 3	40	2481	

[a] Number in parentheses refers to the error term used. The terms were not pooled because of statistically significant differences among them.
* Significant at .001 level.

Es: first, we are dealing with some relatively stable characteristics of three-month-old infants; second, the results may be accepted with confidence; and third, the results of the separate experiments may be pooled for all remaining analyses.

Effect of Experimental Conditions

Table 3.2–1 shows that there was a difference in the effect of the three two-day experimental conditions ($p < .001$), and, also, in the effect of successive days within conditions ($p < .001$). These effects were assessed by t tests (for paired data) on the amount of change from one day to another in the mean number of vocalizations given by individual Ss. The error term was derived only from the scores for the two days being compared. The tests on the pooled sample (21 df) show that:

1. There was no statistically significant difference in the mean number of vocalizations given in a 3-min. period from the first to the second Baseline day ($t = 0.87$, $p > .30$).

2. The mean number of vocalizations increased from the second Baseline day to the first Conditioning day ($t = 2.69$, $p < .01$).

3. A further increase occurred from the first to the second Conditioning day ($t = 3.61$, $p < .001$).

4. On the first Extinction day, vocalizations decreased ($t = 3.19$, $p < .0025$).

5. The mean number of vocalizations on the second Extinction day was smaller than on the first Extinction day, but the difference was not reliable ($t = 1.35$, $p < .10$).

6. There was no statistically significant difference between the mean number of vocalizations given on the second Extinction day and on the second Baseline day ($t = 1.20$, $p > .20$).

The tests between Baseline days and between Baseline and Extinction days were two-sided tests; the others were one-sided.

If final days within conditions are compared, the differences are more marked: the mean for the second Conditioning day is higher than that of the second Baseline day at $p < .0005$ ($t = 4.80$), and the second Extinction day mean is lower than the second Conditioning day mean at $p < .0005$ ($t = 4.08$). Similar differences occur between the means of experimental conditions, obtained by averaging the first- and second-day results for each condition.

Amount of Change in Number of Vocalizations

The treatment effects have been found reliable. It seems in order, therefore, to present the means of vocalizations for each day and to calculate the amount of change produced by the experimental conditions. Under baseline conditions the three-month-old infants gave about 13 to 14 vocalizations in a 3-min. period. Individual differences were wide and ranged from 3 to 37 vocalizations. Using the social reinforcer for one day raised the rate to 18 vocalizations, an increase of 39%. A second day of conditioning elevated the rate to 25, a further increase of 34%. In all, conditioning brought about an increase of 86%. Removing the reinforcer depressed the rate to 17 during the first and to 15 during the second day, the latter approaching very closely the level of baseline performance.

Emotional Behavior

Emotional behavior, while striking when it occurred, was observed infrequently. The largest mean for any day in both experiments was 3.0, the smallest was 1.9. The order of the means by experimental days was identical in the two experiments. It was: first Extinction day, second Extinction day, second Baseline day, second Conditioning day, first Conditioning day, and first Baseline day. The greater number of emotional responses during Extinction agrees with the findings of others (e.g., Brackbill, 1958; Skinner, 1953; Verplanck, 1955). Because the responses labeled emotional occurred so infrequently and because observer-agreement measures were not made, no further statistical analysis seemed warranted.

Additional Findings

Performance of Successive Groups. It will be recalled that in any one experimental week the Ss were studied in groups of three or four. Inspection of the results suggests that in each successive group of each experiment an increasing number of Ss conformed to expectation, showing an increase in vocalizations during Conditioning and a decrease during Extinction. The Es apparently became more adept in executing the reinforcer as each experiment progressed.

Performance of Individual Subjects. Although differences between experimental conditions have been demonstrated for the Ss as a group, the performance of individual Ss is of interest. Of the 22 Ss, 19 showed an increase in vocalizations under Conditioning. For 14 of these 19 the increase was significant at the .05 level, according to the Mann-Whitney Test (1947). Under Extinction, 16 of the 22 Ss showed some decrease, and for 10 of these 16 the decrease was significant at the .05 level.

Three Ss departed widely from the group pattern. For two, not only did Conditioning depress the rate of vocalizing, but Extinction restored it to its Baseline rate. The first chewed her thumb more during Conditioning than before or after. The second strained (in an apparent effort to defecate) during Conditioning whenever anyone, E or the nurse, leaned over his crib. Both activities precluded vocalizing. Both babies were very active, and it is possible, therefore, that in the very first Conditioning period *E* may have inadvertently reinforced these activities. For the third S, in Experiment I the experimental conditions appeared not to affect the frequency of vocalizations. Developmental immaturity seemed the most likely reason, for two weeks later he was studied again in Experiment II (the only S to be used in both experiments) with satisfactory results.

Effect of Baseline Performance upon Conditioning. The Ss tended to maintain their relative positions under Baseline and Conditioning. The rank-order coefficient of correlation (*R*) was .66, $p < .0005$. Further, the amount of gain under Conditioning was not correlated with original position ($R = .24$, $p > .05$).

Sex Differences. The 12 male Ss gave slightly more vocalizations during Baseline and gained more under Conditioning than the 10 female Ss, but the differences were not reliable.

DISCUSSION

The results of these experiments suggest that:

1. Infants' vocal behavior in a social situation can be brought under experimental control; that is, it appears to be conditionable.

2. A social event composed of an everyday complex of acts, performed by an adult who is not a caretaker, can function as a reinforcing stimulus.

3. The incidence of such behavior can be very quickly modified in as young an organism as the three-month-old infant.

Alternative Explanation

The question raised in the introduction may now be considered. Did the reinforcing stimulus function as an arouser of vocalizations? Would infants have vocalized more often because of the stimulation it provided, even if it had *not* been made contingent upon the infant's behavior? Or, did some part of the reinforcing stimulus (say, the smile) act as a social "releaser"? The findings appear to be compatible with the conclusion that conditioning occurred: The rate of vocalizing continued to rise on the second day of Conditioning; the rate did not fall to the Baseline level on the first day of Extinction; it continued to fall on the second day of Extinction; and Ss with low Baseline rates of vocalizing gained under Conditioning, although for them there was often a relatively long time interval (30 sec. or more) between the reinforcing stimulus and the occurrence of the next vocalization. Still, the decisive answer to the question must await an experiment in which the reinforcing stimulus is administered with equal frequency, but never directly after the infant vocalizes.

Nature of the Reinforcer

The results seem to show that some everyday behavior of adults can function as a reinforcing stimulus for an infant. One would like to know from what sources its reinforcing properties arise. In the simplest case, the smiles, sounds, and caresses of adults may be reinforcing only because they provide a change in stimulation. Further information on this matter could be obtained by working with the separate parts of the reinforcing stimulus, one by one; by substituting for them lights or sounds dispensed by a machine; or by using a reinforcer of a less "affectionate" nature than the one used here appears to be. On the other hand, even for the three-month-old infant the smiles, sounds, and caresses of the adults may function as conditioned reinforcers because of their past association with caretaking acts.

It is possible that the Ss of this study, living in an institution, may have had a less rich experience with adults. Institutional babies were used as Ss only because they were more readily available, because more of them could be studied at one time, and because the complicating variable of differences in maternal care could be bypassed. They did not appear however to be "starved" for attention or affection. Indeed, the attendants were often observed responding to babies when they vocalized. While it is possible that mothers would respond more often, in the absence of a comparative study we believe that infants in general would respond as these infants did.

Relation of Results to Theories of Speech

Since this study was limited to the vocalizing of infants in a social situation, attempts to reconcile the results with theories which account for all classes of prelinguistic utterances (babbling is the class frequently mentioned) cannot be complete. Thus, nothing in the findings of this study is incompatible with, for example, Holt's theory (1931) that the sound which the child hears himself make has reinforcing properties; with Lewis' theory (1951) that the adult's speech calls forth the infant's speech (a kind of imitation); or with Piaget's theory (1952) that vocalizing is perpetuated for its own sake by the processes of assimilation and accommodation. These may be labeled circular theories, for they do not postulate the necessity for any class of events prior to the moment when the infant responds to his own or another's vocalization. The theories of Miller and Dollard (1941) and of Mowrer (1950), on the other hand, are based upon the infant's associating the gratification of his needs and the accompanying vocalizations of the caretaker. Again, the results do not contradict this possibility.

The present study, however, does demonstrate the operation of still another principle: that the speech of the infant, if only in a social situation, can be modified by a response from the environment which is contingent upon his vocalizing. Hence, what happens *after* the infant vocalizes has been shown to be important.

Significance of Results

On the basis of the results of these experiments it is seen that responses of adults which do not involve caretaking can affect the vocalizing of the young in a social setting. If the results can be extended to life situations, then mothers might be able to increase or decrease the vocal output of their children by the responses they make when the children vocalize. Other kinds of social behavior in addition to vocalizing behavior should respond similarly to conditioning. Brackbill (1958) has shown that smiling in the four-month-old infant may be increased when followed by a social response from an adult. It is likely that still other kinds of social behavior in babies, such as showing an interest in people, reaching out to them or turning away, perhaps even fear of the stranger, may also be affected by the responses adults make to them.

SUMMARY

Infants often vocalize as part of the response they give to the appearance of an adult. The central question of this study is: Can the frequency of vocalizing be increased if the adult makes a social response contingent upon it?

The Ss were 21 normal infants, three months of age, living in an institution. Eleven of them were studied in Experiment I with one E; 10 different Ss and one S from Experiment I were studied in Experiment II with a different E.

During the first and second Baseline days E leaned over S with an expressionless face, and the number of vocalizations was tallied. During the next two days, the first and second Conditioning days, E reinforced vocalizations by simultaneously smiling, clucking, and touching S's abdomen. During the last two days, the first and second Extinction days, E returned to Baseline conditions.

The results indicated that: (*a*) there was no difference between Experiments, (*b*) Conditioning raised the rate of vocalizing above the Baseline level, (*c*) while Extinction lowered it until it approached the Baseline level.

The results suggest that the social vocalizing of infants and, more generally, their social responsiveness may be modified by the responses adults make to them.

REFERENCES

Brackbill, Y. Extinction of the smiling responses in infants as a function of reinforcement schedule. *Child Develpm.*, 1958, 29, 115–124.

Gewirtz, J. L. A program of research on the dimensions and antecedents of emotional dependence. *Child Develpm.*, 1956, 27, 205–221.

Holt, E. B. *Animal drive.* London: Williams & Norgate, 1931.

Lewis, M. M. *Infant Speech: A study of the beginnings of language.* (2nd ed.) New York: Humanities Press, 1951.

Lindquist, E. F. *Design and analysis of experiments in psychology and education.* Boston: Houghton Mifflin, 1953.

Mann, H. B., & Whitney, D. R. On a test of whether one of two random variables is stochastically larger than the other. *Ann. Math. Statist.*, 1947, 18, 50–60.

Miller, N. E., & Dollard, J. *Social learning and imitation.* New Haven: Yale Univer. Press, 1941.

Mowrer, O. H. *Learning theory and personality dynamics.* New York: Ronald, 1950.

Piaget, J. *The origins of intelligence in children.* New York: Int. Univer. Press, 1952.

Rheingold, H. L. The modification of social responsiveness in institutional babies. *Monogr. Soc. Res. Child Develpm.*, 1956, 21, No. 63 (No. 2).

Skinner, B. F. *Science and human behavior.* New York: Macmillan, 1953.

Verplanck, W. S. The control of the content of conversation: Reinforcement of statements of opinion. *J. abnorm. soc. Psychol.*, 1955, 51, 668–676.

3.3 ELECTRICAL SELF-STIMULATION OF THE BRAIN IN MAN*

Robert G. Heath

At a symposium concerning depth electrode studies in animals and man in New Orleans in 1952, the Tulane investigators described (and illustrated with films of patients treated between 1950-1952) a pleasurable response with stimulation of specific regions of the brain (5). The pleasur-

* Reprinted from *The American Journal of Psychiatry*, 1963, 120, 571–577. Copyright 1963, the American Psychiatric Association, and reproduced by permission. Read at the 119th annual meeting of The American Psychiatric Association, St. Louis, Mo., May 6-10, 1963.

At the time of presentation, a 16 mm. sound film was shown demonstrating the effects of stimulation by the transitorized portable self-stimulator to a number of specific regions of the brain in Patients No. B-7 and No. B-10. The two subjects were interviewed to obtain subjective descriptions of the effects of stimulation.

Supported by funds provided by the Louisiana State Department of Hospitals.

Charles J. Fontana, Electroencephalographic Technologist and Esther Blount, R.N., Research Nurse, Assistants.

able response to stimulation of some deep regions of the brain, first observed with electrical stimulation to the septal region, has proved a consistent finding in continuing studies (6, 7, 12). Since 1952 we have reported various aspects of the phenomenon including demonstration of relief of physical pain by stimulation to this pleasure-yielding area of the brain (11).

With the introduction of ingenious techniques for self-stimulation by Olds (14-17), the need to depend largely upon verbal reports of the subjective response was eliminated and it was possible to study apparent reward and aversive areas of the brain in animals. Subjective data, of course, were lacking in the animal studies.

During the last few years the Tulane researchers have incorporated and modified some animal intracranial self-stimulation (ICSS) methods for human investigation, permitting extension of the pleasurable phenomenon studies in man. An ICSS study recently published (3) was designed to explore human behavior under strict laboratory conditions of the type characteristically employed in animal studies. A study has also been described in which a patient was equipped with a small portable self-stimulator with 3 buttons, permitting delivery of electrical stimuli of fixed parameters to any one of 3 brain sites (8). The primary motivation in these studies, as in all depth electrode studies in man at Tulane, was therapeutic (5).

Study of reward areas in the brain of man, including use of induced reward for therapeutic purposes, is extensive and complex. This presentation will focus on a description of the subjective responses of two patients treated by the self-stimulation technique. Their reports provide information concerning the reasons for repeated ICSS—information that is not available from animal studies.

MATERIAL AND METHODS

Two patients were used in the study. Patient No. B-7, age 28, with a diagnosis of narcolepsy and cataplexy, had failed to respond to conventional treatments. He had electrodes implanted by the method developed in our laboratory (1, 2) into 14 predetermined brain regions and fixed to remain in exact position for prolonged study. These small silver ball electrodes (most of those used in this study consisted of 3 leads each separated by 2 mm.) were placed into the right anterior and posterior septal region, left anterior and posterior septal region, right anterior hypothalamus, mid-line mesencephalic tegmentum, left anterior and posterior hippocampus, left anterior and posterior caudate nucleus and over the right frontal cortex, right and left mid-temporal cortex, and left anterior temporal cortex.

Patient No. B-10, age 25, a psychomotor epileptic with episodic brief periods of impulsive behavior uncontrolled with the usual treatments, had 51 leads implanted into 17 brain sites: left and right centromedian, left caudate nucleus, right ventricle, left and right hippocampus mid-line mesencephalic tegmentum, left and right septal region, left amygdaloid nucleus, left paraolfactory area, and over the left and right temporal cortex, left and right occipital cortex, and left and right frontal cortex. Twenty-four leads were of stainless steel .003 inch in diameter coated with Teflon; 27 were the small silver ball type electrode.[1]

ICSS studies were not initiated until a minimal period of 6 months following operation, assuring elimination of any variables induced by operative trauma, e.g., edema, anesthetic effects.

Stimuli were delivered from a specially constructed transistorized self-contained unit[2] which was worn on the patient's belt. The unit generated a pre-set train of bi-directional stimulus pulses each time that one of the 3 control buttons was depressed. Each button directed the pulse train to a different electrode pair permitting the operator a possible selection of cerebral sites. A mechanical counter was coupled to each button to record the total number of stimuli directed toward a given area. An internal timer limited each pulse train to 0.5 second for each depression, thereby prohibiting the operator from obtaining continuous stimuli merely by keeping the button depressed. An additional feature of the unit provided 3 separate level potentiometers to give wide-range control of stimuli for each electrode pair.

Circuit Details

To minimize the effects of dc polarization, a bi-directional pulse was chosen (Fig. 3.3–1). This pulse permitted restoration of the dc level to zero after each 1.0 millisecond stimulus and maintenance at zero during the entire dead time of 10 milliseconds.

A silicon unijunction timing circuit generated the basic 10 millisecond interval. The output from the unijunction transistor was gated off after 0.5 second operation by a diode gate driven from an R-G charging circuit. When the diode gate was open, the unijunction transistor generator drove two complementary one-shot multivibrators operated serially, permitting the falling edge of the first to trigger the second. The two multivibrators had equal periods of 0.5 millisecond. The multivibrator timing circuits saturated complementary output transistors which fed voltage to the load through isolating capacitors.

Studies conducted on the two patients differed somewhat because of therapeutic considerations. For studies with Patient No. B-7, the narcoleptic, the 3 buttons of the unit were attached to electrodes in the septal region, hippocampus, and mesencephalic tegmentum, and he was free to stimulate any of these sites as he chose. The patient wore the stimulator

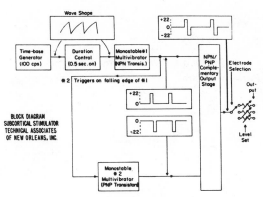

FIGURE 3.3–1   Circuit diagram for transistorized intracranial self-stimulator.

for a period of 17 weeks. Before he was equipped with the unit, baseline data concerning the time he spent sleeping during an arbitrary 6-hour period each day were charted by specific ward personnel. These data were later compared with sleeping time following attachment of the unit. This study was basically therapeutic (treatment results will be presented elsewhere) but from the experimental design we were able to obtain considerable subjective data regarding the effects of ICSS to several regions of the brain.

With Patient No. B-10, the psychomotor epileptic, a number of different experimental designs were employed to investigate the effects of ICSS. For illustrative purposes, the results of one study are presented herein as background for a description of the subjective responses. In the first part of the study a total of 17 different cerebral regions were stimulated. They were selected at random, the unit design permitting 3 sites to be hooked up at any one time. Each electrode was made available to the patient for stimulation for a minimal period of 2 hours. Various combinations of 3 sites were arranged. The purpose in making stimulation to different combinations of sites available was based on well-documented animal studies which indicate that rate of stimulation at a given site will vary somewhat depending upon the site stimulated beforehand. Data are presented in terms of the hourly stimulation to a given site as recorded with the automatic counter of the unit. Additionally, the same site of the brain was attached to different buttons to determine if the patient would relate a response to a given button. He reported, however, a consistent response to stimulation of a given electrode regardless of the button to which it was attached.

In the second part of the study the 3 sites of the brain which the subject had elected to stimulate most frequently during the first part of the study were compared over a 6-hour period.

RESULTS

Patient No. B-7

After randomly exploring the effects of stimulation with presses of each of the 3 buttons, Patient No. B-7 almost exclusively pressed the septal button (Fig. 3.3–2).

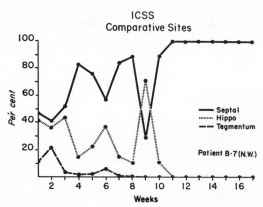

FIGURE 3.3–2   Comparative sites, ICSS. Frequency of stimulation to various intra-cranial sites expressed in percentages in patient with narcolepsy and cataplexy.

Stimulation to the mesencephalic tegmentum resulted in a prompt alerting, but was quite aversive. The patient, complaining of intense discomfort and looking fearful, requested that the stimulus not be repeated. To make certain that the region was not stimulated, he ingeniously modified a hair pin to fit under the button which directed a pulse train to the mesencephalic tegmentum so it could not be depressed.

Hippocampal stimulation was mildly rewarding.

Stimulation to the septal region was the most rewarding of the stimulations and, additionally, it alerted the patient, thereby combatting the narcolepsy. By virtue of his ability to control symptoms with the stimulator, he was employed part-time, while wearing the unit, as an entertainer in a night club.

The patient's narcolepsy was severe. He would move from an alert state into a deep sleep in the matter of a second. Recognizing that button pressing promptly awakened him, fellow patients and friends occasionally resorted to pushing the button if he fell asleep so rapidly that he was unable to stimulate himself.

The patient, in explaining why he pressed the septal button with such frequency, stated that the feeling was "good"; it was as if he were building up to a sexual orgasm. He reported that he was unable to achieve the orgastic end point, however, explaining that his frequent, sometimes frantic, pushing of the button was an attempt to reach the end point. This futile effort was frustrating at times and described by him on these occasions as a "nervous feeling."

Patient No. B-10

Studies conducted on the psychomotor epileptic patient were more varied and provided more information concerning subjective responses. The average number of button presses per hour for various regions of the brain is listed in Tables 3.3–1 and 3.3–2. Regions of the brain are listed in order of the frequency with which they were selectively stimulated by the subject. A summary of the principal subjective feelings is given.

TABLE 3.3–1   ICSS in Man, Reward (?) Sites

Region Stimulated	Average/Hour	Subjective Response
L. Centromedian	488.8	Partial memory recall; anger and frustration
R.P. Septal	394.9	"Feel great"; sexual thoughts; elimination of "bad" thoughts
L. Caudate	373.0	Cool taste; "like it OK"
Mesenceph. Teg.	280.0	"Drunk feeling"; "happy button"; elimination of "bad" thoughts
A. Amygdala	257.9	Indifferent feeling; somewhat pleasant, but feeling not intense
P. Amygdala	224.0	Moderately rewarding; increase of current requested

TABLE 3.3–2   ICSS in Man, Aversive Sites

Region Stimulated	Average/Hour	Subjective Response
R. Hippocampus	1.77	Strongly aversive; "feel sick all over"
L. Paraolfactory	0.36	Moderately aversive
R. Parietal Cortex	0.50 ⎤	
R. Frontal Cortex	0.00 ⎥	No significant subjective response
R. Occipital Cortex	0.00 ⎥	
R. Temporal Cortex	0.00 ⎦	

The button most frequently pushed provided a stimulus to the centromedian thalamus. This stimulus did not, however, induce the most pleasurable response; in fact, it induced irritability. The subject reported that he was almost able to recall a memory during this stimulation, but he could not quite grasp it. The frequent self-stimulations were an endeavor to bring this elusive memory into clear focus.

The patient most consistently reported pleasurable feelings with stimulation to two electrodes in the septal region and one in the mesencephalic tegmentum. With the pleasurable response to septal stimuli, he frequently produced associations in the sexual area. Actual content varied considerably, but regardless of his baseline emotional state and the subject under discussion in the room, the stimulation was accompanied by the patient's introduction of a sexual subject, usually with a broad grin. When questioned about this, he would say, "I don't know why that came to mind—I just happened to think of it." The "happy feelings" with mesencephalic stimulation were not accompanied by sexual thoughts.

Patient No. B-10 also described as "good," but somewhat less in pleasurable-yielding quality, stimuli in two sites, the amygdaloid nucleus and the caudate nucleus. Several other septal electrodes and one other electrode in the amygdaloid nucleus were stimulated a moderate number of times. His reports concerning these stimulations suggested a lesser magnitude of pleasurable response, but definitely not an unpleasant feeling.

Minimal positive response was obtained with stimulation of several other septal electrodes. The most aversive response ("sick feeling") was obtained with stimulation to one hippocampal electrode and one lead in the paraolfactory area. With stimulation of the latter lead, he complained of light flashes, apparently due to spread to the optic nerve, and of general discomfort.

No consistent changes, either significantly aversive or rewarding, were displayed with stimulation to any of 12 cortical leads dispersed widely over the cortical surface, including the frontal, temporal, occipital, and parietal lobes.

In the second part of the study the 3 electrodes which were stimulated most during the first phase of the study were attached to the 3 buttons. The sites of these electrodes were the centromedian thalamus, the septal region, and the mesencephalic tegmentum. Data indicated that the combination of sites available influenced the number of times that a given region of the brain was stimulated (Fig. 3.3–3). When coupled with the subjective reports, the data also suggested that the over-all state of the subject at a given moment was an influential determinant for selecting the region to be stimulated. For example, the centromedian thalamus was stimulated up to 1,100 times per hour when in combination with relatively inactive sites of stimulation and only a maximum of 290 times per hour when in combination with two other highly rewarding areas, the septal region and the mesencephalic tegmentum.

The patient noted that the frustration and anger resulting from stimulation of the centromedian thalamus was alleviated with stimulation to the septal region and to the mesencephalic tegmentum. As Figure 3.3–3 indicates, the patient during the first two hours stimulated the centromedian thalamus most frequently. This was associated with discomfort in his attempt to recapture a fleeting memory. He reported that stimula-

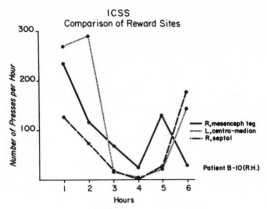

FIGURE 3.3-3   Comparison of frequency of stimulation to reward sites in the brain of patient with psychomotor epilepsy.

tion of the other areas relieved this discomfort. There was little activity during the next two hours. Toward the end of the study, in the 5th and 6th hours, stimulation to septal and tegmental leads increased. During the 5th hour, the mesencephalic tegmentum was stimulated most frequently; during the 6th hour, the septal lead was stimulated most frequently. The patient evolved a pattern coupling the stimulus to the centromedian thalamus (which stirred his curiosity concerning the memory) with stimuli to the more pleasurable areas to lessen the feeling of frustration.[3]

DISCUSSION

Changes in parameters of stimuli to a given region of the brain, including current intensity, wave form, pulse width, and frequency, in many instances altered the patients' responses. This has similarly been reported with animal ICSS.

Information acquired from the patients' reporting of their reasons for button pressing indicates that all ICSS is not solely for pleasure. The highest rate of button pressing occurred with Patient No. B-7 when he was somewhat frustrated in his pleasurable pursuit and as he attempted to achieve an orgastic end point. In Patient No. B-10 the highest rate of button pressing also occurred with frustration, but of a different type, evolving with attempts to bring into focus a vague memory that ICSS had evoked. The subject's emotional state in this instance built into strong anger. It was interesting that the patient would button press to stimulate the region within the centromedian thalamus for a prolonged period, but at a slower rate when buttons providing more pleasurable septal and tegmental stimulation were also available. Depression of the septal button, with resultant pleasant feelings, alleviated the painful emergency state, according to the subject's report, and thereby provided him comfort to pursue his quest for the fleeting memory.

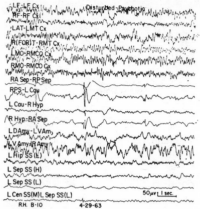

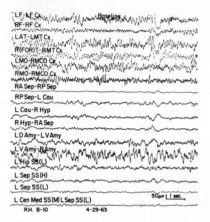

FIGURE 3.3–4 Subcortical and cortical recordings from patient with psychomotor epilepsy during psychotic episode. This record was obtained during the time that the baseline of the last sequence of film (described herein) was taken. Note the predominant spiking localized principally to the septal leads. This has proved to be a consistent physiological correlate with psychotic behavior.

FIGURE 3.3–5 In contrast to the recording in Figure 3.3–4, this is a baseline record of the type displayed by the patient with psychomotor epilepsy during his usual nonpsychotic behavioral state.

With septal stimulation in other patients, as well as the two subjects discussed here, a sexual motive state has frequently been induced in association with the pleasurable response. This sexual state has not developed in association with pleasurable feelings during stimulation to other regions. The consistent observation of a relation between sexual feelings and stimulation to the septal region has been described by MacLean in monkey experiments (13). These reports, in part, answer questions raised by Galambos regarding ICSS when he asked, "What motivates these animals to do such unheard-of-things? Is it some exquisite pleasure they receive, as several students of the problem staunchly contend, or the feeling of utter and complete well-being as others claim?" (4).

The ICSS techniques represent one of several methodologies that the Tulane researchers have used in man to investigate the pleasurable phenomenon associated with certain types of cerebral activity. These studies complement early subcortical electrical stimulation studies (5). The pleasurable response has also been induced in man with introduction of certain chemicals into specific deep brain regions (8-10). It is noteworthy that intense pleasurable responses induced with chemical stimulation of the brain occurred when a high amplitude spindling type of recording was set up in the septal region (Figs. 3.3–6 and 3.3–7).

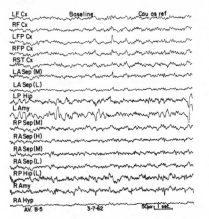

FIGURE 3.3–6 Baseline record of epileptic patient No. B-5.

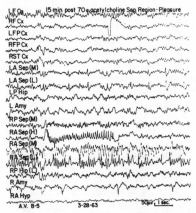

FIGURE 3.3–7 Recording from epileptic patient No. B-5 following injection of acetylcholine into the septal region through intracerebral cannula.

The observation that introduction of a stimulus which induces pleasure immediately eliminates painful emergency states is quite consistent. If our psychodynamic formulations are correct, this basic observation may have widespread implication for the development of therapeutic methods to alter favorably disordered behavior.

SUMMARY

Studies are described of two human patients under treatment with ICSS. Their subjective reports in association with stimulation to reward areas of the brain are presented. The data indicate that patients will stimulate regions of the brain at a high frequency for reasons other than to obtain a pleasurable response. These data extend information obtained from ICSS in animals.

NOTES

1. Stainless steel array constructed of No. 316 stainless steel wire, .003 inch in diameter, with quad Teflon-coated leads and 6 contact points 2 mm. apart. Electrode designed and fabricated by Henry A. Schryver, 110 W. Packard St., Fort Wayne, Indiana.
2. Technical Associates of New Orleans.
3. When the paper was presented, it was here that the 16 mm. sound film was

shown. Clinical effects of stimulation to a variety of deep regions of the brain, as summarized herein, were demonstrated.

In the last sequence of the film, Patient No. B-10, the psychomotor epileptic, was stimulated in the septal region during a period when he was exhibiting agitated, violent psychotic behavior. The stimulus was introduced without his knowledge. Almost instantly his behavioral state changed from one of disorganization, rage, and persecution to one of happiness and mild euphoria. He described the beginning of a sexual motive state. He was unable, when questioned directly, to explain the sudden shift in his feelings and thoughts. This sequence of film was presented to demonstrate a phenomenon which appears to be consistent and which has been repeated in a large number of patients in our laboratories. This phenomenon is the ability to obliterate immediately painful emergency emotional feelings in a human subject through introduction of a pleasurable state by physical or chemical techniques.

BIBLIOGRAPHY

1. Becker, H. C., et al.: In: Studies in Schizophrenia. Cambridge: Harvard Univ. Press, 1954, p. 565.
2. Becker, H. C., et al.: Electroenceph. Clin. Neurophysiol., 9: 533, 1957.
3. Bishop, M. P., et al.: Science, 140: 394, 1963.
4. Galambos, Robert: Fed Proc., 20: 603, 1961.
5. Heath, R. G., et al.: Studies in Schizophrenia. Cambridge: Harvard Univ. Press, 1954, pp. 42, 46, 47, 50, 560.
6. Heath, R. G.: Psychosom. Med., 17: 383, 1955.
7. Heath, R. G.: Confinia Neurol., 18: 305, 1958.
8. Heath, R. G.: In Heath, R. G. (Ed.): The Role of Pleasure in Behavior. New York: Harper & Row, 1964.
9. Heath, R. G., and deBalbian Verster, F.: Am. J. Psychiat., 117: 980, 1961.
10. Heath, R. G., and Founds, W. L.: Electroenceph. Clin. Neurophysiol., 12: 930, 1960.
11. Heath, R. G., et al.: In: Studies in Schizophrenia. Cambridge: Harvard Univ. Press, 1954, p. 555.
12. Heath, R. G., and Mickle, W. A.: In Ramey, R. R., and O'Doherty, D. S. (Eds.): Electrical Studies on the Unanesthetized Brain. New York: Hoeber, 1960.
13. MacLean, P. D., et al.: Trans. Am. Neurol. Ass., 84: 105, 1959.
14. Olds, J.: Physiol. Rev., 42: 554, 1962.
15. ———: Am. J. Physiol., 199: 965, 1960.
16. Olds, J., and Milner, P.: J. Comp. Physiol. Psychol., 47: 419, 1954.
17. Olds, J., and Olds, M. E.: In Heath, R. G. (Ed.): The Role of Pleasure in Behavior. New York: Harper & Row, 1969.

3.4 | USE OF THE PREMACK PRINCIPLE
IN CONTROLLING THE BEHAVIOR
OF NURSERY SCHOOL CHILDREN*

Lloyd Homme, P. C. deBaca, J. V. Devine,
R. Steinhorst, and E. J. Rickert

Premack's principle (Premack. 1959) can be stated: if behavior B is of higher probability than behavior A, then behavior A can be made more probable by making behavior B contingent upon it.

In a preliminary exploration of nursery school procedures, three 3-yr-old subjects (Ss) were available three hours a day, five days a week, for about one month. On the first day, in the absence of any aversive control, verbal instructions usually had little effect on the Ss' behavior. When they were instructed to sit in their chairs, Ss would often continue what they were doing—running around the room, screaming, pushing chairs, or quietly working jigsaw puzzles. Taking Premack seriously, such behaviors were labeled as high probability behaviors and used in combination with the signals for them as reinforcers. These high probability behaviors were then made contingent on desired behaviors. For example, sitting quietly in a chair and looking at the blackboard would be intermittently followed by the sound of the bell, with the instruction: "Run and scream." The Ss would then leap to their feet and run around the room screaming. At another signal they would stop. At this time they would get another signal and an instruction to engage in some other behavior which, on a quasi-random schedule, might be one of high or low probability. At a later stage, Ss earned tokens for low probability behaviors which could later be used to "buy" the opportunity for high probability activities.

With this kind of procedure, control was virtually perfect after a few days. For example, when Ss were requested to "sit and look at the blackboard" (an activity which in the past had intermittently been interrupted by the signal for some higher probability behavior), they were under such good control that an observer, new on the scene, almost certainly would have assumed extensive aversive control was being used.

An examination of high probability behaviors quickly showed that many, if not most of them, were behaviors which ordinarily would be

* Reprinted from the *Journal of the Experimental Analysis of Behavior*, 1963, *6*, 544. Copyright 1963 by the Society for the Experimental Analysis of Behavior, Inc., and reproduced by permission.

173

suppressed through punishment. Extrapolating from this we were able to predict the reinforcing properties of some behaviors which had never been emitted. For example, throwing a plastic cup across the room and kicking a waste basket had never been observed but proved to be highly reinforcing activities after they had once been evoked by instructions. (Some unpredicted behaviors proved to be highly reinforcing, e.g., pushing the experimenter around the room in his caster-equipped chair.)

In summary, even in this preliminary, unsystematic application, the Premack hypothesis proved to be an exceptionally practical principle for controlling the behavior of nursery school Ss.

REFERENCE

Premack, D. Toward empirical behavior laws: I. positive reinforcement. *Psychol. Rev.*, 1959, 66, 219–233.

3.5   SECONDARY REINFORCEMENT IN RATS AS A FUNCTION OF INFORMATION VALUE AND RELIABILITY OF THE STIMULUS*

M. David Egger and Neal E. Miller

Although secondary reinforcement has been of major importance to behavior theory, especially in explanations of complex learning phenomena (e.g., Hull, 1943; Miller, 1951; Skinner, 1938), little is known about the conditions for its occurrence in any but the simplest situations. The first hypothesis explored in the experiments reported here is that in a situation in which there is more than one stimulus predicting primary

* M. David Egger and Neal E. Miller, "Secondary Reinforcement in Rats as a Function of Information Value and Reliability of the Stimulus," *The Journal of Experimental Psychology*, 64, 1962, 97–104. Copyright 1962 by the American Psychological Association, and reproduced by permission. This study was supported by funds from Grant MY647 from the National Institute of Mental Health, United States Public Health Service. We wish to thank Elizabeth Sherwood for her assistance in running the animals.

A portion of the data reported in this paper was presented by Neal Miller in his Presidential Address to the American Psychological Association.

reinforcement, e.g., food, the more informative stimulus will be the more effective secondary reinforcer. Further it is asserted that a necessary condition for establishing any stimulus as a secondary reinforcer is that the stimulus provide information about the occurrence of primary reinforcement; a redundant predictor of primary reinforcement should not acquire secondary reinforcement strength.

A possible situation in which to test this hypothesis is the following: a short stimulus always precedes the delivery of food. But it is made essentially redundant by being overlapped by a longer stimulus of slightly earlier onset which is also invariably followed by food. This situation is summarized in Fig. 3.5–1. The longer stimulus is labeled S_1 and the shorter, S_2. For an S trained with this series of stimulus events, S_2 is a reliable, but redundant, i.e., noninformative, predictor of food. Hence, according to our hypothesis, S_1 should be an effective secondary reinforcer; S_2 should acquire little or no secondary reinforcing strength, even though it is closer in time to the occurrence of food, and therefore in a more favorable position than is S_1 on the gradient of delay of reinforcement.

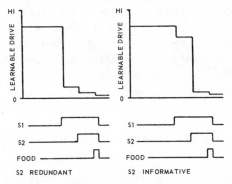

FIGURE 3.5–1   Schematic representation of the theoretical analysis of the two main experiment groups according to a strict interpretation of the drive-reduction hypothesis.

There is a way, however, to make S_2 informative. If S_1 occurs a number of times without S_2, unaccompanied by the food pellet, and randomly interspersed with occurrences of the stimulus sequence shown at the bottom of Fig. 3.5–1, then S_2, when it occurs, is no longer redundant; for now S_2 is the only reliable predictor of food. Thus, it is predicted that for a group of rats who receive the stimulus sequence depicted in Fig. 3.5–1 interspersed with occurrences of S_1 alone, S_2 will be a considerably more effective secondary reinforcer than for the group of rats who receive only the stimulus sequence depicted in Fig. 3.5–1.

It should be noted that both groups will receive exactly the same number of pairings of S_2 with food and in exactly the same immediate stimulus context, so that if a difference were found between the groups in the secondary reinforcing value of S_2, it could not be due to simple patterning, stimulus-generalization decrement, or differences in association with food.

Our predicted results would be compatible with a strict interpretation of the drive-reduction hypothesis of reinforcement (Miller, 1959). Such a theoretical analysis is represented schematically in the upper portion of Fig. 3.5–1. According to the drive-reduction hypothesis, a stimulus acquires secondary reinforcing value by acquiring the ability to elicit a drive-reducing response. The left side of Fig. 3.5–1 illustrates that if most of the learnable drive already has been reduced by S_1, little drive-reduction remains to be conditioned to S_2. On the other hand, if S_1 sometimes fails to predict food, some of the conditioned drive-reduction to it should extinguish. Hence, as is depicted on the right side of Fig. 3.5–1, more of the drive-reduction should occur to, and be conditioned to, S_2.

From Fig. 3.5–1, one can also see that the drive-reduction analysis also demands that the secondary reinforcing value of S_1 should be greater when it is a reliable predictor (making S_2 redundant) than when it is an unreliable predictor (making S_2 informative). Thus we are led to our second hypothesis, namely, that in a situation in which a predictor of primary reinforcement exists which is both reliable and informative, this predictor should become a more effective secondary reinforcer than an unreliable predictor. Note that here we predict the opposite of a partial-reinforcement effect, which would be expected to increase the resistance to extinction of the unreliable predictor, that is, the stimulus which had been paired with food only part of the time. In any prolonged test for secondary reinforcement, this increased resistance to extinction should show up as a greater total secondary-reinforcing effect.

MAIN EXPERIMENT

Method

Subjects. The Ss were 88 male rats of the Sprague-Dawley strain who were approximately 90 days old at the beginning of their experimental training. Owing to deaths and equipment failures, the data from 4 Ss were lost, and the data from another 4, selected at random, were discarded in order to have equal sized groups for an analysis of variance. The Ss, fed once daily following the experimental session, were maintained at approximately 80% of their ad lib. weight.

Apparatus. The apparatus consisted of two identical Skinner boxes, 19 in. long, 8 in. wide, and 6¾ in. high (inside dimensions). The floors of the boxes consisted of six ½ in.-diameter rods running parallel to the side containing the Plexiglas door. Each box was enclosed in a large, light-proof, sound-deadened crate into which a stream of air was piped for ventilation and masking noise. Inside each of the Skinner boxes were two lights, one located 2 in. above the food cup, another located in the middle of the long back wall, opposite the Plexiglas door. The food cup was in the center of the front, 8-in. wall; the bar, a bent steel strip 1½ in. wide, protruded ½ in. into the inner chamber of the box. The entire bar assembly was removable and, when withdrawn, its opening was sealed with a metal panel. The bar was located to the right of and slightly above the food cup. A downward force of at least 12 gm. on the bar activated a microswitch normally connected in the circuit of a Gerbrands feeder which delivered a standard .045-gm. Noyes pellet into the food cup. A loudspeaker was located 3 in. behind and slightly to the left of the front wall of the Skinner box. Both flashing lights (12 per sec.) and tones (750 cps) were used as stimuli.

   Procedure.   All training sessions lasted 25 min. per day. During the first three sessions, Ss were magazine-trained in the absence of the bar. Then the bar was inserted, and, for two sessions, each bar press was followed by a pellet of food. A few rats who did not spontaneously learn to press were given an extra remedial session during which bar pressing was "shaped." Over the next four sessions the required ratio of responses to reinforcements was gradually increased to 4:1.

   Then, for the subsequent five sessions, the bar was removed, and Ss were randomly assigned to Group A (for whom S_2 was reliable but *redundant* and Group B (for whom S_2 was reliable and *informative*). Group A received the following sequence of events during each of its five "stimulus-training" sessions: once every 56 sec, on the average, a pellet of food was delivered into the food cup. The pellet was inevitably preceded by 2 sec. of S_1 and 1½ sec. of S_2. Both stimuli overlapped the delivery of the food pellet by ¼ sec., and both terminated together.

   Group B also received this stimulus sequence immediately preceding the delivery of the food pellet. But in addition, Group B Ss received aperiodically,, interspersed with the stimulus-food sequence, 2 sec. of S_1 alone. The events for Group B occurred on the average of once every 30 sec.

   For half the Ss in each group, S_1 was a flashing light and S_2 was a tone, and for the other half, the conditions were reversed: S_1 was a tone and S_2 was a flashing light.

   During 5 days of such training, each group received 135 pairings of S_1 and S_2 with food, and Group B received in addition about 110 occurrences of S_1 alone. Thus for both groups S_2 was followed 100% of the time by food, while S_1 was followed by food 100% of the time for Group A, but only 55% of the time for Group B.

   The above description of training applies to all but 16 Ss, 8 Group B and 8 Group A. For these Ss, training was exactly as described above except that the stimulus-food pairings occurred for both groups on the average of once every 75 sec. instead of 56 sec., and Group B received a stimulus event on the average of once every 15 sec. instead of 30 sec., so that S_1 was followed by food only 20% of the time for Group B. These 16 Ss were given seven 25-min. "stimulus-training" sessions. The data from these Ss were analyzed separately and not included in the overall analysis of variance.

Testing. On the day following the final stimulus-training session, Ss were tested as follows: the bar was reinserted and Test Session 1 began with each S pressing for food pellets on a fixed ratio of 3:1. The retraining presses continued until S had received 30 pellets. At this point the bar was disconnected and 10 min. of extinction ensued.

At the end of the 10 min., the bar was reconnected, not to the feeder, but to a timer which delivered on the same 3:1 schedule 1 sec. of whatever stimulus was being tested for secondary reinforcing strength. The test session continued until 25 min. had elapsed since the beginning of the extinction period, or until 10 min. after the first occurrence of a stimulus, whichever was longer.

In the foregoing procedure, relearning following experimental extinction was used as the measure of secondary reinforcing strength on the assumption that it would be more rapid and less variable than would de novo learning of the skill of pressing the bar. A preliminary study had validated this technique showing that in such a test more bar presses would occur when followed by a stimulus previously associated with food than when the stimulus had not been associated with food.

After an interval of 1 day, Test Session 2 was conducted, identical to the first, except that this time the stimulus delivered following the 10-min, extinction period was the opposite from that tested in Test Session 1: for half of the Ss, S_2 was tested in Test Session 1 and S_1 was tested in Session 2; for the other half of the Ss, trained and tested subsequent to the first half, the stimuli were tested in the opposite order.

For Ss tested first with S_2 and then with S_1, Test Session 3 followed another intervening day, this time with Ss pressing for S_2 again. Throughout the course of the 10-min. extinction and ensuing "pressing for stimuli" period, the cumulative total number of bar presses for each S was recorded each minute.

Response Measures. The total number of bar presses in a 10-min. period following the first occurrence of the stimulus was the measure of secondary reinforcing strength. Since there were significant between-S and within-S correlations ($r_b = .53$; $r_w = .34$) of this measure with the total number of bar presses in the 10-min. extinction periods, this total number of bar presses in extinction was used as a control variable in analyses of covariance. (It should be noted that most of the bar presses during extinction occurred within the first 2–4 min. of the 10-min. extinction period.)

Furthermore, since it was found that in no case would analyses based only on data from Test Session 1 have led to any substantially different conclusions from those reported below, the means and results of analyses reported (unless otherwise noted) are based on combined data from Test Sessions 1 and 2.

Since by Test Session 3, there no longer appeared to be any differences between the experimental groups, the data from this session were not included in the final analyses.

RESULTS

Overall Analysis. Neither of the hypotheses being tested depended upon the significance of the main effects of the overall analysis, but instead upon comparisons between the means shown in specific subcells of Table 3.5–1. The marginal entries in Table 3.5–1 give the overall means for Groups A and B (rows), and for S_1 and S_2 (columns). The overall mean for each group is based on data from 32 Ss each tested with S_1 and with S_2; the overall means for each stimulus position is based on data from all 64 Ss. As seen from an inspection of Tables 3.5–1 and 3.5–2, Group A responded significantly more than Group B and the position of S_1 was reliably more effective than that of S_2.

TABLE 3.5–1 Mean Responses during 10 Min. of Extinction and 10 Min. of "Pressing for Stimuli"

| | S_1 | | S_2 | | |
Group	Ext.	Pressing	Ext.	Pressing	$S_1 + S_2$
A	110.8	115.1	101.9	65.8	90.5
B	112.1	76.1	112.0	82.6	79.4
A+B		95.6		74.2	

Note.—Test Sessions 1 and 2 combined.

It should be noted that although the groups were identically treated in all other respects, the 32 Ss tested with S_1 first and S_2 second were run subsequent to the 32 Ss tested with S_2 first and with S_1 second. No significant differences between these groups existed in the control variable, total presses in 10 min. of extinction. Nor did an analysis of covariance reveal any significant effects of order of testing (O), or of the interaction of order of testing with experimental group (G), or with stimulus position (P) (see Table 3.5–2).

Across all groups, the Ss responded more for flashing lights than for the tone ($F = 8.45$; $df = 1/55$; $P < .01$, analysis of covariance).

Examination of the minute-by-minute response totals during the "pressing for stimuli" period revealed that the differences between groups tested at 10 min. had generally begun to appear after 3–5 min., and continued to increase out to 15 min., which was the longest period any S was permitted to bar press for stimuli during a given test session.

TABLE 3.5–2   Summary of Analysis of Variance and Covariance: Test Sessions 1 and 2 Combined

Source	Analysis of Variance			Analysis of Covariance		
	df	MS	F	df	MS	F
Between Ss						
Experimental						
Group (G)	1	3,916.12	2.36	1	6,062.17	4.98*
Modality of S_1 (M)	1	7,938.00	4.79*	1	4,792.37	3.93
Order of S_1,S_2 (O)	1	435.13		1	709.44	
G × M	1	2,907.03	1.75	1	573.36	
G × O	1	2,329.03	1.41	1	50.93	
M × O	1	9.03		1	37.41	
G × M × O	1	1,624.50		1	1,382.64	1.14
Error (b)	56	1,657.19		55	1,218.04	(r_b = .53)
Within Ss						
Stimulus Position (P)	1	14,663.28	10.83**	1	12,168.39	9.97**
P × G	1	24,864.50	18.36***	1	21,613.81	17.71***
P × M = St	1	15,664.50	11.56**	1	10,316.32	8.45**
P × O = T	1	52,650.13	38.87***	1	1,594.90	1.31
P × G × M	1	87.78		1	546.78	
P × M × O	1	35.13		1	16.45	
P × G × O	1	5,330.28	3.94	1	3,168.95	2.60
P × G × M × O	1	5,781.27	4.27*	1	6,720.79	5.51*
Error (w)	56	1,354.57		55	1,220.64	(r_w = .34)

Note.—St = modality of stimulus tested; T = test session (1 or 2).
  * $P < .05$.
  ** $P < .01$.
  *** $P < .001$.

As expected from our hypotheses, the (P × G) interaction was highly significant ($F = 17.71$; $df = 1/55$; $P < .001$, analysis of covariance). Hence, we were justified in making within experimental group and stimulus position comparisons.

S_2: Group B vs. Group A.   On the basis of our first hypothesis, we expected that Group B Ss, for whom S_2 was informative, should press more for S_2 than Group A Ss, for whom S_2 was redundant. The difference between the group means on the secondary reinforcing measure was in the predicted direction and significant beyond the .05 level ($F = 4.03$; $df = 1/56$). (The means are given in Table 3.5–1.) However, the effect was not statistically reliable in an analysis of covariance.

As mentioned above, 16 Ss, 8 each in Groups A and B, were trained with the number of occurrences of S_1 alone for Group B increased so that 80% of the stimulus event for Group B were unaccompanied occurrences of S_1. For these Ss, tested with S_2 in Test Session 1, the means on the secondary reinforcing measure were in the predicted direction, 97.5 vs. 88.0, but the difference was short of statistical significance. However, when these data were analyzed in an analysis of covariance and combined by means of a critical ratio test with the data discussed above, the predicted effects was significant beyond the .05 level. ($CR = 1.97$ if the data from these 16 Ss are combined with those from the 64 Ss tested with S_2 in Test Session 1 or Test Session 2; $CR = 2.02$ if the data are combined with those from the 32 Ss tested with S_2 in Test Session 1 only.)

S_1: *Group A vs. Group B.*   Our second hypothesis predicted that S_1 would be a more effective secondary reinforcer for Group A, for whom it was reliable and informative, than for Group B, for whom it was unreliable. This prediction was borne out by the data beyond the .001 level ($F = 15.71$; $df = 1/55$; analysis of covariance).

Group A: S_1 vs. S_2.   As predicted from our first hypothesis, S_1 was a much more effective secondary reinforcer than S_2 for Group A. The difference between the means for these two stimulus positions, 115.1 vs. 65.8, was significant beyond the .001 level ($F = 26.35$; $df = 1/27$; analysis of covariance).

CONTROL EXPERIMENTS

Pseudoconditioned and Unconditioned Control

Fourteen Ss, male albino rats, handled exactly as in the Main Experiment, were trained in groups of 7 Ss each with stimulus sequences identical to those of Groups A and B, except that the stimuli were *never* paired with the occurrence of food, which was delivered at least 10 sec. after the occurrence of the stimuli. The two different patterns of stimuli used in training had no effect upon the pseudoconditioned rate of bar pressing. The mean for the 14 Ss with both test sessions combined was 64.3. These 14 Ss bar pressed for the stimuli significantly less in both Test Session 1 ($t = 3.41$; $df = 28$; $P < .005$) and Test Session 2 ($t = 2.72$; $df = 28$; $P < .02$) than did the 16 Group A Ss bar pressing for the informative stimulus (S_1) in each of the Main Experiment test sessions. Hence, in a group predicted to show a large secondary reinforcing effect, we did indeed find such an effect produced by our training procedure.

Eight Ss were exposed to the stimuli during training exactly as described above, except that the food pellets were eliminated entirely. The unconditioned rate of pressing for the stimuli was comparable to that of the pseudoconditioned group ($M = 73.4$).

The mean for the total group of pseudoconditioned and unconditioned Ss with both test sessions combined was 67.6, indicating that the secondary reinforcing value of the redundant stimulus for Group A of the Main Experiment ($M = 65.8$), once the unconditioned rate of pressing for stimuli is taken into account, was small, if not zero, as we predicted from our first hypothesis. The estimates of the pseudoconditioned and unconditioned scores may be somewhat high, however, since these Ss tended to have higher 10-min. extinction scores than did Ss of the Main Experiment.

Activation Control

To test whether the effects studied in the Main Experiment were related to secondary reinforcement or only to a possible activation effect of a stimulus formerly associated with food (Wyckoff, Sidowski, & Chambliss, 1958), 10 additional Ss were trained exactly as in the Main Experiment, 5 as in Group A and 5 as in Group B. However, during the testing of these Ss, the bar remained nonfunctional once it was disconnected from the feeder. Each S was tested at the same time as an identically trained S used in the Main Experiment. The yoked Activation Control S received only the stimuli earned by his Main Experiment partner. If the Main Experiment S pressed for a stimulus within 7½ sec. of a yoked Activation Control S's response, the stimulus for the Activation Control S was delayed so that it was not delivered until 7½ sec. after his response. Hence spurious pairings of stimuli and pressing could not occur.

Thus, for these 10 Ss, any pressing which occurred during the retraining test period could have been due only to the activation effects of the stimuli plus remaining operant level; the possibility of secondary reinforcement was eliminated.

In Test Session 1, all 10 of the Activation Control Ss pressed less than did their secondary-reinforced partners ($P < .002$, binomial test, two-tailed). In Test Session 2, 9 out of 10 pressed less than did their yoked partners ($P < .02$, binomial test, two-tailed). Hence, we are quite certain that in the Main Experiment we were indeed studying secondary reinforcement.

Partial Reinforcement Effect Control

In the Main Experiment we had found that in the presence of a reliable predictor (S_2), training with partial reinforcement of S_1 produced less total pressing for S_1 as a secondary reinforcer than did 100% reinforcement. This confirmed our hypothesis but was opposite to the effect of increased resistance to extinction usually found with partial reinforcement. In order to see whether the presence of the reliable predictor was indeed the crucial factor, we ran two special control groups of 8 Ss each, one with the usual partial reinforcement procedure and one with 100%

reinforcement. These groups were identical in all respects to those of the Main Experiment, except that the reliable predictor, S_2, was omitted. When these groups were tested, the partial reinforcement group tended to press more for the stimuli than did the continuous reinforcement group (though the difference between the group means, 128.6 vs. 115.6, was not statistically significant). However, the difference between these two groups was in the opposite direction and significantly different ($F = 5.71$; $df = 1/35$; $P < .025$) from the difference found between Test Session 1 means of the 32 Ss of the Main Experiment tested with S_1 during Test Session 1. Thus it appears that the presence of S_2, the reliable predictor of food, did play the crucial role in determining the direction of the results obtained in our tests of the secondary reinforcing value of S_1.

DISCUSSION

Our situation differed from those in which the effect of partial reinforcement on the establishment of secondary reinforcement has been studied (e.g., Klein, 1959; Zimmerman, 1957, 1959) in that during training all our Ss had a reliable predictor of food. The seemingly crucial importance of the presence or absence of a reliable predictor during training may help to explain the apparently conflicting results obtained from single-group vs. separate-group experimental designs in determining the effects of partial reinforcement on the strength of a secondary reinforcer (e.g., D'Amato, Lachman, & Kivy, 1958). It may be that partial reinforcement will increase resistance to extinction of a secondary reinforcer only if training occurs in the absence of a reliable predictor.

It should be noted that our formulation of the conditions necessary for the establishment of a secondary reinforcer is compatible with the well-known "discriminative stimulus hypothesis" of secondary reinforcement (Keller & Schoenfeld, 1950; Schoenfeld, Antonitis, & Bersh, 1950). Furthermore, our results with respect to S_2: Group B vs. Group A could perhaps be considered analogous to those reported by Notterman (1951) in studies using rats as Ss in both a Skinner box and a straight alley.

SUMMARY

Albino rates ($N = 88$, male) were trained to press a bar for food, then divided randomly into two groups and trained as follows for 135 trials in the same Skinner boxes with the bars removed: two stimuli, when paired, ended together and always preceded food. For Group A, the second, shorter stimulus (S_2) was always redundant because the first stimulus (S_1) had already given reliable information that food was to come. But for Group B, S_2 was informative, because for them S_1 also occurred sometimes alone without food.

After the training sessions, the bars were reinserted, bar pressing was retrained with food pellets, extinguished, and then retrained again, this time using 1 sec. of one of the training stimuli as a secondary reinforcer in place of the food. The total number of bar presses in 10 min. following the first occurrence of the secondary reinforcing stimulus was used as the measure of secondary reinforcing strength. The testing procedure was repeated after 48 hr. using the other training stimulus as secondary reinforcer, so that all Ss were tested with both stimuli in a balanced sequence.

Control experiments were run to provide baseline levels for pseudo-conditioned and unconditioned rates of pressing, and for any activating effect of the stimuli.

As predicted, S_2 was a stronger secondary reinforcer when it was informative than when it was redundant; S_1 was a more effective secondary reinforcer than S_2 in that group for which S_2 was a redundant predictor of primary reinforcement. In addition, S_1 was a more effective secondary reinforcer when it had been a reliable predictor of food.

REFERENCES

D'Amato, M. R., Lachman, R., & Kivy, P. Secondary reinforcement as affected by reward schedule and the testing situation. *J. comp. physiol. Psychol.*, 1958, 51, 737–741.

Hull, C. L. *Principles of behavior.* New York: Appleton-Century, 1943.

Keller, F. S., & Schoenfeld, W. N. *Principles of psychology.* New York: Appleton-Century-Crofts, 1950.

Klein, R. M. Intermittent primary reinforcement as a parameter of secondary reinforcement. *J. exp. Psychol.*, 1959, 58, 423–427.

Miller, N. E. Learnable drives and rewards. In S. S. Stevens (Ed.), *Handbook of experimental psychology.* New York: Wiley, 1951. Pp. 435–472.

Miller, N. E. Liberalization of basic S-R concepts: Extensions to conflict behavior, motivation, and social learning. In S. Koch (Ed.), *Psychology: A study of a science.* Vol. 2. New York: McGraw-Hill, 1959. Pp. 196–292.

Miller, N. E. Analytical studies of drive and reward. *Amer. Psychologist*, 1961, 16, 739–754.

Notterman, J. M. A study of some relations among aperiodic reinforcement, discrimination training, and secondary reinforcement. *J. exp. Psychol.*, 1951, 41, 161–169.

Schoenfeld, W. N., Antonitis, J. J., & Bersh, P. J. A preliminary study of training conditions necessary for secondary reinforcement. *J. exp. Psychol.*, 1950, 40, 40–45.

Skinner, B. F. *The behavior of organisms.* New York: Appleton-Century, 1938.

Wyckoff, L. B., Sidowski, J., & Chambliss, D. J. An experimental study of the relationship between secondary reinforcing and cue effects of a stimulus. *J. comp. physiol. Psychol.*, 1958, 51, 103–109.

Zimmerman, D. W. Durable secondary reinforcement: Method and theory. *Psychol. Rev.*, 1957, 64, 373–383.

Zimmerman, D. W. Sustained performance in rats based on secondary reinforcement. *J. comp. physiol. Psychol.*, 1959, 52, 353–358.

3.6 INSTRUMENTAL LEARNING OF VASOMOTOR RESPONSES BY RATS: LEARNING TO RESPOND DIFFERENTIALLY IN THE TWO EARS*

Leo V. DiCara and Neal E. Miller

Abstract. *Curarized and artificially respirated rats were rewarded by electrical stimulation of the brain for changes in the balance of vasomotor activity between the two ears. They learned vasomotor responses in one ear that were independent of those in the other ear, in either forepaw, or in the tail, or of changes in heart rate or temperature. In addition to implications for learning theory and psychosomatic medicine, these results indicate a greater specificity of action in the sympathetic nervous system than is usually attributed to it.*

In previous studies from this laboratory, we have discussed the importance of the instrumental learning of visceral responses for theories of learning and psychosomatic medicine, and have summarized the literature; we have presented evidence that the instrumental learning of cardiac, gastrointestinal, and renal responses can occur in curarized rats, with the use of either the onset of rewarding brain stimulation or the offset of mildly painful electric shock to the tail as reinforcement (1).

DiCara and Miller (2) have shown that vasomotor responses in the tail of the rat can be modified by instrumental learning. The purpose of the experiment we now report was to determine whether such vascular learning can be made specific to a given structure, such as one ear. In order to accomplish this, individual measures of vasomotor responses in the ears of the curarized rat were fed into a bridge circuit so that the differences in vasomotor activity between the two ears could be detected. The output of the bridge circuit was then fed in parallel into two pens of a Grass polygraph. One pen, the tip of which was constructed of a brass ballpoint, traced the between-ear difference over the surface of a plate constructed of 25 strips of brass, each 1.7 mm wide, inlaid into a flat piece of Plexiglas and separated from each other by 0.3 mm. When these strips were appropriately connected to programming equipment, reward consisting of electrical stimulation of the brain (ESB) could be delivered whenever the pen tracing the difference between the two ears was on or beyond a specified "reward criterion" strip. The second pen traced an

* Reprinted from Science, 1968, 159, 1485–1486. Copyright 1968 by the American Association for the Advancement of Science, and reproduced by permission.

185

ink record of the exact movements of the first pen. Other pens recorded the separate responses of each ear.

Subjects were 12 male rats of the Sprague-Dawley strain (394 to 558 g), implanted with permanent monopolar electrodes aimed at the medial forebrain bundle with Krieg stereotaxic coordinates of 1.5 mm posterior to bregma, 8.5 mm below the surface of the skull at 1.5 mm lateral to midline. Subsequent histologic examination showed that all of the electrode tips were located in the medial forebrain bundle at the level of the ventromedial nucleus [for details of general method, see (3)].

During vasomotor conditioning, the subject lay prone in a harness-supported cloth sling, placed in a soundproof, ventilated enclosure equipped with a loudspeaker delivering a 1000-hz tone at 82 db. The sling was cut so as to allow the subject's forepaws to hang down through the opening and rest on a small platform support. Grass photoelectric plethysmograph transducers were used to measure the vasomotor activity in the ears, forepaws, and tail. Recordings were taken at a sensitivity of 0.1 mv/cm for the ears, and 1.0 mv/cm for the forepaws and tail. The transducers were rigidly mounted on swivel arms attached to the metal frame of the harness so that the arms could be adjusted in all directions to place the photocells in homotopic positions on the ears (bisecting the central artery) and forepaws. The photocell used to measure vasomotor activity in the tail was placed at the base of the tail, and the tail was elevated about 3 cm to allow excreted boluses to pass without disturbing the position of the photocell. Heart rate was measured with previously implanted stainless steel electrodes, and temperature was measured by a thermistor probe inserted 4 cm into the rectum. A Grass Model 5 polygraph was used for all recordings.

Three to 4 days before vasomotor training, and approximately 2 weeks after electrode implantation, a current ranging from 30 to 100 μa was adjusted for each subject in order to elicit maximum rates of bar pressing for 0.5 second of 60-cycle a-c ESB. Current was then held constant, and on the next 2 days each subject was trained on fixed-interval schedules. During this training, a 1000-hz tone was turned on whenever bar pressing would secure ESB, and turned off during the time-out intervals (lengthened progressively: 5, 10, 20, 30 seconds), at which time the subject was in silence and ESB was not available.

The day after the above training, subjects were injected intraperitoneally with 3 mg of d-tubocurarine chloride per kilogram of body weight in a solution containing 3 mg/ml; the animals were fitted with a specially constructed face mask and artificially respirated, with the ratio of inhalation to exhalation being 1:1 (70 cycle/min, and a peak pressure of 20 cm-water). Additional d-tubocurarine was infused intraperitoneally at 1.0 mg per kilogram of body weight per hour throughout the experiment.

At the end of a 60-minute habituation period, vasomotor training began. Of the 12 rats used in this experiment, six were rewarded for relatively greater vasodilatation in the right ear (which could also be relatively less vasoconstriction), and the other six were rewarded for relatively greater vasodilatation in the left ear. Assignment to groups was random except for the last two subjects, that had to be assigned to the group rewarded for left-ear dilatation. All subjects had ESB electrodes located on the right side of the brain.

Training consisted of the presentation of trials signaled by the onset of the 1000-hz tone, during which the subject could obtain ESB for making the proper vasomotor response, and time-out or intertrial intervals during which the subject remained in silence and ESB was not available. A total of 300 trials was presented on a variable-interval schedule with a mean intertrial interval of 30 seconds (range: 10 to 50). The fifth trial and every tenth trial thereafter were test trials during which ESB could not be obtained for the first 7.5 seconds of the trial, so that vasomotor performance could be measured without contaminating effects from having the tone turned off or ESB turned on. On the tenth trial and every tenth one thereafter, subjects received so-called blank trials each lasting 7.5 seconds, during which vasomotor activity was recorded, but the subjects remained in silence and could not achieve reward. Throughout training ,each block of 20 trials was analyzed, and the criterion level (that is, the difference in vasomotor activity between the two ears required to obtain ESB) was made more difficult if the time to achieve reward fell below an average of 5 seconds and easier if it was above 10 seconds.

The results are presented in Fig. 3.6–1. Since the resistance of the photocell in the photoelectric transducer depends on the amount of light reaching it, changes in vasomotor activity have been expressed as changes in resistance of the photocell. The subjects rewarded for relatively greater vasodilatation in the right as compared to the left ear showed significant increases in dilatation of the right ear ($P < .01$) and significant decreases in vasodilatation of the left ear ($P < .01$), with the difference between the two ears at the end of training being highly significant ($t = 10.12$, $P < .001$). Subjects rewarded for relatively greater vasodilatation in the left as compared to the right ear showed significant vasodilatation of the left ear ($P < .01$) but did not show a significant change in vasomotor activity in the right ear. However, despite the lack of significant vasomotor changes in the left ear in this group, the increase in the difference between the ears during training, as well as the difference at the end of training ($t = 5.18$, $P < .001$), was highly significant.

During training, the between-paw difference in vasomotor response was not significantly correlated with the between-ear difference ($\rho = -.22$), and at the end of training there was no significant difference between the paws ($t = .32$).

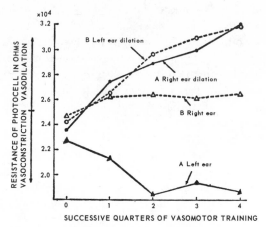

SUCCESSIVE QUARTERS OF VASOMOTOR TRAINING

FIGURE 3.6–1   Learning a difference between the vasomotor responses of the two ears, Group A was rewarded for relatively more dilatation of the right ear; Group B was rewarded for relatively more dilatation of the left ear.

These results indicate that the learned differences between the vaso-motor responses of the two ears were specific to the ears and not to the entire right or left side of the rat's body. Analyses of heart rate, vasomotor activity in the tail, and temperature did not indicate any significant overall changes either between groups at the end of training or within groups during training; however, both groups showed slight increases in vasoconstriction of the tail and in body temperature. In previous experiments on heart rate, rats learned the discrimination of changing their heart rate during the time-in stimulus, when such a response would be rewarded, rather than during the time-out intervals between trials, when it would not. However, analyses of vasomotor responses on blank and test trials in the present experiment did not indicate any evidence of discrimination learning.

The experiment described here adds to an increasing list of successful attempts to secure instrumental learning of visceral responses mediated by the autonomic nervous system, and represents a striking example of the specificity of the learning which can be achieved. Since the vasomotor innervation to the ear of the rat is primarily, if not wholly, sympathetic, the results indicate that the sympathetic nervous system has a greater capacity for specific local activity than usually has been attributed to it. The specificity of visceral learning is further supported by the finding that changes in either heart rate or intestinal contraction can be learned without changes in the other response (4). Furthermore, Miller and DiCara (5) have secured instrumental learning of changes in urine formation, accompanied by changes in renal blood flow but independent of heart rate and blood pressure, and of vasomotor responses in the tail. The specificity of learning of a variety of visceral responses demonstrated in these experiments makes it difficult to salvage the strong traditional belief that the instrumental learning of visceral responses is impossible by trying, as Black (6) has done, to explain the visceral changes produced by training as the indirect effects of somatic learning mediated by the cerebrospinal nervous system.

Finally, if changes in the blood flow to organs other than the kidney can be learned, and if these changes have the specificity that our experiment has demonstrated for the vasomotor responses of the ears, such changes could have significant consequences for psychosomatic medicine.

REFERENCES AND NOTES

1. N. E. Miller, Ann. N.Y. Acad. Sci. 92, 830 (1961); ———, Proc. World Congr. Psychiat. Montreal 3, 213 (1963); ——— and A. Carmona, J. Comp. Physiol. Psychol. 63, 1 (1967); L. V. DiCara and N. E. Miller, ibid., 65, 8, 1968.
2. L. V. DiCara and N. E. Miller, Commun. Behav. Biol., in press.
3. N. E. Miller and L. V. DiCara, J. Comp. Physiol. Psychol. 63, 12 (1967).
4. N. E. Miller and A. Banuazizi, ibid., 65, 1, 1968.
5. N. E. Miller and L. V. DiCara, in preparation.
6. A. H. Black, paper presented at the 7th annual meeting of the Psychonomic Society. St. Louis, 1966.
7. Supported by USPHS grant MH 13189 to N.E.M. One of us (L.V.D.) is an advanced research fellow of the American Heart Association.

3.7 ATTITUDE CHANGE BY RESPONSE REINFORCEMENT: REPLICATION AND EXTENSION*

William A. Scott

Within the framework of S-R learning theory an attitude may be regarded, like a habit, as an implicit anticipatory response which mediates overt behaviors, and arises out of them through reinforcement (6). Such

* Reprinted from Sociometry, 1959, 22, 328–335. Copyright 1959 by the American Sociological Association, and reproduced by permission. The research reported in this article was supported by a grant from the Foundation for Research on Human Behavior (Ann Arbor, Michigan).

a conception provided the basis for an earlier study (9) of the effect on attitudes of rewarding relevant verbal behaviors. The purposes of the present experiment were to substantiate the earlier results with different operations, to investigate the effects of response reinforcement on subjects with neutral, as well as extreme, attitudes, and to determine whether or not the induced attitude change were "permanent."

Briefly, the design of the earlier study (9) was as follows: Pairs of students were selected from a number of general psychology classes and asked to debate any of three different issues on which they had previously expressed their opinions. However, both members were required to defend sides of the issue opposite to those which they actually held. The excellence of their presentations was to be judged by class vote, but this vote was falsified so that a predetermined member of each pair won. Posttests of subjects' attitudes showed that the "winners" had changed in the direction of debate significantly more than the "losers" and more than a group of control S's, while the "losers" did not change significantly more than the controls.

This study had used only S's with initially extreme attitudes, and no provision had been made for a second posttest to determine the extent to which the attitude changes persisted. Therefore, a new experiment was designed to fill these gaps. Although the design was conceptually similar to the previous one, the actual operations differed in several respects: different issues were presented, S's debated under different conditions, and the nature of the reinforcing stimuli was different. Given these innovations in operations (not in conceptualization), it was felt that corroborative results would better serve to substantiate the theory on which the experiments were based than would replication by identical operations.

METHOD

Attitudes of students toward three different controversial issues were assessed in several General Psychology classes, by the following open questions:

    1. *Curriculum.* If you had the job of laying out a curriculum of required courses for all undergraduates at CU, what kinds of courses would you lay most emphasis on—those related to the study of scientific facts and research methods, or courses dealing with social problems and courses which help the student learn more about people?

    2. *Fraternities and sororities.* Some people feel that fraternity and sorority life contributes a great deal to the development of the student during his college career. Others feel that fraternities and sororities work to the detriment of students by taking their attention away from more important academic matters. What do you think about this?

3. *Ideal husband or wife.* If you were thinking of getting married, which kind of a husband or wife would you rather have: One who is mainly interested in people and enjoys being with people, or one who has a wide variety of interests and creative talent in some area?

Immediately after this pretest, a general invitation was addressed to the classes to participate in an elimination debate contest, the winners of which would share a $100 cash prize. The investigator's interest was reported to be "to find out what kinds of people hold what kinds of attitudes." A couple of weeks later volunteers were contacted by phone and asked to take a particular side of one of the three issues for debate. The sides were assigned irrespective of Ss' initial positions, so that some debators defended their own opinions, some the opposite opinions, and some debated "off-neutral" (they expressed no clear opinion on the pretest, but were assigned a definite position in the debate). The only restrictions were to keep these three groups (same, opposite, and off-neutral) approximately equal and to give equal representation to each of the three issues. S's were told that debate positions were being assigned irrespective of actual attitudes, because "the purpose of the study is to see how well people can present opinions they don't actually hold, and how well their opponents can judge their own true attitudes."

The debates took place in a small research room, with the two S's seated at one end of a long table, and three judges at the opposite end. For every debate, two of the judges were professors of psychology, and the third was a mature graduate student; E was one of the judges at every debate, but the other judging professor and the graduate student were changed several times throughout the experiment. Introductions were formal, as was the decorum of the entire procedure. None of the S's had known his opponent prior to that time. It was explained that the winner of this first debate would be contacted for a second debate, and if he won that, as well as a third debate, he would receive a $20 prize. S's presented their initial arguments for five minutes each, followed by two-minute rebuttals in reverse order.

Each judge, in turn, rendered his decision on the relative merits of the two performances. The reasons he offered for his decision were confined to the manner of presentation (style, clarity, convincingness, etc.), rather than to the content of the talk, in order to minimize the possible influences of prestige suggestion which might be entailed if the judgment referred to the substance of the argument (e.g., "that was a good point"). The winner in each case had been predetermined in systematic fashion, so that all the judges had to do during the debate was to jot down plausible reasons for their decisions.

Following the judgment, S's were led to small individual rooms near the debate room, where they filled out questionnaires on the three issues, identical with those from the pretest. E indicated that "we are interested in seeing how you feel about these matters at this time," without explicitly indicating that opinions were expected either to change or to remain constant. In addition there was the question, "How do you think your opponent *really* feels about this issue?" included simply to maintain the pretext previously offered for the study.

Winning S's were called back about ten days later to debate a different issue. Their positions were again assigned irrespective of their true attitudes, and the debating situation was as before, except that judgments of win or loose were based on merit (as the judges saw it).[1] There were no predetermined winners or losers, so occasionally there was a split vote among the three judges; but E always voted last, in order to make the decision as clear and definite as possible. A second posttest of attitudes toward the three issues was obtained. (S's wrote in separate rooms.)

Winners of the second debate were recalled for a third time, to debate the remaining issues of the three. The consequences of this contest were made clear, and S's were given the choice of "winner take all" ($20) or "split the prize" ($15 and $5). Three pairs chose the former division; two, the latter. Again the voting of judges was genuine; a third posttest of attitudes toward all three issues was obtained.

Attitudes expressed in the pretest and on the three posttests were typed on 3″ × 5″ cards, numbered in such a way as to disguise their sources (see 9). These were then coded by E on a seven-point attitude scale, representing a neutral position and three degrees of intensity toward each extreme of the issue—e.g.:

1. Greek organizations are very definitely a help.
2. Greek organizations are a help.
3. Greek organizations are mainly a help, but also some hindrance.
4. Don't know; not ascertained; equally a help and a hindrance; depends on the individual.
5. Greek organizations are mainly a hindrance, but also some help.
6. Greek organizations are a hindrance.
7. Greek organizations are very definitely a hindrance.

Check-coding, by an independent judge, of a sample of these attitudes showed their coding reliability to be .87.

RESULTS

Of principal interest is the comparison of winners and losers on the first round of debates, for in that series they were randomly determined. The results are presented in the top part of Table 3.7–1, which shows that winners tended to change toward the side debated more than did losers or controls. (The control group was composed of those volunteers who could not be scheduled during the first debate series. Their posttest attitudes were assessed just after the third debate series, approximately one month after the pretest.)

Attitude changes following the second and third debates were comparable to those in the first debate (see bottom of Table 3.7–1). It will be recalled that, here, the decisions were not predetermined, but depended on performance as estimated by the judges.

TABLE 3.7–1   Mean Attitude Changes of Winners, Losers, and Controls

Group of Subjects	N	Mean Change*	S.D. of Change	Differences in Mean Changes
First Debate				
(A) Winners	20	+1.67	1.55	A vs. B: $t = 2.76$; $p < .01$
(B) Losers	20	+0.15	1.83	A vs. C: $t = 3.80$; $p < .001$
(C) Controls	15	+0.24	0.47	B vs. C: $t = -0.20$; NS
(D) Winners ten days later	20	+1.20	1.66	D vs. C: $t = 2.40$; $p < .05$
Second Debate				
(A) Winners	10	+1.40	1.80	A vs. B: $t = 1.29$; NS
(B) Losers	10	+0.36	1.62	
Third Debate				
(A) Winners	5	+2.80	1.72	A vs. B: $t = 2.88$; $p < .05$
(B) Losers	5	-0.20	1.17	

* A positive sign indicates a mean change in the direction of debate; or, for control S's, a mean change opposite to their original position. For control S's with initially neutral attitudes the directions of changes were assigned alternatingly positive and negative signs. One-tail tests of significance were used throughout.

Also of interest are the findings concerning "permanence" of the effects of reinforcement. As previously noted, all 20 S's who participated in the second debate were tested concerning their attitudes toward the issue of the first debate. From their responses it is possible to estimate the degree of "savings" from the first posttest to the second posttest— approximately ten days later. It is clear from the data in Table 3.7–1 ("first debate: Winners ten days later") that attitudes expressed on the second posttest are different, both from the pretest attitudes, and from the first posttest attitudes. Thus, there is a significant degree of savings from the first reward experience, even though the reinforcement is not explicitly repeated; but the amount of savings is less than the amount of initial change.

Since S's were assigned debate positions regardless of their own true attitudes, it is possible to see whether or not the response reinforcement

TABLE 3.7–2   Mean Attitude Change as a Function of the Relationship between S's Pretest Attitude and Debate Position

Group of Subjects	N	Mean Change*	S.D. of Change	Differences in Mean Changes
Debating Opposite Side				
(A) Winners	10	+2.77	1.97	
(B) Losers	10	+0.90	1.05	A vs. B: t = 2.53; p < .05
Debating Off-neutral				
(A) Winners	11	+1.47	1.25	A vs. B: t = 1.62; p < .10
(B) Losers	13	+0.54	1.44	
Debating Own Side				
(A) Winners	7	+0.63	0.86	A vs. B: t = 2.15; p < .05
(B) Losers	13	−0.77	1.89	

* A positive sign indicates a mean change in the direction of debate. One-tail tests of significance are reported.

was effective when it operated in the same direction as S's initial attitude, or when it aimed at moving him from a neutral position. Table 3.7–2 shows the results of the debates, grouped according to the relationship between S's initial attitudes and his debate position. When S's debated "opposite sides," the absolute change of winners was largest (2.77 on a seven-point scale). When debating "off-neutral," the mean change was 1.47, and the mean change of winners debating their "own sides" was 0.63 toward a more extreme position in the same direction. A comparison of absolute changes in position is deceptive, however, since S's debating "opposite sides" had the greatest room for movement, and those debating "own sides" had the least. Relative to the amount of movement (in the direction of reinforcement) possible, the three groups showed changes of 55 per cent, 49 per cent, and 63 per cent, respectively. But since there is no way of comparing scale intervals at various points on the dimension, it would be mere sham to conclude anything about the relative effects of response reinforcement under the three circumstances. All one can say is that winners tended to change in the direction of debate more than losers did, regardless of whether they debated their own positions, opposite positions, or off-neutral.

DISCUSSION

The results of this study suggest, first of all, that the effects of response reinforcement on attitude change are not necessarily transitory, but may be preserved up to periods of at least ten days. On the one hand, this may seem surprising, since, during the interval between tests, S's were presumably living within the same social contexts that had supported their initial attitudes. Thus one might expect them to revert to their old positions as soon as they were removed from the reinforcing situation. On the other hand, the occasion for the second posttest was so nearly identical with that for the first posttest, that the cues present could well have served to reintegrate the former response, even though it did not conform to S's true attitude at that time. In a more imaginative study, one might attempt a follow-up assessment of Ss' attitudes in a completely different context, with someone other than E eliciting the relevant response.

A second result suggests that response reinforcement can be effective either in strengthening previously held attitudes, in changing them, or in creating new ones (if those S's debated "off-neutral" can be said to have developed "new" attitudes). There was no evidence to indicate that S's with neutral attitudes were more amenable to change than those with more extreme views. Such an outcome might have been expected in the light of the frequently reported finding that people who hold intense attitudes, or who are quite certain of their opinions, are relatively resistant to pressures to change (1, 2, 5, 7, 8). However, with less than interval-scale measures, it is difficult to compare relative movements at different positions on the attitude scale. Moreover, the status of the initially "neutral" attitudes is by no means clear, since that category included S's who expressed balanced opinions on both sides of the issue as well as those who replied "no opinion." It seems to this writer that neutrality of an attitude as such is probably not the critical feature for predicting susceptibility to change, but rather it is the degree to which the attitude, of whatever direction or strength, is embedded in a cognitive structure of other supporting attitudes and cognitive elements. (This quality of "embeddedness" has been referred to elsewhere as *cognitive consistency* [10, 11].)

The major significance of the study, however, would seem to lie in its confirmation of previously obtained results (9) not by exact replication, but by "methodological triangulation" (3). Whereas the earlier experiment required S's to debate in front of their fellow classmates and "rewarded" them by class vote, the present procedure involved debates in a private setting with reinforcement by judges' decisions and monetary reward. Moreover, the issues debated were different from those previously used. Thus one can safely maintain that the hypothesized relationship is not exclusively dependent on the particular methods chosen to assess it. When a number of different sets of empirical operations yield comparable results, it is reasonable to presume that they reflect a valid relationship (i.e., one that is independent of the measuring procedures), rather than just a reliable relationship (one that depends on a particular instrument or experimental design) (cf., 4).

SUMMARY

S's were invited to participate in a series of debates, in which they defended positions on three different issues irrespective of their own opinions. Comparison of their pretest attitudes with those expressed immediately following the debates indicated that S's who "won" (by judges' decision) tended to change their attitudes in the direction of the position presented. This result confirmed that of a previous experiment in which S's debated under different conditions and were reinforced by vote of their classmates. The effect on "winners" in this study occurred regardless of whether they debated their own side of the argument, the opposite side, or from an initially neutral position. Some permanence of the change was evidenced on a second posttest about ten days after the initial winning. "Losers" in the debate did not change their attitudes significantly more than a control group of non-debaters.

NOTE

1. This shift in the basis for determining winners was largely for ethical reasons. Though a random choice of winners was necessary for purposes of experimental control, once this had been achieved on the first round of debates, there appeared to be no reason why virtue should not be rewarded.

REFERENCES

1. Birch, H. G., "The Effect of Socially Disapproved Labelling upon Well-structured Attitudes," *Journal of Abnormal and Social Psychology*, 1945, 40, 301–310.
2. Burdick, H. A., "The Relationship of Attraction, Need Achievement, and Certainty to Conformity under Conditions of a Simulated Group Atmosphere," *Dissertation Abstracts*, 1956, 16, 1518–1519.
3. Campbell, D. T., *A Study of Leadership among Submarine Officers*, Columbus: Ohio State University, Personnel Research Board, 1953.
4. Campbell, D. T., and D. W. Fiske, "Convergent and Discriminant Validation by the Multitrait-multimethod Matrix," *Psychological Bulletin*, 1959, 56, 81–105.
5. Carlson, E. R., "Attitude Change through Modification of Attitude Structure," *Journal of Abnormal and Social Psychology*, 1956, 52, 256–261.
6. Doob, L. W., "The Behavior of Attitudes," *Psychological Review*, 1947, 54, 135–156.
7. Hochbaum, G. M., "The Relation between Group Members' Self-confidence and their Reactions to Group Pressures to Uniformity," *American Sociological Review*, 1954, 19, 678–687.
8. Osgood, C., and P. H. Tannenbaum, "The Principle of Congruity in the Prediction of Attitude Change," *Psychological Review*, 1955, 62, 42–55
9. Scott, W. T., "Attitude Change through Reward of Verbal Behavior," *Journal of Abnormal and Social Psychology*, 1957, 55, 72–75.
10. Scott, W. A., "Rationality and Non-rationality of International Attitudes," *Conflict Resolution*, 1958, 2, 8–16.
11. Scott, W. A., "Cognitive Consistency, Response Reinforcement, and Attitude Change," *Sociometry*, 1959, 22, 219–229.

Four
The Principles
of Reinforcement

We have seen the use of reinforcers ranging from flashing lights to candy bars, and the modification of responses ranging from vasodilation in the right ear to attitudes toward Greek fraternities. Rather than clarifying the status of reinforcement, however, this evidence sharpens our dilemma: Why is behavior so hard to control when reinforcement is potentially effective in such a wide variety of situations? In this chapter we will examine some of the conditions that determine reinforcement's effectiveness, and we will look at the results that can be obtained when it is used under optimal conditions.

Delay of Reinforcement

One possible explanation for the ineffectiveness of reinforcement is that it normally occurs long after the response has been completed. In our discussion of classical conditioning we saw that the CS and US must be contiguous for learning to occur, and it seems reasonable that a similar relationship might hold for reinforcement, that a response and a reinforcer must occur together if we are to learn their relationship. In order to test this hypothesis the delay of reinforcement was manipulated in several experiments with rats, and the results generally confirmed the importance of delay. There were, however, some puzzling discrepancies.

Wolfe (1934) studied the effects of delayed reinforcement in a T-maze. Subjects were reinforced for choosing the correct arm at a choice point in the maze, but before reaching the goal box containing food they were confined in a delay box. Wolfe varied the delay between making the correct response and being released into the goal box, and found that subjects with longer delays took longer to learn the correct path. Even with reinforcement delays of 20 minutes, however, subjects still showed some signs of learning.

A very different result was reported in 1943 by Perin. He varied the delay of reinforcement after rats pressed a bar inserted into their cage, and found learning to be impossible with a delay of even 30 seconds (instead of bar-pressing, many subjects went to sleep). Why the difference in the results of these experiments? Why was learning still possible with a delay of 20 minutes in Wolfe's T-maze while in Perin's situation a delay of 30 seconds was already too great? A seemingly paradoxical answer was proposed by Kenneth Spence (1947), who said the variability in the effects of delayed reinforcement was due to the fact that there was no delay! The ostensible source of reinforcement, food, was indeed delayed, but Spence said that *secondary* reinforcers were present in both experiments, and occurred immediately after the response. The difference between Wolfe's and Perin's results was due not to variability in the effects of delay but to variability in the strength of the secondary reinforcers.

In the Wolfe study, said Spence, the delay box became a secondary reinforcer because it was immediately followed by the presentation of food. In the Perin study there was no comparable source of *exteroceptive* secondary reinforcement, but there were *proprioceptive* reinforcers. Exteroceptive receptors such as the eye and ear respond to stimuli originating in the external environment, but we also have proprioceptive receptors within the body which are stimulated by muscular contractions. When the rats pressed the bar in the Perin study they would have produced proprioceptive stimuli, and Spence argued that *traces* of that stimulation might still have been present when food occurred. If so, the proprioceptive stimuli would have become secondary reinforcers, and their presence immediately after the response would explain why learning occurred despite short delays of primary reinforcement. The inability of Perin's subjects to learn with the longer delay was attributed by Spence to the absence of secondary reinforcement in that condition. The strength of a secondary reinforcer depends upon its contiguity with the primary reinforcer, and in Perin's 30-second delay condition the proprioceptive traces might have already disappeared by the time food was presented, and so would not have become secondary reinforcers. In the Wolfe study, on the other hand, visual stimuli from the delay box were still present throughout the delay period, so that even with long delays the delay box stimuli were still closely followed by food.

Spence's explanation of the available evidence was ingenious, but it was also completely hypothetical. He offered no direct evidence that Wolfe's delay box had functioned as a secondary reinforcer, much less for the existence of proprioceptive secondary reinforcement in Perin's experiment. Furthermore, if Spence was correct, it was difficult to see how one could ever eliminate immediate proprioceptive reinforcement in order to test the true effects of delays in primary reinforcement.

These problems were overcome in a brilliant experiment by Robert Grice (Article 4.1). Grice recognized that it would be difficult if not impossible to prevent proprioceptive stimuli from becoming secondary reinforcers. Instead of trying to eliminate secondary reinforcement for the correct response, Grice reasoned, a more effective strategy would be to provide equivalent secondary reinforcement for the incorrect response! If both correct and incorrect responses are followed by secondary reinforcement, their effects should be neutralized, and any learning would have to be the result of delayed primary reinforcement. Specifically, Grice designed a brightness discrimination apparatus in which subjects were reinforced for entering whichever of two alleys was the correct brightness. Since the position of the correct alley varied randomly over trials, turns to the left and right were reinforced equally often, and thus the proprioceptive stimuli following both these responses would have become secondary reinforcers. His results showed that learning was significantly slower when reinforcement was delayed for even one second, and became almost impossible after delays of as little as five seconds.

Together, the experiments of Wolfe, Perin, and Grice suggest that reinforcement must occur immediately after a response if learning is to take place. The reinforcer need not be primary—exteroceptive and proprioceptive secondary reinforcers are also effective—but whatever reinforcer is used should be presented as quickly as possible. To some extent this result may seem counterintuitive, since so many of our rewards seem to be effective despite relatively long delays (for example, grades, wages). In part, this appearance of effectiveness may be deceptive (do students and workers really work as hard as they can?), but reinforcement often does seem to control our behavior despite substantial delays. We still know very little about the mechanisms involved, and can only speculate whether covert verbal mediation might play a role similar to that of proprioceptive feedback ("I've got to keep working if I'm going to earn that bonus"). Until these mechanisms are better understood, however, the best practical advice remains to present reinforcement as soon as possible when trying to strengthen behavior.

Schedules of Reinforcement

In the experiments we have discussed up to this point responses were usually reinforced every time they occurred. *Continuous reinforcement* of this kind is often a convenient rule for use in the laboratory, but in the real world reinforcement rarely occurs so consistently. A worker receives his wages once a week or once a month, a child is only occasionally praised when he cleans his room, an undergraduate receives grades only two or three times a term. Even in situations where reinforcement is supposed to be continuous, such as in starting a car on a cold day or operating a vending machine, the all too common experience is *intermittent* or *partial reinforcement*.

Because of the ubiquity of partial reinforcement in everyday life, psychologists have devoted a great deal of effort to trying to understand how it affects behavior. Several partial reinforcement *schedules*, or rules of reinforcement, have been extensively studied in the laboratory, of which the two most common are *ratio* and *interval* schedules. In a ratio schedule, a specified number of responses must be emitted before a response can be reinforced. In piece work, for example, a worker's bonus depends on the precise number of units that have been completed. In an interval schedule, on the other hand, the availability of reinforcement is determined by the passage of time. Trips to the mail box, for example, are usually reinforced every 24 hours, regardless of how many trips occur in the interim.

Further complicating matters, schedules can also be distinguished by whether the requirement for reinforcement is *fixed* or *variable*. In a *Fixed Interval* (FI) schedule, for example, the required interval before reinforcement is always the same, whereas in a *Variable Interval* (VI) schedule the interval varies. Thus in an FI 60-sec schedule sixty seconds must elapse after a reinforcement before another response can be reinforced, whereas in a VI 60-sec schedule the *average* interval will be sixty seconds, but it might sometimes be as short as five seconds and at other times as long as two minutes.

To test your understanding of these schedules, consider the following graph:

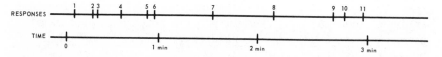

If every vertical mark on the "response" line represents a response, and if Response 1 has already been reinforced, what other responses would be reinforced if the schedule was:

1. FI 60-sec
2. FR 5

The correct answers are given at the end of the chapter.

Learning the distinctions among the various schedules can be tedious, but these differences can have important consequences for behavior. FI 60-sec and VI 60-sec schedules, for example, both reinforce responses on the average of once every minute, so that we might expect fairly similar behavior under the two schedules, but in fact the average response rates and response patterns are very different. The following figure shows typical VI and FI performance plotted as a cumulative response record, where every point represents the total number of responses emitted from the beginning of the session until that point in time. Every diagonal mark represents the occurrence of reinforcement.

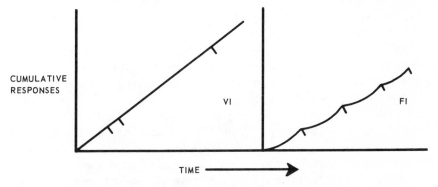

In a VI schedule subjects tend to respond at a moderately high rate throughout the session, but in an FI schedule the average rate is lower, and follows a cyclical pattern. Immediately after reinforcement, the response rate falls to almost zero, and then steadily increases to a maximum value immediately before the next reinforcement. Because of its appearance, this response pattern is called an FI *scallop*.

Why do these schedules produce such different effects even though each delivers reinforcement on the average of once a minute? One possible explanation is that animals, whether pigeons or men, have an innate ability to measure time, and that they quickly learn to use time as a cue for when to respond. In a VI schedule, for example, reinforcement can occur at any time and so subjects maintain a steady rate of responding, whereas in an FI schedule a response is never reinforced immediately after reinforcement and so subjects don't respond then. As time passes, however, the probability of reinforcement increases, and so subjects increase their rate of responding. Reynolds and Catania (Article 4.2) tested this explanation by giving their subjects a discrimination problem in which the only cue was the passage of time. They presented pigeons with stimuli of different durations and reinforced responses after some of these stimuli but not after others. If pigeons can truly discriminate time, they reasoned, they should respond most strongly after the precise time interval that was reinforced and should show progressively less responding as the interval presented was either increased or decreased. This was exactly the result they obtained, suggesting that the passage of time can act as a stimulus controlling responding.

Another possibility, however, is that pigeons use not time but their own behavior as a cue telling them when to respond. If responses in a sequence differed in some discriminable aspect, subjects could use their own responses as cues as to whether reinforcement was likely. In running a mile, for example, racers might use their own state of fatigue as a cue concerning how much farther they had to run, and modulate their behavior accordingly. Similarly for subjects on a Fixed Interval schedule, it is conceivable that some aspects of their own responding might be a cue for the imminence of reinforcement, and Donald Mintz (Article 4.3) has provided evidence that such cues are indeed available. He trained his subjects on a Fixed Ratio schedule and measured not only when responses occurred but the force with which they were emitted. He found that subjects progressively increased their response effort with each response in the sequence, and concluded that the force of each response could well have served as a cue for subsequent behavior.

The experiments of Reynolds and Catania, and of Mintz indicate that either time or response force *could* serve as a cue controlling Fixed Interval behavior, but they do not directly demonstrate such control. In order to determine which of these potential stimuli was truly controlling FI behavior, Dews (Article 4.4) first trained pigeons on an FI schedule, and then periodically turned off the house light during the fixed interval. Darkness reduces the pigeon's tendency to respond, so that if responding was controlled by cues from prior responses, then turning off the house light should disrupt the normal sequence of cues. If time were the cue for responding, however, responses during light periods should be unaffected by the prior periods of darkness. Dews found exactly this result, indicating that FI behavior is primarily controlled by cues originating from the passage of time.

The control of behavior by reinforcement schedules is far more complex than we have been able to indicate by this brief sketch, but hopefully the experiments described give some feeling for the variety of behavior produced and the subtlety of control involved. Simply saying that a response has occasionally been reinforced is not enough: the effects of reinforcement depend on the precise schedule involved. In training a child to work steadily, for example, it would be a mistake to check his progress only at regular, hourly intervals: the all-too-likely result would be work at equally regular hourly intervals.

Motivation

Imagine a mother trying to teach her two sons arithmetic. In previous lessons they have been bored and listless, utterly uninterested in anything but going outside to play. Finally, as a last resort, she decides to use reinforcement, promising them candy whenever they solve a problem. She starts the new strategy with her first son immediately after lunch, but the exasperating result is no progress. He continues to play with his pencil and daydream, requiring more than one hour to solve the ten simple problems she has given him. After a long rest for her nerves, she tries again later in the afternoon with her second son, but now the effect is almost magical—he immediately begins to work hard and solves all of the problems within 15 minutes.

Why did the same reward have such different effects? There could have been differences between the children, between the mother's behavior in the two situations, and so on, but perhaps the simplest explanation is that one child was hungry and the other wasn't! Our willingness to work for food would obviously depend on how hungry we are, and common sense suggests that hunger would have been greater several hours after eating than immediately. In fact, psychologists have reversed this logic and have *defined* hunger in terms of hours of deprivation rather than by the sensations of hunger which may wax and wane in a somewhat random pattern. By definition, then, the twins differed in hunger *drive* and we can explain their behavior by assuming that drive level determines learning.

Before we turn to the experimental evidence on this question, however, consider another situation. Suppose that the next day the twins are tested in school on their knowledge of arithmetic. Should the twin who learned under the high drive now do better? If drive affects learning, the answer is obviously yes; but another possible explanation is that drive affects not learning but performance. Hunger, for example, may play a role in performance or response selection (Should I eat or go to sleep?), but not necessarily in what is learned once a response is made. The hungrier twin might have been more willing to study in order to earn the candy, but as long as both eventually solved all the problems, they might have learned equally.

We have, then, two questions: Does drive affect reinforcement, and if so is the effect on learning or on performance? Hillman, Hunter, and Kimble (Article 4.5) studied the first question by training two groups of rats to run down a maze for food reward. One group was

203

run after 2 hours of food deprivation, the other after 22 hours, and the result was that the 22 hour group ran faster, even though both groups received the same reward. This confirms our earlier hypothesis that drive determines the effect of reinforcement, but of course it does not indicate whether the effect is really on learning or on performance. To find out, Hillman *et al.* then reversed the drive levels for half the subjects in each group. If drive affects learning, the group trained on low drive should have learned less than those trained on high drive, and thus subjects suddenly switched to high drive should do worse than subjects trained on the high drive throughout. If drive only determines performance, however, both low- and high-drive groups should have learned equally during training, and should therefore perform identically once their drives are equalized.

The results were that all groups did perform the same once drives were equalized, indicating that drive's effect is on performance rather than on learning. This is not a trivial effect, since performance is generally what we are most concerned about, but it does suggest certain limitations on the role of drive in learning. In fact, even in the realm of performance high drive is not *necessarily* beneficial. On difficult tasks a very high drive may actually hinder performance, a phenomenon formally recognized as the Yerkes-Dodson Law. Severe hunger, for example, may lead to better performance in training a child to clean his room for food reward, but it may have disastrous effects on teaching him mathematics.

In addition to drive level, a second determinant of motivation is amount of reinforcement. Our willingness to respond increases with the magnitude of the reinforcement we can obtain, but as in the case of drive the effect seems to be on performance rather than learning. Crespi (1944), for example, in the classic study in this area trained rats to run down an alley for food, and gave different groups either a small or a large reward. The large-reward group ran faster, but when the amounts were changed the small-reward group quickly reached the level of the large-reward group. In fact, the group switched from small to large reward actually did *better* than the group trained on large reward throughout! Crespi called this enhanced performance an "elation effect," and found a comparable "depression effect" for subjects suddenly switched from a large to a small reward.

The elation and depression effects, now called *contrast effects*, show that the motivational or *incentive* value of a reinforcer depends heavily on the subject's past history. We sometimes think of rewards as having fixed values—a candy bar is this good, a hot dog is that good—but in fact incentive value is affected by a variety of conditions. The same candy bar may be highly reinforcing to a child used to M & Ms, but a very poor reinforcer for one accustomed to banana splits. This effect is clearly shown in the experiment by DiLollo and Beez (Article 4.6), who were able to dramatically change the incentive value of food by varying the amount of reward given during training. Rats were reinforced for running down a straight alley, with different groups receiving from 1 to 16 pellets during training. The greater the reward during training, the *slower* the subjects ran during the test phase, when they all received the same one pellet reward. The depression effect, in other words, is greater for subjects who are used to larger rewards.

Applications

In the two previous chapters we've looked at a number of powerful techniques for controlling behavior—powerful, at any rate, for controlling the behavior of a rat. Do these principles also apply to human behavior? Can basic aspects of human behavior really be changed through the simple-minded principles of primary and secondary reinforcement?

There are many reasons for thinking not. Most of the research, after all, has been done with rats, and men are simply not rats. We argued in the first chapter that the gulf between rats and men might be narrower than is commonly assumed, but still there *are* differences, and it seems unlikely that the principles of animal and human behavior would be identical. Besides, if reinforcement is so powerful, why is behavior so hard to control? The principles of reward have been known for centuries, but children seem to be as intractable and society as discontented as ever.

One possible explanation for past failures of reinforcement may be ignorance—the importance of *immediate* reinforcement, for example, has not always been obvious, and there are many other aspects of reinforcement which we still understand only vaguely. Perhaps a more important problem, however, has been the failure to apply known principles consistently. Too often reinforcers are presented in an arbitrary and haphazard fashion: the teacher reinforces the favored pupil while ignoring the rest; the parent is attentive and loving one day, irritable and capricous the next. If the principles of reinforcement were used systematically and consistently, psychologists have argued, the results might be very different.

Suppose, for example, that *all* good behavior received immediate secondary reinforcement, perhaps a token that could be exchanged for a variety of primary reinforcers. Could large changes in behavior be produced by such a simple procedure? Atthowe and Krasner (Article 4.7) tested this question by establishing a *token economy* in the psychiatric ward of a hospital. Special privileges such as candy and passes were distributed only in exchange for tokens, and patients earned these tokens by any of a variety of adaptive behaviors, such as cleaning themselves or their rooms, reading, talking to each other, and so forth. Over a one-year period the authors found not only significant changes in the specific behaviors reinforced, but also a general decrease in apathy and withdrawal, and most dramatically a substantial increase in the rate of discharge, this in a ward not previously noted for its success rate (the average patient had already been in the hospital for twenty-two years!).

An attempt to modify the behavior of a rather different subject population was reported by Fred Keller (Article 4.8). Mixing the principles of reinforcement with a little common sense, Keller developed a new system for teaching psychology to undergraduates, and found he was able to dramatically increase not only the students' effort but their grades and even their enjoyment of the course! His system, sometimes called "100 percent mastery," is applicable to virtually any subject matter and, though no statistics are available, it appears to be spreading rapidly throughout the country.

Though more controlled research is obviously necessary, the use of token economies and 100 percent mastery systems appear to have been extremely successful. Token economies, for example, have also been used in institutions for mental retardates (e.g., Baldwin, 1967) and juvenile delinquents (e.g., Phillips, 1969; Cohen, Filipzak, Bis, and Cohen, 1966), and even in classroom situations (e.g., O'Leary and Drabman, 1971), and in almost all cases dramatic improvements have been reported. This success does *not* prove that reinforcement is the only possible teaching technique, nor that men are simply overgrown rats, but it does suggest that we may have underestimated the power of reinforcers in modifying behavior. Reinforcement seems to be an extremely potent principle, as effective for students as for psychotics or retardates.

Answers to the Schedule Problem

1. Responses 7 and 9. In this schedule an interval of 60 seconds must elapse after every reinforcement before another response can be reinforced, and Response 7 is the first response to occur at least 60 seconds

after Response 1 was reinforced. Similarly, Response 9 is the first response to occur at least 60 seconds after Response 7.

2. Responses 6 and 11. In an FR 5 schedule, reinforcement is delivered after every fifth response, and Response 6 is the fifth response after Response 1, and Response 11 is the fifth response after Response 6.

| THE RELATION OF SECONDARY REINFORCEMENT
TO DELAYED REWARD IN VISUAL
DISCRIMINATION LEARNING*

G. Robert Grice

INTRODUCTION

Delayed reward is a problem of central importance for reinforcement theories of learning. In his goal gradient hypothesis, Hull (4) postulated that the strength of the association formed between a response and its accompanying stimuli is inversely related to the length of the delay by which the reward follows the response. The gradient was assumed to be logarithmic in form. This hypothesis was supported by the delayed reward experiments of Hamilton (3) and Wolfe (11), both of which showed learning to be a decreasing function of the delay of reward. These studies indicated also that the gradient extended for a considerable period of time following the response. Subsequently, Hull (5) pointed out the possibility that the learning after long delays in the Wolfe and Hamilton experiments might have been the result of immediate secondary reinforcement. In both of these maze learning experiments the Ss were detained in delay compartments for a period of time prior to entering the goal box. It was suggested that the delay boxes, being followed by reward, might have become secondary reinforcing agents.

In an attempt to minimize secondary reinforcement immediately following the response to be learned, Perin (6, 7) employed a Skinner-type box in which the lever pressing response, the delay, and the reward all occurred in the same compartment. The results of these experiments indicated that learning under such conditions was impossible with delays of about 30 sec. or longer. On the basis of these findings, Hull (5) postulated a short primary delay of reinforcement gradient of about 30 sec. The longer goal gradient was then derived from this by assuming the development of secondary reinforcement within the 30-sec. period, and the gradual moving forward of such secondary reinforcing property in the stimulus response sequence.

* G. Robert Grice, "The Relation of Secondary Reinforcement to Delayed Reward in Visual Discrimination Learning," *The Journal of Experimental Psychology*, 38, 1948, 1–16. Copyright 1948 by the American Psychological Association, and reproduced by permission. A dissertation submitted in partial fulfillment of the requirements for the degree of Doctor of Philosophy in the Department of Psychology in the Graduate College of the State University of Iowa. The writer is indebted to Professor Kenneth W. Spence who directed the investigation.

Further evidence of the importance of secondary reinforcement in delayed reward learning is provided in an experiment by Perkins (8). Perkins employed a covered T-maze of which both the top and bottom were opal-flashed glass, thus eliminating all extra-maze cues. The possibility of secondary reinforcement by the two different delay boxes was eliminated by interchanging the two delay compartments so that each was followed by reward half of the time. When a group for which the delay compartments were interchanged in this manner was trained with 45 sec. delay, it was found to learn significantly more slowly than another 45 sec. delay group for which the same delay box was always followed by food. This difference in rate of learning was attributed by Perkins to the action of secondary reinforcement in the case in which the delay compartments were not interchanged, and to the elimination of differential secondary reinforcement by the shifting procedure. Perkins then went on to study learning in the T-maze as a function of delay with the delay compartments interchanged. He obtained a function which dropped more sharply than that obtained by Wolfe, and which showed only a barely significant amount of learning with 120 sec. delay.

Spence (10), in a recent analysis of this problem, has suggested that even the shortened gradients obtained by Perin and Perkins may be the result of immediate secondary reinforcement. His suggestion is that while these experiments may have succeeded in eliminating differential secondary reinforcing stimuli from the external environment, such stimuli may have existed *within* the animal. Thus the particular pattern of proprioceptive stimulation following the correct response would presumably persist within the organism for a short period, and might still be effective at the time of reward. In such an event, the proprioceptive pattern of stimulation coincident with the reward would acquire secondary reinforcing properties through its association with the immediate food reinforcement. On subsequent occurrences of the response, the proprioceptive stimuli resulting from the act, being similar to the proprioceptive traces persisting until the moment of reinforcement, could, through generalization, provide immediate secondary reinforcement. The length of delay during which learning could occur, would depend then upon the length of time that the changing proprioceptive stimulus trace remained sufficiently similar to that at the time of the response to permit generalization.

Under such an interpretation there is no need for the assumption of a primary delay of reinforcement gradient, as all instances of learning under delayed reward conditions would be accounted for by immediate secondary reinforcement. This formulation relieves the learning theorist of the embarrassing problem of explaining how a reward can work backwards to strengthen a stimulus-response association, when the response was made some time earlier.

One possible experimental test of this interpretation is to introduce delay of reward in a non-spatial type of discrimination learning problem, e.g., visual discrimination learning. In spatial discrimination problems such as the T-mazes used by Wolfe and Perkins, the S is forced to make different spatial responses, turning right or left, which provide very different proprioceptive stimulation. Since one of these responses is consistently followed by reward, and the other is never reinforced, differential proprioceptive secondary reinforcement may be built up so long as the proprioceptive traces of the different acts are discriminably different at the moment of food reward. However, in the non-spatial visual discrimination situation, it is possible to eliminate such immediate secondary reinforcement based on differential proprioceptive stimulation. Since the positions of the positive and negative stimuli are shifted irregularly from left to right, each motor response of turning left or right is correct half of the time and incorrect half of the time. This condition means that neither pattern of proprioceptive stimulation acquires greater secondary reinforcing strength than the other. The remaining possibility of immediate secondary reinforcement in this type of learning problem is that the stimulus traces of the visual stimuli provide the basis of the differential stimulation. So long as a trace of the positive stimulus is effective at the time of reward, this trace may become a secondary reinforcing agent, and the positive stimulus itself might then come to provide immediate secondary reinforcement. The limit within which delayed reward learning could take place in a visual discrimination problem would depend then on the time that the after-effects (stimulus traces) of the positive and negative stimuli remain discriminably different.

A further implication of the above analysis for visual discrimination learning is that it should be possible to improve learning with delayed reward by experimentally introducing immediate secondary reinforcement. For example, if the positive stimulus itself, or stimuli within the range of its generalization gradient, were present at the time of reward, this stimulus should acquire secondary reinforcing properties, and would then provide immediate reinforcement, thus increasing the speed of learning, and lengthening the delay with which learning might occur. Furthermore, if the Ss were *forced* to respond with characteristically different motor patterns to the different choice stimuli, the proprioceptive traces of the response to the correct stimulus should, within limits, acquire secondary reinforcement properties, and extend the delay of reinforcement gradient.

Several investigators have employed delayed reward in visual discrimination situations. Wood (12) using chicks in a brightness discrimination found learning to be a decreasing function of delayed reward up to five min. However, the chicks were delayed only following correct choices. Following errors they received immediate electric shock. Thus, the avoidance of shock on correct trials may have provided immediate reinforcement, and the experiment is not an uncomplicated delayed reward situation. Wolfe (11), in a black-white discrimination experiment with rats, found no learning with delayed reward when the delay followed both correct and incorrect responses. However, when the door was blocked providing immediate frustration of wrong responses, results were obtained similar to those of his T-maze experiment. Like the Wood experiment, this one is also probably not a genuine delayed reward situation. The delay compartment, which after the delay always leads immediately to food, would acquire secondary reinforcing properties. Under Wolfe's procedure, only correct responses are followed by entrance into the delay compartment. Thus, immediate secondary reinforcement is provided for correct responses but not for incorrect responses. Wolfe's incidental finding, that learning is greatly retarded when delays follow choices of both stimuli, has been verified by two other investigators. Riesen (9), using a red-green discrimination with chimpanzees, found greatly retarded learning with one- and two-sec. delays, and one of two Ss failed to learn with four sec. delay. There was no evidence of learning with eight sec. delay. However, several specially trained Ss, trained to respond differentially to the stimuli, were able to learn with eight sec. delay. Gulde (2), in a study with rats in a black-white discrimination, found no evidence of learning in 200 trials with five sec. delay.

In the present experiment, the learning of a black-white discrimination problem was studied as a function of the time of the delay of reward, in order to ascertain the limit and form of this relationship. The function presumably depends on the stimulus traces of the black and white stimuli. Second, the effect of introducing immediate secondary reinforcement was studied. This was accomplished first by the black and white goal boxes, so that following a choice of either black or white, the animal, after the delay, always entered a goal box of the same color as the stimulus chosen. The final experiment was to force the animal to make characteristically different motor adjustments to the black and white stimuli. Learning in this situation was then compared with that in a problem of equal delay of reward in which no such characteristically different motor responses were made.

SUBJECTS AND APPARATUS

The Ss were 75 experimentally naive, female, albino rats from the colony maintained by the department of psychology of the State University of Iowa. Their ages ranged from 80 to 110 days at the beginning of the experiment. They were assigned at random to the experimental groups.

The apparatus consisted of a black-white discrimination box. The ground plan is shown in Fig. 4.1–1. The rat was placed in the starting box from which it passed through a two-in.-wide alley into the choice chamber. From this point it could enter either a black or a white painted alley. The floor of the half of the choice chamber leading to the black alley was painted black and the floor of the half leading to the white alley was white. In each alley two in. from the entrance there were black or white curtains the same color as the alley. The section of the apparatus which made up the black and white alleys and the floor of the choice chamber consisted of three identical alleys with the two outer ones white and the middle one black. By sliding this section back and forth, the black and white alleys could be shifted from right to left. After passing through either the black or white stimulus alley, the animal entered a neutral gray alley which was used as a delay compartment, and could be varied in length from 18 to 72 in. The goal boxes were continuations of these alleys and were 15 in. long. All alleys except the narrow starting alley were four in. wide and four in. high. With the exception of the black and white alleys, the entire apparatus was painted a neutral gray. The choice chamber and the stimulus alleys were covered with clear glass and all others were covered with hardwarecloth. Vertical sliding doors, which prevented retracing, were located at the entrances to the stimulus alleys, at the beginning of the delay compartments and at the entrances to the goal boxes. The doors were operated by E from behind a one-way vision screen at the starting end of the apparatus.

The lighting was indirect from two shaded 200-watt bulbs. The brightness of the floor of the white alley just in front of the curtain was 1.515 apparent foot candles. The brightness of the floor of the black alley at the same point was 0.071 apparent foot candles.

In order to force the animals to make characteristically different motor responses to the black and white alleys, different obstacles could be placed in them. One of these sets of obstacles consisted of a 15-degree incline, nine in. long, which began one in. beyond the curtain. The other

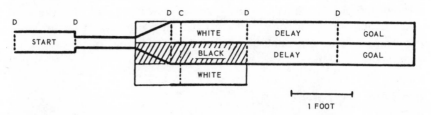

FIGURE 4.1–1 Ground plan of the experimental apparatus. Doors are represented by heavy dotted lines at the points D. Curtains are represented by the light dotted line at C.

consisted of two blocks 2¼ by five in. and the same height as the alley. One block was placed on the left side of the alley one in. beyond the curtain. The second was placed on the right side of the alley two in. beyond the first. This forced the animal, after passing the curtain, to pass through a five-in. section of alley 1¾ in. wide, make a sharp jog to the left, and continue through another narrow five-in. section before entering the delay compartment. Both the blocks and the inclines were available in black and white, so that the blocks could be in the white alley and the incline in the black, or the reverse. Removable black and white goal boxes were made of quarter-in. plywood. These boxes fitted inside of the gray goal boxes and could be shifted from the left to the right side.

PRELIMINARY TRAINING

All animals were adapted to a 24-hour feeding scheldule for at least a week prior to preliminary training. They were fed in individual cages and received eight gm. of Purina Laboratory Chow daily. This diet and feeding procedure were the same throughout the experiment. During the experiment they were fed immediately after the daily runs.

For the preliminary training, neutral gray alleys were substituted for the black and white stimulus alleys. On the first day the rats were placed in the goal box and allowed to eat ten 0.3 gm. pellets of Purina Chow. They remained in the goal box for 15 min. The animals which were assigned to the zero delay group were fed in the removable gray alleys, and all others were fed in the regular gray goal boxes at the end of the 18-in. delay compartment. Next, the animals were placed in the gray alley between the curtain and the door at the entrance to the alley and were allowed to run through the alley and the delay compartment to the goal box where they received one .15 gm. pellet of food, which was the standard reward throughout the experiment. There were four such runs, two on the left side and two on the right. The zero-delay animals received food in the movable alley and did not run through the delay compartment. On the second day there were four more such runs. On the third and fourth days the animals were placed in the starting box and allowed to run through the gray alleys to food. They received 10 runs each day, forced half to the right and half to the left in a random order. The forcing was accomplished by closing one of the doors at the choice point. The purpose of these 20 forced trials was to help equalize position habits. The animals in the differential response group received their forced runs with gray blocks and a gray incline, otherwise identical to the black and white ones, placed in the gray alleys. Runs through the blocks and over the incline were divided equally between left and right.

EXPERIMENTAL PROCEDURE

Gradient Experiment

In the experiment proper, all animals were trained to go to the white alley. All animals had either no initial color preference or a preference for the black. Three animals with initial white preferences were eliminated. There were 10 free choice trials per day for the first 200 trials and 20 trials per day after that. The white alley was alternated from left to right in the order RLRRLLRLLRLRLLRRLRRL. All trials were separated by at least two min. Animals were run until they reached the criterion of learning, which was 18 out of 20 trials correct, with the last 10 perfect. One animal was discontinued after failing to learn in 700 trials and four after failing to learn in 1440 trials.

Groups of animals were run under six different delay of reward conditions. The zero delay group received food immediately in the white alley. The 0.5 sec. delay group was allowed to run through the 18-in. delay compartment with the doors open and was rewarded in the goal box following choices of the white alley. The 1.2 sec. delay group ran through a 36-in. delay alley with the doors open and the 2 sec. delay group ran through a 72-in. alley. The times 0.5, 1.2 and 2 sec. were determined by timing the animals on each run. The time measured was that from the leaving of the black or white alley to the entrance into the goal box. These times are the means for each group, of the median times for each animal in the group. The median times ranged from 0.4 to 0.6 sec. for the 1.5 sec. group, from 1.1 to 1.3 sec. for the 1.2 sec. group, and from 1.5 to 2.4 sec. for the 2.0 sec. group. The distributions of delay times for individual animals were all positively skewed in the manner typical of such time data. The mean semi-interquartile ranges of these distributions were 0.1 sec. for the 0.5 sec. group, 0.2 sec. for the 1.2 sec. group and 0.2 sec. for the 2.0 sec. group. The five-sec. delay group was delayed for five sec. in the 18-in. delay compartment by leaving the goal box door closed for five sec. after the animal entered the delay compartment. The delay for the 10 sec. group was accomplished in a similar manner. In all groups the delay was the same following correct and incorrect choices. Following all choices of the white, the rat received the pellet of food in a glass cup placed at the end of the goal box and was allowed to eat in the goal box. Following choices of the black there was no food or cup in the goal box, and the animal was allowed to remain in the box approximately the same amount of time as in the case of correct choices.[1] There were 10 animals in each group except in the 10 sec. delay group in which there were only five.

Secondary Reinforcement Groups

One group of 10 rats was under the same conditions as the regular five sec. group except that the goal box following choices of the white alley was white with a white food cup, and the box following choices of the black was black with no reward. The delay compartments were gray as in the regular five sec. group. The black and white goal boxes were placed inside the regular gray ones and were shifted from left to right to correspond with the stimulus alleys.

Another group of 10 rats was run under the five sec. delay conditions, with the blocks in one color alley and the incline in the other. Half of the animals had the incline in the white alley with the blocks in the black, and half had the reverse arrangement. White was correct in both cases, and both the delay compartments and the goal boxes were gray as in the original five sec. delay group.

RESULTS

Gradient Experiment

The number of trials required by each S to reach the criterion of learning is shown in Table 4.1–1. The median number of trials for the zero delay group was 20; for 0.5 sec., 95 trials; for 1.2 sec., 200 trials; for 2 sec., 290 trials, and for 5 sec., 580 trials. In the five sec. group one animal was discontinued after failure to learn in 700 trials and another after 1440 trials. No median is available for the 10 sec. delay group since three of the five Ss failed to learn in 1440 trials. It was not possible to apply the t-test of statistical significance to the differences between the groups because the assumptions of normality and homogeneous variance were not fulfilled, and because there were some indeterminate values in cases where animals failed to learn. However, a test proposed by Festinger (1) which makes no assumptions as to the form of the distributions was applied. All differences between adjacent groups were significant at the five percent level of confidence or higher. The results of the test for the comparisons made with this test are shown in Table 4.1–2.[2]

Learning curves for the six groups for 700 trials are shown in Fig. 4.1–2. These curves represent the percent of correct choices for successive blocks of 20 trials. Each S is assumed to continue at the 100 percent level after reaching the criterion. Tests with several animals showed this to be the case with only very slight deviation.

Gradient curves to show learning as a function of delay are shown in Figs 4.1–3 and 4.1–4. In Fig. 4.1–3 the reciprocal of the number of

TABLE 4.1–1 Number of Trials Required by Each Animal to Reach the Criterion, and the Median Number for Each Experimental Group

Sec. of delay	0	0.5	1.2	2	5	10	5 sec. Black and White Goal Boxes	5 sec. Differ- ential Responses
	20	100	220	300	320	840	80	320
	20	110	160	150	350	850	180	380
	10	60	160	190	250	1440+	160	600
	20	140	280	440	560	1440+	130	270
	20	90	230	360	700+	1440+	130	210
	10	40	140	370	350		140	390
	10	100	250	260	600		150	350
	10	90	230	440	650		200	170
	30	130	180	240	1440+		270	140
	20	80	170	280	1260		180	270
Median	20	95	200	290	580	(1440+)	155	295

trials required by each group to reach the level of 75 percent correct choices is plotted against the time of the delay of reward.[3] Fig. 4.1–4 shows a gradient based on the percent of correct choices for each group during trials 141–180. The sigma value, based on the percent correct, is assumed to be a measure of the difference in habit strength between the correct and incorrect responses.[4] The fact that the 10 sec. group is below zero reflects the fact that this group had, at this stage of learning, not yet overcome a slight initial preference for the black alley.

TABLE 4.1–2 Results of the Festinger Test of the Significance of the Differences between the Groups in the Number of Trials Required to Reach the Criterion of Learning

The P-values are the levels of confidence at which the hypothesis may be rejected that the two groups compared were drawn from the same population.

Groups Compared	d	P
0 vs. .5 sec.	5.00	.01
0 vs. 1.2 sec.	5.00	.01
.5 vs. 1.2 sec.	4.05	.01
.5 vs. 2.0 sec.	5.00	.01
1.2 vs. 2.0 sec.	3.25	.05
1.2 vs. 5.0 sec.	4.20	.01
2.0 vs. 5.0 sec.	3.20	.05
5 sec. vs. B & W Boxes	4.90	.01
5 sec. vs. different responses	3.00	.05

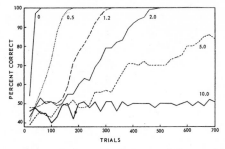

FIGURE 4.1–2 Learning curves for each of the six different delay groups.

Secondary Reinforcement Experiments

The two groups of concern in this portion of the experiment are the five sec. delay group with the black and white goal boxes, and the five sec. delay group in which the animals were forced to make different responses to the two stimulus alleys. These groups may be compared to the five sec. group in the gradient experiment, where no differential secondary reinforcement was present. The numbers of trials required by each animal to reach the criterion are shown in Table 4.1–1. The medians were 155 for the black-white goal box group and 295 for the differential response group as contrasted with 580 trials for the five sec. control group. Again

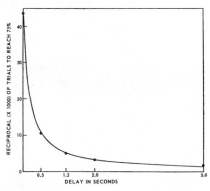

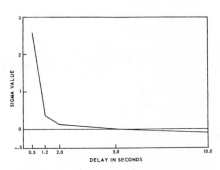

FIGURE 4.1–3 Rate of learning as function of delay of reward. The reciprocal × 1000 of the number of trials to reach the level of 75 percent correct choices is plotted against the time of delay. Experimental values are represented by black dots and the smooth curve is fitted to these data.

FIGURE 4.1–4 Sigma values based on the percent of correct responses during trials 141–180 for each delay group.

the *t*-test of statistical significance could not be applied. According to the test used above, the difference between the black-white goal box group and the five sec. control group is significant at the one percent level of confidence, and the difference between the differential response group and the control group is significant at the five percent level.

The learning curves for the three groups are shown in Fig. 4.1–5. They are plotted as percent correct for blocks of 20 trials. The rate of learning for the black-white goal box group is clearly much more rapid than the other two. The difference between the differential response group and the control group was tested by applying the *t*-test for related measures to the differences between blocks of 20 trials for the 300 trials from 141 to 440. The mean number correct in each block of 20 trials was obtained for each group. Since the differences between these means approximated a normal distribution the *t*-test was appropriate. A *t* of 3.61 was obtained, which for 14 degrees of freedom means that the hypothesis that the mean difference is zero may be rejected at the one percent level of confidence. This means that the two curves differ significantly, and that the differential response group did learn at a significantly faster rate than the rats in the control condition.

DISCUSSION OF RESULTS

One fact of primary interest in the above data is the steepness and short duration of the obtained delay of reinforcement gradient. It should be pointed out that the discrimination problem itself was a very easy one, as shown by the unusually low median number of 20 trials required to learn the problem with no delay. It is significant that a delay of even one-half sec. required almost five times that number of trials, and that

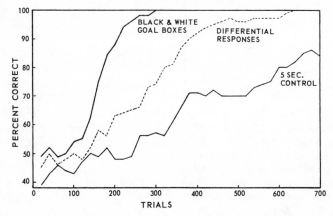

FIGURE 4.1–5   Learning curves for the three different groups with 5-sec. delay.

at five sec., the median trials to learn increased to 580 and two animals failed to learn in 700 and 1440 trials respectively. Ten sec. delay was apparently beyond the limit under which learning was possible for three of the five Ss, and the other two were able to learn only after about 850 trials. The discrepancy between the results of this study and those of Wolfe (11) and Perkins (8) is shown strikingly in Fig. 4.1–6, in which sigma values similar to those of Fig. 4.1–4 are plotted against length of delay. Perkins' experiment differed from Wolfe's in that differential secondary reinforcement in the delay boxes was eliminated by alternating the two delay boxes in a random order and by rotating the maze in the room. However, there was the possibility of secondary reinforcement based on the reinforcement of the proprioceptive trace of the consistently correct turning response. However, this possibility was eliminated in the present experiment, since there was no motor response pattern which was always correct. The difference between Perkins' results and those of this experiment may be accounted for by the presence of such secondary reinforcement in the one but not in the other.

The gradient obtained here is also steeper and shorter than that obtained by Perin (7). The results of the two experiments are compared in Fig. 4.1–7. Both of the gradient curves are based on the slopes of group learning curves which were plotted as percent of correct trials. Perkin's learning curves ranged from zero to 100 percent correct responses. The slopes plotted for his experiment are the slopes of the tangents to the fitted learning curves at the 50 percent point. The learning curves

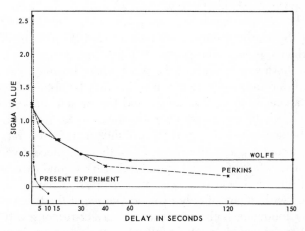

FIGURE 4.1–6   Sigma values from blocks of trails for the various delay groups in the Wolfe, Perkins and present experiments. The blocks of trials included for each of the three experiments are as follows: Wolfe—trials 7, 8, 9, and 10; Perkins—first 36 trials; present experiment—trials 141–180.

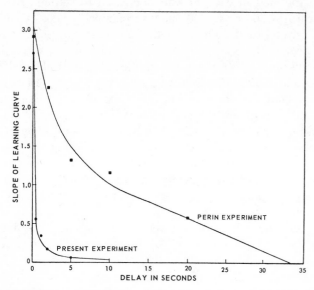

FIGURE 4.1–7 Rate of learning as a function of time of delay in the Perin and present experiments. The slopes of the group learning curves are plotted against the time of delay of reward. The Perin experimental data are represented by black squares and the present data by black circles. The smooth curves are fitted to the empirical data.

of the present experiment range from 50 to 100 percent correct. Since the middle portions of these curves were approximately linear, the slopes plotted in the gradient curve are the slopes of straight lines fitted to the portions of the learning curves between 60 and 90 percent. These two gradients then represent the slopes of the learning curves (the rate of learning) of both experiments at the point where learning was half completed.[5] Perin's results indicate that learning may be obtained in his situation up to about 30 or 35 sec. delay, and the present data suggest that the limit is about 10 sec. or possibly less for most Ss. Again the discrepancy may be accounted for by the possibility that Perin's rats obtained immediate secondary reinforcement from the proprioceptive cues following the act. A fact of interest is that in Perin's second experiment (7), involving a differentiation between two bar-pressing habits, no learning was obtained with delays of only two and five sec. if the bar was removed immediately following both correct and incorrect responses. It was only when the bar remained in place following the incorrect response, but was removed immediately following the correct response, that the 30-sec. gradient was obtained. The result of this difference in procedure was probably to make the difference between the correct and incorrect responses greater. The removal of the bar following response would certainly affect the postural adjustments to the bar and those immediately following the act of pressing the bar. Thus the pattern of response following removal of the bar would always be reinforced, while that following the incorrect response and the bar remaining in place would never be reinforced. Apparently the difference between the two motor patterns was not enough to provide differential secondary reinforcement unless this additional difference were introduced. Another factor is that the occurrence of massed, non-reinforced incorrect responses with the bar in place would tend to eliminate that response through the process of extinction.

If there is no true primary gradient of reinforcement, as previously suggested, the question may be raised as to why even the short gradient effect was obtained in the present experiment. One plausible answer is that the basis of the secondary reinforcement is the perseverative stimulus trace or sensory after-effect from the black or white stimulus. So long as any traces of the black and white stimuli remain discriminably different at the time of reward, there is the possibility of differential secondary reinforcement. The stimulus trace from the positive white stimulus in the choice chamber could thus acquire secondary reinforcing potency through generalization from its perseverative trace which is contiguous with the food reward. The data suggest that the traces or the differences between them decrease rapidly during the first sec., are at a very low level at the end of five sec., and have more or less disappeared at the end of 10 sec. or are sufficiently different from those at the choice point to be beyond the range of generalization.

The black-white goal box experiment demonstrates clearly the effect of secondary reinforcement in delayed reward learning. The stimulus, being present at the time of reward, acquired secondary reinforcing properties. Thus, upon orienting toward and entering the white alley, the S received immediate secondary reinforcement. The result was a marked speeding up of learning, even though the food reward itself was delayed for five sec.

The fact that animals which were forced to make consistently different motor responses to the two stimuli learned at a significantly faster rate than the Ss for which this was not the case, may be interpreted in terms of proprioceptive secondary reinforcement as described in the Perin and Perkins experiments. In this group there were not only different visual traces following the different choices but also entirely different afferent traces resulting from the different postural and motor adjustments required in the two alleys. It is reasonable to assume that in the rat such differential proprioceptive stimulation effects would continue longer than the visual after-effects. As stated above, the limits of delay with which learning may occur would depend on the length of time during which these two proprioceptive traces remain discriminably different. During the period in which this difference between the traces remains, the food reward following correct responses will produce and strengthen secondary reinforcing properties for the trace of the stimuli produced by the correct response. No such reward is associated with the traces of the incorrect response. As long as the trace of the correct response is within the range of the generalization gradient of the proprioceptive pattern stimulating the organism at the time of the response in the white alley, this proprioceptive pattern will acquire secondary reinforcing properties. It is this immediate secondary reinforcement that accounts for the superiority of the differential motor response group over the five sec. delay group with no such differential motor response.

SUMMARY

1. Groups of white rats were run on a black-white discrimination problem with delays of reward of 0, 0.5, 1.2, 2, 5, and 10 sec.

2. A very steep delay of reinforcement function was obtained within this range, with no learning by three of five Ss in the 10 sec. group.

3. When immediate secondary reinforcement was introduced by allowing the animal to eat in a goal box of the same color as the positive stimulus, learning with delayed reward was greatly facilitated.

4. When animals were forced to make characteristically different motor responses to the black and white stimuli, they learned at a significantly faster rate than animals which received equal delay, but made no such characteristically different motor adjustments.

5. The data are consistent with a theory which assumes no "primary" delay of reinforcement gradient, but accounts for learning under delayed reward conditions in terms of some type of immediate secondary reinforcement. Such secondary reinforcement may be based upon proprioceptive stimulation resulting from the response and continuing until the moment of the reward. The proprioceptive pattern accompanying the correct response acts as a secondary reinforcing agent by virtue of its similarity to the traces which on previous trials have lasted until the reward. In the usual visual discrimination learning situation no differential proprioceptive stimuli follow correct and incorrect choices. In such situations, learning is possible with only very short delays of reward. What learning does occur may be attributed to immediate secondary reinforcement from the visual stimuli. This secondary reinforcement is presumably based on traces of the visual stimuli which continue until the time of the primary reward.

NOTES

1. The use of no food cup, rather than an empty one, in the goal box following incorrect responses reduces the possibility of secondary reinforcement following wrong responses, and probably, in part, accounts for the unusually rapid learning of the zero delay group.
2. The test of statistical significance proposed by Festinger (1) is based on a pooled ranking of the measures in the two groups to be compared. It is then possible to make statements of probability about the sum of ranks of one group. The test yields a statistic, 'd,' which may be referred to tables giving the values of 'd' for various N's required for significance at the one and five percent levels of confidence. Strictly speaking, the hypothesis tested is that the two groups of measures are samples drawn from the same population, but the test is believed by Festinger to be most sensitive to differences between means. The only assumptions involved are that the two samples are independent and drawn at random.
3. Mathematically this function may be represented by a hyperbola of the reciprocal type. The equation for the curve fitted to the data of Fig. 4.1–3 is:

$$R = \frac{1}{.023 + .14T}$$

where R is the reciprocal $\times$ 1000 of the number of trials to reach 75 percent correct, and T is the time in sec. of the delay of the reward.
4. This measure, suggested by Hull (5), is based on the assumption that the excitatory strengths of the two competing responses oscillate from moment to moment according to the normal probability function. Consequently, their difference would also oscillate in this manner. The result is that, when the tendencies are equal, there is a 50 percent choice of each response, and as the difference between them increases, the percent of choice of the stronger increases until the ranges of oscillation no longer overlap, and one response is chosen 100 percent of the time. Any percent of occurrence of one response may be converted into an amount of difference value by means of the normal integral table. This gives a standard score representing the difference between the excitatory (habit) strengths of the competing responses.
5. The curve fitted to the data from the present experiment in Fig. 4.1–7 is of the same type as the one in Fig. 4.1–3. The equation is:

$$S = \frac{1}{.3704 + 2.83T}$$

where S is the slope of the learning curve and T is the time of the delay of reward. The equation fitted by Perin to his data and reproduced here is:

$$S = 1.6 \cdot 10^{-.15T} - .043T + 1.45.$$

REFERENCES

1. Festinger, L. The significance of difference between means without reference to the frequency distribution function. *Psychometrika*, 1946, *11*, 97–105.
2. Gulde, C. J. The effects of delayed reward on the learning of a white-black discrimination by the albino rat. Unpublished Master's thesis, Univ. of Iowa, 1941.

3. Hamilton, E. L. The effect of delayed incentive on the hunger drive in the white rat. *Genet. Psychol. Monogr.*, 1929, 5, 131–207.
4. Hull, C. L. The goal gradient hypothesis and maze learning. *Psychol. Rev.*, 1932, 39, 25–43.
5. Hull, C. L. *Principles of behavior.* New York: Appleton-Century, 1943.
6. Perin, C. T. A quantitative investigation of the delay-of-reinforcement gradient. *J. exp. Psychol.*, 1943, 32, 37–51.
7. Perin, C. T. The effect of delayed reinforcement upon the differentiation of bar responses in white rats. *J. exp. Psychol.*, 1943, 32, 95–109.
8. Perkins, C. C. The relation of secondary reward to gradients of reinforcement. Unpublished Ph.D. thesis, Univ. Iowa, 1946.
9. Riesen, A. H. Delayed reward in discrimination learning by chimpanzees. *Comp. Psychol. Monogr.*, 1940, 15, 1–53.
10. Spence, K. W. The role of secondary reinforcement in delayed reward learning. *Psychol. Rev.*, 1947, 54, 1–8.
11. Wolfe, J. B. The effect of delayed reward upon learning in the white rat. *J. comp. Psychol.*, 1934, 17, 1–21.
12. Wood, A. B. A comparison of delayed reward and delayed punishment in the formation of a brightness discrimination habit in the chick. *Arch. Psychol.*, 1933, 24, No. 157, 40 pp.

4.2 TEMPORAL DISCRIMINATION IN PIGEONS*

G. S. Reynolds and A. Charles Catania

Abstract. Pigeons trained to peck a lighted key were presented with a key that was alternately dark and lighted. The key was dark for intervals of from 3 to 30 seconds. Pecking of the lighted key was reinforced only after the shortest or, in a second experiment, the longest interval that the key was dark. The pigeons were able to discriminate the duration of the dark interval.

Previous studies (1) have shown that organisms can discriminate the duration of a stimulus. In a fixed-interval schedule of reinforcement (2), for example, a response is reinforced only after a fixed interval of time has elapsed since the previous reinforcement. The frequency of responding

* Reprinted from *Science*, 1962, 135, 314–315. Copyright 1962 by the American Association for the Advancement of Science, and reproduced by permission.

generally increases throughout the interval between two reinforcements, indicating that the organisms are to some extent sensitive to the passage of time.

Our procedure (3) was a modification of a standard procedure for the simultaneous study of stimulus discrimination and generalization (4). In the standard procedure as applied to pigeons, several different stimuli, lights of different wavelength, for example, are successively presented to the pigeon. Pecks are reinforced with food in the presence of one wavelength and not in the presence of the other wavelengths. The frequency of pecking plotted against wavelength reveals both discrimination of the wavelength associated with reinforcement and generalization to wavelengths adjacent to it on the continuum. This procedure was modified in our work to accommodate a peculiarity of the continuum of duration, namely, that the duration of a stimulus does not have a single, unchanging value until the stimulus has terminated. Accordingly, in order precisely to define the durations to which our pigeons responded, we exposed them to various durations of a stimulus and allowed them to peck after, rather than during, the presentation of each duration. Pecking was reinforced after one duration and was not reinforced after the other durations.

The experiments were conducted in a standard pigeon chamber containing a feeder for delivering grain to the pigeon and a circular plastic key that could be illuminated with orange light. For observing the birds, there was dim overhead illumination throughout each session. The pigeons were maintained at 80 percent of free-feeding weight and had previously been trained to peck a lighted key.

In each daily session, intervals of various durations during which the key was dark were each followed by a 30-second interval during which the key was lighted. The dark-key intervals ranged from 3 to 30 seconds in steps of 3 seconds. They were presented in an irregular order (5). Each duration occurred 12 times per session. In the first experiment, pecks on the lighted key were reinforced only after a dark-key interval of 3 seconds, and were not reinforced after longer dark-key intervals. In the second experiment, pecks on the lighted key were reinforced only after a dark-key interval of 30 seconds, and were not reinforced after shorter dark-key intervals. Reinforcement was a presentation of grain for 3 seconds, according to a variable-interval schedule with an average interreinforcement interval of 20 seconds.

Figure 4.2–1 shows the results of the two experiments for each of four pigeons. The median number of pecks on the lighted key during the last five sessions of each experiment is plotted against the duration of the preceding dark-key interval. The open circles show the frequencies when pecking was reinforced after a dark-key interval of 3 seconds; the solid

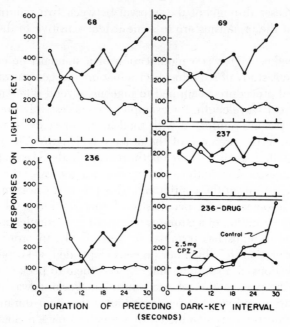

FIGURE 4.2–1 Median number of key-pecks per session during the presentation of a lighted key, as a function of the duration of the preceding dark-key interval for four pigeons. For the open circles, pecking on the lighted key was reinforced only after dark-key intervals of 3 seconds; for the solid circles, only after dark-key intervals of 30 seconds. The bottom right graph shows the effect of 2.5 mg of chlorpromazine on the discrimination of duration by pigeon 236. Reinforcement occurred only after the key was dark for 30 seconds.

circles show the frequency when pecking was reinforced after a dark-key interval of 30 seconds. The lighted key was pecked most frequently after the dark-key interval preceding reinforcement. The frequency of pecking was lower after dark-key intervals that were longer or shorter than the interval preceding reinforcement. The pigeons both discriminated the duration of the dark-key interval and generalized to similar duration.

The relations in Fig. 4.2–1 are adequately fitted by power functions of the form $N = kt^c$, where N is the number of responses and t is the duration of the preceding dark-key period. The functions differ in the value of the constants k and c.

Observation of the birds revealed no systematic changes in their behavior within individual presentations of the dark key. The number of pecks on the dark key never exceeded 40 per session, an average of one peck for every three presentations of the dark key.

The data in Fig. 4.2–1 indicate that pigeons can discriminate a difference as small as 3 seconds in 30 in the duration of a stimulus. Pigeon 236, for example, increased its frequency of pecking from about 300 pecks per session after 27-second intervals to about 550 pecks after 30-second intervals. From this large change in the frequency of pecking, however, it seems certain that the pigeon could discriminate differences in duration of less than 3 seconds in 30. Our procedure could be modified to measure directly, at different points on the continuum of duration, the change in duration that produces a given small change in the frequency of pecking. One duration, always followed by reinforcement, could be held constant, while a second duration is progressively made less different from the first.

A problem encountered with the present series of stimuli was the tendency of the pigeons to peck infrequently after any interval that followed reinforcement. This tendency came from the fact that reinforcement was always followed by nonreinforcement, because two dark-key intervals associated with reinforcement were never presented successively. The low rate of pecking just after reinforcement accounts for the systematic depression in the number of pecks after 21-second stimuli in Fig. 4.2–1. This artifact disappears when the correlation between reinforcement and nonreinforcement is reduced by arranging the sequence of dark-key intervals so that the interval associated with reinforcement recurs two or three times in succession.

Factors that affect the discrimination of duration, such as drugs, may be accurately studied with the present procedure. For example, the bottom graph in the right column of Fig. 4.2–1 shows the performance obtained when 2.5 mg of chlorpromazine was injected into the breast muscle of pigeon 236, 30 minutes before the start of a session (solid circles). Reinforcement occurred only after a dark-key interval of 30 seconds. The open circles show the undrugged, control performance from the previous day. This dosage of chlorpromazine does not abolish pecking, but it attenuates the discrimination of duration of a stimulus.

REFERENCES AND NOTES

1. C. F. Sams and E. C. Tolman, *J. Comp. and Physiol. Psychol.* 5, 255 (1925); H. Woodrow, *ibid.* 8, 395 (1928). Additional citations in P. Fraisse, *Psychologie du Temps* (Presses Universitaires, Paris, 1957), especially pp. 51–59.
2. C. B. Ferster and B. F. Skinner, *Schedules of Reinforcement* (Appleton-Century-Crofts, New York, 1957).
3. Research supported by grant G-8621 from the National Science Foundation.
4. For example, R. Pierrel, *J. Exptl. Anal. Behav.* 1, 303 (1958).
5. The order of presentation of the durations was as follows, the bird starting in a different place in the series each day: 24, 30, 21, 6, 27, 12, 18, 9, 15, 3, 12, 6, 18, 27, 9, 24, 3, 30, 15, 21, 15, 30, 9, 27, 12, 24, 18, 6, 3, 21 seconds.

4.3 FORCE OF RESPONSE DURING RATIO REINFORCEMENT*

Donald E. Mintz

Abstract. Sharp decline in response force after reinforcement and progressive force elevation over a sequence of unreinforced responses were observed for subjects in a fixed-ratio lever-press situation. It is suggested that these systematic variations in force level may provide, through feedback, discriminable cues for behavioral regulation.

When a simple motor response is maintained with a schedule of intermittent food reinforcement, a characteristic and stable pattern of response typically develops (1). Fixed-ratio (FR) is a major class of such reinforcement schedules, involving the reinforcement of every Nth response.

Recent research (2) has shown that properties of behavior such as the peak force of response emission will be greater in magnitude and more variable during extinction than during continuous reinforcement. Since fixed-ratio schedules combine the experimental operations of reinforcement and extinction, peak force of response during reinforcement of this type was examined in order to determine if systematic changes in this response property occurred during the schedule performance.

The procedure involved a modification of the conventional fixed-ratio programming, which typically has single reinforced responses separated by sequences of fixed numbers of unreinforced responses. In order to observe progressive behavioral changes that might occur during reinforcement, sequences of several reinforced as well as unreinforced responses were used. By the convention of specifying the number of reinforced responses with a roman numeral, and the number unreinforced with an arabic numeral, a fixed-ratio schedule involving cycles of four successively reinforced responses and 12 successively unreinforced responses is designated FR(IV)-12. Within the respective sequences each cycle position is identified by the appropriate numeral.

The subjects were male albino rats of the Wistar strain, approximately 110 days of age at the beginning of experimentation. The animals were maintained under a food deprivation regimen, and food pellet reinforcement for a lever-press response was employed (2). A peak force of at least 2.5 g was required for all responses. Continuous reinforcement (approximately 250 responses) was conducted prior to fixed-ratio training.

Figure 4.3–1 shows the mean peak force of response at each ordinal position of the fixed-ratio cycles for four different animals, each under a

* Reprinted from Science, 1962, 138, 516–517. Copyright 1962 by the American Association for the Advancement of Science, and reproduced by permission.

228

different schedule. Each of the schedules required 12 unreinforced responses within a cycle. The number of reinforced responses varied with the subjects, as indicated in Fig. 4.3–1. The means are based on 20 to 25 cycles (20 to 25 responses for each ordinal position). The data represent the 12th consecutive day's performance on the particular schedule.

All subjects, regardless of the number of reinforced responses, show the same trend: The first reinforcement (position I) is followed by a sharp drop in the mean peak force of response. So long as reinforcement continues, the force remains at a low level. Over the sequence of nonreinforced responses, there is a progressive elevation in the mean peak force. The standard deviations of the peak force distributions for each ordinal position (not shown) were correlated with the magnitude of the means.

The systematic changes in the peak force of response within the fixed-ratio cycle were consistently present over the 12 days of conditioning. They have also been observed for these and other subjects with sequences of six and 24 unreinforced responses. In general, the longer the unreinforced sequence, the higher the level of force that was achieved. Conversely, longer reinforced sequences (with number of unreinforced responses held constant) tended to produce less extreme force elevation at the end of the cycle (see Fig. 4.3–1).

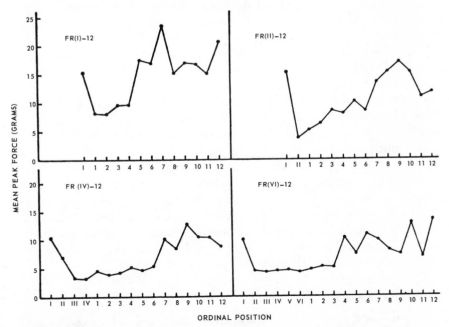

FIGURE 4.3–1   The mean peak force of response during modified fixed-ratio performance. The roman numerals indicate reinforced, and the arabic indicate unreinforced, ordinal positions of the cycle.

It is interesting to note that despite the frequent reinforcement of responses manifesting high peak forces (position I), a subsequent force decline persists. In the cycle positions following each reinforced response (position I), a subsequent force decline persists. In the cycle position following each reinforced response (II through 1) the force levels displayed are of the order of magnitude each animal produced during stable continuous reinforcement performance. The occurrence of reinforcement appears to set the occasion for an immediate return to this formerly reinforced level of responding. An earlier study (3) has shown that the Wistar rat's level of force emission can be brought under the control of an exteroceptive cue (presence or absence of light).

The control exerted by pellet delivery in the present study appears to be analogous to the cueing function served by the light. As was true of the light in the earlier study (3), pellet delivery during fixed-ratio reinforcement provides a stimulus condition following which a particular level of response force was formerly reinforced (during continuous reinforcement). It is therefore possible that the pellet delivery during fixed-ratio reinforcement provides a discriminative basis for the observed force decline, effecting a return to the response force levels characteristic of continuous reinforcement performance.

The force elevation after nonreinforcement appears comparable to "an increase in the vigor of behavior immediately following non-reward," reported by Amsel (4) for the performance of rats in a double runway situation. Notterman and Block have shown that nonreinforced responses during discrimination training are characterized by higher forces than the reinforced responses (5). In the fixed-ratio schedule this increase in force provides a systematic correlate of cycle position. Ferster and Skinner (1) propose that the number of responses an organism has emitted during a fixed-ratio cycle comes to serve a discriminative function. Obviously, they are not referring to any "cognitive" operation of counting (6). It is possible that the "counting" under such circumstances reflects the animal's discrimination of its own level of force emission (7). Systematic variations in behavior such as have been demonstrated for force during fixed-ratio responding may well provide the basis for the cohesive nature of larger and more complicated behavioral units. Even in such an apparently homogeneous chain of responses as those which occur during this type of reinforcement, variations along a discriminable dimension (force) are found (8).

REFERENCES AND NOTES

1. C. B. Ferster and B. F. Skinner, *Schedules of Reinforcement* (Appleton-Century-Crofts, New York, 1957).
2. J. M. Notterman, *J. Exptl. Psychol.* 58, 341 (1959). A description of the apparatus used in this study is included.

3. ―――― and D. E. Mintz, *Science 135*, 1070 (1962).
4. A. Amsel, *Psychol. Bull. 55*, 102 (1958).
5. J. M. Notterman and A. H. Block, *J. Exptl. Anal. Behav. 4*, 289 (1960). They suggest a discriminative basis for the observed force elevation after non-reinforcement.
6. F. Mechner, in *ibid. 1*, 109 and 229 (1958), provides more direct evidence of FR "counting" behavior.
7. T. Marton, in a Ph.D. dissertation (Princeton, 1962), has demonstrated that pharmacological interference with afferent pathways from the rat's paw reduces the precision of force emission in the lever-press. The evidence lends additional credence to the notion that the subjects "discriminate" the force they are emitting.
8. This research was supported by the Office of Naval Research, under contract Nonr 1858 (19). The data are drawn from a portion of my Ph.D. dissertation (Columbia, 1961). The advice and encouragement of Drs. Joseph M. Notterman of Princeton University and Fred S. Keller, William J. McGill, and William N. Schoenfeld of Columbia University are gratefully acknowledged.

4.4 THE EFFECT OF MULTIPLE S^Δ PERIODS ON RESPONDING ON A FIXED-INTERVAL SCHEDULE*

P. B. Dews

The effect of repeated interruption of FI responding by short S^Δ presentations on the pattern of increasing frequency of responding through the interval has been studied. Although the S^Δ profoundly changed the pattern of responding during their presentation, the general scalloped pattern of FI responding survived. The implication of these findings for understanding the role of chaining of responses in FI patterns is discussed. It is suggested that chaining is not a necessary condition for the scalloped pattern.

This is the first of a series of papers on behavior maintained by fixed-interval (FI) schedules of positive reinforcement (Ferster & Skinner, 1957, Chapter 5).

* Reprinted from *The Journal of the Experimental Analysis of Behavior*, 1962, 5, 369–374. Copyright 1962 by the Society for the Experimental Analysis of Behavior, Inc., and reproduced by permission. The experiments described were in collaboration with W. H. Morse, and with the help of Mrs. B. Booth and Mrs. C. Jackson, under Grants M-2094 and 2165 from the National Institute of Mental Health, USPHS, and the Eugene Higgins Trust.

When organisms are exposed to FI schedules of reinforcement, a pattern of responding commonly emerges in which the frequency of responding increases through the interval (Ferster & Skinner, 1957, Chapter 5). This increase gives rise to a scalloped appearance of the cumulative responses: time curves. In discussions as to the genesis and maintenance of this pattern, recourse has been made to the concepts of chained responding and mediating behavior. A chain of responses is a sequence in which each response functions as a discriminative (or eliciting) stimulus changing the probability of occurrence of a further response. Mediating behavior is a sequence of responses between two events that serves to transmit the behavioral influence of one event to that of the other. The events may be responses, and the influence may be "transmitted" in time forward (as in the postulated mediating behavior between recorded responses on a DRL schedule) or backward (as when mediating behavior is suggested to "transmit" to a particular response the reinforcing effects of a delayed reinforcement) (Ferster & Skinner, 1957, p. 729). The two concepts of chained responding and mediating behavior are, of course, closely related. Most mediating behavior is generally considered to be comprised of chained responding, and the early members of a chain of responses affect the later members because the intervening members constitute mediating behavior. To establish a sequence of responses as being chained or as constituting mediating behavior, however, it is not sufficient to demonstrate that the sequence is consistent and *could* so function; it must be explicitly demonstrated that changes in the sequence disrupt the chain or prevent mediation. This paper is concerned with the role of chained responding as mediating behavior in the maintenance of a progressive increase in rate through the interval.

If the orderly progression of rates of responding on FI were mediated by chaining of the recorded response, the rate in any short period, t_i to $t_i + \Delta t$, in the interval should be primarily determined by the rate in the preceding short period, $t_i - \Delta t$ to t_i. Under these circumstances, any influence that disrupts the responding for an appreciable period during the interval should destroy the orderly progression of rates through the interval. It was arranged that an S^Δ was repeatedly presented during each FI. This came to disrupt the pattern of key-pecking responses during the presentation of S^Δ. It has been found that the statistical increase in the tendency to respond through the interval, and even the general scalloped pattern of individual intervals, survived this program of repeated interruptions. Therefore, the chaining of key-pecking responses must not be necessary for the maintenance of this common characteristic of FI responding.

MATERIALS, METHODS, AND PROCEDURES

The subjects were four male White Carneaux pigeons, maintained in the usual way at close to a "running weight" of about 80% of their weight on free feeding. The apparatus, response, and food reinforcer were standard. The key was transilluminated by white lights. The "houselight" (HL) was a 25-watt GE type 101 F bulb projecting from the top of the rear wall (*i.e.*, that opposite to the wall carrying the manipulandum and magazine) of the pigeon compartment. All birds had had extensive and varied exposure to a variety of schedules before these experiments; they had all been subjected to FI procedures for protracted periods.

The basic schedule was FI 500 sec TO 250 sec. That is, the first response made after the key had been transilluminated for 500 sec led to presentation of food; following food presentation, there was a 250-sec period during which there were no lights in the chamber; then the key was transilluminated, and another cycle was in progress. (A 900-sec, limited-hold contingency was included in the program; but because this apparently was never actually operative in concluding an interval during this series of experiments, it will not be considered further.) The daily session consisted of 11 FI — TO cycles. Responses made in the first cycle were not used for computational purposes. Thereafter, responses were cumulated over the 10 fixed intervals in 50-sec compartments; that is, all responses occurring in the first 50 sec following onset of transillumination of the key in all 10 intervals were recorded on one digital counter, then all occurring in the second 50 sec on a second counter, and so on through the 10 compartments comprising the 500-sec fixed interval. These compartments and the corresponding time periods will be referred to by the ordinal numbers of their chronological sequence.

Procedure

In the first part of the experiment (Procedure 1), there was no HL. The birds were subject to the FI 500 sec TO 250 sec for: Bird 40, 64 sessions; Bird 44, 66 sessions; Bird 152, 26 sessions; and Bird 204, 22 sessions.

In the second part of the experiment (Procedure 2), the HL was present during alternate 50-sec periods through the interval; specifically, the HL periods were 2, 4, 6, 8, and 10. At the end of the 10th period, which coincided with the end of the interval, the HL continued until a response occurred. This response was reinforced, of course. Thus, no response made in the absence of the HL was reinforced; and so the periods without HL may be referred to properly as S^Δ periods. This procedure was continued for a number of sessions: Bird 40, 34 sessions; Bird 44, 22 sessions; Bird 152, 37 sessions; and Bird 204, 35 sessions.

On both procedures, there was no clear trend in the day-to-day changes in performance after the first few sessions. Ordinarily, the birds were subjected to five daily sessions per week. Definitive information was assembled from the last 10 "control" days, a "control" day being defined as one that was preceded by a day on which an identical session had been run. At least 10 sessions on each procedure had occurred before the first of the last 10 control days, except for Bird 204 on the simple FI 500 sec TO 250 sec. For this bird, the 10th session was included.

RESULTS

On the simple FI 500 sec to 250 sec procedure, all birds developed the characteristic FI performance (Fig. 4.4–1). Following introduction of alternative periods with HL, the rate of responding gradually fell in the absence of the HL (Fig. 4.4–1).

Figure 4.4–2 shows the mean rates of responding in the successive 50-sec compartments during the last 10 control days. Since there were 10 intervals per session, each bar is the mean of 100 periods of 50 sec. Responding is clearly suppressed in the no-HL periods of Procedure 2. In spite of this, the overall tendency to respond in the successive HL periods shows a progressive increase highly similar to that in the corresponding periods during operation of Procedure 1 when there were no

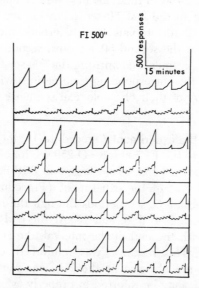

FIGURE 4.4–1 Tracings of complete sessions on Procedure 1 and on Procedure 2 for all four birds. For each bird, the session on Procedure 1 is shown above the session for Procedure 2. The presence of the houselight on Procedure 2 is indicated by the downward off-setting of the cumulative record. The pairs of records are, from above down, respectively, from Birds 40, 44, 152, and 204.

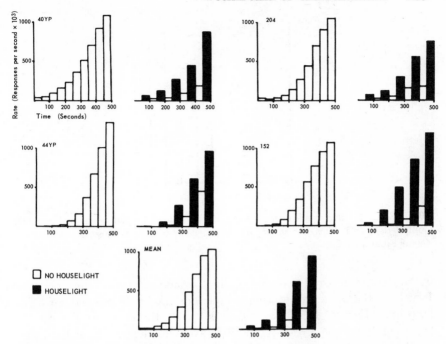

FIGURE 4.4–2 Mean rates in successive 50-sec. compartments of FI. The bar graphs show each bird singly, as labelled; the bottom row shows the simple arithmetic means, period by period, for the four birds.

intervening S^Δ periods. There is even a progressive increase in mean responding during consecutive S^Δ periods. If the rates of responding in the S^Δ periods are multiplied by 3.5, the pattern of the bar graph becomes as shown in Fig. 4.4–3. It crudely reproduces the pattern with no S^Δ periods. The figure 3.5 was obtained from a proportionality formula:

$$\frac{\Sigma\,(\text{R's in periods 1, 3, 5, 7, 9   on Procedure 1})}{\Sigma\,(\text{R's in periods 2, 4, 6, 8, 10 on Procedure 1})} =$$

$$\frac{\Sigma\,(\text{R's in periods 1, 3, 5, 7 on Procedure 2}) \times [S^\Delta]}{\Sigma\,(\text{R's in periods 2, 4, 6, 7, 10 on Procedure 2})}$$

where $[S^\Delta]$ is the S^Δ factor; it is an estimate of the extent to which the stimuli correlated with nonreinforcement suppress the tendency to respond. This formula assumes that the effect of S^Δ is linearly multiplicative with the tendency to respond, that is, that the S^Δ reduces the frequency of responding by a fixed percentage irrespective of the absolute rate of responding. The justification for this assumption is the faithfulness with which the constant factor converts the bar graph of Procedure 2 to resemble that of Procedure 1 at all periods through the interval.

There was no general increase in rate of responding in the presence

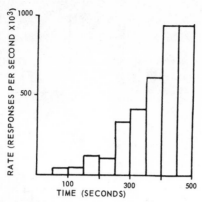

FIGURE 4.4–3   Bar graph of mean rates on Procedure 2 when S^Δ rates have been multiplied by 3.5. This bar graph should be compared with those of the bottom row of Figure 4.4–2.

of the HL as compared to corresponding periods of intervals on Procedure 1 such as those occurring when S^Δ periods are superimposed on a VI base line (Ferster, 1958; Reynolds, 1961). On the contrary, the rate in corresponding (non-S^Δ) 50-sec periods averages slightly lower than that on Procedure 1 (Fig. 4.4–2). The individual 50-sec HL periods tended to show "miniature" FI patterns of responding, as the enlarged sample in Fig. 4.4–4 shows, particularly for Birds 40 and 204. The rates in the terminal parts of the later (in interval) 50-sec periods were frequently higher than any on Procedure 1 (Fig. 4.4–1). This increase in rate may be related to that on other schedules when time outs are introduced.

DISCUSSION

The general pattern of FI responding is not disrupted by the interposition of repeated S^Δ periods during the interval. Therefore, chaining of responses from moment to moment consecutively through the interval is not necessary for maintenance of the overall scalloped pattern characteristic of FI responding.

The rate of responding during the period $t_i + \Delta t$ is not determined predominately by the rate of responding in period $t_i - \Delta t_i$; for many values of t_i, it is much more importantly determined by the absolute position of t_i in the interval. In other words, there appears to be an underlying gradient of increasing tendency to respond that continues through the interval; this gradient is manifest in the responding both in the presence and absence of the HL, even though the absolute response rates differ by a factor of several-fold depending on the stimulus conditions. This is reminiscent of a "goal-gradient" (Hull, 1932) type of hypothesis.

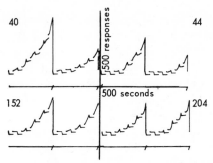

FIGURE 4.4–4 Two consecutive intervals from the final session on Procedure 2 for each of the four birds to show details of distribution of responses within 50-sec. compartments. Conventions as in Figure 4.4–1. Note the miniature FI scallops in individual HL periods (shown most clearly in the record of Pigeon 204) and the desultory responding in individual S^Δ periods. Note also the high terminal rates of individual HL periods late in the FI; these rates exceed any seen on Procedure 1 (cf. Fig. 4.4–1).

It should be noted that here we are concerned specifically with a *temporal* gradient that should be susceptible to quantitative validation.

It may be argued that the FI pattern does depend on "response chaining" but that the response involved is not, or is not only, key pecking. This view would necessitate the further postulate that the response(s) comprising the continuous chain through the interval is compatible with, and uninfluenced by, rate of pecking, while being competent to determine rate of pecking. This is rendered untenable by examination of local changes in rate during the successive periods of the FI. There is a clear indication of scalloping in the S^D periods; miniature FI's emerge. During S^Δ periods, responding tends to be irregular, with some tendency for the rate to fall. A second type of mediating behavior would have to be postulated for the miniature FI and a third for control of S^Δ responding. All these mediating behaviors would have to be mutually independent except for their effects on key-pecking behavior. This stretches the credulity; surely, the burden of proof rests with anyone postulating such a collection of behaviors.

How could FI contingencies operate directly to produce a progressive increase in tendency to respond through the interval? It has been shown that presentation of reinforcing stimuli can have a retroactive enhancing effect on responses (in the sense of making those responses more likely to occur in the future) that occurred as long as 100 sec previously (Dews, 1960). In those experiments, the tendency to respond was severely suppressed by reinforcement postponing contingencies in the schedule. The experiments point to the possibility that reinforcement following a response by periods even longer than 100 sec may lead to the maintenance of substantial rates of responding, provided the tendency to respond was not opposed by other factors. This sort of situation obtains under FI schedules of reinforcement. If reinforcement occurs at time T, responding during the period $T - t_i - {}^\Delta t$ to $T - t_i$ is reinforced, after a delay of t_i, by presentation of the reinforcing stimuli; and so, responding during the corresponding period is maintained in subsequent intervals. If this view is correct, the progressive increase in rate of responding through the fixed interval would be based on a declining retroactive rate-enhancing effect of the reinforcing stimuli as the delay between response and reinforcement is increased (Dews, 1960). Of course, in any particular interval the fixed reference point for the organism must be the start of the interval rather than the future reinforcement; but under ordinary conditions, t_i see from the beginning of the FI uniquely defines an instant that is $T - t_i$ before reinforcement.

Two matters of rather general importance arise out of these findings. First, the view of the basis of the FI scallop just presented is contrary to the general opinion that accords overwhelming importance to the terminal inter-response time (the inter-response time concluded by the reinforced response) in determining the pattern of responding engendered by a schedule. It suggests a re-examination of the interpretations of the *modus operandi* of other schedules that have been based on the assumption of the pre-eminent importance of the final inter-response time. For example, the possibility should be considered that the high rates of responding engendered by fixed-ratio schedules (FR) may come about as follows: The higher the average rate of responding on an FR schedule, the closer, temporally, the initial response and all subsequent responses in the FR are to reinforcement, and, therefore, the greater the retroactive enhancing effect of that reinforcement. This will tend to increase the rate of responding, which in turn will tend to bring the responses closer to reinforcement, which will increase the rate further. Thus, there is, in effect, a positive feedback situation, in which random increases in rate will tend to be self-enhancing. Similar interpretations can be given to other schedule performances that have been described; but their validation depends on specific quantitative information that is not now available. Further speculation is not merited at the present time.

Second, they emphasize the danger of casual attribution of mediating properties to behavior. In the desire to present a continuous causal account, there has been considerable tendency to "fill in" intervals of time with behavior presumed to bridge the gap. Much supposed "mediating behavior" has the status of a hypothetical intervening variable or, at best, as for "proprioception," of an intervening variable with hypothetical properties as a discriminative stimulus. It should be remembered that it is not enough to establish a mediating role to show that behavior occurs and that it could so function. It must be shown that disruption of that behavior abolishes or seriously impairs the consistent relationship of the events between which the behavior is supposed to mediate. Responding through the FI could plausibly function as mediating behavior, but apparently it does not do so importantly.

The information in this paper is based on a single value of FI and a single pattern of introduction of S^Δ periods. The fact that with these particular values the pattern of FI responding persists in the face of interruptions is competent to controvert the proposition that the FI performance is always dependent on "response — chaining"; yet, it would be desirable to have information on other durations of FI and other patterns of interruptions. Such information will be presented later.

A final point of interest, unrelated to FI, concerns the information the data presented give on the operation of stimulus control. It was noted that the bar graph for Procedure 2 could be made to resemble that for Procedure 1 by multiplying the rate of responding in the HL periods by a constant factor of 3.5. It is as though the "S^Δ properties" of the HL reduced the tendency to respond to 1/3.5 of its value in the absence of the HL, more or less independently of what the absolute value of that tendency to respond might be—at any rate over the range from its value at the beginning of the interval to that at the end. It would be of great interest to know whether this simple multiplicative effect of S^Δ control, and, indeed, other varieties of stimulus control, is generally applicable.

REFERENCES

Dews, P. B. Free-operant behavior under conditions of delayed reinforcement. I. CRF-type schedules. *J. exp. Anal. Behav.*, 1960, 3, 221–234.

Ferster, C. B. Control of behavior in chimpanzees and pigeons by time out from positive reinforcement. *Psychol. Monogr.* 1958, 72, No. 8 (Whole No. 461).

Ferster, C. B., and Skinner, B. F. *Schedules of reinforcement.* New York: Appleton-Century-Crofts, 1957.

Hull, C. L. The goal gradient hypothesis and maze learning. *Psychol. Rev.* 1932, 39, 25–43.

Reynolds, G. S. Behavioral contrast. *J. exp. Anal. Behav.*, 1961, 4, 57–71.

4.5 THE EFFECT OF DRIVE LEVEL ON THE MAZE PERFORMANCE OF THE WHITE RAT*

Beverly Hillman, Walter S. Hunter, and Gregory A. Kimble

This experiment was performed to collect data relevant to the following question: Does motivation at the time of training influence habit or merely performance? Methodologically, the previous investigations to which this one is most closely related are those of Finan (4), Kendler (6), MacDuff (7), O'Kelley and Heyer (8), Reynolds (9), Strassburger (10), and Teel (11). The experimental design used in each of these experiments was one in which different groups of Ss were trained at different drive levels and then tested under equated drive in extinction or relearning. By each of these experimenters, differences in behavior in the *test* situation are taken to mean that differential drive during training produced differences in habit or the amount learned. The absence of such differences means that the effect of motivation is upon performance rather than upon learning. Results of the experiments mentioned above fall about equally into these two categories, indicating the desirability of further research on the question.

METHOD

Apparatus

The apparatus was a 10-unit elevated T maze constructed from planks 2 in. thick by 12 in. high. The starting unit was 30 in. long; other units were 36 in. long. Blind alleys in the maze were 9 in. deep, and the distance between choice points was 18 in. The sequence of correct turns was LRRLRLLRL. At the end of the maze was a goal box, into which there extended the nipple of a water bottle attached to the outside of the goal box.

* Beverly Hillman, Walter S. Hunter, and Gregory A. Kimble, "The Effect of Drive Level on the Maze Performance of the White Rat," The Journal of Comparative and Physiological Psychology, 46, 1953, 87–89. Copyright 1953 by the American Psychological Association, and reproduced by permission. This report is a description of a portion of the senior author's Master's thesis, done at Brown University under the joint direction of the other two authors. The junior author (G. A. K.) assumes the responsibility for the interpretation and the results presented in this paper.

Subjects

The Ss in the experiment were 40 male albino rats from the colony maintained by Brown University, 60 days old at the beginning of pretraining. Before beginning the experiment, they were blinded and placed in individual living cages. During the whole experiment, they were on an ad libitum supply of food. Motivation in the experimental situation was controlled by manipulating water deprivation.

Procedure

In experiments involving the thirst drive, such variables as temperature and humidity may seriously affect the motivational level of the S. For this reason it is desirable to run various groups at as nearly the same time as possible. In this experiment, Ss in all groups were run early in the evening, and the investigation was performed in two replications. Since the results of the two replications were the same, and since neither humidity nor temperature showed systematic variation during the experiment, both procedure and results will be described as if the experiment had required just one series of sessions.

The Ss were placed on a 22-hr. drinking schedule two days before pretraining, and kept on it through the pretraining series. Pretraining consisted of 20 trials on a straight runway constructed from three maze units and the same goal box as was used later on in the maze. During pretraining, the Ss were run under 22 hr. of deprivation and were allowed to drink for 30 sec. in the goal box at the end of each run. Trials were administered at the rate of two a day. After ten such days and 20 trials, running time had decreased to about 5 sec., and group variability was low. At this point training on the maze was begun.

In this training, the Ss were given 15 trials on the maze, at the rate of one trial a day to eliminate possible complicating effects of drive reduction produced by the administration of reward. During the first ten trials, 20 Ss were run under 2 hr. of water deprivation and the remaining 20 Ss were run under 22 hr. of deprivation. The 2-hr. group was allowed access to water continuously except for the 2 hr. immediately preceding the experimental period. The 22-hr. group remained on the same schedule as during pretraining. On each trial, S was allowed 45-sec. access to water in the goal box.

After trial 10, the two groups were subdivided and ten Ss from each group assigned at random to a 2-hr. group and a 22-hr. group. Beginning on the evening following trial 10, each of the four subgroups thus produced was given five more *rewarded* trials in the maze on the one-trial-a-day schedule.

The experimental design, it will be seen, is a 2 × 2 factorial, in which motivation during trials 1 to 10 defines one marginal, and motivation during trial 11 to 15 defines the other. Results from a design of this sort are easily treated by the analysis-of-variance technique. An effect on *habit* is demonstrated if the measures obtained on trials 11 to 15 are significantly different for Ss trained on trials 1 to 10 under the two degrees of motivation. An effect on *performance* is demonstrated if the same measures are significantly different for Ss run under the two different levels of motivation on trials 11 to 15. We shall refer to the four experimental groups in this design in terms of the number of hours of deprivation obtaining in the two phases of the experiment. For example, group 22–2 is the group run first under 22 hr. of water deprivation and then shifted to 2 hr. of deprivation. Group 22–22 is that which received all of its trials under 22 hr. of deprivation. The other two groups will be called group 22–2 and group 2–2. Our main interest is in the performance of these four groups on the last five trials of training, in terms of number of errors and amount of time accumulated in each maze run.

RESULTS

Let us consider error scores first. If we use as a measure for performance mean number of errors per trial for each S on trials 11 to 15, averages are 0.9, 0.9, 1.2, and 0.4 errors for groups 22–22, 2–2, 22–2, and 2–22, respectively. Differences assignable to level of motivation either during the first ten trials or the last five trials fail to reach significance at the .05 level. The analysis of variance on which this statement is based is presented in the left-hand portion of Table 4.5–1. Learning curves for the four groups are nearly identical. There is, in short, no evidence that the number of errors is related to strength of motivation at *any* point in learning.

TABLE 4.5–1   Analysis of Variance Performed on Mean Error Score and on Mean Log Running Time during Trials 11 to 15 in the Maze

Source of Variation	df	Error Scores			Time Scores		
		Sum of Squares	Mean Square	F^*	Sum of Squares	Mean Square	F^*
Motivation trials 1–10	1	2.03	2.03	3.08	0.00	0.00	0.00
Motivation trials 11–15	1	2.03	2.03	3.08	1.02	1.02	51.00
Interaction	1	0.07	0.07	0.11	0.06	0.06	3.00
Within groups (error)	36	23.91	0.66	—	0.60	0.02	—

* The F ratio required for significance at the .05 level is 4.17; for significance at the .001 level, 13.29.

The time scores show quite a different picture. Learning curves for the logarithm of this measure are presented in Figure 4.5–1. Note that the groups are clearly different from approximately trial 3 on. Also note that, with the motivational change introduced on trial 11, performance immediately slows up for group 2–2, and that a decrease in the time measure occurs for group 2–22 on trial 12. The fact that the response of this latter group to the change in deprivation is delayed for one trial may represent a residual effect of ten days of nearly continuous free access to water. Finally, observe that the speed of maze traversal seems to depend almost entirely upon motivation during the trials when it is measured. Mean log time scores for groups 2–2, 22–2, 22–22, and 2–22 are 1.66 sec., 1.74 sec., 1.34 sec., and 1.42 sec., respectively. This last fact argues against the idea that drive level during learning has anything to do with the amount learned and is supported by the analysis of variance presented in the right-hand portion of Table 4.5–1. The results of this analysis show that the only significant experimental contribution to variability is that from the motivational level at the time the measures used in the analysis were obtained.

DISCUSSION

The results of this experiment are similar to those of Kendler (6), Strassburger (10), and Teel (11) in showing that drive level at the time of learning has no significant effect on behavior in a test situation when drive is equated. So far as the main question under investigation is con-

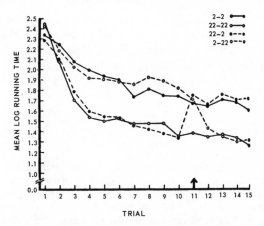

FIGURE 4.5–1 Learning curves showing the mean logarithm of the time score for each experimental groups as a function of practice. The arrow indicates the point at which drive was changed for two of the groups. For the meaning of the legend, see the text.

cerned, they support Hull's (5) guess that motivation is important in response evocation but not in habit formation.

At another level, however, these findings are potentially damaging to one of Hull's fundamental assumptions, that various response measures depend for their value upon a single terminal construct, $_sE_R$. From our results it appears, as Anderson (1) and Bruce (2) have previously found, that measures involving a time dimension are more responsive to motivational changes than measures like number of errors, which are independent of time. Such a result indicates that these two indices of response strength may be reflecting quite different aspects of behavior. In this respect the situation is like that in conditioning where low correlations between response latency and probability of occurrence are typically found (3). Although the response-evocation process described by Hull can accommodate such low correlations, results like those of the present experiment suggest at least a reconsideration of the widely accepted notion that all response variables depend equally upon a single process.

SUMMARY

Four groups of ten male albino rats were given 15 trials in a ten-unit T maze in an experiment designed to determine whether motivation at the time of learning influences the amount learned. Two groups received all their trials under 2 and 22 hr. of water deprivation, respectively. The other two groups received ten trials under these two conditions and then were shifted to the other condition. Analysis of maze performance in the last five trials shows no effect of earlier motivation on either time or error scores. Motivation *at the time of testing*, however, does influence time scores ($p = .001$). This fact supports Hull's hypothesis that the habit-formation process is independent of drive. The finding that time and errors respond differently to motivational changes suggests a re-examination of the relationship postulated by Hull to exist among the response variables.

REFERENCES

1. Anderson, E. E. Interrelationship of drives in the male albino rat: I. Intercorrelations of measures of drives. *Comp. Psychol. Monogr.*, 1937, 24, 73–118.
2. Bruce, R. H. The effect of lessening drive upon performance by white rats in the maze. *J. comp. Psychol.*, 1938, 25, 225–248.
3. Campbell, A. A. The interrelations of two measures of conditioning in man. *J. exp. Psychol.*, 1938, 22, 225–243.
4. Finan, J. L. Quantitative studies in motivation: I. Strength of conditioning in rats under varying degrees of hunger. *J. comp. Psychol.*, 1940, 29, 119–134.
5. Hull, C. L. *Principles of behavior.* New York: D. Appleton-Century, 1943.

6. Kendler, H. H. Drive interaction: II. Experimental analysis of the role of drive in learning theory. *J. exp. Psychol.*, 1945, 35, 188–198.
7. MacDuff, M. M. The effect of retention of varying degrees of motivation during learning in rats. *J. comp. Psychol.*, 1946, 39, 207–240.
8. O'Kelly, L. I., & Heyer, A. W. Studies in motivation and retention. I. Retention of a simple habit. *J. comp. physiol. Psychol.*, 1948, 41, 466–478.
9. Reynolds, B. The relationship between the strength of a habit and the degree of drive present during acquisition. *J. exp. Psychol.*, 1949, 39, 296–305.
10. Strassburger, R. C. Resistance to extinction of a conditioned operant as related to drive level at reinforcement. *J. exp. Psychol.*, 1950, 40, 473–487.
11. Teel, K. S. Habit strength as a function of motivation during learning. *J. comp. physiol. Psychol.*, 1952, 45, 188–191.

4.6 NEGATIVE CONTRAST EFFECT AS A FUNCTION OF MAGNITUDE OF REWARD DECREMENT*

Vincent DiLollo and Victor Beez

Five groups of 12 rats each were given 20 daily training trials in a straight runway and were rewarded with either 1, 2, 4, 8 or 16 20-mg food pellets, respectively. All groups were then shifted to 1 pellet reward for 14 additional trials. Performance during Training was an increasing monotonic function of the amount of reward. The magnitude of the negative contrast effect obtained in post-shift performance was directly related to the magnitude of reward decrement.

Following a sudden decrement in the amount of reward, the performance of a group of animals typically decreases below that of a control group maintained at the lower amount throughout. Although the occurrence of this phenomenon, termed *negative contrast effect*, has been repeatedly demonstrated, little work has been done towards a description of its relation to relevant variables connected with the shift in reward.

* Reprinted from *Psychonomic Science*, 1966, 5, 99–100. Copyright 1966 by the Psychonomic Society, and reproduced with permission. The experimental work reported in this paper was conducted at Indiana University and was supported in part by Grant GE 2904 from the National Science Foundation. Analyses of the data and preparation of this report were supported by the Air Force Office of Scientific Research, Office of Aerospace Research, United States Air Force, under AFOSR Grant Nr AF - AFOSR - 968 - 65.

The effect of magnitude of shift in reward was first studied by Crespi (1942) with inconclusive results. In a more recent study (Gonzales, Gleitman, & Bitterman, 1962) a positive relationship was obtained between magnitude of reward decrement and negative contrast effect; these investigators, however, used only two levels of reward decrement and thus did not obtain an indication of the function relating the two variables. The study here reported investigates the magnitude of the negative contrast effect as a function of the magnitude of decrement in reward over a range of five levels of the independent variable.

METHOD

Apparatus

The apparatus consisted of a straight runway 86 in. long, 3 in. wide and 4 in. high; the length included a 12 in. start box and a 14 in. goal box separated from the alley by clear plastic guillotine doors. A soft-drink bottle top was attached to the floor of the far end of the goal box and acted as a food cup. The apparatus was painted flat black and was covered with clear Plexiglas. Running times were measured by a .01 sec. Standard Electric timer between a photo beam 12 in. past the start door and a second beam located 36 in. from the first.

Subjects and Procedure

Sixty male albino rats, 90 to 100 days old, were allocated randomly to five groups of 12 Ss each. Fourteen days before the beginning of training the Ss were placed on a feeding schedule with food available for 1 hr. each day and water available at all times. During Training each S ran one trial per day for 20 days. The reward consisted of either 1, 2, 4, 8, or 16 20-mg Noyes food pellets for each of the five groups, respectively. On the last day of Training, and for 14 subsequent daily trials, the reward was shifted to one pellet for all groups (Shift stage).

RESULTS AND DISCUSSION

The running time of each S on each trial was transformed logarithmically and then averaged for each group over the last five trials of Training and Shift, respectively, to give the measure of performance shown in Fig. 4.6–1. The one-tailed probability of obtaining an order replication of the five amounts of reward during Training or Shift is $1/5!$ ($p < .01$). Clearly, the magnitude of the negative contrast effect is a monotonic function of the magnitude of reward decrement under the present experimental conditions.

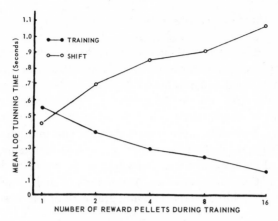

FIGURE 4.6–1   Mean log running time for each group over the last five trials of training and shift, respectively.

During Training, performance was an approximately linear function of the log amount of reward (Fig. 4.6–1). This result is in agreement with earlier work (e.g., Guttman, 1953) and is consonant with predictions from the incentive motivation theory proposed by Bevan & Adamson (1960).

As shown in Fig. 4.6–2, changes in performance during Shift were gradual and, apparently, not quite complete at the end of the experiment. A similarly slow onset of the negative contrast effect was obtained in some earlier studies (Meyer, 1951; Spence, 1956; Collier & Marx, 1959), while rapid shifts were obtained in others (DiLollo, 1965; Vogel, Mikulka, & Spear, 1965). Some of the variables possibly affecting the

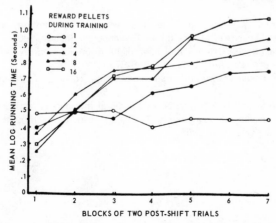

FIGURE 4.6–2   Mean log running time for each group during shift.

rapidity of the shifts have recently been discussed by Ison & Rosen (1965): the issue, however, is complex and has not been resolved.

Although both perceptual–motivational theory (Bevan & Adamson, 1960) and response–motivational theory (Crespi, 1944; Spence, 1956) can account for the graded magnitude of the contrast effect, the gradual onset of the phenomenon is not in agreement with predictions from either formulation. In its present form, each theory predicts converging, rather than diverging, post-shift performance curves. The gradual changes in performance suggest that, under some yet unspecified conditions, the development of the negative contrast effect is governed by learning, as distinct from motivational, variables. A statement of such variables should be encompassed within any theory aiming at a complete account of the phenomenon.

REFERENCES

Bevan, W., & Adamson, R. Reinforcers and reinforcement: their relation to maze performance. *J. exp. Psychol.*, 1960, 59, 226–232.

Collier, G., & Marx, M. H. Changes in performance as a function of shifts in the magnitude of reinforcement. *J. exp. Psychol.*, 1959, 57, 305–309.

Crespi, L. P. Quantitative variations of incentive and performance in the white rat. *Amer. J. Psychol.*, 1942, -55, 467–517.

Crespi, L. P. Amount of reinforcement and level of performance. *Psychol. Rev.*, 1944, 51, 341–357.

DiLollo, V. Runway performance in relation to runway-goal-box similarity and changes in incentive amount. *J. comp. physiol. Psychol.*, 1964, 58, 327–329.

Gonzales, R. C., Gleitman, H., & Bitterman, M. E. Some observations on the depression effect. *J. comp. physiol. Psychol.*, 1962, 55, 578–581.

Guttman, N. Operant conditioning, extinction, and periodic reinforcement in relation to concentration of sucrose used as a reinforcing agent. *J. exp. Psychol.*, 1953, 46, 213–224.

Ison, J. R., & Rosen, A. J. On changes in incentive: some new findings and theoretical speculations. Paper read at meeting of Psychonomic Society, 1965.

Meyer, D. R. The effects of differential rewards on discrimination reversal learning by monkeys. *J. exp. Psychol.*, 1951, 41, 268–274.

Spence, K. W. *Behavior theory and conditioning*. New Haven: Yale University Press, 1956.

Vogel, J. R., Mikulka, P. J., & Spear, N. E. Effects of interpolated extinction and level of training on the "depression effect". Paper read at meeting of the Eastern Psychological Association, 1965.

4.7 PRELIMINARY REPORT ON THE APPLICATION OF CONTINGENT REINFORCEMENT PROCEDURES (TOKEN ECONOMY) ON A "CHRONIC" PSYCHIATRIC WARD*

John M. Atthowe, Jr. and Leonard Krasner

An 86-bed closed ward in a Veterans Administration hospital was used in a 2-yr. study involving the application of a "token economy." For the patients, labeled chronic schizophrenics or brain damaged, every important phase of ward life was incorporated within a systematic contingency program. Patients received tokens for performing specified desirable behaviors involving self-care, attending activities, interacting with others, or demonstrating responsibility. The tokens could be exchanged for the "good things in life" such as passes, movies, and well-located beds. The results at the end of a year indicated a significant increase in the performance of reinforced "desirable" behaviors and a general improvement in patient initiative, responsibility, and social interaction.

Although investigators may disagree as to what specific strategies or tactics to pursue, they would agree that current treatment programs in mental hospitals are in need of vast improvement. Release rates for patients hospitalized 5 or more years have not materially changed in this century (Kramer, Goldstein, Israel, & Johnson, 1956). After 5 yr. of hospitalization, the likelihood of release is approximately 6% (Kramer et al., 1956; Morgan & Johnson, 1957; Odegard, 1961), and, as patients

* John M. Atthowe, Jr. and Leonard Krasner, "Preliminary Report on the Application of Contingent Reinforcement Procedures (Token Economy) on a 'Chronic' Psychiatric Ward," *The Journal of Abnormal Psychology*, 73, 1968, 37–43. Copyright 1968 by the American Psychological Association, and reproduced by permission.

Parts of this paper were presented to the annual meeting of the American Psychological Association, Chicago, September 1965. Supported by the Psychology Research Associate Program of the Veterans Administration at the VA Hospital, Palo Alto, California and United States Public Health Service Grants MH 6191 and MH 11938 to Stanford University and The State University of New York at Stony Brook. The authors wish to acknowledge the following staff members and trainees who participated in the program: Dave Panek, Robert Houlihan, Ralph Sibley, Gordon Paul, Lois Brockhoff, Joseph McDonough, Loraine Ceaglske, Martha May, Rose Peter; psychiatric aides Ed Noseworthy, Donald Bradford, Herbert Bowles, Sam Asbury, Kay Key, Harriet Faggitt, Van Cliett, Calvin Johnson, and Alice Bruce; Arlene Stevens, ward secretary; Martha Smiley; W. G. Beckman, ward psychiatrist; J. J. Prusmack, and Thomas W. Kennelly.

grow older and their length of hospitalization increases, the possibility of discharge approaches zero. Even for those chronic patients who do leave the hospital, more than two out of every three return within 6 mo. (Fairweather, Simon, Gebhard, Weingarten, Holland, Sanders, Stone, & Reahl, 1960). There is certainly need for new programs of demonstrated efficiency in modifying the behavior of long-term hospitalized patients.

In September 1963 a research program in behavior modification was begun which was intimately woven into the hospital's ongoing service and training programs. The objective was to create and maintain a systematic ward program within the ongoing social system of the hospital. The program reported here involves the life of the entire ward, patients, and staff, plus others who come in contact with the patients. The purpose of the program was to change the chronic patients' aberrant behavior, especially that behavior judged to be apathetic, overly dependent, detrimental, or annoying to others. The goal was to foster more responsible, active, and interested individuals who would be able to perform the routine activities associated with self-care, to make responsible decisions, and to delay immediate reinforcement in order to plan for the future.

THE WARD POPULATION

An 86-bed closed ward in the custodial section of the Veterans Administration Hospital in Palo Alto was selected. The median age of the patients was 57 yr. and more than one-third were over 65. Their overall length of hospitalization varied from 3 to 48 yr. with a median length of hospitalization of 22 yr. Most of the patients had previously been labeled as chronic schizophrenics; the remainder were classified as having some organic involvement.

The patients fell into three general performance classes. The largest group, approximately 60% of the ward, required constant supervision. Whenever they left the ward, an aide had to accompany them. The second group, about 25%, had ground privileges and were able to leave the ward unescorted. The third group, 15% of the patients, required only minimal supervision and could probably function in a boarding home under proper conditions if the fear of leaving the hospital could be overcome.

In order to insure a stable research sample for the 2 yr. of the project, 60 patients were selected to remain on the ward for the duration of the study. The patients selected were older and had, for the most part, obvious and annoying behavioral deficits. This "core" sample served as the experimental population in studying the long-term effectiveness of the research program, the token economy.

THE TOKEN ECONOMY

Based on the work of Ayllon and his associates (Ayllon, 1963; Ayllon & Azrin, 1965; Ayllon & Houghton, 1962; Ayllon & Michael, 1959) and the principle of reinforcement as espoused by Skinner (1938, 1953), we have tried to incorporate every important phase of ward and hospital life within a systematic contingency program. The attainment of the "good things in life" was made contingent upon the patient's performance.

If a patient adequately cared for his personal needs, attended his scheduled activities, helped on the ward, interacted with other patients, or showed increased responsibility in any way, he was rewarded. The problem was to find rewards that were valued by everyone. Tokens, which could in turn be exchanged for the things a patient regards as important or necessary, were introduced. As stated in the manual distributed to patients (Atthowe, 1964):

> The token program is an incentive program in which each person can do as much or as little as he wants as long as he abides by the general rules of the hospital, *but*, in order to gain certain ends or do certain things, he must have tokens. . . . The more you do the more tokens you get [p. 2].

Cigarettes, money, passes, watching television, etc., were some of the more obvious reinforcers, but some of the most effective reinforcers were idiosyncratic, such as sitting on the ward or feeding kittens. For some patients, hoarding tokens became highly valued. This latter practice necessitated changing the tokens every 30 days. In addition, the tokens a patient still had left at the end of each month were devaluated 25%, hence the greater incentive for the patient to spend them quickly. The more tokens a patient earned or spent, the less likely he would be to remain apathetic.

In general, each patient was reinforced immediately after the completion of some "therapeutic" activity, but those patients who attended scheduled activities by themselves were paid their tokens only once a week on a regularly scheduled pay day. Consequently, the more independent and responsible patient had to learn "to punch a time card" and to receive his "pay" at a specified future date. He then had to "budget" his tokens so they covered his wants for the next 7 days.

In addition, a small group of 12 patients was in a position of receiving what might be considered as the ultimate in reinforcement. They were allowed to become independent of the token system. These patients carried a "carte blanche" which entitled them to all the privileges within the token economy plus a few added privileges and a greater status. For this special status, the patient had to work 25 hr. per week in special vocational assignments. In order to become a member of the "elite group," patients had to accumulate 120 tokens which entailed a considerable delay in gratification.

The token economy was developed to cover all phases of a patient's life. This extension of contingencies to all of the patient's routine activities should bring about a greater generality and permanence of the behavior modified. One criticism of conditioning therapies has been that the behavior changed is specific with little evidence of carry-over to other situations. In this project plans were incorporated to program transfer of training as well as behavior change, per se. As a major step in this direction, token reinforcements were associated with social approval.

The attainment of goals which bring about greater independence should also result in strong sustaining reinforcement in and of itself. The aim of this study was to support more effective behavior and to weaken ineffective behavior by withdrawal of approval and attention and, if necessary, by penalties. Penalties comprised "fines" of specified numbers of tokens levied for especially undesirable behavior or for *not* paying the tokens required by the system. The fines can be seen as actually representing a high token payment to do something socially undesirable, for example, three tokens for cursing someone.

METHOD

The research program was initiated in September of 1963 when the senior author joined the ward as the ward psychologist and program administrator. The remainder of 1963 was a period of observation, pilot studies, and planning. Steps were taken to establish a research clinic and to modify the traditional service orientation of the nursing staff. In January 1964, the base-line measures were begun. The base-line or operant period lasted approximately 6 mo. and was followed by 3 mo. in which the patients were gradually prepared to participate in the token economy. In October 1964, the token economy was established and, at the time of writing, is still in operation. This report represents results based on the completion of the first year of the program.

The general design of the study was as follows: A 6-mo. base-line period, a 3-mo. shaping period, and an 11-mo. experimental period. During the base-line period, the frequency of particular behaviors was recorded daily, and ratings were carried out periodically. The shaping period was largely devoted to those patients requiring continual supervision. At first, the availability of canteen booklets, which served as money in the hospital canteen, was made contingent upon the amount of scheduled activities a patient attended. It soon became clear that almost one-half of the patients were not interested in money or canteen books. They did not know how to use the booklets, and they never bought things for themselves. Consequently, for 6 wk. patients were taken to the canteen and urged or "cajoled" into buying items which seemed to interest them (e.g., coffee, ice cream, pencils, handkerchiefs, etc.). Then all contingencies were temporarily abandoned, and patients were further encouraged to utilize the canteen books. Next, tokens were introduced but on a noncontingent basis. No one was allowed to purchase items in the ward canteen without first presenting tokens. Patients were instructed to pick up tokens from an office directly across the hall from the ward canteen and exchange them for the items they desired. After 2 wk. the tokens were made contingent upon performance and the experimental phase of the study began.

Within a reinforcement approach, the principles of successive approximation in gradually shaping the desired patient behavior were utilized. Once the tokens were introduced, shaping procedures were reduced. It would be impossible to hold reinforcement and shaping procedures constant throughout the experimental period or to match our ward or our patients with another ward or comparable group of patients. Consequently, a classical statistical design does not suit our paradigm. It is much more feasible, in addition to reducing sampling errors, to use the patients as their own controls. Therefore, we first established a base line over an extended period of time. Any changes in behavior from that defined by the base line must be taken into account. The effects of any type of experimental intervention become immediately obvious. We do not have to rely solely on the inferences teased out of statistical analyses.

Other than an automatic timer for the television set, the only major piece of equipment was the tokens. After a considerable search, a durable and physically safe token was constructed. This token was a 1¾ × 3½ in. plastic, nonlaminated, file card which came in seven colors varying from a bright red to a light tan. Different exchange values were assigned to the different colors. The token had the appearance of the usual credit card so prevalent in our society.

Whenever possible, the giving of the tokens was accompanied by some expression of social approval such as smiling, "good," "fine job," and a verbal description of the contingencies involved, for example, "Here's a token because of the good job of shaving you did this morning."

RESULTS

There has been a significant increase in those behaviors indicating responsibility and activity. Figure 4.7–1 shows the improvement in the frequency of attendance at group activities. During the base-line period,

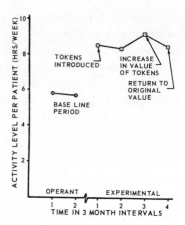

FIGURE 4.7–1   Attendance at group activities.

the average hourly rate of attendance per week was 5.85 hr. per patient. With the introduction of tokens, this rate increased to 8.4 the first month and averaged 8.5 during the experimental period, except for a period of 3 mo. when the reinforcing value of the tokens was increased from one to two tokens per hour of attendance. Increasing the reinforcing value of the tokens increased the contingent behavior accordingly. With an increase in the amount of reinforcement, activity increased from 8.4 hr. per week in the month before to 9.2 the first month under the new schedule This gain was maintained throughout the period of greater reinforcement and 1 mo. thereafter.

Thirty-two patients of the core sample comprised the group-activity sample. Nine patients were discharged or transferred during the project, and the remaining patients were in individual assignments and did not enter into these computations. Of the 32 patients, 18 increased their weekly attendance by at least 2 hr., while only 4 decreased their attendance by this amount. The probability that this is a significant difference is .004, using a sign test and a two-tailed estimate. Of those patients going to group activities, 18% changed to the more token-producing and more responsible individual assignments within 4 mo. of the onset of the token economy.

A widening of interest and a lessening of apathy were shown by a marked increase in the number of patients going on passes, drawing weekly cash, and utilizing the ward canteen. Of the core sample of 60 patients, 80% had never been off the hospital grounds on their own for a period of 8 hr. since their hospitalization. During the experimental period, 19% went on overnight or longer passes, 17% went on day passes, and 12% went out on accompanied passes for the first time. In other words, approximately one-half of those who had been too apathetic to leave the hospital grounds increased their interest and commitment in the world outside. Furthermore, 13% of the core sample left on one or more trial visits of at least 30 days during the token program, although 6 out of every 10 returned to the hospital.

For the entire ward, the lessening of apathy was dramatic. The number of patients going on passes and drawing weekly cash tripled. Twenty-four patients were discharged and 8 were transferred to more active and discharge-oriented ward programs as compared to 11 discharges and no such transfers in the preceding 11-mo. period. Of the 24 patients released, 11 returned to the hospital within 9 mo.

Independence and greater self-sufficiency were shown by an increase in the number of patients receiving tokens for shaving and appearing neatly dressed. Fewer patients missed their showers, and bed-wetting markedly diminished.

At the beginning of the study, there were 12 bed-wetters, 4 of whom were classified as "frequent" wetters and 2 were classified as "infrequent." All bed-wetters were awakened and taken to the bathroom at 11 P.M., 12:30 P.M., 2 A.M., and 4 A.M. regularly. As the program progressed, patients who did not wet during the night were paid tokens the following morning. In addition, they were only awakened at 11 P.M. the next night. After a week of no bed-wetting, patients were taken off the schedule altogether. At the end of the experimental period no one was wetting regularly and, for all practical purposes, there were no bed-wetters on the ward. The aversive schedule of being awakened during the night together with the receiving of tokens for a successful non-bed-wetting night seemed to instigate getting up on one's own and going to the bathroom, even in markedly deteriorated patients.

Another ward problem which had required extra aide coverage in the mornings was the lack of "cooperativeness" in getting out of bed, making one's bed, and leaving the bed area by a specified time. Just before the system of specific contingency tokens was introduced, the number of infractions in each of these areas was recorded for 3 wk. This 3-wk. base-line period yielded an average of 75 "infractions" per week for the entire ward, varying from 71 to 77. A token given daily was then made contingent upon not having a recorded infraction in any of the three areas above. This token was given as the patients lined up to go to breakfast each morning. In the week following the establishment of the contingency, the frequency of infractions dropped to 30 and then to 18. The next week the number of infractions rose to 39 but then declined steadily to 5 per week by the end of 9 wk. (see Figure 4.7–2). During the last 6 mo., the frequency of infractions varied between 6 and 13, averaging 9 per week.

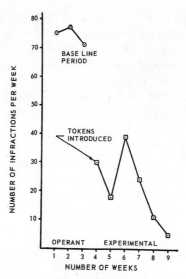

FIGURE 4.7–2   Number of infractions in carrying out morning routines.

A significant increase was shown in measures of social interaction and communication. A brief version of the Palo Alto Group Psychotherapy scale (Finney, 1954) was used to measure social responsiveness in weekly group meetings. The changes in ratings by one group of raters 1 mo. before the introduction of tokens compared with those of a second group of raters 4 mo. later was significant at the .001 level. A simple sign test based upon a two-tailed probability estimate was used. Neither set of raters knew which of their patients was included within the core sample. The rater reliability of the scale is .90 (Finney, 1954). Evidence of enhanced social interaction was dramatically shown by the appearance of card games using tokens as money among some of the more "disturbed" patients and an increased frequency in playing pool together.

DISCUSSION AND CONCLUSION

A detailed description of the entire procedures and results is in preparation. However, we wish to point out in this paper the usefulness of a systematic contingency program with chronic patients. The program has been quite successful in combating institutional behavior. Prior to the introduction of tokens most patients rarely left the ward. The ward and its surrounding grounds were dominated by sleeping patients. Little interest was shown in ward activities or parties. Before the tokens were introduced, the ward was cleaned and the clothing room operated by patients from "better" wards. During the experimental period the ward was cleaned and the clothing room operated by the patients of this ward themselves. Now, no one stays on the ward without first earning tokens, and, in comparison to prior standards, the ward could be considered "jumping."

Over 90% of the patients have meaningfully participated in the program. All patients do take tokens, a few only infrequently. However, for about 10%, the tokens seem to be of little utility in effecting marked behavior change. With most patients, the changes in behavior have been quite dramatic; the changes in a few have been gradual and hardly noticeable. These instances of lack of responsiveness to the program seem to be evident in those patients who had previously been "catatonically" withdrawn and isolated. Although most of the patients in this category were favorably responsive to the program, what "failures" there were, did come from this type of patient. Our program has been directed toward all patients; consequently, individual shaping has been limited. We feel that the results would be more dramatic if we could have dealt individually with the specific behavior of every patient. On the other hand, a total ward token program is needed both to maintain any behavioral gains and to bring about greater generality and permanence. Although it was not our initial objective to discharge patients, we are pleased that the general lessening of apathy has brought about a greater discharge rate. But, even more important, the greater discharge rate would point to the generalized effects of a total token economy.

The greater demands on the patient necessitated by dealing with future events and delaying immediate gratifications which were built into the program have been of value in lessening patients' isolation and withdrawal. The program's most notable contribution to patient life is the lessening of staff control and putting the burden of responsibility, and thus more self-respect, on the patient himself. In the administration of a ward, the program provides behavioral steps by which the staff can judge the patient's readiness to assume more responsibility and thus to leave on pass or be discharged.

The program thus far has demonstrated that a systematic procedure of applying contingent reinforcement via a token economy appears effective in modifying specific patient behaviors. However, the evidence in the literature based on research in mental hospitals indicates that many programs, different in theoretical orientation and design, appear to be successful for a period of time with hospitalized patients. The question which arises is whether the success in modifying behavior is a function of the specific procedures utilized in a given program or a function of the more general social influence process (Krasner, 1962). If it is the latter, whether it be termed "placebo effects" or "Hawthorne effect," then the specific procedures may be irrelevant. All that would matter is the interest, enthusiasm, attention, and hopeful expectancies of the staff. Advocates of behavior-modification procedures (of which the token economy is illustrative) argue that change in behavior is a function of the specific reinforcement procedures used. The study which most nearly involves the approach described in this paper is that of Ayllon and Azrin (1965) whose procedures were basic to the development of our own program. Their study was designed to demonstrate the relationship between contingency reinforcement and change in patient behavior. To do this they withdrew the tokens on a systematic basis for specific behaviors and, after a period of time, reinstated them. They concluded, based upon six specific experiments within the overall design, that

> the reinforcement procedure was effective in maintaining desired performance. In each experiment, the performance fell to a near-zero level when the established response-reinforcement relation was discontinued. On the other hand, reintroduction of the reinforcement procedure restored performance almost immediately and maintained it at a high level for as long as the reinforcement procedure was in effect [Ayllon & Azrin, 1965, p. 381].

They found that performance of desirable behaviors decreased when the response-reinforcement relation was disrupted by: delivering tokens independently of the response while still allowing exchange of tokens for the reinforcers; or by discontinuing the token system by providing continuing access to the reinforcers, or by discontinuing the delivery of tokens for a previously reinforced response while simultaneously providing tokens for a different, alternative response.

In the first year of our program we did not test the specific effects of the tokens by withdrawing them. Rather, we approached this problem in two ways. First, we incorporated within the base-line period of 9 mo. a 3-mo. period in which tokens were received on a noncontingent basis. During this period patients received tokens with concomitant attention, interest, and general social reinforcement. This resulted in slight but nonsignificant change in general ward behavior. The results of the experimental period were then compared with the base line which included the nonspecific reinforcement. The results indicate that the more drastic changes in behavior were a function of the specific procedures involved. The other technique we used was to change the token value of certain specific activities. An increase in value (more tokens) was related to an increase in performance; return to the old value meant a decrement to the previous level of performance (see Figure 4.7–1).

We should also point out that the situation in the hospital is such that the token economy did not mean that there were more of the "good things in life" available to these patients because they were in a special program. The patients in the program had had access to these items, for example, extra food, beds, cigarettes, chairs, television, recreational activities, passes, before the program began, as had all patients in other wards, free of charge. Thus we cannot attribute change to the fact of more "good things" being available to these patients and not available to other patients.

Thus far, a contingent reinforcement program represented by a token economy has been successful in combating institutionalism, increasing initiative, responsibility, and social interaction, and in putting the control of patient behavior in the hands of the patient. The behavioral changes have generalized to other areas of performance. A token economy can be an important adjunct to any rehabilitation program for chronic or apathetic patients.

REFERENCES

Atthowe, J. M., Jr. Ward 113 Program: Incentives and costs—a manual for patients. Palo Alto, Calif.: Veterans Administration Hospital, 1964.

Ayllon, T. Intensive treatment of psychotic behavior by stimulus satiation and food reinforcement. *Behaviour Research and Therapy*, 1963, 1, 53–61.

Ayllon, T., & Azrin, N. H. The measurement and reinforcement of behavior of psychotics. *Journal of the Experimental Analysis of Behavior*, 1965, 8, 357–384.

Ayllon, T., & Houghton, E. Control of the behavior of schizophrenic patients by food. *Journal of the Experimental Analysis of Behavior*, 1962, 5, 343–352.

Ayllon, T., & Michael, J. The psychiatric nurse as a behavioral engineer. *Journal of the Experimental Analysis of Behavior*, 1959, 2, 323–334.

Fairweather, G. W., Simon, R., Gebhard, M. E., Weingarten, E., Holland, J. L., Sanders, R., Stone, G. B., & Reahl, J. E. Relative effectiveness of psychotherapeutic programs: A multicriteria comparison of four programs for three different patient groups. *Psychological Monographs*, 1960, 74(5, Whole No. 492).

Finney, B. C. A scale to measure interpersonal relationships in group psychotherapy. *Group Psychotherapy*, 1954, 7, 52–66.

Kramer, M., Goldstein, H., Israel, R. H., & Johnson, N. A. Application of life table methodology to the study of mental hospital populations. *Psychiatric Research Reports*, 1956, 5, 49–76.

Krasner, L. The therapist as a social reinforcement machine. In H. H. Strupp & L. Luborsky (Eds.), *Research in psychotherapy*. Washington, D. C.: American Psychological Association, 1962. Pp. 61–94.

Morgan, N. C., & Johnson, N. A. The chronic hospital patient. *American Journal of Psychiatry*, 1957, 113, 824–830.

Odegard, O. Current studies of incidence and prevalence of hospitalized mental patients in Scandinavia. In P. H. Hoch & J. Zubin (Eds.), *Comparative epidemiology of the mental disorders*. New York: Grune & Stratton, 1961. Pp. 45–55.

Skinner, B. F. *The behavior of organisms*. New York: Appleton-Century-Crofts, 1938.

Skinner, B. F. *Science and human behavior*. New York: Macmillan, 1953.

4.8 "GOOD-BYE, TEACHER . . ."*
Fred S. Keller

When I was a boy, and school "let out" for the summer, we used to cele-
brate our freedom from educational control by chanting:

> Good-bye scholars, good-bye school;
> Good-bye teacher, darned old fool!

We really didn't think of our teacher as deficient in judgment, or as a
clown or jester. We were simply escaping from restraint, dinner pail in
one hand and shoes in the other, with all the delights of summer before
us. At that moment, we might even have been well-disposed toward our
teacher and might have felt a touch of compassion as we completed the
rhyme.

"Teacher" was usually a woman, not always young and not always
pretty. She was frequently demanding and sometimes sharp of tongue,
ever ready to pounce when we got out of line. But, occasionally, if one
did especially well in home-work or in recitation, he could detect a flicker
of approval or affection that made the hour in class worthwhile. At such
times, we loved our teacher and felt that school was fun.

It was not fun enough, however, to keep me there when I grew older.
Then I turned to another kind of education, in which the reinforcements
were sometimes just as scarce as in the schoolroom. I became a Western
Union messenger boy and, between deliveries of telegrams, I learned
Morse code by memorizing dots and dashes from a sheet of paper and
listening to a relay on the wall. As I look back on those days, I conclude
that I am the only living reinforcement theorist who ever learned Morse
code in the absence of reinforcement.

It was a long, frustrating job. It taught me that drop-out learning
could be just as difficult as in-school learning and it led me to wonder
about easier possible ways of mastering a skill. Years later, after returning
to school and finishing my formal education, I came back to this classical
learning problem, with the aim of making International Morse code less
painful for beginners than American Morse had been for me (Keller,
1943).

* Reprinted from *The Journal of Applied Behavior Analysis*, *1*, 1968, 79–89. Copyright 1968 by the Society for the Experimental Analysis of Behavior, Inc., and
reproduced by permission. President's Invited Address, Division 2, Amer. Psychol.
Assn., Washington, D.C., Sept., 1967.

During World War II, with the aid of a number of students and colleagues, I tried to apply the principle of immediate reinforcement to the early training of Signal Corps personnel in the reception of Morse-code signals. At the same time, I had a chance to observe, at close hand and for many months, the operation of a military training center. I learned something from both experiences, but I should have learned more. I should have seen many things that I didn't see at all, or saw very dimly.

I could have noted, for example, that instruction in such a center was highly individualized, in spite of large classes, sometimes permitting students to advance at their own speed throughout a course of study. I could have seen the clear specification of terminal skills for each course, together with the carefully graded steps leading to this end. I could have seen the demand for perfection at every level of training and for every student; the employment of classroom instructors who were little more than the successful graduates of earlier classes; the minimizing of the lecture as a teaching device and the maximizing of student participation. I could have seen, especially, an interesting division of labor in the educational process, wherein the non-commissioned, classroom teacher was restricted to duties of guiding, clarifying, demonstrating, testing, grading, and the like, while the commissioned teacher, the training officer, dealt with matters of course logistics, the interpretation of training manuals, the construction of lesson plans and guides, the evaluation of student progress, the selection of non-commissioned cadre, and the writing of reports for his superiors.

I did see these things, of course, in a sense, but they were embedded deeply within a special context, one of "training" rather than "education." I did not then appreciate that a set of reinforcement contingencies which were useful in building simple skills like those of the radio operator might also be useful in developing the verbal repertoires, the conceptual behaviors, and the laboratory techniques of university education. It was not until a long time later, by a very different route, that I came to such a realization.

That story began in 1962, with the attempt on the part of two Brazilian and two North American psychologists, to establish a Department of Psychology at the University of Brasilia. The question of teaching method arose from the very practical problem of getting a first course ready by a certain date for a certain number of students in the new university. We had almost complete freedom of action; we were dissatisfied with the conventional approaches; and we knew something about programmed instruction. We were also of the same theoretical persuasion. It was quite natural, I suppose, that we should look for fresh applications of reinforcement thinking to the teaching process (Keller, 1966).

The method that resulted from this collaborative effort was first used in a short-term laboratory course[1] at Columbia University in the winter of 1963, and the basic procedure of this pilot study was employed at Brasilia during the following year, by Professors Rodolfo Azzi and Carolina Martuscelli Bori, with 50 students in a one-term introductory course. Professor Azzi's report on this, at the 1965 meetings of the American Psychological Association and in personal correspondence, indicated a highly satisfactory outcome. The new procedure was received enthusiastically by the students and by the university administration. Mastery of the course material was judged excellent for all who completed the course. Objections were minor, centering around the relative absence of opportunity for discussion between students and staff.

Unfortunately, the Brasilia venture came to an abrupt end during the second semester of its operation, due to a general upheaval within the university that involved the resignation or dismissal of more than 200 teachers. Members of the original psychology staff have since taken positions elsewhere, and have reportedly begun to use the new method again, but I am unable at this time to report in detail on their efforts.

Concurrently with the early Brazilian development, Professor J. G. Sherman and I, in the spring of 1965, began a series of more or less independent applications of the same general method at Arizona State University. With various minor changes, this work has now been tried through five semesters with an increasing number of students per term (Keller, 1967; Sherman, 1967). The results have been more gratifying with each successive class, and there has been as yet no thought of a return to more conventional procedures. In addition, we have had the satisfaction of seeing our system used by a few other colleagues, in other courses and at other institutions.[2]

In describing this method to you, I will start with a quotation. It is from a hand-out given to all the students enrolled in the first-semester course in General Psychology (one of two introductions offered at Arizona State University) during the past year, and it describes the teaching method to which they will be exposed unless they elect to withdraw from the course.

This is a course through which you may move, from start to finish, at your own pace. You will not be held back by other students or forced to go ahead until you are ready. At best, you may meet all the course requirements in less than one semester; at worst, you may not complete the job within that time. How fast you go is up to you.

The work of this course will be divided into 30 units of content, which correspond roughly to a series of home-work assignments and laboratory exercises. These units will come in a definite numerical order, and you must show your mastery of each unit (by passing a "readiness" test or carrying out an experiment) before moving on to the next.

A good share of your reading for this course may be done in the classroom, at those times when no lectures, demonstrations, or other activities are taking place. Your classroom, that is, will sometimes be a study hall.

The lectures and demonstrations in this course will have a different relation to the rest of your work than is usually the rule. They will be provided only when you have demonstrated your readiness to appreciate them; no examination will be based upon them; and you need not attend them if you do not wish. When a certain percentage of the class has reached a certain point in the course, a lecture or demonstration will be available at a stated time, but it will not be compulsory.

The teaching staff of your course will include proctors, assistants, and an instructor. A proctor is an undergraduate who has been chosen for his mastery of the course content and orientation, for his maturity of judgment, for his understanding of the special problems that confront you as a beginner, and for his willingness to assist. He will provide you with all your study materials except your textbooks. He will pass upon your readiness tests as satisfactory or unsatisfactory. His judgment will ordinarily be law, but if he is ever in serious doubt, he can appeal to the classroom assistant, or even the instructor, for a ruling. Failure to pass a test on the first try, the second, the third, or even later, will not be held against you. It is better that you get too much testing than not enough, if your final success in the course is to be assured.

Your work in the laboratory will be carried out under the direct supervision of a graduate laboratory assistant, whose detailed duties cannot be listed here. There will also be a graduate classroom assistant, upon whom your proctor will depend for various course materials (assignments, study questions, special readings, and so on), and who will keep up to date all progress records for course members. The classroom assistant will confer with the instructor daily, aid the proctors on occasion, and act in a variety of ways to further the smooth operation of the course machinery.

The instructor will have as his principal responsibilities: (a) the selection of all study material used in the course; (b) the organization and the mode of presenting this material; (c) the construction of tests and examinations; and (d) the final evaluation of each student's progress. It will be his duty, also, to provide lectures, demonstrations, and discussion opportunities for all students who have earned the privilege; to act as a clearing-house for requests and complaints; and to arbitrate in any case of disagreement between students and proctors or assistants. . . .

All students in the course are expected to take a final examination, in which the entire term's work will be represented. With certain exceptions, this examination will come at the same time for all students, at the end of the term. . . . The examination will consist of questions which, in large part, you have already answered on your readiness tests. Twenty-five percent of your course grade will be based on this examination; the remaining 75% will be based on the number of units of reading and laboratory work that you have successfully completed during the term.

(In my own sections of the course, these percentages were altered, during the last term, to a 30% weighting of the final examination, a 20% weighting of the 10 laboratory exercises, and a 50% weighting of the reading units.)

A picture of the way this method operates can best be obtained, perhaps, by sampling the activities of a hypothetical average student as he moves through the course. John Pilgrim is a freshman, drawn from the upper 75% of his high-school class. He has enrolled in PY 112 for unknown reasons and has been assigned to a section of about 100 students, men and women, most of whom are also in their beginning year. The class is scheduled to meet on Tuesdays and Thursdays, from 9:15 to 10:30 A.M., with a laboratory session to be arranged.

Together with the description from which I quoted a moment ago, John receives a few mimeographed instructions and some words of advice from his professor. He is told that he should cover two units of laboratory work or reading per week in order to be sure of taking an A-grade into his final examination; that he should withdraw from the course if he doesn't pass at least one readiness test within the first two weeks; and that a grade of Incomplete will not be given except in special cases. He is also advised that, in addition to the regular classroom hours on Tuesday and Thursday, readiness tests may be taken on Saturday forenoons and Wednesday afternoons of each week—periods in which he can catch up with, or move ahead of, the rest of the class.

He then receives his first assignment: an introductory chapter from a standard textbook and two "sets" from a programmed version of similar material. With this assignment, he receives a mimeographed list of "study questions," about 30 in number. He is told to seek out the answers to these questions in his reading, so as to prepare himself for the questions he will be asked in his readiness tests. He is free to study wherever he pleases, but he is strongly encouraged to use the study hall for at least part of the time. Conditions for work are optimal there, with other students doing the same thing and with an assistant or proctor on hand to clarify a confusing passage or a difficult concept.

This is on Tuesday. On Thursday, John comes to class again, having gone through the sets of programmed material and having decided to finish his study in the classroom, where he cannot but feel that the instructor really expects him. An assistant is in charge, about half the class is there, and some late registrants are reading the course description. John tries to study his regular text, but finds it difficult to concentrate and ends by deciding to work in his room. The assistant pays no attention when he leaves.

On the following Tuesday, he appears in study hall again, ready for testing, but anxious, since a whole week of the course has passed. He reports to the assistant, who sends him across the hall, without his books and notes, to the testing room, where the proctor in charge gives him a blue-book and one of the test forms for Unit 1. He takes a seat among about 20 other students and starts work. The test is composed of 10 fill-in questions and one short-answer essay question. It doesn't seem particularly difficult and, in about 10 min John returns his question sheet and is sent, with his blue-book, to the proctor's room for grading.

In the proctor's room, in one of 10 small cubicles, John finds his special proctor, Anne Merit. Anne is a psychology major who passed the same course earlier with a grade of A. She receives two points of credit for about 4 hr of proctoring per week, 2 hr of required attendance at a weekly proctors' meeting, and occasional extra duty in the study hall or test room. She has nine other students besides John to look after, so she will not as a rule be able to spend much more than 5 or 10 min of class time with each.

Anne runs through John's answers quickly, checking two of them as incorrect and placing a question mark after his answer to the essay question. Then she asks him why he answered these three as he did. His replies show two misinterpretations of the question and one failure in written expression. A restatement of the fill-in questions and some probing with respect to the essay leads Anne to write an O.K. alongside each challenged answer. She congratulates John upon his performance and warns him that later units may be a little harder to master than the first.

John's success is then recorded on the wall-chart in the proctors' room, he is given his next assignment and set of study questions, and sent happily on his way. The blue-book remains with Anne, to be given later to the assistant or the instructor for inspection, and used again when John is ready for testing on Unit 2. As he leaves the room, John notices the announcement of a 20-min lecture by his instructor, for all students who have passed Unit 3 by the following Friday, and he resolves that he will be there.

If John had failed in the defense of one or two of his answers, he would have been sent back for a minimal period of 30 min for further study, with advice as to material most needing attention. If he had made more than four errors on his test, the answers would not have been considered individually; he would simply have been told that he was not ready for examination. And, if he had made no errors at all, he would probably have been asked to explain one or two of his correct answers, as a way of getting acquainted and to make sure that he was the one who had really done the work.

John did fail his first test on Unit 2, and his first two tests on Unit 4 (which gave trouble to nearly everyone). He missed the first lecture, too, but qualified for the second. (There were seven such "shows" during the term, each attended by perhaps half of the students entitled to be there.) After getting through his first five units, he failed on one review test before earning the right to move on to Unit 6. On the average, for the remainder of the course, he required nearly two readiness tests per unit. Failing a test, of course, was not an unmixed evil, since it permitted more discussion with the proctor and often served to sharpen the concepts involved.

In spite of more than a week's absence from school, John was able, by using the Wednesday and Saturday testing sessions, to complete his course units successfully about a week before the final examination. Because of his cramming for other courses during this last week, he did not review for his psychology and received only a B on his final examination. His A for the course was not affected by this, but his pride was hurt.

Sometime before the term ended, John was asked to comment on certain aspects of the course, without revealing his identity. (Remember, John is a mythical figure.) Among other things, he said that, in comparison with courses taught more conventionally, this one demanded a much greater mastery of the work assignments, it required greater memorization of detail and much greater understanding of basic concepts, it generated a greater feeling of achievement, it gave much greater recognition of the student as a person, and it was enjoyed to a much greater extent.

He mentioned also that his study habits had improved during the term, that his attitude towards testing had become more positive, that his worry about final grades had diminished, and that there had been an increase in his desire to hear lectures (this in spite of the fact that he attended only half of those for which he was qualified). When asked specifically about the use of proctors, he said that the discussions with his proctors had been very helpful, that the proctor's non-academic, personal relation was also important to him, and that the use of proctors generally in grading and discussing tests was highly desirable.

Anne Merit, when asked to comment on her own reactions to the system, had many things to say, mostly positive. She referred especially to the satisfaction of having the respect of her proctees, of seeing them do well, and of cementing the material of the course for herself. She noted that the method was one of "mutual reinforcement" for student, proctor, assistant, and instructor. She suggested that it ought to be used in other courses and at other levels of instruction. She wondered why it would not be possible for a student to enroll in a second course immediately upon completion of the first, if it were taught by the same method. She also listed several changes that might improve the efficiency of the course machinery, especially in the area of testing and grading, where delay may sometimes occur.

In an earlier account of this teaching method (Keller, 1967), I summarized those features which seem to distinguish it most clearly from conventional teaching procedures. They include the following:

(1) The go-at-your-own-pace feature, which permits a student to move through the course at a speed commensurate with his ability and other demands upon his time.

(2) The unit-perfection requirement for advance, which lets the student go ahead to new material only after demonstrating mastery of that which preceded.

(3) The use of lectures and demonstrations as vehicles of motivation, rather than sources of critical information.

(4) The related stress upon the written word in teacher-student communication; and, finally:

(5) The use of proctors, which permits repeated testing, immediate scoring, almost unavoidable tutoring, and a marked enhancement of the personal-social aspect of the educational process.

The similarity of our learning paradigm to that provided in the field of programmed instruction is obvious. There is the same stress upon analysis of the task, the same concern with terminal performance, the same opportunity for individualized progression, and so on. But the sphere of action here is different. The principal steps of advance are not "frames" in a "set," but are more like the conventional home-work assignment or laboratory exercise. "The 'response' is not simply the completion of a prepared statement through the insertion of a word or phrase. Rather, it may be thought of as the resultant of many such responses, better described as the understanding of a principle, a formula, or a concept, or the ability to use an experimental technique. Advance within the program depends on something more than the appearance of a confirming word or the presentation of a new frame; it involves a personal interaction between a student and his peer, or his better, in what may be a lively verbal interchange, of interest and importance to each participant. The use of a programmed text, a teaching machine, or some sort of computer aid within such a course is entirely possible and may be quite desirable, but it is not to be equated with the course itself." (Keller, 1967a.)

Failure to recognize that our teaching units are not as simple as the response words in a programmed text, or the letter reactions to Morse-code signals, or other comparable atoms of behavior, can lead to confusion concerning our procedure. A well-known critic of education in America, after reading an account of our method, sent me a note confessing to "a grave apprehension about the effect of breaking up the subject matter into little packages." "I should suppose," he said, "it would prevent all but the strongest minds from ever possessing a synoptic view of a field, and I imagine that the coaching, and testing, and passing in bits would amount to efficient training rather than effectual teaching."

Our "little packages" or "bits" are no smaller than the basic conceptions of a science of behavior and cannot be delivered all at once in one large synoptic parcel. As for the teaching-training distinction, one needs only to note that it is always the instructor who decides what is to be taught, and to what degree, thus determining whether he will be called a trainer or a teacher. The method he uses, the basic reinforcement contingencies he employs, may be turned to either purpose.

Many things occur, some of them rather strange, when a student is taught by a method such as ours. With respect to everyday student behavior, even a casual visit to a class will provide some novel items. For example, all the students seated in the study hall may be seen studying, undistracted by the presence or movements of others. In the test room, a student will rarely be seen chewing on his pencil, looking at a neighbor's blue-book, or staring out the window. In the crowded proctors' room, 10 pairs of students can be found concurrently engaged in academic interaction, with no couple bothered by the conversation of another, no matter how close by. Upon passing his assistant or instructor, in the corridors or elsewhere, a student will typically be seen to react in a friendly and respectful manner—enough to excite a mild alarm.

More interesting than this is the fact that a student may be tested 40 or 50 times in the course of one semester, often standing in line for the privilege, without a complaint. In one extreme instance, a student required nearly two terms to complete the work of one (after which he applied for, and got, permission to serve as a proctor for the following year).

Another unusual feature of our testing and grading is the opportunity given to defend an "incorrect" answer. This defense, as I noted earlier, may sometimes produce changes in the proctor's evaluation, changes that are regularly checked by the assistant or the instructor. Occasionally, a proctor's O.K. will be rejected, compelling the student to take another test, and sensitizing the proctor to the dangers of leniency; more often, it produces a note of warning, a correction, or a query written by the instructor in the student's blue-book; but always it provides the instructor with feedback on the adequacy of the question he has constructed.

Especially important, in a course taught by such a method, is the fact that any differences in social, economic, cultural, and ethnic background are completely and repeatedly subordinated to a friendly intellectual relationship between two human beings throughout a period of 15 weeks or more. Also, in such a course, a lonesome, ill-favored underprivileged, badly schooled, or otherwise handicapped boy or girl can be assured at least a modicum of individual attention, approval, encouragement, and a chance to succeed. The only prerequisite for such treatment is a well-defined amount and quality of academic achievement.

Another oddity of the system is the production of a grade distribution that is upside down. In Fig. 4.8–1, are the results from a class of 208 students at Arizona State University during the past semester. Note the diminishing relative frequency as one moves from A to D. The category of E, indicating failure, is swollen by the presence of 18 students who failed to take up their option of W (withdrawal from the course). Grades of C and D were due to the failure of students to complete all the units of reading or laboratory before going into the final examination.

Figure 4.8–2 shows data from the class 1 yr earlier. Essentially the same distribution holds, except for the category of Incomplete, which was then too easily obtainable. Discouraging the use of the Incomplete, together with the provision of more testing hours, apparently has the effect of regularizing study habits and equalizing the number of tests taken per week throughout the term.

In Fig. 4.8–3 (filled bars), the grade distribution is for a section of 25 students in an introductory course at Queens College (N.Y.) during the second semester of the past school year. The same method of teaching was employed as at Arizona State, but the work requirement was somewhat greater in amount. The distinctive feature here is the relative infrequency of low grades. Only four students received less than a B rating. Professor John Farmer, who provided me with these data, reports that the two students receiving F had dropped out of the course, for unknown reasons, after seven and eight units respectively.

With this teaching method, students who are presumably inferior may show up better upon examination than presumably superior students taught by more conventional procedures. Figure 4.8–4 shows two distributions of grades on a mid-term examination. The empty bars represent the achievement of 161 students of an Ivy League College, mainly sophomores, in the first semester of a one-year lecture-and-laboratory

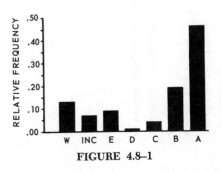

FIGURE 4.8–1

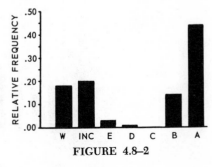

FIGURE 4.8–2

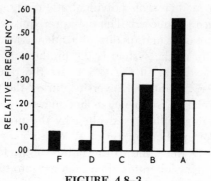

FIGURE 4.8–3

course in elementary psychology. The filled bars represent the achievement of 66 Arizona State University students, mainly freshmen, on an unannounced mid-term quiz prepared by the Ivy League instructor and from which 13% of the questions had to be eliminated on the grounds of differential course coverage.

Relevant to this comparison is that pictured in Fig. 4.8–3. The grade distribution obtained by Professor Farmer (and his associate, Brett Cole) is here compared with one obtained from a section of 46 students in the same course, taught in the conventional manner by a colleague who is described as "a very good instructor." The filled bars show the Farmer-Cole results; the empty ones are those from Professor Brandex.

Such comparisons are of some interest and may relieve the tedium of a lecture, but they raise many questions of interpretation, and their importance should not be over-emphasized. The kind of change needed in education today is not one that will be evaluated in terms of the percentage of A's in a grade distribution or of differences at the 0.01 (or 0.001) level of confidence. It is one that will produce a reinforcing

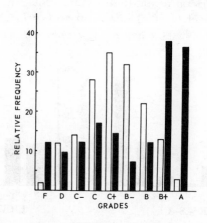

FIGURE 4.8–4

state of affairs for everyone involved—a state of affairs that has here-
tofore been reached so rarely as to be the subject of eulogy in the world's
literature, and which, unfortunately, has led to the mystique of the "great
teacher" rather than a sober analysis of the critical contingencies in
operation.

Our method has not yet required a grant-in-aid to keep it going. On
one occasion we tried to get such help, in order to pay for mimeograph
paper, the services of a clerk, and one or two additional assistants. Our
request was rejected, quite properly, on the grounds that our project was
"purely operational." Almost any member of a present-day fund-granting
agency can recognize "research" when he sees it. I do think, however,
that one should be freed, as I was, from other university demands while
introducing a system like ours. And he should not be asked to teach more
than two such courses regularly, each serving 100 students or less, unless
he has highly qualified assistants upon whom he can depend.

Neither does the method require equipment and supplies that are
not already available to almost every teacher in the country. Teaching
machines, tape recorders, and computers could readily be fitted into the
picture. Moving pictures and television could also be used in one or two
ways without detriment to the basic educational process. But these are
luxuries, based on only partial recognition of our problem, and they
could divert us from more important considerations. (Proctors, like computers, may go wrong or break down, but they can often be repaired and
they are easily replaced, at very little expense.)

The need for individualized instruction is widely recognized, and the
most commonly suggested way of filling this need is automation. I think
that this solution is incomplete, especially when applied to the young;
and I'd like to mention a personal experience that bears upon the matter.

In the summer of 1966, I made numerous visits to a center for the
care and treatment of autistic children.[3] One day, as I stood at the door
of a classroom, I saw a boy get up from his chair at the end of a class
period and give a soft pat to the object on the desk in front of him.
At the same time, he said, with a slight smile, "Good-bye, Teaching
Machine!"

This pseudo-social behavior in this fundamentally asocial child
amused me at the time. It reminded me of Professor Moore's description
of the three-year-old who became irritated when his "talking typewriter"
made a mistake, called the device a "big bambam," requested its name,
and ended by asking, "Who is your mother?" Today, however, I am not
so sure that this is funny. It does suggest that affection may be generated within a child for an electromechanical instrument that has been
essential to educational reinforcement. Unfortunately, such a machine,
in its present form, is unlikely to generalize with human beings in the
boy's world, giving to them a highly desirable reinforcing property. In

fact, the growth of this type of student-machine relation, if it were the only one, would be a poor substitute for a directly social interaction.

In an earlier report upon our method, I mentioned that it had been anticipated, partially or *in toto*, in earlier studies and I described one of these in some detail. As for current developments by other workers in our field, I have not made any systematic attempt to examine the offerings, even those that deal with college or university instruction. However, I have been impressed by several of them which seem to have points in common with ours, which have met with some success, and which will probably be increasingly heard from in the future.

One of these is the Audio-Tutorial Approach to the teaching of botany, developed by S. N. Postlethwait at Purdue University (Postlethwait and Novak, 1967). Another is the Socratic-Type Programming of general psychology by Harry C. Mahan (1967) and his associates at Palomar College, in Californa; and a third is the Interview Technique recently applied by C. B. Ferster and M. C. Perrott (1968) in teaching principles of behavior to graduate students in education at the University of Maryland.

Professor Postlethwait's method places great emphasis upon "independent study sessions" in which students carry out each individual work assignment in the course at their own pace, by means of the extensive use of tapes and films. Teaching assistants provide for oral quizzing on major concepts and help the students with difficult assignments. Weekly "small assembly sessions" are used primarily for recitation and the discussion of problems or small research projects; and "general assembly sessions" deal mainly with motivational materials. Postlethwait reports high student interest and greatly improved performance with the use of this technique. "Grades have risen from 6% A's under the conventional system to as high as 25% A's in some semesters. Failures have decreased from 20% in the conventional system to as few as 4%."

"Socratic-Type Programming" is described by Professor Mahan as "a philosophy and technology of instruction which emphasizes student response rather than presentations by the teacher. Its basic media consist of exercises made up of questions and short answers covering the content of a standard text, the text itself, tapes for recording the questions in the exercises, a classroom tape recorder for administering tests, tape duplicating facilities, a listening center in the college library, and student owned tape recorders for home use whenever possible. Classroom time is devoted largely to the discussion of points covered by the questions. All examinations are the short-answer type and are presented aurally on tape." Students must pass three periodic tests with a score of 85% or better before they are permitted to take a comprehensive final examination. The method does not yet permit "multiple exit" from the course, but Mahan says it is "tending very much in that direction." (1967)

APPLICATIONS 273

The Interview Technique, as described by Ferster and Perrott, does permit students to complete the course at different times, and it also approximates the student-and-proctor feature. Progress through the course is possible by verbalizing successive units of course content in a lengthy series of short interviews. The interviews are conducted mainly between students currently enrolled in the course, and any student is free to leave the course when all of his reading assignments have been adequately covered. The interviewer may sometimes be a staff member, as at the beginning of the course, but generally he is a student who has already been interviewed by someone else on the topic in question. The interviews are highly formalized, with the interviewer playing the role of the listener, checker, appraiser, and summarizer. Each interview is an open-book affair, but of such short and sharply-defined duration (10 min, as a rule) that the student can do no more than cue himself by reference to the printed page.

The goal of this method is nothing less than fluency with respect to each main feature of the course. Lectures, group discussions, and demonstrations are available at certain times, contingent upon a given stage of advance. Inadequate interviews are rejected, in whole or part, without prejudice, and with suggestions for further study. A product of high quality is guaranteed through staff participation at critical points. A modification of this procedure, which is to include written tests and the employment of advanced-student proctors, is planned by Professor Ferster for the introductory course in psychology at Georgetown University during the coming semester.

In systems like these, and in the one I have centered on, the work of a teacher is at variance with that which has predominated in our time. His public appearances as classroom entertainer, expositor, critic, and debater no longer seem important. His principal job, as Frank Finger (1962) once defined it, is truly "the facilitation of learning in others." He becomes an educational engineer, a contingency manager, with the responsibility of serving the great majority, rather than the small minority, of young men and women who come to him for schooling in the area of his competence. The teacher of tomorrow will not, I think, continue to be satisfied with a 10% efficiency (at best) which makes him an object of contempt by some, commiseration by others, indifference by many, and love by a few. No longer will he need to hold his position by the exercise of functions that neither transmit culture, dignify his status, nor encourage respect for learning in others. No longer will he need to live, like Ichabod Crane, in a world that increasingly begrudges him room and lodging for a doubtful service to its young. A new kind of teacher is in the making. To the old kind, I, for one, will be glad to say, "Good-bye!"

I started this paper on a personal note and I would like to end it on one. Twenty-odd years ago, when white rats were first used as laboratory subjects in the introductory course, a student would sometimes complain about his animal's behavior. The beast couldn't learn, he was asleep, he wasn't hungry, he was sick, and so forth. With a little time and a handful of pellets, we could usually show that this was wrong. All that one needed to do was follow the rules. "The rat," we used to say, "is always right."

My days of teaching are over. After what I have said about efficiency, I cannot lay claim to any great success, but my schedule of rewards was enough to maintain my behavior, and I learned one very important thing: *the student is always right.* He is not asleep, not unmotivated, not sick, and he can learn a great deal if we provide the right contingencies of reinforcement. But if we don't provide them, and provide them soon, he too may be inspired to say, "Good-bye!" to formal education.

NOTES

1. With the aid of (Dr.) Lanny Fields and the members of a senior seminar at Columbia College, during the fall term of 1963-64.
2. For example, by J. L. Michael with high-school juniors on a National Science Foundation project at Grinnell College (Iowa), in 1965; and by J. Farmer and B. Cole at Queens College (New York) in a course similar to the one described here.
3. At the Linwood Children's Center, Ellicott City, Maryland.

REFERENCES

Ferster, C. B. and Perrott, M. C. *Behavior principles.* New York: Appleton-Century-Crofts, 1968. Pp. 542.

Finger, F. W. Psychologists in colleges and universities. In W. B. Webb (Ed.), *The profession of psychology.* New York: Holt, Rinehart and Winston, 1962. Pp. 50-73.

Keller, F. S. Studies in international morse code: 1. a new method of teaching code reception. *Journal of Applied Psychology,* 1943, 27, 407-415.

Keller, F. S. A personal course in psychology. In R. Ulrich, T. Stachnik, and J. Mabry (Eds.), *The control of behavior.* Glenview, Ill.: Scott, Foresman, 1966. Pp. 91-93.

Keller, F. S. Neglected rewards in the educational process. *Proc. 23rd Amer. Conf. Acad. Deans,* Los Angeles, Jan., 1967a. Pp. 9-22.

Keller, F. S. Engineering personalized instruction in the classroom. *Rev. Interamer de Psicol.,* 1967b, 1, 189-197.

Keller, F. S. and Schoenfeld, W. N. The psychology curriculum at Columbia College. *American Psychologist,* 1949, 4, 165-172.

Mahan, H. C. The use of Socratic type programmed instruction in college courses in psychology. Paper read at West. Psychol. Assn., San Francisco, May, 1967.

Postlethwait, S. N. and Novak, J. D. The use of 8-mm loop films in individual instruction. *Annals N. Y. Acad. Sci.,* Vol. 142, Art. 2, 464-470.

Sherman, J. G. Application of reinforcement principles to a college course. Paper read at Amer. Educ. Res. Assn., New York, Feb., 1967.

Five
Response
Suppression

Of several responses made to the same situation . . . those which are accompanied or closely followed by discomfort to the animal will, other things being equal, have their connection with the situation weakened, so that, when it recurs, they will be less likely to occur [Edward L. Thorndike, *Animal Intelligence*, 1911].

We are gradually discovering—at an untold cost in human suffering —that in the long run punishment doesn't reduce the probability that an act will occur [B. F. Skinner, *Walden Two*, 1948].

Punishment

Punishment is one of society's oldest techniques for controlling behavior, and also one of the most controversial. Does it really work? Is it ethical? Just as we now consider public floggings and the rack to be cruel and unusual punishment, will we someday condemn spankings as equally senseless and barbaric?

There has been no lack of debate on these issues, but rarely can either side produce any clear evidence to support their position, nor perhaps should we expect them to. How, after all, does one study the long-range effects of punishment? We might compare children from families that use punishment with those that do not, but how could we be sure that the use of punishment was the crucial difference? To control for extraneous variables could we ask parents to punish half their children and spare the other half so that we might compare their behavior in later life? Or could we ask a society to close down its prisons for ten or twenty years in order to determine the effectiveness of its penal code? As important as the effects of punishment may be, they are extremely difficult to study in a complex social environment.

One approach, as we have suggested previously, is to use animals rather than humans as subjects. Even in the confines of the animal laboratory, however, the effects of punishment have proven controversial. The early evidence was largely negative, suggesting that punishment had little or no effect on behavior. Edward L. Thorndike, for example, in his early statements of the Law of Effect accorded punishment equal status with reinforcement as a fundamental process in learning, but his subsequent research led him to drop it completely from later versions. Similarly Skinner was persuaded by his own research with rats that punishment has at best a temporary effect on behavior, and he argued vigorously that any possible advantages were more than outweighed by the potential dangers.

These conclusions were, however, based on very little evidence. Perhaps because of a reluctance to inflict pain, even on rats, most experimenters either avoided punishment or else chose relatively mild punishers. Skinner, for example, at one point used a slap on the paws to punish his rats, and Thorndike's research was largely done with human subjects using the word "No" as the aversive event! Only in the last decade have experiments on punishment been reported in any number, and the effect has been to largely reverse the earlier negative conclusions. At least insofar as the white rat is concerned there is now substantial evidence that punishment produces powerful and enduring suppression of behavior (e.g., Solomon, 1964; Campbell and Church, 1969). In perhaps the most vivid illustration of punishment's potency, Masserman and Pechtel (1953) presented a toy snake to a spider monkey while it was eating. Snakes are extremely frightening to these monkeys, and the result was that the monkey not only immediately stopped eating but never started again, eventually starving to death! The effects of punishment are rarely this dramatic—to be maximally effective, it must be both immediate and moderately strong, and even then its effects may sometimes be peculiar (e.g., Fowler, 1963; Morse and Kelleher, 1970)—but there now seems little question that punishment can be effective in suppressing behavior.

Its effectiveness in the animal laboratory, however, does not necessarily mean that punishment should be used in raising children or rehabilitating criminals. Is punishment as effective with humans as with animals? And even if it is, does it have harmful side effects that might outweigh its advantages? One experiment addressed to these issues was reported by Lovaas, Schaeffer, and Simmons (Article 5.1). Their subjects were children suffering from autism, a form of schizophrenia in which the child becomes totally isolated from the world, having neither verbal nor physical contact with those around him. Typically an autistic child spends his day rocking or fondling himself, occasionally

engaging in bizarre and stereotyped gestures. The twins used
in this study were five years old, and had already spent one year in
psychiatric treatment, with no visible effect. The prognosis, the authors
note, was certain institutionalization, since children who are not
cured by this age "will not improve, despite traditional psychiatric
treatment, including psychotherapy, of the child and/or his family."
Given these conditions, the authors felt that any treatment with a chance
of success was worth trying.

One problem which was considered particularly serious was the
amount of time the children spent in tantrums or self-stimulatory
behavior. Their total absorption in these behaviors made any attempt at
therapy impossible, and in order to eliminate them the authors
decided to try electric shock. The twins were placed barefoot in a
room with a grid floor, and were given electric shocks whenever they
had a tantrum or engaged in self-stimulation. Despite the ingrained
nature of these habits, one half-hour punishment session was enough to
completely suppress them, and they remained totally suppressed over
the next eleven months of intermittent testing.

The results of these and other experiments (e.g., Risley, 1968) clearly
demonstrate punishment's power, but they also suggest some of its
limitations. Lovaas *et al.*, for example, found behavior totally suppressed
in the test room, but over a period of weeks the behavior gradually
reappeared in other situations as the children learned that shock
only occurred in the test room. Such discrimination learning is not
surprising, but it does mean that punishment must occur in a variety of
situations if it is to be effective. Slapping a child with his hand in the
cookie jar, for example, may not suppress cookie-stealing but only
stealing in an adult's presence.

A second, potentially more serious problem with punishment is that
it may elicit aggression. In one of the early experiments on this
phenomenon Ulrich and Azrin (1962) placed pairs of rats into the
same cage. In such situations laboratory rats typically explore their
environment peacefully, circling the cage and sniffing in every corner.
When Ulrich and Azrin began to present brief electric shocks,
however, the previously friendly rats immediately began to attack each
other, rearing up on their hind legs to strike and bite each other. Nor
was this effect limited to rats or even to electric shock. Using a
variety of aversive stimuli, including tail pinches and extreme heat,
pain-elicited aggression has been found in almost every species tested,
ranging from mice to alligators (see Vernon, 1969). Aggression now
appears to be an innate reaction to pain in most animal species,
and it seems at least possible that punishment has a similar effect in man.

Even if punishment does not directly elicit aggression in humans, there is suggestive evidence that the use of force may serve as a *model* for aggressive behavior. Children are highly imitative, and are particularly so when the model is important or influential in their lives (Flanders, 1968). A parent using physical force to control a child's behavior, then, might serve as a potent model for aggressive behavior. Some indirect evidence on this question comes from an experiment by Geen and Berkowitz (Article 5.2), who studied aggressiveness in undergraduates after watching a movie. If the film showed violence (Kirk Douglas in a boxing scene) the students were far more likely to be physically aggressive on a later test than if the film was equally exciting but nonviolent (a race). Similar results have been obtained with children (e.g., Bandura, Ross, and Ross, 1963), suggesting that punishment may lead to aggression indirectly through imitation as well as directly through pain-elicitation. The evidence at this point is still rather weak, but the possible consequences are too serious to ignore. Even aside from the more spectacular incidents of violence in this country, such as assassination, the rate of murder with guns is more than 35 times greater in the United States than in such countries as England or Germany. It is difficult to balance the immediate effectiveness of punishment against its potentially harmful long-range consequences, but clearly punishment should be avoided wherever alternative techniques are available.

Extinction

We can illustrate one alternative to punishment with a case history reported by Carl Williams (Article 5.3). The subject was a two-year-old boy who had been seriously ill for the first 18 months of his life. Even after his recovery, however, he continued to demand special attention from his parents, and threw tantrums whenever he did not get his way. His crying became a severe strain on his parents generally, but perhaps the most trying outbursts came at bedtime. He demanded his parents' continuous presence and complete attention before he fell asleep, and cried bitterly if they attempted to leave the room or even read a book. Since falling asleep typically required from 30 minutes to two hours, his parents were more than a little concerned, and consulted Williams for advice. One solution might have been some form of punishment—for example, a spanking whenever he cried—but Williams reasoned that the boy's crying was being reinforced by the attention it gave him, and he suggested that the parents simply ignore any crying after they put their son to bed. The first night he cried for almost an hour before falling asleep, but within three nights the crying had almost completely disappeared. There was a brief recurrence when an aunt accidentally reinforced it, but it quickly disappeared again, this time permanently. Furthermore, there were no harmful side effects, and observations one year later suggested that he had become a happy and outgoing child.

Extinction, or nonreinforcement of a previously reinforced response, obviously works, but it has been a theoretical puzzle ever since it was first noted by Pavlov.[1] Why should a well-learned response disappear simply because it is followed by nonreinforcement? Nonreinforcement, after all, really means that the response is followed by *nothing*, and how can nothing affect the strength of a response? One explanation is based on the phenomenon of amount contrast which we discussed in the previous chapter. We said then that the incentive value of any reinforcer is reduced by prior experience with a better incentive, so that a child who becomes used to banana splits will then find candy bars far less attractive. If we assume that contrast affects *all* events, whether positive, negative, or neutral, then the principle of contrast could also explain extinction. Experience with reinforcement during training would reduce the incentive value of nonreinforcement, and if we assume nonreinforcement to initially be neutral, then any reduction would mean a negative incentive value. The elimination of banana splits, then, is not simply neutral, but actually aversive, as painful in its way as a spanking.

If this explanation were correct we should expect extinction to have exactly the same properties as any other aversive event. In one of the first studies on this question Amsel and Roussel (1952) hypothesized that extinction produces an aversive drive of frustration, and like any other drive should increase the strength of subsequent behavior. To find out, they trained rats in a double alley apparatus in which there were goal boxes located both in the middle and end of a long runway. During training food was available in both goal boxes, while during the test phase it was available on all trials in the second goal box but on only half the trials in the first goal box. During the test, then, subjects would run down the alley to the first goal box where they would find food on half the trials, and after a fixed delay period were released into the second alley where they always found food. According to Amsel and Roussel, nonreinforcement in the first goal box should produce frustration, and as a drive it should energize

---

[1] In classical conditioning a response is extinguished by presenting the CS while withholding the US.

subsequent behavior. This prediction was confirmed, as running in the second alley was significantly faster after nonreinforcement than after reinforcement.

Further evidence for the aversive nature of extinction comes from an experiment by Azrin, Hutchinson, and Hake (1966). If extinction is aversive, they reasoned, it should elicit aggression in much the same way electric shock does, and they tested this in an experiment with pigeons. Two pigeons were placed in the same cage with one immobilized in a stock-like apparatus and the other free to move about. A key was mounted on one wall of the apparatus and during the control phase pecks on this key had no effect. During the experimental phase, however, pecks were occasionally reinforced and then suddenly extinguished. Literally within seconds of the onset of an extinction period the free pigeon began to peck fiercely at the target pigeon and these attacks continued for several minutes. As described by the authors, the attacks "consisted of strong pecks at the throat and head of the target bird, especially around the eyes. The feathers of the target bird were often pulled out and the skin bruised." During the control phase, on the other hand, when there were no reinforcement periods, nonreinforcement produced no aggression. Nonreinforcement by itself, then, appears genuinely neutral, and it is only when contrasted with reinforcement that it becomes aversive.

Evidence such as this suggests that extinction is an aversive process similar to punishment, and it seems likely that the same theory will ultimately explain both phenomena. There are, however, several puzzling characteristics of extinction that cannot be explained simply by saying that it is aversive. One is *spontaneous recovery*. If a rat is first reinforced for pressing a bar and then extinguished, during the extinction period it initially responds at a high rate and then gradually reduces responding until it stops completely. If removed from the apparatus for several hours, however, and then returned, it will immediately resume responding, and the longer the interruption the greater the recovery in its responding. This partial return of an apparently extinguised response is called spontaneous recovery, and it has been found with classical conditioning as well as reinforcement, humans as well as animals. Several explanations have been proposed, generally based on the stimulus properties of time, and you might enjoy inventing one of your own (Hint: Are the stimuli present at the beginning, middle, and end of a training session identical? Might responses to these stimuli be differentially weakened during the first extinction session?).

A second extinction phenomenon which has struck psychologists as even more peculiar is the effect of partial reinforcement during training. Reinforcement, as we have seen previously, strengthens a response, and nonreinforcement weakens it. One would think, therefore, that reinforcement during training would strengthen a response more than nonreinforcement, and thus that continuous reinforcement would result in a stronger response than intermittent reinforcement. Since a strong response should be harder to extinguish, we should also predict that continuous reinforcement would result in greater responding in extinction than partial reinforcement. Well, we would be wrong. Not only are intermittently reinforced responses not weaker, they are *stronger*, and the less often they were reinforced, the stronger they are! As measured by resistance to extinction, nonreinforcement during training seems to actually *strengthen* responses, a very puzzling result. First discovered by Lloyd Humphreys in 1939, it is now known as Humphreys' Paradox, or, more prosaically, the *Partial Reinforcement Effect* (PRE).

Appalled by the apparent illogic of the PRE, psychologists quickly began searching for some explanation, and of those put forward, perhaps the most influential has been the *discrimination hypothesis*. According to this hypothesis, the amount of responding during extinction depends not only on the strength of the response during training but on the similarity of the stimulus situations during training and extinction. If training and extinction appear identical, then the subject should continue to respond as he did during training, but the more dissimilar they become the less he should respond. If partial reinforcement is more like extinction than is continuous reinforcement, this would explain why it produces greater resistance to extinction.

The discrimination hypothesis thus offers a simple and elegant explanation of the PRE in terms of the similarity between partial reinforcement and extinction, but theorists have differed as to the *basis* of this similarity. Sheffield (1949), for example, emphasized the role of stimuli persisting from the previous trial. In his account nonreinforcement produced certain stimuli whose aftereffects might still be present when the next trial occurred. If that trial was reinforced, then the connection between those stimuli and the response would be strengthened, and the subject would learn to respond in the presence of nonreinforcement cues. A subject trained on continuous reinforcement, however, would not have the benefit of this training, and thus would be less likely to continue responding when faced with nonreinforcement in extinction. Thus for Sheffield the crucial stimuli were traces persisting from the immediately preceding trial, and partial reinforcement increased resistance to extinction because subjects had already learned to respond in the presence of nonreinforcement cues.

A somewhat different interpretation of the discrimination hypothesis emphasized the role of *sequential* cues in learning. According to this hypothesis, subjects remembered the outcomes of a series of trials, rather than only those of the preceding trial, and cues from the entire sequence came to control responding. In emphasizing the memory for a series of trials, however, the sequential hypothesis was suggesting not only a quantitative but a qualitative difference in memory. In his emphasis on stimulus traces, Sheffield assumed that food left some simple, peripheral aftereffect, perhaps taste in the mouth, but the sequential hypothesis assumed a more permanent, central memory trace—"Last trial I was reinforced."

To separate these explanations, Tyler, Wortz, and Bitterman (Article 5.4) gave their subjects food on an average of 50 percent of the trials during training, with half the subjects receiving continuous alternation (food on every other trial) and half receiving random alternation. In the random reinforcement group subjects might receive relatively long runs of nonreinforcement before being reinforced, and if sequences are remembered then they should find the long runs of nonreinforcement in extinction more familiar (that is, similar to training conditions) than subjects on regular alternation. The results supported the sequential hypothesis, as subjects trained on random alternation responded significantly more in extinction than those on regular alternation, even though both groups received the same percentage of reinforcement in training.

More recent theories of the PRE (e.g., Amsel, 1962, Capaldi, 1971) are still based on the discrimination hypothesis, although they continue to differ on the exact nature of the stimuli, and also on the learning mechanisms involved in connecting those stimuli to a response. We will discuss each of these issues at greater length in the following chapters, but for now it's enough to note that seemingly paradoxical phenomena such as the PRE can sometimes be explained very simply through careful analysis of the stimuli present.

Summarizing our discussion of procedures for eliminating behavior, we have seen that punishment can be an extremely powerful technique for response suppression, but that it also produces side effects which may be harmful. Wherever possible extinction may be preferable, if only because it represents a milder form of punishment, and perhaps one less likely to serve as a model for aggression. With some responses, however, such as overeating or smoking, it may be difficult to withhold or perhaps even identify the reinforcer, and some form of punishment or aversive conditioning may be the only alternative. Regardless of what technique is used, it is more likely to be effective if combined with reinforcement of some alternative behavior. Thus whether trying to cure thumb sucking, overeating, or drug addiction, it will be easier if some pleasurable substitute is available.

5.1 | BUILDING SOCIAL BEHAVIOR IN AUTISTIC CHILDREN BY USE OF ELECTRIC SHOCK*

O. Ivar Lovaas, Benson Schaeffer, and James Q. Simmons

Three experimental investigations were carried out on two five-year-old identical twins diagnosed as childhood schizophrenics by using painful electric shock in an attempt to modify their behaviors. Their autistic features were pronounced; they manifested no social responsiveness, speech, nor appropriate play with objects. They engaged in considerable self-stimulatory behavior, and in bizarre, repetitive bodily movements. They had not responded to traditional treatment efforts.

The studies show that it was possible to modify their behaviors by the use of electric shock. They learned to approach adults to avoid shock. Shock was effective in eliminating pathological behaviors, such as self-stimulation and tantrums. Affectionate and other social behaviors toward adults increased after adults had been associated with shock reduction.

Psychological or physical pain is perhaps as characteristic in human relationships as is pleasure. The extensive presence of pain in everyday life may suggest that it is necessary for the establishment and maintenance of normal human interactions.

Despite the pervasiveness of pain in daily functioning, and its possible necessity for maintaining some behaviors, psychology and related professions have shied away from, and often condemned, the use of pain for therapeutic purposes. We agree with Solomon (1964) that such objections to the use of pain have a moral rather than a scientific basis. Recent research, as reviewed by Solomon, indicated that the scientific premises offered by psychologists for the rejection of punishment are not tenable. Rather, punishment can be a very useful tool for effecting behavior change.

* Reprinted from *The Journal of Experimental Research in Personality*, 1965, *1*, 99–109. Copyright 1965 by Academic Press, and reproduced by permission. This study was supported by a grant from the National Institute of Health (HD 00938). The authors express their gratitude to Professor Donald M. Baer of the University of Washington for his help in the design and report of these studies. They are also indebted to Gilbert Freitag, M. I. Kinder, and B. D. Rubenstein for their assistance in carrying out Study 1. Finally, we acknowledge the cooperation of the Staff at the Children's Unit, Department of Child Psychiatry, Neuropsychiatric Institute, U.C.L.A. The substance of these studies was presented in a paper to the American Psychological Association, September, 1964, Los Angeles.

There are three ways pain can be used therapeutically. First, it can be used directly as punishment, i.e., it can be presented contingent upon certain undesirable behaviors, so as to suppress them. This is perhaps the most obvious use of pain. Second, pain can be removed or withheld contingent upon certain behaviors. That is, certain behaviors can be established and maintained because they terminate pain, or avoid it altogether. Escape and avoidance learning exemplify this. The third way in which pain can be used is the least well known, and perhaps the most intriguing. Any stimulus which is associated with or discriminative of pain reduction acquires *positive* reinforcing (rewarding) properties (Bijou and Baer, 1961), i.e., an organism will work to "obtain" those stimuli which have been associated with pain reduction. The action of such stimuli is analogous to that of stimuli whose positive reinforcing properties derive from primary positive reinforcers.

These three aspects of the use of pain can be illustrated by observations on parent-child relationships. The first two are obvious; a parent will punish his child to suppress specific behaviors, and his child will learn to behave so as to escape or avoid punishment. The third aspect of the use of pain is more subtle, but more typical. In this case, a parent "rescues" his child from discomfort. In reinforcement theory terms, the parent becomes discriminative for the reduction or removal of negative reinforcers or noxious stimuli. During the first year of life many of the interactions a parent has with his children may be of this nature. An infant will fuss, cry, and give signs indicative of pain or distress many times during the day, whereupon most parents will pick him up and attempt to remove the discomfort. Such situations must contribute a basis for subsequent meaningful relationships between people; individuals are seen as important to each other if they have faced and worked through a stressful experience together. It may well be that much of a child's love for his parents develops in situations which pair parents with stress reductions. Later in life, the normal child does turn to his parent when he is frightened or hurt by nightmares, by threat of punishment from his peers, by fears of failure in school, and so on.

In view of these considerations, it was considered appropriate to investigate the usefulness of pain in modifying the behaviors of autistic children. Autistic children were selected for two reasons: (1) because they show no improvement with conventional psychiatric treatment; and (2) because they are largely unresponsive to everyday interpersonal events.

In the present study, pain was induced by means of an electrified grid on the floor upon which the children stood. The shock was turned on immediately following pathological behaviors. It was turned off or withheld when the children came to the adults who were present. Thus, these adults "saved" the children from a dangerous situation; they were the only "safe" objects in a painful environment.

STUDY 1

The objectives of Study 1 were (1) to train the children to avoid electric shock by coming to E when so requested; (2) to follow the onset of self-stimulatory and tantrum behaviors by electric shock so as to decrease their frequency; and (3) to pair the word "no" with electric shock and test its acquisition of behavior-suppressing properties.

Method

Subjects.   The studies were carried out on two identical twins. They were five-years old when the study was initiated and were diagnosed as schizophrenics. They evidenced no social responsiveness; they did not respond in any manner to speech, nor did they speak; they did not recognize each other or recognize adults even after isolation from people; they were not toilet trained; their handling of physical objects (toys, etc.) was inappropriate and stereotyped, being restricted to "fiddling" and spinning. They were greatly involved in self-stimulatory behavior, spending 70 to 80 per cent of their day rocking, fondling themselves, and moving hands and arms in repetitive, stereotyped manners. They engaged in a fair amount of tantrum behaviors, such as screaming, throwing objects, and hitting themselves.

It is important to note, in view of the moral and ethical reasons which might preclude the use of electric shock, that their future was certain institutionalization. They had been intensively treated in a residential setting by conventional psychiatric techniques for one year prior to the present study without any observable modification in their behaviors. This failure in treatment is consistent with reports of other similar efforts with such children (Eisenberg, 1957; Brown, 1960), which have suggested that if a schizophrenic child does not have language and does not play appropriately with physical objects by the age of three to five, then he will not improve, despite traditional psychiatric treatment, including psychotherapy, of the child and/or his family.

Apparatus.   The research was conducted in a 12 × 12-foot experimental room with an adjoining observation room connected by one-way mirrors and sound equipment. The floor of the experimental room was covered by one-half inch wide metal tapes with adhesive backing (Scotch Tape). They were laid one-half inch apart so that when the child stepped on the floor he would be in contact with at least two strips, thereby closing the circuit and receiving an electric shock. A six-volt battery was wired to the strips of tape via a Harvard Inductorium. The shock was set at a level at which each of three Es standing barefoot on the floor agreed that it was definitely painful and frightening.

The Ss' behavior and the experimental events were recorded on an Esterline Angus pen recorder by procedures more fully described in an earlier paper (Lovaas et al., 1965). The observer could reliably record both frequency and duration of several behaviors simultaneously on a panel of push-buttons. A given observer recorded at randomly selected periods.

Pre-shock Sessions. The Ss were placed barefoot in the experimental room with two Es, but were not shocked. There were two such pre-experimental sessions, each lasting for about 20 minutes. The Es would invite the Ss to "come here" about five times a minute, giving a total of approximately 100 trials per session. The observers recorded the amount of physical contact (defined as S's touching E with his hands), self-stimulatory and tantrum behavior, the verbal command "come here," and positive responses to the command (coming to within one foot of E within five seconds).

First Shock Sessions. The two pre-experimental sessions were followed by three shock sessions distributed over three consecutive days during which Ss were trained, in an escape-avoidance paradigm, to avoid shock by responding to E's verbal command according to the pre-established criterion. In the escape phase of the training, consisting of fifty trials, the two Es faced each other, about three feet apart, with S standing (held, if necessary) between them so that he faced one of the Es, who would lean forward, stretch his arms out, and say "come here." At the same time shock was turned on and remained on until S moved in the direction of this E, or, if S had not moved within three seconds, until the second E pushed S in the direction of the inviting E. Either type of movement of S toward the inviting E immediately terminated the shock. The S had to walk alternately from one E to the other.

In the avoidance sessions which followed, shock was withheld provided S approached E within five seconds. If S did not start his approach to the inviting E within five seconds, or if he was not within one foot of E within seven seconds, the shock was turned on and the escape procedure was reinstated for that trial.

During these avoidance sessions Es gradually increased their distance from each other until they were standing at opposite sides of the room. At the same time they gradually decreased the number of cues signaling S to approach them. In the final trials, Es merely emitted the command "come here," without turning toward or otherwise signaling S.

Shock was also turned on if S at any time engaged in self-stimulatory and/or tantrum behaviors. Whenever possible, shock was administered at the onset of such behaviors. Shock was never given except on the feet; no shock was given if S touched the floor with other parts of his body. In order to keep S on his feet, shock was given for any behavior which might have enabled him to avoid shock, such as beginning to sit down, moving toward the window to climb on its ledge, etc.

Extinction Sessions. The three shock sessions were followed by eleven extinction sessions distributed over a ten-month period. These sessions were the same as those in the previous sessions, except that shock and the command "no" were never delivered during this period.

The Second Shock Sessions. Three additional sessions terminated Study 1. In the first of these, S was brought into the experimental room and given a two-second shock not contingent upon any behavior of S or E. This was the only shock given. In all other respects these final sessions were similar to the preceding extinction sessions.

Procedure for Establishing and Testing "No" as a Secondary Negative Reinforcer. During the first shock sessions, shock had been delivered contingent upon self-stimulatory and/or tantrum behaviors. Simultaneous with the onset of shock Es would say "no," thereby pairing the word "no" and shock. The test for any suppressing power which the word "no" had acquired during these pairings was carried out in the following manner. Prior to the shock sessions, Ss were trained to press a lever (wired to a cumulative recorder) for M & M candy on a fixed ratio 20 schedule. The sessions lasted for ten minutes daily. A stable rate of lever-pressing was achieved by the twelfth session, at which Es tested the word "no" for suppressing effects on the lever-pressing rate. The E delivered the "no" contingent upon lever-pressing toward the middle of each session, during three sessions *prior* to the shock sessions, and during three sessions *subsequent* to the shock sessions, i.e., after "no" had been paired with shock.

Results and Discussion

Figure 5.1–1 gives the proportion of time Ss responded to Es' commands (proportion of Rs to S^Ds). As can be seen, in the two preshock session Ss did not respond to Es' commands. During the first three shock sessions (Shock I), Ss learned to respond to Es' requests within the prescribed time interval and thus avoided shock. This changed responsiveness of Ss to Es' requests was maintained for the subsequent nine months (no shock sessions). There was a relatively sudden decrease in Ss' responsiveness after nine months, i.e., the social behavior of coming to E extinguished. One non-contingent shock, however, immediately reinstated the social responsiveness (Shock II), suggesting that Ss responded to it as a discriminative stimulus for social behavior.

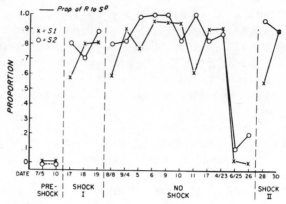

FIGURE 5.1–1 Proportion of time Ss responded to E's commands—proportion of Rs to S^Ds.

The data on Ss' pathological behaviors (self-stimulation and tantrums) and other social behaviors (physical contacts) are presented in Fig. 5.1–2. Prior to shock pathological behaviors occurred 65–85 per cent of the time; physical contacts were absent. Shock I suppressed the pathological behaviors immediately, and they remained suppressed during the following eleven months. In addition, social behaviors replaced the pathological behaviors. This change was very durable (ten to eleven months), but did eventually extinguish. One non-contingent shock reinstated the social responsiveness and suppressed the pathological behaviors.

The data on the acquisition of "no" as a negative reinforcer are presented in Fig. 5.1–3. The records of bar-pressing for candy are presented as cumulative curves. The word "no" was presented contingent upon a bar-pressing response three sessions before and three sessions subsequent to shock, i.e., before and after the pairing of "no" with shock.

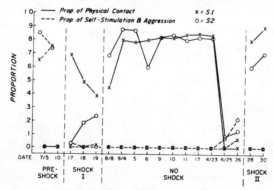

FIGURE 5.1–2 Proportion of self-stimulation and tantrums (pathological behaviors) and physical contact (social behavior).

The cumulative curves of the session immediately preceding and the session following shock to S1 is presented. The curves for the other sessions, both for S1 and S2, show the same effects. It is apparent upon inspection of Fig. 5.1–3 that the word "no" had no effect upon S1's performance prior to its pairing with shock, but that after such pairing it suppressed the bar-pressing response.

Observations of Ss' behaviors in the experimental room indicated that the shock training had a generalized effect; it altered several behaviors which were not recorded. Some of these changes took place within minutes after the Ss had been introduced to shock. In particular, they seemed more alert, affectionate, and seeking of E's company. And surprisingly, during successful shock avoidance they appear happy. These alterations in behavior were only partially generalized to the environment outside the experimental room. The changes in behaviors outside were most noticeable during the first fourteen days of the shock training, after which Ss apparently discriminated between situations in which they would be shocked and those in which they would not. According to their nurse's notes, certain behaviors, such as Ss' responsiveness to "come here" and "no" were maintained for several months, while others, such as physical contact, soon extinguished.

These observations formed the basis for the subsequent two studies. In Study 2 a more objective assessment of the changes in Ss' affectionate behavior toward adults was made, and a technique for extending these effects from the experimental room to the ward was explored. In Study 3 a test was made of any reinforcing power adults might have acquired as a function of their association with the termination of shock.

STUDY 2

Study 2 involved two observations. One attempted to assess changes in Ss' affectionate behavior to E who invited them to kiss and hug him. The other observation was conducted by nurses who rated Ss on behavior

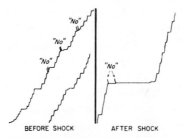

FIGURE 5.1–3 Lever-pressing for candy as cumulative response curves: effect of "no" on lever-pressing by S1 before and after "no" was paired with shock.

change in seven areas (given below). Both observations incorporated measures of transfer of behavior changes to new situations brought about by the use of the remote control shock apparatus. Both observations were conducted immediately following the completion of Study 1.

The "Kiss and Hug" Observations. These observations consisted of six daily sessions. Three of the sessions (3, 5, and 6) are referred to as shock-relevant sessions. Sessions 3 and 5 were conducted in the experimental room where Ss had received shock during avoidance training. Three sessions (1, 2, and 4) are labeled control sessions. They took place in a room sufficiently different from the experimental room to minimize generalization of the shock effect. The last shock-relevant session (session 6) was conducted to test the changes produced by remotely controlled shock. This session was conducted in the same room as the previous control sessions. However, immediately preceding the session Ss received five shock-escape trials similar to those of Study 1. The shock was delivered from a Lee-Lectronic Trainer.[1] The S wore the eight-ounce receiver (about the size of a cigarette pack) strapped on his back with a belt. Shock was delivered at "medium" level over two electrodes strapped to S's buttock.

In order to minimize the effects of a particular observer's recording bias, two observers alternated in recording Ss' behavior. Each observer recorded at least one shock session. The sessions lasted for six minutes each. Every five seconds E would face S, hold him by the waist with outstretched arms, bow his head toward S, and state "hug me" or "kiss me." The E would alternate his requests ("hug me," "kiss me") every minute. The observer recorded (1) embrace (S placing his arms around E's neck), (2) hug and kiss (S hugging E cheek to cheek or kissing him on the mouth), (3) active physical withdrawal by S from E when held by the waist, and (4) E's requests.

Results

Since Ss' behaviors on the test were virtually identical, their behaviors were averaged. The data are presented in Fig. 5.1–4. During the control sessions (sessions 1, 2, and 4) the proportion of time that Ss embraced, or hugged and kissed E was extremely low. Rather, they withdrew from him. During the shock-relevant sessions (sessions 3, 5, and 6) Ss' behavior changed markedly toward increased affection. In a situation where they had received shock-avoidance training they responded with affection to E and did not withdraw from him. The fact that this affectionate behavior maintained itself in session 6 demonstrates that the remotely controlled shock can produce transfer of behavior change to a wide variety of situations.

Nurses' Ratings. The nurses' ratings were initiated at the com-

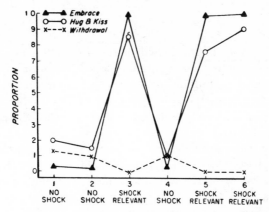

FIGURE 5.1–4 Social reactions of Ss as a function of shock presentations. The "no shock" sessions (1,2,4) were run in a room where Ss had not been shocked. ["Shock" sessions (3,5) were conducted in a room in which Ss had received shock-avoidance training. The last "shock" session (6) was conducted in the same room as the "no shock" sessions, but Ss had received remote controlled shock.]

pletion of the "kiss and hug" sessions. Four nurses who were familiar with Ss but unfamiliar with the experiment, and did not know that shock had been used, were asked to complete a rating scale pertaining to seven behaviors: (1) dependency on adults, (2) responsiveness to adults, (3) affection seeking, (4) pathological behaviors, (5) happiness and contentment, (6) anxiety and fear, and (7) overall clinical improvement. The scale was comprised of nine points, with the midpoint indicating no change. The nurses were asked to indicate whether they considered S to have changed (increased or decreased) in any of these behaviors as compared to S's behaviors the preceding day or morning. The ratings were obtained under two conditions: (1) an experimental condition in which S, wearing the remote control unit on his belt underneath his clothing, was introduced to the nurses who "casually" interacted with him for ten minutes. S was not shocked while with the nurses, but he had been given a one-second, non-contingent shock immediately prior to his interaction with the nurses; (2) a control condition, which was run in the same manner as the experimental condition, except that S had no shock prior to the ratings.

The nurses rated changes in Ss under both conditions. They were not counterbalanced. The ratings from the control conditions were subtracted from the ratings based on the experimental conditions. The difference shows an increase in the ratings of all behaviors following the shock treatment, except for pathological behaviors and happiness-contentment, which both decreased. Only the ratings on dependency and affection seeking behaviors increased more than one point.

STUDY 3

Study 3 showed the degree to which the association of an adult with shock reduction (contingent upon an approach response of the children) would establish the adult as a positive secondary reinforcer for the children. Increased resistance to extinction of a lever-pressing response producing the sight of the adult was used to measure the acquired reinforcing power of the adult.

The study was conducted in two parts. The first part constituted a "pretraining" phase. During this period the children were trained to press a lever to receive M & Ms and simultaneously see E's face. Once this response was acquired, extinction of the response was begun by removing the candy reinforcement, S being exposed only to E's face. The second part of the study constituted a test of the reinforcing power E had acquired as a result of having been associated with shock reduction. This association occurred when, immediately preceding several of the extinction sessions of the lever-press, Ss were trained to come to E to escape shock. The change in rate of responding to obtain a view of E during these sessions was used as a measure of E's acquired reinforcing power.

Method

Study 3 was initiated after the completion of Study 2. It was conducted in an enclosed cubicle, four feet square, in which E and S sat separated by a removable screen. A lever protruded from a box at S's side. Lever-pressings were recorded on a cumulative recorder. An observer (O) looking through a one-way screen recorded the following behaviors of S as they occurred: (1) vocalizations (any sound emitted by S), and (2) standing on the chair or ledge in the booth. The latter measures were taken in a manner similar to that described in Study 1. These additional measures were obtained in an attempt to check on the possibility that an eventual increase in lever-pressing for E might be due to a conceivable "energizing" effect of shock, rather than to the secondary reinforcing power associated with shock reduction. This rationale will be discussed more fully below.

The first ten were labeled *pre-training* sessions. In each, a fifteen-minute acquisition preceded a twenty minute extinction of the lever-pressing response. During acquisition S received a small piece of candy and a five-second exposure to E (the screen was removed momentarily, placing E's face within S's view) on a fixed ratio 10 schedule. During extinction, S received only the five-second exposure to E on the same schedule as before. Both Ss reached a stable rate of about 500 responses during the first acquisition session.

The ten pre-training sessions were followed by S1 by nine *experimental* sessions. In these experimental sessions S never received candy. The sessions consisted only of a twenty-minute extinction period. An S's performance during the last extinction session of pre-training, labeled Session 1 in Fig. 5.1–5, served as a measure of the pre-experimental rate of lever-pressing. Electric shock was administered before the 2nd, 7th, and 9th experimental sessions, as follows: S was placed facing E in the room outside the cubicle. Shock was administered for two to four seconds, at which point E would tell S to "come here." S would invariably approach E and shock would be terminated. The E would then comfort S (fondle and stroke him) for one minute. This procedure was repeated four times. Immediately following this procedure, S was placed within his cubicle. E would repeat S's name every five seconds. On the fixed ratio 10 schedule, the screen would open and E would praise S ("good boy") and stroke him.

The experimental treatment of S2 was identical to that of S1 with the following exceptions: (1) S2 received only seven experimental sessions; (2) shock preceded session 2, 6, and 8; (3) E did not call S2's name while he was in the cubicle; and (4) E was only visually exposed to S2 (E did not stroke or praise S2).

Results and Discussion

The Ss' lever-pressing behavior is presented in Fig. 5.1–5 as cumulative curves. The last extinction curve from the pre-training is labeled one. This curve gives the rate of lever-pressing in the last extinction session preceding E's association with shock reduction. The upward moving

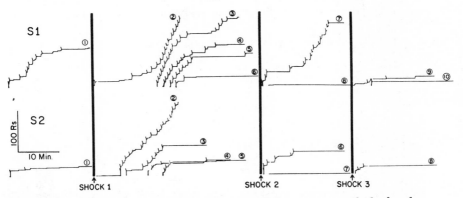

FIGURE 5.1–5 The S's lever-pressing behavior for E's association with shock reduction. [Curve labelled "1" is the last extinction curve from the pretraining. Shock preceded sessions 2, 7, and 9 for S1, and sessions 2, 6, and 8 for S2. The upward moving hatchmarks on the curves indicate occasions at which E was visually presented to S.]

hatchmarks on the curves show the occasions on which E was visually presented to S. The heavy vertical lines labeled shock, show shock-escape training preceding sessions 2, 7, and 9 for S1, and sessions 2, 6, and 8 for S2.

There was a substantial increase in rate of lever-pressing accompanying shock-escape training for both Ss. The curves also show the extinction of this response. The extinction is apparent in the falling rate between shock sessions (e.g., sessions 2 through 6 for S1 show a gradual decrease in rate of responding). A similar extinction is also manifested over the various shock sessions, i.e., the highest rate was observed after the first shock training, the next highest after the second shock training, and so on. The Ss' performances were very systematic and orderly.

Data based on the two additional measures, vocalization and standing on the chair or ledge, are presented in Table 5.1–1. The entries in the column labeled O1 can be compared to those in column O2. These data indicate that there was a high degree of agreement between the two observers rating amount of vocalizations of Ss. The O2's ratings were based on tape recordings taken from Ss while in the booth. It was physically impossible to have a second O assess the reliability of O1's ratings of climbing. However, because of the ease of recording such behavior it was judged unnecessary to check on its reliability. The agreement between Os on vocalizations was judged adequate for the purposes of this study.

If the increase in lever-pressing behavior was correlated with an increase in the two additional behaviors, then it might not be that shock-escape training had led to an increase in behavior toward people *per se*. Rather, it might have led to an "arousal" of many behaviors, asocial as well as social. As Table 1 shows, the two additional measures showed no

TABLE 5.1–1   Per Cent of Total Time Engaged in Vocalization and Climbing

		S1			S2		
		Vocal.		Climb.	Vocal.		Climb.
Session	Shock	01	02	01	01	02	01
1		49		0	27		96
2	S1 and S2	19	19	0	27		0
3		47		0	20		20
4		25		32	23		0
5		18		65	26	29	0
6	S2	22	23	97	22		0
7	S1	22	23	33	23	23	0
8	S2	22		83	22		0
9	S1	11		0			
10		13		75			

systematic relationship to the shock-escape sessions for S2. In the case of S1 there is some possibility of *suppression* of vocalization and climbing subsequent to shock-escape sessions (sessions 2, 7, and 9). It is unlikely, then, that shock-escape training involving other people can be viewed simply as activating many behaviors; rather, such training selectively raised behavior which yielded a social consequence.

Thus it is concluded that this increase in behavior toward E subsequent to shock-escape training came about because E was paired with shock reduction, thereby acquiring reinforcing powers. This conceptualization is consistent with the findings of Studies 1 and 2, both of which demonstrated an increase in social and affectionate behaviors. The findings are similar to those reported by Risley (1964) who observed an increase in acceptable social behavior (eye-to-eye contact) in an autistic child to whom E had administered electric shock for suppression of behaviors dangerous to the child. The data are also consistent with the results of studies by Mowrer and Aiken (1954) and Smith and Buchanen (1954) on animals which demonstrated that stimuli which are discriminative for shock reduction take on secondary positive reinforcing properties. It is to be noted, however, that the data from the studies reported here also fit a number of other conceptual frameworks.

An apparent limitation in these data pertains to the highly situational and often short-lived nature of the effects of shock. This had definite drawbacks when one considers the therapeutic implications of shock. It is considered, however, that the effects of shock can be made much more durable and general by making the situation in which shock is delivered less discriminable from situations in which it is not. The purpose of the present studies was to explore certain aspects of shock for possible therapeutic use. Therefore, only the minimal amount of shock considered necessary for observing reliable behavior changes was employed. It is quite possible that the children's responsiveness to adults would have been drastically reduced if shock had been employed too frequently. It is worth making the point explicitly: a certain use of shock can, as in these studies, contribute toward beneficial, even therapeutic, effects; but it does not at all follow that a more widespread use of the same techniques in each case will lead to even better outcomes. Indeed, the reverse may be true. Recent studies with schizophrenic children in our laboratory have shown, tentatively, that non-contingent shock facilitates performance of a well-learned task; however, such shock interferes with learning during early stages of the acquisition of new behaviors.

Certain more generalized effects of shock training, even though not recorded objectively, were noticed by Es and ward staff. First of all, Ss had to be trained (shaped) to come to E to escape shock. When shock was first presented to S2, for example, he remained immobile, even though adults were in the immediate vicinity (there was no way in which Ss could have "known" that Es presented the shock). This immobility when hurt is consistent with observations of Ss when they were hurt in the play-yard, e.g., by another child. But after Ss had been trained to avoid shock successfully in the experimental room, their nurses' notes state that Ss would come to the nurses when hurt in other settings.

Es had expected considerable expression of fear by Ss when they were shocked. Such fearful behavior was present only in the beginning of training. On the other hand, once Ss had been trained to avoid shock, they often smiled and laughed, and gave other signs of happiness or comfort. For example, they would "mold" or "cup" to E's body as small infants do with parents. Such behaviors were unobserved prior to these experiments. Perhaps avoidance of pain generated contentment.

In their day-to-day living, extremely regressed schizophrenic children such as these Ss rarely show signs of fear or anxiety. The staff who dealt with these children in their usual environments expressed concern about the children's lack of worry or anxiety. There are probably several reasons why children such as these fail to demonstrate anxiety. It is possible that their social and emotional development has been so curtailed and limited that they are unaffected by the fear-eliciting situations acting upon a normal child. For example, they do not appear to be afraid of intellectual or social inadequacies, nor are they known to experience nightmares. Furthermore, by the age of three or four, like normal children, these children appear less bothered by physiological stimuli, and unlike the small infant, are rather free of physiological discomforts. Finally, when these children are brought to treatment, for example in a residential setting, there is much effort made to make their existence maximally comfortable.

If it is the case, as most writers on psychological treatment have stated, that the person's experience of discomfort is a basic condition for improvement, then perhaps the failure of severely retarded schizophrenic children to improve in treatment can be attributed partly to their failure to fulfill this hypothesized basic condition of anxiety or fear. This was one of the considerations which formed the basis for the present studies on electric shock. It is important to note that the choice of electric shock was made after several alternatives for the inducement of pain or fear were tested and found wanting. For example, in the early work with these children we employed loud noise. Even at noise levels well above 100 decibels we found that the children remained unperturbed particularly after the first two or three presentations.

It seems likely that the most therapeutic use of shock will not lie primarily in the suppression of specific responses or the shaping of behavior through escape-avoidance training. Rather, it would seem more efficient to use shock reduction as a way of establishing social reinforcers, i.e., as a way of making adults meaningful in the sense of becoming rewarding to the child. The failure of autistic children to acquire social reinforcers has been hypothesized as basic to their inadequate behavioral development (Ferster, 1961). Once social stimuli acquire reinforcing properties, one of the basic conditions for the acquisition of social behaviors has been met. A more complete argument supporting this thesis has been presented elsewhere (Lovaas et al., 1964). A basic question, then, is whether it is necessary to employ shock in accomplishing such an end or whether less drastic methods might not suffice. In a previous study (Lovaas et al., 1964) autistic children did acquire social reinforcers on the basis of food delivery. However, the necessary conditions for the acquisition of social reinforcers by the use of food were both time-consuming and laborious, and by no means as simple as the conditions which were necessary when we employed shock reduction.

NOTE

1. Lee Supply Co., Tucson, Arizona.

REFERENCES

Bijou, S. W., and Baer, D. M. *Child Development; a systematic and empirical theory.* New York: Appleton-Century-Crofts, 1961.

Brown, Janet L. Prognosis from presenting symptoms of preschool children with atypical development. *American Journal of Orthopsychiatry*, 1960, 20, 382–390.

Eisenberg, L. The course of childhood schizophrenia. *American Medical Association Archives for Neurology and Psychiatry*, 1957, 78, 69–83.

Ferster, C. B. Positive reinforcement and behavioral deficits of autistic children. *Child Development*, 1961, 32, 437–456.

Lovaas, O. I., Freitag, G., Gold, V. J., and Kassorla, I. C. A recording method and observations of behaviors of normal and autistic children in free play settings. *Journal of Experimental Child Psychology*, 1965, 2, 108–120.

Lovaas, O. I., Freitag, G., Kinder, M. I., Rubenstein, D. B., Schaeffer, B., and Simmons, J. O. Experimental studies in childhood schizophrenia—Establishment of social reinforcers. Paper delivered at Western Psychological Association, Portland, April, 1964.

Mowrer, O. H., and Aiken, E. G. Contiguity vs. drive-reduction in conditioned fear: temporal variations in conditioned and unconditioned stimulus. *American Journal of Psychology*, 1954, 67, 26–38.

Risley, Todd. The effects and "side effects" of the use of punishment with an autistic child. Unpublished manuscript, 1964. Florida State University.

Smith, M. P., and Buchanen, G. Asquisition of secondary reward by cues associated with shock reduction. *Journal of Experimental Psychology*, 1954, 48, 123–126.

Solomon, R. L. Punishment. *American Psychologist*, 1964, 19, 239–253.

5.2 | SOME CONDITIONS FACILITATING THE OCCURRENCE OF AGGRESSION AFTER THE OBSERVATION OF VIOLENCE*

Russell G. Geen and Leonard Berkowitz

An increasing body of experimental research has demonstrated that the observation of violence can increase the likelihood of subsequent aggression (Bandura, Ross, & Ross, 1961, 1963; Berkowitz, 1965a; Lovaas, 1961; Walters, Thomas, & Acker, 1962). A good deal has yet to be learned, however, as to how this type of influence arises and what conditions govern the occurrence of the postobservation aggression. Witnessed violence can undoubtedly produce changes in the strength of inhibitions against aggression, as has been suggested by a number of writers (Bandura & Walters, 1963; Wheeler & Caggiula, 1966). Thus, according to several experiments conducted at the University of Wisconsin (Berkowitz, 1965b; Berkowitz, Corwin, & Hieronimus, 1962; Berkowitz & Rawlings, 1963), the audience's attitude toward the observed event may regulate the subsequent aggression by affecting inhibitions against this behavior. In addition to this type of effect, the stimulus properties of the potential targets must also be considered (Berkowitz, 1964, 1965a; Berkowitz & Geen, 1966, 1967; Geen & Berkowitz, 1966). The aggressive tendencies elicited by the film violence apparently lead to the strongest attacks on persons who are associated with the victims of the observed aggression.

The emotional state of the observer is also important. Although some studies have obtained significant film effects with nonangered subjects (e.g., Walters et al., 1962), the Wisconsin experiments have consistently found that the aggression-heightening consequences of observed violence are detectable only when the subjects had previously been angered by the person they are later permitted to attack. The existing anger toward the available target-person evidently facilitates the effects of the film violence; theoretically, the anger energizes the aggressive responses and probably also produces a lowering of inhibitions against aggression in the immediate postobservation situation.

Emotion arousal could also arise from frustrations, and we here

* From Russell G. Geen and Leonard Berkowitz, *The Journal of Personality*, 1967, *35*, 666–676. Reprinted by permission of the publisher. Copyright 1967, Duke University Press, Durham, North Carolina. This experiment was carried out as part of a research program sponsored by NSF grant G-23988 to LB. RGG was primarily responsible for the design and conduct of the study.

inquire into the consequences of nonaggressive frustrations. Berkowitz (1962, 1965a) has advanced a modified frustration-aggression hypothesis. According to this view, the aggressive predisposition does not give rise to aggressive actions unless appropriate cues are present in the situation. Aggression cues are stimuli associated with the frustration source and/or with aggressive behavior generally. Such stimuli presumably elicit the aggressive responses that the frustrated individual is ready to make. Where Buss (1961, 1966) has argued that a nonattacking frustration is not a primary determiner of aggression, the present position holds that the blocking of goal-directed behavior does increase the likelihood of an aggressive response, providing there are the appropriate aggression cues and inhibitions against aggression are weak.

Witnessed violence could well affect the relation between frustration and aggression. If a frustrated observer sees what he believes is justified aggression and then has an opportunity to attack someone associated with the victim of the witnessed aggression, his restraints against aggression would be weak and he would have encountered a target with relatively strong aggressive cue properties. As a result, he should exhibit stronger attacks against this available target than (a) someone seeing the same event who had not experienced the prior frustration, or (b) someone else for whom the available target does not have a high cue value for aggression.

METHOD

Subjects, who were run singly, were 108 male undergraduates enrolled at the University of Wisconsin. The experimenter met the subject and an experimental confederate posing as another subject at the experimental room and introduced them to each other by their last names only. The confederate was always presented as "Mr. Anderson." The two men were then informed by the experimenter that the experiment was designed to test the effects of punishment on learning and that one of them would eventually be given the task of learning a set of relationships. Punishment for failures in the learning task would be electric shocks administered by the other subject.

The experimenter then gave the two men small jigsaw-type puzzles, with the explanation that he wished to test their ability "to form spatial patterns out of their individual parts." This was said to be a test closely related to the relationship-learning problem to follow. The puzzle task actually served to introduce one of three treatments. In every case the confederate was given a puzzle which he was able (after pre-experimental practice) to put together. One-third of the subjects received a puzzle which, although looking like the one given to the confederate, was actually insoluble. The men were informed that they had five minutes to complete the puzzles. At the end of that time, the experimenter returned and picked up the puzzles, remarking that one of them (the confederate) had finished his but that the other (the subject) had not. At no time during this procedure did the confederate seek to interact with the subject; he spoke only when spoken to and treated the subject in a neutral manner throughout. The subject, therefore, was given a frustrating task, in the sense that he could not finish the puzzle (*Task Frustration condition*). This frustration is not an "attack" according to the strict definition employed by Buss (1961, 1966); the confederate does not deliver noxious stimuli to the subject in any direct fashion. However, he implicitly represents an attack on the subject's self-esteem since he completed the task and the subject failed to do so.

Another third of the subjects were given the same insoluble puzzle and allowed five minutes to work on it. In this condition, however, the confederate after successfully completing his puzzle, approached the subject with amusement over his inability to succeed. The confederate told the subject that he was doing his puzzle wrong and that it was probably too difficult for him. When the experimenter returned, the confederate made several disparaging remarks about the subject's lack of ability and boasted about his own skill at problem solving (*Insult condition*). This treatment obviously combines both task frustration and an insulting verbal attack upon the subject.

A final third of the subjects were given puzzles which could be solved easily in five minutes. The confederate treated the subject in the same neutral manner as in the Task Frustration condition. This last will be referred to as the *Control* condition.

After completing the puzzles, the subject and confederate were told they would witness a short motion picture, on the pretext that it contained information later to be used in the learning task. The film shown was either that of a violent prize fight or a one-mile foot race (Berkowitz & Geen, 1966). Half of the subjects viewed each film.

Immediately after the conclusion of the film the experimenter gave each man a mood questionnaire. This questionnaire directed the respondent to indicate his present emotional state by placing a check at the appropriate places on 10 seven-point scales each anchored by polar adjectives.[1] The only scale to yield significant findings was NOT ANGRY–ANGRY. These findings will be reported; the remaining scales will not be referred to again. After picking up the completed mood questionnaires, the experimenter asked the two men for their first names, ostensibly to label their sheets appropriately. In half of the conditions the confederate identified himself as "Kirk Anderson," while in the other half he called himself "Bob Anderson."[2]

At this point the experimenter explained that all of the necessary preliminaries were over and that the learning task was to begin. The apparatus used in this part of the experiment was an "aggression machine" patterned after that originally designed by Buss (1961).

The experimenter arbitrarily designated the confederate as the person who would attempt to learn the stated set of relationships and the subject as the "teacher" who would present to the confederate both information necessary for learning and punishment for failure. After seating the subject at the control panel in the experimental room, the experimenter left the room with the confederate, explaining that he would return after the confederate had been set up in an adjoining room. The experimenter then returned to the subject and handed him a sheet containing a set of 20 random combinations of the letters A through E taken two at a time. The experimenter instructed the subject to present information to the confederate by pushing buttons on his panel labelled A through E according to the combinations on the list. The subject was told to wait until the confederate made a response and to punish incorrect responses by shocking the other man. Shocks were to be given by means of one of 10 buttons which ostensibly governed 10 shock levels of increasing intensity. Choice of intensity was left to the subject's discretion.

The confederate then proceeded to give 12 wrong responses out of the 20 trials, according to a prearranged schedule. The subject's choices of shock intensity were observed by the experimenter and recorded, along with the total duration (in thousandths of a minute) of the 12 shocks. The experimenter then returned to the subject and gave him a final questionnaire on which the subject was asked to state his degree of acceptance or rejection of the confederate on a set of seven-point scales.[3] Finally, the experimenter explained the experimental ruse to the subject, introduced the subject to the confederate, and asked the subject whether he had seen through the deception at any point.

RESULTS

Effectiveness of the Experimental Manipulation

The effectiveness of the Task Frustration–Insult manipulation was ascertained by analysis of responses to the mood questionnaire item on which the subjects rated the degree to which they felt angry. Mean ratings of reported anger are given in Table 5.2–1.

As this table indicates, subjects in the Task Frustration and Insult conditions tended to report themselves as being angrier than did the subjects in the Control condition. The analysis of variance of these data yielded a significant main effect for the arousal treatments ($F = 4.61$, $df = 2/96$, $p < .05$). Inspection of Table 5.2–1 shows clearly, however,

TABLE 5.2–1   Degree of Felt Anger Reported by Subjects

	Boxing film		Track film	
Treatment	Kirk	Bob	Kirk	Bob
Control	3.67_{abc}	3.00_{abc}	2.11_c	2.44_{bc}
Task frustration	4.00_{ab}	3.56_{abc}	3.67_{abc}	3.11_{abc}
Insult	3.67_{abc}	3.78_{abc}	4.22_a	3.89_{ab}

Note.—Means having different subscripts are significantly different from each other as the .05 level of confidence by a Duncan Multiple Range Test. There are nine subjects in each condition. A high score is high felt anger.

that most of the variance is due to the large difference between the Control and Insult groups in the Track Film–Kirk condition. In three of the four columns of Table 5.2–1, nevertheless, the results are in the anticipated direction, with insulted subjects reporting more anger than frustrated ones, who in turn were more angry than controls.

Intensity and Duration of Shocks

The median shock intensity delivered by each subject for the 12 shock trials was calculated. The median was preferred to the mean as a measure of central tendency because several of the subjects gave a few shocks which were either extremely high or extremely low and thus falsely inflated or deflated group means. The mean of the medians for the nine subjects in each condition was then obtained.

The analysis of variance of the data on shock intensity is reported in Table 5.2–2. This analysis shows that the Film $\times$ Treatment interaction was significant ($F = 3.75$, $df = 2/96$, $p < .05$). Table 5.2–3 gives the group means involved in this interaction, along with the results of the Duncan test of differences among the means. The multiple-range tests reveal that in the Track Film condition only the Insult group gave significantly more intense shocks than the Control group. However, in the Boxing Film condition, both arousal treatments led to significantly

TABLE 5.2–2   Analysis of Variance for Shock Intensity Data

Source	df	MS	F	P
1. Film	1	19.97	13.31	.005
2. Name	1	2.78	1.85	
3. Treatment	2	43.66	29.11	.001
4. 1×2	1	2.68	1.79	
5. 1×3	2	5.62	3.75	.05
6. 2×3	2	6.00	4.00	.05
7. $1 \times 2 \times 3$	2	1.78	1.19	
8. Error	96	1.50		
9. Total	107			

TABLE 5.2–3 Mean Intensity of Shocks in the Treatment-by-Film Interaction

Treatment	Boxing film	Track film
Control	2.84$_c$	3.18$_c$
Task frustration	4.16$_b$	3.44$_{bc}$
Insult	5.80$_a$	4.11$_b$

Note.—Means having different subscripts are sugnificantly different from each other at the .05 level of confidence by a Duncan Multiple Range Test. $N = 18$ in each condition.

more intense shocks than those given in the Control group. Insult resulted in the administration of stronger shocks than did task frustration, and task frustration led to the giving of stronger shocks than did neutral behavior. Thus, while insult aroused the greatest degree of aggressive behavior, task frustration also created a readiness for aggression. The socially proper aggression these subjects then witnessed presumably lowered their inhibitions against this form of behavior. The subjects in the Track Film condition, on the other hand, did not receive the inhibition-lowering information, and an extreme provocation was required before these men would commit overt aggressive acts.

But did the witnessed violence do more than lower inhibitions generally? Further analysis of the shock intensity data reveals that the boxing film had effects other than the simple general reduction of inhibitions against aggression. Previous studies have shown that the boxing film produced a specific tendency in insulted subjects: to attack people associated with the victim of the witnessed aggression (Berkowitz & Geen, 1966, 1967; Geen & Berkowitz, 1966). On the basis of these findings, then, the confederate in the present study should receive more intense shocks when his name was "Kirk" rather than "Bob." More than this, we also ask whether this predicted greater volume of aggression against the high-cue target would arise only when the subject is insulted (the arousal treatment employed in the earlier studies), or whether it would also occur when the subject is frustrated (or is the recipient of the indirect blow to his self-esteem). Table 5.2–4 presents the data relevant to this question.

TABLE 5.2–4 Intensity of Shocks Delivered by Subjects

Treatment	Boxing film		Track film	
	Kirk	Bob	Kirk	Bob
Control	3.07$_{de}$	2.60$_e$	3.34$_{cde}$	3.01$_{de}$
Task frustration	4.49$_{bc}$	3.84$_{cde}$	3.91$_{cd}$	2.98$_{de}$
Insult	6.20$_a$	5.41$_{ab}$	3.99$_{cd}$	4.23$_{cd}$

Note.—Means having different subscripts are significantly different from each other at the .05 level of confidence by a Duncan Multiple Range Test. $N = 9$ in each condition.

Looking at Table 5.2–4, there are no reliable differences among any of the four Control groups; the intensity of the electrical attacks was not greatly affected by the target's name or the nature of the film witnessed when the subjects were not emotionally aroused. As expected, the strongest aggression in the experiment was exhibited by the insulted men shown the boxing film who had an opportunity to attack a person with the same name as the film victim. However, this group was not significantly different from the Insult–Boxing Film–Bob group, and both of these insulted boxing film conditions differed reliably from the two nonaggressive film conditions. The task frustration led to significantly weaker attacks than the insult treatment, but only in the Boxing Film and not in the Track Film condition, possibly because a few of the men in the Frustrated–Track Film–Bob group were unusually responsive. In general, however, after the task frustration as after the insult, the most intense aggression was directed against the person having the same name as the victim of the observed aggression. While the Frustrated–Boxing Film–Kirk subjects did not differ significantly from the Bob subjects receiving the same arousal and film treatment, only the former, who had the presumably high-cue target, were significantly different from the Control–Boxing Film conditions. All in all, then, we have at least suggestive evidence here for our theoretical analysis; the task frustration led to stronger aggression than that displayed by a nonaroused group when (1) the thwarted men were given inhibition-lowering information and (2) were then provided with an opportunity to attack a person having high cue value for aggression because of his name-mediated connection with the victim of the observed aggression.

The significant Name × Treatment interaction is difficult to interpret. The name "Kirk" might have an aggressive cue value in itself, leading to greater attacks on Kirk than Bob when the men were frustrated. Since this effect has not been observed in other experiments carried out in this laboratory, and did not arise in the Insult condition of this experiment, the present finding of high intensity shocks to Kirk in the Frustrated–Track Film group may well be only a chance occurrence.

The total duration of all 12 shocks delivered by the subject was noted, and from this an average duration was calculated. Analysis of these results indicated no significant effects. Generally, as we have always found, the best results are obtained with aggressive responses that the subjects are set to make, whether shock number or sheer intensity.

DISCUSSION

If the findings regarding the attacks upon the high-cue target under task frustration are reliable, we would have an easy explanation for the relationship between frustration and aggression: (1) The frustration produces a general arousal or drive state which is capable of energizing whatever response tendencies are elicited in the situation. (2) The highly salient aggressive cues evoke aggressive responses which are strongly energized by the arousal state. (3) The high arousal also results in a decreased responsivity to the peripheral cues in the situation (see Easterbrook, 1959) so that there is a temporary lessening of some possible interferences with the aggressive reaction. Any arousal state, regardless of its origin, could conceivably have these effects. However, to reinterpret the well-known research by Schachter (1964), the individual's cognitions regarding the origin of his emotion might also intervene by inhibiting some actions but not others and by establishing appropriate cues in the environment.

There is also another possibility, however. The arousal state and eliciting cue could function in the manner just described, but certain types of arousal might still have specific consequences lacking in other kinds of states. There may well be a general activation common to all arousal states, but in addition to this there may be some specific components unique to certain states. (This, of course, is the type of observation that Hull had made in his discussion of general and specific drives.) As an example, Roberts and Kiess (cited in Berkowitz, 1965a, p. 320) have demonstrated that electrical stimulation of the hypothalamus of cats did not create a general arousal state which merely intensified whatever response sequence happened to be underway at the time. If the cats were eating when the stimulation was turned on, they would turn to attack a nearby rat rather than consume their food with increased vigor. Berkowitz has observed (1965a, pp. 320–321): "This stimulation at least had a somewhat selective rather than general effect, and it may be that other types of arousal also increase the probability of certain response classes rather than making all actions equally likely."

Some critics of the frustration-aggression hypothesis, of course, have also taken a specificity position. They argue that only certain kinds of emotion-provoking situations, rather than all frustrations generate aggression. Thus, Buss (1961, 1966) has maintained that only attacks produce aggressive reactions, while other writers (see Berkowitz, 1962) have said the specific determinant of aggression is a threat to the individual's ego or self-esteem. Advocates of this point of view could readily interpret the present task frustration as such a blow to the ego: the confederate completed his task while the subject was unable to do so, and therefore, the confederate indirectly deflated the subjects's self-esteem. Additional research obviously is necessary before we can say unequivocally that any arousal situation is capable of producing the aggressive predisposition observed in this study.

SUMMARY

A total of 108 male subjects were assigned to the 12 conditions of a $3 \times 2 \times 2$ factorial design. There were three arousal-treatment groups: one-third of the subjects were given an insoluble puzzle, one-third were insulted by a confederate, and one-third were neither frustrated nor insulted. The subjects then witnessed either a violent prize-fight movie or an exciting but nonviolent racing film. In half of the conditions the confederate's name associated him with the beaten boxer in the fight film, while in the other half he had a name not connected with either film. Subjects were then given an opportunity to aggress against the confederate in what was described as a learning task. Among the subjects who saw the boxing film, insult led to more aggressive behavior than did neutral treatment or task frustration, regardless of whether the target was associated with the film or not. When the target's name connected him with the boxing film, task-frustrated subjects were significantly more aggressive toward him than were the nonaroused controls. There was no reliable difference between the frustrated and control subjects when the available target did not have a name-mediated connection with a violence victim. This latter finding was discussed in terms of (a) the observed aggression lowering inhibitions against subsequent aggression, and also (b) the available target eliciting the aggressive responses because his association with the victim of the observed violence heightened his cue value for aggression.

NOTES

1. See Geen and Berkowitz (1966) for the complete questionnaire.
2. See Berkowitz and Geen (1967) for a complete description of the name manipulation.
3. The four items on the final questionnaire served as a secondary aggression measure. Each of the four scales was preceded by the qualification, "From what you now know about the other subject in this experiment . . . ," followed by the specific question. On these items the subject responded along a continuum from VERY MUCH (1) to NOT AT ALL (7). Item 1 asked, "How much would you like to serve in another experiment with him?" A significant main effect due to the arousal treatment was obtained ($F = 5.07$, $df = 2/96$, $p < .05$), but the findings do not parallel those obtained with shock intensity. There was also a significant main effect for the arousal treatments on the item, "How much would you like to have him for a personal friend?" ($F = 12.43$, $df = 2/96$, $p < .001$). But the results with this measure also do not follow the shock findings. The insulted men expressed more intense hostility than did any of the other subjects, although the differences between the Task Frustration and Control conditions and the target's name did not have any effect on the attacks he received. There are any number of possible explanations for the discrepancy

between the shock and questionnaire results. Most obviously, giving the shocks could have affected the following verbal statements in some unspecifiable manner. There was no simple catharsis operating here. The insulted men, who had delivered the most intense shocks, subsequently expressed the greatest rejection of the confederate as a friend. Rather than producing an emotional purge, the physical attacks could have led to inhibitions against further aggression in some cases and, perhaps, to a self-justifying strong verbal condemnation of the confederate in other instances.

REFERENCES

Bandura, A., Ross, Dorothea, & Ross, Sheila A. Transmission of aggression through imitation of aggressive models. *J. abnorm. soc. Psychol.*, 1961, 63, 575–582.

Bandura, A., Ross, Dorothea, & Ross, Sheila A. Imitation of film-mediated aggressive models. *J. abnorm. soc. Psychol.*, 1963, 66, 3–11.

Bandura, A., & Walters, R. H. *Social learning and personality development.* New York: Holt, Rinehart & Winston, 1963.

Berkowitz, L. *Aggression: A social psychological analysis.* New York: McGraw-Hill, 1962.

Berkowitz, L. Aggressive cues in aggressive behavior and hostility catharsis. *Psychol. Rev.*, 1964, 71, 104–122.

Berkowitz, L. The concept of aggressive drive: Some additional considerations. In L. Berkowitz (Ed.), *Advances in experimental social psychology.* Vol. 2. New York: Academic Press, 1965. Pp. 301–329. (a)

Berkowitz, L. Some aspects of observed aggression. *J. Pers. soc. Psychol.*, 1965, 2, 359–369. (b)

Berkowitz, L., Corwin, R., & Hieronimus, R. Film violence and subsequent aggressive tendencies. *Pub. Opin. Quart.*, 1962, 27, 217–229.

Berkowitz, L., & Geen, R. G. Film violence and the cue properties of available targets. *J. Pers. soc. Psychol.*, 1966, 3, 525–530.

Berkowitz, L., & Geen, R. G. The stimulus qualities of the target of aggression: A further study. *J. Pers. soc. Psychol.*, 1967, 5, 364–368.

Berkowitz, L., & Rawlings, E. Effects of film violence on inhibitions against subsequent aggression. *J. abnorm. soc. Psychol.*, 1963, 66, 405–412.

Buss, A. H. *The psychology of aggression.* New York: Wiley, 1961.

Buss, A. H. Instrumentality of aggression, feedback and frustration as determinants of physical aggression. *J. Pers. soc. Psychol.*, 1966, 3, 153–162.

Geen, R. G., & Berkowitz, L. Name-mediated aggressive cue properties. *J. Pers.*, 1966, 34, 456–465.

Lovaas, O. I. Effect of exposure to symbolic aggression on aggressive behavior. *Child Develpm.*, 1961, 32, 37–44.

Schachter, S. The interaction of cognitive and physiological determinants of emotional state. In L. Berkowitz (Ed.), *Advances in Experimental Social Psychology.* Vol. 1. New York: Academic Press, 1964.

Walters, R. H., Thomas, E. L., & Acker, C. W. Enhancement of punitive behavior by audio-visual displays. *Science*, 1962, 136, 872–873.

Wheeler, L., & Caggiula, A. A. The contagion of aggression. *J. exp. soc. Psychol.*, 1966, 2, 1–10.

5.3 THE ELIMINATION OF TANTRUM BEHAVIOR BY EXTINCTION PROCEDURES*

Carl D. Williams

This paper reports the successful treatment of tyrant-like tantrum behavior in a male child by the removal of reinforcement. The subject (S) was approximately 21 months old. He had been seriously ill much of the first 18 months of his life. His health then improved considerably, and he gained weight and vigor.

S now demanded the special care and attention that had been given him over the many critical months. He enforced some of his wishes, especially at bedtime, by unleashing tantrum behavior to control the actions of his parents.

The parents and aunt took turns in putting him to bed both at night and for S's afternoon nap. If the parent left the bedroom after putting S in his bed, S would scream and fuss until the parent returned to the room. As a result, the parent was unable to leave the bedroom until after S went to sleep. If the parent began to read while in the bedroom, S would cry until the reading material was put down. The parents felt that S enjoyed his control over them and that he fought off going to sleep as long as he could. In any event, a parent was spending from one-half to two hours each bedtime just waiting in the bedroom until S went to sleep.

Following medical reassurance regarding S's physical condition, it was decided to remove the reinforcement of this tyrant-like tantrum behavior. Consistent with the learning principle that, in general, behavior that is not reinforced will be extinguished, a parent or the aunt put S to bed in a leisurely and relaxed fashion. After bedtime pleasantries, the parent left the bedroom and closed the door. S screamed and raged, but the parent did not re-enter the room. The duration of screaming and crying was obtained from the time the door was closed.

The results are shown in Fgure 5.3–1. It can be seen that S continued screaming for 45 min. the first time he was put to bed in the first extinction series. S did not cry at all the second time he was put to bed. This is perhaps attributable to his fatigue from the crying of Occasion 1. By the tenth occasion, S no longer whimpered, or cried when the parent left the room. Rather, he smiled as they left. The parents felt that he made happy sounds until he dropped off to sleep.

* C. D. Williams, "The Elimination of Tantrum Behavior by Extinction Procedures," *The Journal of Experimental Psychology,* 57, 1959, 130–136. Copyright 1959 by the American Psychological Association, and reproduced by permission.

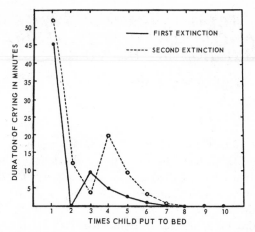

FIGURE 5.3–1   Length of crying in two extinction series as a function of successive occasions of being put to bed.

About a week later, S screamed and fussed after the aunt put him to bed, probably reflecting spontaneous recovery of the tantrum behavior. The aunt then reinforced the tantrum behavior by returning to S's bedroom and remaining there until he went to sleep. It was then necessary to extinguish his behavior a second time.

Figure 5.3–1 shows that the second extinction curve is similar to the first. Both curves are generally similar to extinction curves obtained with subhuman subjects. The second extinction series reached zero by the ninth occasion. No further tantrums at bedtime were reported during the next two years.

It should be emphasized that the treatment in this case did not involve aversive punishment. All that was done was to remove the reinforcement. Extinction of the tyrant-like tantrum behavior then occurred.

No unfortunate side or aftereffects of this treatment were observed. At three and three-quarters years of age, S appeared to be a friendly, expressive, outgoing child.

5.4 | THE EFFECT OF RANDOM AND ALTERNATING PARTIAL REINFORCEMENT ON RESISTANCE TO EXTINCTION IN THE RAT*

D. W. Tyler, E. C. Wortz, and M. E. Bitterman

The greater resistance to extinction which follows partial as compared with consistent reinforcement may be understood in terms of what Mowrer and Jones have called the *discrimination hypothesis*.[1] On the assumption that rate of extinction is inversely related to the similarity between acquisition- and extinction-situations, and on the assumption that the two situations are more similar for partially reinforced than for consistently reinforced animals, it follows that extinction should be more rapid after consistent reinforcement. If this quite reasonable interpretation is accepted, there remains the question of how the similarity between conditions of acquisition and extinction should be assessed. Two solutions to this problem have been proposed, one based on the principle of *stimulus-generalization* (or stimulus-compounding) and a second based on the concept of *serial patterning*.

The principle of stimulus-generalization leads to a trial-by-trial analysis—it directs attention to the similarity between the stimulating conditions present on individual extinction-trials as compared with reinforced training trials. For consistently reinforced animals, the after-effects of previous reinforcement are assumed to be part of the stimulus-compound present on each training trial. After-effects of reinforcement are absent during the extinction series, and this change in stimulating conditions results in relatively rapid extinction. For partially reinforced animals, however, responses to a stimulus-compound which does not contain the afferent consequences of reinforcement are frequently rewarded during training, and these animals are, therefore, expected to extinguish less rapidly.[2] Evidence supporting this interpretation has been provided by Sheffield, who found no difference in the extinction of partially and consistently reinforced groups of rats under conditions of spaced training —a result which follows from the assumption that the after-effects of reinforcement are dissipated during long inter-trial intervals.[3] Evidence that the effects of partial reinforcement cannot be entirely understood in terms of stimulus-generalization has, however, been provided by Crum, Brown, and Bitterman, who substituted delayed reinforcement for non-reinforcement on half the training trials.[4] In these experiments partially delayed animals extinguished less rapidly than consistently and immediately reinforced animals, despite the fact that for both groups the after-effects of reinforcement must be presumed to have been present on all training trials.

The concept of serial patterning directs attention to the similarity between *sequences* of events in training and extinction. The assumption is made that a *series-effect* is generated in training—that the temporal sequence of events is somehow represented in the resulting trace system. The distinction between this conception and the interpretation in terms of stimulus-generalization may be clarified by an experiment of Longenecker, Krauskopf, and Bitterman in which the conditioned galvanic skin response was extinguished following two patterns of partial reinforcement.[5] Two groups of human Ss were reinforced on 50% of the training trials, but in one case reinforcements were randomly administered while in the other case reinforced and unreinforced trials were regularly alternated. In the alternating group, each reinforced response is made to an afferent compound which does not contain the after-effects of reinforcement (because each reinforced trial follows an unreinforced trial). In the random group, only about half the responses to this compound are reinforced, while the remaining reinforcements are administered following responses to an afferent aggregation which contains the after-effects of reinforcement. Since these after-effects are not present during extinction-trials, the principle of stimulus-generalization suggests that the random group should extinguish more rapidly. The concept of serial patterning leads, however, to precisely the opposite prediction. On the assumption that the *sequences* of events during acquisition and extinction differ more markedly for the alternating group than for the random group, the alternating group is expected to extinguish more rapidly—a deduction which was confirmed by the data. The same assumption accounts for the fact that the consistently and immediately reinforced animals of Crum, Brown, and Bitterman extinguished more rapidly than did their partially delayed animals although after-effects were equated by the training procedure. The negative results obtained by Sheffield under conditions of distributed practice may be taken to mean that stimulus-compounding plays some rôle, but the experiment of Longenecker, Krauskopf, and Bitterman (in which the effects of stimulus-generalization and serial patterning were opposed) suggests that the rôle is a secondary one. Perhaps after-effects provide the concrete conditions for serial patterning—as a series of stimuli provide the basis for extrapolation in experiments on concept-formation—although the patterning requires a process of relating which cannot be reduced to a process of discriminating among stimulus-compounds. Sheffield's results may have been due to the absence of differential stimulation—the raw materials for patterning, so to speak; it also is possible, as Mowrer suggested in his analysis of Denny's experiment,[6] that sequential integration may be retarded by the use of long inter-trial intervals. It should be recognized, of course, that factors responsible for the efficacy of partial reinforcement at the human level may be quite different from those which operate at the level of the rat.[7] As Mowrer and Jones suggested,[8] the human ability to count may markedly facilitate discrimination between training- and extinction-situations.

EXPERIMENT

The experiment here reported was designed to compare the effects of alternating and random partial reinforcement at the level of the rat. Both the interpretations which have been discussed suggest that the rat may be able to discriminate between the two conditions of reinforcement, but, as at the human level, they lead to opposed predictions with respect to relative rate of extinction.

Subjects
Thirty experimentally naïve Albino rats were studied. They ranged in age from 3-4 mo. at the outset of the experiment.

Apparatus
The apparatus employed was essentially a combination elevated runway and single-window jumping apparatus. There was a starting box separated from the runway by a guillotine door operated with a string-and-pulley system. The runway itself was 3.75 in. wide and 7.66 ft. long. At its other end was a goal-box, containing a 6×6 in. window, to which the animal gained access by jumping a variable distance to an unfastened card. The purpose of this arrangement was to prevent the animal from seeing the contents of the goal-box prior to the terminal response. The goal-box had funnelled sides and top to discourage abortive jumping. The entire apparatus was painted gray, except the card in the window which was covered with ½-in. vertical black and white stripes.

Preliminary Training
The animals were placed on a 24-hr. feeding schedule on which they were maintained for the duration of the experiment. In the first stage of training the animals were fed in the goal-box, and then taught to jump gradually increasing distances (to a maximum of 9 in.) from the end of the runway, first to the open window and then to the striated card. Of the 30 animals, 25 responded appropriately in the preliminary training. These animals were divided into two groups, one of 12 and the other of 13 animals, which were roughly equated for adjustment to the situation.

Experimental Training

Each animal was given 10 trials per day. Each trial consisted of a run from the starting box to the end of the runway and a jump from there to the goal-box. The animal remained in the goal-box for 10 sec. and was then transferred to a mesh waiting cage for 20 sec. before the beginning of the next trial. (The brevity of the inter-trial interval was designed, in accordance with Sheffield's experiment, to maximize carry-over of the effects of reinforcement.) On each trial the time between the elevation of the door of the starting box and the jump from the end of the runway was measured with a stopwatch. If on any training trial the animal had not reached the goal-box in a period of 180 sec., it was guided in the direction of the goal and manually encouraged to jump from the end of the runway.

All animals were reinforced (10 sec. of feeding with wet mash) on 5 of the 10 trials given on each training day. The *alternate group* ($N = 13$) was reinforced on odd-number trials—reinforcement and non-reinforcement were regularly alternated. For the *random group* ($N = 12$) reinforcements and non-reinforcements were administered in accordance with the following four Gellerman orders:[9] RRRNNRNRNN, RNRRRNNNRRN, RNNRRRNNRN, and RNNNRRNRRN. An examination of these orders shows that 60% of the reinforced trials followed non-reinforcement (including reinforced initial trials), while 40% of the reinforced trials followed reinforcement. For the alternate group, of course, all reinforced trials followed nonreinforcement, and responses following reinforcement were never reinforced. Each group was given 12 series of training trials, with an interval of 48 hr. between series.

Extinction

Extinction-trials also were given in series of 10, with a 48-hr. interval between series. As on unreinforced trials of the training series, no food was present in the goal-box in which the animals were confined for a period of 10 sec., and the 20-sec. interval between trials was spent in the waiting cage. Runs were timed as before, with one exception: if an animal did not reach the goal-box in 90 sec., it was removed from the runway and taken directly to the waiting cage for the usual 20-sec. period. The criterion of extinction was two successive incomplete trials of this kind.

RESULTS

The course of learning in the alternate group is shown in Fig. 5.4–1 which is a plot of median time per trial for the entire training series. The development of patterning can be seen clearly. Early in the series the animals tended to run faster on the unreinforced trials (which in every case

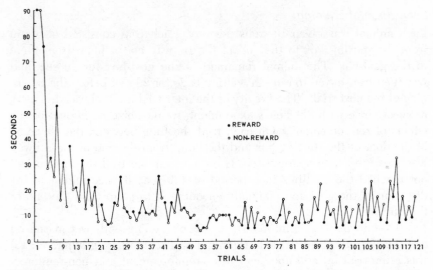

FIGURE 5.4–1   The development of patterning in the alternate group. Median running-time is plotted for each trial of the training series.

followed reinforced trials). In the intermediate stage of training of difference in running speed on trials following reinforcement and trials following non-reinforcement disappeared. Finally, the initial difference was reversed—the animals ran more rapidly after non-reinforcement than after reinforcement.

In Fig. 5.4–2, the two groups are compared with respect to differences in speed of running on trials following reinforcement and on trials following non-reinforcement. For each animal in each group the sum of running times for the five trials following reinforcement was subtracted

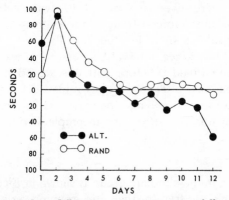

FIGURE 5.4–2   Median differences in running-time following reinforcement and non-reinforcement. The measure employed was the sum of running-times for the five trials following reinforcement minus the sum of running-times for the five trials following non-reinforcement on each day of training.

from the sum of running times for the five trials following non-reinforcement on each day of training. Mean difference-scores for each group are plotted in Fig. 5.4–2. Both curves are positive at first, showing more rapid running after reinforcement, and then fall to zero. The curve for the random group remains at the zero level, while the curve for the alternating group becomes reliably negative. On the final day of training, for example, the mean of the random group does not differ significantly from zero, while the difference from zero of the mean for the alternating group is significant well beyond the 1-% level (Wilcoxon's non-parametric test for paired replicates).[10] These results are precisely what are expected in terms of an analysis of after-effects of reinforcement. In the random group, responses following non-reinforcement (to a stimulus-compound which does not contain after-effects of reinforcement) are not rewarded very much more often than responses following reinforcement (to a stimulus-compound which does contain after-effects of reinforcement). For this reason, runs to the two compounds should be equally rapid. In the alternating group, responses in the presence of after-effects are never reinforced and responses in the absence of after-effects are always reinforced. A significant difference in running times should, therefore, appear. If the delay in extinction which follows partial reinforcement is explained in these terms, however, the alternating group should be expected to extinguish less rapidly than the random.

In Fig. 5.4–3, the course of learning and extinction in both groups is shown in terms of median running times. For every animal the median of the 10 time-scores for each day was computed and the median of these medians plotted for the two groups. After each animal had met the criterion of extinction, it was assigned a score of 90 sec. for each subsequent trial of the seven-day extinction-series. The extinction-curves

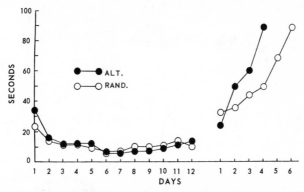

FIGURE 5.4–3   Median running-times during training and extinction. The measure employed was the median of the ten running-times on each day. When each animal reached the criterion of extinction, it was assigned time-scores of 90 sec. for each subsequent "trial."

TABLE 5.4–1 Median Running-Times in Training and Extinction

	Training	Extinction
Alternate	10.75	90.00
Random	10.63	50.25
Diff.	0.12	39.75*

* Significant at the 5% level (Festinger's test).

reach 90 sec. before the end of the seven-day period because more than half the animals in each group had extinguished before that time. The curves for the two groups are quite similar during the training period, but they diverge during extinction—the alternating group tending to extinguish more rapidly.

The performance of each animal during the training series was expressed in terms of the median of the 12 daily medians. Similarly, its performance during extinction was expressed as the median of the seven daily medians. Group medians for training and extinction are compared in Table 5.4–1. The two groups did not differ significantly during training, but during extinction the median running time for the alternating group was significantly higher than that for the random group (Festinger's test[11]).

In Fig. 5.4–4, the course of learning and extinction for the two groups is plotted in terms of mean percentage of response-times below 90 sec. per day. (It will be remembered that the criterion of extinction was two successive time-scores greater than 90 sec.) Again the curves are similar during training but diverge during extinction. In Table 5.4–2, mean values for training and extinction series are given for both groups. No significant difference appears during training, but during extinction the mean frequency for the random group is significantly greater than that for the alternating group (Festinger's test).

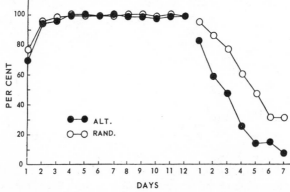

FIGURE 5.4–4 Mean percentage of running-times greater than 90 sec. during training and extinction.

TABLE 5.4–2   Mean Percent of Running-Times below 90 Sec. in Training and Extinction

	Training	Extinction
Alternate	95.96	35.62
Random	96.87	61.31
Diff.	0.91	25.69*

* Significant beyond the 5% level (Festinger's test).

In terms of both measures, then—median running time and mean frequency of response-times below 90 sec.—extinction was found to be more rapid in the alternating group than in the random. The results are in agreement with those obtained by Longenecker, Krauskopf, and Bitterman for the conditioned galvanic skin response to shock in human subjects.[12] Although in both experiments that kind of patterning developed in training which should have been expected in terms of stimulus-generalization to lead to less rapid extinction in the alternating groups, the differences obtained were in the opposite direction. These results provide support for the concept of serial patterning (which suggests that similarity between conditions of training and extinction must be evaluated in terms of sequences of events), on the reasonable assumption that there was greater disparity between training- and extinction-sequences for the alternating than for the random group. Further tests of this interpretation would seem to require the use of a method for the independent evaluation of sequential similarity.

SUMMARY

Two groups of rats were trained on a runway under conditions of partial (50%) reinforcement. For one group (random) reinforced and non-reinforced trials were given according to a haphazard order, while for the second group (alternating) odd-numbered trials were reinforced and even-numbered trials non-reinforced. Significantly greater resistance to extinction was found in the random group. The results are opposed to predictions based on the concept of stimulus-generalization and support the conception of serial patterning.

NOTES

1. O. H. Mowrer and Helen Jones, Habit strength as a function of the pattern of reinforcement, *J. Exper. Psychol.*, 35, 1945, 293–311.
2. The stimulus-compound present on trials following non-reinforcement may differ, not only in that after-effects of reinforcement are absent, but also in that certain after-effects of non-reinforcement (*e.g.* interoceptive stimuli resulting from frustration-responses) are present. Since the same consequences follow from both

differences, exposition in terms of after-effects of reinforcement alone achieves simplicity without doing violence to the theory.

3. V. F. Sheffield, Extinction as a function of partial reinforcement and distribution of practice, *J. Exper. Psychol.*, 39, 1949, 511–526.

4. Janet Crum, W. L. Brown, and M. E. Bitterman, The effect of partial and delayed reinforcement on resistance to extinction, *The Am. J. of Psychol.*, 64, 1951, 228–237.

5. E. D. Longenecker, John Krauskopf, and M. E. Bitterman, Extinction following alternating and random partial reinforcement, *The Am. J. of Psychol.*, 65, 1952, 580–587.

6. Mowrer, *Learning Theory and Personality Dynamics*, 1950, 202.

7. For example, results unlike those of Sheffield were obtained by D. A. Grant, J. P. Hornseth, and H. W. Hake in a study of human expectations (The influence of the inter-trial interval on the Humphreys 'random reinforcement' effect during the extinction of a verbal response, *J. Exper. Psychol.*, 40, 1950, 609–612).

8. Mowrer and Jones, *op. cit.*, 305.

9. L. W. Gellerman, Chance order for alternating stimuli in visual discrimination experiments, *J. Genet. Psychol.*, 42, 1933, 356–360.

10. Frank Wilcoxon, *Some Rapid Approximate Statistical Procedures*, American Cyanamid Co., Stamford, Conn., 1949, 1–16.

11. Leon Festinger. The significance of difference between means without reference to the frequency distribution function, *Psychometrika*, 11, 1946, 97–105.

12. *Op. cit.*, 580–587.

Six

The Stimulus

In Anthony Burgess' *Clockwork Orange* the hero, Alex, is deeply in love with the music of Beethoven, "lovely Ludwig van," and it is one of his major sources of happiness. Unfortunately, his subsidiary pleasures include rape and murder, and he is eventually caught by the authorities and sent to prison. In hopes of curing him of his aggressive tendencies, he is then placed in an experimental program closely modeled on current techniques of aversion therapy. Strapped in a chair with his eyes held open by clips, he is forced to watch movies showing scenes of great violence and cruelty, including an old woman being burned to death by a teenage gang, and assorted scenes of rape. At first Alex reacts with great pleasure, reveling in the ultra-violence, but suddenly he finds himself overcome by pain and nausea, induced by an earlier injection. The therapists hope to condition this illness to the stimuli associated with violence, so that if Alex ever again starts to engage in violence he will be forced to stop by the excruciating pain. The strategem works—nausea later immobilizes him when in a test he is confronted with a gorgeous female—but there is a tragic aftermath. During the conditioning sessions the background music to one of the films was Beethoven's Fifth Symphony, and now Alex's nausea is elicited not only by scenes of violence but by all of Beethoven's music, thereby destroying his greatest pleasure in life.

Burgess' intention in this novel may have been to warn us of the consequences of societal manipulation of behavior, but it can also be interpreted as a warning against *naive* manipulation. The problem with Burgess' therapists is not so much that they are evil as that they are incompetent. Specifically, they ignored one of the most fundamental principles of learning, that *the effects of conditioning depend crucially on the stimuli present during training*. This principle is particularly clear in classical conditioning, where the conditioned response is elicited only by the CS which is presented during conditioning, but it is equally important in reinforcement and punishment. In these *operant conditioning* situations, presentation of a reinforcer or punisher normally depends solely on the subject's response, regardless of the prevailing stimulus situation, and it thus might appear as if no one stimulus should uniquely control responding. Nevertheless, in both types of conditioning responding is eventually controlled by the stimuli present during training. In a Fixed Interval schedule of reinforcement, for example, we have seen that reinforcement results not in a general increase in responding, but only in responding *at those times when reinforcement is likely* (the FI scallop). Similarly in the case of punishment, tantrums were not generally suppressed but *only in the test room where punishment occurred.* In these and other situations, subjects quickly learn to discriminate between those situations in which some consequence is more or less likely, and their behavior is eventually controlled by those stimuli best correlated with the environmental contingencies.

Although all responses do eventually come under stimulus control, analyzing *precisely* what stimuli are controlling behavior is not always easy. In Fixed Interval behavior, for example, the effective stimulus for responding might have been either the time since reinforcement or proprioceptive feedback from earlier responses, and only through careful experimental analysis was time shown to be the crucial variable. And again with the partial reinforcement effect, responding could have been controlled by either the purely physical aftertaste of food or by a true memory for previous trial outcomes, and only recently has the role of long-term memory been fully confirmed (e.g., Capaldi, 1971). If stimulus control is this complex even when dealing with rats in a highly simplified environment such as a wooden alley or a Skinner box, what greater complexities can we expect in the real world? When there are literally thousands of stimuli impinging on our senses at any instant, and traces of thousands of other lights, sounds, odors, and so on, from previous seconds or even hours, which of this bewildering multitude of events will actually come to control our behavior?

Transposition and Generalization

A simple and parsimonious answer was provided by early S-R theorists such as Clark Hull and Kenneth Spence: *all of them.* All stimuli present at the time a response is reinforced will become associated with that response, provided only that they effectively stimulate the subject's receptors. Ultrasonic sound or a light behind our heads might not influence our behavior, but all events which actually do stimulate our receptors will become effective stimuli. Thus Spence (1936) was able to describe how a rat solved a simple brightness discrimination by invoking only the principles of reinforcement and extinction. Imagine, for example, a rat in a T-maze in which the black and white arms alternated positions randomly, and only the white alley led to food. According to Spence, the association between any effective stimulus and a subsequent response is *strengthened* whenever it is followed by reinforcement. Nonreinforcement, on the other hand, *weakens* the preceding S-R association. Over a series of trials, therefore, the cues from the white alley would gradually become associated with the approach response as a result of subsequent reinforcement, while the cues from the black alley would come to inhibit the approach response. The rat's tendency to approach the white side would thus become greater and greater over trials, until eventually he turned to the white side on every trial and thus solved the problem. Cues such as position (right alley versus left), on the other hand, would have no consistent relationship with reinforcement, and approach responses would be reinforced equally often to the opposing cues. Over trials, therefore, the white-black dimension would come to strongly control responding while other cues would become ineffective.

Without any new assumptions beyond reinforcement and extinction, Spence was thus able to simply explain how stimuli come to control behavior, but despite its appealing simplicity, this explanation immediately proved controversial. One source of disagreement was a group of German theoreticians known as *Gestalt* psychologists, who emphasized the *relationships* among stimuli. In our black-white discrimination, for example, Spence treated every stimulus present as an independent element, with each element forming its own association with subsequent responses. By the end of training, therefore, the stimulus controlling the approach response was simply the color white, which had been repeatedly associated with the reinforced response. For the Gestalt psychologist, however, subjects did not react to independent stimuli, but to the relationship between them. Rather than responding separately to the stimuli "black" and "white," they were responding to the relationship between them, approaching the lighter alley and avoiding the darker one. Put another way, S-R theorists said that subjects were responding to the *absolute* properties of a stimulus, independent of the other stimuli present, while for Gestalt theorists, subjects were responding to the *relative* properties of the stimulus, as determined by the stimulus context.

In order to test which of these positions was correct, the Gestalt psychologist Wolfgang Köhler trained two chimps on a size discrimination, 9×12 and 12×16 inch rectangles being present on every trial, with food always located behind the latter. According to

S-R theorists, the chimps should learn to approach the actual stimulus that was reinforced, the 12 × 16 inch rectangle, while Gestalt theorists said that they should simply learn to approach the *larger* rectangle. After the subjects had learned the discrimination, Köhler presented a series of test trials, using 12 × 16 and 15 × 20 inch rectangles. If S-R theory was right the subjects had learned to approach the 12 × 16 inch rectangle during training and should continue to do so during the test. If Gestalt theory was right, however, the subjects had learned to approach the larger rectangle during training and so should now select the 15 × 20 inch rectangle. The results were that both chimps selected the 15 × 20 inch rectangle on more that 85 percent of the test trials, ignoring the 12 × 16 inch rectangle that had actually been reinforced during training. Furthermore, this result could not be attributed to any special intellectual capacity of higher species, since exactly the same results were obtained with brightness problems using baby chicks.

The subjects in these experiments seemed to be transferring or *transposing* the relationship they had learned in training to the test problem, and this transposition seemed to be conclusive evidence against S-R theory. Rather than the simple associational process postulated by S-R theory, in which every stimulus element was directly connected to the response, there now seemed to be a central processing mechanism that abstracted complex relationships such as "brighter" and "larger"; and it was to these relationships rather than the individual stimuli that responses became associated. Or so it seemed until 1937 and the publication by Kenneth Spence of one of the most brilliant and influential papers in psychology (Article 6.1). In his simple but elegant analysis, Spence suggested that transposition could be explained by S-R theory if the effects of *generalization* were taken into account. Pavlov had been the first to notice that if a response was trained to one stimulus, it would also occur to a lesser extent to other, similar stimuli, and that the extent of this generalization depended on the similarity of the stimuli. In an experiment by Hovland (1937), for example, a sweating response classically conditioned to one tone also occurred in weaker form to both higher and lower tones, and the magnitude of the response steadily decreased as the test stimuli became less and less similar to the training tone. To this basic fact, Spence added one new assumption: that there was generalization of inhibitory as well as excitatory tendencies, so that generalization around an inhibitory stimulus might weaken a response in exactly the same way as generalization around a positive stimulus might strengthen it. In fact, Spence had absolutely no evidence for this assumption, and another twenty years would pass before it could be confirmed (see Honig, Boneau, Burstein, and Pennypacker, 1959). Nevertheless, by assuming specific shapes for the spread of generalization around the positive and negative training stimuli (*generalization gradients*) and also a simple algebraic summation rule for combining excitatory and inhibitory tendencies, Spence was able to show that transportation *could* be explained in simple S-R terms, without any reference to relationships.

Perhaps even more remarkable, he was able to use his three simple assumptions to generate totally unique predictions. Regarding transposition, for example, Spence predicted that it should become less likely as the test stimuli became less similar to the training stimuli, even though from a relational point of view transposition should still occur as long as the appropriate relationship still existed. Spence obtained clear evidence for exactly this *distance effect*, suggesting that S-R theory could not only explain transposition but could do a better job of it than any Gestalt theory (but see Zeiler, 1963).

Further support for Spence's theory came from the phenomenon of *peak shift*. Maximal responding in a generalization gradient usually occurs to the stimulus that was reinforced during training, but if training also involves a negative stimulus lying on the same dimension as the positive stimulus, then maximal responding may be displaced in a direction away from the negative stimulus (that is, the peak of the generalization gradient shifts). In a brightness discrimination, for example, in which a pigeon is reinforced for pecking at a 100-millilambert light while simultaneously extinguished for pecks at a 50-millilambert light, maximal responding in a later generalization test might occur not to 100 but to an even brighter stimulus such as 110 or 120 millilamberts. At first, this peak shift might again seem to be evidence against S-R theory—shouldn't maximal responding occur to the training stimulus which was actually reinforced?—but again it can be easily explained if the inhibitory generalization gradient is taken into account. In our brightness discrimination problem, for example, inhibition would generalize from the 50-millilambert light to the 100-millilambert light, thus reducing responding at 100 ml. Inhibition would also generalize to the 110-ml. light, *but less strongly*, since it was less similar to the 50-ml. light. Thus, responding would not be as strongly reduced at 110 as at 100 ml., and depending on the exact shapes of the excitatory and inhibitory generalization gradients, the *net* response strength at 110 ml. might end up being greater than at 100 ml. Peak responding, therefore, would occur not to the positive stimulus during training but to one displaced away from the negative stimulus.

The existence of the distance effect and the peak shift provide strong support for Spence's theory, and are perhaps especially impressive in that they were not simply explained but *predicted* by the theory. Despite the theory's successes, however, there is now considerable evidence that subjects do indeed learn relationships among stimuli under some circumstances. Phenomena such as *behavioral contrast* (see Reynolds, 1961) and the *intermediate size problem* (Gonzales, Gentry, and Bitterman, 1954) provide strong arguments against Spence, but perhaps the most compelling evidence has come from an experiment by Lawrence and DeRivera (Article 6.2). The authors trained a group of rats on a brightness discrimination involving seven cards ranging from white (1) to black (7). During training the mid-grey card (4) was always on the bottom, and one of the other six cards was mounted above it. If the top card was white (1, 2, or 3) responses to the right were reinforced, while if it was black (5, 6, or 7) responses to the left were reinforced. According to relational theory, therefore, subjects should have learned to go right when the top card was lighter and left when it was darker. According to S-R theory, however, the subjects should have learned responses to specific cards: cards 1, 2, or 3, go right; cards 5, 6, or 7, go left. Since both theories predict successful learning, although for different reasons, how can we tell which theory is correct? Lawrence and DeRivera's answer was simple: they reversed the cards! If the problem involved the white card, for example, it was now on the *bottom*, with the mid-grey card now on top (that is, 4 over 1 instead of 1 over 4). According to relational theory, therefore, the subjects should now reverse their responses, since the top card was now darker rather than lighter. S-R theory, on the other hand, predicts no change in responding, since exactly the same stimuli are present as during training. The mid-grey card is presumably neutral, having been previously associated with both right and left turns, and the white card should still elicit a right turn, as it had during training. Unfortunately for Spence's theory, however, over 75 percent of the responses on such problems *were* reversed, suggesting that the relationship among the stimuli was indeed controlling the response.

Spence's theory of discrimination learning now appears wrong, but perhaps more impressive than its ultimate failure were its astonishing successes. Basically employing only three simple assumptions—excitation, inhibition, and generalization—Spence was able to explain and, more important, *predict* a wide variety of behaviors, and these predictions proved remarkably accurate. Thus, although the stimulus does now appear more complex than Spence believed—subjects can respond to relationships among stimuli as well as to individual elements —nevertheless his theory provides a classic demonstration of the power of simple assumptions to explain seemingly complex phenomena.

Attention

A second aspect of the controversy over the stimulus concerned the role of attention. At a subjective level attention refers to our seemingly greater awareness of some stimuli than others, but it may be more objectively defined as the selective control of behavior by a subset of the stimuli present during learning. According to attention theorists our ability to process and store the enormous input to our senses is limited by our neural capacity, and we are thus unable to fully attend to the millions of stimuli impinging on us daily. As a result, we cannot learn about all stimuli, but only about a subset whose size is determined by our processing capacity. According to S-R theorists, on the other hand, there is no need to assume such a selective process. *All* stimuli present at the time of a response become associated to it, provided only that the subject is appropriately oriented to receive them. Some stimuli may be more salient than others, resulting in stronger conditioning, but all stimuli do become associated, and the concept of a central selective mechanism is superfluous.

The implications of this debate extend well beyond the mere existence of attention. In part, it was only one battleground of a larger war over the central versus peripheral nature of learning. For S-R theorists the nature of the stimulus was almost entirely determined by the peripheral receptors of the body, while for the cognitive theorists these peripheral receptors were but the first step in a complex sequence of transformations produced by central processing mechanisms. More fundamentally, the debate was between two conflicting views of behavior: S-R theory, emphasizing the fundamentally simple mechanisms underlying the apparent complexity of behavior, and cognitive theory, unsure of the precise laws underlying behavior but convinced by its obvious complexity that they must be far more sophisticated than the simple laws of association. We will return to this larger debate in the following chapter, but a recognition of the broader implications of attention may help to explain why its existence was such an important issue for learning theorists. For cognitive theorists it was further proof of the complex processing mechanisms involved in learning, while for S-R theorists it was another opportunity to demonstrate the power of simple assumptions in explaining behavior.

The actual debate over attention occupied more than two decades, with first one side and then the other ascendant (for a comprehensive review, see Mackintosh, 1965), but perhaps its simplest resolution came in 1961 in an experiment by George S. Reynolds (Article 6.3).

325

Reynolds trained two pigeons on a discrimination problem in which
pecks in the presence of the positive stimulus were intermittently
reinforced while pecks to the negative stimulus were extinguished. The
positive stimulus was a white triangle projected on a plastic key
against a red background, while the negative stimulus was a white
circle against a green background. According to S-R theory all elements
present at the time of a reinforced response should become associated
to it, so that both the triangular shape and the red color should
elicit pecking. According to attentional theory, however, only a subset of
the stimuli present should become associated, and while this does
not necessarily mean that only *one* stimulus will be associated, it is
possible that the subjects might attend to only the triangle or only the
color red. To test these theories, Reynolds simply presented the
elements separately, illuminating the key with either the triangle or a red
light. The results were that both birds pecked at only one of the two
stimuli, thus demonstrating selective attention, but each chose a
different stimulus, one pecking at red and the other at triangle!

While demonstrating the existence of attention, then, Reynolds'
experiment also illustrates a crucial problem. Given the chaotic flux of
stimuli in the environment, to *which* stimuli will we attend? Is attention
simply a random process, now selecting this stimulus, now that,
or are there systematic principles that can explain the fluctuations
in our attention? Clearly psychologists prefer the assumption
of lawfulness, and a variety of theories of attention have been proposed
(e.g., Sutherland and Mackintosh, 1971; Zeaman and House, 1963;
Lovejoy, 1965). In their simpler form, these theories assume that subjects
attend to only one *dimension* at a time, so that a subject might attend
to color cues or to form cues but not to both simultaneously. Which
dimension will be attended to is determined in part by innate preferences
(color, for example, is a prepotent dimension for monkeys) and in part
by the effects of previous experience. An attentional response is
assumed to have the same properties as any overt response, being
strengthened by reinforcement and weakened by extinction. In Reynolds'
experiment, for example, a pigeon might attend to color on the first
trial, in which case he would then detect all the stimuli on that
dimension which were present (that is, red and green). If he then pecked
at the positive stimulus (red), the resultant reinforcement would
strengthen not only the overt pecking response but the tendency to
attend to color as well.

This model not only explains selective control by dimensions
such as color or shape, but makes some predictions that at first are highly
counterintuitive. If subjects are trained on a two-choice discrimination
problem, for example, and then the positive and negative stimuli are
reversed, one might expect that increasing the number of trials

on the original problem would make it harder for subjects to reverse their choices. The Zeaman and House model, however, predicts that under some circumstances overtraining should actually make the reversal easier, and this *overtraining reversal effect* has in fact been obtained in a number of cases (see Mackintosh, 1965).

A second prediction of the model concerns *intradimensional* vs. *extradimensional shifts*. Consider, for example, two groups of subjects, one of which learns a color discrimination (red versus yellow) and the other a line orientation discrimination (horizontal versus vertical). Suppose both groups are now given the identical problem, a color discrimination involving blue and green stimuli. For the color group, this represents an *intradimensional* shift, since the stimuli within the color dimension have been shifted, but color is still the relevant dimension. For the orientation group, on the other hand, this is an *extradimensional* shift, since the relevant stimuli now come from a new dimension.

According to attentional theory the first group was reinforced during training for attending to color, while the second group learned to attend to orientation. On the test problem, therefore, the first group is more likely to attend to the relevant dimension, and so should learn more quickly. S-R theory, on the other hand, would have to predict equal performance for the two groups, since the test stimuli are identical for both groups, and neither has experienced them before. In fact, in an experiment by Mackintosh and Little (Article 6.4) the intradimensional shift subjects did significantly better, making fewer than half as many errors on the color-test problem as the extradimensional shift subjects. It appears, then, as if subjects do learn to attend to particular dimensions, and that this training can facilitate learning in other situations where the same dimension is still relevant.

Successful predictions such as those concerning the overlearning reversal effect and intradimensional versus extradimensional shifts are by no means the end of the story. As we have seen with Spence's theory of discrimination learning, a theory may initially have great success only to gradually be abandoned as further evidence is accumulated. Already there appear to be serious deficiencies in the attentional explanation of discrimination learning (e.g., Thomas, 1970; Wagner, 1971), but again it may be more appropriate to emphasize the theory's successes than its failures. All theories are wrong: revision and change are inherent in the scientific process, and a theory is never absolutely correct, but only better than its competitors. What is perhaps most impressive, however, is that at this early stage in its development psychology seems to be developing powerful theories that can not only explain but predict behavior. Attentional theory needs revision, but its successes are a hopeful sign that we are slowly beginning to understand the complex stimuli that control our behavior.

6.1 THE DIFFERENTIAL RESPONSE IN ANIMALS TO STIMULI VARYING WITHIN A SINGLE DIMENSION*

Kenneth W. Spence

I

The differential response of animals to stimuli involving differences of degree, such as intensity, size and wave length, has long been regarded as being based on the relational character of the stimulus situation. Prior even to the emphasis given this interpretation by the new gestalt movement, early American investigators of the problem (2, 4, 5, 9) had concluded that animals learn to respond to the relative properties of the stimulus situation rather than to the specific properties of one or other of the stimulus objects. They inferred from these experiments that the animals possessed the ability to perceive the relationship, larger, brighter, etc., and to act in accordance with this ability in new situations in which the same relationship entered. Later, the experiments of Köhler with hen, chimpanzee and human child (12) led to a similar emphasis of the relational aspect. The response of the animal in such instances, he insisted, is not to an isolated "sensation-process" but to a "structure-process." It is responding to properties whose character is a function of the situation as a whole and not to any specific or absolute property of a part or aspect of it.[1] Both his experiments and the theoretical interpretation he placed upon them have received considerable attention and have greatly influenced thinking on the problem (12, 13).

But while the relational viewpoint in one form or another has dominated the attempts at an interpretation of these phenomena, the experimental studies on the problem, almost without exception, have shown that response to relationship is by no means universal. In the transposition tests, in which stimuli of different absolute value but having the same objective relation to one another are employed, the animals sometimes respond in accordance with the relationship, but in a large number of instances they fail to do so. These negative results have led certain psychologists who are opposed to the gestalt viewpoint to be

critical of relational interpretations and to deny that the behavior in such
experiments necessarily involves either "transposition of structure properties" or "abstract relative judgments" (7, 18, 19, 20). Beyond pointing
out, however, that absolute factors, under certain conditions at least, play
an important part, they have had little of a positive nature to offer in the
way of an explanation.

II

In a recent article in this journal (16) a theoretical schema based on
stimulus-response principles and concepts was proposed to explain the
nature of discrimination learning in animals. According to this hypothesis,
discrimination learning is conceived as a cumulative process of building
up the strength of the excitatory tendency of the positive stimulus cue
(i.e., the tendency of this stimulus to evoke the response of approaching
it) by means of the successive reinforcements of the response to it, as
compared with the excitatory strength of the negative stimulus, responses
to which receive no reinforcements. Theoretically, this process continues
until the difference between the excitatory strengths of the two cue
stimuli is sufficiently large to offset always any differences in strength
that may exist between other aspects of the stimulus situation which
happen to be allied in their action with one or other of the cue stimuli.
That is to say, the difference between the excitatory strengths of the cue
stimuli, positive and negative, must reach a certain minimum or threshold
amount before the animal will respond consistently to the positive
stimulus.[2]

The theory as presented in that article was concerned with the discrimination of stimulus objects which differed, objectively at least, in
the single characteristic of form; for example, triangle, circle, or square.
It was explicitly assumed that there was no transfer of the excitatory
tendency acquired by the positive form-character to the negative form-
character, and likewise, that the negative or inhibitory tendency of the
latter was not transferred to the former.[3]

In the case of such continuous dimensions as size and brightness,
however, it would seem reasonable to assume that there is some transfer
of training, at least between nearby members of a series. There is, in fact,
direct experimental evidence in support of such a belief. Thus Pavlov
reports that when an animal is conditioned to a stimulus, e.g., a tone of
a certain wave length, tones of different wave length also acquire the
capacity to evoke the response. His experiments suggest further that the
more unlike the tone is in wave length from the one employed in the
original training, the less will be the transfer or irradiation of the conditioning (14). Bass and Hull (1) have also demonstrated such a spread

or generalization of conditioned excitatory and inhibitory tendencies in human subjects.

The essential characteristics of our hypothesis, as they pertain to the type of discrimination problem involving a stimulus dimension of a continuous nature, can be presented most briefly and clearly in the diagram of Fig. 6.1–1. (1) We shall assume that, as a result of training or successive reinforcements, the positive stimulus, 256,[4] of the combination 256+ and 160—, acquires an excitatory tendency to the response of approaching it of the amount or strength represented by the solid line at that point. (2) We shall assume that there is a generalization of this acquired excitatory tendency to stimulus objects of similar size and that this generalization follows a gradient such as that represented by the upper curved line. (3) We shall postulate also that with failure of reinforcement of response to stimulus 160, experimental extinction will take place and a negative or inhibitory tendency will be developed to the amount indicated by the broken line at the point on the abscissae marked 160. (4) Similarly it will be assumed that there is a generalization of this inhibitory tendency according to the gradient shown by the lower curved line. (5) And, lastly, we shall assume that the effective excitatory strength of a stimulus is the algebraic summation of these two positive (excitatory) and negative (inhibitory) tendencies. This value is indicated graphically by the distance between the upper and lower generalization curves and numerically by the number to the right of each line.

The selection of the curves of generalization has been more or less arbitrary as little experimental evidence bearing on the problem is available. There are, nevertheless, one or two general guiding principles that have been followed. One important assumption that has been made is that sensory process is a logarithmic function of the stimulus dimension (size), and accordingly the latter has been plotted on a logarithmic scale. This assumption is in line with the Weber-Fechner relation between sensory and stimulus dimensions. This relationship has, of course, been found to hold only within a certain middle range of stimulus values. Beyond these points certain modifications would have to be made in this

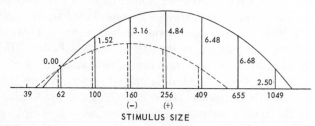

FIGURE 6.1–1   Diagrammatic representation of relations between the hypothetical generalization curves, positive and negative, after training on the stimulus combination 256 (+) and 160 (−).

relationship. Finally, because elaborate mathematical treatment does not seem to be warranted at the present stage of development, our presentation is essentially graphical. The particular curves have been constructed, however, from mathematical equations relating stimulus values and positive and negative tendencies.[5]

Examination of Fig. 6.1-1 reveals the fact that the hypothetical, effective strengths of the various stimuli after the original training on the stimulus pair 256+ and 160— are such that in the transposition test combinations, 409 and 256, and 160 and 100, the effective excitatory strength of the larger stimulus is in each case the greater. Thus the effective strength of 409 is 6.48, as compared with 4.84 for stimulus 256, and the strength of stimulus 160 is 3.16, while that of 100 is only 1.52. The implication of the hypothesis is, that the animal should respond consistently[6] to the larger stimulus in each of these transposition tests. Similarly, as shown in Fig. 6.1-2, subjects trained positively to the smaller stimulus, 160, and negatively to the larger, 256, should respond in each of the test combinations, 100 and 160 and 256 and 409, to the smaller stimulus.

We have shown, then, that it is possible to deduce from stimulus-response concepts and principles that animals will respond to stimulus differences of degree in a manner which has hitherto been interpreted as involving a perception of a relationship or response to a structure-process (larger, brighter, etc.). According to the present hypothesis, however, the animal is responding in each situation to the particular stimulus object which has the greater effective excitatory strength. There is in the preceding account no assumption of a perception of the relational character of the situation.

III

Now let us consider Fig. 6.1-1 further. We have seen that after training in the combination 256+ and 160— the animal's response in the transposition tests with 409 and 256 should be to the larger, 409. In the next

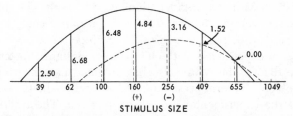

FIGURE 6.1-2 Diagrammatic representation of relations between the hypothetical generalization curves, positive and negative, after training on the stimulus combination 160 (+) and 256 (−).

combination, however, 655 and 409, the difference (.20) is only slightly in favor of the larger stimulus, and the response should be chance. But, in the still larger combination, 1049 and 655, the effective strengths are such that the response would be expected to favor 655, the *smaller* of the two stimuli. The same result, response to smaller, would be expected for the 1678 and 1049 combination. It is apparent then that the results for the transposition tests depend upon the particular stimulus combination employed. The response may be to the larger in some tests, in some to the smaller, and, in some combinations to the larger and smaller equally often—that is, a chance response.

In view of the fact that the point (stimulus pair) at which these changes occur depends upon the extent of the individual generalization curves, it is not possible to make any specific deductions concerning them. The somewhat general implication may be drawn, however, that the amount of transfer will be a function of the absolute change in the test stimuli, the transfer decreasing as the test stimuli are made more different from the training pair. A survey of the experimental literature on discrimination behavior reveals evidence which supports this deduction. Klüver (10) reports an investigation of size discrimination in two Java monkeys which were trained to choose the larger of two rectangles 300 and 150 sq. cms. In critical tests each subject was presented with the following four stimulus combinations: 1536 *vs.* 768, 600 *vs.* 300, 150 *vs.* 75 and 8.64 *vs.* 4.32, and in agreement with the general deduction from our hypothesis we find that the percentage of test responses consonant with the training response, that is, to the larger stimulus, were much less in the extreme pairs than in the combinations nearer to the training pair. In the former, both animals responded approximately only 50 per cent of the time to the larger stimulus, whereas their responses to the larger in the 600 *vs.* 300 and the 150 *vs.* 75 combinations averaged 72 and 97 per cent respectively.

Gulliksen's experiment with white rats (6) also presents data relative to this aspect of our problem. After training them on circular stimuli 9 and 6 centimeters in diameter, he found that the more similar the test combination to the training pair the higher was the percentage of responses consistent with the original training. His results for the various test combinations were as follows: 7½ *vs.* 5 = 97 per cent; 12 *vs.* 9 = 74 percent; 6 *vs.* 4 = 67 per cent; 18 *vs.* 12 = 55 per cent.

In a series of experiments with chimpanzees designed to test various aspects of the theory, the writer also has obtained data bearing on this particular problem. Before presenting these results, however, a brief description of the experimental procedures is given. The discrimination apparatus has been described in detail elsewhere. (17). Briefly, it consisted of two small stimulus (food) boxes which were presented to the animal by pushing the platform on which they were placed up to a position one inch from the cage wall, so that the animal could reach its fingers through the two-inch wire mesh, push open the boxes and obtain the food. The stimulus forms, squares cut from no. 28 galvanized iron and enameled a glossy white, were fitted with a clamp by means of which they could be fastened to the front of the boxes.

In the training series both positive and negative boxes were loaded with food, but the negative one was locked. When the subject responded correctly by opening the box which carried the positive stimulus, it obtained a small piece of banana as a reward. In the case of an incorrect response, the box was found locked and the apparatus was immediately withdrawn so that there was no opportunity to correct the error. Twenty trials, spaced from 20 to 30 seconds apart, were given in each experimental session. Training was continued on a problem until the subject satisfied a criterion of 90 per cent correct in twenty trials, the last ten of which were all correct.

In that part of the experiment concerned with the particular problem with which we are at present concerned, five adult subjects were used. Three of these individuals were trained originally to respond to the larger of two white squares, 160 and 100, while the other two were trained to respond positively to the smaller square of the combination 256 and 409. Beginning on the day after the learning of these discriminations a series of transposition tests (10 trials each) was given daily, followed by 10 trials on the training combination. The subjects trained positively to the larger were given tests on still larger stimuli, and those trained positively to smaller were tested on smaller combinations. All responses in the test series were rewarded.

Table 6.1–1 shows the results for these tests in terms of the percentage of responses consonant with the original training. The upper half of the table presents the results for the three individuals trained originally to the larger stimulus. It will be observed that the average percentage of test responses consistent with the training response decreases from 88.3 per cent to 78.3 per cent as the test combinations are increased in absolute size. The small drop from the second to the third test combination (80.0 per cent to 78.3 per cent) is to be accounted for, in part at least, by the fact that the third test was not given in counterbalanced order, but only after the two series with each of the other two test situations had been given. The order in which each test was given is indicated by the bracketed numbers in the table. If the percentage values in terms of the order of the tests are computed, we find that they increase with each successive test as follows: first—70 per cent, second—76 per cent, third—90 per cent and fourth—100 per cent. The drop to an average of 78 per cent in the fifth and sixth tests is thus seen to be of

TABLE 6.1–1   Showing the Percentage of Responses Consistent with the Original Training, *i.e.*, to the Larger (or Smaller) Stimulus of the Combination

Training Stimuli	Test Stimuli		
160 (+) *vs.* 100 (−)	256 *vs.* 160	320 *vs.* 200	409 *vs.* 256
Pati	100% (2)	80% (1)	80% (5)
	100% (3)	100% (4)	60% (6)
Mona	50% (1)	40% (2)	80% (5)
	100% (4)	70% (3)	60% (6)
Pan	80% (1)	90% (2)	90% (5)
	100% (4)	100% (3)	100% (6)
	Mean = 88.3%	Mean = 80%	Mean = 78.3%
256 (+) *vs.* 409 (−)	160 *vs.* 256	100 *vs.* 160	
Soda	50% (1)	40% (2)	
	70% (4)	50% (3)	
Bentia	40% (2)	30% (1)	
	60% (3)	40% (4)	
	Mean = 55%	Mean = 40%	

considerable significance. A more desirable procedure, of course, would be to use only one test for each subject and have a large number of subjects. The present experiment should be regarded as exploratory and not as offering conclusive results.

The results for the two individuals trained to respond to the smaller of the training pair, 256 and 409, similarly show a decreasing percentage of responses as the smaller test combinations are used. However, a markedly different result was obtained with these subjects, in that the amount of transfer dropped off much more quickly. In fact, in the second test combination, 100 and 160, a slight preference was shown for the larger stimulus over the smaller. That the result for these two subjects was not merely accidental is shown by the results of a further experiment reported below.

Six subjects were used in this part of the investigation; three of which were trained to the smaller stimulus and three to the larger. On the day after the learning of the discrimination a test series of 10 trials was given, in which half of the subjects were tested with the larger of the training stimuli and a still larger stimulus, and half, on the smaller of the training pair and a still smaller one. The next day a second series of test trials was given in which the test stimuli were reversed, *i.e.*, subjects which had had the large stimulus combination were given the small stimuli, and *vice versa*. A retraining series of 10 trials followed each test.

The results for this experiment are shown in Tables 6.1–2 and 6.1–3. It will be seen that the three subjects trained to choose the larger stimulus (Table 6.1–2) responded to the larger stimulus in both test series almost 100 per cent of the time (mean, 93.3 per cent). The data (Table 6.1–3) for the subjects trained originally to the smaller stimulus show a different result. While these individuals responded fairly consistently (86.6 per cent) with their original training in the test series involving the negative stimulus of the training pair (256), and a still larger one (512 or 409) such was not the case in the test series involving the positive stimulus (128 or 160) and a still smaller one (64 or 100). Thus, as will be seen from the last column of table 3, only 16 out of 30, or 53.3 per cent, of the responses were to the smaller stimulus in this test, none of the subjects responding significantly more than a chance number of trials to the smaller stimulus. A second test series of 10 trials with this combination showed a similar result.

TABLE 6.1–2   Showing the Percentage of Responses in the Test Trials Consistent with the Original Training, *i.e.*, to the Larger Stimulus of the Test Pair

Training Stimuli	Test Combination	
256 (+) *vs.* 128 (−)	512 and 256	128 and 64
Cuba	90%	100%
Lia	100%	100%
256 (+) *vs.* 160 (−)	409 and 256	160 and 100
Mimi	90%	80%
	Mean = 93.3%	Mean = 93.3%

TABLE 6.1–3   Showing the Percentage of Responses in the Test Trials Consistent with the Original Training, *i.e.*, to the Smaller Stimulus of the Test Pair

Training Stimuli	Test Stimuli	
128 (+) *vs.* 256 (−)	256 and 512	64 and 128
Jack	80%	50%
Nira	100%	60%
160 (+) *vs.* 256 (−)	256 and 409	100 and 160
Bokar	80%	50%
	Mean = 86.6%	Mean = 53.3%

This failure of transposition to the smaller of two stimuli in the direction of smaller sized stimuli is contrary to the implications not only of the relational theories, but also, of course, to the present hypothesis, *at least in so far as the particular curves of Figs. 6.1–1 and 6.1–2 are concerned.* Either some modification of these curves is required, or some additional factor must be postulated to account for this phenomenon. One possibility of the latter type is that the larger stimuli have, initially, a greater excitatory value than the smaller ones, or that the larger the stimulus the more rapidly do excitatory and inhibitory tendencies develop with training. Tending to support some such belief is the fact that there was a very slight, although not significant, initial preference shown by the subjects for the larger stimuli. Also the individuals trained to the larger stimulus required fewer trials to learn the discrimination than those trained to the smaller, but again the difference was only slight and not statistically significant. Further experimentation involving relatively slighter changes in the size of the test stimuli is required in order to obtain more adequate data on this problem.

In Fig. 6.1–3 is presented a modification of our irradiation curves which fits the experimental data very satisfactorily. The assumption has been made in this figure that the extent of the generalization varies with the size of the stimulus, being greater for large than for small stimuli. Thus, while the positive curve of 160 in Fig. 6.1–3 is the same as that for 160 in Fig. 6.1–2, the negative curve for 256 in Fig. 6.1–3 drops off more slowly than the corresponding curve in Fig. 6.1–2 and, of course, extends farther.

After positive training to 160 and negative to 256, the effective excitatory strengths of 100 and 160 in Fig. 6.1–3 are respectively 4.82 and 4.42. The difference of .40 is considerably below the minimum value for a consistent response to one of the stimuli, which in the present instance is assumed to be 1.00, an amount which is slightly less than the difference (1.26) between the training pair, 100 and 160. With such a

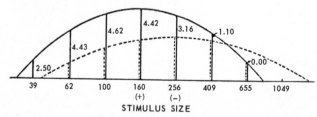

FIGURE 6.1–3 Diagrammatic representation of relations between the hypothetical generalization curves, positive and negative, after training on the stimulus combination 160 (+) and 256 (−). This diagram differs from Figure 6.1–2 in that the negative generalization curve has a more gradual slope and extends farther.

small difference the response to the smaller test stimulus might be expected to be only a chance one, or possibly slightly more. Such a result, it should be noticed, is more closely in line with the data obtained in the present experiments (see Tables 6.1–1 and 6.1–3).

IV

In concluding this paper there are several further points of a theoretical nature that require at least passing mention. A problem of no little importance is the part played by stimulus characteristics other than the cue difference. Stimulus objects have various other aspects, such as form, intensity, wave length, in addition to the cue dimension, size in the present experiments. In so far as these characteristics are the same for both stimulus objects, only one member of each dimension (square form, white, etc.) is present, and, as they receive both reinforcement and non-reinforcement their effective excitatory strengths are not greatly increased. If, however, a considerable amount of overtraining is provided all of the stimulus characteristics are increased in excitatory value since all responses are correct and consequently followed by reinforcement. Just what effect such differences in the level of strength of these non-cue stimulus characteristics may have, it is not possible to say a priori. Possibly they would not affect the differential nature of the response but only the vigor of the reaction. On the other hand, it is possible that the amount of difference between excitatory strengths of the cue aspects necessary to produce a differential response is related to the level of strength of the remaining stimulus aspects. This point is of particular importance in connection with the problem of equivalence of stimuli when more than one stimulus aspect is changed.

Another question that is important from several points of view is the nature of the development of the curves of generalization during training. The theoretical implications of the effects of overtraining would depend to a considerable extent on what happens to these curves, that is, whether the range narrows, broadens or remains unchanged with continued training. The effects to be expected from employing larger differences between the training stimuli would also depend most importantly on the manner in which the generalization curves develop. It is planned to take up the various theoretical aspects of this problem in a subsequent paper.

Similarly, there are very likely numerous other factors that play more or less important parts in this kind of discrimination behavior. As yet, however, only the barest beginning has been made in the experimental analysis of these phenomena. In this connection one cannot help but be struck by the relatively small amount of progress that has been made in this field of research since the initial work of Kinnaman in 1902.

While it is true that the problem was a more or less incidental one in the investigations of the early American psychologists, to the gestalt or configuration psychologists it has been of crucial importance. Instead, however, of a really systematic investigation, the latter seem to have been satisfied to demonstrate the commonness of response on the basis of relational properties as compared with response to absolute factors. Instances of failure of relational response have either been ignored as merely chance occurrences, or vaguely accounted for in terms of a threshold of equivalence of structure-properties.

The gestalt theories have failed to furnish either a satisfactory explanation of these phenomena or an adequate experimental formulation of the problem.[7] The present theoretical scheme, on the other hand, does provide a basis for a systematic experimental attack in this field of study. It possesses, moreover, that most important attribute of a *scientific* theory —the capacity to generate logical implications that can be experimentally tested.

NOTES

1. There is, however, a considerable difference between the views of American investigators and the German gestalters which, unfortunately, has not always been clearly understood by some recent writers on this problem. In a certain sense, indeed, their views may be said to be quite opposed to each other. Thus the American group (and this seems to include the current American configurationists) has held to the notion that the response, in such experiments, represents a fairly high order of mental activity, one involving a relational judgment or a definite experiencing of the relationship in the form of some abstract principle expressible as "food-in-the-larger," "always-in-the-brighter," etc. According to the German gestalt psychologists (11, 12, 13), on the other hand, response to such relations is a very elementary and natural form of reaction rather than an achievement of intelligence. Its occurrence in animals, particularly the more primitive forms, is conclusive evidence of what is to them the fundamental fact that the stimulus situation is from the beginning organized as a "whole" and that response is based on "whole" properties of the stimulus.

2. This is, of course, only a skeletal and purely conceptual outline of the processes that lead to the establishment of the discrimination habit. It is not intended to be, and in no sense should be construed as, a descriptive account of the behavior of the animal in the discrimination situation. Moreover, the animal learns many other responses in addition to the final, selective approaching reaction. Prominent and important among these are what have been termed, for want of a better name, "preparatory" responses. These latter consist of the responses which lead to the reception of the appropriate aspects of the total environmental complex on the animal's sensorium, *e.g.*, the orientation and fixation of head and eyes towards the critical stimuli. That is, the animal learns to "look at" one aspect of the situation rather than another because of the fact that this response has always been followed within a short temporal interval by the final goal response. Responses providing other sensory receptions are not similarly reinforced in a systematic fashion and hence tend to disappear.

3. In the discrimination of stimulus objects differing only in size, the stimulus aspects which the objects have in common, such as brightness, wave length, etc., receive both reinforcement and non-reinforcement. Their effective excitatory strengths do not, then, change greatly, unless considerable overtraining is given. This problem will be discussed briefly in a later portion of the paper.

4. We shall describe the stimulus–object simply by a number which represents its area in square centimeters, ignoring other stimulus characteristics which are the same for all stimuli.

5. The curves of generalization of the positive excitatory tendency all have the equation E (excitatory tendency) $= 10 - 20D^2$ in which D is the distance in logarithmic units between the test stimulus and the training stimulus, i.e., $D = (\log S_1 - \log S_T)$. The curves of generalization of the negative or inhibitory tendency have the equation I (inhibition) $= 6 - 20D^2$ in Figs. 6.1–1 and 6.1–2, $I = 6 - 10D^2$ in Fig. 6.1–3.

6. Whether the response will be consistently, that is 100 per cent, to the larger of the test stimuli will depend on the size of the difference between their effective strengths. This minimum or threshold requirement for a consistent response is a somewhat difficult matter to handle theoretically. One possible indication of it, however, is the amount of the difference between the strengths of the training stimuli, which, in the present instances, is 1.68. Presumably the threshold value would be somewhat less than this difference as training is usually continued, depending upon the criterion of learning adopted, beyond the point at which the animal is just able to respond with 100 per cent consistency. In the present example we shall arbitrarily assume this threshold value at 1.50. A difference less than this would lead, depending on the amount, to the choice of the stronger stimulus somewhere between 50 and 100 per cent of the trials.

7. The writer does not wish to deny the possibility that a theory of this type may be developed which will be capable of accounting for these experimental facts satisfactorily. Such dogmatic denials have no place in the realm of science. At the same time, however, we would emphasize the fact that the burden of the proof devolves on the theory. Its only claim to consideration lies in the extent to which it leads logically to consequences which coincide with empirical events.

REFERENCES

1. Bass, M. J. and Hull, C. L., The irradiation of a tactile conditioned reflex in man, J. Comp. Psychol., 1934, 17, 47–65.
2. Bingham, H. C., Visual perception in the chick, Behav. Monog., 1922, No. 20, Baltimore, Md.: Williams & Wilkins, p. 104.
3. Casteel, D. B., The discriminative ability of the painted turtle, J. Animal Behav., 1911, 1, 1–28.
4. Coburn, C. A., The behavior of the crow, Corvus Americanus Aud, J. Animal Behav., 1914, 4, 185–201.
5. Johnson, H. M., Visual pattern discrimination in the vertebrates, J. Animal Behav., 1914, 4, 319–339, 340–361; 6, 169–188.
6. Gulliksen, Harold, Studies of transfer of response. I. Relative versus absolute factors in the discrimination of size by the white rat, J. Genet. Psychol., 1932, 40, 37–51.
7. Gundlach, Ralph H. and Herington, G. B., Jr., The problem of relative and absolute transfer of discrimination, J. Comp. Psychol., 1933, 16, 199–206.
8. Helson, Harry, Insight in the white rat, J. Exper. Psychol., 1927, 10, 378–396.

9.　Kinnaman, A. J., Mental life of two Macacus rhesus monkeys in captivity, *Amer. J. Psychol.*, 1902, 13, 98–148, 173–218.
10.　Klüver, Heinrich, Behavior mechanisms in monkey, Chicago: University of Chicago Press, 1933.
11.　Koffka, K., The growth of the mind, New York: Harcourt, Brace, 1928, 153–159, 233–242.
12.　Köhler, W., Aus der Anthropoidenstation auf Teneriffa. IV. Nachweis einfacher Strukturfunktionen beim Schimpansen und beim Haushuhn: Über eine neue Methode zur Untersuchung des bunten Farbensystems, *Abh. preuss. Akad. Wiss.*, 1918, Berlin, 1–101.
13.　———, Gestalt psychology, New York: Liveright, 1929.
14.　Pavlov, I., Conditioned reflexes, London: Oxford Press, 1927.
15.　Perkins, F. T. and Wheeler, R. H., Configurational learning in the goldfish, *Comp. Psychol. Monog.*, 1930, 7, 1–50.
16.　Spence, K. W., The nature of discrimination learning in animals, *Psychol. Rev.*, 1936, 43, 427–449.
17.　———, Analysis of formation of visual discrimination habits in chimpanzee, *J. Comp. Psychol.*, 1937, 23, 77–100.
18.　Taylor, Howard, A study of configuration learning, *J. Comp. Psychol.*, 1932, 13, 19–26.
19.　Warden, C. J. and Rowley, J. B., The discrimination of absolute versus relative brightness in the ring dove, *Turtur risorius, J. Comp. Psychol.*, 1929, 9, 317–337.
20.　——— and Winslow, C. N., The discrimination of absolute versus relative size in the ring dove, *Turtur risorius, J. Genet. Psychol.*, 1931, 39, 328–341.

6.2　EVIDENCE FOR RELATIONAL TRANSPOSITION*
Douglas H. Lawrence and Joseph DeRivera

The specification of the stimulus, or more exactly the specification of those characteristics of the stimulus situation to which S reacts, has always been a difficult problem. One aspect of this problem that has attracted considerable attention is the question of whether or not S can react to the relational characteristics in a stimulation situation. The mere fact of transposition is ambiguous with respect to this question, for it can be

* Douglas H. Lawrence and Joseph DeRivera, "Evidence for Relational Transposition," *The Journal of Comparative and Physiological Psychology*, 47, 1954, 465–471. Copyright 1954 by the American Psychological Association, and reproduced by permission. This study was supported in part by a research grant from the Behavioral Sciences Division of the Ford Foundation.

interpreted as favoring either a relational point of view (2) or one that emphasizes reactions to the specific characteristics of the stimulus (4). The present study attempts to show that there are types of transposition behavior that clearly must be interpreted as evidence for relational responding. Theories assuming that such behaviors can be derived from reactions to the absolute values of the stimulus and the generalization of these reactions are incapable of explaining the results.

The procedure used in the present experiment differs greatly from the usual transposition test. The usual test for transposition involves a simultaneous discrimination in which S is first trained, for example, to approach a white and avoid a mid-gray. The S is then tested by means of another simultaneous discrimination involving a mid-gray and a black. If it chooses the former, it is interpreted as evidence for transposition. The procedure used in the present study is similar to this in that it uses a modified Lashley jumping stand and two cues are presented simultaneously on a given trial. But it differs from the usual procedure in that S is actually trained on a successive discrimination.

This seeming paradox is resolved in the following way. On a given trial both cards in the jumping stand are exactly alike. Each card, however, has one gray on the top half and a different gray on the bottom half. If the top gray is lighter than the bottom one, S is forced to jump to the right window to receive the reward and avoid punishment. If the top half is darker than the bottom half, S is forced to jump to the left. The advantages of this method are: (a) a sharp contrast between the two grays is always present so that their relationship should be perceptually clear regardless of which window S is oriented toward; (b) S is always rewarded or punished in the presence of both grays so that no differential reaction to their absolute characteristics is likely to develop; and (c) it is possible to train S on several such pairs of grays with varying degrees of difference between their absolute brightnesses so that it is familiarized with a wide range of such relationships.

This procedure also permits clear-cut contrasts between the predictions about transposition behavior that are derived from theories emphasizing reactions to the relational aspects of the stimulus situation and those derived from theories emphasizing reactions to specific stimulus values. These contrasts were established in the present study by selecting seven grays ranging from white, no. 1, to black, no. 7. On all training trials the bottom half of each card was the mid-gray, no. 4. On any given trial the top half of both cards could be any one of the remaining six grays, 1, 2, 3, 5, 6, and 7. These occurred in a semirandom order on successive trials. Whenever the top half was lighter than the bottom half, S jumped to the right, and whenever it was darker, S jumped to the left.

In terms of a theory emphasizing reactions to the specific values of the stimuli, this should mean that no. 4 remained neutral in that the animal jumped half the time to the right and half the time to the left in its presence. Grays 1, 2, and 3, however, should have become associated with jumping right, because this was the only reaction reinforced in their presence, and grays 5, 6, and 7 should have become associated with jumping left. In terms of a relational theory, on the other hand, the specific gray values would have been of minor importance; rather, S would have learned to react to each of these six values in terms of the relationship it bore to the no. 4 gray on the bottom half of the card. "Darker than" should be associated with jumping left, and "lighter than" should be associated with jumping right. Consequently, if this reference gray, no. 4, were now shifted up or down the brightness continuum, S's reactions to the other six grays should change in accordance with the shift in relationships resulting from this change in the reference stimulus. It is in this sense that we can speak of transposition behavior in this situation.

The differential predictions made by the two theories for this type of transposition can be illustrated as follows. Suppose that during the test trials the top half of the two cards was gray no. 2 and the bottom half was gray no. 3. The specific stimulus theory would predict a jump to the right because both grays had previously been associated with such behavior. Similarly, the relational theory would predict a jump to the right in that the top half was lighter than the bottom half. Both theories would predict the same on such a test. On the other hand if the top half was gray no. 3 and the bottom half was gray no. 2, the specific stimulus theory would still predict a jump to the right for the same reasons as in the previous case, but a relational theory would predict a jump to the left because the top half was now darker than the bottom half. Thus the two theories would make directly opposing predictions on such tests.

It is apparent that several such test pairs leading to differential predictions by the two theories are possible among this set of stimuli. Consequently, this type of transposition experiment should provide a fairly clear-cut answer to the question of whether or not it is necessary to assume that relational responding is a fundamental form of behavior.

METHOD

Subjects

The Ss were 12 albino rats between 60 and 90 days old at the beginning of the experiment. They were tamed and then placed on a food-deprivation schedule during which they were allowed to eat all the food they wanted for 2 hr. each day. This schedule was started two weeks prior to the experiment and continued throughout the training and testing.

TABLE 6.2–1   Reflectances of Seven Grays as Measured by the Illumitronic
Engineering Reflectometer (The illumination of these when in position was 2.5 to 3.0 ft.-candles.)

Gray	Reflectance	
	%	Log.
1	73.0	1.863
2	43.0	1.633
3	30.0	1.477
4	20.0	1.301
5	15.5	1.190
6	9.5	0.978
7	7.0	0.845

Apparatus

The apparatus was a modified Lashley jumping stand painted a flat black. The windows were 7 in. by 9 in. The jumping platform was 8 in. from the windows and at a height such that S's head was on the same plane as the mid-point of the two cards. The back of the platform from which Ss jumped consisted of a box, 12 by 12 by 12 in. The front wall of this box was of milk glass. A 100-w. lamp inside the box provided all the illumination for the apparatus. Because of the diffusion of the light through the milk glass, an even illumination of the two cards without shadows was obtained even though S stood in front of it.

The seven stimulus grays used were obtained by mixing various proportions of flat black and flat white paint, and then painting a large quantity of paper with each mix. In this way several cards all of a constant gray value could be obtained. An attempt was made to have equal brightness steps between adjacent grays in the series, but as the reflectance values in Table 6.2–1 indicate, this equality was not obtained. Stimulus cards were made from these gray papers by covering the top half of the card with one gray and the bottom half with a different gray.

Procedures

The Ss were adapted to the apparatus by first feeding them on it, then teaching them to jump the gap to an open window, and finally to jump the gap when the windows were closed by stimulus cards of gray. Each S was then given a "dry run" of 20 trials to these neutral cards during which either the right or left window was blocked in random order. If it jumped to the blocked one, S was placed back on the jumping stand and forced to jump again until it chose the open one. It was hoped by this method to break the animals of position preferences and to adapt them to the type of punishment involved. However, this procedure seemed to result in partial fixations for some Ss. During this adaptation period, as well as the remainder of the training and testing, S was never forced to jump by beating its tail or similar methods; S was always left on the stand until it had initiated its own choice. It appeared that the heat and light coming from the box behind S increased the motivation to jump even when a series of punishments had occurred on the preceding trials.

The training of Ss was in two stages. During the first stage only two different stimulus cards were used. They were 1/4, i.e., the top half was gray no. 1 and the bottom half gray no. 4, and 7/4. On a given trial both cards were exactly the same. The Ss were rewarded if they jumped to the right when the top half was lighter than the bottom and if they jumped to the left when the top half was darker than the bottom. Otherwise they were punished by a blocked window and fell to a platform below the apparatus. Training was by a correction method; if S made a mistake, it was immediately picked up and forced to jump again until it made a correct choice. A trial consisted of one rewarded response. The stimuli were so arranged that not more than two jumps to the same side occurred on consecutive trials. Half the jumps were to the right and half to the left. Five trials a day, spaced at 20- to 30-min. intervals, were given until Ss reached a criterion of 9 out of 10 consecutive correct responses. If upon reaching the criterion, any S was not jumping readily and directly at the stimulus card, it was given additional training until this condition was corrected.

During the second stage of training, all Ss were presented with the following set of six stimuli: 1/4, 2/4, 3/4, 5/4, 6/4, and 7/4. These stimuli were presented in six different orders with the restriction that not more than two jumps to the same side succeeded each other on consecutive trials. Again Ss had to jump right when the top half was lighter than the bottom half and to jump left when it was darker. Training was continued for 30 trials, with five trials per day. If by that time S had not reached a criterion of going twice through the sequence of six without error, training was continued until S did reach it. One of the 12 Ss showed such a strong position preference that it was discontinued before the test trials.

During the test period five trials a day were given; three were a continuation of the previous training trials and the other two were test trials. On the test trials both cards were unlocked and S was rewarded regardless of which way it jumped. The 24 test stimuli used are shown in Table 6.2–2. The following restrictions were imposed on the test stimuli: (a) each S went through the 24 stimuli in a different order; (b) on a given day 22 different stimuli were tested; (c) the two test stimuli presented to S on a given day were of such a nature that if the animal jumped relationally, one of the jumps would be to the right the other to the left, with the right jump occurring first on half the days and the left occurring first on the remainder; (d) the test trials were given on the third and fifth trials of each day and so interspersed with the training trials that if S reacted relationally to the test stimuli, it would never be rewarded more than two consecutive trials on the same side; and (e) the pair of stimuli presented on a given day always had the same number of brightness units between the two grays, e.g., 1/2 and 6/5 or 3/5 and 7/5.

Five Ss, picked at random, were given posttest training on a successive discrimination. It was assumed that if Ss had been reacting to the specific stimulus values, rather than relationally, they should be able to discriminate between grays no. 3 and 5 even though the reference value no. 4 was absent. They had done so during the original training trials when the bottom half of each card was gray no. 4. Consequently, each of these Ss was trained for 50 trials, 5 trials a day, on a successive discrimination involving grays no. 3 and no. 5. When both cards were no. 3, they had to jump right; when both were no. 5, they had to jump left. Rewards and punishment were correlated with these jumps in the same manner as during the original training.

RESULTS

In order to reach the criterion of 9 correct out of 10 consecutive trials on stimuli 1/4 and 7/4, Ss required on the average 31.5 trials. With the overtraining given them, they averaged a total of 60.8 training trials on these stimuli. When transferred to the training stimuli 1/4, 2/4, 3/4, 5/4, 6/4, and 7/4, they required an average of 7.6 trials to reach the same criterion of 9 correct out of 10 consecutive trials. This indicates a considerable amount of transfer. Each S, however, was continued on these stimuli for at least 30 trials or until it had gone through the sequence of six stimuli two times in a row without error. As a consequence Ss averaged 48.8 training trials on these stimuli.

The Ss' reactions to the 24 test stimuli are shown in Table 6.2–2. It should be noted that in 21 of these cases, the majority of Ss chose the side predicted by the relational theory. The three exceptions are cases in which there is only one step difference in brightness between the top and bottom halves of the stimulus cards, i.e., stimuli 6/7, 5/6, and 4/5. Altogether, 80 per cent of the 264 test jumps are in keeping with a relational hypothesis. The extent of this accuracy can best be appreciated by noting that during this time Ss were reacting to the three training stimuli per day with only 89 per cent accuracy despite all their previous training on these. Table 6.2–2 indicates that relational responding was least evident when the two grays differed by only one unit in brightness and for the darker grays, especially no. 7, which had the same reflectance value as the flat black paint used on the jumping stand.

TABLE 6.2–2   Frequency of Relational Responses to 24 Test Stimuli

Difference in Brightness between Grays	Stimulus and Response	Gray on Bottom Half of Card						
		No. 1	No. 2	No. 3	No. 5	No. 6	No. 7	%
+1	Stimulus	2/1	3/2	4/3	6/5	7/6		
	Relational	8	7	8	10	11		80
	Nonrel.	3	4	3	1	0		20
−1	Stimulus		1/2	2/3	4/5	5/6	6/7	
	Relational		10	9	3	5	2	53
	Nonrel.		1	2	8	6	9	47
+2	Stimulus	3/1	4/2	5/3	7/5			
	Relational	9	10	10	11			91
	Nonrel.	2	1	1	0			9
−2	Stimulus			1/3	3/5	4/6	5/7	
	Relational			11	11	10	6	86
	Nonrel.			0	0	1	5	14
+3	Stimulus	4/1	5/2	6/3				
	Relational	10	10	11				94
	Nonrel.	1	1	0				6
−3	Stimulus				2/5	3/6	4/7	
	Relational				11	10	8	88
	Nonrel.				0	1	3	12
%	Relational	82	84	89	84	82	48	80
	Nonrel.	18	16	11	16	18	52	20

The first statistical test made was to determine if there was any evidence of a progressive change in relational responding as the testing continued. Each S was tested on two stimuli each day, and a different pair of stimuli was used for each S. With the stimulus sets thus balanced from day to day, no evidence was found of a progressive change in the percentage of relational choices on test stimuli during this period nor of any change in the level of accuracy on the three training stimuli per day. Thus, while the continued training during the test period may have helped to maintain the tendency toward relational choices, there is no evidence that Ss were actually learning such behavior during the test period.

In contrasting the predictions of a specific stimulus theory and a relational theory on these test stimuli, it is necessary to consider four different sets of test cards. On stimuli 1/2, 1/3, 2/3, 6/5, 7/5, and 7/6, both theories make the same prediction. For instance, on stimulus 1/2 the specific stimulus theory would predict a jump to the right because S had always been reinforced for jumping right in the presence of both these grays. Similarly, the relational theory would predict this because the top gray is lighter than the bottom one. On these six stimuli 94 percent of the 66 test jumps were as predicted by both theories.

On the second set of stimuli, 2/1, 3/1, 3/2, 5/6, 5/7, and 6/7, the two theories make opposing predictions. For instance, on stimulus 2/1 the specific stimulus theory would predict a right jump because both grays had been associated with this response, whereas the relational theory would predict a left jump because the top gray is darker than the bottom one. On this set of six stimuli, 56 per cent of the responses were in the direction predicted by the relational theory; for six of the Ss the majority of their jumps were relationally determined, for three of them their choices were split equally between the relational and specific directions, and for two the majority of their choices were in the direction predicted by the specific stimulus hypothesis. This percentage in favor of relational responding differs from a chance split between the .10 and .20 levels of significance. It should be noted that the majority of these test stimuli involve two grays that differ by only one step in brightness.

The third set of stimuli, 4/1, 4/2, 4/3, 4/5, 4/6, and 4/7, is that in which gray no. 4, which was always on the bottom half of the cards during training, is now on the top half. In terms of the specific stimulus theory this gray should be neutral, having been equally often associated with jumps to the right and to the left. Consequently, S's response to these test stimuli should be entirely determined by the gray on the bottom half of the card. But this would always lead to just the opposite prediction from that of a relational theory, e.g., on 4/1 the specific stimulus hypothesis would predict a right jump because the gray no. 1 had been associated with this response, whereas the relational theory would predict a left jump because the top was darker than the bottom. On these stimuli 74 per cent of the jumps were relationally determined, which is well beyond the .01 level of significance.

The fourth and final set of stimuli, 2/5, 3/5, 3/6, 5/2, 5/3, and 6/3, is that in which one gray is lighter than the neutral gray no. 4 and the other is darker. On these the predictions from the specific stimulus theory are ambiguous. Presumably the response should be determined by two factors: (a) the gray on the top half of the card should have more influence than the one on the bottom because during training this one was always the determining cue, and (b) the gray of the pair that is farthest removed in brightness from the neutral gray no. 4 should have the greater influence because of generalization. Depending on how these two factors are weighted, a wide variety of predictions can be made. If only the top half of the card is considered, the predictions are exactly the same as for the relational theory. This latter theory makes unambiguous predictions for each stimulus in this set. For this set of stimuli, 95 per cent of the responses were in keeping with the relational prediction, a value significantly different from chance well beyond the .01 level.

If the 12 stimuli of sets 2 and 3 above, for which the two theories make opposing predictions, are combined, 65 per cent of the responses are in accordance with the relational hypothesis, a value significantly different from chance at the .01 level. If, as Table 6.2–2 suggests, part of the failure to show relational behavior on some of these stimuli is due to the difficulty of the discrimination when the two grays are separated by only one unit of brightness, a clearer picture of the predominance of relational responding is shown when this type of stimulus is excluded from the comparison. Considering the 6 stimuli in the above set of 12 in which the pair of grays differs by two or three brightness units, the percentage of relational responding increases to 80.

Five animals were given posttest training on a successive discrimination involving grays no. 3 and no. 5. During the original training these Ss had shown the ability to discriminate between cards 3/4 and 5/4. If, as the specific stimulus theory seems to imply, gray no. 4 was neutral, then according to this theory Ss must have been responding in terms of grays no. 3 and no. 5. Consequently, one would expect that they would continue to respond fairly accurately even though gray no. 4 was removed from the situation. Actually all discrimination between these two grays broke down, and there was little if any sign of learning during the 50 training trials. During the first 10 of these trials, Ss chose correctly 50 per cent of the time, and during the last 10 trials they chose correctly 58 per cent of the time. This supports the idea that this discrimination is very difficult when Ss must react to the stimuli as specific values, but that it is relatively easy when they can relate each of these grays to the reference gray no. 4 of a given trial.

DISCUSSION

In interpreting the results of this experiment, it should be borne in mind that the method of testing for transposition, and therefore the actual definition of the term transposition, in this study differs markedly from the usual method of testing. Usually S is presented during training with two stimuli and taught to approach one of these and avoid the other. Transposition is then tested by presenting S with two new stimuli. The implicit assumption is that the relationship between these new stimuli is the same as it was for the training pair. Thus, in this technique S always must select one of two simultaneously presented stimuli; in addition only the relationship, not the specific stimuli, remains constant from the training to the test situation.

In the present method the procedure is very different. While two stimuli are presented on each trial, S does not choose between them. Rather, S must react to the relationship between them by jumping either right or left. Again all the specific stimulus values that are used during the test situation have been used during the training situation; they are constant. The aspect of the situation that is varied from the training to the test trials is the relationship these specific stimuli bear to each other. The test for transposition is whether or not the behavior varies concomitantly with these changes in relationship. Because of these differences in procedure, it would seem likely that the present method should be a more sensitive test for relational responding than is the usual method. In a sense S is forced to respond relationally from the beginning of training. Furthermore, S is familiar with all the stimulus values used during the test so that these should not introduce any disruptive effect.

There would seem to be little question in terms of the present results that in most instances Ss were reacting to brightness relationships rather than to specific brightness values. A relational hypothesis is able to make a specific, unambiguous prediction about each of the 24 test stimuli used. Eightly per cent of the test responses were in keeping with these predictions, a level of transposition that is almost as great as the level of accuracy these Ss were able to maintain on the training stimuli during this period. Furthermore, it was shown that this level of accuracy was obtained on the very first day of testing and was not the result of learning or continued improvement during this period.

It is true that on the six test stimuli, 2/1, 3/1, 3/2, 5/6, 5/7, and 6/7, for which a relational hypothesis and a specific stimulus hypothesis make directly opposing predictions, only 56 per cent of the responses favor the relational predictions and 44 per cent the specific stimulus hypothesis. This small differential, however, is probably not representative of the true difference. It is especially questionable when it is noted that in the next set of test stimuli involving gray no. 4, where the two theories also make opposing predictions, the difference jumps to 74 per cent versus 26 per cent in favor of relational responding.

The lack of a significant differential in the first case seems to result from the difficulty of the discriminations involved in this set of tests. As can be seen from the logarithmic values for the reflectances in Table 6.2–1, the differences between grays no. 4 and no. 5 and between no. 6 and no. 7 are small as compared with the others. These two pairs of grays were the ones that gave results most opposed to the relational hypothesis, as shown in Table 6.2–2. This latter table also indicates two trends that lowered the percentage of relational responding. First, it indicates that when there was only one unit difference in brightness between the top and bottom half of a test stimulus, relational responding was reduced, suggesting that the grays employed were not spaced properly along the continuum for the most sensitive test of transposition. Secondly, it is evident that when the bottom half of a test card was gray no. 7, the darkest gray, relational responding was minimal. This gray has the same reflectance as the flat black used to paint the entire jumping stand. This suggests the possibility that as one of the grays on the card becomes very similar to the background gray, this similarity may dominate the response and mask the perception of the difference in brightness of the two grays on the card. In a sense the darker gray is amalgamated with the background so that relationship is obscured. If this hypothesis is correct, then this breakdown of relational responding on the dark grays should not have occurred if the background had consisted of stripes or some other distinct pattern.

Although the evidence from this experiment indicates that Ss were responding to the relational aspects of the stimulus situation, this does not imply that this mode of responding is more basic or fundamental than responding to the absolute or particular characteristics of the situation. Certainly the evidence to date indicates that the particular aspects can be the determining factor in behavior in many situations. Rather, this study indicates that when these particular aspects are minimized as reliable cues for behavior in a given training situation, and the relational properties are emphasized, S is perfectly capable of responding to the latter.

It does suggest, also, that even in situations where S is presumably reacting to an absolute characteristic, behavior may be in part determined by the relation between this characteristic and the background stimuli. For instance in the usual successive discrimination involving black and white, this discrimination presumably would be easier to learn if the apparatus were painted a neutral gray than if it were either black or white. In the former case, the differential relations of "lighter than" and "darker than" between the two stimuli and the background should facilitate learning whereas these differential relationships would be lacking if the background was either white or black. The fact that these Ss could discriminate the stimuli 3/4 and 5/4 during original training but were unable to discriminate between grays no. 3 and no. 5 during the posttest training supports this suggestion.

Acceptance of these results as evidence for the perception of, and response to, relationships suggests an alternative interpretation of those studies in which a correlation between mental age and amount of transposition behavior has been shown (1, 3). Usually these studies have been interpreted as evidence that the specific stimulus theories are correct, but that somehow the development of language responses permits more widespread transposition. The present study suggests this alternative. Children can respond relationally prior to the development of language, but do not necessarily do so in all situations. However, the very factors that lead to the development of language behavior also lead to an emphasis on relational responding as the dominant mode of behavior in the child. The result is a correlation between the rate at which language and relational responding develop.

The technique used in the present experiment should be equally applicable to studies of transposition phenomena involving size, form, or like dimensions. It would appear also to have advantages in the study of brightness thresholds. The rate of learning seems to be almost as great as on the usual simultaneous discrimination. At the same time much sharper contrasts between the two brightnesses can be obtained when both are on the same card than when they are spatially separated by the division between the two windows. Therefore, more sensitive measures of differential brightness thresholds should be obtained.

SUMMARY

Eleven albino rats were trained in a new type of transposition situation. The procedure consisted of training Ss on a successive discrimination in which each stimulus card consisted of two grays, one brightness on the top half and a different one on the bottom half. When the top half was lighter than the bottom half, Ss jumped to the right window, and when the top half was darker than the bottom half, they jumped to the left window. When this discrimination had been mastered, Ss were tested on a set of 24 new relationships of this type. These were so selected that in 6 of them both a relational theory and a specific stimulus theory of transposition would make the same prediction, in 12 they would make opposing predictions, and in 6 the relational theory could make an unambiguous prediction whereas the specific stimulus theory could not.

1. For the entire set of 24 test stimuli, 80 per cent of the choices were as predicted by the relational theory.
2. For the set of six on which the two theories make the same prediction, 94 per cent of the choices were in agreement with them.
3. For the set of 12 on which the two theories make opposing predictions, 65 per cent of the choices were as predicted by the relational theory.
4. For the set of six on which only the relational theory could make an unambiguous prediction, 95 per cent of the choices were in this direction.
5. It is suggested that this technique should prove valuable in the study of other forms of transposition behavior and in the study of differential brightness thresholds.

REFERENCES

1. Alberts, Elizabeth, & Ehrenfreund, D. Transposition in children as a function of age. *J. exp. Psychol.*, 1951, 41, 30–38.
2. Köhler, W. *Gestalt psychology.* New York: Liveright, 1929.
3. Kuenne, Margaret R. Experimental investigation of the relation of language to transposition behavior in young children. *J. exp. Psychol.*, 1946, 36, 471–490.
4. Spence, K. W. The differential response in animals to stimuli varying within a single dimension. *Psychol. Rev.*, 1937, 44, 430–444.

6.3 ATTENTION IN THE PIGEON*

George S. Reynolds

Lashley (1938, p. 152) found that a rat that had been reinforced for jumping toward a square and punished for jumping toward a diamond did not jump consistently toward either figure if only the upper halves of the figures were presented. They did, however, jump consistently toward the square if only the lower halves of the figures were presented. This sort of relation between a particular part or aspect of the environment and a response is called *attention* (*cf.* Skinner, 1953). Lashley's rat attended only to the lower parts of the figures, which were shown experimentally to bring about the jump. In general, an organism attends to an aspect of the environment if independent variation or independent elimination of that aspect brings about variation in the organism's behavior. Thus, a gradient of generalization to tones (cps), for example, is a way of showing that the organism was attending to the frequency of the sound in whose presence responding had been reinforced, but a flat generalization function may indicate a lack of attention to the frequency of the sound (*cf.* Jenkins & Harrison, 1960).

The physical parameters of a visual stimulus may be independently varied, but some cannot be independently eliminated. To take specific examples, a triangle against a colored background may be varied without varying the background, and, in addition, the triangle may be eliminated without eliminating the background. The luminance of a visual stimulus may be varied without varying its position or wavelength, but it is not possible to eliminate the luminance without eliminating the entire stimulus. In both sorts of procedures, the experimental study of attention aims at the identification of the stimuli that control responding in a given situation. The present experiments use both the elimination and variation of aspects of a stimulus to study visual attention in the pigeon.

METHOD

Subjects

Two adult male, White Carneaux pigeons, both experimentally naive, were maintained at 80% of their free-feeding body weights.

* Reprinted from *The Journal of the Experimental Analysis of Behavior*, 1961, 4, 203–205. Copyright 1961 by the Society for the Experimental Analysis of Behavior, Inc., and reproduced by permission. Some of the present data were presented at the meetings of the Eastern Psychological Association in April, 1960, under the title "Two examples of 'selective attention' in the pigeon." I am grateful to Dr. A. C. Catania for several careful criticisms of the present manuscript.

Apparatus

The experimental chamber was a modified picnic icebox, similar to that described by Ferster and Skinner (1957). A standard response key, 0.75 inch in diameter, was mounted on one wall of the chamber. The key was operated by a minimum effective force of 15 grams. Below the key was a 2-inch-square opening through which the pigeon was occasionally given access to grain for 3 seconds. The chamber was illuminated by two 6-watt lamps except during periods of access to grain. White noise masked most extraneous sounds.

A projection system[1] allowed transillumination of the key with either red, green, or blue light and, simultaneously, with a white triangle or a white circle. The triangle and circle appeared as white line figures against the colored background. The width of the lines composing each figure was about 0.0625 inch. The circle was 0.5 inch in diameter and the triangle, 0.5 inch high.

During the second experiment only, two Drake No. 51 pilot lights (one yellow and the other green) were mounted one above the other and 2.5 inches to the right of the key. The bulbs extended from their sockets in a plane parallel to the plane of the response key.

Procedure

Both birds were trained to eat grain through the opening in the panel and to peck the response key. On each of 2 days, each of 60 consecutive responses (pecks) was reinforced (3-second access to grain). For 3 hours on each of the next 3 days, responding was reinforced on a variable-interval schedule (mean interval of 3 minutes). Throughout this training the response key was illuminated with a white triangle on a red background.

Experiment I. Each of six daily, 3-hour sessions contained 30 cycles of a two-component multiple schedule. Each cycle consisted of two 3-minute components. During the first component, the key was illuminated with a white triangle on a red background, and responding was reinforced on a VI 3-minute schedule. During the second component, the key was illuminated with a white circle on a green background, and responding was not reinforced. At the end of the sixth session, several cycles with 1-minute components were added. Changing the length of the components from 3 to 1 minute did not alter the rates of responding in the presence of each of the stimuli.

During Sessions 7 and 9, the triangle, circle, red or green light *separately* illuminated the key for 1 minute apiece. A different order of stimulus presentations was used in each session. A total of 52 minutes' exposure to each stimulus separately was given to one pigeon and a total of 69 minutes, to the other pigeon. No responses were reinforced. The procedure during Session 8 was the same as during the first six sessions.

Experiment II. The key was illuminated with either of four stimuli: a white triangle on red or on blue, or a white circle on red or on blue. Each of the four stimuli was presented for 3 minutes in this order: triangle on red, circle on red, triangle on blue, circle on blue, triangle on red, triangle on blue, circle on red, circle on blue. This sequence of eight stimuli (a cycle) was repeated six times during each daily session. During Cycles 1, 3, and 5, the yellow side-lamp (*cf.* Apparatus) was lighted. During Cycles 2, 4, and 6, the green side-lamp was lighted. Thus, the stimulus at a given moment in this procedure consisted of one lighted side-lamp plus a white figure and a background color on the key.

The schedule of reinforcement correlated with each stimulus was either a fixed interval of 3 minutes (no limited hold) or extinction. Which reinforcement schedule was in effect at a particular time depended upon both the side-lamp and the key illuminations. When the yellow side-lamp was lighted, responding was reinforced in the presence of key stimuli containing red. When the green side-lamp was lighted, responding was reinforced in the presence of stimuli containing a triangle. Each bird was exposed to this procedure for about 100 hours over a 2-month period.

After a stable pattern of responding had developed, several modifications of the procedure were introduced for one or two sessions each. Between modifications, the birds were returned to the original procedure for at least two sessions. Responding was never reinforced during a modified procedure.

The modifications of the procedure were:

1. *Extinction:* Responding was extinguished in the presence of the usual pattern of side-lamp and key illuminations.

2. *Both* side-lamps were lighted together, and no responses were reinforced.

3. *No* side-lamps were lighted, and no responses were reinforced.

4. The yellow side-lamp was lighted during Cycles 1, 3, and 5, and responding was reinforced appropriately during the presentation of stimuli containing red. *No* side-lamp was lighted during Cycles 2, 4, and 6, and no responses were reinforced.

5. The green side-lamp was lighted during Cycles 2, 4, and 6, and responding was reinforced appropriately during the presentation of stimuli containing the triangle. *No* side-lamp was lighted during Cycles 1, 3, and 5, and no responses were reinforced.

6. The positions of the original yellow and green side-lamps were reversed, and no responses were reinforced.

7. A lighted *red* side-lamp replaced the green side-lamp during Cycles 2, 4, and 6 only, and no responses were reinforced.

8. A lighted *white* side-lamp replaced the yellow side-lamp during Cycles 1, 3, and 5 only, and no responses were reinforced.

9. The yellow side-lamp was *dimmed* (by increasing the distance between the bulb and the jewel) during Cycles 1, 3, and 5, and no responses were reinforced.

RESULTS

Experiment I

When responding was reinforced (VI 3 minutes) in the presence of a triangle on red and extinguished in the presence of a circle on green, both birds came to respond predominantly in the presence of the triangle on red. The discriminative control acquired by these stimuli is shown in the control (Cont.) histograms in Fig. 6.3–1, which present the average rates of responding for three sessions in the presence of each of the two stimuli (abscissa).

The results of presenting each stimulus—triangle, circle, red, and green—separately are shown in the experimental (Exp.) histograms in Fig. 6.3–1. Pigeon 105 responded (in extinction) at a rate exceeding 20 responses per minute in the presence of the triangle and at a rate of 0.5 response per minute in the presence of a red key (52 minutes in each stimulus). Pigeon 107, however, responded at a rate exceeding 20 responses per minute in the presence of a red key and at a rate less than 0.5 response per minute in the presence of a triangle (69 minutes in each stimulus). Even though each pigeon was reinforced in the presence of a triangle superimposed on a red background, the responding of each

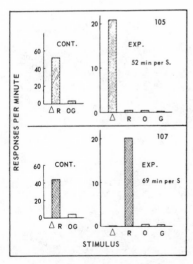

FIGURE 6.3–1 The rate of responding of each pigeon in the presence of each of the key illuminations in the control and experimental phases of Experiment I.

bird was brought under the control of only one of the two aspects of the discriminative stimulus.

The rates of responding in the presence of the two aspects of the stimulus correlated with extinction, a circle and a green key, were typically low for both birds.

Experiment II

When a yellow side-lamp was lighted, responding in the presence of key illuminations containing red was reinforced (FI 3 minutes). When a green side-lamp was lighted, responding in the presence of key illuminations containing a triangle was reinforced. Figure 6.3–2 shows cumulative records of responding from a complete session for each bird. The record was reset to the base line at the end of each cycle of eight 3-minute stimulus presentations. The color of the side lamp during each cycle and the key illumination have been indicated on the records, which have been telescoped (Ferster & Skinner, 1957). A filled circle has been placed above the labels on stimuli during which responding was reinforced (FI 3 minutes). When the side-lamp was yellow, responding occurred predominantly in the presence of stimuli containing red. When the side lamp was green, responding occurred predominantly in the presence of stimuli containing a triangle. The rate of responding during the key stimulus, a triangle on blue, for example, is high when the side-light is green and low when it is yellow. Almost no responses occurred during a circle on blue, in whose presence responding was never reinforced. A high rate of responding occurred during a triangle on red with both

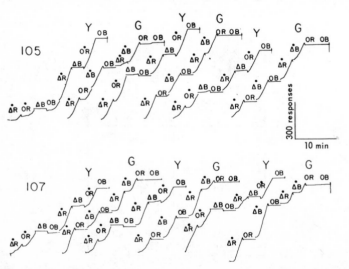

FIGURE 6.3–2 Telescoped cumulative records of the responding of each pigeon during one complete control session Experiment II. Filled circles appear above key stimuli during which responding was reinforced (FI 3 minutes).

yellow and green side-lamps. An acceleration of responding through each interval is noticeable, but not well-developed.

The rate of responding in the presence of each side-lamp and each key illumination is summarized in the Control graph of Fig. 6.3–3. The ordinate is rate of responding, and the abscissa is a nominal scale of stimuli. The solid lines show the responding of Pigeon 105, the dotted lines, the responding of Pigeon 107. Stimuli in whose presence responding was reinforced are indicated by filled circles on the abscissa. The graph shows the same data as the cumulative records: The rate of responding was high only during stimuli in whose presence responding was reinforced.

The graph labeled Extinction in Fig. 6.3–3 shows the pattern of responding when the side lamp and key illuminations are maintained as in the control session but no responses are reinforced. The pattern or ordinal arrangement of the rates of responding in the presence of each side-lamp was not altered by extinction alone.

Figures 6.3–4 and 6.3–5 show the results of the changes in procedure, which were designed to demonstrate the stimuli to which the organisms were attending. Stimuli correlated with reinforcement are indicated by filled circles on the abscissa of each graph. Note that reinforcement was never programmed when the side-lamp illumination was altered. The solid lines show the responding of Pigeon 105, and the dotted lines, the responding of Pigeon 107. The legend for each pair of curves indicates the side-lamp illumination: Y + G means that both side-lamps were lighted; None, that neither side-lamp was lighted; and Y, that only yellow was lighted, etc. The graphs show the responding of each bird on the usual sequence of stimuli under the side-lamp illumination in the

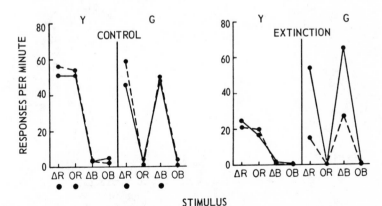

STIMULUS

FIGURE 6.3–3 The rate of responding of Pigeon 105 (solid lines) and Pigeon 107 (dashed lines) in the presence of each of the stimuli on the key during yellow and green side-lamp illuminations. Filled circles along the abscissa designate stimuli in whose presence responding was reinforced.

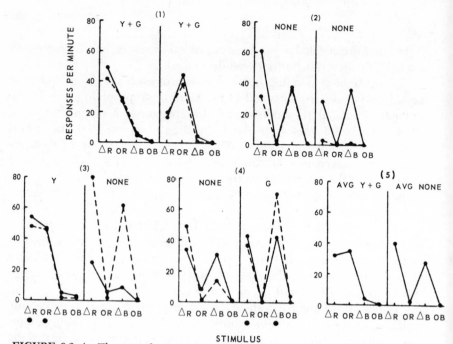

FIGURE 6.3–4 The rate of responding of Pigeon 105 (solid lines) and Pigeon 107 (dashed lines) in the presence of each of the stimuli on the key during the modifications of the side-lamp illumination that are given by the labels of the graphs.

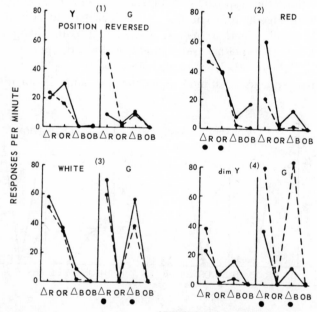

FIGURE 6.3–5 The rate of responding of Pigeon 105 (solid lines) and Pigeon 107 (dashed lines) in the presence of each of the stimuli on the key during the modifications of the side-lamp illumination that are given by the labels of the graphs.

legend. The left half of each graph shows the rate of responding in Cycles 1, 3, and 5; and the right half, that in Cycles 2, 4, and 6.

The graphs in Fig 6.3–4 show generally an invariance in the ordinal arrangement (or pattern) of the rates of responding in the presence of the key illuminations under two changes in the side-lamp illumination. When *no* side-lamp was lighted (indicated by None in Graphs 2, 3, and 4), the pattern of rates usually resembled the pattern when only the green side-lamp was lighted. This may be seen by comparing the pattern of responding under None in Graphs 2 and 3 of Fig. 6.3–4 with the pattern under G in the control graph in Fig. 6.3–3 or with the pattern under G in Graph 4, Fig. 6.3–4. The occasional, very low rates of responding in Cycles 2, 4, and 6, as in the right half of Graph 2 (Fig. 6.3–4), result from rapid extinction, which affects the responding in the later cycles more than in Cycles 1, 3, and 5 (left half of the graph). When *both* side-lamps were lighted (indicated by Y + G in Graph 1, Fig. 6.3–4), the pattern of responding resembled the pattern when only the yellow side-lamp was lighted (compare with Y in control graph, Fig. 6.3–3, and in Graph 3, Fig. 6.3–4). These results of lighting *both* or *none* of the side-lamps are summarized in Graph 5 of Fig. 6.3–4. The left half of Graph 5 shows the average rates of responding of both pigeons in the presence of the key stimuli when *both* side-lamps were lighted. The right half shows the average rates of responding of both pigeons in the presence of the key stimuli when *no* side-lamp was lighted. The patterns of responding in Graph 5 closely resemble the patterns in the control graph, Fig. 6.3–3. To summarize, *both* lamps produce responding as if only yellow were lighted, and *no* lamp produces responding as if only green were lighted. It thus appears that responding was controlled by the presence or absence of the yellow lamp.

Four other modifications of the side-lamp illumination were studied in order to identify further the effective stimulus. The results are shown in Fig. 6.3–5. Reversing the positions of the yellow and green lamps did not alter the pattern of responding (Graph 1, Fig. 6.3–5). A lighted *red* side-lamp (Graph 2), replacing the green lamp, produced a pattern of responding that was ordinally similar to the pattern produced by the absence of the yellow lamp. The functions produced by red may be compared with those produced by green in Fig. 6.3–3 and in Graph 4, Fig. 6.3–5. A lighted *white* side-lamp (Graph 3), replacing the yellow lamp, produced a pattern of responding similar to the pattern produced by the yellow side-lamp (compare with Graph 2, Fig. 6.3–5). A *dimmed* yellow lamp (Graph 4), however, produced a pattern of responding more similar to the pattern produced by the complete absence of the yellow lamp than to the pattern produced by the presence of the original yellow lamp. The intensity, rather than the wavelength or position, of the side-lamps appears to be the effective stimulus.

DISCUSSION AND SUMMARY

In each of the present experiments, the responding of a single pigeon was affected by only one of several aspects of a compound discriminative stimulus. The other aspects of the discriminative stimulus apparently did not control responding and therefore were not discriminative stimuli for the pigeon. In the first experiment, the responding of each bird was reinforced (VI 3 minutes) in the presence of a white triangle with a red background on the response key and extinguished with a white circle on a green background. Subsequently, in extinction, the triangle, circle, red, and green lights were presented separately. Only the presentations of the triangle for Pigeon 105, and only the presentations of a red key for Pigeon 107, resulted in responding. Both aspects of the stimulus correlated with extinction, the circle and the green light, produced typical, low rates of responding.

In the second experiment, reinforcement (FI 3 minutes) or extinction in the presence of stimuli on the key depended upon the color of a side lamp. When the side lamp was yellow, any stimulus on the key containing red was correlated with reinforcement; when it was green, any key stimulus containing a triangle was correlated with reinforcement. Responding appropriate to the reinforcement dependencies developed (Fig. 6.3–2). Changes in the procedure (Fig. 6.3–4 and 6.3–5) revealed that if *both* side-lamps were lighted, the pattern of responding in the presence of the key stimuli was as though only the yellow side-lamp were lighted. If *none* of the side lamps was lighted, the pattern of responding was as though only the green side-lamp were lighted. Only the presence or absence of the yellow light affected the pattern of responding to the stimuli on the key. The discriminative behavior of neither pigeon was based upon the different colors of the side lamps. Reversing the position of the side lamps also did not alter the patterns of responding in the presence of the stimuli on the key.

The results of the additional modifications of the side-lamp illumination suggest that the complex discrimination shown in Fig. 6.3–2 was based predominantly on the intensity, rather than the wavelength or position, of the side-lamps. During the presentation of a *red* side-lamp. about as bright as the green lamp, the key stimuli controlled a pattern of responding similar to the pattern that they controlled during green. During the presentation of a *white* side-lamp, brighter than the yellow, the key stimuli controlled a pattern similar to the pattern that they controlled during yellow. Intensity is further implicated as the effective stimulus since the pattern of responding with a *dimmed* yellow side-lamp turned out to be more similar to the pattern produced by green than to the pattern produced by the original yellow. These results suggest that although pigeons usually can easily discriminate these wavelength bands, these birds were instead responding to the intensity of the stimuli. The present discrimination was certainly not, however, based upon the *relative* intensity of the yellow lamp and the dimmer green lamp, since Graph 4, Fig. 6.3–4, shows that both a green lamp and the dimmer no-lamp condition produced very similar patterns of responding during the same experimental session. Possibly, the effective stimulus was the difference in the effects of the high and low side-lamp intensities upon the form and color combinations as they appeared on the response key.

The present results show that a pigeon may attend to only one of several aspects of a discriminative stimulus. Every part of the environment that is present when a reinforced response occurs may not subsequently be an occasion for the emission of that response. In the present usage, attention refers to the controlling relation between a stimulus and responding. An organism attends to a stimulus when its responding is under the control of that stimulus. In the first experiment, one pigeon attended to the red key and the other to the triangle, even though the responding of each had been reinforced in the presence of the triangle superimposed on the red key. On the other hand, both parts of a compound stimulus correlated with extinction separately produced the low rate of responding typical of extinction. In the second experiment, neither pigeon attended to the color of the side-lamp. Their responding was controlled only by the presence or absence of the yellow side-lamp, or, under further analysis, by the intensity of the side-lamp illumination.

NOTE

1. "One Plane Digital Display Unit," manufactured by Industrial Electronics Engineers, North Hollywood, California.

REFERENCES

Ferster, C. B., and Skinner, B. F. *Schedules of reinforcement.* New York: Appleton-Century-Crofts, 1957.

Jenkins, H. M., and Harrison, R. H. Effect of discrimination training on auditory generalization. *J. exp. Psychol.*, 1960, 59, 246–253.

Lashley, K. S. The mechanism of vision: XV. Preliminary studies of the rat's capacity for detail vision. *J. gen. Psychol.*, 1938, 18, 123–193.

Skinner, B. F. *Science and human behavior.* New York: Macmillan, 1953.

6.4 INTRADIMENSIONAL AND EXTRADIMENSIONAL SHIFT LEARNING BY PIGEONS*

N. J. MacKintosh and Lydia Little

Pigeons were trained consecutively on two simultaneous visual discriminations. For half the Ss, the dimension relevant in the first problem remained relevant in the second (intradimensional shift); for the remainder, the dimension irrelevant in the first problem became relevant in the second (extradimensional shift). As is predicted by two-stage theories of discrimination learning, the intradimensional shift was learned more rapidly than the extradimensional shift.

Several recently proposed theories of discrimination learning have assumed that in order to solve a discrimination problem, Ss must not only learn which value of the relevant dimension is associated with reinforcement, but must also learn to identify, observe, or attend to the relevant dimension itself (Lovejoy, 1968; Sutherland, 1964; Zeaman & House, 1963). One prediction that follows from such a theory is that training on one problem with a given dimension relevant may selectively facilitate the learning of a new discrimination problem involving the same relevant dimension even though no direct transfer based on the response requirements of the two tasks could be expected. Lawrence's experiments on the acquired distinctiveness of cues, in which transfer between successive and simultaneous discriminations was assessed, provided the earliest support for this prediction (Lawrence, 1949); but the procedure has since been criticized by Siegel (1967) on the grounds that some direct transfer might have occurred.

A second appropriate experimental design, used in studies of human concept learning, involves comparing intradimensional shift (IDS) and extradimensional shift (EDS) learning, Ss are trained on a discrimination problem with Dimension A relevant and Dimension B irrelevant; in the second stage of the experiment new values of the two dimensions are chosen, and Ss learning the IDS problem are again trained with A relevant and B irrelevant, while Ss learning the EDS problem are trained with B relevant and A irrelvant. If Ss during Stage 1 learn to attend to A and ignore B, and if these attentional changes transfer to the new values of A and B used in Stage 2, then the IDS problem should be learned more rapidly than the EDS problem.

* Reprinted from *Psychonomic Science*, 1969, *14*, 5–6. Copyright 1969 by the Psychonomic Society, and reproduced by permission. This research was supported by Grant APA-259 from the National Research Council of Canada.

362

Although there is ample evidence that human Ss, from 4-year-old children (Trabasso, Deutsch, & Gelman, 1966) to college students (Isaacs & Duncan, 1962) learn IDS problems more rapidly than EDS problems, only one study with animals (rats) has shown such an effect (Shepp & Eimas, 1964). The present experiment was designed to see whether pigeons would show any difference in rate of learning the two kinds of problems.

SUBJECTS

The Ss were 16 White Carneaux pigeons, six months old. They were maintained at 80% of their ad lib weights.

APPARATUS

The apparatus was a three-key pigeon chamber, with the center key blacked out except during initial shaping. The stimuli were projected onto the rear of the two side keys by means of in-line projectors, and consisted of three colored lines on a white background. The colors were red, yellow, green, or blue; and the orientation of the lines was 0, 90, 45, or 135 deg.

PROCEDURE

After being shaped to peck at a white center key, Ss were given 50 non-correction trials each day for the remainder of the experiment. At the beginning of each trial, the house light was turned off and the two side keys were illuminated. A correct response led to 5-sec access to grain; an error led to 8-sec time-out in darkness. At the end of each trial, the house light was turned on and a 25-sec intertrial interval followed. All events were controlled by external programming equipment, and responses were recorded on counters.

EXPERIMENTAL DESIGN

All Ss learned two simultaneous discriminations. In Stage 1, the stimuli were red and yellow, 0-deg and 90-deg lines. For eight Ss, color was the relevant dimension (half being trained with red positive, half with yellow positive), and orientation irrelevant. For the remaining Ss, orientation was relevant (0-deg positive for half, 90-deg positive for the other half) and color was irrelevant. The position of the positive and negative stimuli, and the values of the irrelevant dimension, were determined by selected Gellermann orders. All Ss received 250 trials.

In Stage 2, the stimuli were blue and green, 45-deg and 135-deg lines. Half of each of the above groups was trained on a color problem (blue positive) with orientation irrelevant, and half was trained on an orientation problem (45-deg positive) with color irrelevant. All Ss were trained to a criterion of 40 correct responses in a day.

There were, therefore, four main experimental groups distinguished by the dimensions relevant in Stages 1 and 2: Color-color, and orientation-orientation (these groups learned an IDS problem in Stage 2); color-orientation, and orientation-color (these groups learned an EDS problem in Stage 2). Within these four groups, equal numbers of Ss had been trained in opposite directions in Stage 1.

RESULTS

Table 6.4–1 shows the average number of errors made during the 250 trials of Stage 1. The color discrimination was substantially easier than the orientation discrimination ($F = 42.71$, df $= 1/12$, p $< .001$), but Ss subsequently learning EDS and IDS problems were closely matched for Stage-1 scores ($F < 1$). All Ss achieved a criterion of 40 correct responses in a day.

Table 6.4–1 also shows the number of errors to criterion in Stage 2. Again, the color discrimination was easier than the orientation discrimination ($F = 49.67$, df $= 1/12$, p $< .001$). The IDS problem was learned faster than the EDS problem ($F = 5.67$, df $= 1/12$, p $< .05$); and there was no interaction between dimensions and type of shift ($F < 1$). Finally there was little sign of any direct (response-based) transfer between the two problems. Of the eight Ss that learned color in Stage 1, those trained with red positive selected blue on 64.5% of trials on the first day of Stage 2, while those trained with yellow positive selected blue on 54% of trials. Similarly, of the Ss trained on orientation in Stage 1, those trained with 0 deg positive selected the 45-deg lines on 58.5% of trials, while those trained with 90 deg positive selected the 45-deg lines on 50% of trials. Neither of these differences approached significance (in both cases, p $> .20$).

TABLE 6.4–1

Groups	Stage 1 Errors in 250 Trials	Stage 2 Errors to Criterion
Color - Color	25.25	13.50
Orientation - Color	77.50	30.50
Orientation - Orientation	74.75	54.00
Color - Orientation	24.50	67.00

In conclusion, therefore, pigeons, like rats and humans, learn IDS problems faster than EDS problems. Although the effect was a relatively small one, the results suggest that transfer between problems may occur which cannot be explained simply in terms of differential response tendencies. It appears that learning to attend to the relevant dimension is part of what is involved in learning a discrimination problem.

REFERENCES

Isaacs, I. D., & Duncan, C. P. Reversal and nonreversal shifts within and between dimensions in concept formation. Journal of Experimental Psychology, 1962, 64, 580–585.

Lawrence, D. H. Acquired distinctiveness of cues: I. Transfer between discriminations on the basis of familiarity with the stimulus. Journal of Experimental Psychology, 1949, 39, 770–784.

Lovejoy, E. Attention in discrimination learning. San Francisco: Holden-Day, 1968.

Shepp, B. E., & Eimas, P. D. Intradimensional and extradimensional shifts in the rat. Journal of Comparative & Physiological Psychology, 1964, 57, 357–361.

Siegel, S. Overtraining and transfer processes. Journal of Comparative & Physiological Psychology, 1967, 64, 471–477.

Sutherland, N. S. The learning of discriminations by animals. Endeavour, 1964, 148–152.

Trabasso, T., Deutsch, J. A., & Gelman, R. Attention in discrimination learning of young children. Journal of Experimental Child Psychology, 1966, 4, 9–19.

Zeaman, D., & House, B. J. The role of attention in retardate discrimination learning. In N. R. Ellis (Ed.), Handbook of mental deficiency: Psychological theory and research. New York: McGraw-Hill, 1963. Pp. 159–223.

Seven

The Response: What Is Learned?

Imagine a rat walking down the straight alley of a T maze, occasionally rearing on his hind legs and sniffing in the air. He eventually reaches the choice point and, after some hesitation, he turns to the right. As luck would have it his right turn takes him to the goal box containing food, and over succeeding trials his tendency to turn to the right becomes greater and greater until eventually he runs to the right goal box immediately and without hesitation on every trial. Why? What is the nature of the learning process that has led him to so totally alter his behavior?

One simple explanation might be that the rat has gradually learned to expect food in the goal box on the right, and since he is hungry, having been deprived of food for many hours, he naturally runs there as quickly as possible in order to obtain food. This explanation is simple and reasonable, and yet it was exactly this kind of explanation that led John B. Watson to spearhead the greatest revolution in psychology, that of *behaviorism*. For Watson, this kind of explanation was not only not reasonable, but the kind of pernicious nonsense that was preventing psychology from becoming a mature science. What, for example, was the meaning of "expect"? How do we know what a rat expects? Or, for that matter, what a human expects? We may see what a man *does* and we may observe his verbal behavior, but do we really know with any certainty what he thinks or expects? If we subjected someone to the closest scrutiny by ten trained observers, whether novelists or psychiatrists, could they possibly hope to agree on what was really in his heart or mind?

Theoretical arguments such as these, combined with the demonstrable failure of introspectionists to agree on even the simplest questions—Is yellow a primary color? Can there be thought without images?—led Watson to call for the total repudiation of mentalistic concepts. Feelings, thoughts, expectations—all of these were states which might or might not exist, but which certainly could not be subjected to scientific analysis. All that we can see is *behavior*, and it is behavior that we must describe and ultimately predict, not consciousness. Behavior for Watson consisted of glandular secretions and muscular movements, and the task of learning psychologists was to predict the changes in these responses with experience.

Is this conception of a muscle twitch psychology, devoid of any mental content, reasonable? The psychologist William McDougall, for example, thought not:

> I come into this hall and see a man on this platform scraping the guts of a cat with hairs from the tail of a horse; and, sitting silently in attitudes of rapt attention, are a thousand persons who presently break out into wild applause. How will the Behaviorist explain these strange incidents: How explain the fact that vibrations emitted by the cat-gut stimulate all the thousand into absolute silence and quiescence; and the further fact that the cessation of the stimulus seems to be a stimulus to the most frantic activity? Common sense and psychology agree in accepting the explanation that the audience heard the music with keen pleasure, and vented their gratitude and admiration for the artist in shouts and hand clappings. But the Behaviorist knows nothing of pleasure and pain, of admiration and gratitude. He has relegated all such "metaphysical entities" to the dust heap, and must seek some other explanation. Let us leave him seeking it. The search will keep him harmlessly occupied for some centuries to come [Watson and McDougall, 1929].

McDougall's point is reasonable as well as amusing—it does seem strange to deny what is so obviously true, the existence of thoughts and feelings—and yet in a sense his argument is irrelevant. The real issue is not whether the mind exists, but whether it can be usefully studied by the analytic tools of science. Science, as opposed to philosophy or art, is based on the ability of all trained observers to agree, and it is this agreement on basic facts that allows science to progress from one question to another, instead of becoming mired down in an endless haggling over the same few issues. Watson believed that a psychology based on mental life could never reach this crucial consensus, and argued instead for an analysis based on observable behavior. The real controversy, then, was not over the mind's existence, but whether studying the mind would help to understand behavior. The crucial scientific criterion for evaluating theories is not how plausible they sound but how accurately they predict, and it is this question—the predictive powers of cognitive versus behaviorist approaches—that will be evaluated in this chapter as we examine their opposing views on the nature of the response.

The Muscle Twitch

For Watson, a response was either muscular or glandular activity, and learning was the formation of an association between a stimulus and a response, such that whenever the stimulus recurred it would again elicit the response. This idea of an *association* of two elements becoming tied together through temporal contiguity is basically a simple extention of the older doctrines of the British Associationists. They had attempted to explain the seemingly random and chaotic nature of thought on the basis of associations between ideas, and Watson now incorporated this same concept into his theory of behavior. Where the British had talked of ideas, Watson substituted stimuli and responses, but underlying the new language of objective behaviorism was the same fundamental concept of an association. Behavior may sometimes appear highly intricate, but underlying its apparent complexity are simple associations, just as the extraordinary diversity of chemical compounds arises from simple associations among a small group of elements.

If associations are formed only between environmental stimuli and muscular responses, then one important implication is that learning should be possible only if a subject responds! If there is no response, no S-R associations can be formed. Beck and Doty (1957) tested this prediction in a classical conditioning experiment with cats. Their CS was a tone and their US was an electric shock to one leg. The normal response to the shock would be flexion of the leg, but the experimenters blocked this response by injecting bulbocapnine, a drug which produces muscular paralysis. In training, therefore, the cats received normal pairings of the CS and US, but their response was effectively blocked so that it could not be associated with the CS. In test trials after the cats had recovered use of their limb, however, they immediately flexed their leg whenever the CS was presented, indicating successful conditioning despite the absence of a response during training. The response learned during training, therefore, must have been some form of *covert* rather than overt behavior.

Similar results have been obtained in experiments on operant conditioning. Learning in the T-maze, for example, is attributed by S-R theorists to an association between the stimuli at the choice point and the correct turning response, so that if there were no response there should be no learning. Blocking the response by injection is impractical in this case, since subjects would then be unable to reach the goal box, so McNamara, Long, and Wike (Article 7.1) instead wheeled their subjects through the maze on a cart! The subjects never moved, since the cart was pulled by the experimenter, and yet in a later test their tendency to choose the correct goal box was indistinguishable from that of control subjects who had literally run during training. Again, therefore, we must conclude that learning does not require any overt behavior.

Fractional Anticipatory Goal Responses

Behaviorism arose out of a growing revulsion against the seemingly endless bickering of the introspectionists, as each observer studied his own private world and no two observers could agree. The solution, as Watson saw it, was to simply eliminate all references to subject states from psychology, allowing as scientific data only those behaviors that could be objectively measured. The evidence for learning without responding, however, meant that learning could no longer be described solely in terms of visible behavior, and created a painful dilemma for behaviorists. Could S-R theory somehow be salvaged? Or did its failure in this instance require a repudiation of behaviorism and a return to introspection and the study of the mind? In fact, there was little thought of repudiation, and the history of science provides few precedents for such abrupt reversals. A theorist develops his theory on the basis of a complex network of assumptions, and while an incorrect prediction may mean that *one* assumption is wrong, it hardly invalidates the entire set. Put less charitably, none of us likes to admit to being totally wrong: a small oversight, perhaps, but surely not a total failure! The practical question confronting S-R theorists, then, was not whether to abandon their theory, but how to modify it so as to account for learning without responding while doing the least damage to the theory's basic structure.

The answer was provided by Clark Hull, and it was breathtaking in its simplicity: If there must be covert behavior, let it have exactly the same properties as overt behavior! Rather than simply abandoning an S-R analysis of behavior, let us extend it to covert as well as overt behavior, assuming that internal responses obey exactly the same S-R laws as their overt counterparts. But how does the assumption of invisible muscle twitches explain such phenomena as latent extinction? And how in any case can a behaviorist assume invisible responses? The very essence of behaviorism is its insistence on objectively measurable behavior, and imaginary muscle twitches clearly do not qualify. Hull argued, however, that untestable assumptions were permissible *so long as they led to testable predictions*. An atom, for example, may never be directly observed, but it is a useful concept so long as its properties are specified clearly enough to lead to testable predictions. It is only when a concept becomes so vague that it can predict *any* outcome that it loses its scientific meaningfulness. The existence of the mind, for example, may seem intuitively obvious, but as long as its properties are left unspecified it can explain behavior only via *post hoc* rationalizations, of no testable value regardless of how plausible they sound. By specifying that covert responses would obey the same laws as overt responses, however, Hull hoped to avoid such ambiguity and to predict not only when such responses would occur but what their consequences would be.

What, then, of his success? Does the assumption of a covert muscle twitch allow S-R theory to handle phenomena that were previously inexplicable? We can illustrate the explanatory power of Hull's theory through an analysis of latent extinction proposed by Howard Moltz (Article 7.2). In latent extinction direct placements in an empty goal box facilitate extinction of running to that goal box, and as we have seen previously, this result is easy to understand in terms of expectations (the rat no longer expects food in the goal box and is therefore less likely to run when placed at the beginning of the maze) but much less comprehensible in terms of overt muscle twitches (since the running response did not occur, how could it have been weakened?). A simple explanation might be to simply assert that *covert* running responses had occurred during latent extinction trials, but Moltz instead adopts a strategy that is less direct but ultimately more flexible. Specifically, he sets out to explain latent extinction in terms of a covert response obeying exactly the same laws as its overt counterpart, but the response he chooses is not running but salivation!

Moltz begins his analysis with the reasonable assumption that food is a US which will elicit some unconditioned response, R_G (goal response). Presentation of food in the goal box, therefore, should result in the conditioning of R_G to the preceding stimuli, namely the goal box cues. We will call this conditioned response r_g, and it may be thought of as some fractional component of eating such as chewing or salivating. If r_g is conditioned to the goal box cues, however, then we know from the principle of generalization that it should also occur to stimuli that are similar to the goal box. The start box, for example, is made from the same material as the goal box, and so we might expect r_g to also be elicited by the start box cues. (r_g is now called a fractional *anticipatory* goal response, since it occurs before the subject actually reaches the goal.) Another property of all responses is that they produce proprioceptive feedback whenever they occur, and so we can also predict that r_g will produce a proprioceptive stimulus, s_g. The start box cues, then, will elicit r_g because of their similarity to the goal box cues, and once r_g occurs it will produce the proprioceptive stimulus s_g.

The next step in Moltz's derivation is one of the most important: He now invokes the principle of reinforcement. As we saw in the previous chapter, S-R theory assumes that reinforcement results in the strengthening of the association between the response and all preceding stimuli, so that when the rat is reinforced running should become conditioned to all previous cues, *including* s_g. In the early phases of training, before r_g has been conditioned, the running response will be associated only to the start box cues, but once r_g is elicited in the start box then s_g will also be present and its association with running will be strengthened on every reinforced trial. By the end of the training, therefore, the running response is elicited not only by the alley cues but by s_g.

During the latent extinction phase the rat is directly placed in the goal box without food. Exposure to the goal box cues (the CS) in the absence of food (the US), however, should result in extinction of any conditioned response. During latent extinction, therefore, r_g should be extinguished to the goal box cues, and as a result it can no longer generalize to the start box stimuli. When the subject is returned to the start box for testing, therefore, r_g will no longer occur, and thus s_g will not be produced. During the final extinction phase latent extinction subjects will thus have one less cue eliciting running than they had during training, and their net response tendency will be less than for control subjects. By simply assuming a little invisible salivation, therefore, and then systematically applying the laws of conditioning, Moltz is again able to explain a seemingly complex phenomenon using only the simple assumptions of association theory (the basic assumption really *are* simple, though you may by now be a little dizzy from trying to follow their combination and application).

It is important to emphasize that the validity of this theory depends solely on its predictive accuracy, and that it is neither enhanced nor diminished by evidence concerning whether r_g really occurs. Nevertheless, it is interesting to note that there is now evidence for a conditioned response of exactly this kind in runway situations. Deaux and Patten (Article 7.3) trained rats to run down a straight alley for water, and used a mobile recording device that allowed them to measure licking in both the goal box and alley. They found that anticipatory licking did occur in the alley, and that it increased significantly as training continued. These results do not directly support S-R theory, but they lend a certain intuitive plausibility to what at first may seem a circuitous and perhaps bizarre explanation.

Expectations

Behaviorism began as an attempt to eliminate all subjective concepts from psychology, replacing them with stimuli and responses that could be objectively measured. In response to the growing evidence for phenomena such as latent extinction, however, a new position, that of *neobehaviorism*, emerged. Neobehaviorists such as Clark Hull and Kenneth Spence still believed in the rigorous exclusion of all subjective data from psychology, but they differed from the earlier behaviorists such as Watson in being willing to incorporate a variety of hypothetical constructs at a *theoretical* level, provided only that these constructs led to objectively testable predictions. Thus Hull introduced the covert response r_g, but in order to be able to generate precise predictions he stipulated that it had the same properties and obeyed the same laws as its more visible counterparts. Learning was still fundamentally a matter of simple S-R associations, but for theoretical purposes the definition of the response was now broadened to include covert as well as overt behavior.

Despite the considerable liberalization of S-R theory produced by this modification, it was still not enough to satisfy cognitive theorists such as Edward C. Tolman. An associative explanation of behavior in terms of muscle twitches, even covert muscle twitches, still seemed to Tolman to be too simple, too mechanical, to account for the flexibility and purposefulness of behavior. Rather than viewing learning as the modification of muscle twitches, Tolman believed that subjects learned cognitive relationships such as "If I press the bar I will obtain food" or "When the tone sounds, I'm going to get a puff of air in my eye." Furthermore, Tolman believed that these expectations might involve complex *cognitive maps* indicating the precise spatial relationships among points in the environment. In one experiment, Tolman trained rats to run down a long alley and then turn to the right into a second alley which led to food. S-R theorists might say that the rat had learned a right turn, but Tolman believed he was also learning the precise spatial relationship between the starting point and the goal box. In the test phase Tolman blocked entry into the first alley and instead offered the rats a choice of test alleys radiating in all directions from the starting point. The most common choice turned out to be the test alley which led directly to where the goal box had been, suggesting that the rats had in fact learned the precise location of the goal box during training (but see Restle, 1957). Details of this and other

ingenious experiments in support of the cognitive viewpoint are contained
in Tolman's classic paper, "Cognitive Maps in Rats and Men"
(Article 7.4).

Further evidence for cognitive processes has come, surprisingly,
from Kenneth Spence (Article 7.5). A puzzling phenomenon in
the extinction of conditioned eyeblink responses in humans is its rapidity,
often occurring after only one trial. One possible explanation is that
human subjects immediately notice the omission of the US, and as
a result form a cognitive set not to blink when the CS is presented.
Extinction, in other words, is normally a slow process but if the subject
notices the altered contingencies, he may form an inhibitory set which
will prevent further responding. If the subject's awareness of the
contingencies could somehow be prevented, however, then human subjects
should extinguish at the same slow rate as animals. To test this
interpretation Spence conditioned two groups of subjects to blink,
using a tone as the CS and a puff of air to the eye as the US. After
50 training trials extinction was begun by lengthening the CS-US interval
from .5 to 2.5 seconds, an interval which does not normally maintain a
conditioned response. For one of the groups, however, extinction
trials occurred while they were occupied with a difficult problem-solving
task. Spence had instructed these subjects that they were participating
in a study on the effects of distraction on problem solving, where
the distractors would be tones and air puffs. Spence hoped that the
subjects would concentrate totally on the problem, and therefore not
notice the change in the tone-air puff contingency. Subsequent interviews
confirmed that these subjects were unaware of the change from
acquisition to extinction, and the result was that their blink rate
decreased only 14 percent, while a comparable control group dropped
45 percent. At least for human subjects, therefore, the effects of classical
conditioning depend heavily on the subject's awareness of the
contingencies.

At this point, if you have been reading this section carefully, you
should be full of righteous indignation. Much of this book has been
devoted to a careful explanation of the evils of introspection and
subjective explanations of behavior, and yet here are Tolman and Spence
talking glibly of "expectations," "cognitive maps," and "cognitive sets."
What do these terms mean? How are they in any way superior to
the "expectation" explanation of a rat's maze behavior that was
so cavalierly dismissed at the beginning of this chapter? The somewhat
complex answer is that Tolman and Spence were indeed using the
same terms as the introspectionists, but they justified their usage
by changing the meanings! By expectation, for example, Tolman did not
mean a conscious state of the mind, but rather an objectively

measurable relationship between environmental conditions and the subject's behavior:

> When we assert that a rat expects food at location L, what we assert is that *if* (1) he is deprived of food, (2) he has been trained on path P, (3) he is now put on path P, (4) path P is now blocked, and (5) there are other paths which lead away from path P, one of which points directly to location L, *then* he will run down the path which points directly to location L.
>
> When we assert that he does *not* expect food at location L, what we assert is that, under the same conditions, he will *not* run down the path which points directly to location L [Tolman, Ritchie, and Kalish, 1946].

An expectation, in other words, is not a mental state, but a behavioral relationship, and the existence of an expectation is to be objectively inferred from the subject's actual behavior. Another sign of an expectation, for example, was *disruption* of behavior if an expected goal was not obtained. In an experiment by Tinklepaugh (1928), a monkey was trained to reach under one of two cups in order to obtain a banana. On one trial, however, Tinklepaugh substituted lettuce for the banana, and then told the monkey to "come and get the food":

> She jumps down from the chair, rushes to the proper container and picks it up. She extends her hand to seize the food. But her hand drops to the floor without touching it. She looks at the lettuce but (unless very hungry) does not touch it. She looks around the cup and behind the board. She stands up and looks under and around her. She picks the cup up and examines it thoroughly inside and out. She has on occasion turned toward observers present in the room and shrieked at them in apparent anger. After several seconds spent searching, she gives a glance toward the other cup, which she has been taught not to look into, and then walks off to a nearby window. The lettuce is left untouched on the floor.

As illustrated by these examples, Tolman was still a *methodological behaviorist*, relying on objectively derived data to test his theory. An expectation was a hypothetical construct, having much the same theoretical status as Hull's r_g. Neither construct could be directly observed, but rather had to be inferred from behavior according to specified rules. The theories differed only in the properties attributed to these covert responses: for Hull they obeyed exactly the same laws as a muscle twitch; for Tolman, they were somehow more complex and purposeful. In Tolman's words, "We feel . . . that the intervening brain processes are more complicated, more patterned, and often . . . more

autonomous than do the stimulus-response psychologists" (Article 7.4).
With S-R theory's increasing reliance on covert mediating responses
such as r_g, however, it has become increasingly difficult to separate
the two positions. Regarding latent extinction, for example, how can we
distinguish between S-R theory, which says that r_g is extinguished,
and cognitive theory, which says that an expectation is weakened?

The crucial problem in trying to distinguish between these
two positions is their ambiguity. Both theories require precise rules for
predicting the effects of their hypothetical constructs, but our ignorance
about the laws of behavior has prevented theorists from developing
these rules. In the experiment in which rats were pulled through
a maze on a cart, for example, a cognitive theorist might predict that
the rats would learn to expect food in the right goal box, since food was
only presented on that side, but he might equally well predict
that they would learn nothing about the correct side, but only to expect
food on half the trials if they sat quietly on the cart! Until we know
more about the development of expectations it is impossible to say which
outcome to expect, and the predictions of S-R theory in this situation
are hardly more determinate. The moral of this discussion is *not*
that S-R and cognitive theories are useless. As originally formulated
there were genuine differences between them, and many of these
differences were ultimately resolved in favor of the cognitive approach,
including the controversies over attention and relational learning.
As S-R theory was modified to meet these developments, however, it
has become increasingly difficult to distinguish between the two theories,
and current theorists often seem as much divided over whether their
theories still differ as over which is really true.

Recognizing the problems produced by the ambiguities in both
theories, psychologists have turned increasingly to mathematical models
of narrower range but greater precision. Rather than vague statements
encompassing all of behavior, these models instead focus on specific,
quantitative assumptions dealing with a highly restricted problem
area. The loss in generality is hopefully offset by the gain in specificity, so
that the model can be unambiguously tested, and then modified
as necessary before being extended to more complex situations.

One example of this approach is the work of Martin Levine on the
role of hypotheses in discrimination learning (Article 7.6). Levine
assumes that subjects form hypotheses about which stimulus is correct,
and then retain or reject that hypothesis depending on the trial
outcome. Only a single hypothesis guides behavior on a given trial, and
the subject learns only about the validity of that hypothesis. In a
typical experiment, Levine presents his subjects with a series of cards
each containing the letters A and B. The subjects are instructed to

say which letter is correct on every trial, and are immediately told whether they were right or wrong. Acording to S-R theory the response in this situation is simply saying "A" or "B," and these responses should be strengthened or weakened depending on whether the experimenter says right or wrong. According to Levine, however, the response is a hypothesis about the trial outcome, and these hypotheses may be simple ("A is always correct") or complex ("A is correct for two trials, then B is correct for three trials").

To distinguish between S-R and cognitive interpretations of what is learned in this situation, Levine presented his subjects with a series of cards in which the position of the letters A and B alternated randomly over trials. "A" was always the correct response, but despite the simple nature of the problem—the response "A" always reinforced, the response "B" always punished—81 percent of the subjects were unable to solve the problem, showing no improvement even after 100 trials! The explanation for this bizarre result lies in the pretraining given the subjects. During this initial phase, subjects were given six problems, with the basis of solution always being a complex position sequence. Using L to indicate "left letter correct" and R to indicate "right letter correct," the basis of solution of one problem was the sequence LLRLLLLRLRR, a sequence which was repeated over and over until the subjects solved the problem. By the end of pretraining, therefore, hypothesis theory predicts that the subjects have learned that the correct hypothesis is always a complex position sequence. On the test problem, therefore, subjects test only position hypotheses, rejecting one after another as they are eventually disconfirmed. Since they never test the letter hypothesis "A is correct," they never notice this simple relationship and therefore never solve the problem.

In Levine's situation, therefore, hypothesis theory is able to explain the subject's inability to solve the problem, while an S-R theory based on the actual choice response "A" or "B" must predict the gradual strengthening of the correct response. Because of Levine's mathematical formulation, moreover, he is able to make quantitative as well as qualitative predictions, and his theory indicates how the vague notions of "expectancies" and "hypotheses" can be rigorously formulated and then tested.

In summary, both the response and our theories describing it have become more sophisticated over the years. For Watson a response was simply the twitching of a muscle fiber, and learning was the process of connecting these twitches to external stimuli. The evidence that learning occurred even when the subject was immobilized, however, meant that whatever response was being associated could not possibly be an overt movement, and thus that activity not only occurs within the hidden depths of the body but cannot be ignored in any adequate theory of learning. The problem, therefore, became how best to describe this covert activity, and how to predict its effects on behavior. For Hull and Spence, this covert behavior was exactly analogous to the muscle twitches described by Watson, having the same properties and obeying the same laws. For Tolman, it was something far more complex, something better described as an expectation or cognitive map than as covert chewing movements. These differences in verbal formulation, however, obscured some important similarities between the two approaches. The real significance of these hypothetical constructs was not in the names given them but in their properties and actual implications for behavior, and these often turned out to be strikingly similar. Thus whether a rat in the start box was said to be expecting food or only chewing a little harder than usual, the prediction that he would run through the maze quickly was the same in both cases. And as theorists have begun to realize the difficulties created by ambiguous formulations, they have turned increasingly toward more precise, quantitative mini-theories dealing with more circumscribed problem areas. One unfortunate result has been to make learning theory less accessible to laymen—Levine's hypotheses have none of the excitement or charm of Tolman's cognitive maps—but the more precise formulations of theories like this should ultimately lead us to a deeper understanding of the complex nature of the response.

7.1 LEARNING WITHOUT RESPONSE UNDER TWO CONDITIONS OF EXTERNAL CUES*

Harold J. McNamara, John B. Long, and Edward L. Wike

In 1946 Thorndike (4) critically examined Tolman's concept of expectancy and proposed a number of experiments to evaluate this viewpoint. Bugelski and his co-workers (1) mention some unpublished research, using Thorndike's situations, which failed to provide support for the expectancy interpretation. More recently, Gleitman (2) has demonstrated place learning without performance in an elevated T maze with rats that had been drawn along a path in a "cable car" and shocked during transit. Learning was observed only when the locus of the T maze coincided with the path which the Ss had traversed.

The first situation suggested by Thorndike was:

> . . . put the rat in a little wire car, in the entrance chamber of a maze, run it through the correct path of a simple maze and into the food compartment. Release it there and let it eat the morsel provided. Repeat 10 to 100 times according to the difficulty of the maze under ordinary conditions. The rat had an opportunity to form expectancies that presence in the food compartment is followed by food, that the correct turn is followed by the food chamber, and so on. Then put it in the entrance chamber free to go wherever it is inclined and observe what it does. Compare the behavior of such rats with that of rats run in the customary manner (4, p. 278).

The present experiments follow rather closely Thorndike's suggested procedure except that the performance on a number of extinction trials is utilized as an indicant of learning. In addition, each S in the experimental ("basket") group is matched with a control S in terms of the number and pattern of rewarded and nonrewarded responses; and, instead of a complex maze, the learning task is a single-unit elevated T maze.

Thus, the experimental question becomes: Is execution of running and turning responses necessary in order for rats to learn the locus of food in an elevated T maze? If learning involves the establishment of S-R connections by means of drive-reduction, then we should expect that the

* Harold J. McNamara, John B. Long, and Edward L. Wike, "Learning without Response under Two Conditions of External Cues," *The Journal of Comparative and Physiological Psychology*, 49, 1956, 477–480. Copyright 1956 by the American Psychological Association, and reproduced by permission.

Ss that are conveyed about the maze in a wire basket would show little or no learning, since the running and turning responses are not made contiguously with the eliciting cues and reinforcement. On the other hand, if the learning consists of the development of field expectancies (5), then there is no obvious reason why the conveyed animals should not acquire a *representation* of the situation if there are sufficient differential cues to serve as environmental supports and the Ss frequently have access to these discriminanda. Accordingly, in experiment I, it is anticipated that Ss which have been transported about an elevated T maze in a basket will go to the correct side as often on the extinction trials as control Ss which have previously learned the maze under normal running conditions.

The purpose of Experiment II is to determine the influence of an extensive reduction in the extramaze cues upon the learning of a basket-transported group and a normally run group of Ss. With the extramaze cues at a minimum, it is expected that the control Ss will select the formerly rewarded side more frequently in extinction than the transported Ss. With decreased external cues the learning is probably dependent to a greater degree on internal, response-produced cues, and since these cues are not available to the conveyed Ss, their extinction performance should be inferior.

EXPERIMENT I

Method

Subjects. Twenty-four experimentally naive Long-Evans strain hooded male rats were used. They were bred in the University of Kansas laboratory and were four to five months of age at the start of the experiment.

Apparatus. The elevated T maze, which was constructed of 3.75-in. black wooden strips, had a 51-in. stem, 31-in. side arms, and stood 30 in. from the floor. A flat black metal tray, 3.75 in. by 3.75 in. by .25 in. served as a food dish. It was clipped to either side arm and was not visible from the choice point.

The basket, which was used to transport the Ss of the experimental group along the maze, had a floor consisting of a 9-in. by 4-in. sheet of transparent plastic. A piece of .5-in.-sq. hardware cloth bent in the shape of a half-cylinder was fastened to the basket floor so as to make a cage with 6-in. walls. The ends of the basket were also constructed of .5-in.-sq. hardware cloth, and one end was hinged to permit the entrance and exit of S.

The maze was placed in the center of a room measuring 10 ft. by 10 ft. by 8.5 ft. Although the walls and ceiling were uniformly white, differential cues were provided by a radiator and window opposite the left arm and a large, black multicelled cage opposite the right arm. The floor of the room provided the possibilities for other gross visual cues since the left half was unpainted while the right half was black. The room was illuminated by the sunlight from the window on the left and by a fluorescent lamp with two 90-w. bulbs which was attached to the ceiling directly over the center of the maze and aligned with the stem.

Procedure. The Ss were placed on a 22-hr. hunger cycle five days before the beginning of maze adaptation by limiting them to a daily 1-hr. feeding session in the living cages. Water was always available in these cages, and Purina Layena pellets were employed as the maintenance food and as an incentive in the maze. During this period, each S was handled for several minutes per day.

In the adaptation phase the Ss were accustomed to the elevated apparatus. The starting half of the stem was detached from the T and aligned in the direction of the stem proper. The purpose of this arrangement was to provide rewarded adaptation without the concurrent induction of directional habits. The reward tray was attached to the end of the stem section, and S was permitted to explore the stem and eat freely for 5 min. daily. After seven days the adaptation was terminated because the Ss ate and moved along the stem without timidity. Four Ss were discarded in this phase when they displayed continued emotionality, leaving a total of 10 Ss in each treatment.

The maze training extended over four days until a group criterion of 95 per cent correct was attained by the control Ss. The control Ss learned a position response by running the maze in the traditional, noncorrection fashion. Four trials were given each day with a 30-sec. intertrial interval. Half the Ss in each group found food on the right side and half on the left. When an S placed all four paws on either side arm, it was prevented from retracing by E's blocking the choice with a wooden paddle. A correct choice resulted in 30-sec. feeding at the food tray, and an incorrect turn led to 60-sec. confinement on that arm of the maze.

The Ss in the experimental group were placed in the basket at the start of the stem, the basket was gently slid along the top of the maze, and they were released from the basket at the end of the side arm. Each experimental S was given the same experiences of right and wrong choices, reward, and confinement, and was rewarded on the same side of the maze as its matched control S. Both groups were subjected to a 30-min. waiting period following the completion of the last trial before being fed their daily ration.

On the following day, extinction trials were administered to both groups in the same manner. The S was placed at the start of the stem, and the direction of choice was recorded. Retracing was again prevented by blocking off the choice point, the same response criterion was utilized, and the Ss were confined on the selected side arm for a 60-sec. period. Whenever S failed to make a choice within 300 sec., it was placed on a side arm by E for the regular confinement period, and the trial was scored as an error. The S was arbitrarily placed on the right arm after the first no-choice trial, on the left arm after the second, and so on. The Ss received eight extinction trials on the first day and eight more trials the second. The intertrial interval of 30 sec. was maintained throughout extinction.

EXPERIMENT II

Method

Subjects. There were three replications with 10 Wistar albino rats, six males and four females, in the first, 12 male hooded rats in the second, and 14 male hooded rats in the third. The albino rats were purchased from a local vender, and the Long-Evans strain Ss were from the University of Kansas laboratory. The Ss had not been used in an experiment previously and were three to five months of age.

Apparatus. The T maze described above was employed. To decrease the extra-maze cues, the total room was painted flat black. The window on the left side of the room was covered completely by a plywood sheet and sealed to prevent the passage of light. The maze was enclosed in a rectangular wooden framework, 8 ft. by 6 ft. by 8.5 ft., and black cheesecloth was fastened to the frame. To reduce the illumination, the overhead fluorescent light was covered by a black cheesecloth panel. The light intensities, as measured by a photoelectric photometer, were 14.4 ft.-c. at the start of the stem, 13.5 ft.-c. at the choice point, 8.8 ft.-c. at the end of the left arm, and 8.5 ft.-c. at the end of the right arm. The greatest intensity difference between corresponding points on the side arms was 0.8 ft.-c. which was present at the mid-point of the side arm.

Procedure. The procedure was almost identical to that of Experiment I except that the Ss in the third replication received three additional days of training after attaining the criterion of 95 per cent correct, and Ss in all replications had only eight extinction trials. One pair of Ss was discarded from the third replication when a control S failed to learn the maze.

RESULTS

The percentages of correct responses for the successive quarters of extinction in experiment I are shown in Table 7.1–1. The average percentage correct was 66.25 for the experimental group and 64.38 for the control

TABLE 7.1–1 Percentages of Correct Responses During Extinction in Experiment I

Group	N	Trials			
		1–4	5–8	9–12	13–16
C (run)	10	65	60	67.5	65
E (carry)	10	60	65	65	75

group. The difference between these two values was evaluated by the sign test (6) and was not significant (p > .30). In addition, none of the tests at the separate quarters of extinction was significant at less than the .30 level. We may conclude that, with the number of correct responses in extinction serving as a measure of previous learning, there were no reliable differences between the Ss that ran the maze and those that traversed the maze in a basket.

A further question which can be raised is: Did the performance of the groups in extinction differ from chance? To answer this question, the number of Ss in the combined groups which ran to the correct side more than eight times and the number of Ss that ran to the correct side equal to, or less than, eight times were found. On an a priori basis, if no learning occurred, we should expect 10 Ss in each category. Actually there were 17 Ss in the "above" category and 3 Ss in the "below." The resulting χ^2 of 8.45 is significant at less than .01 level of confidence—the Ss manifested a significant preference for the formerly rewarded side in extinction.

The three replications of Experiment II were tested for homogeneity of their means and variances. Since the differences among the replications were within the limits of sampling, they were pooled. The combined extinction data in the form of the percentages of correct turns for the four quarters of extinction are presented in Table 7.1–2. When the external cues were reduced, the transported Ss scored 47.75 per cent correct choices in extinction, and the regularly run Ss made 64 per cent correct turns. Eleven of the Ss in the latter condition went to the correct side more often than their matched mates, one regularly run S was inferior to its mate, and in five instances there were no differences between Ss in the two treatments. Disregarding the ties (6), the probability of such an outcome is .01.

TABLE 7.1–2 Percentages of Correct Responses During Extinction in Experiment II

Group	N	Trials			
		1–2	3–4	5–6	7–8
C (run)	17	85	62	50	59
E (carry)	17	44	59	56	32

It is clear from Table 7.1–2 that the experimental Ss did not deviate from chance on the extinction trials. If assignment is made at random of the 5 control Ss that ran to the correct side on half the trials, there were 14 Ss in the above-chance category and 3 Ss in the below-chance category. The significance of this outcome is less than the .02 level of confidence. In summary, then, in Experiment II the regularly run animals gave evidence, in extinction, of learning, whereas the transported Ss did not.

DISCUSSION

The results of Experiment I confirm Gleitman's finding that place learning in an elevated T maze can occur without performance. However, when the extramaze cues are reduced (Experiment II), performance appears to be necessary for place learning. The finding that place learning without performance is demonstrable is congruent with *our* interpretation of Tolman's system as given in the introduction.

This same finding is not readily reconcilable with those aspects of Hull's system which conceive of learning as habit formation via drive reduction. For, in the case of the basket Ss, the response component of the cue pattern-response-reinforcement paradigm is not present. To encompass these findings, the Hullian theorist must, as in some latent learning studies, call upon fractional antedating goal reactions and/or secondary reinforcement to account for the results. To us, at present, the linkages of these constructs with independent and dependent variables seem to be as programmatic as the coordinating definitions of cognitive map, expectancy, etc. The hopeful feature of this situation is, as Hilgard (3) points out, that with an increased emphasis in S-R theory on secondary reinforcement the differences between field and association theory become more blurred and the possibilities for a fruitful *rapprochement* may be seen.

SUMMARY

Two experiments were performed to determine whether or not place learning is possible without performance. In Experiment I ten Ss were regularly run in an elevated T maze, and ten Ss were transported about the maze in a basket. In the extinction trials there were no reliable differences between the two groups in the frequency of correct choices. In Experiment II, carried out under the conditions of reduced external cues, the run Ss displayed significantly more learning than the transported Ss. It was concluded that: (a) Gleitman's finding that place learning can occur without performance was confirmed; and (b) when the extramaze cues are minimized, performance is necessary for learning.

REFERENCES

1. Bugelski, B. R., Coyer, R. A., & Rogers, W. A. A criticism of pre-acquisition and pre-extinction of expectancies. *J. exp. Psychol.*, 1952, 44, 27–30.
2. Gleitman, H. Place learning without prior performance. *J. comp. physiol. Psychol.*, 1955, 48, 77–79.
3. Hilgard, E. R. *Theories of learning.* New York: Appleton-Century-Crofts, 1948.
4. Thorndike, E. L. Expectation. *Psychol. Rev.*, 1946, 53, 277–281.
5. Tolman, E. C. There is more than one kind of learning. *Psychol. Rev.*, 1949, 56, 144–155.
6. Walker, Helen M., & Lev, J. *Statistical inference.* New York: Henry Holt, 1953.

7.2 | LATENT EXTINCTION AND THE FRACTIONAL ANTICIPATORY RESPONSE MECHANISM*

Howard Moltz

I

Most students of learning would agree that in order for an organism to acquire an adaptive behavior pattern, not only must certain appropriate responses be learned, but other inappropriate or nonadaptive ones must be extinguished.[1] It is not surprising, therefore, that the attempt to provide an explanation of the manner in which response extinction occurs is at present a strategic area of concern for current theories of learning. Of importance to such theories is a procedure, employed recently in several studies (11, 32, 36, 38), that was designed to demonstrate that the strength of an instrumental response can be weakened prior to its first nonrewarded performance. This procedure involves placing experimental animals (rats), following the termination of training, directly into a now empty but previously baited goal box for a period judged sufficient to "inform" them of its present nonrewarding character. The effect upon response strength was observed when the subsequent performance of

* Howard Moltz, "Latent Extinction and the Fractional Anticipatory Response Mechanism," *Psychological Review*, 64, 1957, 229–241. Copyright 1957 by the American Psychological Association, and reproduced by permission. The writer wishes to acknowledge with appreciation the helpful comments of his colleagues, Professors Wayne Dennis, Elizabeth Fehrer, and David Raab.

these Ss in approaching the empty goal location was compared with that of control animals which had not received this pre-extinction experience. The procedure whereby an animal is introduced directly into an unbaited goal location after having acquired a response instrumental in securing a reward object previously contained in that location will be referred to as "latent extinction." While some investigators have questioned the effectiveness of this procedure (9, 37), others (10, 11, 23, 29, 32, 38) have demonstrated conclusively, in several different learning situations, that latent extinction does produce a decrement in the strength of the response to be eliminated. The fact that latent extinction has proven effective in this respect has been considered embarrassing to the S-R reinforcement theorist, since the implication appears to be that ". . . all that seems necessary for extinction is for the organism to *perceive* the absence of reinforcement" (12, p. 62). It is the purpose of the present paper to attempt to interpret the effects of latent extinction in a manner consistent with an S-R theoretical approach and, on the basis of this interpretation, to suggest hypotheses for further empirical study. It should be emphasized that the term "latent extinction" will be used throughout to denote a particular experimental procedure and *not* a process or a state of the organism.

Latent extinction has been employed primarily in two essentially different situations. The situation we will hereafter refer to as Type I was designed to measure the effect of latent extinction on the strength of a *previously established* instrumental response. The Type I situation involves training an animal to traverse a straight alley or acquire a position habit in a maze in order to obtain a reward object. Following training, the animal is placed directly into the goal location in the absence of the reward object for a predetermined period (latent extinction) after which "regular" response extinction is administered. The effect of latent extinction in reducing the strength of the instrumental response is indexed by the number of trials required to reach an extinction criterion. An experiment reported recently by Deese (11) serves to illustrate the Type I procedure. Deese trained rats to a position habit in a U maze with food as the reward. Following the termination of training, the experimental Ss were placed in the now empty goal location for four 1-min. periods. When these Ss were subsequently run to extinction, they yielded a significantly smaller proportion of correct responses than control Ss that had not received the latent extinction experience. Deese's results indicate that a response *can* be weakened by placing S in the goal location without the presence of the reward object and that therefore, in at least some learning situations, performance is *not* a necessary condition for extinction.

The procedure that we will hereafter refer to as Type II is concerned with the effect of latent extinction on the capacity of secondary reward stimuli to mediate the learning of a *new response* in the absence of primary reinforcement. The training employed in the Type II situation involves the use of differential reinforcement in a straight alley. By means of this technique, the cues in the baited goal box come to acquire secondary reward value while those of an unbaited goal box of a different color do not. Following the termination of training, the animal is given latent extinction which, as in the Type I situation, consists of introducing him directly into the positive goal box in the absence of the reward object. The two goal boxes are then placed in a T maze and the number of choices to the side of the maze containing the positive goal box is taken as an index of the effect of latent extinction on the capacity of secondary reward stimuli to mediate new learning. The results of a recent experiment by Moltz and Maddi (33), to be discussed in detail below, attest to the efficacy of latent extinction in reducing the acquired reward value of previously neutral stimuli.

II

An expectancy theory of extinction (44) encounters little difficulty in providing an interpretation of the effects of latent extinction, since it places no special requirement on the response to be eliminated. All that appears necessary to decrease an animal's readiness to respond in accordance with an established expectancy is to change the relationship between environmental objects, and to allow the animal to experience the new relationship on one or more occasions. Since the acquisition of a new cognitive pattern only requires that S, when motivated (45), experience stimulus events in spatial and temporal contiguity, response performance as such is not made a necessary component of the extinction process. Thus placing S directly into the goal location, and permitting him to observe that the reward object is no longer present, should weaken his previously acquired cognition concerning the character of the goal location. As a consequence, he will show a decreased tendency to respond in accordance with this cognition.

Hull's inhibition theory of extinction (21), on the other hand, encounters a great deal of difficulty in providing an explanation of the effects of latent extinction (especially when latent extinction is employed within the framework of a Type I situation), since the performance of the response to be eliminated is considered a necessary component of the extinction process. Reactive inhibition (IR) and conditioned inhibition (S^IR), which are assumed to produce extinction by jointly opposing reaction potential (S^ER), develop only in the course of response performance. This implies that either the response to be eliminated or some other response from which extinction effects can generalize must be performed before extinction can take place. Since the latent extinction procedure does not require that an animal perform the response to be eliminated, it could not produce an increase in the inhibitory factors that oppose reaction potential, and consequently could have no effect upon response strength. But while it is clear that Hull's response-induced inhibition theory of extinction requires the performance of the response to be eliminated, and is thus not adequate to account for the effects of latent extinction, Hull's general behavior theory makes no such requirement. In a series of early papers (15, 16, 17, 18, 19, 20), Hull explored the possibility of applying a number of explanatory constructs to complex behavioral relationships in which reasoning, insight, knowledge, and purpose appeared to be operative. One of these constructs—the fractional anticipatory goal response—was used subsequently by others to mediate a wide range of behavior phenomena. For example, Kendler's analysis of switching behavior (25, 26, 27) and Osgood's mediation hypothesis (35) both rely heavily on the explanatory capacity of the fractional anticipatory response mechanism. Following the leads contained in Hull's early theoretical article, Spence (40, 41, 43) has provided a somewhat more rigorous analysis of the role played by this mechanism in the acquisition of a T-maze choice response, and has used this analysis to integrate latent-learning data and data concerned with the acquisition of opposed spatial responses under the simultaneous presence of hunger and thirst. It is the opinion of the present author that the fractional anticipatory goal response possesses the deductive potential necessary to mediate also an interpretation of latent extinction data that is consistent with an S-R reinforcement approach.

Spence has suggested (40) that, as a function of differential reinforcement during training, the stimulus traces of the cues in the positive goal box and those in the alley leading to it become (classically) conditioned to the goal response (e.g., eating or drinking). Through generalization, cues at the entrance to the correct alley acquire the capacity to evoke that fractional component of the goal response (r_g) not in conflict with the overt acts of the behavior sequence. This component produces a characteristic proprioceptive stimulus (s_g) which in turn becomes conditioned to entering and continuing locomotion in the alley leading to the positive goal box. Through the acquisition of this associative connection, s_g becomes a component of the habit strength determining the instrumental response. It has also been suggested that "through the intensity of its trace which . . . increases with the increased strength of r_g as the latter becomes more strongly conditioned, s_g determines the non-associative factor K" (incentive motivation) (40, p. 273). Spence implies that the magnitude of this nonassociative component is an increasing monotonic function of the intensity of s_g. Since the latter, in turn, is assumed to covary positively with the strength of r_g, such variables as the amount of reinforcement and the delay of reinforcement (which presumably affect the strength of r_g) play a role in determining the value of K. If it is recalled that

$$S^E R = f(M \times S^H R),$$

where

$$M = F(K + V + D),$$

it can be seen that r_g and its characteristic proprioceptive cue determine the excitatory strength of the correct response by contributing a component to $S^H R$ and also by determining the value of K.[2]

But while the fractional anticipatory goal response has been considered by some students of learning to be a construct that possesses a great deal of explanatory fertility, it has been considered by others as an *ad hoc* device designed to rescue the S-R theorist from embarrassing experimental data. Koch, for example, maintains that:

> Among the potentially most fruitful items in Hull's bequest to the future are the many ingenious "peripheral" mechanisms which were elaborated in the first instance, in his earlier theoretical articles. . . . It is likely that concepts of this order point to factors which must be ultimately taken into account by any theory of behavior . . . (28, pp. 164–165).

On the other hand, Meehl and MacCorquodale write that ". . . r_g at present . . . is as readily available a *deus ex machina* for nonexpectancy theorists as the concepts of 'attention,' 'emphasis,' or 'perceptual threshold' are for Tolman" (31, p. 232). Since r_g appears to enjoy a somewhat ambiguous epistemological position, it would be well to clarify its meaning before attempting to provide an interpretation of the effects of latent extinction.

The use of a theoretical construct denoting a nonobservable response process carries with it the responsibility of providing a set of symptom relations by which the construct in question can be coordinated with observable events. A number of such reductions to data language is essential if the construct is to acquire univocal intersubjective reference, and if it is to be integrated with other constituents of the theoretical system in which it functions. One way in which a set of reduction symptoms can be provided for r_g is to conceive its relation to certain antecedent manipulable variables to be the same as that of any other molar response with which contemporary behavior theory has been concerned (e.g., bar pressing, spatial responses, salivation, etc.). This conceptualization implies that such variables as, for example, number of reinforced trials, quality and magnitude of the reward object, and hours of deprivation will exert the same effect on the strength of r_g as they have been found to exert on the strength of these molar responses. Once the relations postulated to hold between r_g and certain experimental parameters are clearly set forth it becomes possible to specify the effect upon r_g of variations in the value of any one of these parameters. However, it should be emphasized that, since r_g is an inferred response and as such does not possess a directly observable element, evidence relevant to variations in the strength of r_g can be obtained only by examining the overt behavior of the organism under certain sets of experimental conditions.

III

The Type I Situation

Consider the situation in which an animal is required to turn right in a T maze to obtain a reward object relevant to an existent need state. When the excitatory tendency of the cues in the right alley to evoke a right turn becomes greater than that of the cues in the left alley to evoke a left turn, the animal will respond above chance expectancy in the direction of the goal location. An important factor involved in the growth of the correct excitatory potential $(S^E R_a)$ is the increase in habit strength $(S^H R)$ resulting from each reinforcement. However, as the animal is repeatedly reinforced during the course of training, not only does $S^E R_a$ approach its asymptote but, in addition, the overt consummatory response appropriate to the reward object (i.e., eating or drinking) becomes more strongly conditioned to the stimulus traces of the cues in the goal location. On the basis of the latter it appears reasonable to assume that when latent extinction is administered following the termination of training, that component of the consummatory response which can occur in the absence of the reward object (i.e., r_g) will be evoked by the cues to which its molar counterpart was previously conditioned. Since these cues are constantly present during latent extinction, it would be expected that r_g will be strongly and repeatedly evoked; each latent extinction "trial" providing the occasions for its *free repetition*.[3] Now if r_g is conceived as a response process that obeys the same behavioral laws as most molar systems, then it would follow that these successive nonreinforced emissions of r_g will produce a sharp reduction in its response strength with respect to cues in the goal location. If these cues are similar to those at the choice point, and if delay of reward during training was at a minimum, the extinction effects of r_g will generalize readily to antedating segments of the behavior sequence, so that at the start of the test trials r_g either will not be elicited at the choice point or will be elicited with greatly reduced excitatory potential. If latent extinction is effective in reducing the strength of r_g to the extent that it is subsequently not available at the choice point, then s_g, of course, will also not be available, and the associative connection established during training between s_g and the instrumental response will no longer contribute to the habit strength of that response. As a consequence of the withdrawal of this component of habit strength, the organism will manifest a decreased tendency to enter the correct alley during the test trials.

But assume that r_g was not completely extinguished during the latent extinction period, and that at the start of the test trials the cues at the choice point still possessed some excitatory tendency with respect to r_g. Even if latent extinction only reduced this tendency, a decrease in the strength of the established instrumental response would nevertheless be expected. It will be recalled that the incentive motivational factor K was postulated to be a nonassociative component of $S^E R_a$. Since the relationship between K and s_g is assumed to be monotonically increasing and, furthermore, since the intensity of s_g is a direct function of the r_g evoked, it would follow that any decrease in the strength of r_g will reduce the value of K. This reduction of K will, in turn, reduce the excitatory potential mediating the correct approach response, as a result of which the animal will show a decreased tendency to enter and continue locomotion in the alley leading to the previously positive goal box.

The Type II Situation

The experimental procedures that we have labeled Type I and Type II are similar in that they both involve introducing an animal into an empty goal location after it has acquired a response instrumental in securing a reward object previously contained in that location. The difference between these procedures arises with respect to the responses with which they deal following the latent extinction period. It will be recalled that while the Type I procedure is concerned with the effect of latent extinction on the strength of an established response, the Type II procedure is concerned with the capacity of goal-box stimuli that have acquired secondary reward value to mediate the learning of a *new response* after latent extinction has been administered. It is to the latter procedure that we now turn our attention.

Consider the experimental situation in which an animal is trained to traverse a straight alley in order to obtain a reward object relevant to an existent need state. A differential reinforcement technique is employed by which, on a given number of trials, the animal runs to a white goal box that contains the reward object, while on the remaining trials he runs to an empty black goal box. By the principle of secondary reinforcement the cues in the white goal box will acquire reward value as a function of their association with the reinforcement situation. Hull (21, 22) suggested the factional anticipatory goal response and its proprioceptive cue as providing the mechanism underlying the acquisition of secondary reward properties. The role that r_g plays in this respect develops by virtue of its intimate association with the reinforcement situation, this association establishing s_g as a secondary reinforcer. In order for any neutral stimulus to acquire reward value it must acquire the capacity to elicit r_g either by being conditioned to r_g directly, as in the case of stimuli that are spatially and temporally contiguous with the receipt of the reward object, or through generalization, as in the case of stimulus events that are similar to those actually conditioned. Hull further suggested that a stimulus that has acquired reward value will retain that value as long as it retains the power to evoke r_g. It would appear reasonable on this basis to assume the acquired reward capacity of a stimulus to be some positive function of the strength of the r_g to which it is conditioned, and for any subsequent reduction in this strength to decrease the reinforcing values of the stimulus.

Now with respect to the experimental situation being considered, assume that following training the positive and negative goal boxes are placed on opposite arms of a T maze, and that the animal is given a number of free trials in the *absence of the reward object*. When he first responds correctly and enters the positive goal box, r_g will be evoked by those stimuli to which it was conditioned during the course of training. As a result of the evocation of r_g, and the presence consequently of s_g with its reinforcing capacity, there will occur an increment in the excitatory potential of the correct response. As long as r_g continues to be evoked in the positive goal box, the correct response will be reinforced and will increase in strength relative to the incorrect response. But the excitatory potential of the correct response will not continue to increase unabated until some asymptotic value is reached. Since the reward object is not present during the maze series, the emission of r_g in the positive goal box following each correct choice will reduce its response strength, as a result of which the intensity of s_g and hence the magnitude of available secondary reinforcement will decrease progressively. When the stimuli in the positive goal box no longer elicit a threshold value of r_g, the excitatory potential of the correct response will begin to decrease, so that after several trials the animal will cease to respond correctly in excess of chance.

Now assume that latent extinction is administered at some time between the termination of straight-alley training and the beginning of the maze trials. For reasons presented in connection with the Type I situation, placing an animal in a previously baited goal box provides the occasion for the free nonreinforced repetitions of r_g, each such repetition reducing its response strength. Because of the role that s_g plays as a reinforcing agent, it would be expected that, as the strength of r_g decreases during the course of latent extinction, the intensity of s_g, and hence the secondary reward value of goal-box stimuli, will also decrease. Depending on the duration of latent extinction and the presence of other conditions to be discussed below, r_g either will not be elicited in the positive goal box at the termination of the latent extinction period or it will be elicited with greatly reduced excitatory potential. In the event that r_g is completely extinguished with respect to goal-box stimuli, there will be no secondary reinforcement available to mediate subsequently the learning of a choice response in the maze. On the other hand, if the excitatory strength of r_g had not been eliminated but had been reduced to a near threshold value, then r_g will become completely extinguished *early* in the maze series. In any case, animals that have been given latent extinction would not be expected to show a strong tendency to choose the arm of the maze leading to the positive goal box, as compared with control animals that had not undergone the latent extinction experience.

By employing the fractional anticipatory response mechanism in a manner consistent with the requirements of the neobehavioristic system in which it was developed, we have been able to provide an interpretation of the effects of latent extinction in both the Type I and Type II situations. Within the theoretical framework employed it was necessary only to assume that r_g is repeatedly evoked during latent extinction, and that, as a consequence of this repeated evocation, r_g either becomes completely extinguished with respect to cues in the goal location or that a sharp reduction in its response strength occurs.

IV

The value of a theoretical construct should be measured not only in terms of how well propositions involving that construct explain available data but also in terms of the extent to which these propositions generate novel (i.e., not previously formulated) functional relationships. It must be determined, therefore, whether the fractional anticipatory response mechanism as employed in the present analysis is capable of mediating predictions concerning the influence on behavior of certain selected variations in both the Type I and Type II situations. Unless the present analysis possesses a prospective reference, propositions involving r_g have no value other than as vehicles in providing an economical description of already established empirical relationships. While such descriptions play an important role in science, the constructs involved function simply as analytic devices whose systematic significance is limited to furnishing summary statements of observed facts (5).

On the basis of our analysis of the effect of latent extinction on the strength of r_g we can specify the following general hypothesis: *Latent extinction will reduce the excitatory strength of an instrumental response to the extent that it reduces the excitatory strength of* r_g. Following from this is the implication that if a variable is introduced, during latent extinction, that increases the degree to which r_g is weakened, a greater decrement in subsequent molar performance will occur than if latent extinction is administered in the absence of this variable. It will be recalled that r_g was conceived as a hypothetical response process whose relation to observable antecedent events was assumed to follow the same behavioral laws as molar responses like bar pressing and salivation. This implies that all those experimental operations that have been demonstrated to reduce the strength of a molar response should affect similarly the strength of r_g. Since empirical evidence appears to indicate that reduction in the strength of these molar responses occurs as a monotonic increasing function of the number of nonreinforced evocations, it would follow that the more frequently r_g is evoked during latent extinction the greater will be the reduction in its response strength. On this basis we would be led to expect latent extinction to produce a pronounced decrement in subsequent molar performance under those experimental conditions that produce a rapid rate of emission of r_g during the latent extinction period. We turn now to consider some of these conditions.

Variations in the Strength of the Relevant Drive

The results of several studies have indicated that the higher the level of a relevant (rewarded) drive during a series of extinction test trials the greater the rate of response evocation. For example, Jenkins and Daugherty (24) have shown that following training an increase in drive strength will result in the more frequent emission of a nonreinforced pecking response, while Skinner (39) has presented evidence confirming this relationship with respect to bar pressing. On the assmption that r_g obeys the same behavioral laws as these responses, we would except a higher drive level during latent extinction to result in a greater increase in the number of nonreinforced evocations of r_g.[4] On this basis the following hypothesis can be specified with reference to the Type I situation: If after being trained to a position habit in a T maze under identical motivational conditions, one group of animals is given latent extinction under a high drive and another group under a low drive, the high-drive group will show a greater decrease in the tendency to choose the previously baited goal box when both groups are again run under the motivational level that prevailed during acquisition. A recent experiment by Pliskoff (36) is relevant to the present hypothesis. Animals under 8 hr. of food deprivation were trained in the performance of a T-maze turning response, after which latent extinction was administered under either 0, 8, or 22 hr.

of hunger. When the extinction test trials were subsequently run under acquisition conditions it was found, in accord with expectation, that on the first test trial the 22-hr. group chose the previously correct side of the maze less often than the 0-hr. group. This result suggests a relationship between drive level during latent extinction and reduction in the strength of a previously established response.

The assumption concerning the relation between drive strength and rate of emission of r_g is also relevant to the Type II situation. It will be recalled that the acquired reward capacity of a neutral stimulus was assumed to be some positive function of the excitatory strength of the r_g to which that stimulus was conditioned. This implies that if increasing the drive level during latent extinction serves to increase the number of non-reinforced emissions of r_g (and thereby to decrease the strength of the latter with respect to goal location stimuli), then there should be a more pronounced reduction in secondary reward value the more intense the drive level under which latent extinction is administered. Evidence supporting such a hypothesis was reported recently by Moltz and Maddi (33). They employed a differential reinforcement technique during training which consisted of running animals in a straight alley to a goal box of one color on rewarded trials, and to a goal box of a different color on nonrewarded trials. While all Ss were under the same hunger drive schedule during training (22 hr.), they were under either a 0-, 22-, or 44-hr. drive at the beginning of the latent extinction period. The test trials were subsequently run in a T maze, with all Ss again on the same hunger deprivation schedule imposed during training. It was found that the mean number of responses (in 15 free choices) to the side of the maze containing the positive goal box was 9.30, 7.10, and 6.30 for the 0-, 22-, and 44-hr. groups, respectively.[5] These results are in accord with theoretical expectation, since they indicate a relationship between motivational level during latent extinction and the capacity of goal location stimuli to mediate subsequently the learning of a new response.

Variations in the Strength of an Irrelevant Drive

Hull has proposed that the drive strength available at any given amount is a function not only of the need for which the goal object in the situation is appropriate but also of all irrelevant (nonrewarded) drives operative at the time. It is the total need state, consisting of both relevant and irrelevant drives, that is assumed to combine with $S^H R$ (in addition to the non associative factors V and K) to determine excitatory potential. In *Principles of Behavior* (21) Hull stated as a corollary that, with the number of reinforcements held constant, response strength will increase as some positive function of the magnitude of an irrelevant drive.

Webb (46) reported the results of a study designed to determine the role of an irrelevant drive (thirst) in activating a habit structure when the drive under which the habit was originally developed (hunger) was satiated. He found the strength of a panel-pushing response to be approximately an increasing linear function of the intensity of the irrelevant drive. Brandauer (6) subsequently confirmed this relationship, using a different operant response. Since we have assumed that r_g follows essentially the same behavioral laws as most molar responses, we appear to be in the somewhat uncomfortable position of having to propose that r_g appropriate to a relevant hunger drive will increase in strength in approximately linear fashion with increases in the magnitude of an irrelevant thirst drive. However, the implications of a theory or of a postulate are determined not only by the relations or laws specified but also by the conditions operative in the experimental situation to which these relations or laws are applied. As a case in point, consider the situation into which there is introduced an irrelevant need that provides a drive stimulus which elicits response *incompatible* with a previously established criterion response. Under such conditions it would not appear reasonable to expect the strength of the criterion response to increase as the irrelevant need becomes more intense. Indeed, only when conflicting habit tendencies are not activated would a criterion response, whether it be "molar" or "molecular," be expected to increase with increases in the intensity of an irrelevant drive stimulus.

The results of several studies (1, 2, 7, 13) in the area of secondary motivation provide evidence in support of this contention. For example, Amsel and Maltzman (3) have shown that, when anxiety is added to an existing motivational complex, the strength of a previously established consummatory (drinking) response will increase if the experimental situation is arranged so that responses conditioned to the irrelevant anxiety-drive stimulus (e.g., crouching, face washing, escape response, etc.) cannot compete with the drinking response. On the other hand, if the situation is arranged so that response competition is permitted, the rate of drinking will be sharply reduced. These results, in addition to those provided by Kendler (26) concerning the "incompatibility" of fractional anticipatory eating and drinking responses, make it appear reasonable to assume that anticipatory drinking responses ($r^g d$), when instigated by an irrelevant thirst drive, will complete with anticipatory eating responses ($r^g e$), and consequently will decrease the rate of emission of the latter.[6] Following from this is the implication that after training under moderately intense hunger, the stronger the thirst drive that is subsequently introduced (thereby increasing the strength of $r^g d$) the greater the *reduction* in the rate of evocation of $r^g e$.

This analysis generates an important deduction with respect to both the Type I and Type II situations. Assume that an animal learns to approach a distinctive goal location under moderately intense hunger, and that as a function of this training the cues in the goal location acquire a strong excitatory tendency with respect to $r^g e$. If latent extinction is administered subsequently under both hunger and thirst, the presence of incompatible anticipatory drinking responses should *reduce* the number of nonreinforced evocations of $r^g e$; this reduction being greater the more intense the thirst drive. On this basis, and on the basis of the previously formulated assumption concerning relation between rate of emission of r_g and the influence of latent extinction on molar performance, we can state the following general hypothesis: If an organism is trained to acquire a response under moderately strong hunger but with ad libitum consumption of water, the effectiveness of latent extinction in reducing the strength of this response will *decrease* as the intensity of thirst during latent extinction increases. More specifically, in the Type I situation we would expect that if, after learning a position habit under 22 hr. of hunger, one group of animals is given latent extinction under the same hunger drive but in conjunction with 3 hr. of thirst, and another group in conjunction with 22 hr. of thirst, the latter will yield significantly *more* responses to extinction when the motivational complex of both groups is subsequently made identical with that which prevailed during acquisition.

Since the relation between intensity of an irrelevant thirst drive and the rate of emission of $r^g e$ would be expected to obtain in a Type II situation as well, we may also state the following hypothesis: After an approach response to food is established under moderately intense hunger, a greater reduction in the acquired reward value of goal location stimuli will occur if, in conjunction with the prevailing hunger drive, latent extinction is administered under 3 hr. of thirst as compared with 22 hr. of thirst. Unfortunately there is no empirical evidence relevant either to this hypothesis or to the hypothesis formulated with reference to the Type I situation. Several experiments are, however, being conducted in the writer's laboratory in the attempt to determine the role of drive interaction during latent extinction.[7]

Reward Immediately Prior to Latent Extinction

In the presence of the appropriate drive state, a reward object with which an animal has had previous commerce will serve typically as an "unconditioned" stimulus for the consummatory response, in the sense that the latter will be regularly elicited when the reward object is presented. Since r_g has been conceived as a hypothetical process representing a fractional component of the consummatory response, it appears reasonable to assume that r_g possesses this functional characteristic in common with its molar counterpart. On this basis we would expect that, with the primary drive state remaining relatively constant, the frequency with which r_g is evoked will increase during a period following consumption of an appropriate goal object. However, if a large amount of reward is consumed, a reduction in the primary drive state would occur which, in turn, might offset or prevent entirely an increase in the rate of emission of r_g. On the other hand, a small amount of reward, while not appreciably modifying the drive state, might not be sufficient to effect this increase. Presumably there is an optimal amount of reward that would produce the desired result. With respect to food as the reward object, experimental evidence reported by Maltzman (30) indicates this amount to be within the range of *1000 to 2000 mg.* when the animal is under a hunger drive of approximately 22 hr.[8] On the basis of Maltzman's results, we would be led to expect that if, after training under hunger motivation, an animal is fed about 1500 mg. of food 20 sec. prior to latent extinction, an increase in the rate of emission of r_g will occur during the latent extinction period. This increase in rate of emission will, according to the present analysis, produce a marked reduction in the strength of r_g, as a consequence of which latent extinction should be more effective in reducing subsequent molar performance. Thus in the Type I situation it would be expected that if latent extinction is preceded by the ingestion of a reward object appropriate to the prevailing drive state, a greater decrement in the strength of the established instrumental response will occur, while in the case of the Type II situation a greater decrement in the acquired reward value of goal location stimuli would be expected.

The hypotheses that have been presented in the present paper have been concerned with the relation between certain experimental variables introduced during latent extinction and the rate of emission of r_g. Further experimental work and theoretical analysis might also be directed toward determining whether variations in molar performance following latent extinction can be ascribed to other parameters of r_g function. In addition, the effect of latent extinction might also be investigated with regard to the influence of such training parameters as the quality and magnitude of the reward object, number of reinforced trials, and the nature of contextual stimulus conditions.

V

The present paper represents an attempt to provide an interpretation of latent extinction that is consistent with an S-R reinforcement approach. The effects of latent extinction on the strength of an established instrumental response and on the secondary reward value of goal location stimuli were analyzed. It was found that propositions involving the fractional anticipatory goal response in conjunction with other propositions of neobehavioristic theory are adequate to account for these effects. Several hypotheses were suggested concerning the influence of certain variables on the rate of emission of the anticipatory goal response during the latent extinction period. Evidence relevant to these hypotheses was considered.

NOTES

1. Extinction will be defined as the reduction in response strength that occurs following nonreinforcement. The mechanism mediating this reduction is left open, since in the opinion of the present author much more data are required before a complete and empirically adequate explanation of the extinction process can be formulated.

2. The additive relationship between V, K, and D presented here is consistent with Spence's latest formulation (42). Following Hull, Spence had earlier postulated a multiplicative relationship between these factors, the implication being, of course, that if any one of them is reduced to zero the excitatory strength of the instrumental response would also be reduced to zero.

3. Failure to conceive of latent extinction as providing the occasions for the *free repetition* of r_g led Gleitman, Nachmias, and Neisser (14) to dismiss the possibility of employing r_g to interpret the results of those experiments in which a Type I procedure was used.

4. The relation between drive strength and response evocation also follows readily from Hull's 1943 (21) and 1952 (22) postulate sets.

5. The F ratio for the difference between these drive levels was significant well below .01. No significant difference in maze performance was found between control groups which were not given latent extinction but which were made differentially hungry during the latent extinction period.

6. On the assumption that anticipatory drinking responses are in some manner "incompatible" with anticipatory eating responses, Kendler has attempted to explain what he has called the switching phenomenon, i.e., ". . . the tendency of rats after learning to go to one end of a T maze to obtain dry food to switch their spatial responses when made thirsty" (26, p. 179). He tested several deductions based on this assumption, one of which was that the conflict between $r_g e$ and $r_g d$ would be intensified (and hence the amount of switching increased) when S is shifted to a strong as compared with a weak thirst drive. The results obtained were consistent with this deduction.

7. These studies are being carried out in collaboration with Miss Nina Tokarow and Mr. Leonard Rosenblum.

8. Maltzman found that hungry rats fed about 1200 mg. of food approximately 20 sec. before being run in a straight alley tended to run significantly faster than a control group that was not pre-fed. Several other investigators (4, 8, 34) have also reported that small amounts of preliminary reward will facilitate the performance of an instrumental response. Maltzman has indicated how these results can be interpreted in terms of the fractional anticipatory response mechanism.

REFERENCES

1. Amsel, A. The effect upon level of consummatory response of the addition of anxiety to a motivational complex. *J. exp. Psychol.*, 1950, 40, 709–715.
2. Amsel, A., & Cole, K. F. Generalization of fear-motivated interference with water intake. *J. exp. Psychol.*, 1953, 46, 243–247.
3. Amsel, A., & Maltzman, I. The effect upon generalized drive strength of emotionality as inferred from the level of consummatory response. *J. exp. Psychol.*, 1950, 40, 563–569.

4. Anderson, E. E. The externalization of drive. IV. The effect of prefeeding on the maze performance of hungry rats. *J. comp. physiol. Psychol.*, 1941, 31, 349–352.

6. Beck, L. W. Constructions and inferred entities. In H. Feigl and May Brodbeck (Eds.), *Readings in the philosophy of science.* New York: Appleton-Century-Crofts, 1953.

6. Brandauer, C. M. A confirmation of Webb's data concerning the action of irrelevant drives. *J. exp. Psychol.*, 1953, 45, 150–152.

7. Brown, J. S., Kalish, H. I., & Farber, I. E. Conditioned fear as revealed by magnitude of startle response to an auditory stimulus. *J. exp. Psychol.*, 1951, 41, 317–328.

8. Bruce, R. H. An experimental investigation of the thirst drive in rats with especial reference to the goal-gradient hypothesis. *J. gen. Psychol.*, 1937, 17, 49–60.

9. Bugelski, B. R., Coyer, R. A., & Rogers, W. A. A criticism of pre-acquisition and pre-extinction of expectancies. *J. exp. Psychol.*, 1952, 44, 27–30.

10. Coate, W. B. Weakening of conditioned bar-pressing by prior extinction of its subsequent discriminated operant. *J. comp, physiol. Psychol.*, 1956, 49, 135–138.

11. Deese, J. The extinction of a discrimination without performance of a choice response. *J. comp. physiol. Psychol.*, 1951, 44, 362–366.

12. Deese, J. *The psychology of learning.* New York: McGraw-Hill, 1952.

13. Estes, W. K., & Skinner, B. F. Some quantitative properties of anxiety. *J. exp. Psychol.*, 1941, 29, 390–400.

14. Gleitman, H., Nachmias, J., & Neisser, U. The S-R reinforcement theory of extinction. *Psychol. Rev.*, 1954, 61, 23–33.

15. Hull, C. L. Knowledge and purpose as habit mechanism. *Psychol. Rev.*, 1930, 37, 511–525.

16. Hull, C. L. Goal attraction and directing ideas conceived as habit phenomena. *Psychol. Rev.*, 1931, 38, 487–506.

17. Hull, C. L. The concept of the habit-family hierarchy and maze learning. *Psychol. Rev.*, 1934, 41, 33–54, 134–152.

18. Hull, C. L. The mechanism of the assembly of behavior segments in novel combinations suitable for problem solution. *Psychol. Rev.*, 1935, 42, 219–245.

19. Hull, C. L. Mind, mechanism, and adaptive behavior. *Psychol. Rev.*, 1937, 44, 1–32.

20. Hull, C. L. Fractional antedating goal reactions as pure stimulus acts. In *Psychological Memoranda*, 1940–1944. Bound mimeographed material on file in the libraries of the Univer. of Iowa, Univer. of North Carolina, and Yale Univer., Oct. 24, 1941.

21. Hull, C. L. *Principles of behavior.* New York: Appleton-Century-Crofts, 1943.

22. Hull, C. L. *A behavior system.* New Haven: Yale Univer. Press, 1952.

23. Hurwitz, H. M. B. Response elimination without performance. *Quart. J. exp. Psychol.*, 1955, 7, 1–7.

24. Jenkins, W. O., & Daugherty, Georgette. Drive and the asymptote of extinction. *J. comp. physiol. Psychol.*, 1951, 44, 372–377.

25. Kendler, H. H., & Levine, S. Studies of the effect of change of drive: I. From hunger to thirst in a T-maze. *J. exp. Psychol.*, 1951, 41, 429–436.

26. Kendler, H. H., Levine, S., Altchek, E., & Peters, H. Studies of the effect of change of drive: II. From hunger to different intensities of a thirst drive in a T-maze. *J. exp. Psychol.*, 1952, 44, 1–3.

27. Kendler, H. H., Karasik, A. D., & Schrier, A. M. Studies of the effect of change

of drive: III. Amounts of switching produced by shifting from thirst to hunger and from hunger to thirst. *J. exp. Psychol.*, 1954, 47, 179–182.

28. Koch, S. Clark L. Hull. In W. K. Estes, S. Koch, K. MacCorquodale, P. E. Meehl, C. G. Mueller, Jr., W. N. Schoenfeld, and W. S. Verplanck, *Modern learning theory*. New York: Appleton-Century-Crofts, 1954. Pp. 1–176.

29. Levy, N. Latent extinction of a jumping response. *Amer. Psychologist*, 1955, 10, 416. (Abstract)

30. Maltzman, I. The process need. *Psychol. Rev.*, 1952, 59, 40–48.

31. Meehl, P. E., & MacCorquodale, K. Some methodological comments concerning expectancy theory. *Psychol. Rev.*, 1951, 58, 230–233.

32. Moltz, H. Latent extinction and the reduction of secondary reward value. *J. exp. Psychol.*, 1955, 49, 395–400.

33. Moltz, H., & Maddi, S. R. Reduction of secondary reward value as a function of drive strength during latent extinction. *J. exp. Psychol.*, 1956, 52, 71–76.

34. Morgan, C. T., & Fields, P. E. The effect of variable preliminary feeding upon the rat's speed of locomotion. *J. comp. Psychol.*, 1938, 26, 331–348.

35. Osgood, C. E. *Method and theory in experimental psychology*. New York: Oxford Univer. Press, 1953.

36. Pliskoff, S. S. Response elimination as a function of generalization, motivation and number of non-response extinction trials. Unpublished doctor's dissertation, New York Univer., 1955.

37. Scharlock, D. P. The effects of a preextinction procedure on the extinction of place and response performance in a T maze. *J. exp. Psychol.*, 1954, 48, 31–36.

38. Seward, J. P., & Levy, N. Sign learning as a factor in extinction. *J. exp. Psychol.*, 1949, 39, 660–668.

39. Skinner, B. F. Are theories of learning necessary? *Psychol. Rev.*, 1950, 47, 193–216.

40. Spence, K. W. Theoretical interpretations of learning. In C. P. Stone (Ed.), *Comparative psychology*. New York: Prentice-Hall, 1951. Pp. 239–291.

41. Spence, K. W. Theoretical interpretations of learning. In S. S. Stevens (Ed.), *Handbook of experimental psychology*. New York: Wiley, 1951. Pp. 690–729.

42. Spence, K. W. Current interpretations of learning data and some recent developments in stimulus-response theory. In *Learning theory, personality theory, and clinical research. The Kentucky Symposium*. New York: Wiley, 1954.

43. Spence, K. W., Bergmann, G., & Lippitt, R. A study of simple learning under irrelevant motivational-reward conditions. *J. exp. Psychol.*, 1950, 40, 539–551.

44. Tolman, E. C. *Purposive behavior in animals and men*. Berkeley: Univer. of California Press, 1932.

45. Tolman, E. C. There is more than one kind of learning. *Psychol. Rev.*, 1949, 56, 144–155.

46. Webb, W. B. The motivational aspect of an irrelevant drive in the behavior of the white rat. *J. exp. Psychol.*, 1949, 39, 1–14.

7.3 MEASUREMENT OF THE ANTICIPATORY GOAL RESPONSE IN INSTRUMENTAL RUNWAY CONDITIONING*

Edward B. Deux and Richard L. Patten

Abstract. Seven rats were run to water reinforcement in a straight
runway while a measure was taken of anticipatory licking in the runway
and consummatory licking in the goal box. Licking rate was shown to
increase in a positively accelerated manner as S approached the goal
box and to increase in a negatively accelerated manner with training.
The results are discussed in relation to Spence's r_g-s_g mechanism.

PROBLEM

In the learning theories of Hull (1931) and Spence (1951, 1956), the r_g-s_g
mechanism plays a large role in the explanation of appetitional instrumental conditioning. In the runway situation, stimulation by cues at the
beginning of the alley are assumed to evoke such components of the consummatory response as can occur without the actual presence of the goal
object. The interoceptive cues produced by this classical conditioned
response in turn are assumed to become conditioned to the instrumental locomotor response and thus become a determiner of its excitatory
strength (Spence, 1951, 1956). Development of a technique by which
licking can be recorded from a moving rat has made it possible to measure
anticipatory goal responses in the runway and thus to test these assumptions. This paper is a report of the research conducted with this technique.

METHOD

Figure 7.3–1 shows the device used to detect the licking responses and
present the water to the rat in the goal box. A small elastic harness held
a bit made of 1/16-in brass tubing which fit in the S's mouth and held
the headset in place. Fastened to the headset was a piece of 3/32-in
aluminum tubing to which a wire from the contact side of a Hunter
contact relay was connected. A grounding electrode was implanted sub-
dermally on S's back, and with each contact with the aluminum tube a
circuit was made through the animal. A Brush penmotor was used to

* Reprinted from Psychonomic Science, 1964, 1, 357–358. Copyright 1964 by the
Psychonomic Society, and reproduced by permission. The authors would like to thank
Dr. Kenneth W. Spence for his advice and critical reading of this paper.

give a graphic record of the licking rate in each foot of the runway and in the goal box where water was fed through the aluminum tube for 8 sec. (.20 ml). The unit allowed complete mobility without any variation in the distance from the tubing to S's mouth and consequently with no variation in the accuracy of the licking count.

The straight runway employed was 5 ft 1 in long, 11 in high, and 2 3/4 in wide and was painted flat black. The end wall of the goal box was illuminated by a 15-w bulb behind a sheet of Plexiglas, also painted black. Time measures were taken from the opening of the start box door to the end of the first foot, from the first to the second foot, and for each following foot down to 1 in from the end wall of the goal box, at which point the water was presented.

The Ss were seven naive female hooded rats, approximately 130 days of age, and were deprived of water for 22 hr. before each session. Each was adapted to the harness and headset for two 15-min. sessions prior to the start of training. During both acquisition and extinction phases Ss were given seven trials a day with an intertrial interval of 15 min.

RESULTS

Running speed in the second foot of the runway for each of the seven 7-trial sessions is shown in Fig. 7.3–2 and gives an indication of the strength of the instrumental locomotor response. Figure 7.3–3 presents the anticipatory goal response data for the first, third, and fifth acquisition sessions. It can be seen that the slope of the licking gradient increases greatly from Day 1 to Day 3 and that there is little change from Day 3 to Day 5. The licking rate in the goal box increases accordingly to a mean of 3.02 licks per second for the fifth session.

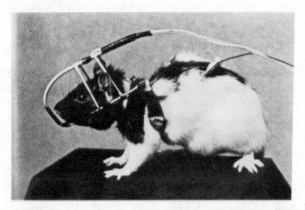

FIGURE 7.3–1   Illustration of the technique used for detecting licking responses.

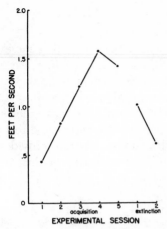

FIGURE 7.3–2 Running speed in the second foot of the runway for each seven-trial session.

In the first extinction session there was a significant decrease in the licking rate in the alley (F, 35.20; df, 1/12; p < .05), and the goal box licking rate dropped to 1.07 licks per second. On the second day of extinction the gradient of licking in the alley was essentially flat, and the goal box rate decreased further to .48 licks per second.

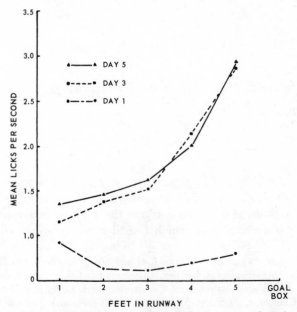

FIGURE 7.3–3 Rate of licking in each foot of the runway and in the goal box.

DISCUSSION

The results indicate that anticipatory licking increases in the runway as S approaches the goal box and that the increase in rate is a negatively accelerated function of the amount of training, consistent with the predictions made by Spence (1951). Whereas previous studies have interpreted their results with an inferred r_g-s_g mechanism (e.g., Wike & Barrientos, 1957), the present technique of directly recording anticipatory goal responses in the runway situation provides an operational reference for this mechanism. The adequacy of this reference remains to be tested.

REFERENCES

Hull, C. L. Goal attraction and directing ideas conceived as habit phenomena. *Psychol. Rev.*, 1931, 38, 487–506.

Spence, K. W. Theoretical interpretations of learning. In C. P. Stone (Ed.), Comparative psychology. (3rd ed.) New York: Prentice-Hall, 1951.

Spence, K. W. Behavior theory and conditioning. New Haven: Yale University Press, 1956.

Wike, E. L., & Barrientos, G. Selective learning as a function of differential consummatory activity. *Psychol. Rep.*, 1957, 3, 255–258.

7.4 | COGNITIVE MAPS IN RATS AND MEN*
Edward C. Tolman

I shall devote the body of this paper to a description of experiments with rats. But I shall also attempt in a few words at the close to indicate the significance of these findings on rats for the clinical behavior of men. Most of the rat investigations, which I shall report, were carried out in

* Edward C. Tolman, "Cognitive Maps in Rats and Men," *Psychological Review*, 55, 1948, 189–208. Copyright 1948 by the American Psychological Association, and reproduced by permission. 34th Annual Faculty Research Lecture, delivered at the University of California, Berkeley, March 17, 1947. Presented also on March 26, 1947 as one in a series of lectures in Dynamic Psychology sponsored by the division of psychology of Western Reserve University, Cleveland, Ohio.

the Berkeley laboratory. But I shall also include, occasionally, accounts of the behavior of non-Berkeley rats who obviously have misspent their lives in out-of-State laboratories. Furthermore, in reporting our Berkeley experiments I shall have to omit a very great many. The ones I *shall* talk about were carried out by graduate students (or underpaid research assistants) who, supposedly, got some of their ideas from me. And a few, though a very few, were even carried out by me myself.

Let me begin by presenting diagrams for a couple of typical mazes, an alley maze and an elevated maze. In the typical experiment a hungry rat is put at the entrance of the maze (alley or elevated), and wanders about through the various true path segments and blind alleys until he finally comes to the food box and eats. This is repeated (again in the typical experiment) one trial every 24 hours and the animal tends to make fewer and fewer errors (that is, blind-alley entrances) and to take less and less time between start and goal-box until finally he is entering no blinds at all and running in a very few seconds from start to goal. The results are usually presented in the form of average curves of blind-entrances, or of seconds from start to finish, for groups of rats.

All students agree as to the facts. They disagree, however, on theory and explanation.

(1) First, there is a school of animal psychologists which believes that the maze behavior of rats is a matter of mere simple stimulus-response connections. Learning, according to them, consists in the strengthening of some of these connections and in the weakening of others. According to this 'stimulus-response' school the rat in progressing down the maze is helplessly responding to a succession of external stimuli—sights, sounds, smells, pressures, etc. impinging upon his external sense organs—plus internal stimuli coming from the viscera and from the skeletal muscles. These external and internal stimuli call out the walkings, runnings, turnings, retracings, smellings, rearings, and the like which appear. The rat's central nervous system, according to this view, may be likened to a complicated telephone switchboard. There are the incoming calls from sense-organs and there are the outgoing messages to muscles. Before the learning of a specific maze, the connecting switches (synapses according to the physiologist) are closed in one set of ways and produce the primarily exploratory responses which appear in the early trials. *Learning*, according to this view, consists in the respective strengthening and weakening of various of these connections; those connections which result in the animal's going down the true path become relatively more open to the passage of nervous impulses, whereas those which lead him into the blinds become relatively less open.

It must be noted in addition, however, that this stimulus-response school divides further into two subgroups.

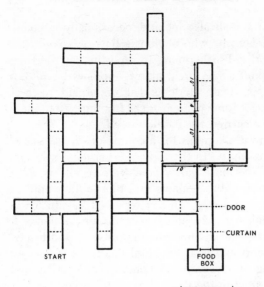

FIGURE 7.4–1 Plan of maze, 14-unit T-alley maze. (From M. H. Elliott, The effect of change of reward on the maze performance of rats. *Univ. Calif. Publ. Psychol.*, 1928, 4, p. 20.)

FIGURE 7.4–2 14-Unit T-elevated mazes. (From C. H. Honzik, The sensory basis of maze learning in rats. *Compar. Psychol. Mongr.*, 1936, 13, No. 4, p. 4. These were two identical mazes placed side by side in the same room.)

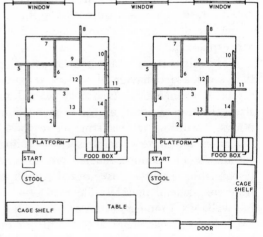

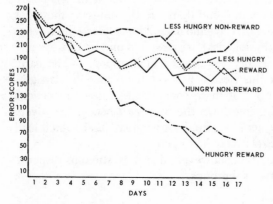

FIGURE 7.4–3 Error curves for four groups, 36 rats. (From E. C. Tolman and C. H. Honzik, Degrees of hunger, reward and non-reward, and maze learning in rats. *Univ. Calif. Publ. Psychol.*, 1930, 4, No. 16, p. 246. A maze identical with the alley maze shown in Figure 7.4–1 was used.)

(a) There is a subgroup which holds that the mere mechanics involved in the running of a maze is such that the crucial stimuli from the maze get presented simultaneously with the correct responses more frequently than they do with any of the incorrect responses. Hence, just on a basis of this greater frequency, the neural connections between the crucial stimuli and the correct responses will tend, it is said, to get strengthened at the expense of the incorrect connections.

(b) There is a second subgroup in this stimulus-response school which holds that the reason the appropriate connections get strengthened relatively to the inappropriate ones is, rather, the fact that the responses resulting from the correct connections are followed more closely in time by need-reductions. Thus a hungry rat in a maze tends to get to food and have his hunger reduced *sooner* as a result of the true path responses than as a result of the blind alley responses. And such immediately following need-reductions or, to use another term, such 'positive reinforcements' tend somehow, it is said, to strengthen the connections which have most closely preceded them. Thus it is as if—although this is certainly not the way this subgroup would themselves state it—the satisfaction-receiving part of the rat telephoned back to Central and said to the girl: "Hold that connection; it was good; and see to it that you blankety-blank well use it again the next time these same stimuli come in." These theorists also assume (at least some of them do some of the time) that, if bad results—'annoyances,' 'negative reinforcements'—follow, then this same satisfaction-and-annoyance-receiving part of the rat will telephone back and say, "Break that connection and don't you dare use it next time either."

So much for a brief summary of the two subvarieties of the 'stimulus-response,' or telephone switchboard school.

(2) Let us turn now to the second main school. This group (and I belong to them) may be called the field theorists. We believe that in the course of learning something like a field map of the environment gets established in the rat's brain. We agree with the other school that the rat in running a maze is exposed to stimuli and is finally led as a result of these stimuli to the responses which actually occur. We feel, however, that the intervening brain processes are more complicated, more patterned and often, pragmatically speaking, more autonomous than do the stimulus-response psychologists. Although we admit that the rat is bombarded by stimuli, we hold that his nervous system is surprisingly selective as to which of these stimuli it will let in at any given time.

Secondly, we assert that the central office itself is far more like a map control room than it is like an old-fashioned telephone exchange. The stimuli, which are allowed in, are not connected by just simple one-to-one switches to the outgoing responses. Rather, the incoming impulses are usually worked over and elaborated in the central control room into a tentative, cognitive-like map of the environment. And it is this tentative map, indicating routes and paths and environmental relationships, which finally determines what responses, if any, the animal will finally release.

Finally, I, personally, would hold further that it is also important to discover in how far these maps are relatively narrow and strip-like or relatively broad and comprehensive. Both strip-maps and comprehensive-maps may be either correct or incorrect in the sense that they may (or may not), when acted upon, lead successfully to the animal's goal. The differences between such strip maps and such comprehensive maps will appear only when the rat is later presented with some change within the given environment. Then, the narrower and more strip-like the original map, the less will it carry over successfully to the new problem; whereas, the wider and the more comprehensive it was, the more adequately it will serve in the new set-up. In a strip map the given position of the animal is connected by only a relatively simple and single path to the position of the goal. In a comprehensive-map a wider arc of the environment is represented, so that, if the starting position of the animal be changed or variations in the specific routes be introduced, this wider map will allow the animal still to behave relatively correctly and to choose the appropriate new route.

But let us turn,. now, to the actual experiments. The ones, out of many, which I have selected to report are simply ones which seem especially important in reinforcing the theoretical position I have been presenting. This position, I repeat, contains two assumptions: First, that learning consists not in stimulus-response connections but in the building up in the nervous system of sets which function like cognitive maps, and second, that such cognitive maps may be usefully characterized as varying from a narrow strip variety to a broader comprehensive variety.

The experiments fall under five heads: (1) "latent learning," (2) "vicarious trial and error" or "VTE," (3) "searching for the stimulus," (4) "hypotheses" and (5) "spatial orientation."

1. "LATENT LEARNING" EXPERIMENTS

The first of the latent learning experiments was performed at Berkeley by Blodgett. It was published in 1929. Blodgett not only performed the experiments, he also originated the concept. He ran three groups of rats through a six-unit alley maze, shown in Fig. 7.4–4. He had a control group and two experimental groups. The error curves for these groups appear in Fig. 7.4–5. The solid line shows the error curve for Group I, the control group. These animals were run in orthodox fashion. That is, they were run one trial a day and found food in the goal-box at the end of each trial. Groups II and III were the experimental groups. The ani-

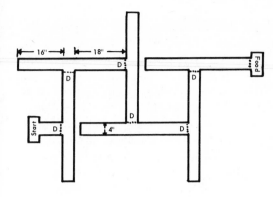

FIGURE 7.4–4 6-Unit alley T-maze. (From H. C. Blodgett, The effect of the introduction of reward upon the maze performance of rats. *Univ. Calif. Publ. Psychol.*, 1929, 4, No. 8, p. 117.)

FIGURE 7.4–5 From H. C. Blodgett, The effect of the introduction of reward upon the maze performance of rats. *Univ. Calif. Publ. Psychol.*, 1929, 4, No. 8, p. 120.

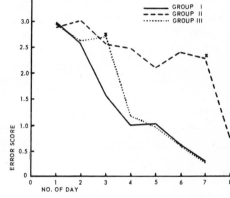

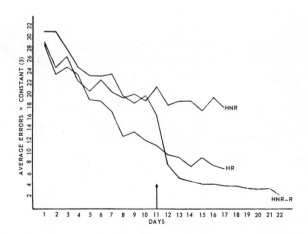

FIGURE 7.4–6 Error curves for HR, HNR, and HNR-R. (From E. C. Tolman and C. H. Honzik, Introduction and removal of reward, and maze performance in rats. *Univ. Calif. Publ. Psychol.*, 1930, 4, No. 19, p. 267.)

mals of Group II, the dash line, were not fed in the maze for the first six days but only in their home cages some two hours later. On the seventh day (indicated by the small cross) the rats found food at the end of the maze for the first time and continued to find it on subsequent days. The animals of Group III were treated similarly except that they first found food at the end of the maze on the third day and continued to find it there on subsequent days. It will be observed that the experimental groups as long as they were not finding food did not appear to learn much. (Their error curves did not drop.) But on the days immediately succeeding their first finding of the food their error curves did drop astoundingly. It appeared, in short, that during the non-rewarded trials these animals had been learning much more than they had exhibited. This learning, which did not manifest itself until after the food had been introduced, Blodgett called "latent learning." Interpreting these results anthropomorphically, we would say that as long as the animals were not getting any food at the end of the maze they continued to take their time in going through it—they continued to enter many blinds. Once, however, they knew they were to get food, they demonstrated that during these preceding non-rewarded trials they had learned where many of the blinds were. They had been building up a 'map,' and could utilize the latter as soon as they were motivated to do so.

Honzik and myself repeated the experiments (or rather he did and I got some of the credit) with the 14-unit T-mazes shown in Fig. 7.4–1, and with larger groups of animals, and got similar results. The resulting curves are shown in Fig. 7.4–6. We used two control groups—one that never found food in the maze (HNR) and one that found it throughout (HR). The experimental group (HNR–R) found food at the end of the maze from the 11th day on and showed the same sort of a sudden drop.

But probably the best experiment demonstrating latent learning was, unfortunately, done not in Berkeley but at the University of Iowa, by Spence and Lippitt. Only an abstract of this experiment has as yet been published. However, Spence has sent a preliminary manuscript from which the following account is summarized. A simple Y-maze (see Fig. 7.4–7) with two goal-boxes was used. Water was at the end of the right arm of the Y and food at the end of the left arm. During the training period the rats were run neither hungry nor thirsty. They were satiated for both food and water before each day's trials. However, they were willing to run because after each run they were taken out of whichever end box they had got to and put into a living cage, with other animals in it. They were given four trials a day in this fashion for seven days, two trials to the right and two to the left.

In the crucial test the animals were divided into two subgroups one made solely hungry and one solely thirsty. It was then found that on the first trial the hungry group went at once to the left, where the food had been, statistically more frequently than to the right; and the thirsty group went to the right, where the water had been, statistically more frequently than to the left. These results indicated that under the previous non-differential and very mild rewarding conditions of merely being returned to the home cages the animals had nevertheless been learning where the water was and where the food was. In short, they had acquired a cognitive map to the effect that food was to the left and water to the right, although during the acquisition of this map they had not exhibited any stimulus-response propensities to go more to the side which became later the side of the appropriate goal.

There have been numerous other latent learning experiments done in the Berkeley laboratory and elsewhere. In general, they have for the most part all confirmed the above sort of findings.

Let us turn now to the second group of experiments.

2. "VICARIOUS TRIAL AND ERROR" OR "VTE"

The term Vicarious Trial and Error (abbreviated as VTE) was invented by Prof. Muenzinger at Colorado[1] to designate the hesitating, looking-back-and-forth, sort of behavior which rats can often be observed to indulge in at a choice-point before actually going one way or the other.

Quite a number of experiments upon VTEing have been carried out in our laboratory. I shall report only a few. In most of them what is called a discrimination set-up has been used. In one characteristic type of visual discrimination apparatus designed by Lashley (shown in Fig. 7.4–8) the animal is put on a jumping stand and faced with two doors which differ in some visual property say, as here shown, vertical stripes vs. horizontal stripes.

One of each such pair of visual stimuli is made always correct and the other wrong; and the two are interchanged from side to side in random fashion. The animal is required to learn, say, that the vertically striped door is always the correct one. If he jumps to it, the door falls open and he gets to food on a platform behind. If, on the other hand, he jumps incorrectly, he finds the door locked and falls into a net some two feet below from which he is picked up and started over again.

Using a similar set-up (see Fig. 7.4–9), but with landing platforms in front of the doors so that if the rat chose incorrectly he could jump back again and start over, I found that when the choice was an easy one, say between a white door and a black door, the animals not only learned sooner but also did more VTEing than when the choice was difficult, say between a white door and a gray door (see Fig. 7.4–10). It appeared further (see Fig. 7.4–11) that the VTEing began to appear just as (or just before) the rats began to learn. After the learning had become established, however, the VTE's began to go down. Further, in a study of

FIGURE 7.4–7 Ground plan of the apparatus. (Taken from K. W. Spence and R. Lippitt, An experimental test of the sign-gestalt theory of trial and error learning. *J. Exper. Psychol.*, 1946, 36, p. 494. In this article they were describing another experiment but used the same maze.)

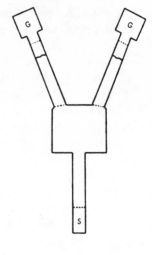

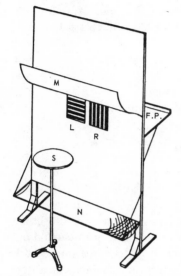

FIGURE 7.4–8 Apparatus used for testing discrimination of visual patterns. (From K. S. Lashley, The mechanism of vision. I. A. method for rapid analysis of pattern-vision in the rat. *J. Genet. Psychol.*, 1930, 37, p. 454.)

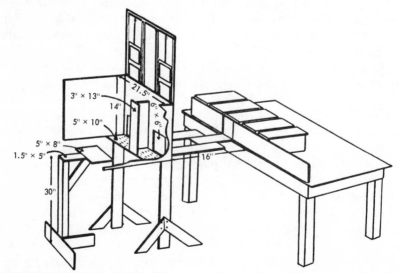

FIGURE 7.4–9 From E. C. Tolman, Prediction of vicarious trial and error by means of the schematic sowbug, *Psychol. Rev.*, 1939, 46, p. 319.

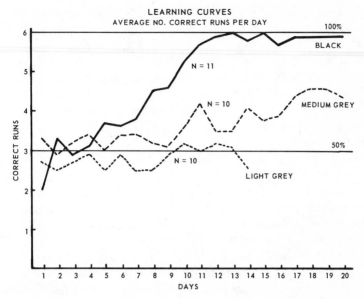

FIGURE 7.4–10 Learning curves (From E. Tolman, Prediction of vicarious trial and error by means of the schematic sowbug, *Psychol. Rev.*, 1939, 46, p. 319.)

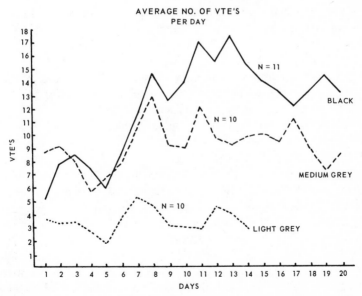

FIGURE 7.4–11 Average number of VTE's. (From E. C. Tolman, Prediction of vicarious trial and error by means of the schematic sowbug, *Psychol. Rev.*, 1939, 46, p. 320.)

individual differences by myself, Geier and Levin[2] (actually done by Geier and Levin) using this same visual discrimination apparatus, it was found that with one and the same difficulty of problem the smarter animal did the more VTEing.

To sum up, in *visual discrimination* experiments the better the learning, the more the VTE's. But this seems contrary to what we would perhaps have expected. We ourselves would expect to do more VTEing, more sampling of the two stimuli, when it is difficult to chose between them than when it is easy.

What is the explanation? The answer lies, I believe, in the fact that the manner in which we set the visual discrimination problems for the rats and the manner in which we set similar problems for ourselves are different. We already have our 'instructions.' We know beforehand what it is we are to do. We are told, or we tell ourselves, that it is the lighter of the two grays, the heavier of the two weights, or the like, which is to be chosen. In such a setting we do more sampling, more VTEing, when the stimulus-difference is small. But for the rats the usual problem in a discrimination apparatus is quite different. They do not know what is wanted of them. The major part of their learning in most such experiments seems to consist in their discovering the instructions. The rats have to discover that it is the differences in visual brightness, not the differences between left and right, which they are to pay attention to. Their VTEing appears when they begin to 'catch on.' The greater the difference between the two stimuli the more the animals are attracted by this difference. Hence the sooner they catch on, and during this catching on, the more they VTE.

That this is a reasonable interpretation appeared further, from an experiment by myself and Minium (the actual work done, of course, by Minium) in which a group of six rats was first taught a white vs. black discrimination, then two successively more difficult gray vs. black discriminations. For each difficulty the rats were given a long series of further trials beyond the points at which they had learned. Comparing the beginning of each of these three difficulties the results were that the rats did more VTEing for the easy discriminations than for the more difficult ones. When, however, it came to a comparison of amounts of VTEing during the final performance after each learning had reached a plateau, the opposite results were obtained. In other words, after the rats had finally divined their instructions, then they, like human beings, did more VTEing, more sampling, the more difficult the discrimination.

Finally, now let us note that it was also found at Berkeley by Jackson[3] that in a maze the difficult maze units produce more VTEing and also that the more stupid rats do the more VTEing. The explanation, as I see it, is that, in the case of mazes, rats know their instructions. For them it is

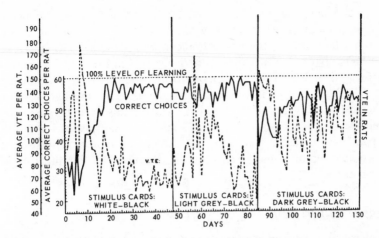

FIGURE 7.4–12   From E. C. Tolman and E. Minium, VTE in rats: overlearning and difficulty of discrimination, *J. Comp. Psychol.*, 1942, 34, p. 303.

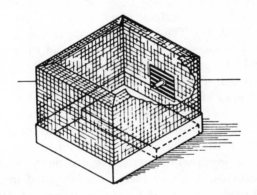

FIGURE 7.4–13   From Bradford Hudson. Ph.D. thesis: One trial learning: A study of the avoidance behavior of the rat. On deposit in the Library of the University of California, Berkeley, California.

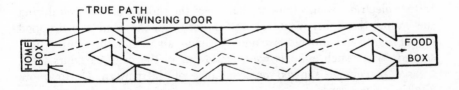

FIGURE 7.4–14   From I. Krechevsky (now D. Krech), The genesis of "hypotheses" in rats. *Univ. Calif. Publ. Psychol.*, 1932, 6, No. 4, p. 46.

natural to expect that the same spatial path will always lead to the same outcome. Rats in mazes don't have to be told.

But what, now, is the final significance of all this VTEing? How do these facts about VTEing affect our theoretical argument? My answer is that these facts lend further support to the doctrine of a building up of maps. VTEing, as I see it, is evidence that in the critical stages—whether in the first picking up of the instructions or in the later making sure of which stimulus is which—the animal's activity is not just one of responding passively to discrete stimuli, but rather one of the active selecting and comparing of stimuli. This brings me then to the third type of experiment.

3. "SEARCHING FOR THE STIMULUS"

I refer to a recent, and it seems to me extremely important experiment, done for a Ph.D. dissertation by Hudson. Hudson was first interested in the question of whether or not rats could learn an avoidance reaction in one trial. His animals were tested one at a time in a living cage (see Fig. 7.4–13) with a small striped visual pattern at the end, on which was mounted a food cup. The hungry rat approached this food cup and ate. An electrical arrangement was provided so that when the rat touched the cup he could be given an electric shock. And one such shock did appear to be enough. For when the rat was replaced in this same cage days or even weeks afterwards, he usually demonstrated immediately strong avoidance reactions to the visual pattern. The animal withdrew from that end of the cage, or piled up sawdust and covered the pattern, or showed various other amusing responses all of which were in the nature of withdrawing from the pattern or making it disappear.

But the particular finding which I am interested in now appeared as a result of a modification of this standard procedure. Hudson noticed that the animals, anthropomorphically speaking, often seemed to look around *after* the shock to see what it was that had hit them. Hence it occurred to him that, if the pattern were made to disappear the instant the shock occurred, the rats might not establish the association. And this indeed is what happened in the case of many individuals. Hudson added further electrical connections so that when the shock was received during the eating, the lights went out, the pattern and the food cup dropped out of sight, and the lights came on again all within the matter of a second. When such animals were again put in the cage 24 hours later, a large percentage showed no avoidance of the pattern. Or to quote Hudson's own words:

> Learning what object to avoid . . . may occur exclusively during the period *after* the shock. For if the object from which the shock was

actually received is removed at the moment of the shock, a significant number of animals fail to learn to avoid it, some selecting other features in the environment for avoidance, and others avoiding nothing.

In other words, I feel that this experiment reinforces the notion of the largely active selective character in the rat's building up of his cognitive map. He often has to look actively for the significant stimuli in order to form his map and does not merely passively receive and react to all the stimuli which are physically present.

Turn now to the fourth type of experiment.

4. THE "HYPOTHESIS" EXPERIMENTS

Both the notion of hypotheses in rats and the design of the experiments to demonstrate such hypotheses are to be credited to Krech. Krech used a four-compartment discrimination-box. In such a four-choice box the correct door at each choice-point may be determined by the experimenter in terms of its being lighted or dark, left or right, or various combinations of these. If all possibilities are randomized for the 40 choices made in 10 runs of each day's test, the problem could be made insoluble.

When this was done, Krech found that the individual rat went through a succession of systematic choices. That is, the individual animal might perhaps begin by choosing practically all right-hand doors, then he might give this up for choosing practically all left-hand doors, and then, for choosing all dark doors, and so on. These relatively persistent, and well-above-chance systematic types of choice Krech called "hypotheses." In using this term he obviously did not mean to imply verbal processes in the rat but merely referred to what I have been calling cognitive maps which, it appears from his experiments, get set up in a tentative fashion to be tried out first one and then another until, if possible, one is found which works.

Finally, it is to be noted that these hypothesis experiments, like the latent learning, VTE, and "looking for the stimulus" experiments, do not, as such, throw light upon the widths of the maps which are picked up but do indicate the generally map-like and self-initiated character of learning.

For the beginning of an attack upon the problem of the width of the maps let me turn to the last group of experiments.

5. "SPATIAL ORIENTATION" EXPERIMENTS

As early as 1929, Lashley reported incidentally the case of a couple of his rats who, after having learned an alley maze, pushed back the cover near the starting box, climbed out and ran directly across the top to the goal-box where they climbed down in again and ate. Other investigators have reported related findings. All such observations suggest that rats really develop wider spatial maps which include more than the mere trained-on specific paths. In the experiments now to be reported this possibility has been subjected to further examination.

In the first experiment, Tolman, Ritchie and Kalish (actually Ritchie and Kalish) used the set-up shown in Fig. 7.4–15.

This was an elevated maze. The animals ran from A across the open circular table through CD (which had alley walls) and finally to G, the food box. H was a light which shone directly down the path from G to F. After four nights, three trials per night, in which the rats learned to run directly and without hesitation from A to G, the apparatus was changed to the sun-burst shown in Fig. 7.4–16. The starting path and the table remained the same but a series of radiating paths was added.

The animals were again started at A and ran across the circular table into the alley and found themselves blocked. They then returned onto the table and began exploring practically all the radiating paths. After going out a few inches only on any one path, each rat finally chose to run all the way out on one. The percentages of rats finally choosing each of the long paths from 1 to 12 are shown in Fig. 7.4–17. It appears that there was a preponderant tendency to choose path No. 6 which ran to a point some four inches in front of where the entrance to the food-box had been. The only other path chosen with any appreciable frequency was No. 1—that is, the path which pointed perpendicularly to the food-side of the room.

These results seem to indicate that the rats in this experiment had learned not only to run rapidly down the original roundabout route but also, when this was blocked and radiating paths presented, to select one pointing rather directly towards the point where the food had been or else at least to select a path running perpendicularly to the food-side of the room.

As a result of their original training, the rats had, it would seem, acquired not merely a strip-map to the effect that the original specifically trained-on path led to food but, rather, a wider comprehensive map to the effect that food was located in such and such a direction in the room.

Consider now a further experiment done by Ritchie alone. This experiment tested still further the breadth of the spatial map which is acquired. In this further experiment the rats were again run across the table—this time to the arms of a simple T. (See Fig. 7.4–18.)

Twenty-five animals were trained for seven days, 20 trials in all, to find food at F_1; and twenty-five animals were trained to find it at F_2. The L's in the diagram indicate lights. On the eighth day the starting path and table top were rotated through 180 degrees so that they were

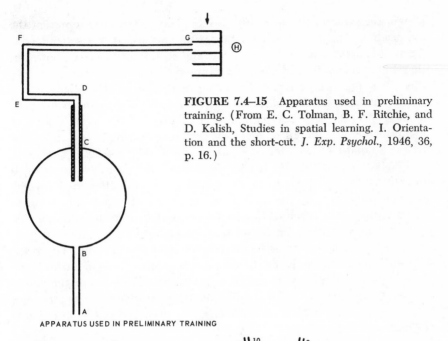

FIGURE 7.4–15   Apparatus used in preliminary training. (From E. C. Tolman, B. F. Ritchie, and D. Kalish, Studies in spatial learning. I. Orientation and the short-cut. *J. Exp. Psychol.*, 1946, 36, p. 16.)

APPARATUS USED IN PRELIMINARY TRAINING

FIGURE 7.4–16   Apparatus used in the test trial. (From E. C. Tolman, B. F. Ritchie, and D. Kalish, Studies in spatial learning. I. Orientation and short-cut. *J. Exp. Psychol.*, 1946, 36, p. 17.)

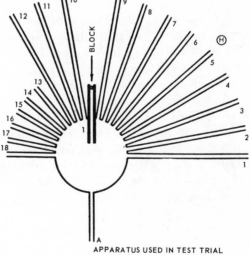

APPARATUS USED IN TEST TRIAL

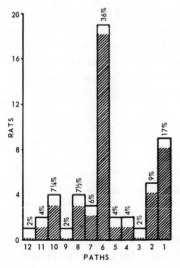

FIGURE 7.4–17   Number of rats which chose each of the paths. (From E. C. Tolman, B. F. Ritchie, and B. Kalish, Studies in spatial learning. I. Orientation and the short-cut. *J. Exp. Psychol.*, 1946, 36, p. 19.)

now in the position shown in Fig. 7.4–19. The dotted lines represent the old position. And a series of radiating paths was added. What happened? Again the rats ran across the table into the central alley. When, however, they found themselves blocked, they turned back onto the table and this time also spent many seconds touching and trying out for only a few steps practically all the paths. Finally, however, within seven minutes, 42 of the 50 rats chose one path and ran all the way out on it. The paths finally chosen by the 19 of these animals that had been fed at F_1 and by the 23 that had been fed at F_2 are shown in Fig. 7.4–20.

This time the rats tended to choose, not the paths which pointed directly to the spots where the food had been, but rather paths which ran perpendicularly to the corresponding sides of the room. The spatial maps of these rats, when the animals were started from the opposite side of the room, were thus not completely adequate to the precise goal positions but were adequate as to the correct sides of the room. The maps of these animals were, in short, not altogether strip-like and narrow.

This completes my report of experiments. There were the *latent learning experiments*, the *VTE experiments*, the *searching for the stimulus experiment*, the *hypothesis experiments*, and these last *spatial orientation experiments*.

And now, at last, I come to the humanly significant and exciting problem: namely, what are the conditions which favor narrow strip-maps and what are those which tend to favor broad comprehensive maps not only in rats but also in men?

There is considerable evidence scattered throughout the literature bearing on this question both for rats and for men. Some of this evidence was obtained in Berkeley and some of it elsewhere. I have not time to present it in any detail. I can merely summarize it by saying that narrow strip maps rather than broad comprehensive maps seem to be induced: (1) by a damaged brain, (2) by an inadequate array of environmentally presented cues, (3) by an overdose of repetitions on the original trained-on path and (4) by the presence of too strongly motivational or of too strongly frustrating conditions.

It is this fourth factor which I wish to elaborate upon briefly in my concluding remarks. For it is going to be my contention that some, at least, of the so-called 'psychological mechanisms' which the clinical psychologists and the other students of personality have uncovered as the devils underlying many of our individual and social maladjustments can be interpreted as narrowings of our cognitive maps due to too strong motivations or to too intense frustration.

My argument will be brief, cavalier, and dogmatic. For I am not myself a clinician or a social psychologist. What I am going to say must

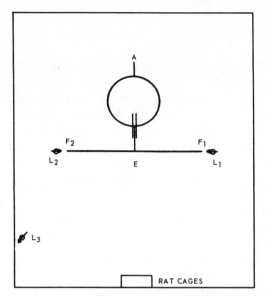

FIGURE 7.4–18 From B. F. Ritchie, Ph.D. thesis: Spatial learning in rats. On deposit in the Library of the University of California, Berkeley, California.

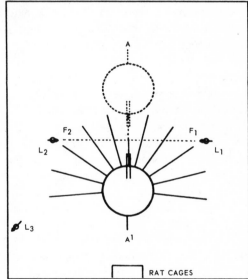

FIGURE 7.4–19 From B. F. Ritchie, Ph.D. thesis: Spatial learning in rats. On deposit in the Library of the University of California, Berkeley, California.

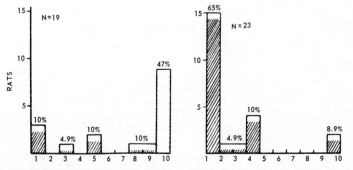

PATHS CHOSEN BY RATS IN THE F_1 GROUP   PATHS CHOSEN BY RATS IN THE F_2 GROUP

FIGURE 7.4–20 From B. F. Ritchie. Ph.D. thesis: Spatial learning in rats. On deposit in the Library of the University of California, Berkeley, California.

be considered, therefore, simply as in the nature of a *rat* psychologist's *rat*iocinations offered free.

By way of illustration, let me suggest that at least the three dynamisms called, respectively, "regression," "fixation," and "displacement of aggression onto outgroups" are expressions of cognitive maps which are too narrow and which get built up in us as a result of too violent motivation or of too intense frustration.

(a) Consider *regression*. This is the term used for those cases in which an individual, in the face of too difficult a problem, returns to earlier more childish ways of behaving. Thus, to take an example, the overprotected middle-aged woman (reported a couple of years ago in *Time Magazine*) who, after losing her husband, regressed (much to the distress of her growing daughters) into dressing in too youthful a fashion and into competing for their beaux and then finally into behaving like a child requiring continuous care, would be an illustration of regression. I would not wish you to put too much confidence in the reportorial accuracy of *Time*, but such an extreme case is not too different from many actually to be found in our mental hospitals or even sometimes in ourselves. In all such instances my argument would be (1) that such regression results from too strong a present emotional situation and (2) that it consists in going back to too narrow an earlier map, itself due to too much frustration or motivation in early childhood. *Time's* middle-aged woman was presented by too frustrating an emotional situation at her husband's death and she regressed, I would wager, to too narrow adolescent and childhood maps since these latter had been originally excessively impressed because of overstressful experiences at the time she was growing up.

(b) Consider *fixation*. Regression and fixation tend to go hand in hand. For another way of stating the fact of the undue persistence of early maps is to say they were fixated. This has even been demonstrated in rats. If rats are too strongly motivated in their original learning, they find it very difficult to relearn when the original path is no longer correct. Also after they have relearned, if they are given an electric shock they, like *Time's* woman, tend to regress back again to choosing the earlier path.

(c) Finally, consider the *"displacement of aggressions onto outgroups."* Adherence to one's own group is an ever-present tendency among primates. It is found in chimpanzees and monkeys as strongly as in men. We primates operate in groups. And each individual in such a group tends to identify with his whole group in the sense that the group's goals become his goals, the group's life and immortality, his life and immortality. Furthermore, each individual soon learns that, when as an individual he is frustrated, he must not take out his aggressions on the other members of his own group. He learns instead to displace his aggressions onto outgroups. Such a displacement of aggression I would claim is also a narrowing of the cognitive map. The individual comes no longer to distinguish the true locus of the cause of his frustration. The poor Southern whites, who take it out on the Negroes, are displacing their aggressions from the landlords, the southern economic system, the northern capitalists, or wherever the true cause of their frustration may lie, onto a mere convenient outgroup. The physicists on the Faculty who criticize the humanities, or we psychologists who criticize all the other departments, or the University as a whole which criticizes the Secondary School system or, vice versa, the Secondary School system which criticizes the University—or, on a still larger and far more dangerous scene—we Americans who criticize the Russians and the Russians who criticize us, are also engaging, at least in part, in nothing more than such irrational displacements of our aggressions onto outgroups.

I do not mean to imply that there may not be some true interferences by the one group with the goals of the other and hence that the aggressions of the members of the one group against the members of the other are necessarily *wholly* and *merely* displaced aggressions. But I do assert that often and in large part they are such mere displacements.

Over and over again men are blinded by too violent motivations and too intense frustrations into blind and unintelligent and in the end desperately dangerous hates of outsiders. And the expression of these their displaced hates ranges all the way from discrimination against minorities to world conflagrations.

What in the name of Heaven and Psychology can we do about it? My only answer is to preach again the virtues of reason—of, that is, broad cognitive maps. And to suggest that the child-trainers and the world-planners of the future can only, if at all, bring about the presence of the required rationality (*i.e.*, comprehensive maps) if they see to it that nobody's children are too over-motivated or too frustrated. Only then can these children learn to look before and after, learn to see that there are often round-about and safer paths to their quite proper goals —learn, that is, to realize that the well-beings of White and of Negro, of Catholic and of Protestant, of Christian and of Jew, of American and of Russian (and even of males and females) are mutually interdependent.

We dare not let ourselves or others become so over-emotional, so hungry, so ill-clad, so over-motivated that only narrow strip-maps will be developed. All of us in Europe as well as in America, in the Orient as well as in the Occident, must be made calm enough and well-fed enough to be able to develop truly comprehensive maps, or, as Freud would have put it, to be able to learn to live according to the Reality Principle rather than according to the too narrow and too immediate Pleasure Principle.

We must, in short, subject our children and ourselves (as the kindly experimenter would his rats) to the optimal conditions of moderate motivation and of an absence of unnecessary frustrations, whenever we put them and ourselves before that great God-given maze which is our human world. I cannot predict whether or not we will be able, or be allowed, to do this; but I *can* say that, only insofar as we *are* able and *are* allowed, have we cause for hope.

NOTES

1. *Vide:* K. F. Muenzinger, Vicarious trial and error at a point of choice: I. A general survey of its relation to learning efficiency. *J. genet. Psychol.*, 1938, 53, 75–86.
2. F. M. Geier, M. Levin & E. C. Tolman, Individual differences in emotionality, hypothesis formation, vicarious trial and error and visual discrimination learning in rats. *Compar. Psychol. Monogr.*, 1941, 17, No. 3.
3. L. L. Jackson, V. T. E. on an elevated maze. *J. comp. Psychol.*, 1943, 36, 99–107.

7.5 | COGNITIVE FACTORS IN THE EXTINCTION
OF THE CONDITIONED EYELID RESPONSE
IN HUMANS*

Kenneth W. Spence

Abstract. Rate of extinction of the conditioned eyelid response in humans is a function of the degree of discriminability of the procedural changes that occur with shift from acquisition to extinction. Extinction is greatly retarded when these changes are minimized or the subject is distracted by another task.

Experimental extinction of the conditioned eyelid response in human subjects has typically been found to be extremely rapid. Thus, when extinction curves are plotted in terms of the number of previously non-reinforced trials, performance may reach its minimum (asymptotic) level in as few as six to eight trials, with many individuals ceasing to respond after the first nonreinforcement. Questioning of subjects from some of our

* Reprinted from *Science*, 1963, *140*, 1224–1225. Copyright 1963 by the American Association for the Advancement of Science, and reproduced by permission.

studies has suggested that a possible factor underlying this rapid extinction might be the subject's recognition of the change in the experimental conditions with shift from acquisition to extinction. Even when not aware of the fact that their eyelids have been conditioned to respond to the conditioned stimulus (CS) most subjects appear to become aware of it when, with the onset of extinction, the unconditioned stimulus (UCS) is suddenly discontinued. Under such conditions the response decrement is probably, in part, a function of some higher order process, some kind of inhibitory set that is more or less immediately adopted by the subject upon recognition of the change. The present report is a preliminary account of a study which shows that the response decrement in extinction is much slower when the change in conditions from acquisition to extinction is reduced and, hence, is more difficult for the subject to recognize.

A number of techniques designed to reduce the difference in the conditions of acquisition and extinction have been employed in previous studies done in our laboratory. McAllister (1), after demonstrating that an extended CS–UCS interval of 2500 msec did not lead to conditioning, showed that a conditioned response established with a CS–UCS interval of 500 msec became extinguished when this interval was extended to 2500 msec. He found, furthermore, that extinction under this extended interval proceeded more slowly than when the UCS was discontinued. Subsequent studies (2), however, have shown that this relatively slower extinction under the extended CS–UCS interval holds only when the original conditioning is conducted under a partial reinforcement schedule. After 100-percent reinforcement, no difference is obtained in the rate of extinction under the extended CS–UCS interval and the condition of no UCS. Extinction is extremely rapid with both procedures.

In these earlier studies the conditioning procedure that was used involved a CS duration of 550 msec. With the shift to extinction with the extended CS–UCS interval, this duration was increased to 2550 msec. Finding that subjects readily reported noticing this change in the duration of the CS, we decided to try to reduce recognition of the change in conditions from conditioning to extinction by keeping the CS duration constant at 2550 msec for both acquisition and extinction.

Three groups were run. In group 1 the UCS was omitted in extinction. In groups 2 and 3 the UCS was continued during extinction but at a CS–UCS interval of 2500 msec. In the case of group 3 a second learning task was introduced into the situation. It was believed that this procedure would decrease still further the likelihood that the subjects would observe the changes in the stimulus events related to extinction. Also, it was presumed that this technique would prevent the subject from recognizing that he was being conditioned.

The learning task used for this purpose was the light-guessing or probability-learning task designed by Estes and Straughan (3). The situation involved a centrally placed signal light which, when it came on, was a signal for the subject to anticipate within its duration (2 seconds) which of two small bulbs, one to the left and one to the right of the signal light, would subsequently light up. The subjects were given a set of instructions to the effect that the experiment was concerned with the effects of distraction on performance in a difficult problem-solving situation. They were instructed that their task was to predict which of the two small lamps was going to light up and to signify their prediction by pressing the push button located on the left or right arm of their chair. They were told further that distracting stimuli in the form of a tone and air puff to their eye would be given in between their response of pressing a button and the lighting up of one of the lamps. The onset of the tone coincided with the turning off of the signal light. The subjects were urged to predict to the best of their ability and to attempt to improve their prediction with practice. The small lamps lighted up according to a prearranged schedule. For half the subjects, the left lamp lit up seven times in each block of 10 trials, the right lamp three times. In the other half, these frequencies were reversed.

The acquisition phase involved 50 trials, the last of which was not reinforced. Thirty extinction trials were then given. The CS, a 500–cy/sec tone, had a duration of 2550 msec. The CS–UCS interval during conditioning was 500 msec and the UCS was a 1.0 lb/in.^{2} air puff, 50 msec in duration. Each group contained 25 subjects from an introductory psychology course.

Figure 7.5–1 presents the extinction curves for the three groups. Clearly evident are the markedly different rates with which the decrement in conditioned responses occurs during the extinction trials. Group 1, extinguished with no UCS, dropped precipitously to a random level of responding (10 percent) after two nonreinforced trials. The curve of group 2, which was extinguished with a 2500-msec CS–UCS interval, also dropped quite rapidly, but somewhat slower than that of group 1. In terms of the number of conditioned responses in the first ten extinction trials the difference between these two groups was significant at the .01 level. This finding differs, it will be noted, from that of earlier studies (2) which obtained no difference between groups extinguished with no UCS and with an extended CS–UCS interval after continuous reinforcement. The only difference in the experimental conditions is that in the present experiment the CS duration was 2550 msec during acquisition, whereas in the previous studies it was increased from 550 msec to 2550 msec in the case of the group extinguished with the extended CS–UCS interval.

In sharp contrast to the findings for groups 1 and 2, the extinction

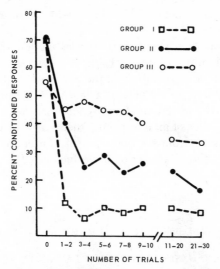

FIGURE 7.5–1 Percentage of conditioned responses during extinction as a function of number of previous nonreinforced trials.

curve of group 3, which was conditioned and extinguished in the context of the probability-learning task, exhibited a very gradual decrease. Thus, by the ninth and tenth extinction trials, this group's performance level had decreased only 14.4 percent from its final acquisition level, whereas the corresponding decrements for groups 1 and 2 were 56 percent and 45.2 percent, respectively. The differences between the performance levels of group 3 and the other two groups during the first ten extinction trials were highly significant, at the .01 level in the case of group 2 and the .005 level for group 1.

After the experiment the subjects were questioned as to whether they noticed any change in the experimental procedure during the course of the experiment. If the subject replied "yes," further questions were asked to ascertain if the change in the CS–UCS interval or the cessation of the UCS in the case of group 1 was noted. The results of these questions indicated considerable differences among the groups. Twenty-one subjects of group 1, 19 of group 2, but only one of group 3, reported noticing the procedural change. Correlated with this absence of recognition on the part of group-3 subjects is the strikingly slower extinction. The slight difference between groups 1 and 2 in the number of subjects that recognized a difference in procedure with extinction indicates that some other factor than difference in proportion of subjects that observed the change must be appealed to in order to account for the difference in mean rate of extinction of these two groups. A possible interpretation is that the lesser change in the case of group 2 than group 1 required, on the average, more extinction trials before the difference in procedure was recognized.

It is apparent from these data that extinction of the conditioned eyelid response in humans is to a considerable degree a function of cognitive factors relating to observation on the part of the subject of procedural changes with the shift to extinction, a finding that suggests support for some version of the discrimination hypothesis. Attempts to infer the quantitative properties of an intervening theoretical variable, for example, inhibition that results from the operation of nonreinforcement, will need to take account of these potent cognitive factors (4).

NOTES AND REFERENCES

1. W. R. McAllister, *J. Exptl. Psychol.* 45, 423 (1953).
2. W. F. Reynolds, *ibid.* 55, 335 (1958); K. W. Spence, E. Rutledge, J. Talbott, *ibid.*, in press.
3. W. K. Estes and J. H. Straughan, *J. Exptl. Psychol.* 47, 225 (1954).
4. This study was carried out as part of a project concerned with classical conditioning in humans under contract Nonr-1509(04) between the University of Iowa and the Office of Naval Research. M. J. Homzie and E. Rutledge assisted in the research.

7.6 HYPOTHESIS THEORY AND NONLEARNING DESPITE IDEAL S–R-REINFORCEMENT CONTINGENCIES*

Marvin Levine

Hypothesis theory generates a few theorems about adult humans failing to reach criterion in discrimination-learning tasks. First, their performance should match behavior on tasks which are intrinsically insoluble but otherwise comparable to the normal tasks. Second, for certain stimulus sequences, performance on both the unsolved and insoluble problems

* Marvin Levine, "Hypothesis Theory and Nonlearning Despite Ideal S–R-Reinforcement Contingencies," *Psychological Review*, 78, 1971, 130–140. Copyright 1971 by the American Psychological Association, and reproduced by permission. The experiments described here and the preparation of this article were supported by Research Grant MH 11857 from the National Institute of Mental Health. I wish to express my appreciation to William Glassman who performed the first experiment and to O. Ernest Andrews who supervised the last set of experiments.

should be below the chance level. The data confirmed both of these predictions. The theory also stipulates the conditions for producing nonlearning by motivated Ss. According to the theory, as long as S is sampling from a set of incorrect hypotheses (i.e., a set lacking the solution) he will show no learning. No response strengthening will occur in this circumstance even if the solution consists in the simplest contingencies (e.g., E says "right" when S says "A," and "wrong" when S says "B"). A series of experiments validated the prediction. The relation of these results to random-feedback effects, the awareness controversy, and the Einstellung phenomenon is discussed.

A college student appears at the laboratory and is given a simple learning task. He is instructed to respond to each of a series of stimuli with any one of a limited set of responses. After some (preselected) response the experimenter (E) says "right," after the others he says "wrong." The well-known experimental result is that the selected response increases in relative frequency.[1] For more than half a century this finding has been so ubiquitous that it has been twice codified, as the Law of Effect and as the Reinforcement Principle.

The phenomenon, however, is not absolutely reliable. There are at least two classes of results indicating that learning does not always take place. The first comes from studies concerned with the role of awareness in learning. Several authors (e.g., Dulaney, 1961; Spielberger & DeNike, 1966) have identified subsets of subjects (Ss) showing no change in response probability throughout the task. The second comes from investigations of transfer of learning from a first to a second discrimination problem (e.g., the reversal-shift procedure). The authors typically report the elimination of several Ss who, after an inordinately long number of trials still had not learned the first problem. It appears, then, that nonlearning certainly occurs. The experiments below will demonstrate that it occurs even with well-motivated Ss for whom all the relevant information is available and unambiguous. The purpose of this article, however, is not merely to substantiate this finding, but to present a theory which accounts for this and related results.

Hypothesis (H) theory has been vigorously developed in recent years (for reviews see Levine 1969; Trabasso & Bower, 1968). The work suggests that in discrimination- or concept-learning laboratory tasks, adult human behavior is the result of H testing. Novel analyses (backward learning curves; blank-trial probes) imply that S has a set of Hs from which he repeatedly samples until he selects the correct H. Some detailed specifications of the theory will be given below, along with a review of the data on which the specifications are based. However, it will be useful first to have a clear description of the initial task to which the theory will be applied.

Several 12-trial multidimensional simultaneous-discrimination problems were constructed. Each trial was initiated by the display of two stimulus patterns (cf. Figure 7.6–1). One pattern consisted of a set of values from each of eight two-valued dimensions; the other pattern consisted of the complementary values of the dimensions. From trial to trial the dimension values shifted from one pattern to the other so that on some trial the T might be large, surrounded by one solid circle, etc. The shifting of values from trial to trial followed these rules: (*a*) on each pair of adjacent trials, values from four dimensions remained paired together (i.e., were on the same side for both trials) while the values from the other four dimensions were changed (shifted sides from one trial to the next); (*b*) no two dimension values stayed paired with each other for more than three consecutive trials (e.g., A's could not be large more than three times in a row, circles could not be paired with the solid underline more than three times in a row, etc.); (*c*) for any dimension value there was one and only one other value paired for the three trials.

The experimental problems were basically of two types: 12-trial 8-dimensional (8-D) problems with legitimate solutions and 12-trial 7-D insoluble problems. The latter were formed by selecting the solution from 8-D stimuli and by then eliminating the relevant dimension. Suppose, for example, that (before the experiment began) "single spot" was selected to be the solution. The *E* noted on which side the single spot occurred on each of the 12 trials—choice of this side would be correct. He then made 12 new stimuli, identical to the old except that the spots were omitted from both of the stimulus patterns. The *S* received eight such insoluble problems distributed throughout 24 legitimate problems.

The Ss were first shown examples of the stimuli and were carefully instructed about the eight dimensions. They were told that they were to select one of the two patterns and that after each choice *E* would indicate the correctness of that response. They were further told that the solution (i.e., the basis for responding correctly) on any one problem was one of

FIGURE 7.6–1 A simultaneous-discrimination stimulus constructed from eight dimensions (letter, A-T; letter size, large-small; letter color, black-white; underline, solid-dashed; border shape, circle-square; border number, one-two; border texture, solid-dashed; spots, one-two).

the 16 attribute values (8 dimensions $\times$ 2 values per dimensions) and that they were to try to be correct as often as possible. The S was then given several practice problems (both 7-D and 8-D—all soluble) followed by the 32 (24 soluble, 8 insoluble) experimental problems.[2]

In the results, three types of problems can be characterized: legitimate 8-D problems which are solved (defined as having correct responses on Trials 10, 11, and 12)—these will hereafter be ignored; legitimate 8-D problems which are unsolved (defined as having an error on one of Trials 10, 11, or 12); and insoluble 7-D problems, which, of course, S cannot solve. It is the comparison of performance on these last two types of problems which is of interest. Before presenting this comparison, however, the theory will first be reviewed.

THE THEORY OF INSOLUBLE AND UNSOLVED PROBLEMS

The necessary assumptions are:

1. The basic assumption: The S selects an H from some universe and responds on the basis of that H. For example, S may predict that circles are the basis for choosing. He would then choose the side containing the circle. This is a primitive axiom, although support for the second part, that the H directs the response, is found by inserting blocks of blank (i.e., no feedback) trials into normal problems. Frankel, Levine, and Karpf (1970) have shown that Ss virtually always respond to a single attribute value for as many as 30 consecutive blank trials.

2. The composition assumption: The universe from which S samples contains only those Hs corresponding to the stimulus levels. The S predicts that "large" or "T," etc., is correct. He does not employ Hs about conjunctions of cues or about complex sequences. This assumption, clearly, is a function of E's instructions and of the preliminary practice problems. By altering these, the assumption can be changed without affecting the rest of the theory. The last set of experiments described below employs a different composition assumption (and, concomitantly, entails different pretraining). The important feature of the present assumption is that for insoluble 7-D problems. S's universe consists of 14 Hs.

3. Presolution responding: Prior to solving the problem (as manifested by a string of successive correct responses) S samples neither the correct H nor the other H on the same dimension. Thus, if "large letter" is the solution, before the criterion run—or during unsolved problems—S tries neither the H "large letter" nor "small letter." This assumption is based on fairly direct experimental support. Levine, Miller, and Steinmeyer (1967), probing for S's H after each trial, showed that prior to solving, Hs from the relevant dimension virtually never appeared. The

important feature of this assumption is that during unsolved 8-D problems, S's universe consists of 14 Hs.

It is hoped that the reader has noticed the congruity between the last two assumptions: During both insoluble 7-D and unsolved 8-D problems, the S is sampling from a universe of 14 wrong (irrelevant) Hs. In both cases, the correct H (H+) and the complement of H+ are outside the set from which S is sampling. This similarity in theoretical state in turn implies that the behavior under the two conditions should be similar. This, then, is the first prediction of the model, that the trial-by-trial behavior should be the same during both an insoluble 7-D problem and an unsolved 8-D problem.

The next two assumptions will permit further refinement of this prediction and some specification of the details of that trial-by-trial behavior.

4. Affirmative feedback: If S's response is followed by a positive outcome (e.g., E says "correct"), he keeps his H for the next trial. Probing for the H after each trial, Levine (1969) showed that, with the present procedure, this assumption almost always held ($p \approx .95$).

5. Negative feedback: If S's response is followed by a negative outcome (e.g., E says "wrong"), he abandons his last H and resamples. Levine (1969) showed that this assumption also virtually always held ($p \approx .99$). Several proposals have been made concerning S's mode of resampling following a "wrong." A few of these will be described here. All of these alternatives can be ordered along a memory continuum describing how much S remembers from past trials. Each proposal will be illustrated by an S sampling from a universe of 14 wrong Hs.

(a) Reject 0: At one extreme, S might remember nothing, not even the H just disconfirmed. He would, in effect, return this H to the set and would resample from the full universe of 14 Hs. This assumption, first made by Restle (1962), has been shown to be generally false (Levine, 1966; Restle & Emmerich, 1966). It is included here, however, as one end of the memory continuum.

(b) Reject 7: The S might remember all the Hs corresponding to the stimulus pattern he just chose and might recognize that they are all disqualified by the negative feedback. He resamples, in effect, from the seven Hs consistent with the information on the trial just past. Also, he does not utilize information from earlier trials. Gregg and Simon (1967) dubbed this the "local consistency" rule. Trabasso and Bower (1968) have employed this assumption.

(c) Reject 11: The S might sample from Hs consistent not only with the just-past trial but with the preceding trial as well. With the stimulus sequences of the present experiment, this always means that S ignores 11 Hs when resampling after a "wrong." This two-trial consistency check is part of an assumption proposed by Trabasso and Bower (1966).

(*d*) Reject all: The S might remember more than just two previous trials and could, therefore, eliminate more incorrect *H*s. At the extreme, his memory would be perfect and he would always sample among logically correct *H*s. This corresponds to the performance of focusers as described by Bruner, Goodnow, and Austin (1956, pp. 129–134). This poses an interesting psychological problem in the present context. The stimulus sequences are such that by the fourth trial of a problem all 14 *H*s are disconfirmed. The focuser facing an insoluble problem has an empty universe after Trial 4. Some suggestions concerning the behavior of S in this circumstance will be made later.

This is all the theory necessary to derive additional properties of S's behavior during insoluble and unsolved problems. The prediction was already stated that during both types of problems, the protocols should match each other. Further predictions come from applying the theory to the sequence of stimuli employed. Within a problem, the stimuli, it will be recalled, were selected not completely randomly, but to fit stringent counterbalancing requirements. Because this counterbalancing held for every problem, it is possible to derive a predicted performance curve when the response rules described in the theory are applied to these stimulus sequences. In general, the predicted performance curve depends on the memory assumption held for a resampling S (i.e., upon variants *a–d* of Assumption 5). The family of memory assumptions generates a corresponding family of predicted curves. Figure 7.6–2 shows the curves predicted using each of the four variants.[3] The most striking feature of the predictions is that for all the variants of the memory assumption, the theory predicts that during both insoluble and unsolved problems, performance will be below chance. The theory, then, predicts that not only will the curves from both types of problems be the same, but that for

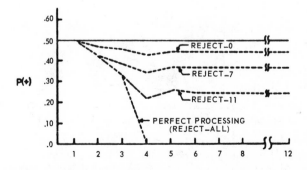

FIGURE 7.6–2   The family of theoretical curves, each of which corresponds to the particular memory assumption added to the theory.

both, fewer than half of the responses will be correct. Furthermore, correct responding will decrease during the first four trials and will then show an upswing. Again, these predictions hold regardless of S's memory, that is, they hold for all the curves in Figure 7.6–2. The details of performance following Trial 4 is currently a matter for some speculation and will be discussed later.

The data comparing 12-trial insoluble and unsolved problems are shown in Figure 7.6–3. It is seen there that the predictions are verified precisely. The curves show below-chance responding and the initial decrease. Most importantly, the curves are closely matched: At no trial do the pairs of points differ at the .01 level; at only one trial do they differ at the .05 level. This similarity holds despite the fact that the .05 confidence interval (indicated by the shaded band in Figure 7.6–3) is fairly narrow. The conclusion is compelling, therefore, that the relevant dimension is not being sampled by an S when he is faced with a soluble problem which he is not solving.

THE EMPTY SET

The S who does not solve a soluble problem was described above with a general conception: He samples from a finite set of Hs (14, in the particular case considered), and the correct H is outside this set. A basic question for the learning process concerns how S might eventually abandon this incorrect set and turn, at some later point, to sample the correct H. This question is intertwined with a question raised earlier. It was noted above that if S's memory for disqualified Hs is good enough, his set, which contains only incorrect Hs, will soon become empty. What alternatives are open to an S when this happens, when the last remaining H proves to be wrong? Consider a homey example—a person is looking

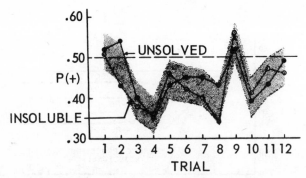

FIGURE 7.6–3 The trial-by-trial proportion correct during unsolved and insoluble problems (the shaded band shows the .05 confidence interval around the pair of points at each trial).

for his car keys. He thinks, "Perhaps I left them in one of my jacket pockets." He opens his closet and checks the pockets of the jackets hanging there (the pockets constitute his H set). Suppose a rapid check of all the pockets reveals no clinking sound of keys (the set goes to zero). One possibility is that he thinks "Did I skip some pockets? Perhaps I should have checked each pocket more carefully." That is, one possibility is that he goes through the set again. A hint that this is happening in the experiment just reported (see Figure 7.6–3) is in the cyclic pattern during the insoluble problems. A perfect processor starts with the full set of Hs at the first trial and reduces the set until, by the third trial, he has eliminated everything but the one H correlated with the (absent) correct H for the first three trials. By the nature of the stimulus constraints, the probability that this H will lead to a correct choice on Trial 4 is zero. The perfect processor selects this H after Trial 3, is told "wrong" at Trial 4, and then has an empty set. If S checks again through the set at this point, one should see a rise in the proportion correct at Trial 5 followed by another minimum a few trials later. The cyclic character of the curves in Figure 7.6–3 suggest that this resurvey of the set might be occasionally occurring.

Another hint that Ss review the H set after it becomes empty comes from an experiment by Erickson (1968), who used four-dimensional stimuli. Erickson presented blocks of three blank trials before each feedback trial as a technique for probing for S's H. He disconfirmed the first H by indicating that the response to the first feedback trial was wrong. Both Erickson (1968) and Levine (1966, 1969) (also cf. Assumption 5, above) showed that Ss do not immediately return this H to the set, where it may be resampled. The H, then, is out of the set. The twist in Erickson's experiment was that this H, for all remaining trials, was made the correct H. Thus, an S might select the large stimulus for the first four trials. After the fourth trial (i.e., the first feedback trial) the E says "wrong." Choice of the large stimulus is then the correct response for all remaining trials.[4] Conditions of the experiment facilitated information processing: not only was there a small number of dimensions, but the stimulus stayed on when feedback was presented, and there was a long intertrial interval (cf. Bourne, Guy, Dodd, & Justesen, 1965, for the effectiveness of these variables). In fact, in a standard control condition, in which feedback was consistent throughout the whole problem, the mean number of feedback trials to criterion was 4.1. In the experimental condition (with the first-trial reversal), 48 of 50 Ss solved the problem. They required on the average only 2.3 feedback trials more than the control condition, approximately the result one might expect if Ss typically reviewed the H set a second time. One reaction, then, when a set goes to zero is to go through it again.

For another reaction let us return to our friend bereft of his car keys. Suppose that he again goes through his jacket pockets for the keys, this time more systematically (i.e., in such a way as to retain in memory that every H was tried and rejected). The set is again empty. What other alternative is open to him? He can leave this set of Hs and look for a new one. He can do this by scanning his memory ("What was I doing the last time I saw those keys?") or the present situation ("Could they be among that clutter of things on my desk?"). That new set may be fairly large ("Maybe they're in one of my pants pockets") or be very small consisting of virtually only the correct H (Of course! I was wearing my raincoat yesterday; they must be in my raincoat pocket"). A parallel within the experimental situation would occur if S, convinced that he is overlooking something, thinks back to E's instructions, in an effort to retrieve some possibly forgotten dimensions.

Another reaction, then, when a set goes to zero is to abandon this set and to look for a new one. It is proposed that this is one important process underlying the shift from nonsolution to solution behavior. The description, while it is probably in keeping with everyday experience, is frankly speculative. Nevertheless, it is sufficiently important to the learning process that it warrants the status of an assumption, along with the five assumptions presented above.

6. Changing of sets (or subsets): The reduction of a set to zero Hs serves as a signal to select a new set. As indicated above, this search for a new set may follow one or more reviews of the old set.

THE INFINITE SET

A mechanism was just provided permitting an S who starts a problem with the wrong H set to eventually solve the problem. That set will go to zero and S, perhaps after one or more reviews of the set, will look for a new one. Suppose the initial incorrect set can never go to zero? Suppose, that is, that S is sampling from a set which is infinitely large yet which does not contain the correct H? According to the theory above, S will never abandon that incorrect set. Only Assumption 6 allows for a change of H set, but it requires that the incorrect set become empty. An S, therefore, sampling from an incorrect but infinite set, will never solve the problem no matter how easy it is, that is, no matter how obvious the S–R and feedback contingencies are.

This implication was first explored by Ress (1965; for a summary see Ress & Levine, 1966). To realize the simplicity of the task employed, consider first the control group: Thirty Ss each received a two-dimensional simultaneous discrimination. They went through a deck containing 115 cards, each card showing one large (2.5 centimeter) and one small (1.3

centimeter) circle. In typical fashion, for half of the cards, the large circle was (randomly) located on the right (or left) side. The S was instructed that he should touch the center of one of the two circles on each card, that E would say "right" or "wrong" after each response, and that he (S) was to try to be right as often as possible. The E said "right" whenever S touched the large circle, "wrong" whenever the small. In short, it was formally identical to the discrimination problem one gives to monkeys in the Wisconsin General Test Apparatus or to rats in the Lashley jumping stand. It is not surprising that these adult humans solved the problem in a mean of three trials.

The experimental Ss received the same task. This was preceded, however, by a series of experiences intended to start the Ss sampling from an infinite and incorrect H set. Sixty Ss each received a series of preliminary problems using decks identical (except for shuffling) to the one for the main problem. The solution to these preliminary problems was always a position sequence. The sequences 2L-2R (two left-side responses followed by two right-side responses), 3L-2R, 1L-4R, 5L-1R, 2L-4R, and 3L-3R were presented.[5] The E announced the correct solution after each of these problems. It was assumed that this series of preliminary problems would fulfill the composition assumption that S was sampling from an infinite set containing Hs dealing only with position sequences.

After the preliminary problems, E announced, as he had prior to each of the preliminaries, "Here is another problem" and presented S the reshuffled deck. This time, of course, the correct H was "touch 'large,'" an H not in the set of position sequences. The Ss were run until they either gave 15 consecutive correct responses or made an error after Trial 100. The results were that these Ss required a mean of 62 trials to solve this problem. Twenty-eight of the 60 Ss did not solve it in 115 trials.

The Ss, incidentally, were clearly motivated to solve these problems, and the feedback ("right" and "wrong") qualified as effective reinforcers. The preceding six sequence problems showed a typical learning set effect. The mean trials to solution went from 65 trials on the first problem to 16 trials on the sixth.

At first glance it appears that the theory is strongly confirmed. The operations employed (i.e., the preliminary problems) for fulfilling the composition assumption that S is sampling from an infinte and incorrect set seemed clearly effective: The Ss required an average of 62 trials to learn a discrimination any self-respecting monkey learns in a few trials. Corroborating testimony comes from postexperimental comments by Ss. Virtually all acknowledged starting the final problem searching for sequence solutions. The results, however, do contain a puzzle for the theory. According to the theory, Ss should not solve at all. If they are sampling from an infinite (and incorrect) set, from a set which does not become empty, then they should never select a new set. Yet more than half of the Ss (32/60) solved the problem, that is, somehow selected a new set containing the correct H.

The puzzle can be resolved in one of two ways: (a) One may look for an additional assumption, postulating some other process by which an H outside the set can be sampled; or (b) one may question whether the composition assumption was fulfilled, whether the preliminary problems really did orient Ss to sample from an *infinite* set of position sequences. A resolution to this puzzle, favoring the second alternative, was suggested in an analysis of sequence structures by Restle (1967). He noted that binary sequence cycles consisting of a single change (true of all the sequence solutions employed by Ress & Levine—cf. above) formed a particular subset of all sequences. The S could code these by what Restle called mandatory rules. More complex sequences, involving several changes in (binary) state within a cycle, required what he called optional rules. His analysis suggested that Ress and Levine trained the Ss with only a subset of sequences, those having short cycles with a single shift within the cycle. This implies that at the final problem the Ss might have held not an infinite set of all possible position sequences, but a finite set of similar and simple sequences. This set, of course, could go to zero. Some Ss might then try a different incorrect H set (e.g., "Maybe it's a more complicated sequence") whereas others might come up with the set containing the correct H (e.g., "Maybe it has something to do with the circle").

The best hunch, then, was that Ress and Levine failed to obtain ideal results because the composition assumption had not been fulfilled. The obvious next step was to repeat the experiment employing more complex sequences. This, accordingly, was done. Two groups of 20 Ss each received six preliminary sequence problems followed by the final test problem. The simple group received the same sequences as those employed by Ress and Levine; the complex group had sequences of varying complexity, the most complex sequence consisting of a cycle of 10 trials with five shifts during the cycle (e.g., LLRLLLRLRR). Except for this variation between the two groups, the task was identical to that employed by Ress and Levine.

Thirteen of 20 Ss in the simple group solved the final problem, thereby replicating the earlier results; in the complex group, however, only 3 of the 20 Ss solved the problem. The difference is significant ($\chi^2 = 8.44, p < .01$). This experiment, then, suggests that the complex sequences produce more successful fulfillment of the composition assumption. Also, this dramatic demonstration of Ss failing to learn the most obvious associations, further validates the H model described above as a description of the learning (and nonlearning) process.

Before considering the results of the complex group in greater detail, an additional experimental variation will be described. In the experiments above, S touched one of two circles. One of these circles (e.g., the larger) was the stimulus entering into the contingencies. One might propose an exceedingly simple reason why S failed to learn: he did not look at these circles. The S might, by this line of reasoning, touch the right or left side of the card without seeing the circles. To put it another way, Spence's (1945) criterion, that an observing response must occur before the data can be considered relevant to any learning theory, may not have been met.

Another experiment, therefore, was undertaken. The primary change from the preceding experiments was the replacement of the two circles on each card by two letters, A and B. Also, every S received the six complex sequences employed with the complex group, above. Two groups of 16 Ss each were run. The touching group, as before, was told to touch one of the two letters; the speaking group was told to indicate each choice by saying one of the two letters. Note two features about the speaking group during the final problem: First, there is no way then they can avoid seeing the stimuli; second, the contingencies are even more simplified. Instead of discrimination learning, this is now the reinforcement paradigm in its simplest form: Whenever S says "A" E says "right"; whenever S says "B" E says "wrong."

There was essentially no difference between the two groups. Four Ss in the touching group and three Ss in the speaking group solved the problem. This result, along with the observation that Ss in the touching group virtually always directed their gaze toward the letters, eliminates any concern that the nonlearning was an artifact of nonstimulation.

Three groups, then (the complex, touching, and speaking), were run in which the composition assumption appeared to be fulfilled. Of a total of 52 Ss, 81% (42 out of 52) did not reach the criterion of 15 successive correct responses within 115 trials. It is possible, of course, that these 42 Ss, though they failed this fairly extreme criterion, may nevertheless have shown some response strengthening. There is, however, no indication of anything but chance ocurrence of the correct response during the 100 trials of the problem. On Trials 91–100, for example, 53% of the responses were correct. Despite a large N (42 Ss $\times$ 10 responses per S), this is not significantly different from 50%. It appears clear that these Ss had not switched to the set containing the correct H.

The remaining 10 Ss did solve the problem. Why these Ss might have been exceptional is suggested by comments made by two of them. One said that the whole experiment had reminded her of Luchins' water-jug experiment, which had recently been reviewed in her course; the other said that he had been looking for a trick—"psychologists always trick you." These comments imply that the preliminary problems did not always succeed in restricting S's H set to position-sequence Hs.

DISCUSSION

Two types of experiments have been presented demonstrating nonlearning. The first experiment showed that an S who had not learned behaved as though the relevant stimuli were literally absent. The second set of experiments, by reducing stimulus complexity to a minimum and by guaranteeing that S observed the relevant stimuli, demonstrated nonlearning in a more dramatic form. Nonlearning was shown also to be not a sporadic occurrence by an occasional S, but rather an outcome of definite problem-solving processes, susceptible to theoretical analysis and to manipulation. According to the analysis, nonlearning can be produced —despite a well-motivated S and consistent S–R feedback contingencies— by making S sample from an H set which does not contain the correct H.

It should be stressed that the theory employed was not ad hoc. A "theory of nonlearning" was not improvised to account for the data. Rather the data conformed to predictions derived from a general theory of hypothesis-testing behavior. The theory had already been employed to account for behavior during blank trials, for the discontinuity in the percentage of correct responses during simple learning, for cue redundancy and cue reversal, etc. The theory was here enlarged to include the concepts of empty and infinite sets, but this broadening followed plausible lines.

This expanded theory and the experimental results have relevance to three other research topics: the effects of random feedback on subsequent discrimination learning, the awareness controversy, and the Einstellung effect.

Random feedback: Levine (1962) demonstrated that the learning of very simple discriminations was clearly retarded if E said "right" or "wrong" randomly for the first few trials. This result was also shown to hold for concept learning by Mandler, Cowan, and Gold (1964) and for complex (6-D) discrimination learning by Holstein and Premack (1965). Levine suggested that some Ss rejected the simple Hs (including the solution) during the random feedback phase and were sampling from another subset (e.g., sequence Hs) well into the discrimination phase. Holstein and Premack made a similar suggestion. Behind these suggestions was the tacit assumption that if Ss were testing Hs from an incorrect set, then they would not learn the correct contingencies. No attempt was made to demonstrate either that random feedback caused S to sample from an incorrect H set or that such a sampling would hinder the subsequent simple learning. The second type of experiment presented above, however, relates directly to the latter assumption. It demonstrated that by setting S to sample Hs from an incorrect set, the learning of a simple contingency was indeed delayed. The operation of random feedback is well viewed, then, as a gross technique for manipulating the sets from which S samples. The resulting retardation in simple learning follows from H theory as outlined above.

The awareness controversy: In recent years several hundreds of Es have challenged or defended the reinforcement principle under the banners of the awareness controversy. Two extreme partisan positions in this controversy may be discerned. One (Dulaney, 1968; Spielberger & DeNike, 1966) is that the reinforcement principle is irrelevant, that only when S becomes "aware" of the contingencies will performance increase. The other (Dixon & Oakes, 1965; Verplank 1962) holds that the response strengthening occurs automatically, that awareness is an irrelevant or, at best, an independent process. Postman and Sassenrath (1961) took up a middle position, as have recently several other theorists (Bandura, 1969; Kanfer, 1968; Krasner, 1967). The view of Postman and Sassenrath is that both reinforcement and awareness contribute to the response-strengthening process, the former weakly but persistently, the latter strongly but rapidly, that is, in a discontinuous way. The results presented above are relevant not only to the extreme views but to this last moderate statement as well. These results demonstrated unequivocally that the reinforcement principle can be completely nullified. Establishing effective contingencies is not a sufficient condition for producing learning, that is, for increasing the probability of the contingent response.

The principle, so long a bastion of learning theory, may be defended in two ways. Silver, Saltz, and Modigliani (1970) suggest that learning via H testing and learning automatically via reinforcement may both occur but are mutually exclusive processes. According to this view, the procedures of the present experiments evoke the H-testing mechanism and thereby switch off automatic strengthening. These experiments, of course, cannot negate this possibility. Nor can any laboratory experiments which S might interpret as a problem-solving task. It may be, however, that the Silver et al. formulation will provide the ultimate resolution of the controversy.

The second defense of the principle comes through redefining the response. This is most easily seen in the second set of experiments. One may argue that because of the preliminary problems, saying "A" was no longer the functional response. Rather, the functional response, that is, that which was affected by the reinforcement, was S's covert formulation of a position sequence. These covert formulations were so strengthened in the preliminary problems that they did not extinguish over the 100 trials of the test problem. Far from rebutting this defense; one need only note that it is a major conversion to H theory. Indeed, H theory may be regarded as the theory of these covert formulations. In the early stages of the development of H theory, Levine (1959, 1963) suggested that its most important feature was the redefinition of the response—"The H, rather than the specific choice response on a particular trial, is regarded as the dependent variable, i.e., as the unit of behavior affected by the reinforcements [Levine, 1963, p. 270]". Subsequently, H theory has had considerable refinement (e.g., the all-or-none character of H strengthening and weakening, the changes in strength of several Hs simultaneously, the encoding mode—visual and verbal—of information, etc.), but the redefinition of the response remains the foundation on which the theory has been built.

Einstellung: The reader, like one S mentioned above, has undoubtedly noticed the similarity of the second set of experiments to the Einstellung experiment (cf. Luchins, 1942). In this experiment also, S has preliminary experiences which render him functionally blind to a subsequent simple solution. For example, Luchins presented Ss with a series of paper-and-pencil maze problems. For the first nine problems, S was given a picture of a maze consisting of both a direct straight path leading from the start toward the goal box and other long circuitous paths. During these problems, the straight path always was blocked, that is, visibly ended as a cul-de-sac just before the goal box. One of the circuitous paths leading off from the right of the start box always eventually led to the goal. On the tenth problem, the direct path was connected to the goal. Nevertheless, the Ss typically chose the roundabout alley leading off from the right. In H terms, the analysis is clear: the preliminary problems led S to sample Hs dealing with alleys off to the right. Until this set is exhausted, the S is insensitive to direct central alleys. This theory, incidentally, has an obvious implication not yet tested within the older Einstellung tradition. The theory implies that the larger the incorrect H set, the longer it takes that set to become empty, and the more durably is S functionally blind to the simple solution. This, in turn, implies that for the critical (tenth) maze, the larger the number of incorrect right-hand circuitous paths, the longer will S fail to see the correct direct path.

For decades the Einstellung effect has been treated in isolation from learning theory, primarily because that theory was based on conditioning principles. This deficiency vanishes when the effect is viewed from the perspective of H theory. The Einstellung-like results in the second set of experiments were predicted from the basic principles of H testing. By the straightforward development of H theory, one suddenly realized that the theory encompassed one form, at least, of the Einstellung effect: The S appears functionally blind as long as he is sampling from an incorrect H set. This easy, natural treatment of a hitherto isolated phenomenon further attests, along with the confirmed predictions, to the validity of the H model described above.

NOTES

1. More typically, *E* says "right" only to certain responses in the presence of certain stimuli. For example, *E* may say "right" to *S*'s response "alpha" only if triangles are part of the stimulus complex. Otherwise he says "right" only to the response "beta." While it is always more accurate to speak of *E*'s feedback as contingent on certain responses *in the presence of certain stimuli*, the italicized phrase will generally be omitted. It should, however, be understood as given throughout.
2. For a more complete review of this experiment, see Glassman (1970).
3. A representative derivation of this type of theoretical curve may be found in Levine, Yoder, Kleinberg, and Rosenberg (1968).
4. This is a loose parallel to Erickson's procedure. He, in fact, used a successive discrimination procedure. The description correctly conveys the relevant features, however, without laboring over the irrelevant differences.
5. Two other variables were manipulated: The Ss had either three or six preliminary problems; the sizes of the circles differed (2.5 vs. 1.3 centimeters and 2.5 vs. 2.0 centimeters). These variables had no significant effects. The data are combined here.

REFERENCES

Bandura, A. *Principles of behavior modification.* New York: Holt, Rinehart & Winston, 1969.

Bourne, J. E., Jr., Guy, D. E., Dodd, D. H., & Justesen, D. R. Concept identification: The effects of varying length and informational components of the intertrial interval. *Journal of Experimental Psychology,* 1965, 69, 624–629.

Bruner, J. S., Goodnow, J. J., & Austin, G. A. *A study of thinking.* New York: Wiley, 1965.

Dixon, P. W., & Oakes, S. F. Effects of intertrial activity on the relationship between awareness and verbal operant conditioning. *Journal of Experimental Psychology,* 1965, 69, 152–157.

Dulaney, D. E., Jr. Hypotheses and habits in verbal "operant conditioning." *Journal of Abnormal and Social Psychology,* 1961, 63, 251–263.

Dulaney, D. E., Jr. Awareness, rules, and propositional control: A confrontation with S–R behavior theory. In T. R. Dixon & D. L. Horton (Eds.), *Verbal behavior and general behavior theory.* Englewood Cliffs, N. J.: Prentice-Hall, 1968.

Erickson, J. R. Hypothesis sampling in concept identification. *Journal of Experimental Psychology,* 1968, 6, 12–18.

Frankel, F., Levine, M., & Karpf, D. Human discrimination learning: A test of the blank-trials assumption. *Journal of Experimental Psychology,* 1970, 85, 342–348.

Glassman, W. E. Unsolved- and insoluble-problem behavior. Unpublished master's thesis, State University of New York at Stony Brook, 1970.

Gregg, L. W., & Simon, H. A. Process models and stochastic theories of simple concept formation. *Journal of Mathematical Psychology,* 1967, 4, 246–276.

Holstein, S. B., & Premack, D. On the different effects of random reinforcement and presolution reversal on human concept identification. *Journal of Experimental Psychology,* 1965, 70, 335–337.

Kanfer, F. H. Verbal conditioning: A review of its current status. In T. R. Dixon & D. L. Horton (Eds.), *Verbal behavior and general behavior theory.* Englewood Cliffs, N. J.: Prentice-Hall, 1968.

Krasner, L. Verbal operant conditioning and awareness. In K. Salzinger & S. Salzinger (Eds.), *Research in verbal behavior and some neurophysiological implications*. New York: Academic Press, 1967.

Levine, M. A model of hypothesis behavior in discrimination learning set. *Psychological Review*, 1959, 66, 353–366.

Levine, M. Cue neutralization: The effects of random reinforcements upon discrimination learning. *Journal of Experimental Psychology*, 1962, 63, 438–443.

Levine, M. Mediating processes in humans at the outset of discriminating learning. *Psychological Review*, 1963, 70, 254–276.

Levine, M. Hypothesis behavior by humans during discrimination learning. *Journal of Experimental Psychology*, 1966, 71, 331–338.

Levine, M. Neo-noncontinuity theory. In G. H. Bower & J. T. Spence (Eds.), *The psychology of learning and motivation*. New York: Academic Press, 1969.

Levine, M., Miller, P., & Steinmeyer, C. H. The none-to-all theorem of human discrimination learning. *Journal of Experimental Psychology*, 1967, 73, 568–573.

Levine, M., Yoder, R. M., Kleinberg, J., & Rosenberg, J. The presolution paradox in discrimination learning. *Journal of Experimental Psychology*, 1968, 77, 602–608.

Luchins, A. S. Mechanization in problem solving: The effect of *Einstellung*. *Psychological Monographs*, 1942, 54 (6, Whole No. 248).

Mandler, G., Cowan, P. A., & Gold, C. Concept learning and probability matching. *Journal of Experimental Psychology*, 1964, 67, 514–522.

Postman, L., & Sassenrath, J. The automatic action of verbal rewards and punishments. *Journal of General Psychology*, 1961, 65, 109–136.

Ress, F. C. The effect of previous sequence problems on simple discrimination learning. Unpublished master's thesis, Indiana University, 1965.

Ress, F. C., & Levine, M. Einstellung during simple discrimination learning. *Psychonomic Science*, 1966, 4, 77–78.

Restle, F. The selection of strategies in cue learning. *Psychological Review*, 1962, 69, 329–343.

Restle, F. Grammatical analysis of the prediction of binary events. *Journal of Verbal Learning and Verbal Behavior*, 1967, 6, 17–25.

Restle, F., & Emmerich, D. Memory in concept identification: Effects of giving several problems concurrently. *Journal of Experimental Psychology*, 1966, 71, 794–799.

Silver, D. S., Salz, E., & Modigliani, V. Awareness and hypothesis testing in concept and operant learning. *Journal of Experimental Psychology*, 1970, 84, 198–203.

Spence, K. W. An experimental test of the continuity and noncontinuity theories of discrimination learning. *Journal of Experimental Psychology*, 1945, 35, 253–266.

Spielberger, C. D., & DeNike, L. D. Descriptive behaviorism versus cognitive theory in verbal operant conditioning. *Psychological Review*, 1966, 73, 306–326.

Trabasso, T., & Bower, G. H. Presolution dimensional shifts in concept identification: A test of the sampling with replacement axiom in all-or-none models. *Journal of Mathematical Psychology*, 1966, 3, 163–173.

Trabasso, T., & Bower, G. H. *Attention in learning*. New York: Wiley, 1968.

Verplank, W. S. Unaware of where's awareness: Some verbal operants—notates, monents, and notants. In C. W. Eriksen (Ed.), *Behavior and awareness*. Durham, N. C.: Duke University Press, 1962.

Eight
The Role
of Reinforcement

In the previous two chapters we have traced the major battles in a long and sometimes confusing war over the nature of learning. On the one hand, S-R theorists argued that learning was fundamentally a simple process based on associations between stimuli and responses. Arrayed against them were cognitive theorists, contemptuous of the simple-minded views of their opponents, convinced that learning was "more complex (and) patterned" than was dreamed of in their associational philosophy. But as the two sides fought over The Stimulus and then again over The Response, a curious thing began to happen. At first, their positions were clearly separated, and each battle ended decisively. Attention, and Learning without Responding, for example, appeared to be clear victories for a cognitive approach to learning. As each controversy was resolved, however, the theorists in both camps modified their positions, and with each successive encounter their strategies grew not only more sophisticated but more similar. This trend was accentuated by the advent of technological warfare, as both sides began to move from verbal formulations to more precise mathematical equations. It became very difficult indeed to say whether a particular equation seemed to more accurately reflect a cognitive or an S-R orientation!

Unlike real war, however, these theoretical controversies resulted not in the wholesale destruction of the combatants (though there was some damage to reputations) but in a healthy increase in the sophistication and power of both theories. In this chapter we will trace this development in the context of still one more controversy, that over Reinforcement. We know that reinforcement is effective—the probability of the reinforced response usually does increase—but why? If we make a child's allowance contingent on making his bed, for example, why does the frequency of this response increase? One possible explanation is *associative*, that is, that reinforcement directly strengthens the association between the sight of an unmade bed and the response of bed-making. According to this explanation learning occurs only if there is a subsequent reinforcer, so that like a coin-operated Xerox machine the brain's copying mechanism is activated only when a reinforcer is presented. Alternatively, we might assume that learning is a continuous process, with the brain constantly noticing and storing environmental relationships, and that reinforcement affects not the learning of a response but only its performance. Reinforcement in this view acts to *motivate* a subject, acting like hunger or thirst to increase the vigor of certain behaviors. And finally, we can take our machine metaphor even more seriously, and talk of the brain's *information-processing* capacities. In this view the brain is essentially a highly sophisticated computer, performing a complex sequence of operations on the information fed into it. The presentation of a reinforcer is simply one more bit of information, one more fact about the problem, to be used in calculating the optimal response.

We have, then, three different views of the mechanisms involved in reinforcement or, adopting the cautious strategy suggested by our earlier analyses, three views that *sound* different. In this chapter we will consider each of these interpretations in turn, and try to evaluate how reinforcement affects behavior.

Reinforcement Theory

According to reinforcement theory, presentation of a reinforcer directly triggers the learning process, resulting in an incease in the association between the preceding stimulus and response. Furthermore, at least in its strong form, reinforcement theory says that *all* learning is due to reinforcement, or at least all forms of classical and operant conditioning. But how could this be? What is the reinforcer in classical eyelid conditioning, for example, or in punishment? At first it may seem implausible or even bizarre to attribute learning in these situations to reinforcement, but in fact careful analysis *does* reveal possible sources of reinforcement in both these cases. Consider, for example, a rat who has been trained to press a bar to obtain food. Why does making electric shock contingent on that response result in its suppression? Perhaps because a painful shock directly suppresses behavior, but alternatively perhaps because the *termination* of shock acts as a reinforcer! The termination of shock might be expected to be reinforcing in much the same way as the termination of hunger, and in fact rats will learn to run down an alley to terminate shock just as readily as to obtain food, a procedure called *escape* training. Since in punishment situations shock termination often follows responses that are incompatible with bar-pressing (for example, the shock is turned off when the rat releases rather than presses the bar), these incompatible responses will gradually become stronger than bar-pressing and therefore replace it. The effects of punishment, then, may be due not to any direct suppression of the punished response, but rather to the reinforcement of some incompatible response.

This analysis becomes even more powerful if we take into account a second source of reinforcement, the reduction of conditioned fear. We saw in Chapter 2 that if a stimulus is paired with an aversive event such as shock, then that stimulus may itself become aversive, eliciting strong fear responses. If we now invoke the learning theorist's favorite weapon, proprioceptive feedback, we can predict that every time the rat begins to press the bar he will produce a proprioceptive stimulus which in turn will be followed by shock. This stimulus should therefore become aversive and now *its* termination should be reinforcing. If the rat stops moving just as he begins to bar-press, therefore, by stopping he will eliminate the aversive feedback from the response, and stopping should therefore be reinforced by the reduction in conditioned fear (see Dinsmoor, 1954).

This analysis suggests that punishment should affect not the *initiation* of a punished response but only its termination, so that subjects may start to make a punished response but should then stop before they complete it. In an experiment by Millenson and Macmillan (1972), for example, rats were first trained to hold down a bar for ten seconds in order to earn food, and only after this response was well established was punishment introduced. Punishment resulted in the nearly total elimination of responding as measured by successful completions, but the rate of response initiation—pressing the bar down and holding it for one or two seconds—remained unchanged, exactly as predicted by reinforcement theory. You may have experienced the same phenomenon if as a child you were ever punished for stealing a cookie or, to use a somewhat more adult example, cheating on an exam. The next time you tried that response you may have started out confidently—casually walking into the kitchen and approaching the cookie jar, for example—but the closer you came to the goal, the more anxious you became, until eventually you may have come to a complete halt, immobilized between advance and retreat. For reinforcement theorists the explanation is simple: the stimuli nearer to the goal elicited more fear, and thus the reinforcement for incompatible behavior was progressively greater as you came closer to the goal.

In the hands of an ingenious theorist, then, reinforcement is an extremely powerful principle, able to explain behavior in a variety of situations that at first appear to contain no possible source of reinforcement. Problems have arisen, however, in trying to demonstrate that these explanations are not only plausible but correct. It is one thing to say that a reinforcer *might* have been present; it is another to demonstrate that it really was. Arguments over the role of reinforcement have erupted in a variety of areas (e.g., Perkins, 1968; Herrnstein, 1969) but perhaps the most influential controversy has been over *latent learning*. The original issue was simple: is reinforcement really necessary for learning? To find out, Blodgett (Article 8.1) trained two groups of rats to run through a maze, but provided food in the goal box only for the control group. Reinforcement theory therefore predicts that only the control group should learn, and indeed only this group showed any improvement during the training phase. The failure of the experimental group to *perform* the correct response, however, did not necessarily prove that they hadn't learned it. Learning might have been equal in both groups, but the experimental group might not have selected the shorter path to the goal because of a lack of any motivation to do so. In the crucial test phase, therefore, Blodgett also introduced reward for the experimental group. If the experimental subjects had already learned the correct path during training, then they should immediately begin to take it once reward was contingent on their performance. If reinforcement is necessary for learning, on the other hand, these reward trials should provide their first opportunity to learn the correct path, and their perfomance should follow the same gradual acquisition curve initially shown by the control subjects. Reinforcement theory, then, predicts gradual learning after the introduction of reward, while a motivational interpretation predicts an immediate change to optimal performance. The results were that the experimental subjects switched almost immediately to the correct path, suggesting that they had learned the correct path during training, but that this learning had remained *latent* until food was introduced. Reinforcement, in other words, is not necessary for learning a response but only for its performance.

But is this evidence conclusive? Can we be sure that no reinforcers were present during training? It is possible, after all, that the rat was reinforced by satisfaction of an exploratory drive, or by his eventual removal from the confining maze apparatus, and there is plausible evidence from other situations that events such as these *can* act as reinforcers (see Fowler, 1971). The counterargument, of course, is that the fact that they can act as reinforcers does not necessarily mean that they did so in Blodgett's situation. If reinforcement really was present, why didn't the performance of the experimental group improve during the training phase? And even if it had, if running in a maze produces sensory reinforcement, then what value is the concept of reinforcement in predicting whether a response will or will not occur?

Arguments like these are very difficult to resolve empirically—how can one ever prove that a reinforcer was *not* present—but in recent years psychologists seem to have drifted away from a strong version of reinforcement theory. Particularly when we examine human behavior, it is difficult to believe that all learning is due to reinforcement. Children, for example, are very likely to remember and then imitate the actions of certain models, particularly parents, but it is difficult in many cases to identify any external reinforcement for this behavior (see Bandura, 1971). More generally, there is the phenomenon of *perceptual learning*, in which our ability to discriminate among stimuli seems to improve simply as a result of exposure to them. Subjects in psychophysical experiments rapidly improve in their ability to hear a very soft tone, or to discriminate between two similar tones, and you may have experienced similar improvement with experience in your ability to recognize fine wines or the characteristic sounds of different rock groups (see Gibson, 1969). And finally, consider your memory for recent events. Was there some reinforcer that followed your reading of the previous words which explains your ability to remember them? It is impossible to prove in such cases that there was no reinforcer (for example, the novelty of the words might have been reinforcing), but as the difficulty of demonstrating such reinforcers has become more apparent, support for a strong version of reinforcement theory has correspondingly weakened (see Glaser, 1971).

Incentive Motivation

Reinforcement may sometimes enhance learning, but the evidence from latent learning suggests that its more important role is in determining performance. Promising a child a dollar for solving a math problem, for example, seems likely to affect not his ability to solve the problem but his willingness to work at it. The question remains, however, as to why reinforcement has this effect. How does reinforcement determine what responses will be performed? One explanation is based on the notion of *incentive motivation*. In our section on motivation (see Chapter 4) we discussed how a drive might enhance or energize performance. Rats, for example, run down an alley leading to food much faster after 22 hours of food deprivation than after 2. Furthermore, and this is one of the crucial defining characteristics of a drive, its energizing effects are not specific to one response but rather affect a broad class of behaviors. Hull (1943), for example, believed that a drive such as hunger increased the vigor of *all* behavior, whether or not it was related to food. Alternatively, a drive may be assumed to energize only those responses related to its satisfaction, so that hunger would motivate all food-seeking responses but not those related to water. In either case, however, a drive is assumed to facilitate some broad class of behavior, not just a single response.

The concept of incentive motivation is similar to that of motivation based on a drive, except that it emphasizes *learned* motives acquired through a process of classical conditioning. Specifically, whenever a reinforcer is presented it is assumed to result in the conditioning of a motivational state to whatever stimuli were present. On subsequent trials these stimuli then elicit the motivational state, and as a result they energize responding. When a bell is paired wih food, for example, incentive theory assumes that it elicits not only a specific response such as salivation but a general motivational state which we may call, after Mowrer (1960), *hope*. As a result, the bell will elicit hope on subsequent trials, and hope will act in much the same way as hunger to increase the vigor of responding.

Incentive theory, then, emphasizes the role of reinforcement in establishing motivational states. To understand how these motivational states mediate the effect of reinforcement on performance, imagine a latent learning experiment run in a straight alley. For the first ten trials the subject is simply removed from the alley after he reaches the goal box, but starting on the eleventh trial he is given food there. According to incentive theory, the presentation of food in the goal box results in the conditioning of hope to the goal box stimuli, and this motivational state then generalizes to the similar cues of the start box. When the rat is returned to the start box on the next trial, therefore, these cues should elicit hope, and the rat should run down the alley faster. The start box cues, in other words, would not specifically elicit running, but rather would elicit a general motivational state that would energize whatever response was most likely in that situation.

One interesting implication of this analysis is that a reinforcer should be able to strengthen a response without ever following it! In latent learning, for example, running normally increases after it is followed by food, but according to incentive theory the major effect of food is not in strengthening the preceding S-R association, but in conditioning hope to the goal box and, via generalization, to the start box. Even if the rat did not run on reward trials, therefore, but was instead placed directly into the goal box, hope should still be conditioned and running should still be enhanced on subsequent trials, and exactly this result has been obtained (Gonzalez and Shepp, 1965; Senkowski, Porter, and Madison, 1968).

Just as the presentation of food is assumed to result in the conditioning of hope, the presentation of an aversive event is assumed to result in the conditioning of the motivational state of fear. A stimulus paired with shock, therefore, should also acquire motivational properties, and should increase the vigor of responses in its presence. Rescorla and LoLordo (1965) tested this prediction in an avoidance experiment in which dogs were trained to jump over a barrier in order to avoid electric shock. Classical conditioning trials were then given in which a tone was paired with the shock, and then the tone was presented during a subsequent session in which the dogs were again responding in the avoidance apparatus. Presentation of the tone caused a significant increase in avoidance responding, despite the fact that the dogs were already avoiding nearly all the programmed shocks.

It might be argued, however, that the pairings of tone and shock in this experiment resulted not in the conditioning of a general fear state but rather of a particular motor response, and it was this motor response which facilitated responding in the avoidance test. For example, during the tone-shock pairings the dogs might have learned to jump in the air to minimize the shock delivered through the grid floor, and it might have been this jumping response to the tone which facilitated leaping over the barrier in the avoidance test. To eliminate this possibility, Overmeir, Bull, and Pack (Article 8.2) ran a transfer experiment employing two major groups, each trained to press a bar in the presence of a tone. For one group pressing produced food, while for the other group it avoided shock. At the end of training both groups were transferred to a shuttle-box avoidance task, in which they had to cross from one side of the box to the other to avoid shock. When behavior in this second stage had stabilized, the tone used in the first stage was introduced. If all that was learned during tone-shock conditioning trials was a specific motor response, then the two groups should show equivalent transfer, since they had both learned the same bar-pressing response during training. In testing, however, presentation of the tone produced a significant increase in avoidance responding for the shock group, but a significant decrease for the food group. The motivational properties of the tone, therefore, cannot be attributed simply to the specific response learned during training, but rather depend on the incentive that the tone was associated with.

This evidence suggests that a stimulus associated with food or shock does acquire motivational properties which then allow it to modify responding. Exactly how incentive motivation controls responding, however, is not well understood. Why, for example, does a stimulus associated with food acquire the capacity to *reduce* avoidance behavior?

If pairing a stimulus with food gives it motivational properties, one would think that it should energize or *increase* avoidance behavior. We can explain this seeming paradox, however, if we assume that: (1) Fear and hope each affect only a particular class of responses (for example, fear affects only avoidance responses, hope only food responses), and (2) Fear and hope are mutually incompatible. We have already considered the possibility that motivational states are specific in our discussion of drive (for example, that hunger motivates only food-seeking responses), and we have also encountered the concept of motivational incompatibility in our discussion of systematic desensitization. There it was relaxation that was assumed to be incompatible with fear, but it is only a small step to extend that account to the relationship between hope and fear. It seems reasonable to assume, therefore, that a stimulus eliciting hope might simultaneously reduce a subject's fear, and insofar as avoidance behavior is specifically motivated by fear it would also reduce avoidance responding. If this analysis were correct, however, then we should also expect the converse result: fear should reduce hope, and thus a stimulus previously paired with shock should reduce responding for food. This result has in fact been obtained (e.g., Estes and Skinner, 1941), lending some support to this version of incentive theory (see also Rescorla and Solomon, 1967).

A more serious problem for incentive theory is how incentive motivation selectively strengthens the response that was reinforced. We have suggested that incentive motivation "energizes" whatever response occurs in its presence, with the initial occurrence of that response presumably depending on the associative strengths of the stimuli presented. This approach works reasonably well in situations involving a single response, such as a straight alley where running is the dominant behavior. Reinforcement in this situation is assumed to condition motivational properties to the start-box cues, and these cues then increase the vigor of the running response. The picture is far less clear, however, in choice situations where a variety of responses are possible. How, for example, does the introduction of reward in Blodgett's latent learning experiment uniquely increase the probability of the *correct* response? Incentive motivation clearly predicts increased vigor of responding, but why is the correct response enhanced more than the incorrect response? Explanations of choice behavior have been offered for some situations (e.g., Hull, 1952) but they have generally been so awkward and cumbersome that they have rarely been used by any save the theorists who proposed them. Incentive motivation, then, has proven an extremely useful concept in suggesting that reinforcement may result in the conditioning of general motivational states, but somewhat less successful in explaining the effects of these states on behavior.

Information Processing

Reinforcement theorists assumed that reinforcement strengthened the association between a stimulus and a particular response, and that all learning was due to reinforcement. Demonstrations of latent learning, however, were a serious source of embarrassment to this position, suggesting that reinforcement was *not* necessary for learning but only for performance. Faced with this evidence, reinforcement theorists like Hull and Spence began to modify their positions, shifting from an associative to a motivational interpretation of the effects of reinforcement. These interpretations, however, are not necessarily incompatible: the presentation of reward could result in both the reinforcement of a specific S-R association and also the classical conditioning of a general motivational state. In fact, *two-process* theorists have argued that *both* processes must be assumed if we are to explain the effects of rewards. Our explanation of punishment, for example, was really a two-process theory: Fear was developed through a process of *classical conditioning*, and response termination was then *reinforced* by a reduction in this learned fear.

In addition to these associative and motivational interpretations of reward, a third approach is based on the concept of *information processing*. In this outgrowth of cognitive theory, the brain is viewed as a sophisticated computer, and its functions are described and analyzed in the terminology of computer programming. Information processing thus represents a general approach rather than a specific theory of behavior, but its perspective is sometimes very different from that of reinforcement or incentive theory. The basic task of the brain is seen as processing information; the brain must first perceive or *code* its stimulus input, and then memorize or *store* it until it is needed. What response will be made depends upon the brain's *decision processes*, and how they analyze and interpret the available input. Reinforcement, in this view, is just one more stimulus input to the brain, providing information about the external environment and thereby aiding decision making.

One experiment illustrative of this view was reported by Buchwald (Article 8.3). He trained human subjects on a *paired-associate* task in which they were given a series of words as stimuli and to each word they had to respond with a number. If they gave the correct response the experimenter immediately said "Right," whereas if they gave an incorrect response he said "Wrong." The results of the experiment were hardly surprising: The frequency of correct responses steadily increased over trials.

The explanation according to reinforcement theory was that "Right" was a secondary reinforcer, so that its presentation was strengthening the association between the verbal stimulus and the correct response. "Wrong," on the other hand, was a secondary punisher, so that it weakened preceding associations. Buchwald's analysis of this situation, however, was rather different. According to Buchwald the word "Right" does not facilitate memorization, *but is itself an event that must be remembered.* Confronted by the stimulus "Cat," for example, the subject might respond with the number "3," and then be told "Right" by the experimenter. In order to be correct on the next trial he must then remember not only his response but its outcome: He may make an error if he forgets his prior response *or* if he remembers the response but forgets whether or not it was correct. The sequence "Cat-3" is remembered equally well whether the experimenter says "Right" or "Wrong"; these outcomes affect not learning, but the subject's subsequent decision whether to repeat the response. Buchwald's explanation is therefore again a performance theory, but instead of assuming some general motivational mechanism such as hope or fear he simply assumes that the subject will behave rationally and repeat whatever response led to a desirable goal (in this case, being correct).

To distinguish between the reinforcing and informative effects of "Right," Buchwald introduced a condition in which the outcome of a particular trial was not revealed until just before the *following* trial. According to reinforcement theory, delaying reinforcement in this way should severely impair the learning of the S-R sequence, but Buchwald predicted that it would actually enhance performance! A subject can make an error if he forgets his response or its outcome, but by delaying the outcome we ensure that it will not be forgotten. Subjects in the Delayed Outcome condition, therefore, need to remember only their response, and their performance should be facilitated relative to the control subjects who must remember both their response and its outcome. This prediction was confirmed, as performance was significantly better when the trial outcome was delayed (see also Buchwald, 1969). "Right" or "Wrong," then, seem to provide information which guides a subject's performance, but do not directly affect his memory for preceding events.

A somewhat similar approach has been taken by Leon Kamin (Article 8.4) to explain the results of classical conditioning. According to Kamin, the presentation of an unconditioned stimulus (US) does not automatically produce conditioning, but rather initiates an active search through memory in an attempt to identify cues that might have predicted the US. Furthermore, this active search through memory does not occur on every trial, but only on those when the US is unexpected. Once the subject learns that the CS predicts the US, its occurrence is no longer surprising, and therefore the subject devotes no more of his limited processing capacity to searching for predictive cues. After the initial conditioning trials, therefore, it is as if the learning mechanism were shut off, and stimuli introduced after this point should not be conditioned. To test this prediction, Kamin first paired a noise with shock, and then after conditioning was well established he presented the shock with a light as well as the noise. Later test trials with the light indicated that no conditioning had occurred. Kamin called this effect *blocking*, since conditioning to the light was apparently blocked by the previous conditioning to the noise. Whether conditioning occurs, therefore, seems to depend on whether the occurrence of the US is surprising or, in information terminology, whether it provides information. Kamin's approach differs from Buchwald's, however, in that he assumes an effect on learning as well as on performance. The effects of the US are now phrased in terms of initiating a memory search rather than directly strengthening an association, but the effect in both cases is on learning, and Kamin's analysis provides an interesting bridge between cognitive and reinforcement theories of learning (see also Rescorla and Wagner, 1972).

We have, then, three rather different interpretations of rewards: as reinforcers, as motivators, and as sources of information. It would be a mistake, however, to view these different approaches as mutually exclusive. In some situations a reward may simply give us information that we then use rationally in making decisions. In other situations, however, it may also elicit strong emotional reactions of hope or fear and these may lead our behavior in directions that are not necessarily quite so "rational" (for example, the use of alcohol or drugs to alleviate the anxiety produced by school or work). Finally, in some situations reinforcement does seem to function in the way envisioned by reinforcement theory, automatically strengthening the connection between certain stimuli and responses. Hefferline, Keenan, and Harford (1959) exposed human subjects to periodic bursts of static superimposed over music, but allowed their subjects to prevent the static by moving an invisible small muscle in their thumb (its occurrence was detected through electrodes). Subjects later reported that they had not noticed any contingency between their own behavior and the static, and were also unaware of having moved their thumb, but nevertheless their rate of muscle twitching increased significantly whenever the avoidance contingency was in effect (but see also Spielberger and DeNike, 1966; Rosenfeld and Baer, 1969).

Predicting the effects of reinforcement, then, is not as simple as it may at first appear. Reinforcement is clearly a powerful procedure for modifying behavior, and we are usually on safe ground when we predict that making a reinforcer contingent on a response will increase the probability of that response (but see the following chapter). If we try to specify how its effects are mediated, however, or predict its consequences in other situations, then its "simple" effects quickly prove elusive. To take just one example, the effects of a reward on behavior may depend heavily on the balance between its reinforcing and motivating properties. A child of low motivation promised a reward for an "A" in school may do significantly better, but promising that same reward to a child already highly motivated might have no effect, or might even injure his performance by increasing his motivational level to such an extreme that it becomes paralyzing. Questions abut the mechanisms of reinforcement, then, are not simply idle speculation, and hopefully as we gain a better understanding of the principles involved our ability to use reinforcement wisely will show a corresponding increase.

8.1 THE EFFECT OF THE INTRODUCTION OF REWARD UPON THE MAZE PERFORMANCE OF RATS*

Hugh Carlton Blodgett

PROBLEM

The purpose of this investigation was to study the efficiency of units of practice when unaccompanied by reward. The method devised was that of running two groups of rats through the maze: an *experimental group* which received no reward during the first part of learning, but which suddenly had reward introduced in the latter part of learning, and a *control group* which received reward throughout the whole of learning. The answer to the question as to the efficiency of non-reward units of practice was sought in a comparison of the learning curve of the experimental group (both before and after the introduction of reward) with that of the control group.

LITERATURE

Most of the previous experimental work on rewards and their relation to learning has been concerned with a comparison of the effectiveness of different incentives as such. The incentives have been sometimes different in quality, as food and escape, and sometimes the same in quality, as two kinds of food, or two strengths of induction shock.

In addition to the general experiments indicating different strengths of reward without much attempt to analyze further what really may be involved, there are three experiments or parts of experiments strictly germane to our present study.

Lashley (1918), in a maze experiment upon distribution of practice, throws some light upon our problem. There were only 25 rats in all, divided into four groups: group A was allowed to run about in the maze for 20 minutes the day before the first run. During training, this group was given reward at the end of the run. Group B was a control, run once a day with the incentive of food; Group C was run the same as A but was not allowed to correct errors; and group D was run with the incen-

* *University of California Publications in Psychology*, 1932, 4, 113–134. Originally published by the University of California Press; reprinted by permission of the Regents of the University of California. Used in excerpted form. This paper is an abridgment of a report entitled "The Relation of Reward to Animal Learning" submitted in partial fulfillment of the requirements for the Ph.D. degree in the Department of Psychology of the University of California and deposited in the Library of the University of California, May, 1925.

tive of food screened in the food box. The quickest learning was made by group A, the group which explored the maze for 20 minutes before the first run. The record of the control group, group B, was next best, group C was third, and group D, last.

Szymanski (1918) has published a series of articles upon the learning of maze habits with various kinds of reward. One of his experiments is closely related to our problem. Three rats were run through a maze to their home cage in which food had been placed. The rats were not hungry. At the end of 61 trials there was no reduction in time and error scores. Then the condition of experiment was changed so that the rats were run when they were hungry. They ran the maze perfectly in one or two trials.

Simmons (1924), in an article on relative effectiveness of various incentives, ran a group of 10 animals under conditions which she designated as delayed incentive. This group was run for five days without incentive. At the beginning and the end of the sixth trial, the animals were given a taste of food, such as was given the control group. In comparing the learning curves for this group and the control group, Simmons unfortunately combined the scores of her rats in groups of five days each. It is impossible, therefore, to determine the precise nature of the difference in the time and error scores for the two groups immediately after the incentive was given to the delayed-incentive group on the sixth day. This can be made clear by an analysis of the error curves given in her monograph.

As will be seen from the curve (fig. 8.1–1), the mean number of errors during the first five days, for the delayed group, was approximately 28 against an approximate 10 for the control group.

Day 6, which is averaged with four following days, was without incentive. As a result, the second point on the curve is a composite of the scores of one run which was made before incentive was introduced at the end of the run, and four runs which were made after incentive had been introduced. Obviously this procedure masks any sudden change on the run following the first reward.

Simmons then compared the total number of trials required by the control group and by the delayed-incentive group to reach the learning criterion, the total number of errors for the groups, and the total amount of time. She found that the delayed-incentive group required fewer runs but that the error score and the time score were greater. This is because the errors and time scores made during the first six runs are figured in the total. She then made the same comparisons, leaving out the first five runs. Again she found the same results. This time, however, the superiority of the control group, in time and error scores, was less, because only one non-reward run (the sixth) was figured in the total. Finally, she compared trials, time, and errors, leaving out of account the first eight runs. In this

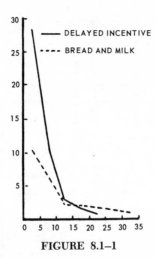

FIGURE 8.1–1

case the delayed-incentive group reached the learning criterion in fewer trials, and made fewer errors and shorter times. This shows that a very marked change in time scores and error scores must have taken place in the delayed-incentive group between the fifth run and the eighth run. And one may assume that this change took place on the seventh run, after reward had been given at the end of the sixth run.

Attention should also be called to the fact that comparisons of scores for the latter part of the learning periods of the control group and the delayed-incentive group contain a spurious feature, namely, that practice for the two groups is not constant because of the much greater number of retracings made by the delayed incentive group during the non-reward period. And so the better final scores of the delayed-incentive group may be due to a different practice effect in the first six runs.

MATERIALS AND METHODS

Mazes

[Two] mazes, A and B were used. Ground plans are shown in figures 8.1–2 and 8.1–3. . . . Maze A and maze B had ordinary blinds.

All three mazes contained a feature not hitherto used in mazes. At each choice point, doors were installed which could be closed behind the animal. These doors were hinged at the top and, when open, lay along the top of the alley. They prevented retracings from one section of the maze to another, they were noiseless, and they caused no excitement in the animals. Their positions in the mazes are shown by the dotted lines, D. The value of this feature is fourfold: (1) it reduces the time of the experiment; (2) it standardizes each run by preventing the rat from running through the maze several times before entering the food box; (3) it equalizes practice in different parts of the maze; (4) it tends

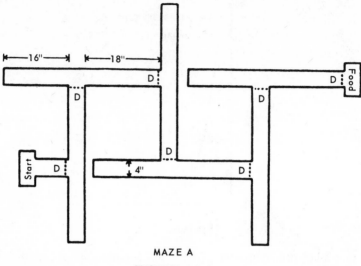

MAZE A

FIGURE 8.1–2

to cause a more symmetrical distribution curve of errors for a group of animals. For retracing tends, as such, to give some unduly large scores.

It may perhaps be argued that this introduction of doors was unsound because it introduced an artificial limit into the problem. Every experiment is necessarily artificial. Thus, for example, in the ordinary maze, the experimenter "artificially" excludes certain "normal" cues as, for example, odors and distinguishing tactual factors. All that has been done, in this case, is to restrict our conclusions to types of maze which do not allow retracings.

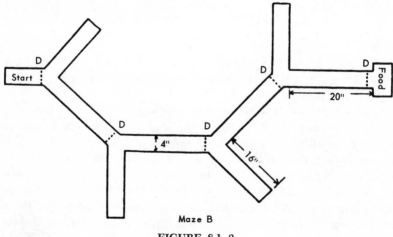

Maze B

FIGURE 8.1–3

A second feature of importance which holds for mazes A and B is the fact that all the blind alleys in the same maze have the same dimensions and the same angular relationships to the true path. This is believed to be an improvement over the usual maze, in that the error scores (number of entrances into blinds) are more definitely scaled.

The mazes were constructed of wood painted dark brown. The walls were 8 inches high and ⅞ inch thick. The tops of the alleys were covered with ¼ inch mesh wire screen. The alleys had no permanent bottom but were placed on a heavy piece of linoleum. The wire covers and the linoleum were painted the same color as the sides.

Animals

The rats were of mixed strain, black and white. They were raised, four to six in a group, in wire cages 10 × 14 inches in a room varying in temperature from 55 to 85 degrees Fahrenheit. They were accustomed to occasional handling at feeding time and when their cages were cleaned, and so they were not wild. They were approximately three months of age when the experiment was begun. The number of males and females was nearly even.

Food

Their food during the pre-experimental stage consisted of a mash of ground barley, bran, and table scraps. Beginning three days before the experiment and throughout the experimental period the animals were fed approximately one-tenth their weight of food saturated with water. They were given no other water. The food was a mixture of four parts dry bread, ground up in fine bits, one part bran, one part sunflower seed, and three-fourths part powdered skim milk.

Scoring

With mazes A and B, a rat was counted as having made one error if it made one (or more) entrances of as much as a body's length (not counting tail) into a blind, while in a given segment of the maze. That is, even though the rat entered and reëntered a given blind before passing to the next segment, it was counted as having made only *one* error. . . .

Time was measured by a stopwatch, in seconds from the time the rat left the starting box until the door of the food box was closed behind it.

PROCEDURE AND RESULTS

Maze A: Groups I, II, and III

Group I. Control. This group consisted of 36 rats run once a day for seven days and allowed to eat for *three minutes in the food box at the end of each run.* They were then removed to another cage (not the living cage) and allowed to finish their day's ration, after which they were returned to their living-cages.

Group II. Experimental. This group also consisted of 36 rats. (They were litter mates of group I. Of each original litter, half the number were put in group I, and half in group II.) *For the first six days,* group II found no food in the food box and were kept in it without reward for two minutes. They were then removed to another cage (not the living-cage) where they were fed after an interval of approximately one hour. Only then were they returned to their living-cages. *For day seven and the two subsequent days* they were treated exactly like group I; that is, they found food in the food box for three minutes and finished their day's ration immediately afterward in another cage.

Group III. Experimental. This group consisted of 25 rats. Like group II, they began with no reward at the end of the maze. But for them such reward was introduced at the end of the third day rather than at the end of the seventh day.

Figures 8.1–4 and 8.1–5 present the error curves and the time curves, for each of these three groups. And tables 8.1–1 and 8.1–2 indicate the differences and the reliability of these differences between the three curves on each successive day.

Examining the error curves and tables, two points appear:

1. The experimental groups (II and III), so long as they were *without reward*, did very much worse than the control group (I). In fact, the curves for groups II and III stayed almost horizontal until after the day (indicated by the cross) when food was introduced.

2. On the day after this first reward (i.e., on day 8 for group II and on day 4 for group III), errors dropped greatly. And on the second

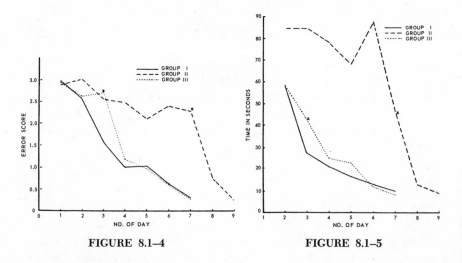

FIGURE 8.1–4   FIGURE 8.1–5

day after reward (i.e., on day 9 for group II and on day 5 for group III) the curves had dropped almost to the level of the curve for the control group.

Examining the time curves and tables, a similar picture appears, save that in the case of time the sudden drops seem to have come on the day of the introduction of the reward rather than on the day after. It appears, in other words, that, although the rats had not yet, on that day, actually experienced the finding of the food, their times were shortened by the fact of its presence in the food box (though their errors, as has been seen, were not reduced). The explanation which suggests itself is that the odor of the food caused greater general activity and hence a shorter running time although it did not cause fewer errors. (For the rats had yet to learn *just where* the food was.)

A further question now arises. Do these sudden drops in errors which come after the introductions of reward indicate that something to be called a *latent learning* developed during the non-reward period—a latent learning which made itself manifest after the reward had been presented? Obviously, if this is to be answered in the affirmative, one must show that the drops which occurred immediately subsequent to the reward were larger than "normal," that is, that they were bigger than drops in the control curve.

The first way of checking this was to compare the drops made by group II between days 7 and 8 and by group III between days 3 and 4 with the *largest* drop made by group I between any two days, which latter (see fig. 8.1–4) was obviously between days 2 and 3.

The results of this comparison are shown in table 8.1–3.

The critical ratio of 1.338 when interpreted in terms of probability means that if there were no real difference between the drops shown by group II, days 7–8, and that shown by group I, days 2–3, a difference

TABLE 8.1–1   Mean Errors

Day	Group I	Group II	Group III	Group II–Group I Diff.	Group II–Group I σ Diff.	Group II–Group I Critical ratio	Group III–Group I Diff.	Group III–Group I σ Diff.	Group III–Group I Critical ratio
1	2.97	2.89	2.96	−.08	.23	.35	−.01	.28	.04
2	2.56	3.03	2.64	.47	.28	1.66	.08	.30	.28
3	1.58	2.56	2.72	.97	.28	3.48	1.14	.27	4.27
4	1.03	2.47	1.20	1.44	.26	5.62	.17	.24	.71
5	1.08	2.08	.96	1.00	.24	4.26	.12	.30	.41
6	.69	2.42	.60	1.72	.28	6.17	.09	.20	.47
7	.30	2.28	.28	1.97	.20	12.72	.02	.13	.19
8		.86							
9		.25							

TABLE 8.1–2   Time (Seconds)

Day	Group I	Group II	Group III	Group II–Group I Diff.	Group II–Group I σ Diff.	Group II–Group I Critical ratio	Group III–Group I Diff.	Group III–Group I σ Diff.	Group III–Group I Critical ratio
2	58.19	84.58	57.60	26.39	10.42	2.53	.59	7.38	.08
3	27.50	84.86	42.60	57.36	19.73	2.91	15.10	3.11	4.86
4	21.39	77.72	25.44	56.34	14.53	3.88	4.05	5.15	.79
5	16.22	67.64	23.32	51.42	8.54	6.02	7.10	5.07	1.40
6	13.06	87.22	12.76	73.97	19.20	3.85	.30	1.77	.17
7	9.97	46.70	8.84	36.72	4.04	9.09	1.13	1.07	1.06
8		12.46							
9		8.61							

between these two drops as large as that obtained and shown in the table would occur by chance 904 times out of 10,000, or a little less than one-tenth of the time. It therefore seems probable, although not certain, that group II dropped more on this day than did group I (control) on the day of its greatest drop.

Similarly, the critical ratio of 1.544, when interpreted in terms of probability, means that, if there were no real difference between the drop shown by group III, days 3–4, and that shown by groups I, days 2–3, a difference as large as that shown in the table would occur by chance 612 times out of 10,000, or between one-fifteenth and one-sixteenth of the time. It again, therefore, seems probable, although not certain, that group III dropped more on this day than did group I on the day of its greatest drop.

Taking these two results together, the hypothesis that the periods of non-reward in groups II and III really produced *latent learning* which became manifest when a reward was introduced seems well supported.

A second way, however, of testing the validity of this hypothesis is suggested. It appears that it might be fair to compare the drops in group II and III not with the one biggest actual drop made anywhere by group I, but rather with the interpolated drops made by group I from the *levels* corresponding to those from which the drops in groups II and III begin. In order to obtain these, an interpolative procedure was required. This (in the case of group II) was as follows: in figure 8.1–4 a horizontal was drawn to the left from the point on curve II corresponding

TABLE 8.1–3   Mean Errors

	Drop in errors	Difference between drop and that shown in Group I	σ Differ-ence	Critical ratio
Group I—Days 2–3	.972			
Group II—Days 7–8	1.416	.444	.332	1.338
Group III—Days 3–4	1.520	.548	.355	1.544

to day 7, until this horizontal intersected curve I. A vertical was then dropped from this intersection to the X-axis. And a distance was thence measured off to the right, equal to the unit of one day. Another vertical was erected from this new point until curve I was again intersected, and the vertical distance between the two intersections on curve I was taken as the demanded drop. A similar procedure was followed with respect to group III.

Finally, however, in order to compare these interpolated drops on curve I and the corresponding drops on curves II and III, it was found necessary to estimate sigmas for the interpolated drops. The sigmas obtained for the actually measured drops on curve I, that is, for the drops between days 1–2, 2–3, 3–4, 4–5, 5–6, 6–7, were as follows: .237, .239, .247, .228, .190, and .187. It would seem, therefore, that to assume a sigma of .275 for an interpolated drop is more than fair.

Comparing, now, the drops in group II, days 7–8, and in group III, days 3–4, with the interpolated drops in group I corresponding to them, we have the results shown in table 8.1–4.

The critical ratio of 1.497, when interpreted in terms of probability, means that, if there were no real difference between the drop shown by group II, days 7–8, and that interpolated on the same level in group I, a difference as large as that shown in the table would occur by chance 671 times out of 10,000. This again suggests rather strongly that the drop between days 7–8 in group II is really greater than any corresponding drop in group I. It suggests, in short, that the drop between days 7–8 was evidence of a real *latent* learning which had already developed and was here being brought to light by the introduction of the reward.

Similarly, the critical ratio, 2.047, when interpreted in terms of probability, means that, if there were no real difference between the drop shown by group III, days 3–4, and that interpolated at the same level of the curve for group I, a difference as large as that shown in the table would occur by chance only 173 times out of 10,000. This is a very strong indication that the drop between days 3–4 was evidence of a true latent learning having occurred in group III which was brought to light by the introduction of the reward.

TABLE 8.1–4   Mean Errors

	Drop in errors	σ Drop	Difference between drop and that of Group I	σ Differ- ence	Critical ratio
Group II—days 7–8	1.416	.232			
Group I—interpolated	.877	.275	.539	.360	1.497
Group III—days 3–4	1.520	.263			
Group I—interpolated	.740	.275	.780	.381	2.047

Maze B: Groups I and II

To make sure that the differences just discussed were not due to any differences between the two groups arising from sampling, one of our experimental groups and the control group were tested in a second maze.

Thus, 22 rats of group II and 23 rats from group I were, subsequent to their practice in maze A, run in maze B. Both groups were run once a day and given food for two minutes in the food box at the end of each run. The learning curves are shown in figure 8.1–6, and are practically identical. We conclude that the differences in the groups in maze A were due to the *experimental conditions* and not to native differences between the groups.

Maze A: Group IV

Granted that the results so far discussed indicate that groups II and III acquired a latent learning during their non-reward periods which was made manifest when reward was introduced, questions still remains as to the nature of this latent learning. Was it the acquisition of mere general familiarity with the maze? Or was it the acquisition of a something more specific? To throw some light on these questions a fourth group of rats was run in maze A, viz., group IV.

Group IV consisted of 10 rats. Like group II, they were run for seven days without reward and then reward was introduced. But instead of being run during the non-reward period in the forward direction, they

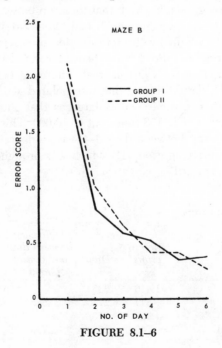

FIGURE 8.1–6

were, during this period, run in a *reverse direction*. That is, they were started at the food box (in this case empty, of course) and run to the starting box, where they received no reward. On the eighth day, their direction was changed to the *normal one* and they were given reward in the food box, as with group I. The hypothesis was that, if, upon being reversed to the normal direction and given reward, they then did decidedly better than the control group, it would suggest that the latent learning which showed itself in groups II and III upon reward may have been no more than a mere general familiarity which might have been acquired just as well through running the maze in the backward direction. If, on the contrary, they did *not* do decidedly better than the control, group I, when being run in the normal fashion, this would suggest that the latent learning developed by groups II and III was in part at least something more specific; something which could be developed only by the forward-going practice.

Table 8.1–5 gives the results of comparing errors for group IV (when running in the forward direction) with those for group I. Figure 8.1–7 gives the corresponding curves for group IV and group I, and for group II (after reward had been introduced).

It would appear that day 2 is the only one on which there is any significant superiority of group IV over group I. On that day the critical ratio of the difference in favor of group IV is 1.647. This, interpreted in terms of probability, means that, if there were no real difference between the groups, a difference as great as the one obtained would occur by chance 498 times out of 10,000.

One is therefore led to conclude that the increased familiarity with the maze gained by group IV in running backward probably did help to a *slight* extent on the second day of forward running. That is, group IV were somewhat better able than group I (probably because less distracted) to make use of their first day's experience in the forward direction. This superiority, however, did not persist. The initial advantage of familiarity possessed by group IV had disappeared on the third day, when their record was no better than that of group I.

TABLE 8.1–5   Mean Errors

Day	Group I	Day	Group IV	Difference	σ Difference	Critical ratio
1	2.97	8	2.80	.17	.46	.37
2	2.56	9	1.80	.76	.46	1.65
3	1.58	10	1.40	.18	.27	.68
4	1.03	11	1.10	.07	.38	.19
5	1.08	12	1.10	.02	.28	.06
6	.69	13	.50	.19	.27	.70
7	.30	14	.30	.005	.17	.03

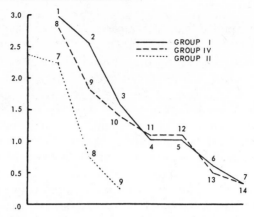

FIGURE 8.1–7 The point of origin for the abscissae is different for each curve. The numeral beside each point indicates the corresponding number of the day.

Compare, now, in figure 8.1–7,[1] group IV with group II after the latter were rewarded. Group IV ran the maze for seven days without the "expectation" of reward in the backward direction. Group II ran it for seven days without the "expectation" of reward in the forward direction. Comparing day 8 of group IV with day 7 of group II, it seems evident that the non-reward forward-running is the more helpful.[2] Six days of it is more valuable than seven days of backward-running. Further, not only does the non-reward forward-running give group II a decided head-start over group IV (which had had only backward non-reward running), but it also seems to cause them to continue to learn faster. In only two days group II accomplished an error elimination which it took group IV six days to achieve. Evidently the latent learning which group II developed as a result of their non-reward forward-running was decidedly more than the *general familiarity* which group IV seems to have acquired from their non-reward backward-running.

CONCLUSIONS

1. Non-reward running definitely develops a *latent learning*, and such latent learning is made manifest when reward is introduced.

2. Furthermore, it is evident that this latent learning is something more than a general familiarity such as might be acquired by backward-running through the maze. . . .

NOTE

1. A comparison in terms of sigmas of the differences and critical ratios of the differences indicated in the figure was not presented in the table because at the time this final report was written, the original data for making such a comparison were no longer available.

2. Although, as just mentioned, we have not the critical ratio for the difference.

LITERATURE CITED

Kuo, Z. Y. 1922. "The Nature of Unsuccessful Acts and their Order of Elimination in Animal Learning." *Jour. Comp. Psychol.*, 2:1–27.

Lashley, K. S. 1918. "A Simple Maze: with Data on the Relation of the Distribution of Practice to the Rate of Learning." *Psychobiology*, 1:353–367.

Peterson, Joseph. 1918. "Effect of Length of Blind Alleys on Maze Learning." *Behav. Monogr.*, 3:1–53.

Sams, C. F., and Tolman, E. C. 1925. "Time Discrimination in White Rats." *Jour. Comp. Psychol.*, 5:225–264.

Simmons, R. 1924. "The Relative Effectiveness of Certain Incentives in Animal Learning." *Comp. Psychol. Mon.*, 2:1–79.

Szymanski, J. S. 1918. "Versuche über die Wirkung der Faktoren, die als Antrieb zum Erlernen einer Handlung dienen können." *Pflüger's Archiv f. d. gesamte Physiologie*, 171:374–385.

Thorndike, E. L. 1911. *Animal Intelligence*, p. 244.

Watson, J. B. 1914. *Behavior*, chap. vii.

8.2 | ON INSTRUMENTAL RESPONSE INTERACTION AS EXPLAINING THE INFLUENCES OF PAVLOVIAN CS⁺s UPON AVOIDANCE BEHAVIOR*

8.2 ON INSTRUMENTAL RESPONSE INTERACTION AS EXPLAINING THE INFLUENCES OF PAVLOVIAN CS^+s UPON AVOIDANCE BEHAVIOR*

J. Bruce Overmier, John A. Bull III, and Kenneth Pack

The finding that Pavlovian signals for food or shock influence avoidance responding might be explained either by interaction of conditioned central mediational states or interaction of learned instrumental responses. Using three groups of dogs, the two hypotheses were pited one against the other in a three-stage transfer-of-control experiment. In the initial conditioning phase, tones were established as signals for food, shock, or neither; additionally the tones also cued a common instrumental response. Following avoidance training, the tone was tested for its influence upon avoidance. If the tone had signaled food, avoidance was

* Reprinted from *Learning and Motivation*, 1971, 2, 103–112. Copyright 1971 by Academic Press, Inc., and reproduced by permission. This research was supported by a grant from the National Institute of Mental Health (MH-13558) to J. Bruce Overmier and by grants from the National Science Foundation (GS-1761), National Institute of Child Health and Human Development (HD-01136), and the Graduate School, University of Minnesota, to the Center for Research in Human Learning, University of Minnesota. The authors thank M. A. Trapold for his helpful critical comments.

suppressed; if shock, avoidance was facilitated; if neither, avoidance was unaffected. This was interpreted as supporting the hypothesis that interaction of central states mediates the transfer-of-control.

In transfer-of-control experiments, stimuli established by Pavlovian conditioning as CSs for either shock or food subsequently modulate the performance of independently established active avoidance behavior. Such demonstrations are of central importance to two-process mediational theories of learning (cf. Rescorla & Solomon, 1967; Trapold & Overmier, 1971). The prototypic transfer-of-control experiment consists of three phases: (a) Pavlovian phase in which CS–US pairings are presented independent of S's behavior, (b) instrumental phase in which an avoidance response is trained by contingent reinforcement, and (c) a transfer test phase in which the CS is tested for its power to control the performance of the instrumental avoidance response.

Using basically this experimental design, Rescorla and LoLordo (1965) and Bull and Overmier (1968) have demonstrated that a CS for shock increases the rate of avoidance responding when superimposed on Sidman avoidance or when compounded with a cue for avoidance. In contrast, Grossen, Kostansek, and Bolles (1969) and Bull (1970) have demonstrated that a CS for food depresses the rate of avoidance responding when superimposed on Sidman avoidance or when compounded with a cue for avoidance. These kinds of demonstrations of transfer, wherein control of a specific avoidance response is immediately transferred to Pavlovian CSs with which it has never before been associated have lead two-process theorists to infer that the influence exerted by the Pavlovian CSs is due to the interaction of response-independent, Pavlovianly conditioned mediational states (Rescorla & Solomon, 1967). Theorists have attributed motivational properties (Rescorla & Solomon, 1967), or cue properties (Logan & Wagner, 1965), or both (Trapold & Overmier, 1971) to these response-independent central mediational states.

However, there is a viable alternative to the central mediational state hypotheses. With some thought one can imagine that some instrumental response may have been acquired (perhaps superstitiously) during the *Pavlovian* phase which later mechanically interacts with the avoidance response to produce the observed change in behavior. Just because one is carrying out Pavlovian operations does not rule out the possibility of learning such mediating instrumental responses. Therefore, it is important to two-process theory that efforts be directed towards reducing the viability of this mechanical interaction of instrumental responses hypothesis.

The experiment to be reported represents one such effort; in it, the question of acquisition of a possible mediating instrumental response during the Pavlovian conditioning phase was not left to chance; such a response was explicitly established in the initial conditioning phase, and this response was mechanically identical for all groups. The present experiment makes use of two facts: (a) that the elements for Pavlovian conditioning are imbedded within every discrete trial instrumental conditioning operation and (b) that the actual performance of a particular instrumental response cannot be simultaneously facilitated and impeded by a second instrumental response. Each S underwent a sequence of three treatment phases: (a) initial instrumental conditioning in a booth using a tone as a cue (S+) for either food or shock in different groups (This corresponds to the Pavlovian conditioning phase of more familiar transfer-of-control experiments to establish the stimuli as Pavlovian cues for food or shock by means of the imbedded Pavlovian contingencies.); (b) instrumental avoidance training in a shuttlebox with a visual S^D; (c) transfer testing in the shuttlebox to determine the influence of the S+s on the performance of the barrier jumping avoidance response to S^D. If the transfer-of-control effects previously observed are due to CS-controlled instrumental responses acquired during the Pavlovian phase mechanically interacting with the avoidance response, then the effect of the S+ upon avoidance responding should be the *same* for both of our experimental groups. If, on the other hand, the influences of the S+ for the two groups are different or even *opposite*, then we shall have to look beyond the instrumental-response–mechanical-interaction hypothesis for explanation of the transfer-of-control phenomena, perhaps to a central mediational state hypothesis.

METHOD

Subjects
Ten mongrel dogs 38–48 cm high at the shoulder and weighing between 10.9 and 13.6 kg served as Ss. These were arbitrarily assigned to 3 groups (Aversive conditioning, $N = 4$; Appetitive conditioning, $N = 4$; and Control, $N = 2$) and housed in individual cages. The Appetitive conditioning and Control groups were food deprived and maintained at approximately 80% body weight throughout all experimental phases. The Aversive conditioning group was maintained on a free feeding schedule. Water was continually available to all.

Apparatus
The initial conditioning phase took place in a white, partially sound proofed booth 1.5 × 1.7 × 2.0 m high. The dogs stood on a .86 × .43-m plywood floor approximately .76 m above ground level and were surrounded by a .86 × .43-m metal pipe frame .36 m above the plywood floor. The dogs were further restrained by a collar loosely fastened by light chains to the ceiling and the two side pipes. A rotary food dispenser operating with an audible click dropped food pellets (Dog Yummies or

Prime) into a chute which delivered the pellets to a food cup on an aluminum tray supported under S's head by the pipe frame. Electric shock was regulated by E at 4 mA and was delivered through two 3.2 × 1.9-cm. stainless steel electrodes coated with electrode paste and attached to the shaved sides of the upper right foreleg (two Ss) or to the sides of the upper right hindleg (two Ss). A 100 kΩ current-limiting resistor was in series with Ss.

A pedal was located 5.1 cm above the floor and 5.1 cm in front of the right foreleg. The pedal surface was 11.4 × 15.2 cm and sloped toward S at an angle of 45° from the horizontal; a force of 227 g operated the pedal which emitted an audible click. The pedal was not visible to S because of the tray beneath its head.

Two speakers provided a background of white noise at approximately 75 dB (re: .0002 dynes/sq. cm). A third speaker was used to present the auditory cue, 2300 Hz, at about 12 dB above the white noise level. The booth was well illuminated.

The second and third phases of the experiment took place in two-way shuttlebox with two compartments separated by an adjustable barrier. Each compartment was 1.14 × .61 × 1.01 m high with black interior walls. Compartment ceilings were made of expanded metal grating. Above each compartment ceiling was a 7.5 W. light, a 150 W. light and two speakers. Extinguishing the 150 W. lamps resulted in a marked decrease in illumination and served as the visual cue (S^D) for avoidance in the shuttlebox. One speaker provided a background of white noise at approximately 70 dB, while the other was used during the transfer test phase to present the auditory cue (S^+) at about 15 dB above the white noise level. Electric shock was administered through a grid floor of 3.2-cm flat aluminum bars placed 1.6 cm apart. A grid scrambler shifted the polarity patterns of the bars six times per sec. The shock was regulated at 4.5 mA by E; a current limiting resistor of 100 kΩ was in series with S.

Trial duration was measured to the nearest .01 sec using an electric timer. Responses were detected by two photocells located 35.5 cm above the grid floor and 27.9 cm on each side of the barrier. Responses were continually recorded on a cumulative recorder and on a multiple event recorder.

Stimulus presentation and contingencies for both apparatus units were controlled by automatic relay circuitry housed in an adjacent room.

Treatments

Sessions took place on consecutive days. Ss were placed in the appropriate apparatus unit approximately 5 min before the start of the daily session and remained there for 5 min after the session.

Initial Conditioning Phase—Appetitive. After reaching the appropriate deprived weight, S was placed in the booth stand for 45-min adaptation periods for 2 or 3 days. Then, magazine training was begun in which 21 food pellets were presented on a 2-min VI schedule; this training continued until S quickly consumed each pellet upon delivery. Magazine training was followed by sessions in which S was shaped to press the pedal with its right foot. After the complete pedal pressing response was attained, continuous reinforcement of free operant pedal pressing was continued until S earned and consumed 21 pellets as delivered in less than 10 min. The time required from the initiation of magazine training to reaching this criterion varied between 8 and 14 sessions (mean = 10.25).

The final stage of appetitive conditioning involved bringing the pedal press response under discrete stimulus control. A trial began with the onset of the auditory cue (ApS$^+$) and was terminated by a pedal pressing response which was reinforced. Trials were scheduled according to a variable intertrial interval (ITI); the mean ITI was 30 sec on the first day and 80 sec thereafter. Intertrial responding was not reinforced and in fact delayed presentation of a scheduled ApS$^+$ for 30 sec, which rapidly eliminated intertrial responses. This appetitive conditioning continued until S completed two consecutive sessions in which all food pellets were quickly earned and eaten *and* in which five or fewer intertrial responses occurred. Conditioning to this strict criterion required from 17 to 50 sessions (mean = 30).

Initial Conditioning Phase—Control. The treatment of the Controls was identical to the preceding except for the final discrete trial stage. In the final stage for the Controls, food pellets were scheduled and earnable on the same VI schedule and in the same number (21) as that for the Appetitive group, but the availability of the reinforcements was not signaled. There were also 21 10-sec auditory cue presentations (ApS^0), but the availability of food was not contingent upon the prior occurrence of ApS^0. Rather both the food and the ApS^0 were scheduled by equal but independent VI programs.

Initial Conditioning Phase—Aversive. Following adaptation to the booth and stand, discrete trial aversive conditioning was begun. A trial began with the onset of the auditory cue (AvS$^+$) which was followed 10 sec later by shock to the leg which continued for a maximum of 50 sec. Pressing the pedal terminated the trial and the AvS$^+$ or the AvS$^+$ plus shock complex, whichever was present. There were 30 such trials per session. Sessions continued until S prevented all ten shocks on the first 10 trials of a session; the session and the aversive conditioning phase were then terminated. Conditioning to this criterion required from three to five sessions (mean = 3.75).

Instrumental Avoidance Training Phase. All Ss from all three groups were given instrumental avoidance training in the shuttlebox. The goal was to get the Ss to perform the barrier crossing response reliably and repeatedly so long as the visual avoidance S^D was being presented. This was achieved by stages. In the first stage of training 21 trials were presented each day; the trials were initiated by the onset of the visual S^D and if S did not cross the barrier within 10 sec, shock was presented continuously until S crossed the barrier or until 50 sec had elapsed. Crossing the barrier terminated the trial and the S^D (i.e., avoidance) or the S^D plus shock complex (i.e., escape), whichever was present. Average ITI was 80 sec. These training sessions continued until S made ten consecutive avoidances in one daily session; all Ss required three such sessions.

Then each S was given a second stage of avoidance training on what amounts to a discrete trial variable interval schedule. This second stage was characterized by a "hold" period during which the S^D was on but responses had no consequences. At the end of the hold period, the next barrier jumping response terminated the trial and the S^D. If no response was made within 5 sec of the termination of the hold period, a shock of 0.5-sec duration was delivered. This VI hold period could be 0, 3, 6, 12, or 18 sec long. A session consisted of seven trials with each of three selected hold periods. The first sessions of this schedule used hold periods of 0, 3, and 6 sec, later sessions used 0, 6, and 12 sec, while the final sessions used 0, 6, and 18 sec. The hold periods were increased in duration when Ss received five or fewer shocks in one session; training was continued on the final hold period values until a criterion of one or fewer shocks during both of two consecutive daily sessions was met. It required between five and seven sessions (mean = 6.25) for all Ss to meet the VI-hold avoidance training criterion. This training schedule resulted in a continuous stable rate of barrier jumping controlled by the discrete trial visual S^D.

Transfer Testing

No food or shock was presented at any time during the testing which was carried out in the shuttlebox. Testing consisted of 24 trials, 12 with each of two different stimuli: (a) the visual S^D alone and (b) the visual S^D compounded with the auditory cue from the initial conditioning phase (either ApS^+, ApS^0, or AvS^+). The trials were presented in a randomized sequence counterbalanced over blocks of 12 trials.

The test trials used a fixed 10-sec hold period during which responses were not effective, and the first response after the end of the hold period resulted in the termination of the test stimulus and ended the trial. If no response was made within 30 sec of the end of the hold period, the trial was automatically terminated.

RESULTS

It should first be noted that the initial conditioning phases for the AvS^+ and ApS^+ groups resulted in what appeared to be essentially identical pedal pressing behavior. The mean pedal pressing response latency for the AvS^+ group on the last 10 trials was 1.90 sec with a range of individual trial latencies of 0.7 to 6.7 sec. The mean pedal pressing response latency for the ApS^+ group on the last 10 trials was 2.09 sec with a range of individual trial latencies of 0.9 to 10.5 sec. An analysis of variance of these response latencies revealed no significant differences between the two groups (Groups $F < 1.00$, n.s.). Furthermore, intertrial pedal press responses were judged to occur only infrequently as AvS^+ and ApS^+ Ss reached criterion in the initial conditioning phase.

Rates of barrier jumping during the 10-sec hold period of each test stimulus presentation provide the primary data of this experiment. The individual S's daily mean rates of jumping under each of the two kinds of test trials were subjected to an analysis of variance. Figure 8.2–1 presents these daily group means. Avoidance responding was differentially affected in the three groups by compounding the S^D with the cue from the initial conditioning phase (Group $\times$ Stimuli $F(2,14) = 8.48, 14, p < .01$). Compounding S^D with ApS^+, the tone which had served as a signal for food, markedly suppressed the rate of avoidance ($t(14) = 4.4, p < .01$).[1] Compounding S^D with the ApS^0, the tone which had no signal value, did not influence the rate of avoidance ($t = .08$, n.s.). And compounding S^D with AvS^+, the tone which had served as a cue for impending shock, increased the rate of avoidance ($t(14) = 2.27, p < .05$). This was observed on all three test days in spite of the general decrease in rate of avoidance (extinction) across days (Days $F(2,4) = 15.67, p < .05$).

To take into account any effects of differences in the base rates of responding in S^D, an analysis of the percentage change in avoidance responding produced by the compound

$$\left(\text{i.e., } \frac{S^D \text{ plus S compound rate} - S^D \text{ rate}}{S^D \text{ rate}} \right)$$

was carried out. This second analysis (see Fig. 8.2–2) confirmed that the groups differed in the change in avoidance responding produced by adding the AvS^+, ApS^0, and ApS^+, respectively, to the S^D $F(2,7) = 5.48, p < .05$. Further comparison also confirmed that the ApS^+ and the AvS^+ resulted in significantly different (and opposite) changes in the S^D-controlled avoidance behavior $t(7) = 3.05, p < .05$.

DISCUSSION

Our findings that the ApS^+ reduced the rate of S^D-controlled avoidance while the AvS^+ increased the rate of the S^D-controlled avoidance

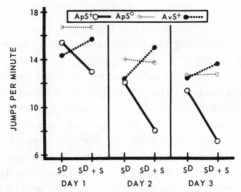

FIGURE 8.2–1 Group daily mean rates of avoidance responding during the fixed 10-sec hold period in the presence of the S^D alone and the compound of the S^D plus the ApS+, ApS°, or AvS+, depending upon the group.

agree with the earlier compounding experiment of Bull and Overmier (1968) and Bull (1970). The present experiment differs from these, however, in that an explicit instrumental response was required of S during the establishment of ApS+ and AvS+, whereas the earlier experiments established ApS+ and AvS+ by merely pairing them with food and shock.

One might wish to attribute the suppressing effect of the ApS+ to an incompatibility between pedal pressing and barrier jumping. But, we see that the AvS+ which also controlled pedal press responding *increased* the rate of S^D controlled shuttlebox avoidance responding. This second effect argues against the possibility that any evoked pedal pressing tendency is mechanically incompatible with barrier jumping.

On the other hand, the argument that the facilitated barrier jumping to the S^D plus AvS+ compound is attributable to a facilitory relationship between pedal pressing and barrier jumping is also untenable. This is

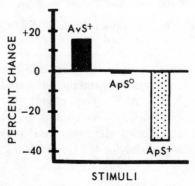

FIGURE 8.2–2 Mean of overall daily percentage changes in avoidance response rates when the S^D was compounded with the ApS+, ApS°, or AvS+ for the respective groups.

because the ApS$^+$ which also controlled pedal press responding *depressed* the rate of S^D controlled shuttlebox avoidance responding. Obviously, both effects cannot be explained by reference to the same simple mechanical mechanism because a given instrumental response cannot simultaneously mechanically facilitate *and* impede a second specific instrumental response.

The finding that the ApS^0 of the control group did not influence the rate of avoidance controlled by the S^D indicates that neither of the effects of the Aps$^+$ or the AvS$^+$ are due to intrinsic tone properties (e.g. novelty, external inhibition, external disinhibition, etc.) or to simply having learned to press the pedal or to having learned to eat from a food cup.

The transfer experiments by Grossen, Kostansek, and Bolles (1969) and Bull and Overmier (1969) showing that a CS for food would suppress avoidance behavior and the experiments by Solomon and Turner (1962) and Leaf (1964) showing that a CS shock would facilitate avoidance behavior did indeed include efforts to rule out the mediating instrumental response hypothesis for the specific effect they observed. Grossen, Kostansek, and Bolles (1969) trained a motor response in the initial "Pavlovian" phase which was hypothetically compatible with the test response; Bull and Overmier (1969) tested the effects of the Pavlovian stimuli on the test response acquired under different motivation; Solomon and Turner (1962) and Leaf (1964) pharmacologically blocked overt motor responses during the Pavlovian phase. However, no single technique for controlling for instrumental mediation (so far at least) is without criticism (cf. Trapold & Overmier, 1971, for a detailed analysis). Therefore, the accumulation of several different lines of evidence against the instrumental-response–mechanical-interaction hypothesis is important to the corroboration of two-process mediational theories. The present experiment meets this need simultaneously for both the facilitative and suppressive transfer effects by utilizing different control and analytical techniques.

The results of this experiment, coupled with the earlier efforts serve to reduce markedly the likelihood that the transfer-of-control demonstrations which are central to two-process theories of learning are explainable by reference to interaction of instrumental responses. In doing so, the present results corroborate those theories suggested by Logan and Wagner (1965), Mowrer (1960), Rescorla and Solomon (1967), Trapold and Overmier (1971), and others which impute the observed transfer-of-control to centrally mediated, response-independent learning established by Pavlovian operations.

NOTE
1. All t tests are based upon the analyses of variance and the p values are based upon two-tailed tests.

REFERENCES

Bull, J. A., III. An interaction between appetitive Pavlovian CSs and instrumental avoidance responding. *Learning and Motivation*, 1970, 1, 18–26.

Bull, J. A., III, & Overmier, J. B. Additive and subtractive properties of excitation and inhibition. *Journal of Comparative and Physiological Psychology*, 1968, 66, 511–514.

Bull, J. A., III, & Overmier, J. B. The incompatibility of appetitive and aversive conditioned motivation. *Proceedings 77th Annual Convention of the American Psychological Association*, 1969, 4, 97–98.

Grossen, N. E., Kostansek, D. J., & Bolles, R. C. Effects of appetitive discriminative stimuli on avoidance behavior. *Journal Experimental Psychology*, 1969, 81, 340–343.

Leaf, R. C. Avoidance response evocation as a function of prior discriminative fear conditioning under curare. *Journal of Comparative and Physiological Psychology*, 1964, 58, 446–449.

Logan, F. A., & Wagner, A. R. *Reward and Punishment*. Boston: Allyn & Bacon, 1965. Pp. 69–74.

Mowrer, O. H. *Learning Theory and Behavior*. New York: Wiley, 1960. Pp. 63–252.

Rescorla, R. A., & LoLordo, V. M. Inhibition of avoidance behavior. *Journal of Comparative and Physiological Psychology*, 1965, 59, 406–412.

Rescorla, R. A., & Solomon, R. L. Two process learning theory: Relationships between Pavlovian conditioning and instrumental learning. *Psychological Review*, 1967, 74, 151–182.

Solomon, R. L., & Turner, L. H. Discriminative classical conditioning under curare can later control discriminative avoidance responses in the normal state. *Psychological Review*, 1962, 69, 202–219.

Trapold, M. A., & Overmier, J. B. The second process in instrumental learning. In A. H. Black & W. F. Prokasy (Eds.), *Classical Conditioning: A Symposium*. New York: Appleton-Century-Crofts, 1971.

8.3 EFFECTS OF IMMEDIATE VERSUS DELAYED OUTCOMES IN ASSOCIATIVE LEARNING*

Alexander M. Buchwald

College student Ss were given two trials on each of 3 lists of stimulus words with either 2 or 4 digits as response alternatives. On immediate outcome items, E said "Right" or "Wrong" immediately after S's response. On delayed outcome items, E informed S that his response

* Reprinted from *The Journal of Verbal Learning and Verbal Behavior*, 1967, 6, 317–320. Copyright 1967 by Academic Press, Inc., and reproduced by permission. This research was conducted under grant HD 920–02 from the National Institutes of Health. Margaret Frye collected the data reported here.

*had been "Right" or "Wrong" the next time the item was presented.
On no-information items E gave no information on either trial. Delayed
"Wrong" led to significantly less response repetition than all other
conditions. Differences among other conditions were generally
not significant.*

An announcement that a response is right or wrong may be used to pro-
mote, or to produce, learning of paired associates, but when is the best
time to make these announcements? This paper presents an experiment
designed to compare the effects of making such announcements immediately after the response has occurred, with the effects of delaying such
announcements until the stimulus items are presented on the next trial.
The rationale for believing that the delayed announcements might lead
to better performance than immediate announcements is the following.

In some earlier experiments (Buchwald, 1962) it was found that
whether calling a response *Right* or calling it *Wrong* had a "reinforcing
effect" seemed to depend upon how many response alternatives S was
allowed to choose from. The attempt to account for such findings led to
the development of an alternative account of the way in which outcomes
affect behavior in this kind of associative learning situation (Buchwald,
1963, 1966). In this theoretical account it is postulated that there are
separate memory processes for responses and for outcomes. Further, outcomes are assumed to have no influence on the stimulus-response associative process.

More explicitly, the following assumptions are made about memory
processes:

(1) The response made to a given stimulus on one trial may be
either recalled or forgotten by the time the stimulus is presented on the
next trial. The probability of the response being recalled is assumed to
be independent of the outcome.

(2) The outcome that followed a stimulus-response sequence on one
trial may be either recalled or forgotten by the time the stimulus is presented on the next trial. The probability of the outcome being recalled
is assumed to be independent of which outcome occurred.

(3) For a given stimulus item, S may recall either his response, or
the outcome, or both of these, or neither of these.

Dand (1946) and Bower (1962) have both noted Ss' reports that
for some items they could remember *either* their responses or the outcomes of these responses, but not both.

There are also two assumptions made concerning the probability of
repeating responses from one trial to the next. (It is here that outcomes
are assumed to influence responding.) (1) If the response to some item
is not recalled it can only be repeated by chance, regardless of whether
the outcome is recalled or not. (2) For an experiment in which the S

must respond each time a stimulus is presented, *if* the previous response to a stimulus is recalled the response will be repeated (a) with probability equal to one, *if* the outcome was *Right*, and the outcome is recalled; (b) with a probability equal to zero, if the outcome was *Wrong*, and the outcome is recalled; (c) with a probability which depends upon the experimental situation and the instructions, if the outcome is not recalled *or* if the outcome gave no information about the correctness of the response.

One implication of these assumptions concerns the most effective time to inform S whether his response to some item was correct or not. If the outcome is given immediately after the response it may be forgotten when that item is next presented. If the outcome of a previously given response is not presented until the same item is presented again, it will insure that the information will be available at the point at which it is needed. Hence the present theory predicts that the use of delayed outcomes, of the type just described, will lead to fewer repetitions of responses called *Wrong* and more repetitions of responses called *Right*, than will the immediate outcome procedure. This prediction contrasts with the usual belief that the most effective time to reinforce a response is immediately after it occurs.

METHOD

Subjects

Forty-eight women and 25 men college students served as Ss in this experiment. These Ss had answered an advertisement for students to serve in verbal learning experiments. None of them had previously served in an experiment of the present type.

Materials

Three lists of common English words were randomly selected from the A and AA lists of Thorndike and Lorge (1944) to serve as stimulus materials. Each list had 44 words. The first two words and the last two words in each list were buffer words not used in gathering data. The other 40 words were arranged in two randomly chosen permutations. Within each list there were five subsets of eight words each. Twenty-four women and 13 men Ss had the digits 7 and 9 available as response alternatives, while the other Ss had the digits 1, 3, 5, and 7 as response alternatives.

Procedure

Each S was given two trials on each of the three lists of words. A different permutation of the words on the list was used on each of the trials. Each S was given both trials on a single list before being exposed to the next list.

Two of the subsets of stimulus items were immediate outcome sets. On the immediate *Right* items *E* said *Right* immediately after any response on Trial 1. On the immediate *Wrong* items *E* said *Wrong* immediately after any response on Trial 1. On Trial 2 *E* said *respond* immediately after presenting any of these immediate outcome items. Two of the subsets of items were delayed outcome sets. On these *E* said nothing after responses on Trial 1. On the delayed *Right* items *E* said *Right* immediately after presenting each item on Trial 2. On the delayed *Wrong* items *E* said *Wrong* immediately after presenting each item on Trial 2. On the fifth subset of items *E* said nothing after responses on Trial 1, and said *respond* after presenting each item on Trial 2. These will be referred to as "nothing" items. The items of these five subsets were intermingled in a single list.

All items were presented orally. Before presenting the next item, or before saying *Right* or *Wrong* if either was called for, *E* waited for *S* to respond. The time between successive item presentations, obtained by timing trials with a stopwatch, was approximately 3 sec.

All *Ss* were told that when *E* said nothing after a response on Trial 1 it meant *S* was being given no information about the correctness of his response, and that when *E* said *Right* or *Wrong* after presenting an item on Trial 2 it meant that the response previously given to that item was correct or incorrect, respectively. They were told that Trial 2 was a test trial to see how much they had learned on Trial 1 and that they should try to give as many correct answers as they could on this trial.

RESULTS AND DISCUSSION

Each of the five subsets of items constituted a separate experimental treatment. For each treatment separately, the number of items to which *S* gave the same response on both trials was summed over the three lists. Since interactions of sex of *Ss* and experimental variables have appeared in earlier experiments (Buchwald, 1962), and since the sexes were not equally represented in the present experiment, data for male and female *Ss* were treated separately. The magnitude of the effects can best be seen by examining the proportion of responses repeated under the various treatments. These are shown in Table 8.3–1. It is apparent that delayed *Wrong* resulted in markedly less repetition of responses than immediate *Wrong*, or any other condition. In contrast, differences between delayed *Right* and immediate *Right* were small and inconsistent. For each of the four groups of *Ss*, a single classification analysis of variance for repeated measures yielded an *F*-ratio for treatments, which was significant at the .01 level. The Newman-Keuls test was used to evaluate the differences between pairs of conditions, the test being carried out for each group of *Ss* separately. The results were markedly consistent from group to

TABLE 8.3–1 Proportion of Responses Repeated Under Various Experimental Conditions

		Outcome events				
		Wrong		Right		
Sex of Ss	Number of alternatives	Delayed	Immediate	Delayed	Immediate	Nothing
Female	2	.42	.52	.60	.59	.56
Male	2	.39	.60	.71	.62	.66
Female	4	.26	.34	.36	.37	.36
Male	4	.22	.37	.46	.49	.36

group. The delayed *Wrong* condition differed from the immediate *Wrong* condition at the .01 level of significance in three cases, and at the .03 level for women Ss with four response alternatives. The delayed *Wrong* condition differed from each of the other conditions at the .01 level of significance in each of the groups. In contrast, none of the differences between delayed *Right* and immediate *Right* reached the .05 level of significance, a finding that would not be altered even by the use of the less conservative *t*-test rather than the Newman-Keuls procedure. For each group of Ss there were five other unplanned contrasts. In general these were nonsignificant, the two exceptions occurring among men Ss with four response alternatives. Here the immediate *Right* condition differed from both the immediate *Wrong* condition, and from the *Nothing* condition, at the .05 level of significance.

The difference between the delayed *Wrong* and immediate *Wrong* conditions supports the present theory. According to the theory, equal numbers of responses will be recalled in both conditions. In the immediate *Wrong* condition many of these responses should be repeated on the test trial because S failed to recall that they had been called *Wrong*. In the delayed *Wrong* condition there was very little opportunity to forget the outcome, hence responses that were recalled should not be repeated.

On the other hand, the lack of a difference between the delayed *Right* condition and the immediate *Right* condition contradicts the predicted result. This need not be a contradiction of the theory. The virtual lack of differences among all of the conditions except for delayed *Wrong* suggests a possible explanation. Suppose when delayed outcomes and immediate outcomes are mingled in a single list Ss repeat all recalled responses whose correctness or incorrectness is not known. Then when a response has been followed by the outcome *Right* it should make no difference whether this outcome is recalled or not since recalled responses will be repeated in either case. This explanation can be directly tested by comparing the performance of groups of Ss given only delayed outcomes with groups of Ss given only immediate outcomes.

These results have important implications concerning the effects of so-called "verbal rewards" and "verbal punishments." Numerous experiments (Postman, 1962) have indicated that Ss show an increased frequency of usage of responses called *Right* but not a corresponding decrease in the frequency of usage of responses called *Wrong*. The data of this experiment show that under certain conditions an announcement that a response was *Wrong* can be quite effective in altering behavior, if the announcement is made at a point in time when the response might be made again. The present theory indicates that this should hold when S is unable to recall whether a given response was correct or incorrect for a particular stimulus.

REFERENCES

Bower, G. An association model for response and training variables in paired-associate learning. *Psychol. Rev.*, 1962, 69, 34–53.
Buchwald, A. M. Variations in the apparent effects of "right" and "wrong" on subsequent behavior. *J. verb. Learn. verb. Behav.*, 1962, 1, 71–78.
Buchwald, A. M. A family of mathematical models for the effectiveness of *right* and *wrong* in altering behavior. *Tech. Rep. No. 2*, NIMH M5283 and MSP-18223. Indiana Univ., 1963.
Buchwald, A. M. The effect of some variations in procedure on response repetition following verbal outcomes. *J. verb. Learn. verb. Behav.*, 1966, 5, 77–85.
Dand, A. 'Reward' and 'punishment' in learning. *Brit. J. Psychol.*, 1946, 36, 83–87.
Postman, L. Rewards and punishments in human learning, in Leo Postman (Ed.), *Psychology in the making*. New York: Knopf, 1962.
Thorndike, E. L., and Lorge, I. *The teacher's word book of 30,000 words*. New York: Teacher's College, Columbia Univ. Press, 1944.

8.4 | PREDICTABILITY, SURPRISE, ATTENTION, AND CONDITIONING*

Leon J. Kamin

The experiments to be described here have no special relevance to the problem of punishment. The studies to be reported do employ the CER procedure (Estes & Skinner, 1941). This procedure, within which an

* From: *Punishment and Aversive Behavior*, edited by Byron A. Campbell & Russell M. Church. Copyright © 1969. By permission of Appleton-Century-Crofts, Educational Division, Meredith Corporation. Used in excerpted form. The research reported here was supported by a research grant from the Associate Committee on Experimental Psychology, National Research Council of Canada.

aversive US follows a warning signal regardless of the animal's behavior, has been contrasted to the arrangements employed in response-contingent punishment (Hunt & Brady, 1955). This type of comparison, however, is not germane to the present research. The kinds of results considered in this chapter derive from rats in a CER procedure, with shock as the US; but very similar results have been obtained in the McMaster laboratory by H. M. Jenkins, using pigeons in a food-reinforced operant discrimination. What appears to be involved in these studies is a concern with phenomena often referred to as examples of "selective attention." To the degree that punishment contingencies may be brought under stimulus control, the present work might be related to other contributions in this volume.

The present work arose from an interest in the possible role of attention in Pavlovian conditioning. The usual statement of the conditions sufficient for a Pavlovian CR asserts simply that a neutral, to-be-conditioned CS must be presented in contiguity with a US. What happens, however, when a compound CS consisting of elements known to be independently conditionable is presented in contiguity with a US? Are all elements of the CS effectively conditioned? Does the animal attend, and thus condition, more to some elements than to others? What kinds of experimental manipulations might direct the animal's attention to one or another element?

The first experimental approach to these questions was, in overview, as follows. First, condition an animal to respond to a simple CS, consisting of Element A. Then condition the animal to respond to a compound, consisting of Element A plus a superimposed Element B. Finally, test the animal with Element B alone. Will it respond to Element B? Put very naively, our primitive notion was that, because of the prior conditioning to Element A, that element might so "engage the animal's attention" during presentation of the compound that it would not "notice" the added Element B. The failure to notice the superimposed element might preclude any conditioning to it. To conclude that the prior conditioning to Element A was responsible for a failure to respond to Element B we must, of course, show that animals conditioned to the compound without prior conditioning to A do respond when tested with B. To control for amount of experience with the US, and variables correlated with it, we ought also to show that, if compound conditioning is followed by conditioning to A alone, the animal will respond when tested with B.

This relatively simple design has since expanded in a number of unexpected directions, and our original primitive notions about attention have been forcibly revised, if not refined. To date, we have utilized over 1200 rats as subjects in more than 110 experimental groups. There has been an earlier report of the first stages of this work (Kamin, 1968); in the present chapter, we shall review the basic preliminary findings, then focus on some of the more recent developments.

The basic CER procedure utilized in all these studies employs naive hooded rats as subjects, reduced to 75% of *ad libitum* body weight and maintained on a 24-hour feeding rhythm. The rats are first trained to press a bar for a food reward in a standard, automatically programmed operant conditioning chamber. The daily sessions are 2 hours in length, with food pellets being delivered according to a 2.5-minute variable-interval reinforcement schedule. The first five sessions (10 hrs.) produce stable bar-pressing rates in individual rats, and CER conditioning is then begun. During CER conditioning, the food-reinforcement schedule remains in effect throughout the daily 2-hour session, but four CS–US sequences are now programmed independently of the animal's behavior. The CS, typically, has a duration of 3 minutes and is followed immediately by a .5-second US, typically a 1-ma. shock. For each CER trial (four trials daily), a suppression ratio is calculated. The ratio is $B/A + B$, where B represents the number of bar presses during the 3-minute CS, and A the number of bar presses during the 3-minute period immediately preceding the CS. Thus, if the CS has no effect on the animal's bar pressing, the ratio is .50; but as the CS, with repeated trials, begins to suppress bar pressing, the ratio drops toward an asymptote very close to .00. We regard the learned suppression produced by the CS as an index of an association between CS and US, much as conditioned salivation to a metronome may be regarded as such an index.

The CS in the experiments to be described was either a white noise (typically 80 db), the turning on of an overhead house light (7.5-w. bulb diffused through milky plastic ceiling), or a compound of noise-plus-light presented simultaneously. The normal condition of the chamber is complete darkness. The various experimental groups received CER conditioning to various CS's, in different sequences. The precise sequences of CS's are detailed in the body of this report. Typically, following the CER conditioning, the animal was given a single test day, during which a non-reinforced CS was presented four times within the bar-pressing session. The data to be presented are suppression ratios for the first test trial. While no conclusions would be altered by including the data for all four test trials, the fact that the test CS is not reinforced means that test trials following the first contribute relatively little to differences between experimental groups.

The characteristic outcome of our basic conditioning procedure is depicted in Fig. 8.4–1, which presents median suppression ratios, as a function of acquisition trial, for three representative groups of subjects. The groups have been conditioned with either noise, light, or the compound as a CS. The major point to note at present is that after a very few

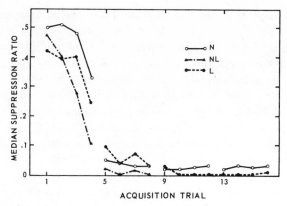

ACQUISITION TRIAL

FIGURE 8.4–1 Acquisition of CER by trial, for three groups of rats, trained with either light, noise, or compound CS.

trials all groups approach asymptotic suppression. It can also be observed that light has a slightly suppressing effect on the very first trial so that the light group tends to acquire slightly more rapidly than the noise group. Finally, the compound group acquires significantly more rapidly than either of the others.

The first experimental approach to attention is illustrated in the design outlined below. The code letter for an experimental group is indicated at the left of the paradigm. Then the CS employed with that group during consecutive phases of CER conditioning is noted; L, N, and LN refer, respectively, to a light, a noise, or a compound CS. The number of reinforced trials with each type of CS is indicated in parentheses immediately following the CS notation; four reinforced trials are given daily. Finally, the CS employed during the test trial is indicated, together with the median suppression ratio for the group on the test trial. The number of animals per experimental group varies, in the studies to be reported, between 8 and 20.

Group A:	LN (8)	N (16)	Test L	.25
Group B:	N (16)	LN (8)	Test L	.45
Group G:	—	LN (8)	Test L	.05
Group 2-B:	—	N (24)	Test L	.44

There are a number of relevant comparisons which can be made within the above set of four experimental treatments. The basic comparison is that between Groups G and B. The test result for Group G indicates, as a kind of base line, the amount of control normally acquired by the light as a result of eight reinforced compound conditioning trials. This is very significantly different from the result for Group B, within which the same compound conditioning trials have been preceded by prior conditioning to the noise element. Thus, our speculation that prior conditioning to an element might block conditioning to a new, superimposed element receives support. When we next compare Groups A and B, we again observe a significant difference. These two groups have each received the same number of each type of CER conditioning trial, but in a different sequence. Group B, for whom the noise conditioning preceded compound conditioning, is less suppressed on the test trial than is Group A, for whom the noise conditioning followed compound conditioning. This again supports the notion that prior conditioning to A blocks conditioning to the B member of the compound. The further fact that Group A is not as suppressed as Group G is not to be regarded as produced by interpolation of noise conditioning after compound conditioning. It must be remembered that four days elapse for Group A between the last compound trial and the test; appropriate control groups have established that Group A's poor performance on the test, relative to Group G's, can be attributed to the passage of time. This *recency effect*, of course, works counter to the direction of the significant difference we have observed between Groups A and B. The failure of Group B to suppress to light as much as does Group A, even with a strong recency effect working to Group B's advantage, suggests a fundamental failure of conditioning to the light in Group B. This is confirmed when we compare the test results of Group B and 2-B. These groups each experience 24 times noise followed by shock, but for Group B light is superimposed during the final eight trials. The fact that the test trial to light yields equivalent results for B and 2-B indicates that the superimpositions have produced literally no conditioning to the light. The test ratios for both these groups are slightly below .50, indicating again that, independent of previous conditioning, an initial presentation of light has a mildly disruptive effect on ongoing bar-pressing behavior.

The blocking effect demonstrated by the experimental treatments described above is not specific to the particular sequence of stimuli employed. When four new groups of rats were trained, reversing the roles of the light and noise stimuli, a total block of conditioning to the noise member of a compound was produced by prior conditioning to the light element (Kamin, 1968). Further, it should be pointed out that we have tested many rats, after *de novo* conditioning to the light–noise compound, to each element separately. We have never observed a rat which did not display some suppression to each element. Thus, granted the present intensity levels of light and noise, the blocking effect depends upon prior conditioning to one of the elements; when conditioned from the outset to the compound, no animal ignores completely one of the elements.

We should also note that animals conditioned to noise alone after previous conditioning to light alone acquire at the same rate as do naive animals conditioned to noise alone. Prior conditioning to noise alone also does not affect subsequent conditioning to light alone. It seems very probable that this lack of transfer between the two stimuli, as well as some degree of equivalence between the independent efficacies of the stimuli, are necessary preconditions for the kind of symmetrical blocking effect which we have demonstrated.

The results so far presented indicate that, granted prior conditioning to an element, no conditioning occurs to a new element which is now superimposed on the old. This might mean, as we first loosely suggested, that the animal does not notice (or perceive) the superimposed element; the kind of peripheral gating mechanism popularized by Hernandez-Peon (Hernandez-Peon et al., 1956) is an obvious candidate for theoretical service here. To speak loosely again, however, we might suppose that the animal does notice the superimposed stimulus but does not condition to it because the stimulus is redundant. The motivationally significant event, shock, is already perfectly predicted by the old element. The possible importance of redundancy and informativeness of stimuli in conditioning experiments has been provocatively indicated by Egger and Miller (1962). We thus decided to examine whether, in the case when the superimposed stimulus predicted something new (specifically, nonreinforcement), it could be demonstrated that the animal noticed the new stimulus. The following two groups were examined.

| Group Y: | N (16) | LN, nonreinforced (8) | N, nonreinforced (4) |
| Group Z: | N (16) | N, nonreinforced (12) | |

The results for both groups during nonreinforced trials are presented in Fig. 8.4–2.

Through the first 16 CER conditioning trials these groups are treated identically, and on the sixteenth trial the median ratio to noise was .02 for each group. When Group Y was presented with the compound on its next trial, its ratio increased to .18; on the equivalent trial, Group Z, presented with the familiar noise, had a ratio of .01. The difference between groups on this trial fell short of significance, but it is certainly suggestive. The animals in Group Y seem to notice the superimposed light, even before the compound is followed by nonreinforcement. It must be remembered that, until the moment of nonreinforcement on Trial 17, Group Y is treated identically to the blocked Group B in the original experiment. Thus, if this result can be replicated, we have evidence that animals do notice the superimposed element, at least on the first trial of its introduction. The evidence is in the form of an attenuation of the suppression which would have occurred had not the new element been superimposed.

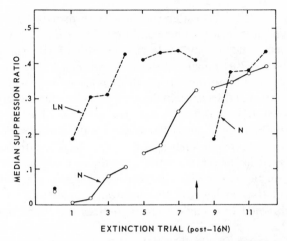

FIGURE 8.4–2   Extinction of CER, by trial, following conditioning to noise. The groups were extinguished either to noise alone or to the compound. The arrow in the abscissa indicates points at which group extinguished to compound is switched to noise alone.

To return to the comparison between Groups Y and Z, on the second nonreinforced trial Group Y's ratio was .31, Group Z's was .02. This difference was significant. Thus a single nonreinforced presentation of the compound was sufficient for Group Y to discriminate between noise (always reinforced) and the compound (nonreinforced). Clearly, the light element had been perceived by Group Y. The very rapid extinction in Group Y cannot be attributed to the mere failure to reinforce the noise element, as Group Z's performance makes perfectly clear. The nature of the discrimination formed by Group Y is further illustrated by comparing performance of the two groups throughout the extinction phase of the experiment. By the eighth nonreinforced trial, the ratios were .41 for Group Y and .33 for Group Z. Then, on the next trial, the stimulus for Group Y was changed to noise alone. The Group Y ratio on this trial was .17, the Group Z ratio was again .33. This was a significantly lower ratio for Group Y than had been observed on the preceding trial. Thus, to some degree, animals in Group Y had learned that it was the compound which was nonreinforced; the noise element per se had been protected from extinction.

We now see that, if the superimposed element provides new information, the animal not only notices the element but can utilize the information which it provides with truly impressive efficiency. Further, the attenuated suppression noted on the transitional trial, when the new element is first superimposed on the old, suggested that, even in the earlier experiments in which the new element was redundant, the animals may have noticed it. This suggestion was confirmed by examining all of our data. We had at last count conditioned 153 animals with 16 trails of noise alone, followed by at least one trial of the compound. The median ratio of these animals on the sixteenth noise trial was .02; on the transitional trial (before reinforcement or nonreinforcement of the compound can exert any differential effect) the median ratio was .15. (When the transitional trial was reinforced, the median ratio on the second compound trial was again .02). There were 106 subjects which displayed higher ratios on the transitional trial than on the sixteenth noise trial; 17 which displayed lower ratios on the transitional trial; and 30 which had equal ratios on the two trials. This is a highly significant effect. There is thus no doubt that, at least on the first transitional trial, an animal previously conditioned to a single element notices the superimposition of a new element.

This observation is clearly fatal to our original theoretical notions. There remains the possibility, however, that in the case when the transitional trial proves the superimposed stimulus to be redundant, some gating mechanism is activated at that point such that the new element is not perceived on subsequent compound trials. Thus, it is at least conceivable that perceptual gating (deficient attention) provides the mechanism through which redundant stimuli are made nonconditionable. This view can be contrasted to the notion that redundant stimuli, though perceived in an intact manner, are simply not conditioned. We shall return to this problem a little later, after reviewing briefly some of the parameters of the blocking effect.

The data gathered to date, much of which has been more fully described elsewhere (Kamin, 1968), indicates such facts as the following. The blocking effect, granted prior conditioning to Element A, remains total even if the number of compound conditioning trials is very substantially increased; on the other hand, if conditioning to Element A is terminated before suppression has become asymptotic, a partial block of conditioning to the B member of the compound occurs. The amount of blocking is very smoothly related to the amount of prior conditioning to Element A. The block can be eliminated by extinguishing suppression to A prior to beginning compound conditioning; if suppression to A is extinguished following compound conditioning (A having been conditioned prior to the compound), the block remains. When blocking experiments were conducted with new groups of animals, holding constant the intensity value of Element B, while varying for different groups the intensity of Element A, the amount of blocking was a clear function of the relative intensities of the two elements. That is, more blocking of conditioning to B occurs if A is physically intense than if A is physically weak. This, however, is confounded with the fact that the level of suppression achieved by conclusion of the conditioning trials to A varies with the intensity of A; and we have already indicated that blocking varies with the level of suppression conditioned to A.

We have, as well, examined the blocking effect under a large number of procedural variations which have had no effect whatever on the basic phenomenon. Thus, for example, if the standard experiment is repeated employing a 1-minute, rather than a 3-minute, CS, a complete block is obtained. The same outcome is observed if the experiment is performed employing a 3-ma., rather than a 1-ma., US throughout. And again, complete blocking is obtained if the first CS, on which light onset is superimposed as a new element, is the turning off of a background 80-db noise, rather than the turning on of an 80-db noise. To put matters simply, the blocking phenomenon is robust, and easily reproducible. . . .

We return now to some further experimental analyses of the basic blocking effect. Within the work previously reported, substantial prior conditioning to an element has invariably given rise to no evidence of conditioning to the superimposed element. Thus the block has appeared to be a dramatically all-or-none affair. We now ask whether the total block which we observed in our basic Group B was in part an artifact of the relatively blunt measure of conditioning which we employed. The test trial to light, following compound conditioning, measures transfer from the compound to the element. The savings method is known to be extremely sensitive in demonstrating transfer, much more so than is the recall method represented by our test. We now repeated the basic experiment, but the test was no longer a single test trial to light; instead, all animals were given four reinforced conditioning trials to light at the end of the experiment. The focus of interest is on rate of acquisition during this conditioning to light. The two basic groups are outlined below.

| Group 2-A: | N (16) | LN (8) | L (4) |
| Group 2-B: | — | N (24) | L (4) |

While Groups 2-A and 2-B have each experienced noise followed by shock 24 times before the conditioning to light alone, the difference is of course that Group 2-A has on the last eight trials experienced the light superimposed on the noise. Will Group 2-A therefore show any savings, relative to Group 2-B, when conditioned to the light alone? Or have the eight superimpositions of light literally left no effect on the animal?

There was, as our earlier results would have suggested, no significant suppression to the light by either group on the first conditioning trial to light. However, Group 2-A displayed significantly more suppression on each of trials 2, 3, and 4 than did Group 2-B. Thus, it is clear that the eight light superimpositions did indeed leave some trace, which was manifested in a significant savings effect. However, we are reminded that our earlier data already demonstrated that, in groups conditioned similarly to Group 2-A, the animals did notice the superimposed light at least on the first, transitional trial. Can it be the case that the significant savings exhibited by Group 2-A is entirely attributable to the first trial on which light is superimposed? Or, do the compound trials following the first also contribute to the savings effect?

To answer this question, Group 2-N was examined. The procedure is sketched below, and should be compared to those diagrammed in the immediately preceding paradigm.

Group 2-N: N (16)   LN (1)   N (7)   L (4)

Group 2-N differs from Group 2-B only on the transitional trial; though the total number of reinforced experiences of noise is equated across Groups 2-A, 2-B, and 2-N, Group 2-N receives seven fewer light superimpositions than does Group 2-A. Nevertheless, the acquisition curves to light alone in the final phase of the experiment are virtually identical for Groups 2-N and 2-A; like Group 2-A, Group 2-N is significantly more suppressed than Group 2-B on each of Trials 2, 3, and 4. If we compute median suppression ratios over the four trials of light conditioning for each group, they are .28 for each of Groups 2-A and 2-N, but .38 for Group 2-B. Thus it is clear that the savings which we have demonstrated can be entirely attributed to the first, transitional trial. We had in any event independent evidence that the animal noticed the light on that trial, and it is now clear that the reinforcement at the termination of that trial does produce an increment in the associative connection between light and shock. There still, however, is nothing in the data which can allow us to conclude that the animal notices a redundant, superimposed element on any trial after the transitional trial; or at least, we have no indication that reinforced presentations of the superimposed element after the transitional trial in any way affect either the contemporaneous or the subsequent behavior of the animal. These results are obviously consistent with a perceptual gating concept, so long as the gating mechanism is not activated until after the transitional trial.

Where then do we stand now? The fact that the superimposed element proves to be redundant (that the US is already perfectly predicted by Element A) seems to be central to any interpretation of the blocking effect. Presumably, then, blocking would not occur if the superimposed element were made informative. We have earlier demonstrated that, if the compound is nonreinforced, the animal utilizes the information provided by Element B very efficiently. The strategy at this point was to perform a study within the blocking paradigm, reinforcing the compound trials, but at the same time making Element B informative. This was accomplished by radically increasing US intensity during the compound trials above the level employed during the prior conditioning to Element A, as with Group 2-M in the set of experimental treatments outlined below.

Group B:	N-1 ma. (16)	LN-1 ma. (8)	Test L	.45
Group 2-M:	N-1 ma. (16)	LN-4 ma. (8)	Test L	.14
Group 3-U:	N-4 ma. (8)	LN-4 ma. (8)	Test L	.36

The comparison between Groups B and 2-M is instructive. Here at last is a simple procedure which can virtually eliminate the blocking effect. Within Group 2-M, shock intensity is radically increased during the compound trials. The effect of this operation is to allow the formation of a clear association between the superimposed element and the US; Group 2-M, on the test trial, is significantly more suppressed than the standard Group B. This effect is not a simple consequence of employing an intense US during the compound trials. With Group 3-U, the same intense US is employed throughout the experiment, and a clear blocking effect is manifested: the test ratio of 3-U does not differ significantly from that of B, but does from that of 2-M. Thus, it is the change of shock intensity during the compound trials from that employed during prior conditioning which seems responsible for eliminating the block. These results provide clear support for the assumption that blocking occurs because of the redundancy of the superimposed element. The question remains, how does redundancy prevent the formation of an association between a CS element and a US with which it is contiguously presented?

The most recent conception at which we have arrived seems capable of integrating all the data already presented. The notion is this: perhaps, for an increment in an associative connection to occur, it is necessary that the US instigate some mental work on the part of the animal. This mental work will occur only if the US is unpredicted, if it in some sense surprises the animal. Thus, in the early trials of a normal conditioning experiment, the US is an unpredicted, surprising event of motivational significance and the CS–US association is formed. Within the blocking experiment, the occurrence of the US on the first compound trial is to some degree surprising. This can be deduced, circularly, from the empirical observation that, on the transitional trial only, suppression is moderately attenuated; and some little learning about Element B can be demonstrated to have occurred on the transitional trial, but on no other compound trial. Finally, if in the blocking experiment US intensity is radically increased when compound training is begun, the new US is obviously surprising and no block is observed.

Precisely what mental work is instigated by a surprising US? The language in which these notions have been couched can be made more respectable, as well as more specific. Thus, as a first try, suppose that, for an increment in an associative connection to occur, it is necessary that the US provoke the animal into a backward scanning of its memory store of recent stimulus input; only as a result of such a scan can an association between CS and US be formed, and the scan is prompted only by an unpredicted US, the occurrence of which is surprising. This sort of speculation, it can be noted, leaves perception of the superimposed CS element intact. The CS element fails to become conditioned not because its input has been impeded, but because the US fails to function as a reinforcing stimulus. We have clearly moved some distance from the notion of attention to the CS, perhaps to enter the realm of retrospective contemplation of the CS.

These notions, whatever their vices, do suggest experimental manipulations. With the backward scan concept in mind, an experiment was performed which employed the blocking paradigm, but with an effort to surprise the animal very shortly after each presentation of the compound. Thus, animals were first conditioned, in the normal way, to suppress to the noise CS, with the usual 1-ma., .5-second US. Then, during the compound trials, the animal received reinforced presentations of the light-noise compound, again with a 1-ma., .5 second US. However, on each compound trial, 5 seconds following delivery of the US, an extra (surprising) shock (again 1 ma., .5 sec.) was delivered. When, after compound training, these subjects were tested with the light CS, they displayed a median ratio of .08. That is, the blocking effect was entirely eliminated by the delivery of an unpredicted shock shortly following reinforced presentation of the compound.

We have emphasized the close temporal relation between the unpredicted extra shock and the preceding compound CS. This emphasis is, of course, consistent with the backward scanning notion. There are, however, several alternative interpretations of the efficacy of the unpredicted shock in eliminating the blocking effect. There is the obvious possibility that the extra shock combines with the shortly preceding normal US to form, in effect, a US more intense than that employed during the prior conditioning to the noise element. We have already indicated that a radical increase of US intensity during the compound trials will eliminate the blocking effect. There is in the data, however, a strong indication that the extra shock functions in a manner quite different from that of an intense US. It is true that, if US intensity is increased from 1 ma. to 4 ma. during the compound trials, the blocking effect is eliminated; but it is also true that, if independent groups of naive rats are conditioned, with either a light, noise, or compound CS, paired with a 4-ma. US, they acquire the CER significantly more rapidly than do equivalent groups conditioned with a 1-ma. US. That is, acquisition of the CER is a clear positive function of US intensity. We have conditioned naive groups of animals, with either light or noise CS's, delivering the extra shock, 5 seconds after the normal US, from the outset of conditioning. In each case, the acquisition curve of rats conditioned with the extra shock was virtually superimposed on that of rats conditioned with the normal US. Thus, the extra shock does not appear to increase effective US intensity.

We have stressed the notion that the second, extra shock might cause the animal to scan the preceding sensory input, and that conditioning to the superimposed CS element occurs as a consequence of this scanning. There remains, however, the plausible alternative that the effect of the unpredicted, extra shock is to alert the animal in such a way that it is more attentive or sensitive to subsequent events; i.e., to the following compound trials. Thus, in this latest view, the extra shock does not increase the amount of conditioning taking place to the superimposed CS element on the first compound trial, but it does increase the amount of such conditioning taking place on all subsequent compound trials. Within the experiment already performed, there is unfortunately no way of deciding whether the extra shock facilitates conditioning to the CS which precedes it or to the CS which follows it. We do know, from appropriate control groups, that the extra shock does not cause the animal to suppress to extraneous exteroceptive stimuli which are subsequently presented.

There should be no great experimental difficulty in localizing the effect of the extra shock. We can, for example, deliver the extra shock to different groups at varying temporal intervals following the compound trials. Presumably, backward scanning should be less effective in forming an association when the extra shock is remote in time from the preceding trial. This approach, however, has the disadvantage that moving the extra shock away from the preceding trial moves it toward the subsequent trial. This problem in turn might be overcome by presenting only one compound trial a day. The sensitivity of the procedure seems to be such that, employing a savings technique, we might demonstrate the facilitating effect of a single extra shock, delivered on a single compound trial, with no subsequent compound conditioning. This effect in turn might be related to the temporal interval between the compound trial and the extra shock. There is no dearth of potential experiments to be performed, and not much sense in attempting to anticipate their outcomes.

To sum up, the blocking experiment demonstrates very clearly that the mere contiguous presentation of a CS element and a US is not a sufficient condition for the establishment of a CR. The question, very simply is: What has gone wrong in the blocking experiment? What is deficient? The experiment was conceived with a primitive hunch that attention to the to-be-conditioned stimulus element was a necessary precondition, and many of the results to date are consistent with the notion that the deficiency is perceptual, having to do with impeded input of the CS element. This blocked input was at first conceived as a consequence of a kind of competition for attention between the previously conditioned element and the new element. The results to date, however, make it clear that, if such an attentional deficit is involved, the redundancy of the new element is critical for producing it. The extra shock experiment, most recently, has suggested an alternative conception. The input of the new CS element can be regarded as intact, but the predictability of the US might strip the US of a function it normally subserves in conditioning experiments, that of instigating some processing of the memory store of recent stimulus input, which results in the formation of an association. There is also the possibility, of course, that the predictability of the US, by the time compound training is begun in the blocking experiment, strips the US of the function of alerting the animal to subsequent stimulus input.

There seems little doubt that, as experimentation continues, still other conceptions will be suggested. The experimental procedures are at least capable of discarding some conceptions and of reinforcing others. The progress to date might encourage the belief that ultimately these studies could make a real contribution toward answering the fundamental question toward which they are addressed: What are the necessary and sufficient conditions for the establishment of an association between CS and US within a Pavlovian paradigm?

REFERENCES

Egger, M. C., & Miller, N. E. Secondary reinforcement in rats as a function of information value and reliability of the stimulus. *Journal of Experimental Psychology*, 1962, 64, 97–104.

Estes, W. K., & Skinner, B. F. Some quantitative properties of anxiety. *Journal of Experimental Psychology*, 1941, 29, 390–400.

Hernandez-Peon, R., Scherrer, H., & Jouvet, M. Modification of electrical activity in cochlear nucleus during "attention" in unanesthetized cats. *Science*, 1956, 123, 331–332.

Hull, C. L. *Principles of behavior*. New York: Appleton-Century, 1943.

Hunt, H. F., & Brady, J. V. Some effects of punishment and intercurrent "anxiety" on a single operant. *Journal of Comparative and Physiological Psychology*, 1955, 48, 305–310.

Kamin, L. J. Temporal and intensity characteristics of the conditioned stimulus. In W. F. Prokasy (Ed.), *Classical conditioning*. New York: Appleton-Century-Crofts, 1965. Pp. 118–147.

Kamin, L. J. "Attention-like" processes in classical conditioning. In M. R. Jones (Ed.), *Miami symposium on the prediction of behavior, 1967: Aversive stimulation*. Coral Gables, Fla.: University of Miami Press, 1968. Pp. 9–31.

Pavlov, I. P. *Conditioned reflexes*. (Tr., G. V. Anrep.) London: Oxford University Press, 1927. (Reprinted, New York: Dover, 1960.)

Nine
Biological Constraints on Conditioning

Give me a dozen healthy infants, well-formed, and my own specified world to bring them up in, and I'll guarantee to take any one at random and train him to become any type of specialist I might select—a doctor, lawyer, artist, merchant-chief and, yes, even into a beggar-man and thief, regardless of his talents, penchants, tendencies, abilities, vocations and race of his ancestors [John B. Watson, 1926].

We have argued throughout this book for the importance of learning in shaping our lives and, potentially, in reshaping them. Watson expressed this faith in perhaps its most extreme form, but to some degree it is implicit in activities ranging from a parent's spanking a child to Mao Tse-tung's efforts to completely transform Chinese society. It would be a mistake, however, to conclude this book without some acknowledgement of the *limitations* of conditioning. We are not composed, after all, of endlessly malleable putty, but of semirigid flesh and bones, our form determined in large part by our genetic inheritance. Behavior too is shaped by heredity, and there may be important limitations on how extensively it can be modified.

Some evidence suggesting the importance of biological constraints on learning comes from observations of animal behavior in the wild. Rats, for example, display a behavior called *bait-shyness*, in which having once eaten from a poisoned bait set out by an exterminator they thereafter avoid it assiduously. This learned aversion seems to be due to classical conditioning: the poisoned bait produces toxicosis, and this illness becomes conditioned to the preceding cues, making them aversive. An anomaly, however, is that while the rats totally avoid food with a taste similar to that of the bait, they show no reluctance to return to the *place* where they were poisoned. It is as if they are selectively prepared to learn relationships between nausea and gustatory cues, but not environmental cues such as light or sound. Thus although all previous laboratory experience had suggested that "any natural phenomenon chosen at will may be converted into a conditioned stimulus (Pavlov, quoted in Garcia, McGowan, and Green, 1972), naturalistic observations suggested that toxicosis might not be conditionable to visual cues.

To test this hypothesis under controlled laboratory conditions, Garcia and Koelling (Article 9.1) allowed rats to drink flavored water while being simultaneously exposed to a light and tone. The conditioned stimulus, then, was a gustatory-audiovisual compound, and after several minutes of exposure to it the rats were poisoned. After allowing the rats to recover, the authors tested which of the compound elements had become conditioned by presenting them separately, and observing their effects on drinking. Drinking was severely depressed by the presence of the flavor, suggesting that it had become aversive as a result of conditioning, but was unaffected by the audiovisual cues. These results suggested that visual cues and nausea cannot be associated in the rat, but a plausible alternative might have been that the visual cue used was simply too weak, and could not have been associated with any US. Garcia and Koelling therefore ran another group which received the same stimulus compound during training, but were then exposed to electric shock rather than poisoning as the US. The result was that it was now the audiovisual stimulus which suppressed later drinking while the taste stimulus had no effect! The audiovisual compound, therefore, was an effective stimulus when paired with shock, but totally ineffective when paired with poisoning.

In our earlier discussion of classical conditioning we implied that it was a completely general process in which any two contiguous stimuli could be associated. The phenomenon of bait-shyness, however, suggests that we don't learn all possible stimulus relationships, but only those for which we are biologically predisposed. In the course of evolution a rat that avoided foods that had been followed by nausea was likely to avoid further poisonings, and thus was more likely to survive and reproduce. Rather than one central learning process which evolved as a unit, therefore, specialized learning mechanisms may have evolved independently, each with its own neural centers and characteristics. The conditioning of nausea, for example, seems to differ from other instances of classical conditioning not only in the stimuli that may be conditioned but in its rapidity and its temporal characteristics. Thus whereas eyelid conditioning is normally a relatively slow process, requiring as many as 100 or more trials to reach asymptote, strong aversions based on illness may be conditioned after only a single trial (e.g., Garcia, McGowan, and Green, 1972). Even more striking are the effects of the delay between the CS and the US. Eyelid conditioning is impossible with a delay of even 2 seconds, whereas successful nausea conditioning has been reported after a delay

of 12 hours (Smith and Roll, 1967)! We have, then, the strong
suggestion that classical conditioning is not a unitary phenomenon,
but one built up of separately acquired subsystems, each shaped by
the species' evolutionary history.

Nor are biological limitations on learning unique to classical
conditioning. Reinforcement was also once assumed to be a totally
general process, capable of modifying any response, but this faith was
challenged in 1961 in a fascinating article by Keller and Marion
Breland (Article 9.2). Trained originally as experimental psychologists,
the Brelands left Harvard to establish a company which trained
animals to perform for commercial exhibits. At first their efforts met
with considerable success, and they were able to train complex behavioral
sequences using the techniques of reinforcement. A raccoon, for
example, was reinforced with food first for picking up a coin, and then
for carrying it over to a piggy bank and dropping it in. Training
progressed quickly at first, but then the raccoon developed a disconcerting
tendency to hold onto the coin, starting to lower it into the piggy bank
but then lifting it out and rubbing it between its hands. The rubbing
behavior became worse and worse, until eventually the trick had to
be abandoned because of the raccoon's refusal to release the coin. The
Brelands found this loss of control by reinforcement to be a common
phenomenon, as the typography of responses learned through
reinforcement gradually began to drift toward that of instinctive
behavior (a tendency to rub or wash potential food in the case of the
raccoon). This *instinctive drift* occurred despite the fact that it delayed
(and, in extreme form, prevented) reward, and it suggests important
limitations on the modifiability of behavior.

Despite the compelling nature of the Brelands' examples, acceptance
of their arguments was slow in coming. Psychologists have traditionally
been reluctant to accept anecdotal evidence based on the casual
observation of individual subjects, but even beyond this factor was the
conservatism inherent in scientific progress. Scientists are reluctant
to accept new ideas which contradict already well-established theories,
and while this conservatism serves the positive function of insulating
science from random fluctuations with every new hypothesis, it may
also delay investigation of radically new ideas (see Kuhn, 1970).
Gradually, however, experimental evidence in support of the Brelands'
hypothesis began to accumulate, and the focus of experimental research
began to shift from demonstrating the generality of the laws of learning
to determining their limitations. This evidence is ably reviewed by
Seligman (Article 9.3), and it suggests significant limitations on
the modifiability of behavior.

The existence of biological limitations on learning does not mean that we must abandon our efforts to apply the principles of learning. Applications such as systematic desensitization and the token economy have already demonstrated the potential of such efforts, and as these techniques are refined their effectiveness should increase. It does suggest, however, that the unbounded optimism of Watson was premature, and that it is still too early to speculate on the limits of social change. Can we learn to love one another and to share our lives together in a free and creative environment? Or are we innately selfish and aggressive, doomed to inevitable conflict and perhaps mutual extermination? We have no way of specifying the limits of social improvement at present, but hopefully future research will enable us to approach these limits as closely as possible.

9.1 RELATION OF CUE TO CONSEQUENCE IN AVOIDANCE LEARNING*

John Garcia and Robert A. Koelling

An audiovisual stimulus was made contingent upon the rat's licking at the water spout, thus making it analogous with a gustatory stimulus. When the audiovisual stimulus and the gustatory stimulus were paired with electric shock the avoidance reactions transferred to the audiovisual stimulus, but not the gustatory stimulus. Conversely, when both stimuli were paired with toxin or x-ray the avoidance reactions transferred to the gustatory stimulus, but not the audiovisual stimulus. Apparently stimuli are selected as cues dependent upon the nature of the subsequent reinforcer.

A great deal of evidence stemming from diverse sources suggests an inadequacy in the usual formulations concerning reinforcement. Barnett (1963) has described the "bait-shy" behavior of wild rats which have survived a poisoning attempt. These animals utilizing olfactory and

* Reprinted from Psychonomic Science, 1966, 4, 123–124. Copyright 1966 by the Psychonomic Society, and reproduced by permission. This research stems from doctoral research carried out at Long Beach V. A. Hospital and supported by NIH No. RH00068. Thanks are extended to Professors B. F. Ritchie, D. Krech and E. R. Dempster, U. C. Berkeley, California.

gustatory cues, avoid the poison bait which previously made them ill. However, there is no evidence that they avoid the "place" of the poisoning.

In a recent volume (Haley & Snyder, 1964) several authors have discussed studies in which ionizing radiations were employed as a noxious stimulus to produce avoidance reactions in animals. Ionizing radiation like many poisons produces gastrointestinal disturbances and nausea. Strong aversions are readily established in animals when distinctively flavored fluids are conditionally paired with x-rays. Subsequently, the gustatory stimulus will depress fluid intake without radiation. In contrast, a distinctive environmental complex of auditory, visual, and tactual stimuli does not inhibit drinking even when the compound stimulus is associated with the identical radiation schedule. This differential effect has also been observed following ingestion of a toxin and the injection of a drug (Garcia & Koelling, 1965).

Apparently this differential effectiveness of cues is due either to the nature of the reinforcer, i.e., radiation or toxic effects, or to the peculiar relation which a gustatory stimulus has to the drinking response, i.e., gustatory stimulation occurs if and only if the animal licks the fluid. The environmental cues associated with a distinctive place are not as dependent upon a single response of the organism. Therefore, we made an auditory and visual stimulus dependent upon the animal's licking the water spout. Thus, in four experiments reported here "bright-noisy" water, as well as "tasty" water was conditionally paired with radiation, a toxin, immediate shock, and delayed shock, respectively, as reinforcers. Later the capacity of these response-controlled stimuli to inhibit drinking in the absence of reinforcement was tested.

METHOD

The apparatus was a light and sound shielded box (7 in. × 7 in. × 7 in.) with a drinking spout connected to an electronic drinkometer which counted each touch of the rat's tongue to the spout. "Bright-noisy" water was provided by connecting an incandescent lamp (5 watts) and a clicking relay into this circuit. "Tasty" water was provided by adding flavors to the drinking supply.

Each experimental group consisted of 10 rats (90 day old Sprague–Dawley males) maintained in individual cages without water, but with *Purina Laboratory chow ad libidum.*

The procedure was: A. One week of habituation to drinking in the apparatus without stimulation. B. Pretests to measure intake of bright-noisy water and tasty water prior to training. C. Acquisition training with: (1) reinforced trials where these stimuli were paired with reinforcement during drinking, (2) nonreinforced trials where rats drank water without stimuli or reinforcement. Training terminated when there was a reliable difference between water intake scores on reinforced and nonreinforced trials. D. Post-tests to measure intake of bright-noisy water and tasty water after training.

In the x-ray study an audiovisual group and a gustatory group were exposed to an identical radiation schedule. In the other studies reinforcement was contingent upon the rat's response. To insure that both the audiovisual and the gustatory stimuli received equivalent reinforcement, they were combined and simultaneously paired with the reinforcer during acquisition training. Therefore, one group serving as its own control and divided into equal subgroups, was tested in balanced order with an audiovisual and a gustatory test before and after training with these stimuli combined.

One 20-min. reinforced trial was administered every three days in the x-ray and lithium chloride studies. This prolonged intertrial interval was designed to allow sufficient time for the rats to recover from acute effects of treatment. On each interpolated day the animals received a 20-min. nonreinforced trial. They were post-tested two days after their last reinforced trial. The x-ray groups received a total of three reinforced trials, each with 54 r of filtered 250 kv x-rays delivered in 20 min. Sweet water (1 gm saccharin per liter) was the gustatory stimulus. The lithium chloride group had a total of five reinforced trials with toxic salty water (.12M lithium chloride). Nontoxic salty water (.12 sodium chloride) which rats cannot readily distinguish from the toxic solution was used in the gustatory tests (Nachman, 1963).

The immediate shock study was conducted on a more orthodox avoidance schedule. Tests and trials were 2 min. long. Each day for four consecutive acquisition days, animals were given two nonreinforced and two reinforced trials in an NRRN, RNNR pattern. A shock, the minimal current required to interrupt drinking (0.5 sec. at 0.08-0.20 ma), was delivered through a floor grid 2 sec. after the first lick at the spout.

The delayed shock study was conducted simultaneously with the lithium chloride on the same schedule. Non-toxic salty water was the gustatory stimulus. Shock reinforcement was delayed during first trials and gradually increased in intensity (.05 to .30 ma) in a schedule designed to produce a drinking pattern during the 20-min. period which resembled that of the corresponding animal drinking toxic salty water.

RESULTS AND DISCUSSION

The results indicate that all reinforcers were effective in producing discrimination learning during the acquisition phase (see Fig. 9.1–1), but obvious differences occurred in the post-tests. The avoidance reactions

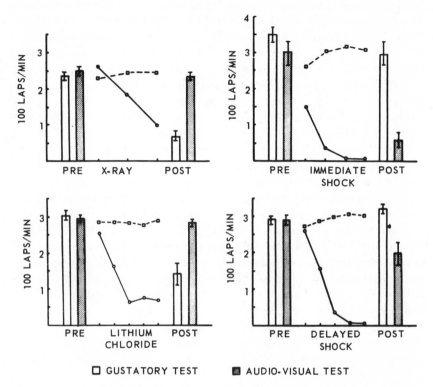

FIGURE 9.1–1   The bars indicate water intake (± St. Error) during a gustatory test (a distinctive taste) and an audiovisual test (light and sound contingent upon licking) before and after conditional pairing with the reinforcers indicated. The curves illustrate mean intake during acquisition.

produced by x-rays and lithium chloride are readily transferred to the gustatory stimulus but not to the audiovisual stimulus. The effect is more pronounced in the x-ray study, perhaps due to differences in dose. The x-ray animals received a constant dose while the lithium chloride rats drank a decreasing amount of the toxic solution during training. Nevertheless, the difference between post-test scores is statistically significant in both experiments ($p < 0.01$ by ranks test).

Apparently when gustatory stimuli are paired with agents which produce nausea and gastric upset, they acquire secondary reinforcing properties which might be described as "conditioned nausea." Auditory and visual stimulation do not readily acquire similar properties even when they are contingent upon the licking response.

In contrast, the effect of both immediate and delayed shock to the paws is in the opposite direction. The avoidance reactions produced by electric shock to the paws transferred to the audiovisual stimulus but not to the gustatory stimulus. As one might expect the effect of delayed shocks was not as effective as shocks where the reinforcer immediately and consistently followed licking. Again, the difference between post-test intake scores is statistically significant in both studies ($p < 0.01$ by ranks test). Thus, when shock which produces peripheral pain is the reinforcer, "conditioned fear" properties are more readily acquired by auditory and visual stimuli than by gustatory stimuli.

It seems that given reinforcers are not equally effective for all classes of discriminable stimuli. The cues, which the animal selects from the welter of stimuli in the learning situation, appear to be related to the consequences of the subsequent reinforcer. Two speculations are offered: (1) Common elements in the time-intensity patterns of stimulation may facilitate a cross modal generalization from reinforcer to cue in one case and not in another. (2) More likely, natural selection may have favored mechanisms which associate gustatory and olfactory cues with internal discomfort since the chemical receptors sample the materials soon to be incorporated into the internal environment. Krechevsky (1933) postulated such a genetically coded hypothesis to account for the predispositions of rats to respond systematically to specific cues in an insoluble maze. The hypothesis of the sick rat, as for many of us under similar circumstances, would be, "It must have been something I ate."

REFERENCES

Barnett, S. A. The rat: a study in behavior. Chicago: Aldine Press, 1963.
Garcia, J., & Koelling, R. A. A comparison of aversions induced by x-rays, toxins, and drugs in the rat. Radiat. Res., in press, 1965.
Haley, T. J., & Snyder, R. S. (Eds.) The response of the nervous system to ionizing radiation. Boston: Little, Brown & Co., 1964.
Krechevsky, I. The hereditary nature of 'hypothesis'. J. comp. Psychol., 1932, 16, 99–116.
Nachman, M. Learned aversion to the taste of lithium chloride and generalization to other salts. J. comp. physiol. Psychol., 1963, 56, 343–349.

9.2 THE MISBEHAVIOR OF ORGANISMS*
Keller Breland and Marian Breland

There seems to be a continuing realization by psychologists that perhaps the white rat cannot reveal everything there is to know about behavior. Among the voices raised on this topic, Beach (1950) has emphasized the necessity of widening the range of species subjected to experimental techniques and conditions. However, psychologists as a whole do not seem to be heeding these admonitions, as Whalen (1961) has pointed out.

Perhaps this reluctance is due in part to some dark precognition of what they might find in such investigations, for the ethologists Lorenz (1950, p. 233) and Tinbergen (1951, p. 6) have warned that if psychologists are to understand and predict the behavior of organisms, it is essential that they become thoroughly familiar with the instinctive behavior patterns of each new species they essay to study. Of course, the Watsonian or neobehavioristically oriented experimenter is apt to consider "instinct" an ugly word. He tends to class it with Hebb's (1960) other "seditious notions" which were discarded in the behavioristic revolution, and he may have some premonition that he will encounter this bete noir in extending the range of species and situations studied.

We can assure him that his apprehensions are well grounded. In our attempt to extend a behavioristically oriented approach to the engineering control of animal behavior by operant conditioning techniques, we have fought a running battle with the seditious notion of instinct.[1] It might be of some interest to the psychologist to know how the battle is going and to learn something about the nature of the adversary he is likely to meet if and when he tackles new species in new learning situations.

Our first report (Breland & Breland, 1951) in the *American Psychologist*, concerning our experiences in controlling animal behavior, was wholly affirmative and optimistic, saying in essence that the principles derived from the laboratory could be applied to the extensive control of behavior under nonlaboratory conditions throughout a considerable segment of the phylogenetic scale.

When we began this work, it was our aim to see if the science would work beyond the laboratory, to determine if animal psychology could stand on its own feet as an engineering discipline. These aims have been

* Keller Breland and Marian Breland, "The Misbehavior of Organisms," *The American Psychologist*, 16, 1961, 681–683. Copyright 1961 by the American Psychological Association, and reproduced by permission.

realized. We have controlled a wide range of animal behavior and have made use of the great popular appeal of animals to make it an economically feasible project. Conditioned behavior has been exhibited at various municipal zoos and museums of natural history and has been used for department store displays, for fair and trade convention exhibits, for entertainment at tourist attractions, on television shows, and in the production of television commercials. Thirty-eight species, totaling over 6,000 individual animals, have been conditioned, and we have dared to tackle such unlikely subjects as reindeer, cockatoos, raccoons, porpoises, and whales.

Emboldened by this consistent reinforcement, we have ventured further and further from the security of the Skinner box. However, in this cavalier extrapolation, we have run afoul of a persistent pattern of discomforting failures. These failures, although disconcertingly frequent and seemingly diverse, fall into a very interesting pattern. They all represent breakdowns of conditioned operant behavior. From a great number of such experiences, we have selected, more or less at random, the following examples.

The first instance of our discomfiture might be entitled, What Makes Sammy Dance? In the exhibit in which this occurred, the casual observer sees a grown bantam chicken emerge from a retaining compartment when the door automatically opens. The chicken walks over about 3 feet, pulls a rubber loop on a small box which starts a repeated auditory stimulus pattern (a four-note tune). The chicken then steps up onto an 18-inch slightly raised disc, thereby closing a timer switch, and scratches vigorously, round and round, over the disc for 15 seconds, at the rate of about two scratches per second until the automatic feeder fires in the retaining compartment. The chicken goes into the compartment to eat, thereby automatically shutting the door. The popular interpretation of this behavior pattern is that the chicken has turned on the "juke box" and "dances."

The development of this behavioral exhibit was wholly unplanned. In the attempt to create quite another type of demonstration which required a chicken simply to stand on a platform for 12–15 seconds, we found that over 50% developed a very strong and pronounced scratch pattern, which tended to increase in persistence as the time interval was lengthened. (Another 25% or so developed other behaviors—pecking at spots, etc.) However, we were able to change our plans so as to make use of the scratch pattern, and the result was the "dancing chicken" exhibit described above.

In this exhibit the only real contingency for reinforcement is that the chicken must depress the platform for 15 seconds. In the course of a performing day (about 3 hours for each chicken) a chicken may turn out over 10,000 unnecessary, virtually identical responses. Operant behaviorists would probably have little hesitancy in labeling this an example of Skinnerian "superstition" (Skinner, 1948) or "mediating" behavior, and we list it first to whet their explanatory appetite.

However, a second instance involving a raccoon does not fit so neatly into this paradigm. The response concerned the manipulation of money by the raccoon (who has "hands" rather similar to those of the primates). The contingency for reinforcement was picking up the coins and depositing them in a 5-inch metal box.

Raccoons condition readily, have good appetites, and this one was quite tame and an eager subject. We anticipated no trouble. Conditioning him to pick up the first coin was simple. We started out by reinforcing him for picking up a single coin. Then the metal container was introduced, with the requirement that he drop the coin into the container. Here we ran into the first bit of difficulty: he seemed to have a great deal of trouble letting go of the coin. He would rub it up against the inside of the container, pull it back out, and clutch it firmly for several seconds. However, he would finally turn it loose and receive his food reinforcement. Then the final contingency: we put him on a ratio of 2, requiring that he pick up both coins and put them in the container.

Now the raccoon really had problems (and so did we). Not only could he not let go of the coins, but he spent seconds, even minutes, rubbing them together (in a most miserly fashion), and dipping them into the container. He carried on this behavior to such an extent that the practical application we had in mind—a display featuring a raccoon putting money in a piggy bank—simply was not feasible. The rubbing behavior became worse and worse as time went on, in spite of nonreinforcement.

For the third instance, we return to the gallinaceous birds. The observer sees a hopper full of oval plastic capsules which contain small toys, charms, and the like. When the S_D (a light) is presented to the chicken, she pulls a rubber loop which releases one of these capsules onto a slide, about 16 inches long, inclined at about 30 degrees. The capsule rolls down the slide and comes to rest near the end. Here one or two sharp, straight pecks by the chicken will knock it forward off the slide and out to the observer, and the chicken is then reinforced by an automatic feeder. This is all very well—most chickens are able to master these contingencies in short order. The loop pulling presents no problems; she then has only to peck the capsule off the slide to get her reinforcement.

However, a good 20% of all chickens tried on this set of contingencies fail to make the grade. After they have pecked a few capsules off the slide, they begin to grab at the capsules and drag them backward into the cage. Here they pound them up and down on the floor of the cage. Of course, this results in no reinforcement for the chicken, and yet some chickens will pull in over half of all the capsules presented to them.

Almost always this problem behavior does not appear until after the capsules begin to move down the slide. Conditioning is begun with stationary capsules placed by the experimenter. When the pecking behavior becomes strong enough, so that the chicken is knocking them off the slide and getting reinforced consistently, the loop pulling is conditioned to the light. The capsules then come rolling down the slide to the chicken. Here most chickens, who before did not have this tendency, will start grabbing and shaking.

The fourth incident also concerns a chicken. Here the observer sees a chicken in a cage about 4 feet long which is placed alongside a miniature baseball field. The reason for the cage is the interesting part. At one end of the cage is an automatic electric feed hopper. At the other is an opening through which the chicken can reach and pull a loop on a bat. If she pulls the loop hard enough the bat (solenoid operated) will swing, knocking a small baseball up the playing field. If it gets past the miniature toy players on the field and hits the back fence, the chicken is automatically reinforced with food at the other end of the cage. If it does not go far enough, or hits one of the players, she tries again. This results in behavior on an irregular ratio. When the feeder sounds, she then runs down the length of the cage and eats.

Our problems began when we tried to remove the cage for photography. Chickens that had been well conditioned in this behavior became wildly excited when the ball started to move. They would jump up on the playing field, chase the ball all over the field, even knock it off on the floor and chase it around, pecking it in every direction, although they had never had access to the ball before. This behavior was so persistent and so disruptive, in spite of the fact that it was never reinforced, that we had to reinstate the cage.

The last instance we shall relate in detail is one of the most annoying and baffling for a good behaviorist. Here a pig was conditioned to pick up large wooden coins an deposit them in a large "piggy bank." The coins were placed several feet from the bank and the pig required to carry them to the bank and deposit them, usually four or five coins for one reinforcement. (Of course, we started out with one coin, near the bank.)

Pigs condition very rapidly, they have no trouble taking ratios, they have ravenous appetites (naturally), and in many ways are among the most tractable animals we have worked with. However, this particular problem behavior developed in pig after pig, usually after a period of weeks or months, getting worse every day. At first the pig would eagerly pick up one dollar, carry it to the bank, run back, get another, carry it rapidly and neatly, and so on, until the ratio was complete. Thereafter, over a period of weeks the behavior would become slower and slower. He might run over eagerly for each dollar, but on the way back, instead of carrying the dollar and depositing it simply and cleanly, he would repeatedly drop it, root it, drop it again, root it along the way, pick it up, toss it up in the air, drop it, root it some more, and so on.

We thought this behavior might simply be the dilly-dallying of an animal on a low drive. However, the behavior persisted and gained in strength in spite of a severely increased drive—he finally went through the ratios so slowly that he did not get enough to eat in the course of a day. Finally it would take the pig about 10 minutes to transport four coins a distance of about 6 feet. This problem behavior developed repeatedly in successive pigs.

There have also been other instances: hamsters that stopped working in a glass case after four or five reinforcements, porpoises and whales that swallow their manipulanda (balls and inner tubes), cats that will not leave the area of the feeder, rabbits that will not go to the feeder, the great difficulty in many species of conditioning vocalization with food reinforcement, problems in conditioning a kick in a cow, the failure to get appreciably increased effort out of the ungulates with increased drive, and so on. These we shall not dwell on in detail, nor shall we discuss how they might be overcome.

These egregious failures came as a rather considerable shock to us, for there was nothing in our background in behaviorism to prepare us for such gross inabilities to predict and control the behavior of animals with which we had been working for years.

The examples listed we feel represent a clear and utter failure of conditioning theory. They are far from what one would normally expect on the basis of the theory alone. Furthermore, they are definite, observable; the diagnosis of theory failure does not depend on subtle statistical interpretations or on semantic legerdemain—the animal simply does not do what he has been conditioned to do.

It seems perfectly clear that, with the possible exception of the dancing chicken, which could conceivably, as we have said, be explained in terms of Skinner's superstition paradigm, the other instances do not fit the behavioristic way of thinking. Here we have animals, after having been conditioned to a specific learned response, gradually drifting into behaviors that are entirely different from those which were conditioned. Moreover, it can easily be seen that these particular behaviors to which the animals drift are clear-cut examples of instinctive behaviors having to do with the natural food getting behaviors of the particular species.

The dancing chicken is exhibiting the gallinaceous birds' scratch pattern that in nature often precedes ingestion. The chicken that hammers capsules is obviously exhibiting instinctive behavior having to do with breaking open of seed pods or the killing of insects, grubs, etc. The raccoon is demonstrating so-called "washing behavior." The rubbing and washing response may result, for example, in the removal of the exoskeleton of a crayfish. The pig is rooting or shaking—behaviors which are strongly built into this species and are connected with the food getting repertoire.

These patterns to which the animals drift require greater physical output and therefore are a violation of the so-called "law of least effort." And most damaging of all, they stretch out the time required for reinforcement when nothing in the experimental setup requires them to do so. They have only to do the little tidbit of behavior to which they were conditioned—for example, pick up the coin and put it in the container—to get reinforced immediately. Instead, they drag the process out for a matter of minutes when there is nothing in the contingency which forces them to do this. Moreover, increasing the drive merely intensifies this effect.

It seems obvious that these animals are trapped by strong instinctive behaviors, and clearly we have here a demonstration of the prepotency of such behavior patterns over those which have been conditioned.

We have termed this phenomenon "instinctive drift." The general principle seems to be that wherever an animal has strong instinctive behaviors in the area of the conditioned response, after continued running the organism will drift toward the instinctive behavior to the detriment of the conditioned behavior and even to the delay or preclusion of the reinforcement. In a very boiled-down, simplified form, it might be stated as "learned behavior drifts toward instinctive behavior."

All this, of course, is not to disparage the use of conditioning techniques, but is intended as a demonstration that there are definite weaknesses in the philosophy underlying these techniques. The pointing out of such weaknesses should make possible a worthwhile revision in behavior theory.

The notion of instinct has now become one of our basic concepts in an effort to make sense of the welter of observations which confront us. When behaviorism tossed out instinct, it is our feeling that some of its power of prediction and control were lost with it. From the foregoing examples, it appears that although it was easy to banish the Instinctivists from the science during the Behavioristic Revolution, it was not possible to banish instinct so easily.

And if, as Hebb suggests, it is advisable to reconsider those things that behaviorism explicitly threw out, perhaps it might likewise be advisable to examine what they tacitly brought in—the hidden assumptions which led most disastrously to these breakdowns in the theory.

Three of the most important of these tacit assumptions seem to us to be: that the animal comes to the laboratory as a virtual *tabula rasa,* that species differences are insignificant, and that all responses are about equally conditionable to all stimuli.

It is obvious, we feel, from the foregoing account, that these assumptions are no longer tenable. After 14 years of continuous conditioning and observation of thousands of animals, it is our reluctant conclusion that the behavior of any species cannot be adequately understood, predicted, or controlled without knowledge of its instinctive patterns, evolutionary history, and ecological niche.

In spite of our early successes with the application of behavioristically oriented conditioning theory, we readily admit now that ethological facts and attitudes in recent years have done more to advance our practical control of animal behavior than recent reports from American "learning labs."

Moreover, as we have recently discovered, if one begins with evolution and instinct as the basic format for the science, a very illuminating viewpoint can be developed which leads naturally to a drastically revised and simplified conceptual framework of starting explanatory power (to be reported elsewhere).

It is hoped that this playback on the theory will be behavioral technology's partial repayment to the academic science whose impeccable empiricism we have used so extensively.

NOTE

1. In view of the fact that instinctive behaviors may be common to many zoological species, we consider *species specific* to be a sanitized misnomer, and prefer the possibly septic adjective *instinctive.*

REFERENCES

Beach, F. A. The snark was a boojum. *Amer. Psychologist,* 1950, 5, 115–124.
Breland, K., & Breland, M. A field of applied animal psychology. *Amer. Psychologist,* 1951, 6, 202–204.
Hebb, D. O. The American revolution. *Amer. Psychologist,* 1960, 15, 735–745.
Lorenz, K. Innate behaviour patterns. In *Symposia of the Society for Experimental Biology.* No. 4. *Physiological mechanisms in animal behaviour.* New York: Academic Press, 1950.
Skinner, B. F. Superstition in the pigeon. *J. exp. Psychol.,* 1948, 38, 168–172.
Tinbergen, N. *The study of instinct.* Oxford: Clarendon, 1951.
Whalen, R. E. Comparative psychology. *Amer. Psychologist,* 1961, 16, 84.

9.3 | ON THE GENERALITY OF THE LAWS OF LEARNING

Martin E. P. Seligman

That all events are equally associable and obey common laws is a central assumption of general process learning theory. A continuum of preparedness is defined which holds that organisms are prepared to associated certain events, unprepared for some, and contraprepared for others. A review of data from the traditional learning paradigms shows that the assumption of equivalent associability is false: in classical conditioning, rats are prepared to associate tastes with illness even over very long delays of reinforcement, but are contraprepared to associate tastes with foodshock. In instrumental training, pigeons acquire key pecking in the absence of a contingency between pecking and grain (prepared), while cats, on the other hand, have trouble learning to lick themselves to escape, and dogs do not yawn for food (contraprepared). In discrimination, dogs are contraprepared to learn that different locations of discriminative stimuli control go–no go responding, and to learn that different qualities control directional responding. In avoidance, responses from the natural defensive repertoire are prepared for avoiding shock, while those from the appetitive repertoire are contraprepared. Language acquisition and the functional autonomy of motives are also viewed using the preparedness continuum. Finally, it is speculated that the laws of learning themselves may vary with the preparedness of the organism for the association and that different physiological and cognitive mechanisms may covary with the dimension.

Sometimes we forget why psychologists ever trained white rats to press bars for little pellets of flour or sounded metronomes followed by meat powder for domestic dogs. After all, when in the real world do rats encounter levers which they learn to press in order to eat, and when do our pet dogs ever come across metronomes whose clicking signals meat powder? It may be useful now to remind ourselves about a basic premise which gave rise to such bizarre endeavors, and to see if we still have reason to believe this premise.

* Martin P. Seligman, "On the Generality of the Laws of Learning," *Psychological Review*, 77, 1970, 406–418. Copyright 1970 by the American Psychological Association, and reproduced by permission. The preparation of this manuscript was supported in part by National Institute of Mental Health Grant MH 16546-01 to the author. The author gratefully acknowledges the helpful comments of R. Bolles, P. Cabe, S. Emlen, J. Garcia, E. Lenneberg, R. MacLeod, H. Rachlin, D. Regan, R. Rosinski, P. Rozin, T. A. Ryan, R. Solomon, and F. Stollnitz.

THE GENERAL PROCESS VIEW OF LEARNING

It was hoped that in the simple, controlled world of levers and mechanical feeders, of metronomes and salivation, something quite general would emerge. If we took such an arbitrary behavior as pressing a lever and such an arbitrary organism as an albino rat, and set it to work pressing the lever for food, then *by virtue of* the very arbitrariness of the environment, we would find features of the rat's behavior general to real-life instrumental learning. Similarly, if we took a dog, undistracted by extraneous noises and sights, and paired a metronome's clicking with meat, what we found about the salivation of the dog might reveal characteristics of associations in general. For instance, when Pavlov found that salivation stopped occurring to a clicking that used to signal meat powder, but no longer did, he hoped that this was an instance of a *law*, "experimental extinction," which would have application beyond clicking metronomes, meat powder, and salivation. What captured the interest of the psychological world was the possibility that such laws might describe the general characteristics of the behavior acquired as the result of pairing one event with another. When Thorndike found that cats learned only gradually to pull strings to escape from puzzle boxes, the intriguing hypothesis was that animal learning in general was by trial and error. In both of these situations, the very arbitrariness and unnaturalness of the experiment was assumed to guarantee generality, since the situation would be uncontaminated by past experience the organism might have had or by special biological propensities he might bring to it.

The basic premise can be stated specifically: In classical conditioning, the choice of CS, US, and response is a matter of relative indifference; that is, any CS and US can be associated with approximately equal facility, and a set of general laws exist which describe the acquisition, extinction, inhibition, delay of reinforcement, spontaneous recovery, etc., for all CSs and USs. In instrumental learning, the choice of response and reinforcer is a matter of relative indifference; that is, any emitted response and any reinforcer can be associated with approximately equal facility, and a set of general laws exist which describe acquisition, extinction, discriminative control, generalization, etc., for all responses and reinforcers. I call this premise the assumption of equivalence of associability, and I suggest that it lies at the heart of general process learning theory.

This is not a straw man. Here are some quotes from three major learning theorists to document this assumption:

> It is obvious that the reflex activity of any effector organ can be chosen for the purpose of investigation, since signalling stimuli can get linked up with any of the inborn reflexes [Pavlov, 1927, p. 17].

any natural phenomenon chosen at will may be converted into a conditional stimulus . . . any visual stimulus, any desired sound, any odor, and the stimulation of any part of the skin [Pavlov, 1928, p. 86].

All stimulus elements are equally likely to be sampled and the probability of a response at any time is equal to the proportion of elements in S' that are connected to it. . . . On any acquisition trial all stimulus elements sampled by the organism become connected to the response reinforced on that trial [Estes, 1959, p. 399].

The general topography of operant behavior is not important, because most if not all specific operants are conditioned. I suggest that the dynamic properties of operant behavior may be studied with a single reflex [Skinner, 1938, pp. 45–46].

A REEXAMINATION OF EQUIVALENCE OF ASSOCIABILITY

The premise of equivalence places a special premium on the investigations of arbitrarily related, as opposed to naturally occurring, events. Such events, since they are supposedly uncontaminated by past experience or by special propensities the organism brings to the situation, provide paradigms for the investigations of general laws of learning. More than 60 years of research in both the instrumental and classical conditioning traditions have yielded considerable data suggesting that similar laws hold over a wide range of arbitrarily chosen events: the shape of generalization gradients is pretty much the same for galvanic skin responses classically conditioned to tones when shock is the US (Hovland, 1937), and for salivating to being touched at different points on the back when food is the US (Pavlov, 1927), Partial reinforcement causes greater resistance to extinction than continuous reinforcement regardless of whether rats are bar pressing for water or running down alleyways for food. Examples of analogous generality of laws could be multiplied at great length.

Inherent in the emphasis on arbitrary events, however, is a danger: *that the laws so found will not be general, but peculiar to arbitrary events.*

THE DIMENSION OF PREPAREDNESS

It is a truism that an organism brings to any experiment certain equipment and predispositions more or less appropriate to that situation. It brings specialized sensory and receptor aparatus with a long evolutionary history which has modified it into its present appropriateness or inappropriateness for the experiment. In addition to sensory-motor capacity, the organism brings associative apparatus, which likewise has a long and specialized evolutionary history. For example, when an organism is placed in a classical conditioning experiment, not only may the CS be more or less perceptible and the US more or less evocative of a response, *but also the CS and US may be more or less associable.* The organism may be more or less prepared by the evolution of its species to associate a given CS and US or a given response with an outcome. If evolution has affected the associability of specific events, then it is possible, even likely, that the very *laws* of learning might vary with the preparedness of the organism from one class of situations to another. If this is so, investigators influenced by the general process view may have discovered only a subset of the laws of learning: the laws of learning about arbitrarily concatenated events, those associations which happen in fact to be equivalent.

We can define a continuum of preparedness operationally. Confront an organism with a CS paired with US or with a response which produces an outcome. Depending on the specifics, the organism can be either prepared, unprepared, or contraprepared for learning about the events. *The relative preparedness of an organism for learning about a situation is defined by the amount of input* (e.g., numbers of trials, pairings, bits of information, etc.) *which must occur before that output* (responses, acts, repertoire, etc.), *which is construed as evidence of acquisition, reliably occurs.* It does not matter how input or output are specified, as long as that specification can be used consistently for all points on the continuum. Thus, using the preparedness dimension is independent of whether one happens to be an S-R theorist, a cognitive theorist, an information processing theorist, an ethologist, or what have you. Let me illustrate how one can place an experimental situation at various points on the continuum for classical conditioning. If the organism makes the indicant response consistently from the very first presentation of the CS on, such "learning" represents a clear case of instinctive responding, the extreme of the prepared end of the dimension. If the organism makes the response consistently after only a few pairings, it is somewhat prepared. If the response emerges only after many pairings (extensive input), the organism is unprepared. If acquisition occurs only after very many pairings or does not ocur at all, the organism is said to be contraprepared. The number of pairings is the measure that makes the dimension a continuum, and implicit in this dimension is the notion that "learning" and "instinct" are continuous. Typically ethologists have examined situations in the prepared side of the dimension, while general process learning theorists have largely restricted themselves to the unprepared region. The contraprepared part of the dimension has been largely uninvestigated, or at least unpublished.

The dimension of preparedness should not be confused with the notion of operant level. The frequency with which a response is made in a given situation is not necessarily related to the associability of that response with a given outcome. As will be seen later, frequent responses may not be required when they are reinforced as readily as infrequent responses. Indeed, some theorists (e.g., Turner & Solomon, 1962) have argued that high-probability, fast-latency responding may actually antagonize operant reinforceability.

The first empirical question with which this paper is concerned is whether sufficient evidence exists to challenge the equivalence of associability. For many years, ethologists and others (for an excellent example, see Breland & Breland, 1966) have gathered a wealth of evidence to challenge the general process view of learning. Curiously, however, these data have had little impact on the general process camp, and while not totally ignored, they have not been theoretically incorporated. In view of differences in methodology, this is perhaps understandable. I do not expect that presenting these lines of evidence here would have any more effect than it has already had. More persuasive to the general process theorist should be the findings which have sprung up within his own tradition. Within traditional conditioning and training paradigms, a considerable body of evidence now exists which challenges the premise. In reviewing this evidence, we shall find the dimension of preparedness to be a useful integrative device. It is not the intent of this article to review exhaustively the growing number of studies which challenge the premise. Rather, we shall look within each of the major paradigms which general process learning theorists have used and discuss one or two clear examples. The theme of these examples is that all events are not equivalent in their associability: that although the organism may have the necessary receptor and effector apparatus to deal with events, there is much variation in its ability to learn about relations between events.

CLASSICAL CONDITIONING

The investigation of classical aversive conditioning has been largely confined to the unconditioned response of pain caused by the stimulus of electric shock (cf. Campbell & Church, 1969), and the "laws" of classical conditioning are based largely on these findings along with those from salivary conditioning. Recently, Garcia and his collaborators (Garcia, Ervin, & Koelling, 1966; Garcia, Ervin, Yorke, & Koelling, 1967; Garcia & Koelling, 1966; Garcia, McGowan, Ervin, & Koelling, 1968), and Rozin and his collaborators (Rodgers & Rozin, 1966; Rozin, 1967, 1968, 1969) have used illness as an unconditioned response and reported some intriguing findings. In the paradigm experiment (Garcia & Koelling, 1966), rats received "bright-noisy, saccharin-tasting water." What this meant was that whenever the rat licked a drinking tube containing saccharin-flavored water, lights flashed and a noise source sounded. During these sessions the rats were X-irradiated. X-irradiation makes rats sick, but it should be noted that the illness does not set in for an hour or so following X-raying. Later the rats were tested for acquired aversions to the elements of the compound CS. The rats had acquired a strong aversion to the taste of saccharine, *but had not acquired an aversion to the "bright-noise."* The rats had "associated" the taste with their illness, but not the exteroceptive noise-light stimuli. So that it could not be argued that saccharin is such a salient event that it masked the noise and light, Garcia and Koelling ran the complementary experiment: "Bright and noisy saccharin-tasting water" was again used as a CS, but this time electric shock to the feet was the US. The rats were then tested for aversion to the elements of the CS. In this case, the bright noise became aversive, but the saccharin-tasting water did not. This showed that the bright noise was clearly perceptible; but the rats associated only the bright noise with the exteroceptive US of footshock, and not the taste of saccharin in spite of its also being paired with shock.

In the experiment, we see both ends as well as the middle of the preparedness continuum. Rats are prepared, by virtue of their evolutionary history, to associate tastes with malaise. For in spite of a several-hour delay of reinforcement, and the presence of other perceptible CSs, only the taste was associated with nausea, and light and noise were not. Further, rats are contraprepared to associate exteroceptive events with nausea and contraprepared to associate tastes with footshock. Finally, the association of footshock with light and sound is probably someplace in the unprepared region. The survival advantage of this preparedness seems obvious: organisms who are poisoned by a distinctive food and survive, do well not to eat it again. Selective advantage should accrue, moreover, to those rats whose associative apparatus could bridge a very long CS-US interval and who could ignore contiguous, as well as interpolated, exteroceptive CSs in the case of taste and nausea.

Does such prepared and contraprepared acquisition reflect the evolutionary results of selective pressure or does it result from experience? It is possible that Garcia's rats may have previously learned that tastes were uncorrelated with peripheral pain and that tastes were highly correlated with alimentary consequences. Such an argument involves an unorthodox premise: that rats' capacities for learning set and transfer are considerably broader than previously demonstrated. The difference between a position that invokes selective pressure (post hoc) and the experiential set position is testable: Would mating those rats who were most proficient at learning the taste–footshock association produce offspring more capable of such learning than an unselected population? Conversely, would interbreeding refractory rats select out the facility with which the taste–nausea association is made?

Supporting evidence for preparedness in classical conditioning has come from other recent experiments on specific hungers and poisoning. Rodgers and Rozin (1966) and Rozin (1967, 1968) have demonstrated that at least part of the mechanism of specific hungers (other than sodium) involves conditioned aversion to the taste of the diet the rats were eating as they became sick. Deficient rats spill the old diet and will not eat it, even after they have recovered. The association of the old taste with malaise seems to be made in spite of the long delay between taste of the diet and gradual onset of illness. The place and the container in which the old diet was set, moreover, do not become aversive. The remarkable ability of wild rats who recover from being poisoned by a novel food, and thereafter avoid new tastes (Barnett, 1963; Rozin, 1968), also seems to result from classical conditioning. Note that the wild rat must be prepared to associate the taste with an illness which does not appear for several hours in only one trial; note also that it must be contra-prepared to associate some contiguous CSs surrounding the illness with malaise.

Do these findings really show that rats can associate tastes and illness when an interval of many minutes or even hours intervenes or are they merely a subtle instance of contiguity? Peripheral cues coming either from long-lasting aftertastes or from regurgitation might bring the CS and US into contiguity. Rozin (1969) reported evidence against aftertaste media-tion: rats received a high concentration of saccharin paired with apo-morphine poisoning. Later, the rats were given a choice between the high concentration and a low concentration. The rats preferred the low concen-tration, even though the aftertaste that was purportedly contiguous with malaise should be more similar to the low concentration (since it had been diluted by saliva) than the high concentration.

Not only do rats acquire an aversion for the old diet, on which they got sick, but they also learn to prefer the taste of a new diet containing the needed substance. This mechanism also seems to involve prepared conditioning of taste to an internal state. Garcia et al. (1967) paired the taste of saccharin with thiamine injections given to thiamine deficient rats, and the rats acquired a preference for saccharin. So both the rejection of old foods and acceptance of new foods in specific hungers can be explained by prepared conditioning of tastes to internal state.

INSTRUMENTAL LEARNING

E. L. Thorndike, the founder of the instrumental learning tradition, was by no means oblivious to the possibility of preparedness in instrumental learning, as we shall see below. He also hinted at the importance of pre-paredness in one of his discussions of classical conditioning (Thorndike, 1935, p. 192–197): one of his students (Bregman, 1934) attempted to replicate the results of Watson and Rayner (1920), who found that little

Albert became afraid of a white rat, rabbit, and dog which had been paired with a startling noise. Bregman was unable to show any fear conditioning when she paired more conventional CSs, such as blocks of wood and cloth curtains, with startling noise. Thorndike speculated that infants at the age of locomotion were more disposed to manifest fear to objects that wiggle and control themselves than to motionless CSs.

Thorndike's parallel views on instrumental learning rose from his original studies of cats in puzzle boxes. As every psychologist knows, he put cats in large boxes and investigated the course of learning to pull strings to escape. What is less widely known is that he put his cats in not just one puzzle box, but in a whole series of different ones (incidentally in doing this he seems to have discovered learning set—Thorndike, 1964, pp. 48–50). In one box the cats had to pull a string to get out, in another a button had to be pushed, in another a lever had to be depressed, etc. One of his boxes—box Z—was curious: it was merely a large box with nothing but a door that the experimenter could open. Thorndike opened the door in Box Z whenever cats licked themselves or scratched themselves. The cat is known to use both of the frequently occurring responses instrumentally: it scratches itself to turn off itches, and licks itself to remove dirt. In addition, Thorndike had established that getting out of a puzzle box was a sufficient reward for reinforcing the acts of string pulling, button pushing, and lever clawing. In spite of this, Thorndike's cats seemed to have a good deal of trouble learning to scratch themselves or lick themselves to get out of the boxes.

A reanalysis of the individual learning curves presented by Thorndike (1964) for each of the seven cats who had experience in Box Z documents the impression: of the 28 learning curves presented for these seven cats in the boxes other than Z, 22 showed faster learning than in Z, three showed approximately equal learning, and only three showed slower learning. While all of the cats eventually showed improved speeds of licking or scratching for escape, such learning was difficult and irregular. Thorndlike noted another unusual property of licking and scratching:

> There is in all these cases a noticeable tendency . . . to diminish the act until it becomes a mere vestige of a lick or scratch . . . the licking degenerated into a mere quick turn of the head with one or two motions up and down with tongue extended. Instead of a hearty scratch, the cat waves its paw up and down rapidly for an instant. Moreover, if sometimes you do not let the cat out after the feeble reaction, it does not at once repeat the movement, as it would do if it depressed a thumb piece, for instance, without success in getting the door open [Thorndike, 1964, p. 48].

Contemporary investigators have reported related findings. Konorski (1967, pp. 463–467) attempted to train "reflex" movements, such as anus licking, scratching, and yawning, with food reinforcement. While reporting success with scratching and anus licking, like Thorndike, he observed spontaneous simplification and arhythmia in the responses. More importantly, he reported that reinforcement of "true yawning" with food is very difficult, if not impossible. Bolles and Seelbach (1964) reported that rearing could be reinforced by noise offset, but not punished by noise onset, exploration could be modified by both, and grooming by neither. This difference could not be accounted for by difference in operant level, which is substantial for all these behaviors of the rat.

Thorndike (1964) speculated that there may be some acts which the organism is not neurally prepared to connect to some sense impressions:

> If the associations in general were simply between situation and impulse to act, one would suppose that the situation would be associated with the impulse to lick or scratch as readily as with the impulse to turn a button or claw a string. Such is not the case. By comparing the curves for Z on pages 57–58 with the others, one sees that for so simple an act it takes a long time to form the association. This is not the final reason, for lack of attention, a slight increase in the time taken to open the door after the act was done, or *an absence of preparation in the nervous system for connections between these particular acts and definite sense impressions* [italics added] may very well have been the cause of the difficulty in forming the associations [p. 113].

This speculation seems reasonable: after all, in the natural history of cats, only behavior such as manipulating objects which maximized chances for escaping traps would be selected, and licking is not in the repertoire which maximizes escape. At minimum, Thorndike demonstrated that the emission of licking paired with an event which could reinforce other emitted acts was not sufficient to reinforce licking equally well. In the present terms, Thorndike had discovered a particular instrumental training situation for which cats are relatively contraprepared.

Brown and Jenkins (1968, Experiment 6) have reported findings which appear to come from the opposite end of the dimension. Pigeons were exposed to a lighted key which was paired with grain delivered in a lighted food hopper below the key. But unlike the typical key-pecking situation, the pigeons' pecking the key did not produce food. Food was contingent only on the key's being lit, not on pecking the key. In spite of this, all pigeons began pecking the key after exposure to the lighted key, followed by grain. Moreover, key pecking was maintained even though it had no effect on food. One can conclude from these "auto-shaping" results that the pigeon is highly prepared for associating the pecking of a lighted key with grain.

There is another curiosity in the history of the instrumental learning literature which is usefully viewed with the preparedness dimension: the question of why a reinforcer is reinforcing. For over 20 years, disputes raged about what monolithic principle described the necessary and sufficient conditions for learning. Hull (1943) claimed that tissue-need reduction must occur for learning to take place, while Miller (1951) held that drive reduction was necessary and sufficient. Later, Sheffield, Roby, and Campbell (1954) suggested that a consummatory response was the necessary condition. More recently, it has become clear that learning can occur in the absence of any of these (e.g., Berlyne, 1960). I suggest that when CSs or responses are followed by such biologically important events as need reducers, drive reducers, or consummatory responses, learning should take place readily because natural selection has prepared organisms for such relationships. The relative preparedness of organisms for these events accounts for the saliency of such learning and hence the appeal of each of the monolithic principles. But organisms *can* learn about bar pressing paired with light onset, etc.; they are merely less prepared to do so, and hence, the now abundant evidence against the earlier principles was more difficult to gather.

Thus, we find that in instrumental learning paradigms, there are situations which lie on either side of the rat's bar pressing for food on the preparedness dimension. A typical rat will ordinarily learn to bar press for food after a few dozen exposures to the bar press—food contingency. But cats, who can use scratching and licking as instrumental acts in some situations, have trouble using these acts to get out of puzzle boxes, and dogs do not learn to yawn for food even after many exposures to the contingency. On the other hand, pigeons acquire a key peck in a lighted key–grain situation, even when there is no contingency at all between key pecking and grain. These three instrumental situations represent unprepared, contraprepared, and prepared contingencies, respectively. Later we shall discuss the possibility that they obey different laws as a function of different preparedness.

DISCRIMINATION LEARNING

The next two paradigms we consider—discrimination learning and avoidance learning—combine both classical and instrumental procedures. In both of these paradigms, findings have been reported which challenge the equivalence of associability. We begin with some recent Polish work on discrimination learning in dogs. Lawicka (1964) attempted to train dogs in either a go right–go left differentiation or a go–no go differentiation. Whether such differentiation could be acquired depended on the specific discriminative stimuli used. For the left–right differentiation, if the S— and the S+ differed in location (one speaker above the dog; one speaker below), the dog readily learned which way to go in order to receive food. If, however, the stimuli came from the *same* speaker and differed only in pitch, the left–right differentiation was exceedingly difficult. Topographical differences in stimuli, as opposed to qualitative differences, seem to aid in differentiating two topographically different responses. The dog seems contraprepared, moreover, for making a left–right differentiation to two tones which do not also differ in direction. Lest one argue that the two tones coming out of the same speaker were not discriminable, Lawicka (1964; like Garcia & Koelling, 1966) did the complementary experiment: dogs were trained to go and receive food or stay with two tones coming out of the same speaker. One tone was the S+ and the other tone the S−. The dogs learned this readily. Thus, using the same tones which could not be used to establish a left–right differentiation, a go–no go differentiation was established. The author then attempted to elaborate the go–no go differentiation to the same tone differing in location of speakers. As the reader should expect by now, the dogs had trouble learning the go–no go differentiation to the difference in location of S+ and S−. Dogs, then, are contraprepared for learning about different locations controlling a go–no go differentiation although they are not contraprepared for learning that the same locations control a left–right differentiation. Dogs are contraprepared for learning that qualitative differences of tone from the same location control a left–right differentiation, but not contraprepared for using this difference to govern a go–no go differentiation. Dobrzecka and Konorski (1967, 1968) and Szwejkowska (1967) have confirmed and extended these findings.

Emlen (personal communication, 1969) reported discrimination (or at least perceptual) learning that is prepared. It is known from planetarium experiments that adult indigo buntings use the northern circumpolar constellations for migration, since blocking these from view disrupts directed migration. One might have thought that the actual constellations were represented genetically. If young birds are raised under a sky which rotates around a fictitious axis, however, they use the arbitrarily chosen circumpolar constellations for migration and ignore the natural circumpolar constellations. Thus, it appears that indigo buntings are prepared to pay attention to and learn about those configurations of stars which rotate most slowly in the heavens.

AVOIDANCE LEARNING

Data from avoidance learning studies also challenge the equivalence of associability. Rats learn reasonably readily to press bars to obtain food. Rats also learn very readily to jump (Baum, 1969) and reasonably readily to run (Miller, 1941, 1951) from a dangerous place to a safe place to avoid electric shock. From this, the premise deduces that rats should learn readily to press bars to avoid shock. But this is not so (e.g., D'Amato & Schiff, 1964). Very special procedures must be instituted to train rats to depress levers to avoid shock reliably (e.g., D'Amato & Fazzaro, 1966; Fantino, Sharp, & Cole, 1966). Similarly, pigeons learn readily to peck lighted keys to obtain grain: too readily, probably, for this to be considered an unprepared or arbitrary response (see Brown & Jenkins, 1968). But it is very difficult to train pigeons with normal laboratory techniques to key peck to avoid shock. Hoffman and Fleshler (1959) reported that key pecking was impossible to obtain with negative reinforcement; Azrin (1959) found only temporary maintenance of key pecking in but one pigeon; and Rachlin and Hineline (1967) needed 10–15 hours of patient shaping to train key pecking to remove shock. This probably attests more to a problem specific to the response and reinforcer than to some inability of the pigeon to learn about avoidance contingencies. Ask anyone who has attempted to kill pigeons (e.g., by electrocution or throwing rocks at them), how good pigeons are at avoiding. Pigeons learn to fly away to avoid noxious events (e.g., Bedford & Anger, 1968; Emlen, 1970). In contrast, it is hard to imagine a pigeon flying *away* from something to obtain food.

Bolles has recently (1970)—and quite persuasively—argued that avoidance responses as studied in laboratory experiments are not simple, arbitrary operants. In order to produce successful avoidance, Bolles argues, the response must be chosen from among the natural, *species-specific* defensive repertoire of the organism. Thus, it must be a response for which the organism is prepared. Running away for rats and flying away for pigeons make good avoidance responses, while key pecking and bar pressing (which are probably related to the appetitive repertoire) do not.

It might be argued that these difficulties in learning avoidance are not due to contrapreparedness but to competing motor responses. Thus, for example, rats have trouble pressing levers to avoid shock because shock causes them to "freeze" which is incompatible with bar pressing. A word of caution is in order about such hypotheses: I know of no theory which specifies in advance what competes with what; rather, response competition (or facilitation) is merely invoked post hoc. When, and if, a *theory* of topographical incompatibility arises it may indeed provide an *explanation* of contrapreparedness, but at the present time, it does not.

Let us review the evidence against the equivalence of associability premise: in classical conditioning, rats are prepared to associate tastes with nausea and contraprepared to associate taste with footshock. In instrumental learning, different emitted responses are differentially associable with different reinforcers: pigeons are prepared to peck lighted keys for food, since they will acquire this even in the absence of any contingency between key pecking and food. Cats are contraprepared for learning to scratch themselves to escape, and dogs for yawning for food. In discrimination learning, dogs are contraprepared to learn that different locations control a go–no go differentiation, and contraprepared for different qualities controlling a left–right response. In avoidance learning, those responses which come from the natural defensive repertoire of rats and pigeons are prepared (or at least unprepared) for avoiding shock. Those responses from the appetitive repertoire seem contraprepared for avoidance.

TWO FAILURES OF GENERAL PROCESS LEARNING THEORY: LANGUAGE AND THE FUNCTIONAL AUTONOMY OF MOTIVES

The interest of psychologists in animal learning theory is on the wane. Although the reasons are many, a prominent one is that such theories have failed to capture and bring into the laboratory phenomena which provide fertile models of complex human learning. This failure may be due in part to the equivalence premise. By concentrating on events for which organisms have been relatively unprepared, the laws and models which general process learning theories have produced may not be applicable beyond the realm of arbitrary events, arbitrarily connected. This would not be an obstacle if all of human learning consisted of learning about arbitrary events. But it does not. *Homo sapiens* has an evolutionary history and a biological makeup which has made it relatively prepared to learn some things and relatively contraprepared to learn others. If learning varies with preparedness, it should not be surprising that the laws for unprepared association between events have not explained such phenomena as the learning of language or the acquisition of motives.

Lenneberg (1967) has recently provided an analysis of language, the minimal conclusion of which is that children do not learn language the way rats learn to press a lever for food. Put more strongly, the set of laws which describe language learning are not much illuminated by the laws of the acquisition of arbitrary associations between events, as Skinner (1957) has argued. Unlike such unprepared contingencies as bar pressing for food, language does not require careful training or shaping for its acquisition. We do not need to arrange sets of linguistic contingencies carefully to get children to speak and understand English. Programmed training of speech is relatively ineffective, for under all but the most impoverished linguistic environments, human beings learn to speak and understand. Children of the deaf make as much noise and have the same sequence and age of onset for cooing as children of hearing parents. Development of language seems roughly the same across cultures which presumably differ widely in the arrangement of reinforcement contingencies, and language skill is not predicted by chronological age but by motor skill (see Lenneberg, 1967, especially pp. 125–158, for a fuller discussion).

The acquisition of language, not unlike pecking a lighted key for grain in the pigeon and the acquisition of birdsong (Petrinovich, 1970), is prepared. The operational criterion for the prepared side of the dimension is that minimal input should produce acquisition. One characteristic of language acquisition which separates it from the bar press is just this: elaborate training is not required for its production. From the point of view of this paper, it is not surprising that the traditional analyses of instrumental and classical conditioning are not adequate for an analysis of language. This is not because language is a phenomenon *sui generis*, but because the laws of instrumental and classical conditioning were developed to explain unprepared situations and not to account for learning in prepared situations. This is not to assert that the laws which govern language acquisition will necessarily be the same as those governing the Garcia phenomenon, birdsong, or the key peck, but to say that species-specific, biological analysis might be fruitfully made of these phenomena.

It is interesting to note in this context the recent success that Gardner and Gardner (1970) have had in teaching American sign language to a chimpanzee. The Gardners reasoned that earlier failures to teach spoken English to chimpanzees (Hayes & Hayes, 1952; Kellogg & Kellogg, 1933) did not result from cognitive deficiencies on the part of the subjects, but from the contraprepared nature of vocalization as a trainable response. The great manual dexterity of the chimpanzee, however, suggested sign language as a more trainable vehicle. Hayes (1968) has recently reanalyzed the data from Vicki (the Hayes' chimp) and confirmed the suggestion that chimpanzees' difficulty in using exhalation instrumentally may have caused earlier failures.

Language is not the only example of human learning that has eluded general process theory. The extraordinary persistence of acquired human motives has not been captured in ordinary laboratory situations. People, objects, and endeavors which were once unmotivating to an individual acquire and maintain strongly motivating properties. Fondness for the objects of sexual learning long after sexual desire is gone is a clear example. Acquisition of motives is not difficult to bring into the laboratory, and the extensive literature on acquired drives has often been taken as an analysis of acquired human motivation. A rat, originally unafraid of a tone, is shocked while the tone is played. Thereafter, the rat is afraid of the tone. But the analogy breaks down here; for once the tone is presented several times without shock, the tone loses its fear-inducing properties (Little & Brimer, 1968; Wagner, Siegel, & Fein, 1967). (The low resistance to extinction of the conditioned emotional response should not be confused with the high resistance to extinction of the avoidance response. This inextinguishability probably stems from the failure of the organism to stay around in the presence of the CS long enough to be exposed to the fact that shock no longer follows the CS, rather than a failure of fear of the CS to extinguish.) Yet, acquired motivators for humans retain their properties long after the primary motivation with which they were originally paired is absent. Allport (1937) raised the problem for general process theory as the "functional autonomy of motives." But in the 30 years since the problem was posed, the failure of acquired human motives to extinguish remains unanalyzed experimentally.

The notion of preparedness may be useful in analyzing persistent acquired motivation. Typically, investigations of acquired drives have paired arbitrary CSs with arbitrary primary motivators. It seems possible that if more prepared CSs were paired with primary motivators, the motivational properties of such CSs might be unusually resistant to extinction. Seligman, Ives, Ames, and Mineka (1970) conditioned drinking by pairing compound CSs with injections of hypertonic saline-procaine in rats. When the CS consisted only of exteroceptive stimuli (white box, white noise), conditioning occurred, but extinguished in a few days. When the interoceptive CS of one-hour water deprivation was added to the compound, conditioning occurred and persisted unabated for two months. It seems possible that preparedness of mild thirst for association with rapidly induced strong thirst may account for the inextinguishability of acquired drinking.

Are humans prepared to associate a range of endeavors and objects with primary motivators, and are such associations unusually persistent after the original motivators have left the scene? Here, as for language, viewing persistent acquired motives as cases of preparedness may make human motivation—both adaptive and maladaptive—more amenable to study.

PREPAREDNESS AND THE LAWS OF LEARNING

The primary empirical question has been answered affirmatively: The premise of equivalence of associability does not hold, *even in the traditional paradigms for which it was first assumed.* But does this matter? Do the same laws which describe the learning of unprepared events hold for prepared, unprepared, and contraprepared events? Given that an organism is prepared, and therefore learns with minimal input, does such learning have different properties from those unprepared associations that the organism acquires more painstakingly? Are the same mechanisms responsible for learning in prepared, unprepared, and relatively contraprepared situations?

We can barely give a tentative answer to this question, since it has been largely uninvestigated. Only a few pieces of evidence have been gathered to suggest that once a relatively prepared or contraprepared association has been acquired, it may not display the same family of extinction curves, values for delay of reinforcement, punishment effects, etc., as the lever press for food in the rat. Consider again the Garcia and Koelling (1966) findings: the association of tastes with illness is made with very different delays of reinforcement from ordinary Pavlovian associations. Unlike salivating to sounds, the association will be acquired with delays of up to one hour and more. Detailed studies which compare directly the delay of reinforcement gradients, extinction functions, etc., for prepared versus unprepared associations are needed. It would be interesting to find that the extinction and inhibition functions for prepared associations were different than for unprepared associations. If preparation underlies the observations of functional autonomy, prepared associations might be highly resistant to extinction, punishment, and other changes in instrumental contingencies. Breland and Breland (1966) reported that many of the "prepared" behaviors that the organisms they worked with acquired would presist even under counterproductive instrumental contingencies. To what extent would the autoshaped key pecking responses of Brown and Jenkins (1968) be weakened by extinction or punishment, as bar pressing for food is weakened? Williams and Williams (1969) reported that autoshaped key-pecking responses persist even when they actually "cost" the pigeon reinforcement.

Does contraprepared behavior, after being acquired, obey the same laws as unprepared behavior? Thorndike (1964) reported that when he finally retained licking for escape, the response no longer looked like the natural response, but was a pale, mechanical imitation of the natural response. Would the properties of the response differentiation and shaping of such behavior be like those of unprepared responses? The answer to this range of questions is presently unknown.

Preparedness has been operationally defined, and it is possible that different laws of learning may vary with the dimension. How can the dimension be anchored more firmly? Might different cognitive and physiological mechanisms covary with dimension?

Acquired aversions to tastes following illness is commonplace in humans. These Garcia phenomena are not easily modified by cognition in constrast to other classically conditioned responses in humans (e.g., Spence & Platt, 1967). The knowledge that the illness was caused by the stomach flu and not the Sauce Bearnaise does not prevent the sauce from tasting bad in the future. Garcia, Kovner, and Green (1970) reported that distinctive tastes can be used by rats as a cue for shock avoidance in a shuttlebox; but the preference for the taste in the home cage is unchanged. When the taste is paired with illness, however, the preference is reduced in the home cage. Such evidence suggests that prepared associations may not be cognitively mediated, and it is tempting to speculate that cognitive mechanisms (expectation, attention, etc.) come into play with more unprepared or contraprepared situations. If this is so, it is ironic that the "blind" connections which both Thorndike and Pavlov wanted to study lie in the prepared realm and not in the unprepared paradigms they investigated.

We might also ask if different neural structures underlie differently prepared learning. Does elaborate prewiring mediate prepared associations such as taste and nausea, while more plastic structures mediate unprepared and contraprepared associations?

We have defined the dimension of preparedness and given examples of it. To anchor the dimension we need to know the answers to three questions about what covaries with it: (a) Do different laws of learning (families of functions) hold along the dimension? (b) Do different cognitive mechanisms covary with it? (c) Do different physiological mechanisms also covary with preparedness?

PREPARATION AND THE GENERAL PROCESS VIEW OF LEARNING

If the premise of equivalence of associability is false, then we have reason to suspect that the laws of learning discovered using lever pressing and salivation may not hold for any more than other simple, unprepared associations. If the laws of learning for unprepared association do not hold for prepared or contraprepared associations, is the general process view salvageable in any form? This is an empirical question. Its answer depends on whether *differences* in learning vary systematically along the dimension of preparedness; the question reduces to whether the preparedness continuum is a nomological continuum. For example, if one finds that the families of extinction functions vary systematically with the dimension, then one might be able to formulate *general* laws of extinction. Thus, if prepared CRs extinguished very slowly, unprepared CRs extinguished gradually, and contraprepared CRs extinguished precipitously, such a systematic, continuous difference in *laws* would be a truly general law of extinction. But before such general laws can be achieved, we must first investigate what the laws of prepared and contraprepared associations actually are. If this were done, then the possibility of general laws of learning would be again alive.

REFERENCES

Allport, G. The functional autonomy of motives. *American Journal of Psychology*, 1937, 50, 141–156.

Azrin, N. J. Some notes on punishment and avoidance. *Journal of the Experimental Analysis of Behavior*, 1959, 2, 260.

Barnett, S. *The rat: A study in behavior*. London: Methuen, 1963.

Baum, M. Dissociation of respondent and operant processes in avoidance learning. *Journal of Comparative and Physiological Psychology*, 1969, 67, 83–88.

Bedford, J., & Anger, D. Flight as an avoidance response in pigeons. Paper presented at the meeting of the Psychonomic Society, St. Louis, October 1968.

Berlyne, D. E. *Conflict, arousal, and curiosity*. McGraw-Hill: New York, 1960.

Bolles, R. Effects of escape training on avoidance learning. In F. R. Brush (Ed.), *Aversive conditioning and learning*. New York: Academic Press, 1970, in press.

Bolles, R., & Seelbach, S. Punishing and reinforcing effects of noise onset and termination for different responses. *Journal of Comparative and Physiological Psychology*, 1964, 58, 127–132.

Bregman, E. An attempt to modify the emotional attitude of infants by the conditioned response technique. *Journal of Genetic Psychology*, 1934, 45, 169–198.

Breland, K., & Breland, M. *Animal behavior*. New York: Macmillan, 1966.

Brown, P., & Jenkins, H. Autoshaping of the pigeon's key-peck. *Journal of the Experimental Analysis of Behavior*, 1968, 11, 1–8.

Campbell, E. A., & Church, R. M. *Punishment and aversive behavior*. New York: Appleton-Century-Crofts, 1969.

D'Amato, M. R., & Fazzaro, J. Discriminated lever-press avoidance learning as a function of type and intensity of shock. *Journal of Comparative and Physiological Psychology*, 1966, 61, 313–315.

D'Amato, M. R., & Schiff, J. Long-term discriminated avoidance performance in the rat. *Journal of Comparative and Physiological Psychology*, 1964, 57, 123–126.

Dobrzecka, C., & Konorski, J. Qualitative versus directional cues in differential conditioning. I. Left leg-right leg differentiation to cues of a mixed character. *Acta Biologiae Experimentale*, 1967, 27, 163–168.

Dobrzecka, C., & Konorski, J. Qualitative versus directional cues in differential conditioning. *Acta Biologiae Experimentale*, 1968, 28, 61–69.

Emlen, S. The influence of magnetic information on the orientation of the indigo bunting. *Animal Behavior*, 1970, in press.

Estes, W. K. The statistical approach to learning theory. In S. Koch (Ed.), *Psychology: A study of a science*. Vol. 2. New York: McGraw-Hill, 1959.

Fantino, E., Sharp, D., & Cole, M. Factors facilitating lever press avoidance. *Journal of Comparative and Physiological Psychology*, 1966, 63, 214–217.

Garcia, J., Ervin, F., & Koelling, R. Learning with prolonged delay of reinforcement. *Psychonomic Science*, 1966, 5, 121–122.

Garcia, J. Ervin, F., Yorke, C., & Koelling, R. Conditioning with delayed vitamin injections. *Science*, 1967, 155, 716–718.

Garcia, J., Kovner, R., & Green, K. F. Cue properties versus palatability of flavors in avoidance learning. *Psychonomic Science*, 1970, 20, 313–314.

Garcia, J., & Koelling, R. Relation of cue to consequence in avoidance learning. *Psychonomic Science*, 1966, 4, 123–124.

Garcia, J., McGowan, B., Ervin, F., & Koelling, R. Cues: Their relative effectiveness as a function of the reinforcer. *Science*, 1968, 160, 794–795.

Gardner, B., & Gardner, A. Two-way communication with an infant chimpanzee. In A. Schrier & F. Stollnitz (Eds.), *Behavior of nonhuman primates*. Vol. 3. New York: Academic Press, 1970, in press.

Hayes, K. J. Spoken and gestural language learning in chimpanzees. Paper presented at the meeting of the Psychonomic Society, St. Louis, October 1968.

Hayes, K. J., & Hayes, C. Imitation in a home-raised chimpanzee. *Journal of Comparative and Physiological Psychology*, 1952, 45, 450–459.

Hoffman, H. S., & Fleshler, M. Aversive control with the pigeon. *Journal of the Experimental Analysis of Behavior*, 1959, 2, 213–218.

Hovland, C. The generalization of conditioned responses. I. The sensory generalization of conditioned responses with varying frequencies of tone. *Journal of Genetic Psychology*, 1937, 17, 279–291.

Hull, C. L. *Principles of behavior*. New York: Appleton-Century-Crofts, 1943.

Kellogg, W. N., & Kellogg, L. A. *The ape and the child*. New York: McGraw-Hill, 1933.

Konorski, J. *Integrative activity of the brain*. Chicago: University of Chicago Press, 1967.

Lawicka, W. The role of stimuli modality in successive discrimination and differentiation learning. *Bulletin of the Polish Academy of Sciences*, 1964, 12, 35–38.

Lenneberg, E. *The biological foundations of language*. New York: Wiley, 1967.

Little, J., & Brimer, C. Shock density and conditioned suppression. Paper presented at the meeting of the Eastern Psychological Association, Washington, D. C., April 1968.

Miller, N. E. An experimental investigation of acquired drives. *Psychological Bulletin*, 1941, 38, 534–535.

Miller, N. E. Learnable drives and rewards. In S. S. Stevens (Ed.), *Handbook of experimental psychology*. New York: Wiley, 1951.

Pavlov, I. P. *Conditioned reflexes*. New York: Dover, 1927.

Pavlov, I. P. *Lectures on conditioned reflexes*. New York: International Publishers, 1928.

Petrinovich, L. Psychobiological mechanisms in language development. In G. Newton & A. R. Riesen (Eds.), *Advances in psychobiology*. New York: Wiley, 1970, in press.

Rachlin, H. C., & Hineline, P. N. Training and maintenance of key pecking in the pigeon by negative reinforcement. *Science*, 1967, 157, 954–955.

Rodgers, W., & Rozin, P. Novel food preferences in thiamine-deficient rats. *Journal of Comparative and Physiological Psychology*, 1966, 61, 1–4.

Rozin, P. Specific aversions as a component in specific hungers. *Journal of Comparative and Physiological Psychology*, 1967, 63, 421–428.

Rozin, P. Specific aversions and neophobia resulting from vitamin deficiency or poisoning in half wild and domestic rats. *Journal of Comparative and Physiological Psychology*, 1968, 66, 82–88.

Rozin, P. Central or peripheral mediation of learning with long CS-US intervals in the feeding system. *Journal of Comparative and Physiological Psychology*, 1969, 67, 421–429.

Seligman, M. E. P., Ives, C. E., Ames, H., & Mineka, S. Conditioned drinking and its failure to extinguish: Avoidance, preparedness, or functional autonomy? *Journal of Comparative and Physiological Psychology*, 1970, 71, 411–419.

Sheffield, F. D., Roby, T. B., & Campbell, B. A. Drive reduction versus consummatory behavior as determinants of reinforcement. *Journal of Comparative and Physiological Psychology*, 1954, 47, 349–354.

Skinner, B. F. *The behavior of organisms.* New York: Appleton-Century-Crofts, 1938.

Skinner, B. F. *Verbal behavior.* New York: Appleton-Century-Crofts, 1957.

Spence, K. W., & Platt, J. R. Effects of partial reinforcement on acquisition and extinction of the conditioned eye blink in a masking situation. *Journal of Experimental Psychology,* 1967, 74, 259–263.

Szwejkowska, G. Qualitative versus directional cues in differential conditioning. II. Go–no go differentiation to cues of a mixed character. *Acta Biologiae Experimentale,* 1967, 27, 169–175.

Thorndike, E. L. *Animal intelligence.* New York: Hafner, 1964. (Originally published: New York: Macmillan, 1911.)

Thorndike, E. L. *The psychology of wants, interests, and attitudes.* New York: Appleton-Century, 1935.

Turner, L., & Solomon, R. L. Human traumatic avoidance learning: Theory and experiments on the operant-respondent distinction and failures to learn. *Psychological Monographs,* 1962, 74 (40, Whole No. 559).

Wagner, A., Siegel, L., & Fein, G. Extinction of conditioned fear as a function of the percentage of reinforcement. *Journal of Comparative and Physiological Psychology,* 1967, 63, 160–164.

Watson, J. B., & Rayner, R. Conditioned emotional reactions. *Journal of Experimental Psychology,* 1920, 3, 1–14.

Williams, D. R., & Williams, H. Auto-maintenance in the pigeon: Sustained pecking despite contingent non-reinforcement. *Journal of the Experimental Analysis of Behavior,* 1969, 12, 511–520.

Bibliography

Adler, N., and Hogan, J. A. Classical conditioning and punishment of an instinctive response in *Betta splendens*. *Animal Behavior*, 1963, *11*, 351–354.

Amsel, A. Frustrative nonreward in partial reinforcement and discrimination learning: Some recent history and a theoretical extension. *Psychological Review*, 1962, *69*, 306–328.

Amsel, A., and Roussel, J. Motivational properties of frustration: I. Effect on a running response of the addition of frustration to the motivational complex. *Journal of Experimental Psychology*, 1952, *43*, 363–368.

Azrin, N. H., Hutchinson, R. R., and Hake, D. F. *Extinction-induced aggression*. *Journal of the Experimental Analysis of Behavior*, 1966, *9*, 191–204.

Baldwin, V. L. Development of social skills in retardates as a function of three types of reinforcement programs. *Dissertation Abstracts*, 1967, *27* (9-A), 2865.

Bandura, A. *Social learning theory*. New York: General Learning Press, 1971.

Bandura, A., Ross, D., and Ross, S. A. Imitation of film-mediated aggressive models. *Journal of Abnormal and Social Psychology*, 1963, *66*, 3–11.

Beecroft, R. S. *Classical conditioning*. Goleta, Calif.: Psychonomic Press, 1966.

Beck, E. C., and Doty, R. W. Conditioned flexion reflexes acquired during combined catalepsy and de-efferentiation. *Journal of Comparative and Physiological Psychology*, 1957, *50*, 211–216.

Boring, E. G. *A history of experimental psychology* (2d ed.). New York: Appleton-Century-Crofts, 1950.

Buchwald, A. M. Effects of "right" and "wrong" on subsequent behavior: A new interpretation. *Psychological Review*, 1969, *76*, 132–143.

Butler, R. A. Incentive conditions which influence visual exploration. *Journal of Experimental Psychology*, 1954, *48*, 19–23.

Campbell, B. A., and Church, R. M. (Eds.). *Punishment and aversive behavior*. New York: Appleton-Century-Crofts, 1969.

Capaldi, E. J. Memory and learning: A sequential viewpoint. In W. K. Honig and P. H. R. James (Eds.), *Animal memory*. New York: Academic Press, 1971.

Carmichael, L. A further study of the development of behavior in vertebrates experimentally removed from the influence of external stimulation. *Psychological Review*, 1927, *34*, 34–47.

Cohen, H. L., Flilpczak, J. A., Bis, J. S., and Cohen, J. E. *Contingencies applicable to special education of delinquents*. Silver Spring, Md.: Institute for Behavioral Research, 1966.

Cowles, J. T. Food-tokens as incentives for learning by chimpanzees. *Comparative Psychology Monographs*, 1937, *14*, No. 71.

Crespi, L. Amount of reinforcement and level of performance. *Psychological Review*, 1944, *51*, 341–357.

Dinsmoor, J. A. Punishment: I. The avoidance hypothesis. *Psychological Review*, 1954, *61*, 34–46.

Estes, W. K., and Skinner, B. F. Some quantitative properties of anxiety. *Journal of Experimental Psychology*, 1941, *29*, 390–400.

Farris, H. E. Classical conditioning of courting behavior in the Japanese quail, *Coturnix coturnix japonica*. *Journal of the Experimental Analysis of Behavior*, 1967, *10*, 213–217.

Flanders, J. P. A review of research on imitative behavior. *Psychological Bulletin*, 1968, *69*, 316–337.

Fowler, H. Facilitation and inhibition of performance by punishment: The effects of shock intensity and distribution of trials. *Journal of Comparative and Physiological Psychology*, 1963, *56*, 531–538.

Fowler, H. Implications of sensory reinforcement. In Glaser, R. (Ed.). *The nature of reinforcement*. New York: Academic Press, 1971.

Franks, C. M. (Ed.). *Behavior therapy: Appraisal and status*. New York: McGraw-Hill, 1969.

Garcia, J., McGowan, B. K., and Green, K. F. Biological constraints on conditioning. In A. H. Black and W. F. Prokasy (Eds.), *Classical conditioning II: Current research and theory*. New York: Appleton-Century-Crofts, 1972.

Gibson, E. J. *Principles of perceptual learning and development*. New York: Appleton-Century-Crofts, 1972.

Gibson, E. J. *Principles of perceptual learning and development*. New York: Appleton-Century-Crofts, 1969.

Glaser, R. (Ed.). *The nature of reinforcement*. New York: Academic Press, 1971.

Gonzalez, R. C., Gentry, G. V., and Bitterman, M. F. Relational discrimination of intermediate size in the chimpanzee. *Journal of Comparative and Physiological Psychology*, 1954, *71*, 742–746.

Gonzalez, R. C., and Shepp, B. The effects of endbox-placement on subsequent performance in the runway with competing responses controlled. *American Journal of Psychology*, 1965, *78*, 441–447.

Grice, G., Masters, L., and Kohfeld, D. L. Classical conditioning without discrimination training: A test of the generalization theory of CS intensity effects. *Journal of Experimental Psychology*, 1966, *72*, 510–513.

Hefferline, R. F., Keenan, B., and Harford, R. A. Escape and avoidance conditioning in human subjects without their observation of the response. *Science*, 1959, *130*, 1338–1339.

Herrnstein, R. J. Method and theory in the study of avoidance. *Psychological Review*, 1969, *76*, 49–69.

Hoffman, H. S., Searle, J. L., Toffey, S., and Kuzma, F., Jr. Behavioral control by an imprinted stimulus. *Journal of the Experimental Analysis of Behavior*, 1966, *9*, 177–189.

Hovland, C. I. The generalization of conditioned responses: I. The sensory generalization of conditioned responses with varying frequencies of tone. *Journal of General Psychology*, 1937, *17*, 125–148.

Hull, C. L. *Principles of behavior: An introduction to behavior theory*. New York: Appleton-Century-Crofts, 1943.

Hull, C. L. *A behavior system*. New Haven, Conn.: Yale University Press, 1952.

Humphreys, L. G. Acquisition and extinction of verbal expectations in a stituation analogous to conditioning. *Journal of Experimental Psychology*, 1939, *25*, 294–301.

Jones, M. C. The elimination of children's fears. *Journal of Experimental Psychology*, 1924, *7*, 382–390.

Jones, A., Wilkinson, H. J., and Braden. I. Information deprivation as a motivational variable. *Journal of Experimental Psychology*, 1961, *62*, 126–137.

Kettlewell, H. B. D. Darwin's missing evidence. *Scientific American*, 1959, *200*, 48–53.

Kish, G. B. Studies of sensory reinforcement. In W. K. Honig (Ed.), *Operant behavior: Areas of research and application*. New York: Appleton-Century-Crofts, 1966.

Kuhn, T. S. *The structure of scientific revolutions*. Chicago: University of Chicago Press, 1970.

Lieberman, D. A. Secondary reinforcement and information as determinants of observing behavior in monkeys (*Macaca mulatta*). *Learning and Motivation*, 1972, *3*, 341–358.

Lovejoy, E. P. An attention theory of discrimination learning. *Journal of Mathematical Psychology*, 1965, *2*, 342–362.

Mackintosh, N. J. Selective attention in animal discrimination learning. *Psychological Bulletin*, 1965, *64*, 124–150.

Masserman, J. H., and Pechtel, C. Neuroses in monkeys: A preliminary report of experimental observations. *Annals of the New York Academy of Science*, 1953, *56*, 253–265.

Millenson, J. R., and Macmillan, A. St. C. Abortive responding during punishment of bar holding. Paper presented at Psychonomics Society Convention, St. Louis, 1972.

Miller, N. E., and DiCara, L. V. Instrumental learning of heart rate changes in curarized rats: Shaping and specificity to discriminative stimulus. *Journal of Comparative and Physiological Psychology*, 1967, *63*, 12–19.

Montgomery, K. C. The role of the exploratory drive in learning. *Journal of Comparative and Physiological Psychology*, 1954, *47*, 60–64.

Morse, W. H., and Kelleher, R. T. Schedules as fundamental determinants of behavior. In W. N. Schoenfeld (Ed.), *The theory of reinforcement schedules*. New York: Appleton-Century-Crofts, 1970.

Mowrer, O. H. *Learning theory and behavior*. New York: Wiley, 1960.

O'Leary, K. D., and Drabman, R. Token reinforcement programs in the classroom: A review. *Psychological Bulletin*, 1971, *75*, 379–398.

Paul, Gordon L. Outcome of systematic desensitization II: Controlled investigations of individual treatment, technique variations, and current status. In C. M. Franks (Ed.), *Behavior therapy: Appraisal and status*. New York: McGraw-Hill, 1969.

Perin, C. J. A quantitative investigation of the delay-of-reinforcement gradient. *Journal of Experimental Psychology*, 1943, *32*, 37–51.

Perkins, C .C., Jr. An analysis of the concept of reinforcement. *Psychological Review*, 1968, *75*, 155–172.

Phillips, E. L. Achievement place: Token reinforcement procedures in a home-style rehabilitation setting for "pre-delinquent" boys. *Journal of Applied Behavior Analysis*, 1968, *1*, 213–224.

Premack, D. Reversibility of the reinforcement relation. *Science*, 1962, *136*, 255–257.

Razran, G. The observable unconscious and the inferable conscious in current Soviet psychophysiology. *Psychological Review*, 1961, *68*, 81–147.

Rescorla, R. A., and LoLordo, V. M. Inhibition of avoidance behavior. *Journal of Comparative and Physiological Psychology*, 1965, *59*, 406–412.

Rescorla, R. A., and Solomon, R. L. Two-process learning theory: Relationships between Pavlovian conditioning and instrumental learning. *Psychological Review*, 1967, *74*, 151–182.

Rescorla, R. A., and Wagner, A. R. A theory of Pavlovian conditioning: Variations in the effectiveness of reinforcement and nonreinforcement. In A. H. Black and W. F. Prokasy (Eds.), *Classical conditioning II: Current research and theory.* New York: Appleton-Century-Crofts, 1972.

Restle, F. Discrimination of cues in mazes: A resolution of the "place-vs.-response" question. *Psychological Review*, 1957, *64*, 217–228.

Revusky, S. The role of interference in association over a delay. In W. K. Honig and P. H. R. James (Eds.), *Animal memory.* New York: Academic Press, 1971.

Reynolds, G. S. Behavioral contrast. *Journal of the Experimental Analysis of Behavior*, 1961, *4*, 57–71.

Risley, T. R. Effects and side effects of punishing the autistic behaviors of a deviant child. *Journal of Applied Behavior Analysis*, 1968, *1*, 21–34.

Rosenfeld, H. M., and Baer, D. M. Unnoticed verbal conditioning of an aware experimenter by a more aware subject: The double-agent effect. *Psychological Review*, 1969, *76*, 425–432.

Schein, M. W. On the irreversibility of imprinting. *Zeitschrift für Tierpsychologie*, 1963, *20*, 462–467.

Schein, M. W., and Hale, E. B. The effect of early social experience on male sexual behavior and androgen injected turkeys. *Animal Behaviour*, 1957, *7*, 189–200.

Senkowski, P. C., Porter, J. J., and Madison, H. L. Goal gradient effect of incentive motivation (K) manipulation through prior goal box placements. *Psychonomic Science*, 1968, *11*, 29–30.

Sheffield, V. F. Extinction as a function of partial reinforcement and distribution of practice. *Journal of Experimental Psychology*, 1949, *39*, 511–526.

Siqueland, E. R., and DeLucia, C. A. Visual reinforcement of non-nutritive sucking in human infants. *Science*, 1969, *165*, 1144–1146.

Smith, J. C., and Roll, D. L. Trace conditioning with X-rays as the aversive stimulus. *Psychonomic Science*, 1967, *9*, 11–12.

Solomon, R. L. Punishment. *American Psychologist*, 1964, *19*, 239–253.

Spence, K. W. The nature of discrimination learning in animals. *Psychological Review*. 1936, *43*, 427–449.

Spence, K. W. The role of secondary reinforcement in delayed reward learning. *Psychological Review*, 1947, *54*, 1–8.

Spielberger, C. D., and DeNike, L. D. Descriptive behaviorism versus cognitive theory in verbal operant conditioning. *Psychological Review*, 1966, *73*, 306–326.

Sutherland, N. S., and Mackintosh, N. J. *Mechanisms of animal discrimination learning.* New York: Academic Press, 1971.

Tinklepaugh, O. L. An experimental study of representative factors in monkeys. *Journal of Comparative Psychology*, 1928, *8*, 197–236.

Thomas, D. R. Stimulus selection, attention, and related matters. In J. H. Reynierse (Ed.), *Current issues in animal learning.* Lincoln: University of Nebraska Press, 1970.

Tolman, E. C., Ritchie, B. F., and Kalish, D. Studies in spatial learning I. Orientation and the short cut. *Journal of Experimental Psychology*, 1946, *36*, 13–24.

Ulrich, R., and Azrin, N. H. Reflexive fighting in response to aversive stimulation. *Journal of the Experimental Analysis of Behavior*, 1962, *5*, 511–520.

Vernon, W. M. Animal aggression: Review of research. *Genetic Psychology Monographs*, 1969, *80*, 3–28.

Vernon, W., and Ulrich, R. Classical conditioning of pain-elicited aggression. *Science*, 1966, *152*, 668–669.

Wagner, A. R. Elementary associations. In H. H. Kendler and J. T. Spence (Eds.), *Essays in neobehaviorism*. New York: Appleton-Century-Crofts, 1971.

Watson, J. B. Experimental studies on the growth of the emotions. In C. Murchison (Ed.), *Psychologies of 1925*. Worcester, Mass.: Clark University Press, 1926.

Watson, J. B., and McDougall, W. *The battle of behaviorism*. New York: Norton, 1929.

Weisberg, P. Social and nonsocial conditioning of infant vocalizations. *Child Development*, 1963, *34*, 377–388.

Wike, E. L. *Secondary reinforcement*. New York: Harper & Row, 1966.

Wolfe, J. B. The effect of delayed reward upon learning in the white rat. *Journal of Comparative Psychology*, 1934, *17*, 1–21.

Zeaman, D., and House, P. J. The role of attention in retardate discrimination learning. In N. R. Ellis (Ed.), *Handbook in mental deficiency: Psychological theory and research*. New York: McGraw-Hill, 1963.

Zeiler, M. D. The ratio theory of intermediate size discrimination. *Psychological Review*, 1963, *70*, 516–533.